This

Volume

Belongs

To:

_____

The Lord's Prayer

Our Father which art in heaven,
Hallowed be thy name.

Thy kingdom come. Thy will be done in earth,
as it is in heaven.

Give us this day our daily bread.
And forgive us our debts,
as we forgive our debtors.

And lead us not into temptation,
but deliver us from evil: For thine is the kingdom, and
the power, and the glory,
for ever. Amen.

Matthew 6:9-13

Get wisdom, get understanding: forget it not; neither
decline from the words of my mouth.

Wisdom is the principal thing; therefore get wisdom;
and with all thy getting get understanding.
Proverbs 4: 5,7

Through wisdom is an house builded; and by
understanding it is established.
Proverbs 24:3

CRUDEN'S

Condensed

CONCORDANCE

How to use the Concordance

This Concordance contains many of the important words in the Old and New Testaments, arranged in alphabetical order with the phrase in which it is used and the book, chapter and verse in which it is found.

We have heard the term *"Abba"* but, do not know in which verse of the Bible it is located. By means of the concordance, we can easily locate it. Find the word *"Abba"*, alphabetically, in the concordance. It is found in **Bold-Face** type. Under that heading are the verses in the Bible in which the word is used (The letter a. being an abbreviation for Abba). In the second line below Abba we find Gal. 4:6 *crying a. father* and turning to Galatians chapter 4 verse 6 in the Bible we read: *and because ye are sons, God hath sent forth the spirit of his son into your hearts, crying, Abba, Father.*

The abbreviations used in this concordance for the books of the Bible will be readily understood, with the possible exception of *Cant.*, which is used for Canticles, or the Song of Solomon.

We hope this volume will be of great value and assistance to your study and understanding of the Bible and your spiritual growth.

Dugan Publishers

CONCORDANCE

A.
AARON
Luke 1:5 wife of daughters of A.
ABASED
Mat. 23:12 exalt, shall be a.
Luke 14:11; 18:14
Phil. 4:12 I know how to be a.
ABBA
Mark 14:36 a. Father, all things
Gal. 4:6 crying a. Father
ABEL, person, or place.
1 Sam. 6:18 stone of A. they set
2 Sam. 20:18 ask counsel at A.
Mat. 23:35 blood of A. Luke 11:51
ABHOR
Prov. 24:24 nations shall a. him
Jer. 14:21 do not a. us
Rom. 12:9 a. that which is evil
ABIDE
Ps. 15:1 shall a. in tabernacle? 61:4
I will a. in thy tabernacle
1 John 2:24 let that a. in you 27 ye
shall a.;28 children a.
ABIDETH
2 John 9 whoso a. not in the
ABIGAIL
1 Sam. 25:3 Nabal's wife A.
ABIMELECHI
Gen. 20:2 A. king of Gerar sent
ABINADAB
1 Sam. 7:1 into the house of A.
16:8 Jesse called A. made him
2 Sam. 6:3 out of house of A.
1 Chr. 13:7
1 K. 4:11 A. had Sol. daughter
ABLE
Dan. 3:17 our God is a. to deliv.
9:28 believe ye I am a. to do
Matt. 20:22 are ye a. to drink
John 10:29 no man is a. to pluck
Rom 4:21 he was a. to perform
11:23 for God is a. to graff them
15:14 ye are a. also to admonish
2 Cor. 3:6 made us a. ministers of
9:8 God is a. to make all grace
Phil. 3:21 he is a. to subdue all
2 Tim. 1:12 he is a. to keep that I
15 scriptures a. to make wise

Heb. 2:18 he is a. to succor them
7:25 is a. to save to uttermost
Jam. 1:21 which is a. to save
Jude 24 to him that is a. to keep
Rev. 5:3 no man was a. to open
Be ABLE
2 Chr. 32:14 should be a. to deliv.
Eze. 33:12 righteous be a. to live
Rom. 8:39 be a. to separate us
Eph. 3:18 be a. to comprehend
6:11 that ye may be a. to stand
Not be ABLE
Luke 13:24 seek, n. be a.; 21:15 to
Not ABLE
Ps. 18:38 wounded not a. to rise
Luke 12:26 not a. to do that is l.
John 21:6 not a. to draw for the f.
Acts 6:10 not a. to resist the w.
ABNER
1 Sam. 14:51 Ner father of A.
ABODE, Verb.
John 1:32 Spirit and it a. on him 39
they came and a. with him
Acts. 1:13 room where a. Peter
14:3 long time a. they speaking
18:3 Paul a. with them and w.
21:7 came and a. with brethren 8
house of Philip and a. with
Gal. 1:18 and a. with Peter
ABOLISHED
Leb. 7:21 touch any a. thing
Deut. 14:3 eat any a. thing
Tit. 1:16 deny him being a.
1 Pet. 4:3 walked in a. idolatries
ABOMINATION
Gen. 43:32 is an a. to Egyptians
Ex. 8:26 sacrifice the a. of Egypt.
Deut. 7:25 it is a. to the Ld.
Prov. 3:32 froward is an a. 6:16
seven things are an a. 12:22 lying
lips are a. to
Prov. 15:8 sacrifi. of w. is a. 21:27
9 of the wicked is an a. 26 of
wicked are a. to L. 16:5 one proud
in heart is a.
Is. 1:13 incense is an a. to me 32:35
that they should do this a.
Ezek. 16:50 and committed a.

1

18:12 to idols and committed a.
Mat. 24:15 a. of desol.

Luke 16:15 is a. with God
Reb. 21:27 enter that worketh a.
These ABOMINATIONS.
Jer. 4:1 wilt put away thine a.
ABOVE
John 8:23 I am from a. ye of
19:11 were given from a.
Col. 3:1 seek things which are a. 2
set your affection on things a.
ABOVE all.
John 3:31 from heaven is a. all
Eph. 3:20 a. all that we ask 4:6 one
God a. all
ABOUND
Prov. 28:20 faithful a. with
Mat. 24:12 iniquity shall a.
Rom 5:20 the offence might a.
6:1 in sin, that grace may a.
Phil. 1:9 love may a. more
1 Thes. 3:12 make you to a. in love
ABOUNDED
Prov. 8:24 no fount a. with
Rom 3:7 of God hath more a.
Co. 2:7 a. therein with thanksg.
2 Thes. 1:3 charity to ea. other a.
ABRAHAM *with* father
Gen. 26:3 the oath to A. thy f.
ABRAHAM *joined with* seed.
2 Chr. 20:7 gavest it to seed of A.
ABROAD.
Rom. 5:5 love of God shed a in
ABSENT
Co. 2:5 I be a. in the flesh
ABSTAIN
1 Pet. 2:11 a. from fleshly lusts
ABUNDANCE
1 Sam. 1:16 out of a. of my
Ps. 72:7 shall be a. of peace
Mat. 12:34 a. of heart. Luke 6:45
Rom. 5:17 receive a. of grace
2 Cor. 8:2 a. of their joy.
ABUNDANT
2 Cor. 4:15 a. grace might
1 Pet. 1:3 his a. mercy
ABUNDANTLY
John 10:10 have life more a.
ACCEPT
1 Sam. 26:19 him a. an offering

2 Sam 32:21 not a. any man's per,
42:8 shall pray, him will I a.
Ps. 20:3 and a. thy burnt-sac.
Prov. 18:5 not good to a. the
ACCEPTABLE
Ps. 19:14 med. of my heart be a.
Phil. 4:18 sac. a. well-pleasing
1 Tim. 2:3 a. in the sight of God
ACCEPTED
Acts 10:35 righteousness is a.
Rom 15:31 service may be a.
ACCESS
Rom. 5:2 also we have a.
Eph. 2:18 have a. to the Father
ACCOMPLISH
Luke 9:31 should a. at Jerusalem
ACCOMPLISHED
Is. 40:2 her warfare is a.
Luke 1:23 his ministration a.
John 19:28 things were now a.
Acts 21:5 had a. those days
ACCORD
Acts 1:14 with one a. in prayer, 2:1
all with one a. in one place - 46
daily with one a. in temple
ACCORDING
Ps. 7:8 judge a. to my righteous,
28:4 give them a. to their deeds,
62:12 to every man a. to his work,
Prov. 24:12, 29
ACCOUNT, Substantive
Ps. 144:3 son of man that thou
Luke 16:2 an a. of stewardship,
Heb. 13:17 that must give a.
ACCOUNT
Luke 20:35 be a. worthy, Rom 8:36
we are a. as sheep
ACCURSED
1 Cor. 12:3 spirit called Jesus a.
Gal. 1:8 gospel, let him be a.
ACCUSATION
1 Tim. 5:19 receive not an a.
ACCUSE
Luke 3:14 nor a. any falsely, 1 Pet.
3:16 falsely a. your good
ACCUSED
Tit. 1:6 not a. of riot, or unruly
ACCUSERS
John 8:10 those thine a.
ACCUSETH
John 5:45 there is one that a. you

ACKNOWLEDGE
Deut. 21:17 a. son of hated, Prov.
3;6 in all thy wyas a. him
1 John 2:23 he that a. the Son
ADAM
Gen. 2:20 A. gave names to all
Deut. 32:8 separated sons of A.
Job 31:33 transgressions as A.
Rom. 5:14 death reigned from A.
1 Cor. 15:22 for as in A. all die
1 Tim. 2:13 A. was first formed
Jude 14 Enoch the 7th from A.
ADD
2 Pet. 1:5 a. to your faith virtue
ADDED
Mat. 6:33 shall be a. to you
Acts 2:41 were a. 3,000 souls
ADMIRATION
Jude 16 men's persons in a.
ADMONISH, ED.
Acts 27:9 Paul a. them
Rom. 15:14 to a. one another
ADMONITION
Eph. 6:4 bring them up in the a.
ADOPTION
Eph. 1:5 predestinated us to a.
ADORN
1 Pet. 3:3 whse a. not outward a.
ADULTERER
Heb. 13:4 a. God will judge
ADULTEROUS
Mat. 12:39 an a. generation, 16:4
ADULTERY
Ex. 20:14 thou shalt not com. a.
Ezek. 16:32 a wife that com. a.
Mat. 5:28 a. in his heart
Mark 10:11 his wife and marry
John 8:3 woman taken in a.
Rom. 2:22 should not commit a.
Gal. 5:19 flesh manifes a.
2 Pet. 2:14 having eyes full of a.
Rev. 2:22 cast them that com. a.
ADVENTURE
Acts 19:31 not a. into the theatre
ADVERSARY
1 Pet. 5:8 your a. the devil
ADVERSARIES
Ps. 38:20 evil for good are my a.
Heb. 10:27 shall devour the a.
ADVOCATE
1 John 2:1 have an a. with the

AFAR, AFAR OFF
Gen. 37:18 say Joseph a. off.
Ps. 65:5 are a. off on the sea
Mark 5:6 he saw Jesus a. off
AFFAIRS
Phil. 1:27 I may hear of your a.
AFFECT
Acts 14:2 their minds evil a.
AFFECTION
Rom. 1:31 without natural a.
Co. 3:2 your a. on things above
AFFECTIONS
Gal. 5:24 crucified flesh with a.
AFFIRMED
Acts 12:15 Rhoda constantly a.
AFFLICTED
Prov. 15:15 days of the a. are evil
Jam. 4:9 a. and mourn and weep
5:13 is any among you a. ? let
AFFLICTION
2 Sam. 16:12 L. look on my a.
Ps. 25:18 my a. and pain
Is. 30:20 L. give water of a.
Jer. 16:19 refuge in days of a.
Lam. 1:7 Jerusa. remem'd in a.
Hos. 5:15 in a. seek me early
Mark 4:17 a. ariseth
Acts 7:11 a dearth and great a.
2 Cor. 2:4 out of much a. I wrote
Phil. 1:16 to add a. to my
1 Thes. 1:6 word in much a.
Heb. 11:25 rather to suffer a.
Jam. 1:27 to visit fatherless in a.
AFFLICTIONS
Acts 7:10 deliver out of all his a.
Co. 1:24 behind of a. of Christ
2 Tim. 1:8 of the a. of the gospel
AFFRIGHT
Job 18:20 that went before a.
AFOOT
Mark 6:33 many ran a. thither
AFORETIME
Rom. 15:4 things were written a.
AFRAID
Ex. 34:30 were a. to come nigh
Neh. 6:9 all made us a.
Job 9:28 a. of all my sorrows
Ps. 56:3 what time I am a.
Mark 5:15 in right mind were a.
Luke 8:25 being a. wondered
Acts 9:26 were all a. of Saul

Gal. 4:11 I am a. of you lest
1 Pet. 3:6 not a. with amazem
2 Pet 2:10 a. to speak evil of dig.
Be AFRAID
Deut. 1:29 nei. be a. of them
Ps. 27:1 of whom shall I be a. ?
Not be AFRAID
Deut. 1:17 not be a. of face
Ps. 3:6 not be a. of ten thous., 56:11
not be a what man can do
Ps. 112:7 not be a. of evil tidings
Rom. 13:3 not be a. of the power
Be not AFRAID
Prov. 3:25 be not a. of sudden
Mat. 17:7 Jesus said, Arise, be not a.
1 Pet. 3:14 be not a. of their
Sore AFRAID
Mark 9:6 for they were sore a.
Was AFRAID
Dan. 8:17 was a. and fell
Hab. 3:2 thy speech and was a.
Mat. 2:22 was a. to go thither
John 19:8 was the more a.
Acts 10:4 Corn's looked, he w.a.
AFTER that
1 Cor. 15:6 a. t. was seen of 500
AFTERWARD
Ps. 73:24 a. receive me to glory
Prov. 29:11 keepeth it in till a.
1 Cor. 15:23 a. that are Christ's
Heb. 12:11 a. yieldeth fruit
AGAINST
Mat. 10:35 man a. his f.
Acts 19:36 cannot be spoken a.
AGE
Gen. 47:28 a. of Jacob 147 years
Ps. 39:5 my a. is as nothing
AGED
Tit. 2:2 that the a. men be sober
Phile. 9 such a one as Paul the a.
AGO
Mat. 11:21 long a.
AGONY
Luke 22:44 in a. he prayed
AGREE
Amos 3:3 walk except they be a.
Mat. 5:25 a. with adversary
1 John 5:8 blood, these a. in one
Rev. 17:17 a. to give their kingd.

AGRIPPA
Acts. 25:13 A. and Bernice came
Acts 26:28 A. said, almost thou per.
AHAB
1 K. 16:30, 33; 18:6, 9, 42, 46
AHIJAH
1 K. 11:29; 12:15; 14:2, 4, 6
AHIKAM
2 K. 22:12 Josiah commanded A.
AHIMELECH
1 Sam. 21:1 A. was afraid at the
AHITHOPHEL
2 Sam. 15:12 Absalom sent for A.
AHOLAH, AHOLIBAH
Ezek. 23:4 Sama. is A. Jerus. A.
AI, OR HAI.
Gen. 13:3 betw. Beth-el and A.
AIR.
2 Sam. 21:10 birds of the a.
Mat. 8:20 birds of a. have nests
Acts 22:23 threw dust into the a.
ALARM
Num. 10:5 when ye blow an a.
2 Chr. 13:12 trumpets to cry an a.
ALAS
Num 24:23 a. who shall live
Joel 1:15 a. for the day of the L.
ALEXANDER
Mark 15:21 Simon, father of A.
Acts 4:6 Annas, Caiaphas, A.
2 Tim. 4:14 A. the coppersmith
ALIEN
Ex. 18:3 been a. in a strange
Ps. 69:8 a. to my mother's child
Is. 61:5 of a. your ploughmen
ALIENATE
Exe. 23:17 her mind was a. from
ALIKE
1 Sam. 30:24 they shall part a.
Ps. 33:15 fashion, their hearts a
Ec. 9:2 all things come a. to all
ALIVE
Gen. 7:23 Noah remained a. and
Lev. 10:16 he was angry with
Jud. 8:19 saved them a. I would
2 K. 5:7 G. to kill and make a.?
Ps. 30:3 L. thou hast kept me a.
Prov. 1:12 swal. a. as the grave
Dan. 5:19 whom would, kept a.
Luke 15:24 was dead and is a
Acts 1:3 a. after his passion

4

Rom. 6:11 a. to God through C.
1 Cor. 15:22 Christ all be made a.
1 Thes. 4:15 are a. and remain, 17
Rev. 1:18 I am a. forevermore

ALL

1 Sam. 9:19 tell thee a. in thy h.
1 K. 20:4 I am thin, and a. I
Job 34:19 they a. are works of his
Ps. 14;3 are a: gone aside, a.
Prov. 22:2 L. is maker of them a.
Ezek. 20:40 a. of them shall serve
Dan. 1:19 among a. none like D.
Mal. 2:10 have we not a. one F.
Luke 4:7 if thou worship me, a.
John 4:39 told me a. ever I did
Acts 4:33 great grace was on a.
Phil. 4:18 I have a. and abound
1 Pet. 3:8 be ye a. of one mind

According to ALL

Gen. 6:22, N. did accor. to a.
Jos. 11:23 took the land ac. to a

For ALL

Phil. 2:21 for a. seek their own
Heb. 8:11 for a. shall know me

In ALL

Gen. 21:12 in a. Sarah hath said
1 Cor. 12:6 God worketh all in a.
Eph. 1:23 him that fill, all in a.

Over ALL

2 Sam. 3:21 mayest reign over a.
John 17:2 giv. him power over a.
Rom. 9:5 over a. God blessed for

To or Unto ALL.

Ec. 2:14 one event to a. 9:3 11
Acts 2:39 promise is to a. afar off
1 Cor. 9:19 a servant unto a.

ALL these

Mat. 6:33 a. t. shall be, Lu. 12:31

ALL this.

Deut. 32:27 hath not done a. this
Ps. 44:17 a. this is come upon us
Ec. 8:9 a. this have I seen and
Mat. 1:22 a. t. was done that
prophets

ALL that he had

Mat. 18:25 he sold a. t. he had
Mark 5:26 she spent a. t. she had

ALLEGORY

Ga. 4:24 which things are an a.

ALLELUIAH

Rev. 19:1 great voice say a. 3, 4, 6

ALLURE

Hos. 2:14 a. her into the wild

ALMIGHTY

Gen. 17:1 I am the a. God, walk
Ex. 6:3 appeared by name God a.
Num 24:4 saw the vision of a. 16
Ruth 1:20 a. hath dealt bitterly
Job 5:17 desp. not chasten. of a.
Ps. 91:1 the shadow of the a.
Exek. 1:24 voice of the a. 10:5
Rev. 1:8 was and is to come, a.

ALMOND

Num. 17:8 rod of Aaron yield a.
Jer. 1:11 I see a rod of an a. tree

ALMOST

Ps. 73:2 my feet were a. gone
Prov. 5:14 I was a. in all evil

ALMS

Mat. 6:1 do not your a. before
Acts 3:3 seeing P. and J. ask a.

ALMSDEEDS

Acts 9:36 Dorcas full of a.

ALOES.

Ps. 45:8 garments smell of a.
John 19:39 brought a mix. of a.

ALONE

Gen. 2:18 good man should be a.
Ps. 83:18 whose name a. is Jeh
Mat. 4:4 live by bread a. Lu. 4:4
Luke 5:21 forgive sins but G. a
Acts 19:26 that not a. at Ephesus
Rom. 4:23 written for his sake a.
Jam. 2:17 faith is dead, being a

Left ALONE

Is. 49:21 I was left a. these where
John 8:9 Jesus was left a and w

Let ALONE

Hos. 4:17 join, to idols, l. him a.
Mat. 15:14 let them a. blind lead
Mark 14:6 Jesus said, let her a.

ALOOF

Ps. 38:11 my friends stand a.

ALPHA

Rev. 1:8 I am a. 11; 21:6; 22:13

ALPHEUS

Mat. 10:3 James, the son of A.

ALREADY

Phil 3:16 we have a. attained
Rev. 2:25 that ye have a. hold f

ALSO

1 Sam. 14:44 S. answ. God do so

John 5:19 these a. doth the Son
1 Cor. 15:8 he was seen of me a.
2 Tim. 1:5 persuaded in thee a.

ALTAR
Gen. 8:20 Noah builded an a.
Gen. 35:1 Beth-el, make there an a.
Lev. 6:9 fire of a. shall be burn.
Num. 7:84 dedication of the a.
Jud. 6:25 throw down a. of B.
2 Sam. 24:18 rear an a. to the L.
2 K. 18:22 shall worship before
Ps. 26:6 will I compass thine a.
Is. 19:19 an a. in midst of Egypt
Amos 2:8 to pledge by every a.
Mat. 5:23 thou bring gift to the a.
Acts 17:23 a. with this inscript.
1 Cor. 9:13 partak. with a. 10:18
Heb. 7:13 attendance at the a.

ALTARS
Ps. 84:3 even thine a. O Lord.
Jer. 17:1 sin graven on horns of a
Hos. 8:11 a. to sin a. shall be
Rom. 11:3 digged down thine a.

ALTER
Ezr. 6:11 whoso. shall a. this
Ps. 89:34 not a. the thing gone

ALTOGETHER
Ps. 14:3 a. filthy, Ps. 53:3 19:9
judgments are righteous a.

ALWAY, S.
Ps. 16:8 have set L. a. before me
Mat. 28:20 I am with you a.
John 8:29 I do a. those things
Phil. 1:4 a. in every prayer

AM I.
Mat. 18:20 there am I in the m.

I AM, I AM that I AM
Ex. 3:14 I am that I am hath
Luke 22:70 ye say that I am
Acts 26:29 altog. such as I am
1 Cor. 15:10 of G. I am what I am
Gal. 4:12 be as I am, for I am as

AMALEK
Gen 36:12 T. bare to Eliphaz A.

AMAZED
Is. 13:8 be a. one at another
Ezek. 32:10 people a. at thee
Mat. 19:25 the disciples were a.
Luke 4:36 all a. and spake among
Acts 9:21 all that heard S. were a.

AMAZEMENT
Acts 3:10 filled with a. at what
1 Pet. 3:6 not afraid with any a.

AMBASSADOR
Prov. 13:17 a faithful a. is health
Eph. 6:20 I am an a. in bonds

AMBASSADORS
Jos. 9:4 as if they had been a.
2 Chr. 35:21 he sent a. saying
Is. 18:2 sendeth a. by the sea
2 Cor. 5:20 we are a. for Christ

AMBUSH
Jos. 8:2 an a. for the city

AMBUSHMENT.
2 Chr. 13:13 Jerob. caused an a.

AMEN
Num 5:22 woman shall say a. a.
1 Chr.16:36 people said a. and
Ps. 41:13 everlasting, a. and a.
Jer. 28:6 even Jeremiah said a.
Mat. 6:13 the glory for ever, a.
2 Cor. 1:20 in him yea and a
Rev. 1:18 alive for evermore a.

AMMON
Gen. 19:38 f. of children of A.

AMMONITE
Deut. 23:3 A. not enter congreg.

AMNON
2 Sam. 3:2 D's first-born was A.

AMORITE
Gen 15:16 iniq. of A. not full

AMOS, OR AMOZ.
2 K. 19:2 Is. the son of A. 20
Amos 7:14 A. said I was no prop.

AMRAM
1 Chr. 1:41 sons of Dishon, A.

ANANIAS
Acts 5:5 A. hearing fell down

ANATHEMA
1 Cor. 16:22 be a. maran-atha

ANATHOTH
Is. 10:30 thy voice, O poor A.

ANCIENT
Dan. 7:9 the a. of days did sit

ANCIENTS
1 Sam. 24:13 proverb of the a.
Is. 3:14 into judgment with a.

ANCLE-BONES
Acts 3:7 a.-b. received strength

ANDREW
Mark 13:3 a. asked privately

ANGEL

Gen. 22:11 a. said, Abraham
Ex. 23:20 send a. before thee,
Num. 20:16 sent an a.
Jud. 13:19 a. did wondrously
2 Sam. 24:16 the a. stretched out
1 K. 13:18 a. spake by the word
1 Chr. 21:15 G. sent an a. to Jeru.
2 Chr. 32:21 an a. which cut off
Ec. 5:6 bef. a. it was an error
Is. 63:9 the a. of his presence
Dan. 3:28 God who hath sent a.
Hos. 12:4 had power over the a.
Zec. 1:9 a. that talked, 4:5
Mat. 28:5 a. answer the women
Luke 1:13 a. said, fear not, ach.
30 the a. said, Fear not, Mary
35 a. answ., Holy Ghost shall
2:10 a. said to the shepherds
13 suddenly with a. a multit.
21 so named of the a.
22:43 an a. strengthening him
John 5:4 a. went down at a c. s.
Acts 6:15 as the face of an a.
7:35 a. that appear. in the bush
10:7 a. which spake to Cornel.
22 warned by a holy a. to send
11:13 he had seen a. in house
12:8 the a. said to Peter, bind
9 true which was done by a.
10 the a. departed from him
11 sent his a. and delivered me
15 then said they, it is his a.
23:8 say, neither a. nor spirit
9 if an a. hath spoken to him
2 Cor. 11:14 transf. into a. of l.
Gal. 1:8 though we or an a.
Rev. 1:1 sig. it by a. to John
5:2 I saw strong a. proclaiming
7:2 a. ascending from the east
8:3 a. came and stood at the al.
4 ascended out of the a. hand
5 a. took the censer
7 first a. sounded; 8 second a.
8:10 third a.; 12 fourth a.
13 I heard an a. flying through
9:1 fifth a. s. 13 sixth a.
11 the a. of the bottomless pit
14 sixth a. loose the four angs.
10:1 a. come down, 18:1; 20:1
5 a. which I saw stand on sea

7 in days of voice of seventh a.
8 take the book in hand of a.
11:15 seventh a. sounded
14:6 a. fly in the midst of heav.
8 another a. saying, Babylon is
19 the a. thrust in his sickle
16:1 a. poured out vial, 3, 4, etc. 5
a. of the waters
17:7 a. said, wherefore marvel?
18:21 mighty a. took up a stone
19:17 an a. standing in the
21:17 of a man, that is of the a.
22:16 I Jesus have sent mine a.

ANGEL of God.

Ex. 14:19 a. of God removed
Jud. 13:6 counten. of a. of God
1 Sam. 29:9 good as an a. of God
Acts 27:23 by me the a. of G.
Gal. 4:14 rec. me as an a. of God

ANGEL of the Lord

Gen. 16:7 a. of the L. found Hag.
Jud. 5:23 Meroz, said a. of L.
16 he was an a. of L. 21
20 a. of the L. ascended
2 Sam. 24:16 a. of the L. was by
the thresh-pl. 1 Chr. 21:15
2 K. 19:35 a. of the L. smote in
1 Chr. 21:12 a. of the L. destroy. 18
a. of the L. commanded G. 30
because of s. of a. of the L.
Ps. 34:7 a. of the L. encampeth
Mat. 1:20 a. of L. ap. in dm. 2:13,·
Luke 1:11 Zacharias an a of L.
Acts 5:19 a. of L. opened prison
8:26 a. of the L. spake to Philip
12:23 a. of the L. smote Herod.

ANGELS

Gen. 19:1 came two a. to Sodom
Ps. 8:5 low. than a. Heb. 2:7,9
68:17 are thousands of a.
78:25 man did eat a.'s food
49 sending evil a. among them
Mat. 4:11 a. ministered. Mk. 1:13
13:39 the reapers are the a. 49 the
a. shall sever the wick.
18:10 their a. behold face of G.
24:36 a. of heaven, Mark 13:32
25:31 all the holy a. with him
26:53 twelve legions of a.
Mark 8:38 Son of man comet with
the holy a. Luke 9:26

7

12:25 are as the a. in heaven
Luke 2:15 as the a. were gone
16:22 was carried by the a.
20:36 equal unto the a.
24:23 also seen a vision of a.
John 20:12 seeth two a. in white
Acts 7:53 by disposition of a.
Rom. 8:38 nor a. able to separate
1 Cor. 4:9 spect. to world, to a.
6:3 that we shall judge a.?
11:10 power because of the a.
13:1 tongues of men and a.
Gal. 3:19 ordained by a.
2 Thes. 1:7 rev. with mighty a.
1 Tim. 3:16 of a. preached to Ge.
5:21 before G. and the elect a.
Heb. 1:4 much better than the a. 5
to which of the a. said he, 13 7 who
maketh his a. spirits
2:2 word spoken by a. steadfast
5 to the a. not put in subject. 16 not
nature of a. but seed
12:22 innum. company of a.
13:2 entertained a. unawares
1 Pet. 1:12 a. desire to look into
3:22 a. and powers beinf subj.
2 Pet. 2:4 if God spared not the a.
11 whereas a greater in power
Jude 6 a. kept not first estate
Rev. 1:20 stars a. of churches
5:11 voice of many a. about th.
7:1 four a. on the four corners
2 with loud voice to the four a.
11 the a. stood round the th.
8:13 trumpet of a. yet to sound
9:14 loose the four a. bound
15 the a. were loosed
14:10 torment in pres. of h. a.
21:12 and the gates twelve a.

ANGELS of God

Gen. 28:12 a. of G. asc. John 1:51
32:1 Jacob went his way, and a of
God met him
Mat. 22:30 but as a. of God in
heaven, Mark 12:25
Luke 12:8 him shall the Son
confess before a. of God
Heb. 1:6 the a. of God worship

His ANGELS

Job 4:18 his a. charged with
Ps. 91:11 give his a. chrage, Mat.

4:6; Luke 4:10
Mat. 13:41 shall send forth his a.

ANGER

Gen. 27:45 thy brother's a. turn
Ex. 32:19 Moses' a. waxed hot
Deut. 9:19 I was afraid of the a.
Job 9:13 G. will not withdraw a.
Ps. 21:9 oven in time of thine a.
90:7 consumed by thine a.
Prov. 15:1 griev. words stir up a.
21:14 a gift in secret pacifieth a.
Is. 5:25 his a. is not turned away
Jer. 2:35 his a. shall turn
Dan. 9:16 let thine a. be turned
Hos. 11:9 not execute mine a.
Amos 1:11 his a. did tear
Jon. 3:9 God turn from firece a.
Mic. 7:18 his a. for ever
Mark 3:5 looked on them with a.

ANGER of the Lord

Num. 25:4 fierce a. of the L.
Deut. 29:20 a. of the L. shall s.
2 K. 24:20 thro' the a. of the L.
Jer. 4:8 a. of the L. is not t.
Lam 4:16 a. of the L. hath
Zep. 2:2 before a. of the L. come

In ANGER

Gen. 49:6 in a. they slew a man
Deut. 29:23 L. overthrew in a.
Job 9:5 overturn them in his a.
Ps. 6:1 not in a. Jer. 10:24
27:9 put not thy serv. away in a.
Is. 13:3 called mighty ones in a.
Jer. 21:5 against you, even in a.
Lam. 2:1 Lord overed Zion with
Ezek. 5:15 execute judgm. in a.

ANGER kindled

Deut. 6:15 lest a. be k. against
2 Sam. 6:7 a. of the Lord was k.

Provoke or Provoked to ANGER

Jud. 2:12 and pr. L. to a.
2 K. 21:15 pr. to a. since day
Ps. 78:58 pro. him to a. with high
Prov. 20:2 whoso pro. to a.
Is. 1:4 pro. Holy One of Is. to a.
Col. 3A:21 pro. not your chil. to a.

Slow to ANGER

Ps. 103:8 slow to a. 145:8
Prov. 15:18 he s. to a. appeaseth

ANGRY

Lev. 10:16 Moses a. with Eleazar

8

Deut. 1:37 L. a. with me 4:21
Prov. 14:7 soon a. dealeth fool
Joh. 4:1 Jonah was very a.
Mat. 5:22 is a. with brother
Eph. 4:26 be a. and sin not
Tit. 1:7 a bishop not soon a.
Rev. 11:18 the nations were a.

ANGUISH
Deut. 2:25 tremble, and be in a
Job 7:11 I will speak in a. of spir.
Ps. 119:143 and a. have taken
Prov. 1:27 when distress and a.
Is. 8:22 and behold dimness of a.
Jer. 4:31 the a. as of her that
John 16:21 no more her a. for joy
Rom. 2:9 tribulation and a. upon
2 Cor. 2:4 out of a. of heart

ANOINT
Ex. 28:41 shalt a. 30:30; 40:15
29:7 take oil and a. hime, 40:13
Jud. 9:8 trees went to a. a king
1 Sam. 9:16 a. him captain
2 Sam. 14:2 a. not thys. with oil
Is. 21:5 princes, a. the shield
Amos 6:6 a. themselves
Mic. 6:15 the olives, but not a.
Mat. 6:17 when thou fastest a.
Mark 14:8 is come to a. my body
Luke 7:46 head thou didst not a.

ANOINTED
1 Chr. 11:3; 14:8
2 Sam. 2:7 Judah have a. me k.
Is 61:1 a. me to preach, Lu. 4:18
Luke 7:38 kissed his feet and a.
John 9:6 he a. the eyes with clay
Acts 4:27 child J. thou hast a.
2 Cor. 1:21 hath a. us is God

ANOINTED Ones.
Zec. 4:14 a. ones which stand

His ANOINTED
1 Sam. 2:10 exalt horn of his a.
2 Sam. 22:51 showeth mercy to
Is 2:2 and against his a.

Lord's ANOINTED
1 Sam. 16:6 Lord's a. is before
10 my hand against Lord's a.

Mine ANOINTED
1 Chr. 16:22 touch not mine a.

ANOINTED with Oil
2 Sam. 1:21 though not a. with o.
Ps. 45:7 a. w. o. of glad. Heb 1:9

Mark 6:13 a. with oil many sick

Thine ANOINTED
2 Chr. 6:42 turn not away the
Ps. 84:9 look on face of thine a.

ANOINTING Oil
Jam. 5:14 a. with o. in name of L.

ANOTHER
2 Cor. 11:4 a. Jesus, a. spirit, or a.

One against ANOTHER
1 Cor. 4:6 puffed up one a. a.

One for ANOTHER
1 Cor. 11:33 tarry one for a.
Jam. 5:16 pray one for a. that ye

ANSWER
Prv. 15:1 soft a. turneth away

ANSWERED
Jud. 8:8 a. as men of Succoth a.
1 Sam. 3:4 he a Here am I, 16

ANSWEREDST
Ps. 99:8 thou a. them, O Lord
138:3 when I cried thou a. me

ANSWEREST
1 Sam. 26:14 a. thou not, Abner?

ANT, S.
Prov. 6:6 the a. thou sluggard
30:25 a. are a people not strong

ANTICHRIST, S.
1 John 2:18 there are many a.
22 a. denieth Father and Son
4:3 spir. of a. whereof ye heard
2 John 7 is a deceiver and an a.

ANTIOCH
Acts 11:26 called Christian first in A.

APOLLOS
1 Cor. 1:12 and I of A. 3:4; 3:5
3:6 I planted, A. watered

APOSTLE
Rom 1:1 Paul, called to be an a.
1 Cor. 9:1 am I not an a. ? 2
15:9 not meet to be called an a.
2 Cor. 1:1 Paul an a. Eph. 1:1;
Col. 1:1; 1 Tim. 1:1; 2 Tim. 1:1;
Gal. 1:1
12:12 the signs of an a.

APOSTLES
Mat. 10:2 names of the twelve a.
2 Pet. 3:2 command. of us the a.

APOSTLESHIP
Acts 1:25 take part of this a.

APPAREL
Acts 1:10 men stood in white a.

9

1 Tem. 2:9 women in modest a.

APPEAL.

Acts 25:11 I a. unto Cesar, 21

APPEAR

Gen. 1:9 let the dry land a.
Mat. 6;16 may a. to men to fast
23:28 ye outwardly a. righteous
24:30 a. the sign of the Son
Rom. 7:13 that it might a. sin
2 Cor. 5:10 a. before judg. seat
Co. 3:4 Christ our life shall a.
1 John 2:28 when he shall a.

APPEAR, referred to God.

Lev. 9:4 to-day L. will a. 6
2 Chr. 1:7 did God a. to Solomon

APPEARANCE

2 Cor. 5:12 which glory in a.
10:7 things after the outward a.

APPEARED

Heb. 9:26 he a. to put away sin

APPEARETH

Jam. 4:14 life as a vapor that a.

APPEARING

1 Pet. 1:7 to praise at the a. of J.

APPLE of the eye

Ps. 17:8 keep me as a. of eye

APPLE-TREE

Joel 1:12 and a.-tree are withered

APPLES

Prov. 25:11 like a. of gold in pic.

APPLIED

Ec. 7:25 I a. my heart to know

APPOINTED

Luke 3:13 exact what is a. you
10:1 Lord a. other seventy
22:29 as Father a. me
Acts 1:23 they a. two, Joseph and
17:31 he hath a. a day in which
1 Cor. 4:9 apostles last, a. to d.
1 Thes. 3:3 that we are a. thereto
5:9 God hath not a. us to wrath
2 Tim. 1:11 I am a. a preacher
Heb. 3:2 faithful to him that a.
9:27 a. to men once to die
1 Pet. 2:8 whereunto they were a.

APPROVE

Phil. 1:10 that ye may a. things

APPROVED

Acts 2:22 Jesus, a man a. of God
Rom. 14:18 accept to G. a. of m

2 Tim 2:15 thyself a. unto God

ARABIA

1 K. 10:15 had kings of A

ARCHANGEL

1 Thes. 4:16 with voice of a.
Jude 9 Michael the a. contend

ARGUMENTS

Job 23:4 fill my mouth with a.

ARIMATHEA

Mat. 27:57 Joseph of A. who

ARISE

Mat. 9:5 easier to say a. Mark 2:9
24:24 shall a. false Christs
Mark 7:41 damsel, a. Luke 8:54
Luke 7:14 L. said, young man a.
Acts 9:40 said, Tabitha, a.
20:30 own selves shall men a.
22:16 a. and be baptized
2 Pet. 1:19 till the day-star a.

ARK

Gen. 6:14 an a. of gopher-wood
7:18 a. went on face of waters
Ex. 2:3 took an a. of burlrush
Heb. 11:7 Noah prepared an a.
Rev. 11:19 in his temple the a.

Before the ARK

Ex. 40:5 set altar of gold a.
Jos. 4:7 w. of Jordan cut off a.
7:6 J. fell on his face be. the a.
1 Sam 5:3 D. was fallen be. the a.

ARK of the covenant

Num 10:33 a. c. of L. went bef.
Deut. 31:26 inside of a. c.
Jos. 4:7 waters cut off before a. c.

ARK of God

1 Sam. 3:3 where a. of G. was
1 Chr. 13:12 bring the a. home

ARMS

Luke 2:28 S. took C. in his a.
ARMEGEDDON Rev. 16:16

ARMED

Prov. 6:11 as an a. man 24:34
Luke 11:21 a strong man a.

ARMIES

Ex. 12:17 your a. out of E.
Num. 33:1 their a. under Mos.
1 Sam. 17:10 defy the a. of Israel

ARMOR

1 Sam 17:54 Goliah's a. in his
Eph. 6:11 put on the a. of God
13 take the whole a. of God

ARMOR-BEARER
Jud. 9:54 Abim. called his a.-b.
ARMY
Rev. 9:16 of a. of horsemen
AROSE
Jud. 2:10 a. a generation that knew not the Lord
5:7 till I Deborah a. a mother
AROSE and went
Jon. 3:3 so Jonah a. to Nineveh
Acts 9:39 Peter a. and went
ARRAY, Verb.
1 Tim. 2:9 not with costly a.
ARRAYED
Mat. 6:29 was not a. like one of
Rev. 7:13 these a. in white
ARROGANCY
Prov. 8:13 pride and a. do I hate
ARROWS
1 Sam 20:20 will shoot three a.
ARTIFICER
Gen. 4:22 T.-Cain an instr. of a.
ASA
1 K. 15:11 A. did right, 2 Chr. 14:2
ASCEND
John 6:62 Son of man a. up
22:17 I a. to my Father
Rev. 17:8 shall a. out of pit
ASCENDING
Gen. 28:12 the angels of God a.
Ps. 74:21 not oppressed turn a.
Rom 1:16 not a. of the gospel
2 Cor. 7:14 I am not a.
2 Tim. 1:12 neverth. I am not a. 16
O. was not a. of my chain
Heb. 2:11 not a. to call them 11:16
not a. to be called
Be ASHAMED
Ps. 6:10 let my enemies be a. 25:3
that wait on thee be a.
2 Cor. 9:4 we (that we say not)
Not be, or Be not ASHAMED
2 Tim. 1:8 a. of testimony of L.
2:15 that needeth not be a.

ASIA
Acts 6:9 of A. disputing Stephen
19:10 all they in A. heard 27 whom
all A. worshippeth
ASK
Mat. 6:8 need of, before ye a.

7:7 a. and it shall be, Luke 11:9 9
his son a. bread, Luke 11:11 11
good things to them that a.
14:7 whatsoever she would a.
18:19 touch, any thing they a.
20:22 what ye a. Mark 10:38
21:22 whatsoever ye a.
22:46 a. him more questions
1 John 3:22 we a. we receive
5:14 we a. according to his will 15
heareth us, whatever we a. 16 not
unto death, he shall a.
ASS
Num 16:15 not taken one a. 22:23
a. saw the angel, 25, 27, 28 opened
the mouth of a. 30
Jud. 15:16 jawbone of an a.
Mat 21:2 shall find an a. tied
ASSEMBLING
Heb. 10:25 forsake not the a.
ASSURE
1 John 3:19 shall a. our hearts
ASSURED
Jer. 14:13 give you a. peace
2 Tim. 3:14 thou hast been a.
ASSYRIA
Gen. 2:14 toward the east of A.
ASTONISHED
Luke 24:22 certain women made us a.
Acts 9:6 Saul trembling and a.
10:45 which believed were a.
12:16 saw Peter, they were a.
ATHENS
Acts 17:15 bro't Paul to A. 16, 22
ATHIRST
Mat. 25:44 when saw we thee a.
Rev. 21:6 give to him that is a.
22:17 let him that is a. come
ATONEMENT
Ex. 30:16 shalt take a. money
Lev. 4:20 a. for them, 26, 31, 35;
5:6;6:7; 8:34; 12:8; 14:18; Num 15:25
9:7 name a. for thyself, 16:24
16:10 the scape-goat to maek a.
34 to make a. once a year 23:28 no
work, it is a day of a. 25:9 day of a.
make trumpet
Num 16:46 make a. for wrath
2 Sam. 21:3 wherewith make a.

11

Rom. 5:11 we have rec. a.
ATTAIN
Ps. 139:6 I cannot a. unto it
Prov. 1:5 man of u. a. wisdom
Hos. 8:5 they a. to innocency?
Phil. 3:11 might a. to resurrec.
ATTAINED
Gen. 47:9 not a. to days of fath.
Rom 9:30 G. have a. to right
31 Is. hath not a. to law
Phil 3:12 I had already a.
ATTENTIVELY
Job 37:2 hear a. noise of his v.
ATTIRE
Prov. 7:10 with a. of harlot
Jer. 2:32 a bride forget her a.?
AUDIENCE
1 Chr. 28:8 in a. of our God
Luke 7:1 his sayings in the a.
Acts 13:16 ye that fear G. give a.
AUGUSTUS
Luke 2:1 decree from Cesar A.
AUTHOR
1 Cor. 14:33 not a. of confusion
Heb. 5:9 became a. of salvation
12:2 Jesus, the a. and finisher
AUTHORITY, IES.
Prov. 29:2 righteous are in a.
Mat. 7:29 having a. Mark 1:22
8:9 a man under a. Luke 7:8
20:25 exercise a. Mark 10:42
21:23 by what a. Mark 11:28
Mark 1:27 for with a. com.
Luke 9:1 power and a. over
John 5:27 a. to execute judgm.
Acts 8:27 eunuch of great a.
1 Cor. 15:24 put down all a.
1 Tim 2:2 suppli. for all in a.
Tit. 2:15 rebuke with all a.
1 Pet. 3:22 and a. made subject to
Rev. 13:2 gave him great a.
AVAILETH
Jam. 5:16 prayer of right a.
AVENGE
Lev. 19:18 thou shalt not a.
Rom. 12:19 a. not yourselves
AVENGED
Gen. 4:24 Cain be a. seven-fold
Acts 7:24 a. him oppressed
Rev. 18:20 God hath a. you
AVENGER

1 Thes. 4:6 Lord is a. of all such
AVOID
Rom. 16:17 divisions, and a.
2 Tim. 2:23 unl. questions a.
Tit. 3:9 a. foolish questions
AVOIDING
1 Tim. 6:20 a. profane babblings
AWAKE
Jud. 5:12 a. a. Deb., a. a. utter
Luke 9:32 when a. saw his glory
John 11:11 that I may a. him
Rom. 13:1 it is high time to a.
1 Cor. 15:34 a. to righteousness
Eph. 5:14 a. thou that sleepest

B

BAAL
Num. 22:41 to high places of B.
1 K. 16:31 B. and worshipped
BAASHA
1 K. 15:16, 19, 27; 16:1, 6, 11, 12
BABBLER
Ec. 10:11 and a b. is no better
Acts 17:18 what will this b. say
BABE, S
Ex. 2:6 behold the b. wept
Luke 1:41 b. leaped in her womb
44 b. leaped in my womb
2:12 find b. wrapped in swad.
16 the b. lying in a manger
Ps. 8:2 mouth of b. Mat. 21:16
17:14 leave substance to their b.
Is. 3:4 princes and b. shall rule
Mat. 11:25 rev. t. to b. Luke 10:21
Rom. 2:20 a teacher of b.
1 Cor. 3:1 as unto b. in Christ
1 Pet. 2:2 as new-born b. desire
BABYLON
Rev. 14:8 B. is fallen, is fallen
16:19 B. came in remembrance
17:5 B. the mother of harlots
BACK, Adjective
Ex. 33:23 shalt see my b. parts
BACKBITERS
Rom. 1:30 b. haters of God
BACKBITETH
Ps. 15:3 that b. not with his
BACKBITING, S
Prov. 25:23 a b. tongue
2 Cor. 12:20 there be debates, b.
BACKSLIDER

Prov. 14:14 b. in heart be filled

BACKWARD

Lam. 1:8 sigheth and turn. b.
John 18:6 went b. and fell to

BAD

1 K. 3:9 discern good and b.
Mat. 13:48 but cast the b. away

BADNESS

Gen. 41:19 never saw in E. for b.

BAG

Hag. 1:6 wages to put in a b. w.
John 12:6 a thief, and had the b.
13:29 because Judas had the b.

BAKE

Lev. 24:5 and b. twelve cakes 26:26
ten women shall b.

BAKETH

Is. 44:15 he b. bread, yea, he

BALAAM

Num. 22:5, 9, 14, 25, 31, 35; 23:4

BALD

2 K. 2:23 go up thou b. head

BALANCE

Job 31:6 be weighed in even b.

BALM

Jer. 8:22 is there no b. in Gilead?

BAND, S

Acts 16:26 every one's b. were lo.
22:30 loosed Paul from his b.

BANDED

Acts 23:12 certain of the Jews b.

BANK

Sam. 20:15 a b. ag. the city
Dan. 12:5 one on this side, other on
that side of the b.

BANKS

Jos. 3:15 Jord. overfl. his b. 4:18

BANNER

Cant. 2:4 his b. over me was

BANQUETING

Cant. 2:4 brought me to the b.

BAPTISM, S

Mat. 3:7 Pharisees come to his b.
20:22 bapt. with b. Mark 10:38
21:25 the b. of J., whence was it?
Mark 11:30; Luke 20:4
Mark 1:4 J. did baptize, and pre.
the b. of repent., Luke 3:3
Luke 7:29 publicans with b. of J.
12:50 a b. to be baptiz. with
Acts 1:22 beginning from b. of J.

10:37 after b. which J. preached
13:24 J. prea. b. of repentance
18:25 Apollos knowing only b.
19:3 they said unto John's b.
4 John bap. with b. of repent.
Rom 6:4 buried with him by b.
Eph. 4:5 one L., one faith, one b.
Col. 2:12 buried with him in b.

BAPTIST

Mat. 3:1 came John b. preaching
11:11 hath not risen a greater than
J. the b. Luke 7:28
12 the days of John the b.
14:2 this is J. the b. he is resen
8 given me John the b. head
16:14 art John b. Mark 8:28
17:13 he spake of John the b.
Mark 6:14 John the b. was risen
25 given me head of John the b.
Luke 7:20 John the b. hath sent 33
J. the b. eating nor drink.
9:19 answering said, J. the b.

BAPTIZE

Mat. 3:6 were b. in J. Mark 1:5
13 then cometh Jesus to be b.
14 I have need to be b. of thee
16 J. when he was b. went up
Mark 1:9 Jesus was b. of John
10:39 baptism I am b. withal
16:16 believeth and is b. shall
Luke 3:7 mult. came to be b.
12 came publicans to be b. 7:29
21 Jesus being b. and praying
7:30 lawyers, being not b.
John 3:22 he tarried, and b.
23 and they were b.
4:1 J. made and b. more disct.
2 though Jesus himself b. not
10:40 place where J. at first b.
Acts 1:5 J. b. with water, but ye
shall be b. with H. G. 11:16
2:28 be b. every one of you
41 received his word were b
8:12 were b. both men and w.
13 Simon, and when he was b.
16 were b. in the name of J.
36 w. doth hinder me to be b.?
38 P. and eunuch, and he b.
9:18 Saul arose and was b.
10:47 these should not be b.
48 P. commanded them to be b.

13

16:15 Lydia when she was b.
33 jailer was b. and all his
18:8 C. believed, and were b.
Acts 19:3 to what were ye b.
5 w. they heard this, were b.
22:16 arise, and be b. and wash
Rom 6:3 b. into Jesus, b. into
1 Cor. 1:13 b. in the name of P.?
14 thank God that I b. none
16 I b. household of S. not b.
10:2 and were all b. to Moses
12:13 one Spirit b. into one body
15:29 are they b. for the dead
Gal. 3:27 as many as b. into Ch.

BARE
Gen. 31:8 the cattle b. speckled

BARE Fruit
Luke 8:8 and b. f. a hundred-fold

BARE and record
Rev. 1:2 b. r. of the word of God

BARK
Is. 56:10 dumb dogs cannot b.

BARLEY
John 6:9 hath five b. loaves

BARN
Luke 12:24 no storehouse nor b.

BARNABAS
Acts 4:36, 11:22, 25, 30; 12:25;
13:1, 2 50; 14:12; 15:2, 12, 37

BARREN
Gen. 11:30 but Sarai was b.

BASIN
1 Chr. 28:17 gold for every b.

BASKET
Ex. 29:23 b. of unleavened bread

BASKETS
Mat. 14:20 twelve b. Mark 6:43;
Luke 9:17; John 6:13

BATTLE
Deut. 20:3 O Israel you ap. to b.
1 Chr. 5:20 cried to God in the b.
Ps. 18:39 girded with str. to b.
24:8 the Lord mighty in b.
Ps. 89:43 not made to st. in the b.
Ec. 9:11 nor b. to the strong
Is. 9:5 every b. of the warrior
1 Cor. 14:8 shall prep. to the b.
Rev. 9:7 like houses prepare to b.

BATTLEMENT.
Deut. 22:8 a b. for thy roof

BAY-TREE
Ps. 37:35 w. like a green b.-t.

BE
Rom. 4:17 things which be not

BEACON
Is. 30:17 left as ab. on the top

BEAM
Mat. 7:3 not b. Luke 6:41, 42 4 a b.
is in thine own eye

BEAR-carry or endure
Gen. 4:13 is greater than I can b.
13:6 not able to b. them, 36:7
Ps. 75:3 I b. pillars of the earth
Prov. 30:21 for four which it cannot
b.
Mat. 3:11 shoes not worthy to b.
Luke 14:27 doth not b. his cross
Rom. 15:1 b. infirm. of the weak
1 Cor. 3:2 hitherto not able to b.
2 Cor. 11:1 would to G. ye could b.
Gal. 6:2 b. one another's burd.
5 shall b. his own burden
17 b. in my body the marks

BEAR - bring forth
Luke 1:13 Elisah, shall b. a son

BEAR rule
Est. 1:22 every man should b. r. in
his own house
Prov.12:24 of dilignet b. r.

BEAR witness
Ex. 20:16 not. b. false w. ag. thy
1 John 1:2 have seen it, and b. w.
5:8 three that b. witness

BEARING
Gen. 1:29 every herb b. seed
16:2 hath restrained me from b.
Jos. 3:3 b. the ark, 14; 2 Sam. 15:24
Ps. 126:6 forth b. precious seed

BEAR.
1 Sam 17:34 came a lion and a b.
36 thy servant slew lion and b.
Prov. 17:12 a b. robbed of whelps

BEARD.
1 Sam. 17:35 caught him by b.

BEAST
Gen. 1:24 earth bring forth b.
Rev. 4:7 first b. like a lion, see. b.
6:3 second b. say, Come
Rev. 11:7 b. that ascendeth out of
13:1 a b. rise up out of the sea 11 b.
coming out of the earth 15:2 got the

victory over the b.
16:13 unclean spirits out of b.
17:8 b. that was, and is not, 11
20:10 the b. and false prophet
EVERY BEAST
Gen. 1:30 to ev. b. I have given
7:2 every clean b. by sevens, 8
14 and every b. after his kind
8:19 every b. went out
9:2 shall be on every b.
Lev. 11:26 ev. b. which divideth
BEASTS.
Gen. 31:39 torn of b. ex. 22:31;
Ex. 11:5 the first b. of b.
Lev. 11:2 b. eat, Deut. 14:4
3 chew cud among b. Deut. 14:6
Rom. 1:23 image made like to b.
1 Cor. 15:32 I have fought with b.
Jam. 3:7 b. is tamed, but tongue
2 Pet. 2:12 as natural brute b.
Jude 10 naturally as brute b.
Rev. 4:6 four b. full of eyes
Rev. 7:11 stood about four b.
BEASTS of the Field,
Ex. 23:11 leave, b. may eat.
WILD BEASTS
1 Sam. 17:46 earc. of Phil. to w. b.
Ps. 50:11 the w. b. are mine
Is. 13:21 w. b. shall lie there
BEAT.
Prov. 23:14 b. him with the rod
Is. 2:4 b, their swords, Mic. 4:3
BEATEN.
Luke 12:47 did not shall be b.
Acts 5:40 apostles and b. them
2 Cor. 11:25 thrice was I b.
BEAUTY.
Ex 28:2 for glory and b.
2 Sam. 1:19 the b. of Israel
14:25 praised as Absalom for b.
Ps. 27:4 behold the b. of the L.
Ps. 96:6 and b. in sanctuary
Prov. 6:25 lust not after her b.
20:29 the b. of old is gray head
31:30 favor is deceitful, b. is v.
BEAUTIES
Ps. 110:3 in the b. of holiness
BEAUTIFUL
Gen. 29:17 Rachel was b.
Ps. 48:2 b. for situation is Zion
Acts 3:2 at the gate called b. 10

BECKONING.
Acts 12:17 Peter b. unto them
BECOME.
John 1:12 to b. the sons of God
2 Cor. 5:17 all things are b. new
BECOMETH.
Ps. 93:5 holiness b. thy house
Prov. 10:4 b. poor that dealeth
Mat. 3:15 it b. us to fulfil
Rom. 16:2 receive P. as b. saints
Phil. 1:27 as b. gospel
1 Tim 2:10 as b. women
BEDCHAMBER.
Ex. 8:3 frogs come into thy b.
BEDS.
Ps. 149:5 sing aloud on b.
Is. 57:2 rest in their b. each
Hos. 7:14 they howled on b.
Amos 6:4 lie on b. of ivory
BEE
Jud. 14:8 swarm of b. in the lion
BEFALL.
Deut. 31:17 evils shall b. them
Ps. 91:10 there shall no evil b.
Acts 20:22 things that shall b.
Come BEFORE.
Ps. 100:2 c. b. presence
BEFORE the people.
Ex. 13:22 pillar of fire from b.
BEFOREHAND.
Mark 13:11 take no thought b.
2 Tim. 1:9 in Christ before the
world b. Tit. 1:2
Heb. 2:3 at first b. to be spoken
BEGAT.
Jam. 1:18 his own will b. he us
1 John 5:1 loveth him that b.
BEGET.
Ec. 6:3 if a man b. 100 children
BEGETTETH.
Prov. 17:21 b. a fool, doeth it
BEG.
Prov. 20:4 sluggard b. in harvest
BEGINNING, Substantive.
Gen. 49:3 Reuben, b. of my st.
At the BEGINNING.
Ruth 3:10 kindness than at b.
From the BEGINNING
2 Pet. 3:4 continue as fr. t. begin.
1 John 2:7 ye have heard b. 3:11

In the BEGINNING.

Gen. 1:1 i. t. b. God created h.

BEGOTTEN.

John 1:14 the only b. of the F.

18 only b. Son, he hath declar.

3:16 he gave his only b. Son

18 not believed in only b. Son

Heb. 11:17 A. offered only b. Son

BEGUN.

2 Cor. 8:6 had b. so would finish

10 for you who have b. before

Gal. 3:3 having b. in the Spirit

Phil. 1:6 hath b. a good work

1 Tim. 5:11 b. to wax wanton

BEHAVE.

1 Cor. 13:5 not b. unseemly

1 Tim. 3:15 how thou oughtest

to b. in the house of God

BEHAVETH.

1 Cor. 7:36 think he b. uncomely

BEHAVIOR.

1 Tim. 3:2 a bishop of good b.

BEHEADED.

Mat. 14:10 b. John, Mark, 6:16,

27; Luke 9:9

BEHELD.

John 1:14 we b. his glory

Acts 1:9 they b. J. was taken up

17:23 and b. your devotions

Rev. 5:6 I b,. and lo a lamb

BEHEMOTH.

Job 40:15 behold now b.

BEHOLD

1 John 3:1 b. what manner of love

Rev. 3:20 b. I stand at the door

BEHOLD, Verb.

Ec. 11:7 pleasant it is to b.

Mat. 18:10 their angels b. face

Luke 14:29 all that b. it mock

John 17:24 they may b. my glory

Acts 7:31 he drew near to b. it.

2 Cor. 3:7 Is. could not b. face

1 Pet. 2:12 works they shall b.

BEHOLDING.

Ps. 119:37 mine eyes from b.

Prov. 15:3 b. the evil and good

Mat. 27:55 women b. Luke 23:49

Acts 4:14 and b. man healed

2 Cor. 3:18 b. as in a glass the g.

Jam. 1:23 b. his natural face

BELIEF.

2 Thes. 2:13 of Spirit and b.

BELIEVE.

Ex. 4:5 may b. L. hath appeared

Luke 8:12 the word lest they b.

John 1:7 all thro' him might b.

Acts 8:37 I b. J. C. is the S. of G.

Rom. 3:22 on all that b.

2 Cor. 4:13 we b. therefore speak

Gal. 3:22 promise to them that b.

Eph. 1:19 to us who b.

Phil. 1:29 given not only to b.

1 Thes. 1:7 ensamples to all th. b.

2 Thes. 1:10 admi. in all that b.

1 Tim. 1:16 pat. to them that b.

Heb. 10:39 b. to saving of soul

Jam. 2:19 devils also b.

1 Pet. 1:21 by him do b. in God

John 3:23 com. that we b.

BELIEVE not, or not BELIEVE.

2 Tim. 2:13 if we b. not, be abid.

1 John 4:1 b. not every spirit

BELIEVED.

2 Tim. 1:12 whom I have b.

Tit. 3:8 which have b. in God

Heb. 4:3 we which b. do enter

1 John 4:16 b. the love of God.

Many BELIEVED.

John 2:23 at the pass, many b.

Acts 19:18 m. b. confess, their d.

BELIEVERS.

Acts 5:14 b. were the more added

1 Tim. 4:12 an example of the b.

BELIEVEST.

Luke 1:20 dumb, bec. thou b. not

BELIEVETH.

1 John 5:1 whoso b. J. is the C.

5 overcometh, but he that b.

10 b. on the Son; he that b. n.

G. bec. he b. not the record

BELIEVING.

Mat. 21:22 ask b. ye shall receive

Acts 16:34 b. in God

Rom. 15:13 joy and peace in b.

1 Tim. 6:2 that have b. masters

1 Pet. 1:8 yet b. ye rejoice

BELLY.

Gen. 3:14 on thy b. shalt thou go

Lev. 11:42 goeth on the b.

BELONG.

Prov. 24:2 these b. to the wise

Dan. 9:9 to the Lord b. mercies
Mark 9:41 bec. ye b, to Christ
Luke 19:42 which b. to thy p.]
1 Cor. 7:32 things b. to Lord
BELONGETH.
Deut. 32:35 to me b. vengeance,
   Ps. 94:1; Heb. 10:30
Ps. 3:8 salvation b. unto the L.
BELOVED.
Eph. 1:6 accepted in the b.
  6:21 T. a b. brother. Col. 4:7
Col. 3:12 elect of G. holy and b.
1 Thes. 1:4 kn. b. your election
1 Tim. 6:2 serv. bec. they are b.
Phile. 16 a servant a brother b.
Heb. 6:9 b. we are persuaded
2 Pet. 3:8 b. be not ignorant
1 John 3:2 b. now we are the sons
  4:1 b. believe not every spirit
  7 b. let us love one another
  11 b. if God so loved us, we
3 John 11 b. follow not evil,
Jude 20 but ye b, building up
BEND.
Ps. 11:2 wicked b, their bow
BENDING.
Is. 60:14 that afflicted thee shall
  come b. to thee
BENEFIT.
Phile. 14 b. not be of necessity
BENEVOLENCE.
1 Cor. 7:3 render to the w. due b.
BENJAMIN.
Gen. 35:18 his f. called him B.
BENJAMITES.
Jud. 19:16 men of pl. were B.
BEREAVE.
Jer. 15:7 I will b. them, 18:21
Ezek. 5:17 send evil beasts, and
  they shall b. thee
BEREAVED.
Gen. 42:36 ye have b. of my ch.
Hos. 13:8 meet them as a bear b.
BESEECH.
Amos 7:2 forgive I b. thee
Mal. 1:9 b. God, he be gracious
Rom. 12:1 I b. you by mercies
1 Cor. 4:16 I b. ye followers
BESOUGHT.
2 Cor. 12:8 for this I b. the Lord

BEST.
1 Cor. 12:31 covet the b. gifts
BESTEAD.
Is. 8:21 pass thro' it hardly b.
BESTOW.
1 Cor. 12:23 on these we b. more
  13:3 though I b. all my goods
BESTOWED.
1 John 3:1 manner of love F. b.
BETHABARA. John 1:28
BETHANY.
Mat. 21:17 went into B. 26:6
BETH..EL.
Gen. 28:19 c. the place B. 35:15
  31:13 I am God of B.
BETH LEHEM.
2 Sam, 23:15 well of B. 1 Ch.
11:17
Mat. 2:1 Jesus born in B. 6, 16
BETHSAIDA.
Mat. 11:21 thee, B, 1 Luke 10:13
BETRAY.
1 Chr. 12:17 come to b. me
Mat. 24:10 shall b. one another
Mark 13:12 brother shall b. bro.
John 6:64 should b. him, 13:11
  13:2 into heart of Judas to b.
BETRAYED.
Mat. 10:4 J. who b. him, Mark
  3:19
17:22 S. of m. shall be b. 20:18;
  26:2, 45; Mark 14:41
26:24 Son of man is b. Mark
  14:21; Luke 22:22
  48 he that b. Mark 14:44
27:4 I b. innocent blood
Luke 21:16 be b. both by parents
BETROTHED.
Ex. 22:16 entice a maid not b.
BETTER.
18:6 b. that a millstone, Mark
  9:42; Luke 17:2
Rom. 3:9 are we b. than they?
Phil. 2:3 esteem other b. than
Heb. 1:4 much b. than the angels
BETTER is.
Prov. 15:16 b. is little with f. of L
Is BETTER, or is it BETTER.
Prov. 3:14 wisdom is b.
9:4 a liv. dog is b. than a d. lion
16 wisdom is b. than strength

18 wisd. is b. than w. of war
Phil. 1:23 with C. wh. is far b.
**It is BETTER, or BETTER
it is.**
Ps. 118:8 it is b. to trust in L. 9
Prov. 16:19 b. to be of humble
BEWARE
Mark 12:38 b. of s. Luke 20:46
Luke 12:15 b. of covetousness
Acts 13:40 b. lest that come
Phil. 3:2 b. of dogs, b. of evil w.
Col. 2:8 b, lest any man spoil
2 Pet. 3:17 b. lest being led
BEWITCHED.
Acts 8:9 Simon b. the people, 11
BEYOND.
Gal. 1:13 b. measure I persecut.
1 Thes. 4:6 that no man go b.
BID.
1 Cor. 10:27 any that bel. not o
2 John 10 nor b. him God speed
BIND.
Prov. 3:3 b. them about thy neck
6:21 b. them upon thy heart
Ezek. 34:16 I will b. up broken
Hos. 6:1 smitten and will b. us
Mat. 12:29 first b. the strong
13:30 b. tares to burn them
16:19 shall b. on earth, 18:18
Acts 9:14 authority to b. all that
BIRD.
Gen. 7:14 every b. went into
Amos 3:5 a b. fall where no gin
Rev. 18:2 every unclean b.
BIRTH.
Mat. 1:18 the b. of Jesus Christ
Luke 1:14 shall rejoice at his b.
Gal. 4:19 I travail in b.
Rev. 12:2 she cried, trav. in b.
BIRTHDAY
Gen. 40:20 which was Ph.'s b.
BIRTHRIGHT.
Gen. 25:31 this day thy b.
33 sold his b. to Jacob
1 Chr. 5:1 R.'s b. to sons of Jos.
BISHOP
1 Tim. 3:1 desire the office of a b.
BITE.
Ec. 10:8 a serpent bite b.
BITTER.
Gen. 27:34 E. cried with b. cry

Ex. 1:14 made their lives b.
12:8 with b. herbs, Num. 9:11
Jam. 3:14 if ye have b. envying
Rev. 8:11 men died of waters b.
BITTERLY.
Jud. 5:23 curse ye b. the inhab.
Ruth 1:20 Almighty hath dealt b.
Mat. 26:75 P. wept b. Luke 22:62
BITTERNESS.
1 Sam. 1:10 Hannah was in b.
Prov. 14:10 heart knoweth his b.
17:25 a foolish son is b. to her.
Is. 38:15 softly in b. of my soul.
Eph. 4:31 let all b. be put away
Heb. 12:15 lest any root of b.
BLACK.
Prov. 7:9 in the b. and dark n.
Rev. 6:5 and lo, a b. horse
BLACKNESS.
Is. 50:3 clothe heavens with b.
Joel 2:6 shall gath. b. Nah. 2:10
BLAME.
Eph. 1:4 holy and without b.
BLAMELESS.
Luke 1:6 in ordin. of the L. b.
1 Cor. 1:8 b. in the day of our L.
Phil. 2:15 be b. and harmless
1 Thes. 5:23 body be preserved b.
2 Pet. 3:14 ye may be found b.
BLASPHEME.
Mark 3:28 they shall b.
29 that shall be ag. Holy G.
BLASPHEMED.
Rom. 2:24 name of God is b.
1 Tim. 6:1 his doctrine be not b.
BLASPHEMEST,ETH.
Lev. 24:16 whoso b. the Lord
Ps. 44:16 voice of him that b.
BLASPHEMING.
Acts 13:45 J. contradicting and b.
BLASPHEMER
Acts 19:37 are not b. of your god.
BLASPHEMY.
Mat. 12:31 all manner of b. shall
Mark 7:22 out of heart proceed b.
BLASPHEMIES.
Luke 5:21 who is this speak. b.?
Rev. 13:5 speaking b.
BLEMISH.
Eph. 5:27 holy and without b.
1 Pet. 1:19 of a lamb without b.

18

BLESS.

1 Cor. 10:16 cup of bless. we b.

BLESS, God being agent.
Gen. 12:2 I will b. thee, 16:3, 24
Num. 6:24 Lord b. and keep thee
Deut. 7:13 b. the fruit of thy w.
2 Sam 7:29 to b. the hous of
1 Chr. 4:10 wouldst b. me indeed
Ps. 5:12 wilt b. the righteous
 13 he will b. them that fear L.
132.15 abundantly b. her prov.
Is. 19:25 L. of hosts shall b.
Hag. 2:19 from this day will I b.
Acts 3:26 sent him to b. you

BLESS, God being the object.
Ps. 16:7 b. L. who hath given
26:12 in the cong. will I b. Lord
34:1 b. the Lord at all times
63:4 will I b. thee while I live
66:8 O b. our God
103:1 b. L. O my soul, 2,22;
 104:1, 35
22 b. the Lord all his works
115:18 will b. L. from this time
135:19 b. the L. O house of Is.
Jam. 3:9 therewith b. we God

BLESS, man agent and object.
Gen. 27:4 b. thee before I die, 25
 34 b. me, O my father, 38
Num. 6:23 on this wise b. Israel
Deut. 10:8 separ. Levi to b. 21:5
1 Sam. 9:13 doth b. the sacrifice
2 Sam. 6:20 David returned to b.
1 K.1:47 came to b. our lord k.D.
1 Chr. 23:13 to b. in his name
Rom. 12:14 b. and curse not
1 Cor. 4:12 being reviled we b.

BLESSED, Man agent and
 object.
Gen. 14:19 Melchized. b. Abra.
Ps. 49:18 lived he b. his soul
 72:17 men be b. in him
118:26 b. be he that cometh in
 name of the L. we ha. b. you
Prov. 31:28 children call her b.
Is. 66:3 as if he b. an idol
Jer. 20:14 let not the day be b.
Mal. 3:12 all nations call you b.
Mark 11:10 b. be king, of our f.
Luke 1:48 gen. shall call me b.
Acts 20:35 it is more b. to give

Tit. 2:13 looking for that b. hope
Heb. 7:1 met Abraham b. him, 6
 7 the less is b. of the better

BLESSED, God the agent.
Gen. 1:22 b. Be fruitful, 28; 5:2
Num. 22:12 for the people are b.
Deut. 2:7 thy God hath b. thee,
 119:1 b. are the undefiled
Ps. 128:1 b, is every one that fear.
Prov. 5:18 let thy fountain be b.
Mat. 5:3 b. poor in spirit, 5 meek
 7 merciful, 8 pure in heart
 9, peacemakers, 10 persecuted
13:16 b. are y. eyes, Luke 10:23
14:19 b. and br. 26:26; Mark
 6:41; 14:22; Luke 9:16; 24:39
16:17 b. art thou, S. Bar-jona
24:46 b. is that serv. Luke 12:43
25:34 come, ye b. of my Father

BLESSED, God the object.
Gen. 14:20 b. be most high God
Jos. 22:33 children of Is. b. God
2 Sam. 22:47 b. be my r. Ps. 18:46
1 Chr. 29:10 D. b. the L. b. be L
2 Chr. 20:26 for there they b. L.
Job 1:21 b. be name, Ps. 113:2
Ps. 66:20 b. be G. 68:35; 2 Cor. 1:3
 119:12 b. art thou, O Lord
Dan. 2:19 b. the G. of heaven, 20
 4:34 Nebuch. b. the Most High
Luke 2:28 in his arms and b. God
John 12:13 b. is theKing of Is.
Rom. 1:25 who is b. for ever
Eph. 1:3 b. be the F. 1 Pet. 1:3
1 Tim. 1:11 gospel of the b. God

BLESSED are they.
Ps. 2:12 b. a. t. that trust
Prov. 8:32 b. a. t. that keep my w.
Mat. 5:4 b. are they that mourn
Luke 11:28 rather b. hear the w.
John 20:29 b. have not seen
Rom. 4:7 b. are they whose iniq.

BLESSED are ye.
Mat. 5:11 b. when m. shall revile
Luke 6:21 b. are ye that hunger,
 be filled; b. a. ye that weep

BLESSED is he.
Num. 24:9 b. is he that blesseth
Ps. 32:1 b. is he who transg.
Mat. 11:6 b. is he whoso. shall not
21:9 b. is he that cometh in the

19

name of the Lord, 23:39;
Rev. 1:3 b. is he that readeth

BLESSED is the man.
Ps. 1:1 b. is the m. that walk, not
Jam. 1:12 b. that end, temptation

BLESSING, Substantive.
Zec. 8:13 and ye shall be a b.
Mal. 3:10 and pour you out a b.
1 Cor, 10:16 the cup of b. we bless
1 Pet. 3:9 but contrariwise b. that

BLESSINGS.
Prov. 10:6 b. are upon the just
28:20 shall abound with b.
Mal. 2:2 and will curse your b.
Eph. 1:3 with all spiritual b.

BLIND, Adjective.
Ex. 4:11 who maketh the b.?
Lev. 19:14 stumb,-block before b.
Jer. 31:8 the b. and lame
Lam. 4:14 wandered as b. men
Zep. 1:17 walk like b. men
Mat. 9:27 two b men. 20:30
Mark 8:23 took b. man by the h.
Luke 4:18 recovery of sight to b.
John 5:3 a great multitude of b.
Acts 13:11 thou shalt be b.
Rom. 2:19 art & guide to the b.
2 Pet. 1:9 lack, these things is b.
Eph. 4:18 because of b. of their h.

BLOOD.
Where marked with + it is in the
 original BLOODS.
Gen. 4:10 + thy brother's b.
Prov. 28:17 violence to b. of any
Is. 1:15+ hands are full of b.
Mat. 9:20 w. with an issue of b.
Luke 13:1 whose b. P. mingled
44 sweat as great drops of b.
John 1:13 born not of b.
55 and my b. is drink indeed
19:34 forth. came there out b.
Acts 5:28 to bring this man's b.
Col. 1:20 through b. of his cross
Heb. 2:14 partak, of flesh and b.
1 Pet. 1:2 sprinkling of the b.
1 John 1:7 b. of J. C. cleanseth
5:6 came by water and b.
8 the Spirit, water, and b.

BLOOD of Christ.
1 Cor. 10:16 com, of b. of C.
Eph. 2:13 made nigh by b. of C.

Heb. 9:14 shall b. purge?
1 Pet. 1:19 with precious b. of C.
1 John 1:7 the b. of C. cleanseth

BLOOD of the Covenant.
Ex. 24:8 M, said Behold the b.
Zec. 9:11 for thee also by b. of c.
Heb. 10:29 b. of cov. unholy thing
13:20 b. of the everlasting cov.

His BLOOD.
Gen. 37:26 and conceal his b.
Acts 20:28 ch. purchased with h. b.
Rom. 3:25 thro' faith in his b.
5:9 justified by his b.

Innocent BLOOD.
Jon 1:14 L, lay not on us inno. b.
Mat. 27:4 I betrayed innocent b.

Shed BLOOD.
10 reveng. b. of thy servants sh.
Prov. 1:16 b. to shed b. Rom. 3:15
Lam. 4:13 shed the b. of the just
Mat. 23:35 the righteous b. s.
Mark 14:24 this is my b. which
 is shed, Luke 22:20

With BLOOD.
Ex. 30:10 A. make atone. with b.
Lev. 19:26 not eat any th. with b.
1 K. 2:9 bring thou down with b.

BLOOD-THIRSTY.
Prov. 29:10 b. th. hate upright

BLOT out.
2 K. 14:27 would b. out name
Ps. 51:1 b. out rransgress.

BLOTTED.
Neh. 4:5 let not their sin be b.
Ps. 69:28 b. out of book of the l.

BOAST, Substantive.
Ps. 34:2 shall make her b.
Rom. 2:17 makest thy b. of God
28 makest thy b. of the law

BOAST, Verb.
1 K. 20:11 not b. as he
Prov. 27:1 b. not of to-morrow

BOASTING, Substantive.
Rom. 3:27 where is b. then?
2 Cor. 7:14 our b. before Titus
Jam. 4:16 ye rejoice in your b.

BOAT, S.
John 6:22 no other b. there, Jesus
Ruth 2:1, 19, 3:2; 4:1; Lu. 3:32

BODY.
Mat. 5:29 b. be cast into hell, 30

Mark 5:29 she felt in her b.
John 20:12 b. of Jesus had lain
Rom. 6:6 b. of sin be destroyed
2 Cor. 5:8 to be absent from b.
Eph. 3:6 heirs of the same b.
16 from whom the whole b.
5:23 he is the Savior of the b.
Col. 1:18 head of the b. the ch

HIS BODY.
John 2:21 temple of his b.
Acts 19:12 from his b. were br.
Phil. 3:21 like his glorious b.
1 Pet. 2:24 bare our sins in his b.

In BODY.
Rom. 6:12 in your mortal b.
1 Cor. 5:3 I verily as absent in b.
2 Cor. 4:10 in b. the dy. of the L.
Gal. 6:17 I bear in b. the marks

One BODY.
Rom. 12:4 members in one b.
Col. 3:15 also called in one b.

BODIES
Amos 8:3 d. in every place

BODILY.
Col. 2:9 fulness of the Godh. b.

BOIL.
Job 41:31 the deep to b. like a pot

BOLD.
Prov. 28:1 right, are b. as a lion
Phile. 8 I might be much b. in C.

BOLDLY.
Mark 15:43 Joseph went in b.
Heb. 4:16 b. to the thr. of grace

BONDS
Eph. 6:20 am an ambassa. in b.
Phil. 1:7 in b. ye are all partak.

BONDAGE.
Ex. 1:14 bitter with hard b.

BONES.
Ex. 13:19 M. took b. of Joseph
Ps. 51:8 b. thou hast broken
Prov. 3:8 marrow to thy b.
15:30 good report maketh b. fat
17:22 broken spirit drieth the b.
Is. 58:11 shall make fat thy b.
Mat. 23:27 full of dead men's b.
Luke 24:39 a spirit hath not b.

His BONES.
Prov. 12:4 rottenness in his b.

MY BONES.
Ps. 6:2 heal me, my b. are vexed

Is. 38:13 will he break all my b.

BOOK.
Ezek. 2:9 roll of a b. was therein
Dan. 12:1 ev. one writ. in the b.
4 O Daniel, seal the b.
Nah. 1:1 b. of vision of Nahum
Mal. 3:16 a b. of remembrance
Mat. 1:1 b. of the gen. of Jesus
Luke 3:4 written in the b. of E.
Acts 7:42 in b. of the prophets
Heb. 9:19 sprinkled the b. and
Rev. 1:11 write in a b.

BOOK of the Law.
Deut. 31:26 b. of l. put it in ark

BOOK of Life.
Phil. 4:3 writ, in the b. of life
Rev. 3:5 name out of b. of l.

BOOTH.
Jon. 4:5 Jonah made him a b.

BORDER, Verb.
Zeg. 9:2 H. shall b. thereby

BORDERS.
Cant. 1:11 will make b. of gold

BORN, for brought forth.
Gen 17:17 b. him 100 yrs. old, 21:5
Ec. 3:2 a time to be b.
1 Pet. 2:2 as new b. babes desire
1 John 2:29 righte, is b. of him

BORN again.
John 3:3 except a man be b. a. 5

BORN of God.
John 1:13 b. n. of blood, but of G.'

BORN of a woman
Job 14:1 man b. of a w.

BORNE, carried.
Is. 46:3 b. by me from the belly
Jer. 10:5 they must be b. because
Amos 5:26 have b. tab. of Moloch
Mark 2:3 one sick of palsy was b.

BORNE, endured.
Job 34:31 I have b. chastisement
Ps. 55:12 then I could have b.
Mat. 20:12 b. burden and heat

BORROW.
Ex. 3:22 ev. wom. shall b. 11:2
Deut. 15:6 shalt not b. 28:12
2 K. 4:3 E. said, Go b. vessels
Mat. 5:42 him that would b.

BORROWER.
Prov. 22:7 b. is servant to lender

BOSOM.

Mic. 7:5 lieth in thy b.
Luke 6:38 good m. into your b.
  16:22 by angel's into Ab,'s b.
John 1:18 the b. of the Father

BOTTLE.

Gen. 21:14 b. of water gave it H.

BOTTLES.

Mat. 9:17 new wine into old b.

BOTTOM.

Mat. 27:51 veil rent from top to b.
Mark 15:38

BOTTOMLESS.

Rev. 9:1 to him key of the b. pit

BOUGHT.

Mat. 13:46 sold all, b. that field
1 Cor. 6:20 ye are b. 7:23

BOUND, actively

Gen. 22:9 b. Isaac his son

BOUND up.

Luke 10:34 he b. up his wounds

BOWS.

1 Sam. 2:4 the b. of mighty
Neh. 4:16 half of them held b.
Ps. 37:15 b. shall be broken

BOW, Verb.

Eph. 3:14 b. my knees to the F.

BOW knee.

Phil. 2:10 every knee shall b.

BOWED head.

John 19:30 Jesus b. his head

BOWL.

Zec. 4:2 candlestick with a b.

BRANCH.

Prov. 11:28 shall flour, as a b.
Is. 4:2 shall b. of the L. be beau.
  9:14 Lord will cut off b.
Mal. 4:1 it shall leave root n or b.
Mat. 24:32 b. yet t. Mark 13:28
John 15:2 every b. that beareth

BRANCHES.

Joel 1:7 b. thereof are m. white
Nah. 2:2 marred their vine b.

Iron and BRASS.

Dan. 2:35 was iron b. broken, 45

Vessels of BRASS.

Jos. 6:19 all v. of b. are consec.

BRAVERY.

Is. 3:18 will take away their b.

BRAWLING.

Prov. 25:24 a b. woman, 21:19

BRAZEN.

2 K. 18:4 brake the b. serpent

BREAD.

Deut. 8:3 man doth not live by b.
  only, Mat. 4:4; Luke 4:4
Ps. 37:25 his seed begging b.
  78:20 can he give b.?
Prov. 9:17 b. eaten in secret
  11:1 cast thy b. upon the waters
Mat. 4:3 st. be made b. Luke 4:3
  6:11 our daily b. Luke 11:11
  7:9 if his son ask b. will he give
Acts 2:42 con. in breaking of b.
1 Cor. 10:16 b, we break is it not

Leavened BREAD.

Ex. 13:3 shall no l. b. eaten
Chr. 16:3 to every one l. of b.

Piece, or Pieces of BREAD.

1 Sam. 2:36 I may eat a p. of b.
Prov. 6:26 to a piece of b.

Unleavened BREAD.

Ex. 12:18 eat w. u. b. Num 9:11
Deut. 16:8 six days sh. eat un. b.
Ezek. 45:21 passover of un. b.
Mark 14:12 first day of un. b.

BREADTH.

Eph. 3:18 the b. and length
Rev. 20:9 up on b. of the earth
  21:16 length of city is as the b.

BREAK.

Mat. 5:19 b. one of least com.
  9:17 the bottles b. and the wine
Acts 20:7 came tog. to b. bread.
  21:13 mean ye to b. my heart?
1 Cor. 10:16 bread we b. is it not

BREAK covenant.

Lev. 26:44 I will not b. my cov.
Deut. 31:16 will b. my c. 20
Jud. 2:1 I will never b. my c.

BREAKER

Mic. 2:13 b. is come up before

BREAST

John 13:25 lying on J.'s b. 21:20

BREASTPLATE.

Eph. 6:14 the b. of righteousness
1 Thes. 5:8 the b. of faith and lo.

BREATH.

Gen. 2:7 into his nostrils b. of l.
Ec. 3:19 they have all one b.
Is. 2:22 b. in his nostrils
Jer. 10:14 no b. in them, 51:17

22

Lam. 4:20 the b. of our nostrils
Ezek. 37:5 b. to enter you
Dan. 5:23 in whose hand thy b.
BREATHED.
Gen. 2:7 b. into nostrils b. of life
BRETHREN
Prov. 6:19 soweth discord am. b.
17:2 shall have part among b.
Mat. 4:18 Jesus saw two b. 21
Mark 10:29 no man hath left b.
Luke 14:26 hate not children b.
John 21:23 went among the b.
Rom. 1:13 not have you ignor. b.
11:25; 1 Cor. 10:1; 12:1; 1 Thes.
4:13
Gal. 1:2 b. with me to churches
Eph. 6:23 peace be to the b. and
Col. 1:2 to faithful b. in Christ
1 Thes. 4:1 we beseech you b. 10;
His BRETHREN.
Mat. 12:46 his b. stood without,
Mark 3:31; Luke 8:19
John 7:5 his b. believe in him
Acts 7:13 was made known to h.b.
23 into M.'s heart to visit h. b.
Men and BRETHREN.
Acts 1:16 m. b. this scripture.
MY BRETHREN.
Mat. 12:48 are my b. Mark 3:33
Our BRETHREN.
Num. 20:3 when our b. died
1 Chr. 13:2 let us send to our b.
Neh 5:5 as flesh of our b.
Your BRETHREN.
Gen. 42:33 leave one of your b.
Lev. 10:4 carry y. b. from sanct.
Mat. 5:47 if ye salute your b.
1 Cor. 6:8 defraud that your b.
1 Pet. 5:9 same afflic. in your b.
BRIBE, S.
1 Sam. 8:3 Samuel's sons took b.
BRIDE.
Is. 49:18 bind them, as a b. doth
61:10 as a b. adorn. with jewels
John 3:29 he that hath the b. is
Rev. 18:23 voice of b. heard
21:2 b. adorned for her husband
9 show the b. the Lamb's wife.
BRIDEGROOM.
Mat. 9:15 while the b. is with
them, Mark 2:19; Luke 5:34

25:1 ten virgins to meet the b.
BRIDLE
2 K. 19:28 b. in thy lips, Is. 37:29
BRIGHT.
Job 37:11 scattereth his b. cloud
Rev. 22:16 b. and morning star
BRIMSTONE.
Rev. 21:8 part in the lake which
burneth with fire and b.
BRING.
Gen. 6:17 b. a flood on the earth
19 two of every sort b. into ark
2 Sam. 3:12 to b. all Israel to thee
13 except thou b. Michal when
Prov. 29:8 scornful b. a city
Ec. 3:22 shall b. him to see
2 Cor. 11:20 if a man b. you
Gal. 3:24 schoolm. to b. us to C
BRING again.
Zep. 3:20 at that time b. you a
Zec. 10:6 b. them again to place
10 I will b. them a. out of E.
BRING down.
Gen. 42:38 b. d. gray h. 44:29, 31
BRING forth.
Rom. 7:4 that we shall b. f. fruit
5 motions of sin to b. f.
BRING up.
Hos. 9:12 they b. up children
Rom. 10:7 to b. up C. from the d.
BRINGETH.
Mat. 3:10 every tree that b. not
forth g. fruit, 7:19; Luke 3:9
7:17 good tree b. forth g. fruit
Jam. 1:15 b. forth sin, and sin b.
BROAD.
Neh. 3:8 they fortified Jerusalem
to the b. wall, 12:38
Mat. 7:13 b. way to destruction
BROKEN.
1 Cor. 11:24 my body b. for you
Rev. 2:27 as ves. shall they be b.
BROKEN-HEARTED.
Is. 61:1 to bind up the b.-h.
Luke 4:18 to heal the b. - h.
BROOD.
Luke 13:34 hen doth gather b.
BROOK.
John 18:1 went over b. Cedron
BROOKS.
Ps. 42:1 hart pant. after wat.-b.

23

His BROTHER.

1 John 2:9 and hateth his b. 11

10 loveth his b. abideth in lig.

My BROTHER.

Gen. 4:9 C, said, Am I my b. kee.

Thy BROTHER.

Mat. 5:23 that t. b. hath aught

24 first be reconciled to thy b.

BROTHERLY.

Heb. 13:1 let b. love continue

2 Pet. 1:7 to godliness b. kindness

BROUGHT.

2 Tim. 1:10 b. life and immortal.

1 Pet. 1:13 grace that is b. to you

2 Pet. 2:19 of same is he b.

BROUGHT back.

1 K. 13:23 prophet he had b. back

BROUGHT down.

Ps. 20:8 they are b. d. and fallen

107:12 he b. d. their heart

Is. 5:15 mean man shall be b. d.

14:11 thy pomp is b. down

15 shall be b. down to hell

BROUGHT forth.

Mat. 1:25 she had b. f. first-born

BROUGHT into.

1 Tim. 6:7 b. nothing into world

BRUISE, Verb.

Gen. 3:15 b. thy head, b. his heel

BRUISED.

53:5 he was b. for our iniquities

BUDDED.

Heb. 9:4 ark wherein rod that b?

1 Chr. 17:10 will b. thee a house

BUILD, Man the Agent

Luke 12:18 barns and b. greater

1 Cor. 8:12 b. on this foundation

BUILD, joined with House, s.

1 Chr. 17:12 shall b. ah. 2Chr.6:9

22:8 not b. a h. thou shed blood.

BUILDER, S.

Heb. 11:10 city whose b. is God

1 Pet. 2:7 the stone b. disallowed

BUILT altar.

Ex. 17:15 b. a. 24:4; 32:5 Aaron

BUILT city.

Luke 4:29 hill whereon c. was b.

BUILT house, or houses.

Deut. 8:12 when hast b. goodly h.

20:5 what man hath b. new h.

1 K. 3:2 no h. b. to name of Lord

6:9 Sol. b. h. 14;8:13 b. th a h.

Zec. 1:16 my h. shall be b. in it.

Mat. 7:24 b. h. on a r. Luke 6:48

26 b. his h. on sand, Luke 6:49

Acts 7:47 Solomon b. him a h.

1 Pet 2:5 b. up a spiritual house

BULRUSHES.

Ex. 2:3 an ark of b.

BULWARKS.

Deut. 20:20 b. against the city

BURDEN, Substantive.

Mat. 11:30 and my b. is light

21:3 ship was to unlade her b.

Gal. 6:5 man bear his own b.

Mat. 23:4 heavy b. Luke 11:46

Gal. 6:2 bear ye one another's b.

BURIAL.

Mat. 26:12 she did it for my b.

Acts 8:2 carried Stephen to his b.

BURIED.

Gen. 25:10 there was Abraham b.

2 Sam. 4:12 b. head of Ish-bosh.

21:14 bones of Saul b. in Zelah

Rom. 6:4 b. with him by baptism

1 Cor. 15:4 that he was b. and r.

Col. 2:12 b. with him in baptism

BURN.

Gen. 44:18 let not thine anger b.

BURN joined with fire.

Mat. 3:12 b. up the chaff with

unquench. fire, Luke 3:17

BURNETH.

Rev. 21:8 lake which b. with fire.

BURNT-OFFERING.

Gen. 22:7 where is l. for a b.o.

8 G. will provide lamb for b. o.

Continual BURNT-OFFERING

Ex. 29:42 a con. b.o. Num. 28:3,

6, 10, 15, 24, 31; 29:11, 16, 19,

22; Ezr. 3:5; Neh. 10:33;

Ezek. 46:15

BURNT-OFFERINGS.

Gen. 8:20 N. offered b.o. on altar

Num. 10:10 trumpets over b. o.

1 Sam. 15:22 delight in b. o.

1 K. 3:15 Solomon offered b. o.

2 Chr. 2:4 b. a house for b. o.

Offer BURNT-OFFERINGS.

2 Sam. 24:24 o. b. o. of that cost

me nothing, 1 Chr. 21:24

BURNT-SACRIFICE.
Num. 23:6 he stood by his b.s.
BURNT up.
2 Pet. 3:10 earth and w. be b. up
Rev. 8:7 third part of trees and
all green grass was b. up.
BUSINESS.
Prov. 22:29 a man dilig. in his b.
Ex. 5:3 through mult. of b.
Rom. 12:11 not slothful in b.
1 Thes. 4:11 to do your own b.
BUSYBODY, IES.
2 Thes. 3:11 are b. 1 Tim. 5:13
1 Pet. 4:15 let none suffer as a b.
BUTLER
Prov. 30:33 churn. of milk bri. b.
BUY.
John 4:8 were gone to b. meat
6:5 whence shall we b. break
13:29 b. things we have need of
1 Cor. 7:30 b. as though they pos.
Jam. 4:13 b. and sell and get gain
BUY poor.
Amos 8:6 may b. the poor for sil.
BUY truth.
Prov. 23:23 b. truth, sell it not
BUYETH.
Prov. 31:16 consider, field, b. it.
Mat. 13:44 he selleth all, b. field
BY-WAYS.
Jud. 5:6 walked through b.w.
BYWORD.
Ps. 44:14 a b. among heathen

C.

CABINS.
Jer. 37:16 when J. entered into c.
CAGE
Jer. 5:27 as a c. is full of birds
CAIN.
Gen. 4:2, 5, 15, 25; Jos. 15:57
1 John 3:12 not as C. who was of
CAKES.
Lev. 24:5 bake twelve c. thereof
CALAMITY, IES.
Job 6:2 my c. laid in balances
Ps 57:1 until these c. be overp.
Prov. 1:26 I will laugh at your c.
6:15 his c. shall come suddenly

CALEB.
Num. 13:6, 30; 14:24, 38; 34:19
Jos. 14:13 Joshm gave C. Hebron
CALF.
Gen. 18:7 Abraham fetched a c.
Ex. 32:20 Moses burnt c.
Deut. 9:16 made you a molten c.
Neh. 9:18; Ps. 106:19
CALL.
Gen. 2:19 what A. would c. them
1 Sam. 3:6 thou didst c. me, 8
1 K, 8:52 hearken in all they c.
Lam. 2:15 men c. perfection
Jon. 1:6 sleeper c. on thy God
Zec. 3:10 c. ev. man his neighbor
Mal. 3:15 we c. the proud happy
Mat. 9:13 not come to c. righte-
ous, Mark 2:17; Luke 5:32
Luke 6:46 why c. me Lord
John 13:13 ye c. me Master
Acts 9:14 all c. on thy name
Rom. 10:12 to all that c. on him
2 Cor. 1:23 I c. God for a record
2 Tim. 2:22 peace wi. th. c. on L.
Jam. 5:14 let him c. the elders
1 Pet. 1:17 if ye c. on the Father
CALL on the name of the Lord.
Gen. 4:26 began men to c. on L.
1 Cor. 1:2 in every place c. L
Shall, or shalt CALL.
Mat. 1:21 shalt c. his name Jesus
Luke 1:13 shalt c. his name John
Acts 2:39 as many as the L. s.c.
WILL CALL.
1 Sam. 12:17 I will c. to Lord.
2 Sam. 22:4 I will c. Lord, Ps. 18:3
Job 27:10 will hypocrite c. on G.
Ps. 55:16 I will c. on God, 86:7
Is. 22:20 that I w. c. my ser. E.
Rom. 9:25 I w. c. them my peo.
CALL upon me.
Ps. 50:15 c. u. m. in d. of trouble
CALLED.
2 Sam. 6:2 name is c. by name
12:28 city be c. after my name
61:3 be c. trees of righteousness
Mat. 1:16 Jesus who is c. Christ
Luke 1:61 none of thy kind, is c.
15:19 worthy to be c. thy son, 21
John 1:48 before Phillip c. thee I

25

Acts 9:11 go into str. c. Straight
Rom. 1:1 P.c. to be apos. 1 Cor. 1:1
Col. 3:15 to the which ye are c.
2 Thes. 2:4 exalteth above all c.
Jam. 2:7 name by wh. ye are c.
1 Pet. 2:9 c. you out of darkness
2 Pet. 1:3 that hath c. us to glory
1 John 3:1 sh. be c. the sons of G.

CALLED, joined with God or
LORD.

Gen. 1:5 God c. the light Day
1 Sam. 3:4 L. c. Samuel, 6,8,10
Ps. 50:1 c. earth from the rising
Is. 41:2 Lord c. him to his foot
2 Tim. 1:9 c. us with a holy call.
Heb. 5:4 c. of God as was Aaron

HE CALLED.

Mat. 10:1 c. twelve; 15:10 mult.

I CALLED, or I have
CALLED.

Ps. 31:17 not be ashamed, I have c.
Is. 43:1 I c. thee by thy name, 45:4

CALLED by my name.

2 Chr. 7:14 if my people which
   are c. by my name humble

SHALT BE CALLED.

Is. 1:26 s. c. city of righteousness

They CALLED.

Luke 1:59 t. c. him Zacharias
John 9:18 t. c. parents of him
   24 c. they man that was blind

Was CALLED.

Heb. 11:8 A. wh. he w. c. obeyed
Jam. 2:23 w. c. the friend of God
Rev. 19:11 sat on him w. c. faith.

CALLETH.

Hos. 7:7 none that c. to me
Amos 5:8 c. for waters of sea, 9:6
Rom. 4:17 c. things which be not
   9:11 election m. stand of him c.
1 Cor. 12:3 by Spirit c. Jesus

CALLING, Substantive.

Heb. 3:1 partakers of heavenly c.
9 Pet. 1:10 your c. and election

CALLING, Participle.

Is. 41:4 c. gen. from beginning
46:11 c. ravenous bird from east
Acts 7:59 stoned Stephen c. on G.

CALM.

Mat. 8:26 gr. c. Mark 4:39; Lu 8:24

CALVES.

1 K. 12:28 king made 2 c. of gold

CAME.

John 1:11 he c. to his own

CAME again.

Jud. 13:9 angel c. a. to the wom.

CAME down.

Gen. 11:5 L. c. down to see tower
Ex. 19:20 L. c.d. on mount Sinai
Dan. 4:13 holy one c. d. from h.
Mic. 1:12 evil c. down from the L.

CAME forth.

Jud. 14:14 out of eater c. f. meat
2 Sam. 16:11 son which c. f. of
Prov. 7:15 c. I forth to meet thee
Jer. 20:18 c. I f. out of womb?

I CAME.

1 Cor. 2:1 I c. not with excellency
2 Cor. 1:23 to spare you I c. not

CAME in.

Est. 2:14 c. in to king no more
Luke 1:28 angel c. in to Mary

CAME near.

Acts 9:3 as he c. n. Damascus

CAME nigh.

Mat. 15:29 Jesus c. n. to sea of G.

CAME out.

Mat. 8:34 whole city c. o.
   12:44 return to m. house whence
   I c. out, Luke 11:24
   27:32 they c. out found Simon
   53 c. o. of graves after his res.
Mark 1:26 unc. spirit c. out, 9:26
Rev. 7:14 these c. o. of great trib.

CAME over.

Jos. 4:22 Is. c. o. J. on dry land

Word of the Lord CAME.

Gen. 15:1 the w. L. to Abr. 4
1 Sam. 15:10 w. L. c. to Samuel
Hos. 1:1 Hosea; Joel 1:1 Joel

CAMEL.

Mat. 19:24 is easier for a c. Mark

CAMEST.

Gen. 16:8 Hagar, whence c. thou
John 6:25 Rabbi, when c. hither
   16:30 we believe thou c. from G.
Acts 9:17 in the way as thou c.

CAMP.

2 King 19:35 angel of L. smote in
   c. of Assyr. 185,000 Is. 37:36
Ps. 78:28 let it fall in midst of c.
   106:16 envied M. also in the c.

CAMPHIRE.
Cant. 1:14 my beloved is as c.

CAN.
John 15:4 no more c. ye except

How CAN.
John 2:1 marriage in C. 11

CANAAN.
Gen. 9:18, 22, 25; 10:15; 28:1
Ex. 15:15 the inhabitants of C.

Land of CANAAN.
Gen. 12:5 to go into land of C.

CANAANITE.
Ex. 23:28 drive out C. 33:2; 34:11

CANDLE.
Mat. 5:15 put c. under a bushel.

CANDLESTICK.
Lev. 24:4 lamps on c. continually

CANKER-WORM.
Joel 1:4 c. eat, and c. w. left, 2:25

CANST.
Mat. 8:2 thou c. make me clean
CAPERNAUM. Mat. 4:13; 8:5;

CAPTAIN.
Gen. 37:36 sold him to Potiph. c.
2 Chr. 13:12 God himself is our c.
Is. 3:3 doth take away c. of fifty
Acts 5:26 c. with officers brought
Heb. 2:10 c. of their salvation

CAPTAINS.
1 Sam. 8:12 he will appoint him c.
22:7 son of Jesse make you c.
Jer. 13:21 taught them to be c.

CAPTIVE.
Amos 6:7 c. with first that go c.

Carry or carried CAPTIVE, or CAPTIVES.
Dan. 11:8 also c. c. into Egypt
Amos 1:6 bec. they c. c. captivity
Ob. 11 in day strangers car. c.

Lead or led CAPTIVE.
Jud. 5:12 lead thy captivity c.
1 K. 8:48 return unto thee in land
of enemes which l. them c.
2 Tim. 3:6 lead c. silly women

CAPTIVES.
1 Sam. 30:5 David's two wives c.
2 K. 24:14 from Jerus. 10,000 c.
2 Chr. 28:11 deliver the c. again

CAPTIVITY.
Num. 21:29 his daughters into c.

Bring CAPTIVITY.
Joel 3:1 b. again c. of Judah
Amos 9:14 b. again c. of my peo.

CARCASS.
Lev. 5:2 touch c. unclean thing
Jud. 14:8 to see c. of lion honey
1 \K. 13:22 thy c. not come
2 K. 9:37 c. of Jez. be as dung

CARE.
1 Tim. 3:5 how take c. of church
1 Pet. 5:7 casting your c. on him

CARE, ED.
2 Sam. 18:3 if we flee, not c. for
Ps. 142:4 no man c. for my soul

CAREFUL
Tit. 3:8 c. to maintain good w.

CAREFULLY.
Phil. 2:28 I sent him the more c.

CAREFULNESS.
1 Cor. 7:32 have you without c.
2 Cor. 7:11 what c. it wrought

CARELESSLY.
Zep. 2:15 rejoicing city dwelt c.

CARES.
Mark 4:19 c. of this world choke
Luke 8:14 chok, with c. and rich.

CARMEL.
Jer. 46:18 as C. by the sea

CARMELITE.
1 Sam. 30:5 N. C. 2 Sam. 2:2; 3:3

CARNAL.
Rom. 7:14 I am c. sold under sin
Heb. 7:16 law of a c. command.

CARNALLY.
Rom. 8:6 c. minded is death

CARPENTER, S.
Zec. 1:20 Lord showed me four c.
Mark 6:3 is not this the c.

CARRY.
Lev. 10:4 c. your breth. out of c.
Ec. 10:20 a bird shall c. the v.
Is. 23:7 own feet c. her afar off
Luke 10:4 c. nef. purse nor scrip
John 5:10 not lawful to c.

CARRIED.
1 Sam. 5:8 let ark be c. to Gath
Joel 3:5 c. into your temples
Luke 7:12 dead man c. out
16:22 was c. by the angels
Acts 3:2 one lame from womb c.
Eph. 4:14 c. with every wind

Heb. 13:9 c. with divers doctrines
2 Pet. 2:17 c. with a tempest
Jude 12 clouds without water c.

CARRIED away.

1 Cor. 12:2 G. c. a. dumb idols
Gal. 2:13 Barnabas c. a.

CART.

1 Chr. 13:7 Uzziah drave the c.
Amos 2:13 as a c. is pressed

CARVED

Jud. 18:18 fetched the c. image
2 Chr. 33:7 c. image in house G.
Prov. 7:16 my bed with c. work

CASE, S.

Ps. 144:15 happy p. in such a c.
1 Cor. 7:15 bondage in such c.

CAST, passive.

Ps. 22:10 I was c. on thee
Prov. 16:33 the lot is c. into lap
Is. 25:7 covering c. over all
Rev. 8:7 hail and fire c. on earth
 8 mountain burning c. into sea
20:10 the devil was c. into lake
 15 not found in book of life, c.

CAST, active.

Num. 35:23 c. it on him
Deut. 29:28 L. c. into an. land.
 19:19 E. c. his mantle on him
2 K. 2:16 c. him on some mount.
 21 spring, and c. salt in there
Ps. 55:3 they c. iniquity on me
 22 c. thy burden on the Lord
Prov. 1:14 c. in thy lot among us
Ec. 11:1 c. thy bread on waters
Jon. 2:3 c. me into the deep
Mic. 4:7 I will make her c. off
Mal. 3:11 nor vine c. fruit before
Mat. 3:10 is c. into fire, 7:19
7:6 nor c. pearls before swine
17:27 c. a hook and take up fish
18:30 c. into prison till he pay
27:44 c. same in his teeth
Mark 9:22 c. him into fire
12:4 and at him they c. stones
 43 widow hath c. more in, 44
Luke 12:5 to c. into hell
 19:43 enemies shall c. a trench
John 8:7 first c. a stone at her
2:7 Peter c. himself into sea
Acts 12:8 c. garment about thee
16:23 c. Paul and S. into prison

1 Cor. 7:35 may c. a snare on you
Rev. 2:10 devil c. some into pris.

CAST away.

Hos 9:17 God will c. them a.
Mat. 13:48 but c. the bad away
Luke 9:25 if a man be c. away
Rom. 11:1 God c. a. his people?
 2 not c. away people
Heb. 10:35 c. not a. your confid.

CAST down.

Ex. 7:10 Aaron c. down his rod
Jud. 6:28 Baal was c. down
1 K. 18:42 Elijah c. himself d.
Neh. 6:16 c. d. in their own eyes
Prov. 7:26 c. d. many wounded
Is. 28:2 shall c. d. with his hand
Lam. 2:1 c. d. the beauty of Isr.
Ezek. 6:4 c. d. your slain
Dan. 7:9 the thrones were c. d.
Mat. 4:6 c. thyself d. Luke 4:9
Luke 4:29 c. Jesus d. headlong
2 Cor. 4:9 c. d. but not destroyed
2 Pet . 2:4 c. angels down to hell

CAST forth.

John 1:15 c. f. Jonah into sea

CAST lots.

Is. 34:17 he hath c. lots
Joel 3:3 c. lots for my people

CAST off.

2 K. 23:27 I will c. off Jerusa.
Amos 1:11 bec. he c. off all pity
Zec. 10:6 tho' I not c. them off
Rom. 13:12 let us c. off works
1 Tim. 5:12 c. off their first faith

CAST out.

Ps. 5:10 c. them out in trans.
 18:42 did c. them out as dirt in
Is. 14:19 art c. out of thy grave
Jer. 7:15 c. you out of my sight
Ezek. 16:5 wast c. o. in open field
Mat 5:13 unsav. c. o. Luke 14:35
7:5 first c. out beam, Luke 6:42
8:12 child, of kingdom be c. out
 16 c. out spirits with his word
9:33 devil was c. o. dumb spake
10:1 power against spir. to c. o.
 8 raise dead, c. out devils

CASTEST, ETH.

Mat. 9:34 he c. out devils Mark
 3:22; Luke 11:15
1 John 4:18 per. love c. out fear

Rev. 6:13 fig-tree c. untimely figs

CASTING.

Mat. 27:35 c. lots, Mark 15:24

Mark 9:38 c. out dev. Luke 9:49

CATCH.

1 K. 20:33 men did hastily c.

2 K. 7:12 we shall c. them alive

Ps. 10:9 in wait to c. the poor

35:8 let his net c. himself

Jer. 5:26 set a trap they c. men

Mark 12:13 to c. him in his wo.

Luke 5:10 from hencef. c. men

CATCHETH.

Mat. 13:19 c. what was sown

John 10:12 wolf c. the sheep

CATTLE.

Gen. 1:25 God made the c.

8:1 God remembered c. in ark

9:10 establish covenant with c.

13:2 Abram was rich in c.

Ps. 50:10 c. on a thousand hills

Much CATTLE.

Gen. 30:43 Jacob had much c.

Your CATTLE.

Gen. 47:16 bread for your c.

CAUGHT.

1 Sam. 17:35 I c. him by his bea.

2 Sam. 2:16 c. every one his fellow

18:9 Absalom's head c. hold of

1 Thes. 4:17 we shall be c, up to.

Rev. 12:5 child was c. up to God

CAUSE, Substantive.

Ex. 22:9 c. of both before judges

Num. 16:11 for which c. thou

and all thy company are ga.

Deut. 1:17 the c. too hard for you

1 K. 8:45 maintain their c. 49, 59.

1 Chr. 21:3 a c. of tresp. to Is?

2 Chr. 19:10 what c. shall come

Job 5:8 would I commit my c.

Ps. 9:4 hast maintained my c.

Prov. 18:17 he first in his own c.

Jer. 5:28 judge not c. of fatherl.

Lam. 3:36 subv. a man in his c.

Jon. 1:7 for whose c. 8

Luke 23:22 no c. of death in him

Acts 10:21 c. where. ye are come

2 Cor. 4:16 which c. we faint not

2 Cor. 7:12 his c. that h. done w.

Phil. 2:18 same c. do ye joy

2 Tim. 1:12 for which c. I suffer

Heb. 2:11 c. he is not ashamed to

Plead CAUSE.

1 Sam. 24:15 Lord plead my c. Ps.

Ps. 74:22 plead thine own c.

Prov. 22:23 will plead their c.

Jer. 30:13 none to plead thy c.

Mic. 7:9 until he plead my c.

For this CAUSE.

Ex. 9:16 f. t. c. raised up Ph.

Rom. 15:9 f. c. I will confess

1 Cor. 11:30 f. this c. many

Eph.-3:14 f. this c. I bow

1 Thes. 2:13 f. this c. thank we

1 Tim. 1:16 f. t. c. I obtained

Heb. 9:15 f. this c. he is med.

1 Pet. 4:6 f. t. c. was gospel pr.

Without CAUSE.

1 Sam. 19:5 slay D. without a c.

CAUSE.

2 Sam. 13:13 c. my shame to go

Ps. 10:17 wilt c. thine ear

Prov. 4:16 unless c. some to fall

Ec. 5:6 to c. thy flesh to sin

Cant. 8:13 voice, c. me to hear it

Ps. 3:12 lead c. thee to err, 9:16

Jer. 3:12 not c. mine anger

7:3 c. to dwell in this place, 7

23:27 c. people forget my name

31:2 I went to c. him to rest

9 c. to walk by rivers of waters

Lam. 3:32 but though he c. grief

Ezek. 20:37 c. to pass under rod

Dan. 9:17 G. c. thy face to shine

Mat. 10:21 c. par. to be put to d.

CAUSED.

Gen. 2:21 Lord c. a deep sleep

2 Sam 7:11 c. thee to rest

Job 31:16 c. eyes of widow

Is. 19:14 have c. Egypt to err

Jer. 12:14 c. my people to inher.

Zec. 3:4 c. thy iniquity to pass

2 Cor. 2:5 if any have c. grief

CAUSETH.

Job 20:3 spirit of under c. me

Ps. 135:7 he c. vapors to ascend,

Prov. 10:5 son c. sh. 17:2; 19:26

Mat. 5:32 c. her to commit adul.

CAVE,S.

Gen. 19:30 Lot dwelt in a c. he

Jos. 10:16 kings hid in a c. 17

1 Sam. 13:6 Israel did hide in c.

1 K. 18:4 prophets hid in c. 13
Heb 11:38 they wandered in c.

CEASE.
Gen. 8:22 day and night not c.
Deut. 15:11 poor shall never c.
Jos. 22:25 child. c. from fearing
Jud. 15:7 after that I will c.
Job 3:17 c. from troubling
Ec. 12:3 grinders c. bec. few
Is. 1:16 c. to do evil
Jer. 14:17 let tears not c.
Lam. 2:18 apple of thine eye c.
Ezek. 6:6 that your idols may c.
Eph. 1:16 I c. not to give thanks
Col. 1:9 not c. to pray for you
2 Pet. 2:14 cannot c. from sin

Cause to CEASE.
Dan. 9:27 shall c. oblation to c.
11:18 cause reproach offered to c.

CEASED.
Jud. 2:19 c. not from their d.
Gal. 5:11 offence of cross c.
Heb. 4:10 c. from his own words.
1 Pet. 4:1 hath c. from sin

CEASETH.
Ps. 12:1 for the godly man c.

CEASING.
1 Thes. 2:13 we think G. w. c.
5:17 pray without c.

CEDAR-TREES.
Num. 24:6 Is. tabernac. as c. t.
2 Sam. 5:11 H sent c. t. to Dav

CEDARS.
Zec. 11:1 fire may devour thy c.

CEDARS of Lebanon.
Jud. 9:15 bramble dev. c. of Leb.
Ps. 104:16 c. of Leb. he planted
Is. 2:13 Lord on all c. of Leb.
14:8 c. of Leb. rejoice at thee

CELESTIAL.
1 Cor. 15:40 c. bodies, glory of c.

CENSER.
2 Chr. 26:19 Uzziah had a c.

CENTURION.
Mat. 8:5 came unto him a c.
8 c. said, L. I am not worthy

CEPHAS.
John 1:42 shalt be called C.

CERTAIN, some.
Deut. 13:13 c. men children of B.
John 5:4 went at a c. season

Acts 9:19 Saul c. days with disc.
Rom. 15:26 to make a c. contrib.
Gal. 2:12 before c. came from J.
Heb. 2:6 one in a c. place testified;

CERTAIN, sure.
Deut. 13:14 the thing c. 17:4
1 K. 2:37 kn. for c. 42; Jer. 26:15
Dan. 2:45 the dream is c.
Acts 25:26 no c. thing to write
1 Cor. 4:11 no c. dwelling-place
1 Tim. 6:7 it is c. we can carry

CERTAINLY.
Ex. 3:12 c. I will be with thee
1 K. 1:30 so will I c. do this day
2 K. 8:10 thou mayest c. recover
Lam. 2:16 c. this day looked

CERTAINTY.
Acts 22:30 would have known c.

CERTIFY
Gal. 1:11 I c. you the gospel

CESAR.
Mat. 22:17 tribute to C. Mark
Luke 2:1 a decree from C.

CESAREA.
Mat. 16:13 into coasts of C.
Acts 8:40; 9:30; 10:24; 23:23; 25:4

CHAFF.
Job 21:18 as c. storm carrieth
Is. 5:24 as flame consumeth c.
Jer. 23:28 what is c. to the wheat
Dan. 2:35 c. of threshing floor

CHAIN.
Gen. 41:42 put a gold c. about his
2 Tim, 1:16 O, not ashamed of c.
Rev. 20:1 angel c. in his hand

CHAINS.
Jud. 8:26 c. about camels' necks
Ps. 149:8 to bind kings with c.
Prov. 1:9 instruction shall be c.
Is. 3:19 L. will take away thy c.
Acts 12:7 Peter's c. fell off
2 Pet. 2:4 deliv. into c. of dark.
Jude 6 reserved in everlasting c.

CHALDEA.
Jer. 50:10 C. shall be a spoil

CHALDEAN.
Dan. 2:10 such things at any C.

CHALDEANS.
Dan. 1:4; 2:2; 3:8; 4:7; 5:7; 11

CHALDEES.
2 K. 24:2 of the C. 25:4, 10, 26

CHAMBER.
2 K. 4:11 Elisha turned into c.
Ps. 19:5 as bridegroom out of c.
Jer. 36:10 book in c. of Gemariah
Joel 2:16 bridegr. go forth of c.
Inner CHAMBER.
1 K. 20:30 Benh. came into in c.
Upper CHAMBER.
Acts 9:37 Dorcas in an upper c.
CHAMBERS.
Ps. 104:3 beams of c. in waters
Prov. 7:27 down to c. of death
CHAMELEON.
Lev. 11:30 be unclean, the c.
CHAMPAIGN.
Deut. 11:30 in c. over against G.
CHAMPION.
1 Sam. 17:4 there went out a c.
CHANCELLOR.
Ezr. 4:8 Rehum the c. 9, 17
CHANGE.
Heb. 7:12 of necessity a c. of law
CHANGE, Verb.
Job 17:12 c. the night into the day
Ps. 102:26 as vesture c. them
Dan. 7:25 think to c. times
Mal. 3:6 I am the Lord I c. not
CHANGED.ETH.
Gen. 31:7 your father c. wages
Mic. 2:4 c. portion of my people
Acts 28:6 barbarians c. their m.
1 Cor. 15:51 we shall all be c. 52
2 Cor. 3:18 c. into same image
Heb. 7:12 for priesthood being c.
CHANGERS.
Mat. 21:12 tables of money c.
CHARGE, Substantive.
Gen. 26:5 Abraham kept my c.
28:6 Isaac gave Jacob a c.
1 K. 11:28 Jeroboam ruler over c.
1 Chr. 9:27 bec. c. was on them
Job 34:13 c. over the earth?
Ps. 35:11 c. things I knew not
Jer. 39:11 c. concerning Jeremiah
Ezek. 9:1 I have c. over the city
44:8 not kept c. of holy things
Acts 7:60 lay not sin to their c.
23:29 to his c. worthy of death
Rom. 8:33 to c. of God's elect?
1 Cor. 9:18 gospel without c.
1 Tim. 1:18 c. I commit to thee

2 Tim. 4:16 not be laid to their c.
Give CHARGE.
1 Tim. 5:7 these things give in c.
6:13 give thee c. in sight of God
CHARGE, Verb.
Mark 9:25 I c. thee, come out
CHARGED.
Gen. 26:11 Abimelech c. his peo.
1 Thes. 2:11 c. every one of you
1 Tim. 5:16 let not church be c.
CHARGES.
Acts 21:24 be at c. with them
CHARGING.
Acts 16:23 c. jailer to keep safely
CHARIOT.
2 K. 2:11 appeared a c. of fire
12 cried, c. of Israel, 13:14
5:21 from c. to meet Gehazi
9:16 J. rode in c.; 27 smite in c.
28 carried him in a c. 23:30
2 Chr. 35:24 took him out of c.
His CHARIOT.
2 K. 5:9 Naaman came with h. c.
9:21 went out each in his c.
Acts 8:28 in his c. read Esaias
CHARIOTS.
Gen. 50:9 went with Joseph c.
Ex. 14:7 Pharaoh took 600 c.
Jos. 17:16 c. of iron 18; Jud. 1:19:
4:3
Jud. 5:28 wheels of his c.
1 Sam. 8:11 king appoint for his c.
13:5 to fight Israel 30,000
1 K. 10:26 Solomon had 1,400 c.
Ps. 68:17 c. of God are 20,000
Is. 2:7 nor any end of their c.
31:1 woe to them that trust in c.
66:15 with c. like whirlwind.
Rev. 9:9 sound of wings as of c.
CHARIOTS with horses.
Ps. 20:7 trust in c. some in h.
CHARITABLY
Rom. 14:15 now walkest not c.
CHARITY.
1 Cor. 8:1 but c. edifieth
13:1 and have not c. 2, 3
4 c, suffereth long, c. env. not
13 faith, hope, c. greatest is c.
14:1 follow c. desire spir. gifts
16:14 let all be done with c.
Col. 3:14 above all put on c.

31

1 Thes. 3:6 good tidings of your c.
1 Tim. 1:5 end of command. is c.
2 Tim. 2:22 follow righteous. c.
Tit. 2:2 aged men be sound in c.
1 Pet. 4:8 fervent c. c. cover sins
5:14 greet with a kiss of c.
2 Pet. 1:7 brotherly kindness c.
3 John 6 borne witness of thy c.
Jude 12 spots in your feasts of c.
Rev. 2:19 I know thy works, c.

CHASTE.

2 Cor. 11:2 pres. you as c. virgin
Tit. 2:5 young women be c.
1 Pet. 3:2 your c. conversation

CHASTEN.

2 Sam. 7:14 c. with rod of men
Ps. 6:1 c. me in hot displ. 38:1
Prov. 19:18 c. son while hope
Dan. 10:12 c. thyself before God.

CHASTENED.

1 Cor. 11:32 c. that we be not
2 Cor. 6:9 as c. and not killed
Heb. 12:10 for a few days c. us

CHASTENEST, ETH, ING.

Ps. 94:12 bless, is whom thou c.
Prov. 13:24 lov. him. c. betimes
Heb. 12:6 whom Lord loveth he c.
Heb. 12:7 if ye end, c. what son

CHASTISE, ED

Luke 23:16 c. him and release, 22

CHASTISEMENT.

Deut. 11:2 have not seen the c.

CHECKER-WORK.

1 K. 7:17 Hir. made nets of c.

CHEEK.

Mat. 5:39 right c. turn other
Luke 6:29 to him smiteth one c.

CHEER.

Ec. 11:9 thy heart c. thee

Good CHEER.

Mat. 9:2 son, be of g. c.
14:27 be of g. c. Mark 6:50.
John 16:33 be of g. c. I have

CHEERFUL.

Prov. 15:13 a c. countenance
2 Cor. 9:7 God loveth a c. giver

CHEERFULNESS.

Rom. 12:8 showeth mercy with c.
2 Chr. 18:23

CHERISH, ED.

1 K. 1:2 let her c. him, and lie

Eph. 5:29 c. flesh, as L. church
1 Thes 2:7 as a nurse c. children

CHERUBIM

Ex. 37:7 made two c. of gold
8:7 c. covered ark, 2 Chr. 5:8;
Heb. 9:5
2 Chr. 3:10 most holy house two c.
Ezek. 10:16 c. went wheels went

CHEW

Lev. 11:4 c. the cud, Deut. 14:7

CHICKENS.

Mat. 23:37 hen gathereth her c.

CHIEF.

Gen. 40:21 restored the c. butler
1 Tim. 1:15 of whom I am c.
1 Pet. 5:4 c. Sheph. shall appear

CHIEF captain.

2 Sam. 5:8 he shall be c. and cap.
Acts 21:31 came to c. captain

CHIEF fathers.

Num. 31:26 c. f. of the congreg.
1 Chr. 9:34 c. fathers of Levites
26:32 2, 700 c. f. D. made rulers
2 Chr. 26:12 number of c. fathers
Ezr. 1:5 rose up c. fath. of Jud.

CHIEF house.

Jos. 22:14 c. h. a prince was sent

CHIEF man, or men.

Lev. 21:4 not defile hims. a c. m.
Is. 41:9 I called thee from c. m.
Acts 13:50 Jews stirred up c. m.

CHIEF priest.

2 K. 25:18 took Ser. the c. priest
1 Chr. 27:5 Benaiah a c. priest

CHIEF priests.

Ezr. 10:5 c. p. and all Israel
Mat. 16:21 suffer of the c. priests
Mark 14:1 c. p. sought 55; Mat.
Luke 23:23 voices of c. p. prev.
Acts 9:14 auth. from c. p. 26:10

CHIEF prince, or princes.

Dan. 10:13 Michael one of c. p.

CHIEF singer, or singers.

Hab. 3:19 to c. singer on instru.

CHIEFEST.

2 Chr. 32:33 in c. of sepulchres
Cant. 5:10 the c. among 10,000
Mark 10:44 c. shall be servant

CHILD.

Gen. 21:16 not see death of c.
42:22 do not sin against the c.

Ex. 2:8 maid called c. mother
Jud. 11:34 his daughter, only c.
1 Sam. 1:25 brought the c. to Eli
2 Sam. 12:14 the c. born shall die
    16 David besought God for c.
1 K. 3:25 divide living c. in two
2 K. 4:31 told c. is not awaked
Prov. 23:13 correction from c.
    15 second c. that shall stand
Is. 3:5 c. shall behave proudly
65:20 c. shall die 100 years old
Jer. 4:31 bring, forth her first c.
31:20 Eph. is he a pleasant c.?
44:7 cut off man, woman, and c.
Mat. 10:21 deliver c. to death
    17:18 c. was cured from that h.
    23:15 more the c. of hell
Luke 1:59 came to circumcise c.
    1:66 what manner of c.
    76 c. called prophet of Highest
    80 c. grew, waxed strong, 2:40
2:27 parents brought in c. Jesus
9:38 look on my son, only c.
John 4:49 come down ere c. die
Acts 4:27 against thy holy c. **J.**
    30 done by name of thy c. **J.**
13:10 Saul said, Thou c. of devil
Rev. 12:4 to devour her c. as soon
A CHILD.
Gen. 18:13 bear a c. who am old?
Ps. 131:2 as a c. as a weaned c.
Prov. 20:11 a c. is known
    22:6 train up a. c. in way he
Ec. 4:18 better is a wise c. than
Is. 9:6 for unto us a c. is born
Hos. 11:1 Is. a. c. I loved him
Mark 9:21 he said of a c.
1 Cor. 13:11 a e. I spake as a. c.
Gal. 4:1 as long as he is a c.
2 Tim. 3:15 from a c. known sc.
Heb. 11:11 S. deliv. of a c. past a.
Rev. 12:5 a man c. to rule nations
Little CHILD.
1 K. 3:7 I am but a l. c.
2 K 5:14 the flesh of a little c.
Is. 11:6 a little c, shall lead them
Sucking CHILD.
Is. 11:8 suck, c. play on hole
    49:15 woman forget suck, c.
This CHILD.
Luke 2:17 told concerning this c.

9:48 receive t. c. in my name
With CHILD.
Gen. 16:11 Hagar thou art w. c.
Ex. 21:22 hurt a woman w. c.
2 K. 8:12 wilt rip up their wo-
    men with c. 15:16
Is. 26:17 with c. that draweth
Amos 1:13 rip, up women, w. c.
Mat. 1:18 with c. of the H. Ghost
    23 a virgin shall be with c.
24:19 woe to them that are w. c.
    Mark 13:17 ; Luke 21:23
Luke 2:5 Mary, great with c.
1 Thes. 5:3 travail on wom. w. c.
Rev. 12:2 and she being with c.
Young CHILD.
1 Sam. 1:24 the c. was young
Mat. 2:8 search dilig. for y. c.
    13 take young c. and his moth.
CHILDISH.
1 Cor. 13:11 I put away c. things
CHILDLESS.
Lev. 20:20 they shall die c.
1 Sam. 15:33 as thy sword made
    women c, so thy mother b c.
Luke 20:30 sec. took her, died c.
CHILDREN.
Gen. 3:16 in sorrow bring forth c.
Ex. 20:5 iniq. of fath. on c. 34:7;
2 Sam. 7:10 c. of wickedness affi.
    any more, 1 Chr. 17:9
1 K. 21:13 came in two c. of Bel.
2 Chr. 13:7 to Jeroboam c. of B.
Ezra 10:44 by whom had c.
Job 19:17 I entreated for c. sake
Prov. 4:1 hear, ye c. the instruc-
    tion, 5:7; 7:24; 8:32
17:6 glory of c. are their fathers
31:28 her c. call her blessed
Ec. 6:3 if a man beget 100 c.
Is. 1:2 brought up c. they reb.
    4 c. that are corrupters
3:4 give c. to be their princes
8:18 c. Lord hath giv. Heb. 2:13
13:18 eyes shall not spare c.
30:1 woe to rebellious c.
    9 lying c. c. will not hear law
Mal. 4:6 heart of fathers to c. of c.
    to fathers, Luke 1:17
Mat. 2:16 Herod slew all the c.
    3:9 to raise up c. Luke 3:8

5:45 be the c. of your Father
8:12 but the c. shall be cast out
9:15 c. of bridechamber mourn,
　　Mark 2:19; Luke 5:34
10:21 c. ag. parents, Mark 13:12
11:19 justi. of her c. Luke 7:35
13:38 good seed are c. of kingd.
15:26 c. bread, Mark 7:27
17:26 then are the c. free
19:29 forsaken c. Mark 10:29
20:20 mother of Zebedee's c.
21:15 saw c. crying in temple
Mark 7:27 let the c. first be filled
　28 dogs eat of the c. crumbs
9:37 receive one of such c. 41
Luke 6:35 shall be c. of Highest
16:8 c. of this world are wiser
20:29 the first died without c.
　34 the c. of this world marry
John 8:39 were Abraham's c.
Acts 3:25 ye are c. of prophets
Rom. 8:17 if c. then heirs, heirs
　9:7 seed of Abra. are they all c.
　11 the c. being not yet born
1 Cor. 14:20 not c. in understand.
2 Cor. 12:14 c. not lay up
Gal. 3:7 of faith, are c. of Abra.
Eph. 1:5 to the adoption of c.
1 Tim. 5:4 if any widow have c.
Heb. 2:14 as c. are partakers
1 Pet. 1:14 as obedient c.
2 Pet. 2:14 cursed c.

CHILDREN of Benjamin.
Jud. 20:13 c. of B. would not

Children's CHILDREN.
Gen. 45:10 thou and thy c. c.
Ps. 103:17 righteousness to c. c.
128:6 shalt see thy c. c.
Prov. 13:22 inherit. to his c. c.
17:6 child. c. crown of old men

Fatherless CHILDREN.
Ps. 109:12 to favor his f. c.

CHILDREN of God.
Mat. 5:9 peacemakers c. of God
Luke 20:36 c. of God being c.
John 11:52 in one the c. of God
Rom. 8:16 we are the c. of God.
　21 glor. liberty of the c. of G.
9:8 c. of the flesh, not c. of G.
　26 called c. of the living God
Gal. 3:26 c. of God by faith in C.

John 3:10 c. G. manifest, c. of d.

His CHILDREN.
Job 5:4 his c. are far from safety
Ps. 89:30 if his c. forsake
103:13 as a father pitieth his c.
109:9 let his c. be fatherless
　10 let his c. be vagabonds
Prov. 14:26 his c. shall have ref.
20:7 his c. are blessed after him
1 Thes. 2:11 ch. you as fath. h. c.
1 Tim. 3:4 his c. in subjection

CHILDREN of Israel.
Rom. 9:27 c. of I. be as the sand
Rev. 7:4 sealed 144,000 of c. of I.
21:12 twelve tribes of c. of I.

CHILDREN of Judah.
Num. 1:26 c. of J. by their gen.
Joel 3:19 for violence ag. c. of J

CHILDREN of light.
Luke 16:8 wiser than c. of light
John 12:36 ye may be the c. of l.
Eph. 5:8 walk as c. of light
1 Thes. 5:5 ye are all the c. of l.

Little CHILDREN.
Mat. 18:3 except bec. as little c.
19:13 brought to him little c.
　14 suffer l. c. to come unto me,
Mark 10:14; Luke 18:16
John 13:33 l. c. yet a little while
Gal. 4:19 l. c. of whom I travail
1 John 2:1 my little c. 12, 13
Mat. 14:21 eaten, were 5,000 m.
beside women and c. 15:38

My CHILDREN.
3 John 4 that my c. walk in truth

No CHILDREN.
1 Sam. 1:2 but Hannah had no c.

Our CHILDREN.
Neh. 5:5 our c. as their children
Mat. 27:25 his blood be on our c.

CHILDREN of promise.
Rom. 9:8 c. prom. counted
Gal. 4:28 as Isaac, are c. of prom.

Strange CHILDREN.
Ps. 144:7 rid me from str. c. 11

Thy CHILDREN.
Jos. 14:9 be thine and thy c.
1 Sam. 16:11 are here all thy c.
Job 8:4 if thy c. have sinned
Ps. 45:16 inst. of fathers be thy c.
Is. 49:17 thy c. shall make haste

34

54:13 all thy c. be taught of L.
Jer. 5:7 thy c. have forsaken me
Ezek. 16:36 by the blood of thy c.
Hos. 4:6 I will also forget thy c.
Mat. 23:37 how oft. would I have
Luke 19:44 lay thy c. within thee
2 John 4 thy c. walking in truth

Your CHILDREN.
Ex. 12:26 your c. shall say
  22:24 your c. shall be fatherless
11:2 I speak not with your c.
Jos. 4:22 then let your c. know
Ps. 115:14 you and your c.
Mat. 7:11 gifts to y.c. Luke 11:13
Luke 23:28 weep for y. and y. c.
Acts 2:39 is to you and y. c.
1 Cor. 7:14 were your c. unclean
Eph. 6:4 pro. not y. c. Col. 3:21

Young CHILDREN.
Mark 10:13 brought y. c. to him
Acts 7:19 they cast out y. c.

CHOKE.
Mat. 13:22 deceitfulness of riches
  c. the word, Mark; 4:19

CHOOSE, as an act of God.
Neh 9:7 God who didst c. Abram
Ps. 25:12 teach in way he shall c.
Zec. 1:17 Lord shall c. Jer. 2:12

CHOOSE.
Prov. 1:29 did not c. fear of L.
Ezek. 21:19 c. a place c. it
Phil. 1:22 what I shall c. I wot n.

CHOOSEST, ETH, ING.
Job 7:15 my soul c. strangling
Ps. 65:4 blessed is man thou c.
Is. 40:20 c. a tree will not rot
Heb. 11:25 c. to suffer affliction

CHOSE.
1 K. 8:16 I c. no city to build a
1 Chr. 28:4 Lord c. me before all
Is. 66:4 c. that I delighted not
Luke 6:13 he c. twelve apostles
Acts 6:5 c. Stephen, full of faith
15:40 Paul c. Silas and departed

CHOSEN.
Num. 16:5 him c. cause to come
Job 36:21 c. rather than affliction
Ps. 33:12 c. for his inheritance
Prov. 16:16 underst. rather c.
  22:1 a good name rather c.
1 Pet. 2:9 ye are a c. generation

Rev. 17:14 they are called, and c.

CHOSEN of God.
Luke 23:35 if C. the c. of God
Acts 10:41 witnesses c. bef. of G.
1 Pet. 2:4 living stone c. of God

I HAVE CHOSEN.
Hag. 2:23 I have c. thee
John 13:18 whom I have c.
  15:16 ye have not c. me. I h. c.
  19 I have c. you out of world

Lord hath CHOSEN.
Deut. 7:6 L.h.c. thee a sp. peo. 14:2

CHOSEN men.
Jud. 20:16 700 c. m. left-handed
Acts 15:22 to send c. men, 25

CHRIST.
Mat. 2:4 where C. sh. be born
16:16 thou art C. the Son
23:8 one is Master, even C. 16
24:5 saying I am C. Mark 13:6'
  Luke 21:8
Mark 9:41 bec. ye belong to C.
  15:32 let C. descend from cross
Luke 2:26 before he had seen C.
  4:41 devils knew he was C.
23:35 save himself, if he be C.
24:26 ought not C. to have suff.
John 4:25 Mes. cometh called C.
  41 C. come out of Galilee?
  42 C. cometh of seed of David
9:22 did confess he was C.
12:34 heard C. abideth for ever
Acts 2:30 would raise up C. to sit
  36 Jesus both Lord and C.
3:18 showed C. should suffer
8:5 Philip preached C. to them
9:20 straightway preached C.
17:3 C. must needs have suff.
26:23 C. should suffer
Rom. 5:6 in due time C. died
  8 yet sinners, C. died for us
6:4 C. was raised from dead
  9 C. being raised dieth no m.
7:4 by the body of C.
8:9 have not the spirit of C.
  10 if C. be in you, body is d.
  11 raised up C. from dead
9:3 accursed from C.
  5 of whom C. came
10:4 C. is end of law for right
  6 to bring C. down from above

7 that is, to bring C. up again
14:9 to this end C. both died
15 not him for whom C. died
18 in these things serveth C.
15:3 C. pleased not himself
7 as C. also received us
15:18 wh. C. not wrought
20 not where C. was named
16:5 Epenetus first-fruits to C.
1 Cor. 1:23 we preach C. crucif.
24 C. the power of God, and
3:23 ye are C. and C. is God's
5:7 C. our passover sacrificed
8:11 perish, for whom C. died
9:21 under law to C. that I m.
10:4 and that Rock was C.
9 nor let us tempt C.
15:3 how C. died for our sins
12 if C. be preached
16 rise not, is not C. raised
17 if C. not raised, faith is v.
23 in his order, C. first-fruits
2 Cor. 3:4 thro' C. to God-ward
5:16 known C. after flesh
6:15 what concord C. with B
11:2 as a chaste virgin to C.
Gal. 2:20 C. liveth in me.
21 then C. is dead in vain
3:13 C. redeemed us from curse
24 schoolmaster to br. us to C.
29 if ye be C. then Abr.'s seed
4:7 heir of God through C.
19 till C. be formed in you
5:1 wherewith C. m. us free
2 if circum. C. profit nothing
4 C is none effect unto you
24 that are C. have crucified
Eph. 2:12 without C.
3:17 that C. may dwell by faith
4:15 which is the head, even C.
20 ye have not so learned C.
5:2 as C. also loved us
14 C. shall give thee light
23 as C. is head of the church
24 as church is subject to C.
25 love wives as C. loved ch.
32 concerning C. and church
6:5 singlen, of heart as to C.
Phil. 1:15 some preach C.
16 preachC. of contention
18 C. is preached, and I rejoice

20 C. be magnified in my body
3:8 dung that I may win C.
4:13 I can do all through C.
Col. 2:8 world, and not after C.
3:1 C. sitteth on right hand
4 C. who is our life shall ap.
11 but C. is all and in all
13 as C. forgave you, so do ye
24 for ye serve the Lord C.
Heb. 3:6 C. as a son
5:5 so C. glorified not himself
9:11 so C. a high priest of good
24 C. is not entered into holy
28 C was once offered to bear
1 Pet. 2:21 C also suffered for us
3:18 C. once suffered for sins
4:1 as C. suffered in the flesh
Rev. 11:15 kingdom of L. and C.
12:10 is come power of his C.
Against CHRIST.
Acts 4:26 kings gath. a. his C.
1 Cor. 8:12 brethren, ye sin a. C.
1 Tim. 5:11 wax wauton a. C.
By CHRIST.
2 Cor. 1:5 aboundeth by C.
Gal. 2:17 to be justified by C.
Eph. 3:21 glory in church by C.
For CHRIST.
1 Cor. 1:17 C. sent me not to b.
4:10 we are fools for C. sake
2 Cor. 5:20 ambassadors for C.
12:10 in distresses for C.
Eph. 4:32 as God for C. sake
Phil. 3:7 I counted loss for C.
2 Thes. 3:5 patient waiting for C
Jesus, with CHRIST.
Mat. 1:16 J. called C. 27:17, 22
John 1:17 and truth by J. C.
17:3 may know thee, and J. C.
Acts 2:38 in name of J.C.
3:6 in name of J.C. rise up
20 . J.C. who was preached
4:10 of J.C. doth this man
5:42 ceased not to preach J. C. 8:12
Philip preach. things concern, the name of J. C.
37 I believe J. C. is Son of God
9:34 J.C. maketh thee whole
10:36 preaching peace by J. C.
16:18 in name of J. C. come out
17:3 Jesus I preach to you is C.

18:5 testified that Jesus was C.
28 by scripture, Jesus was C.
19:4 should believe on C. Jesus
Rom. 1:1 serv. of J. C. Phil. 1:1
3 concerning his son J. C.
6 are ye the called of Jesus C.
8 I thank God through J. C.
2:16 secrets of men by J. C.
3:22 by faith of J. C.
24 redemption in Jesus C.
Rom. 5:15 gr. by one man J. C.
17 reign in life by one J. C.
6:3 baptized into Jesus C.
8:1 to them in C. Jesus
2 C. J. made me free
16:3 my helpers in C. Jesus
1 Cor. 1:1 J. C. 2 Cor. 1:1 Eph. 1:1
2 call on name of J. C.
4 grace given you by J. C.
20 of him are ye in C. Jesus
2:2 save J. C. crucified
4:15 in C. J. have I begotten
2 Cor. 4:6 in face of J. C.
5:18 reconciled us by J. C.
13:5 that Jesus C. is in you
Gal. 2:16 justified by faith of J. C.
3:14 blessings on G. through J. C.
28 ye are all one in C. Jesus
4:14 me as an angel, as C. J.
Eph. 2:6 heav. places in C. J.
20 J. C. chief corner-stone
Phil. 1:8 I in bowels of Jesus C.
2:5 mind in you, was in C. J.
11 J. C. is Lord to glory of G.
21 seek not th. wh. are J. C.
3:8 for excellency of C. J.
12 I am apprehended of C. J.
4:19 riches in glory by C. J.
Col. 2:6 rec. C. J. so walk ye
1 Tim. 1:15 C. J. ca. to save sin.
2:5 one mediator, the man C. J.
6:13 C. Jesus who witnessed
2 Tim. 1:9 grace given us in C. J.
13 faith and love in C. Jesus
Phile. 1 P. a priso, of J. C. 9, 23
Heb. 13:8 Jesus C. the same yes.
1 John 1:7 blood of Jesus C.
2:1 an advocate Jesus C.
5:6 by water and blood J. C.
20 even in Jesus C.

Lord Jesus CHRIST.
Acts 11:17 believed on L. J. C.
15:11 through grace of L. J. C.
16:31 believe on L. J. C.
20:21 faith toward L. J. C.
Rom. 5:1 p. with G. thro' L.J.C.
11 joy in God through L. J. C.
6:23 eternal life through L. J. C.
8:39 love of G. in C. J. our L.
13:14 put ye on the L. J. C.
16:20 grace of L. J. C. be w. you.
24; 2 Cor. 13:14; Gal. 6:18;
2 Thes. 3:18; Rev. 22:21
1 Cor. 1:7 coming of our L. J. C.
8:6 one L. J. C. by whom are
15:57 victory thro' our L. J. C.
16:22 if any love not L. J. C.
2 Cor. 1:2 from G. and L. J. C.
Gal. 1:3; Eph. 1:2; Col. 1:2
8:9 ye know grace of L. J. C.
Gal. 6:14 in cross of L. J. C.
Eph. 1:3 Father of L. J. C.
17 God of L. J. C.
1 Thes. 1:3 hope in L. J. C.
16 our L.J.C. who hath
1 Tim. 5:21 I charge thee before
L. J. C. 2 Tim. 4:1
2 Tim. 4:22 L. J. C.. be with thy
2 Pet. 1:11 kingdom of L.J.C.
3:18 in knowledge of L. J. C.
IN CHRIST.
Acts 24:24 concerning faith in C.
Rom. 9:1 I say the truth in C.
12:5 manyh, are one body in C.
16:7 were in C. before me
9 Urbane our helper in C.
10 Apelles approved in C.
1 Cor. 3:1 as unto babies in C.
4:10 but ye are wise in C.
15:18 asleep in C.
19 in this life hope in C.
22 in C. all be made alive
2 Cor. 1:21 establish us in C.
2:14 to triumph in C.
17 in sight of God speak in C.
3:14 Veil is done away in C.
5:17 in C. he is a new creature
19 in C. reconciling the world
20 in C . stead be reconciled
12:2 a man in C. 14 years
19 we speak before God in C.

Gal. 1:22 to Churches of J. in C.
3:17 confirmed of God in C.
27 as many as baptized in C.
Eph. 1:3 spiritual bless, in C.
10 in one all things in C.
12 who first trusted in C.
20 in C. when he raised
3:6 his promise in C.
Phil. 1:13 my bonds in C.
2:1 if any consolation in C.
Col. 2:5 your faith in C.
1 Thes. 4:16 dead in C. rise first
1 Tim. 2:7 I speak the truth in C.
1 Pet. 3:16 good conversation in C.

In CHRIST.

Mat. 24:23 h. is C. Mark 13:21
Mark 12:35 C. is son. Luke 20:41
Luke 2:11 a Savior, wh. is C.
23:2 saying, that he is C.
John 7:41 said this is the C.
Acts 9:22 Saul proving this is C.
17:3 Jesus I preach to you is C.
Rom. 8:34 it is C. that died
1 Cor. 1:13 is C. divided?
7:22 being free is C. servant
11:3 head of every man is C.
12:12 are one body, so is C.
15:13 if dead rise not, is C. 16
20 now is C. risen from dead
2 Cor. 10:7 if any trust he is C.
Gal. 2:17 is C. minister of sin?
3:16 to thy seed, which is C.
Phil. 1:21 to live is C.
Col. 1:27 is C. in you hope

Of CHRIST.

Mat. 11:2 John heard works of C.
22:42 what think ye of C.?
Rom. 8:9 any have not S. of C.
35 sep. us from love of C?
14:10 judgment- seat of C.
1 Cor. 1:17 cross of C. be made
2:16 we have the mind of C.
6:15 your bodies members of C.
10:16 Communion of blood of C.
11:1 be foll. of me as I of C.
3 the head of C. is God
12:27 ye are the body of C.
2 Cor. 1:5 as sufferings of C.
2:10 forgave I it in person of C.
15 we are a sweet savor of C.
3:3 epistle of C. ministered

4:4 light of gospel of C. shine
5:14 love of C. constraineth us
8:23 they are glory of C.
10:1 by the meekness of C.
5 bringing to obedience of C.
11:10 the truth of C. is in me
12:9 power of C. Rev. 12:10
13:3 proof of C. speaking
Gal. 1:10 be servant of C.
2:16 be justified by faith of C.
6:12 persecution for cross of C.
Eph. 2:13 by the blood of C.
3:4 in mystery of C.
8 the unsearching riches of C.
19 love of C. which passeth
4:7 measure of gift of C.
5:5 inheritance in King, of C.
6:6 as servants of C.
Phil. 1:10 till the day of C.
29 it is given in behalf of C.
2:16 rejoice in the day of C.
30 work of C. nigh to death
3:18 enemies of the cross of C.
Col. 1:24 afflictions of C.
2:2 mystery of God, and of C.
17 but the body is of C.
3:16 let the word of C. dwell
4:3 to speak the mystery of C.
2 Tim. 2:19 the name of C.
Heb. 3:14 made partakers of C.
9:14 more, blood of C. purge
11:26 reproach of C. greater
1 Pet. 1:11 Spirit of C. did signify
19 with precious blood of C.
4:13 partakers of C. sufferings
14 reproached for name of C.
Rev. 20:6 priests of G. and of C.

That CHRIST.

John 1:25 if thou be not that C.
6:69 sure that thou art that C.

The CHRIST.

Mat. 16:20 he was the C.
26:63 whether thou be the C.
Mark 8:29 saith, thou art the C.
14:61 the C. son of the B.?
Luke 3:15 whether he were t. C.
9:20 Peter said thou art the C.
22:67 saying art thou the C.
John 1:20 I am not the C.
41 found the Messais, the C.
3:28 I said I am not the C.

4:29 is not this the C.?
42 this is indeed the C. 7:26
7:41 others said, this is the C.
10:24 be the C. tell us plainly
11:27 I believe thou art the C.
20:31 believe Jesus is the C.

With CHRIST.
Rom. 6:8 if we be dead with C.
8:17 then joint-heirs with C.
Gal. 2:20 I am crucified with C.
Eph. 2:5 quickened us tog. w. C.
Phil. 1:23 a desire to be with C.
Col. 2:20 if dead with C.
3:1 if risen w. C. seek things
Col. 3:3 your life is hid with C.
Rev. 20:4 reigned with C.

CHRISTIAN, S.
Acts 11:26 called c. at Antioch
26:28 almost pers. me to be a c.
1 Pet. 4:16 if any suffer as a c.

CHRISTS.
Mat. 24:24 false c. Mark 18:22

CHURCH.
Mat. 16:18 on this rock b. my c.
18:17 tell it to the c.
Acts 2:47 added to c. daily such
5:11 great fear came on c.
8:1 persecution against c.
11:26 assembled with the c.
14:23 ordained elders in every c.
27 had gathered c. together
15:3 brought on way by the c.
22 it pleased elders with the c.
18:22 when he had saluted c.
Rom. 16:5 greet c. in their house
1 Cor. 4:17 as I teach in every c.
14:4 prophesieth edifieth c.
5 that c. may receive edifying
23 if c. be come into one place
16:19 c. in their house
Eph. 1:22 head over all to the c.
3:10 known by c. wisdom of G.
5:24 as c. is subject to Christ
25 as Christ loved the c.
27 might present a glorious c.
29 cherisheth it, as Lord the c.
32 speak concern, Christ and c.
Phil 3:6 persecuting the c.
4:15 no c. communicated
Col. 1:18 head of the body the c.
24 for his body's sake, the c.

4:15 salute c. in Nymphas' ho.
1 Tim. 5:16 let not c. be charged
Phile. 2 Paul to c. in thy house
Heb.12:23 to c. of first-born
1 Pet 5:13 c. at Babylon saluteth
3 John 6 thy charity before c.
9 I wrote to the c. but Diotre

In the CHURCH.
Acts 7:38 that was in the c.
13:1 proph. in the c. at Antioch
1 Cor. 6:4 least esteemed in the c.
11:18 come together in the c.
12:28 hath set some in the c.
14:19 yet in the c. I had rather
28 keep silence in the c.
35 sh. for wo. to speak in the c.
Eph. 3:21 be glory in the c.
Col. 4:16 to be read in the c.

Of the CHURCH.
Acts 8:3 S. made havoc of the c.
11:22 came to ears of the c.
12:1 H. vexed certain of the c.
5 prayer was made of the c.
15:4 were received of the c.
20:16 Paul called elders of the c.
Rom. 16:1 P. a servant of the c.
23 Gains my host and of the c.
1 Cor. 14:12 excel to edify, of c.
Eph. 5:23 as C. is head of the c.
Heb. 2:12 in midst of the c.
3 John 10 D. casteth out of c.
Rev. 2:1 angel of c. of Ephesus
8 Smyrna; 12 Perga; 18 Thya.
3:1 Sardis; 7 Philad; 14 Laodi.

CHURCH of God.
Acts 20:28 feed the c. of God
1 Cor. 1:2 to c. of God at Corinth
10:32 none offence to c. of God
11:22 despise ye the c. of God
15:9 I pers. c. of God, Gal. 1:13
1 Tim. 3:5 take care of c. of God

CHURCHES.
Acts 9:31 then had the c. rest
15:41 Paul confirming the c.
16:5 c. established in the faith
19:37 these neither robbers of c.
Rom. 16:4 all c. gave thanks
16 the c. of Christ salute you
1 Cor. 7:17 so ordain I in all c.
11:16 such custom, nei, the c.
14:33 author of peace as in all c.

34 women keep silence in c.
2 Cor. 8:1 grace bestow, on the c.
19 chosen of the c. to travel
28 they are messengers of c.
14:8 I robbed other c.
2 Cor. 11:28 the care of all the c.
12:13 inferior to other c.?
Gal. 1:29 unknown by face to c.
1 Thes. 2:14 fol. of the c. of God
2 Thes. 1:4 glory in you in c.
Rev. 1:4 John to the seven c.
11 send it to the seven c.
20 seven stars are angels of c.
candlesticks are the seven c.
2:7 what the Spirit saith unto
the c. 11,17,29; 3:6 13, 22
23 c. know I am he searcheth
22:16 testify these things in c.

CINNAMON.
Ex. 30:23 sweet c.
Prov. 7:17 perf. bed with c.

CIRCUMCISE.
Gen. 17:11 ye shall c. foreskin
Jos. 5:2 c. again children of Isr.
Acts 15:5 needful to c. them

CIRCUMCISED.
Gen. 17:10 every man-child be c.
26 Abraham was c. and Ishm.
Jos. 5:3 J. c children of Israel
Jer. 9:25 punish all c. with uncir.
Acts 15:1 except c. not saved, 24
Rom. 4:11 though not c.
1 Cor. 7:18 being c.? in uncircum.
Gal. 2:3 Titus compelled to be c.
5:2 if c. C. shall profit nothing
6:12 they constrain you to be c.
13 they c. keep not the law
Phil. 3:5 c. eighth day
Col. 2:11 in whom also ye are c.

CIRCUMCISION.
John 7:22 M. gave unto you c.
Rom. 2:25 c. profiteth, if thou
3:30 shall justify c. by faith
4:9 this blessedness on c. only?
10 when he was in c.? not in c.
1 Cor. 7:19 c. is keeping of com.
Gal. 2:9 they should go unto c.
Eph. 2:11 by that called c.
Phil. 3:3 c which worship God
Col. 2:11 c. without hands, by c.

Of CIRCUMCISION.
Ex. 4:26 bloody hus. bec. of c.
Acts 7:8 Abrah. covenant of c.
15:8 J. C. was a minister of c.
Gal. 2:7 gospel of c. com. to Pa,
Col. 4:11 who are of the c. salute
Tit. 1:10 unruly, especially of c.

CISTERN.
Prov. 5:15 drink of thine own c.
Is. 36:16 every one of own c.
Jer. 2:13 hewed out c. of brok. c.

CITY.
Gen. 4:17 Cain builded a c.
Jud. 6:27 he feared men of c.
Ruth 1:19 all the c. was moved
1 Sam. 1:3 out of c. yearly to w.
2 Sam. 12:1 two men in one c.
Ps. 48:2 c. of gr. king, Mat. 5:35
Is 1:26 c. of right, faithful c. 21
62:12 a c. not forsaken
Jer. 3:14 take you one of a c.
Amos 4:7 to rain on one c.
Zec. 8:3 Jerusalem a c. of truth
Zec. 14:2 the c. shall be taken
Mat. 5:14 a c. set on hill cannot
35 Jerusalem is c. of great King
15 that c. Mark 6:11; Luke 10:12
John 4:39 many of th. c. believed
Acts 8:8 was great joy in that c.
19:29 c. was filled with confus.
Heb. 11:10 c. that hath found.
16 hath prepared for them a c.
13:14 we have no continuing c.
Jam. 4:13 will go into such a c.
Rev. 20:9 comp. the beloved c.
21:14 wall of c. had foundations

CITY of David.
2 Sam. 5:9 c. of D. 1 Chr. 11:7
1 K. 2:10 D. was buried in c. D
3:1 Sol. brought her to c. of D.
2 K. 8:24 J. bur. c. D. 2 Chr. 21:20
Luke 2:4 Joseph went to c. of D.

Every CITY.
Mat. 12:25 e. c. divided ag. itself
Luke 10:1 two into every c.
Acts 15:21 in e. c. them that p.

CITY of God.
Ps. 46:4 make glad c. of God
Heb. 12:22 c. of living God
Rev. 3:12 name of c. of my God

Great CITY.

Jos. 10:2 Gibeon was great c.
Neh. 7:4 c. was large and great
Rev. 11:8 in street of great c.

HOLY CITY.
Neh. 11:1 Jerusalem the holy c.
Rev. 11:2 holy c. shall they tread
21:2 John saw the h. c. coming

CITY of the Lord.
Ps. 101:8 cut off all wicked doers
from c. of the Lord.
Is. 60:14 call thee c. of Lord.

Out of the CITY.
Acts 7:58 cast Steph. out of the c.

CITY of Refuge.
Num. 35:25 rest. him to c. of ref.
Jos. 21:13 c. of r. 1 Chr. 6:57
21 Shech; 27 Golan; 32 Ked.

This CITY.
Gen. 19:14 L. will destroy this c.
Mat. 10:23 persecute in this c.

CITIES of Judah.
2 Sam. 2:1 I go up to c. of J.?

CLAMOR, OUS.
Prov. 3:13 a foolish woman is c.
Eph. 4:31 let all c. be put away

CLAP hands.
Job 27:23 shall c. their hands
Ps. 47:1 c. your h. all ye people
98:8 let the floods c. their hands
Is. 55:12 trees of field c. their h.

CLAY.
Ps. 40:2 up out of the miry c.
Is. 41:25 as potter treadeth c.
Rom. 9:21 potter power over c.?

CLEAN, Adjective.
Prov. 16:2 c. in his own eyes
Ec. 9:2 alike to c, and unclean
Is. 1:16 wash ye, make you c.
Mat. 8:2 thou canst make me c.
Luke 11:41 all things are c.
John 13:11 Ye are not all c.

CLEAN heart.
Ps. 51:10 create in me a c. heart
73:1 God is good to such of c. h.
Prov. 20:9 made my heart c.?

Is CLEAN.
Ps. 19:9 fear of the Lord is c.
Prov. 14:4 no oxen are, crib is c.

CLEANSE.
Ps. 19:12 c. from secret faults
Mat. 10:8 heal the sick, c. lepers

1 John 1:9 c. us from unright.

CLEANSED.
Luke 4:27 none c. save Naaman

CLEAR.
Rev. 21:11 c. as crystal, 22:1

CLEARNESS.
Exod. 24:10 body of heaven in c.

CLOAK.
Is. 50:17 clad with zeal as a c.
Mat. 5:40 let him have c. also

CLOSER.
Prov. 18:24 a friend sticketh c.

CLOTHE.
Mat. 63:0 if God so c. the grass,
much more c. you, Lu. 12:28

CLOTHED.
Prov. 31:21 c. with scarlet
Is. 61:10 c. me with garm. of ssl.
Mat. 11:8 c. in soft, Luke 7:25
Mark 1:6 c. with camel's hair.
Luke 16:19 rich man c. in purple
2 Cor. 5:2 desiring to be c. upon
1 Pet. 5:5 be c. with humility
Rev. 3:18 that thou mayest be c.

CLOTHED, with linen.
Rev. 15:6 c. in wh. l. 18:16; 19:14

CLOTHES.
Mark 5:28 if I touch but his c. I
Luke 2:7 in swaddling c. 12
John 11:44 bound with grave-c.
19:40 and wound it in linen c.
20:7 napkin not with linen c.
Acts 7:58 laid their c. at S.'s feet

Rent CLOTHES.
2 Sam. 3:31 r. gird with sack.
2 K. 11:14 Atha. 2 Chr. 23:13
19:1 Hezekiah rent c. Is. 37:1

CLOUD.
Gen. 9:13 set my bow in the c.
Ex. 14:20 it was a c. to them
16:10 glory of L. appeared in c.
19:9 lo, I come in a thick c.
24:15 a c. covered the mount
16 God called to
Mos. out of c.
34:5 L. desc. in c. Num. 11:25
40:34 a c. covered tent of cong.
38 c. on tabernacle by day
Lev. 16:2 I will appear in the c.
21:27 Son of man coming in c.
Acts 1:9 a c. received him

1 Cor. 10:1 our fathers under c.

2 baptized to Moses in the c.

Heb. 12:1 so great a c. of witn.

Rev. 10:1 angel clothed with a c.

Pillar of CLOUD.

Ex. 13:21 in a pillar of c.

CLOUDS.

1 Thes 4:17 caught up in c.

COALS.

Prov. 6:28 can one go on hot c.

COAT.

Gen. 37:3 c. of many colors, 32

1 Sam. 2:19 made him a little c.

Mat. 5:40 take away thy c.

Luke 6:29 forbid not to take c.

John 19:23 c. was without seam

COATS.

Gen. 3:21 God made c. of skins

Mat. 10:10 neither provide two c.

Acts 9:39 c. which Dorcas made

COCK.

John 13:38 c. not crow till thou

hast denied me thrice.

COLD.

Rev. 3:15 neither c. nor hot, 16

COLOR.

Ezek. 1:4 midst as c. of amber

7 like c. of brass, Dan. 10:6

16 like c. of beryl, Dan. 10:9

22 firmament as c. of crystal

COLT.

Zec. 9:9 riding upon a c. Mat.

Mat. 21:2 find an ass tied, a. c.

Mark 11:2; Luke 19:30

COME.

Ps. 42:2 when shall I c. and app.

Is. 13:5 c. from a far country

6 day of L. c. as destruction

35:4 your G. will c. with veng.

44:7 things coming, and shall c.

45:20 assem. and c. draw near

51:11 redeemed shall c. to Z.

Jer. 2:31 will c. no more to thee

Ezek. 21:27 till he c. whose right

Hos. 6:1 c. let us return to Lord

Joel 1:15 as destruction sh. it c.

2:31 be terrible day of Lord c.

Mat. 2:6 out of thee c. Governor

6:10 thy kingdom c. Luke 11:2

28 c. all ye that labor

16:24 if any man will c. after me

42 know not hour Lord doth c.

Mark 8:34 if any will c. after me,

19:13 occupy till I c.

John 1:39 he saith, c. and see

37 if any man thirst, let him c.

21:22 I will he tarry till I c. 23

Acts 1:11 this Jesus shall so c. as

8:24 pray none of these things c.

9:38 he would not delay to c.

Rom. 3:8 do evil th. good may c.

1 Cor. 4:5 judg nothing till L. c.

2 Thes. 1:10 shall c. to be glori.

Heb. 4:16 c. boldly to throne.

Rev. 2:5 else I will c. quickly

3:11 I c. quickly, 22:7, 20

COME forth.

John 11:43 he cried, Lazarus, c.

forth

COME in or into.

Gen. 19:31 not a man to c. in.

Mat. 24:5 many sh. c. in my name,

Mark 13:6; Luke 21:8

Luke 14:23 compel them to c. in

John 5:43 I am c. in my Father's

Rom. 11:25 fulness of G. be c. in

1 Cor. 14:23 c. in those unlearned

Jam. 2:2 there c. in a poor man

COME out.

John 1:46 any good c. out of N.

COME short.

Rom. 3:23 all c. sh. of glory of G.

COME, passive.

1 Cor. 13:10 when that perf. is c.

I am COME, or am I COME.

Ex. 18:6 I jethro am c. to thee

Num. 22:38 Bal.said. lo, I am c.

2 Sam. 14:32 am I c. fr. Gesh.?

Ps. 69:2 I am c. into deep wat.

Dan. 9:23 I am c. to show, 10:14

10:12 I am c. for thy words

Mat. 5:17 I am c. to destroy law

9:13 I am not c. to call right

10:34 not I am c. to send peace

35 I am c. to set at variance

Luke 12:51 I am c. to give peace?

John 1:31 therefore am I c.

5:43 I am c. in my F.'s name

7:28 I am not c. of myself

9:39 for judgment I am c.

10:10 I am c. th. might ha. life

12:46 I am c. a lifht into world

42

16:28 I am c. again I leave wor.

COME, joined with Time.

Ps. 102:13 the set time is c.
Prov. 31:25 rejoice in t. to c.
Cant. 2:12 t. of sing, of birds c.
Is. 13:22 her time is near to c.
  30:8 be for time to c.
  42:23 will hear for time to c.?
Ezek. 7:7 t. is c. 12; Hag. 1:2
  not c.
Luke 9:51 t. c. he sh. be received
Gal. 4:4 when fulness of t.w.c.
1 Tim. 6:19 founda. aga. t. to c.
1 Pet. 4:17 t. is c. judgm. must b.

Yet COME.

Deut. 12:9 not yet c. to the rest
John 2:4 my hour is not yet c.
7:6 my time is not yet c.
  11:30 J. was not y. c. into town
Rev. 17:10 the other is not yet c.

COMELINESS.

Is. 53:2 hath no form nor c.
Ezek. 16:14 perfect through my c.
  27:10 they of Lud set fo. thy c.
Dan. 10:8 my c. into corruption
1 Cor. 12:23 more abundant c.

COMELY.

1 Sam. 16:18 David a c. person
Job. 41:12 con. his c. proportion
Ps. 33:1 praise is c. fo, 147:1
Prov. 30:29 four are c. in going
Cant. 1:5 I am black, but c.
  10 cheeks are c. with jewels
2:14 thy countenance is c
  4:3 thy speech is c.
  6:4 art c. O my love, as Jerus.
Is. 4:2 the fruit shall be c.
Jer. 6:2 daugh. of Zion to a c.w.
1 Cor. 7:35 I speak for that c.
  12:24 c. parts have no need

COMFORT.

Acts 9:31 walking in c. of H.G.

COMFORT, Verb.

Job 2:11 friends came to c. him
Ps. 23:4 thy staff, they c. me
2 Thes. 2:17 L. J. c. your hearts

COMFORTABLY.

Hos. 2:14 I will speak c. to her

COMFORTED.

Jer. 31:15 Rachel refused to be c.
Ezek. 5:13 fury to rest, I w. be c.

Mat. 2:18 not be c. bee, were not
  5:4 mourn, for they shall be co.
1 Cor. 14:31 and all be c.
Rom. 1:12 I may be c. with you
2 Cor. 1:4 we are c. of God.
Col. 2:2 hearts be c. being knit
1 Thes. 2:11 know how he c. you

COMFORTER.

John 14:16 give you another C.
  26 C. which is the Holy Ghost
15:26 when the C. is come
16:7 C. will not come

COMFORTETH.

Job 29:25 as one that c. mourners
Is. 51:12 I am he that c. you

COMFORTLESS.

John 14:18 I will not leave you c.

COMING.

Mal. 3:2 abide day of his c.?
Mat. 16:28 till see Son of man c.
1 Cor. 1:7 waiting for c. of L. J.
15:23 that are Christ's at his c.
Jam. 5:7 be patient to c. of Lord
  8 c. of Lord draweth nigh

COMMAND, Verb.

Is. 45:11 work of my hands, c.
Jer. 27:4 c. to say to masters
Lam. 1:10 c. should not enter
Mark 10:3 what did Moses c. you
1 Tim. 4:11 these things c.

I COMMAND.

John 15:14 if ye do what I c. you
  17 I c. you, that ye love

COMMANDED.

Mat. 28:20 teac. to observe all I c.
1 Cor. 14:34 c. to be under obed.
1 Thes. 4:11 work as we c.

God COMMANDED.

Deut. 5:32 observe to do as God c.
  6:1 God c. to teach 20; 13:5

Lord COMMANDED.

2 Sam. 24:19 D. went up as L. c.

Lord or God COMMANDED

Acts 10:42 he c. us to preach

COMMANDETH.

Mark 1:27 c. spirits, Luke 4:36
Acts 17:30 c. all men to repent

COMMANDMENT.

Prov. 6:23 the c. is a lamp
  8:29 waters not pass his c.
Jer. 35:14 obey their father's c.

43

Eph. 6:2 first c. with promise
Keep COMMANDMENT.
Ps. 19:8 the c. of the Lord is pure
New Commandment..
John 13:34 a new c. I give
COMMANDMENTS.
Gen. 26:5 Abraham kept my c.
Ex. 15:26 if give ear to his c.
31:28 ten c. Deut. 4:13; 10:4
Ps. 89:31 if they keep not my c.
Mat. 5:19 whoso, break least c.
Mark 10:19 thou knowest c.
Luke 18:20
Luke 1:6 walking in c. blameless
John 14:21 he that hath my c.
2 John 6 this is love, walk after c.
Do COMMANDMENTS
Num. 15:40 do all my c.
Deut. 6:25 to do all c. 15:5
1 Chr. 28:7 to do my c.
Ps. 103:18 that rem, his c. to do
111:10 understanding that do c.
Rev. 22:14 blessed are they do c.
COMMEND.
Luke 23:46 into thy hands I c.
COMMENDETH.
Rom. 5:8 God c. his love tow, us
COMMIT.
Ex. 20:14 not c. adult, Deut. 5:18;
Luke 12:48 c. worthy of stripes
Rom. 1:32 c. such worthy of d.
1 Cor. 10:8 nei. let us c. fornica.
COMMITTED
2 Tim. 1:12 to keep what I c.
Jam. 5:15 if he c. sins be forgiv.
1 Pet. 2:23 c. himself to him jud.
Jude 15 ungodly deeds they c.
COMMITTEST,ETH, ING.
Ps. 10:14 c. himself to thee
Hos. 4:2 by lying, c. adultery
1 Cor. 6:18 c. fornication sinneth
1 John 3:4 c. sin transgresseth L.
COMMON.
Ec. 6:1 there is an evil, it is c.
Jer. 31:5 eat them as c, things
Acts 2:44 had all things c. 4:32
28 should not call any man c.
1 Cor. 10:13 no temptation but c.
Jude 3 to write of c. salvation
COMMUNICATE.
Gal. 6:6 c. to him that teacheth

COMMUNICATION.
1 Cor. 15:33 evil c. corrupt good
Eph. 4:29 no corrupt c. Col. 3:8
Phile. 6. c. of thy faith effectual
COMMUNION.
1 Cor. 10:16 c. of blood, c. of body
2 Cor. 6:14 wh. c. light with dark.
COMPANY, Substantive.
2 Thes. 3:14 have no c. with him
Great COMPANY.
Ps. 68:11 g. was c. of those pub.
COMPANION.
Prov. 13:20 c. of fools be destroy.
COMPARE, ING.
1 Cor. 2:13 c. spiritual things
2 Cor. 10:12 c. ours, with some
that com. c. thems. amongst
COMPASS, Verb.
Hab. 1:4 wicked c. righteous
COMPASSION.
1 Pet. 3:8 hav. c. one of another
1 John 3:17 shut, his bowels of c.
Full of COMPASSION.
Ps. 78:38 he being full of c.
Have or had COMPASSION.
Ex. 2:6 babe wept, she had c.
1 Sam. 23:21 for ye have c. on me
Is. 49:15 she not have c. on son
Mark 5:19 how L. had c. on thee
Luke 7:13 L. saw her, he had c.
Rom. 9:15 will have c. on whom
Heb. 5:2 can have c. on ignorant
Jude 22 of some have c. making
COMPASSIONS.
Lam. 3:22 because his c. fail not
Zec. 7:9 show c. ev. man to bro.
COMPEL.
Mat. 5:41 c. thee to go a mile go
COMPLAINERS
Jude 16 these are murmurers, c.
COMPLETE.
Col. 2:10 and ye are c. in him
COMPREHEND.
Eph. 3:18 able to c.
COMPREHENDED.
John 1:5 the darkness c. it not
CONCERNING.
Rom. 9:5 as c. flesh Christ came
11:28 as c. gospel enemies for
2 Cor. 11:21 I sp. as c. reproach
CONCORD.

2 Cor. 6:15 what c. Ch. with B.
CONDEMN.
1 John 3:20 if our heart c. us
  21 if our heart c. us not, we
CONDEMNATION.
Rom. 5:18 judgment came to c.
  8:1 there is no c. to them in C.
CONDEMNED.
1 Cor. 11:32 not be c. with world
Tit. 2:8 speech that cannot be c.
CONFESS.
Phil. 2:11 every tongue should c.
Jam. 5:16 c. your faults
1 John 1:9 if we c. our sins
2 John 7 c. not Jesus Christ
Rev. 3:5 c. his name bef. my Fa.
CONFESSETH
1 John 4:2 spirit that c. Christ
  3 c. not Jesus Christ is come
CONFESSION.
Rom. 10:10 with mouth c. is m.
1 Tim. 6:13 witnessed a good c.
CONFIDENCE.
Prov. 3:26 Lord shall be thy c.
Acts 28:31 preaching with all c.
2 Cor. 1:15 in this c. minded
Gal. 5:10 I have c. in you
Eph. 3:12 access with c. by faith
Phil. 1:25 having this c.
2 Thes. 3:4 c. in L. touching you
Phile. 21 c. in thy obedience
1 John 2:28 we may have c.
3:21 them have we c. toward G.
CONFIDENT.
Prov. 14:16 fool rageth and is c.
Rom. 2:19 art c. thou art a guide
CONFIRM.
2 Cor. 2:8 ye would c. your love
CONFIRMATION.
Phil. 1:7 in the c. of the gospel
CONFIRMED.
Acts 15:32 exhorted and c. them
1 Cor. 1:6 testim. of C. c. in you
Gal. 3:15 if c. no man disannul.
CONFORMED.
Rom. 8:29 c. to image of his Son
12:2 be not c. to this world
CONFOUND.
Gen. 11:7 c. their language, 9
CONFUSION.
1 Cor. 14:33 God not author of c.

Jam. 3:16 where strife is, is c.
CONQUERORS.
Rom. 8:37 we are more than c.
CONSCIENCE.
John 8:9 convicted by own c.
Acts 23:1 I have lived in good c.
Rom. 2:15 c. bearing witness
1 Cor. 8:7 with c. of idol eat it
2 Cor. 1:12 testimony of our c.
1 Tim. 1:5 and of a good c.
  4:2 c. seared with a hot iron
2 Tim. 1:3 whom I serve with c.
Tit. 1:15 but their c. is defiled
Heb. 9:9 as pertaining to c.
1 Pet. 2:19 for c. endure grief
CONSECRATE.
Mic. 4:13 I will c. their gain
CONSECRATED.
Heb. 7:28 Son, who is c, evermore
CONSENT, ED, ING.
Luke 23:51 same had not c.
Acts 8:1 c. to his death, 22:20
  18:20 to tarry longer, he c. not
Rom. 7:16 I c. to law
1 Tim. 6:3 c. not to whole, words
CONSIDER.
Deut. 4:39 c. it in thy heart
Job. 11:11 will he not then c. it?
37:14 c. wondrous works of God
Ps. 5:1 c. my meditation
  9:13 c. my trouble
48:13 c. her palaces, that ye
50:22 c. this, ye that forget God
  153 c. mine affliction, deliver
  159 c. how I love thy precepts
Ec. 5:1 c. not that they do evil
Is. 14:16 shall narrowly c. thee
Mat. 6:28 c. the lilies, Lu. 12:27
Luke 12:24 c. the ravens
Heb. 3:1 brethren c. the Apostle
10:24 let us c. one another
12:3 c. him endured such con.
CONSIDERED
Ps 31:7 hast c. my trouble
Prov. 24:32 then I c. it well
Acts 12:12 when Peter had c.
Rom. 4:19 c. not his body dead
CONSOLATION.
Jer. 16:7 nor give them cup of c.
Luke 2:25 Simeon waiting for c.
  6:24 woe to you rich, rec. yo. c.

Acts 4:36 interpreted, son of c.
15:31 they rejoiced for the c.
Rom. 15:5 God of c. grant you
2 Cor. 1:5 our c. aboundeth by C.

CONSPIRACY.

2 Sam. 15:12 Absalom's c. strong
2 K 12:20 a c. and slew Joash
Jer. 11:9 c. among men of Judah
Ezek. 22:25 a c. of her prophets
Acts 23:13 forty which made c.

CONSPIRED.

Gen. 37:18 c. ag. Jos. to slay him
1 Sam. 22:13 c. thou and son of J.
1 K. 15:27 Baasha c. aga. Nadab
2 K. 9:14 Jehu c. against Joram
Amos 7:10 Amos hath c. ag. thee

CONSTRAIN, ED, ETH.

Job 32:18 the spirit in me c. me
Luke 24:29 c. him, saying, Abide
Acts 16:15 Lydia c. us to come
2 Cor. 5:14 love of Christ c. us

CONSUME.

Ex. 33:3 lest I c. thee in way, 5
Deut. 5:25 this fire will c. us
Jos. 24:20 c. after done you good
2 K. 1:10 let fire c. thy fifty, 12
Ps. 37:20 c. into smoke shall c.
  39:11 his beauty to c. away
Is. 7:20 it shall c. the beard
Ezek. 4:17 c. away for iniquity
2 Thes. 2:8 whom L. shall c.
Jam. 4:3 may c. it on your lusts

CONSUME them.

Num. 16:21 c. t. in a moment, 45
Ps. 59:13 c. t. in wrath, c. them
Luke 9:54 fire to c. them

CONSUMED.

Gen. 19:15 be c. in the iniquity
Ex. 3:2 behold, bush was not c.
Num. 11:1 c. them were in utter.
Jud. 6:21 fire out of rock c. flesh
Job 1:16 fire of God c. sheep
  7:9 as cloud is c. and vanisheth
Ps. 6:7 mine eye c. 31:9
  10 my bones c. 102:3
Jer. 5:3 c. refused correction
  44:18 we have been c. by sword
Lam. 2:22 those I swad, enemy c.
Mal. 3:6 sons of Jacob are not c.

Shall be CONSUMED.

Is. 1:28 that forsake L. sh. be c.

Jer. 16:4 s. be c. by sw. 44:12, 27
Ezek. 5:12 with famine shall be c.

CONTAIN.

1 K. 8:27 heaven of heav. cannot
  c. thee, 2 Chr. 2:6 6:18
1 Cor. 7:9 if cannot c. marry

CONTEMPT.

Prov. 18:3 wicked com. then c.

CONTENT.

Luke 3:14 be c. with you wages
Phil. 4:11 in every state to be c.
1 Tim. 6:8 raiment, let us be c.

CONTENTION.

Prov. 13:10 by pride cometh c.
Phil. 1:16 preach Christ of c.
1 Thes. 2:2 speak gospel with c.

CONTENTIONS.

Prov. 18:18 causeth c. to cease
1 Cor. 1:11 there are c. am. you
Tit. 3:9 avoid c. and strivings

CONTENTIOUS.

Prov. 21:19 with c. woman
  27:15 dropping and c. woman
Rom. 2:8 to them that are c.
1 Cor. 11:16 if any seem to be c.

CONTENTMENT.

1 Tim. 6:6 godli. with c. is gain.

CONTINUAL.

Jer. 48:5 c. weeping shall go up
Ezek. 39:14 men of c. employm.
Luke 18:5 lest by her c. coming
Rom. 9:2 c. sorrow in my heart

CONTINUALLY.

1 Chr. 16:11 seek his face c.
Job. 1:5 thus did Job c.
Ps. 34:1 his praise be c. 71:6
  38:17 sorrow c. before me
  40:11 truth c. preserve me
Prov. 6:14 deviseth mischief c.
Acts 6:4 ourselves c. to prayer
Rom. 13:6 c. on this very thing

CONTINUE.

1 Tim. 2:15 if they c. in faith
  4:16 doctrine, c. in them
2 Tim. 3:14 c. in things hast
Heb. 7:23 not suffer to c.
  18:1 let brotherly love c.
Jam. 4:13 c. there a year
2 Pet. 3:4 things c. as they were
1 John 2:24 ye shall c. in the Son.

CONTRADICTING.
Acts 13:45 with envy c. blasph.
CONTRARY.
Rom. 11:24 graffed c. to nature
  16:17 c. to doctrine ye learned
Gal. 5:17 c. one to the other
Col. 2:14 handwriting c. to us
1 Thes. 2:15 and are c. to all men
1 Tim. 1:10 c. to sound doctrine
Tit. 2:8 he of a c. part be asham.
CONTRITE.
Ps. 34:18 such as of c. spirit
  51:17 c. heart, wilt not despise
Is. 57:15 of a c. spirit, to revive
  heart of the c. ones
66:2 of c. spirit and trembleth
CONVERSATION.
Ps. 37:14 as be of upright c.
2 Cor. 1:12 in godly sinc. had c.
Gal. 1:18 ye have heard of my c.
Eph. 2:3 had our c. in times past
Phil. 1:27 as becometh gospel
  3:20 for our c. is in heaven
1 Tim. 4:12 be an example in c.
Heb. 13:5 c. be without covet.
Jam. 3:13 show out of a good c.
1 Pet. 1:15 in all manner of c.
  18 not redeemed from vain c.
  2:12 c. honest among Gentiles
CONVERSION.
Acts 15:3 declaring c. of Gentiles
CONVERT, ED.
Mat. 13:15 be c. Mark 4:12
  18:3 c. and become as children
Acts 3:19 repent ye and be c.
Jam. 5:19 do err, and one c. him
CONVERTETH, ING.
Ps. 19:7 law is perfect, c. soul
Jam. 5:20 he which c. a sinner
CONVICTED.
John 8:9 c. by their conscience
COOL.
Gen. 3:8 walking in c. of day
CORD.
Jos. 2:15 let spies down by a c.
CORDS.
Jud. 15:13 Samson with new c.
CORINTH.
Acts 18:1 after, Paul came to C.
1 Cor. 1:2; 2 Cor. 1:1, 23

CORINTHIANS.
Acts 18:8 of the C. 2 Cor. 6:11
CORN.
Gen. 41:57 all came to buy c.
Deut. 16:9 put sickle to c.
  25:4 not muzzle ox treadeth c.
Ruth 3:7 lie down at heap of c.
1 Sam. 17:17 for breth. parched c.
  25:18 Abigail took of parched c.
John 12:24 except c. of wheat
Ears of CORN.
Gen. 41:5 seven ears of c. came
Ruth 2:2 glean ears of c.
CORN and wine.
Gen. 27:28 G. gave plenty of c. w
Zec. 9:17 c. make men cheer. w.
CORNELIUS. Acts 10:1, 7, 25,31
CORNER.
Mat. 21:42 same is bec. head of c.
  Ps. 118:22; Mark 12:10; Luke
  20:17; Acts 4:11; 1 Pet. 2:7
CORNER-STONE, S.
Job 38:6 who laid c.-s. thereof?
Is. 28:16 in Zion a c.-s, 1 Pet. 2:6
Eph. 2:20 Christ being chief c.-s.
CORNERS.
Deut. 32:26 I will scatter into c.
Ezek. 7:2 end is come upon four c.
Mat. 6:5 they love to pray in c.
Rev. 7:1 four angels on four c.
CORRECTION.
Prov. 3:11 nei. be weary of his c.
Hab. 1:12 establish them for c.
CORRUPT, Adjective.
Gen. 6:11 the earth also was c. 12
Ps. 14:1 they are c. 53:1; 73:8
Mat. 7:17 a c. tree evil fruit
Eph. 4:22 put off the old man c.
1 Tim. 6:5 disputings of men of c.
2 Tim. 3:8 men of c. minds
CORRUPT, Verb.
Deut. 4:16 lest ye c. yours. 25
Mat. 6:19 moth and rust doth c.
Rev. 19:2 c. earth with her fom.
CORRUPTIBLE.
1 Cor. 9:25 to obtain a c. crown
  15:53 c. must put on incorrup.
CORRUPTION.
Dan. 10:8 comeliness into c.
Jon. 2:6 br. up my life from c.
Rom. 8:21 from bondage of c.

47

1 Cor. 15:42 is sown in c. raised
Gal. 6:8 of the flesh reap c.
2 Pet. 1:4 escaped the c. that is

COST.

Luke 14:28 and counteth the c.

COSTLY.

1 Tim. 2:9 not with c. array

COUNCIL.

Mark 15:1 c. bound Jesus
Luke 22:66 led Jesus into their c.
John 11:47 gather c. Acts 5:21
Acts 4:15 com. to go out of c.
   5:27 and set them before c.

COUNSEL.

Ex. 18:19 I will give thee c.
Num. 27:21 Eleazar ask c.
Deut. 32:28 a nation void of c.
Jos. 9:14 asked not c. at the L.
Ezr. 10:8 accord, to c. of princes
Neh. 4:15 brought c. to naught
Prov. 8:14 c. is mine, and wisd.
   11:14 where no c. is, people fall
Is. 5:19 c. of Holy One
Mark 3:6 c. ag. Jes. John 11:53
Luke 23:51 not consented to c. of
John 18:14 now Caiaphas gave c.
Acts 4:28 thy c. determined bef.
Acts 27:42 soldiers c. to kill pris.
Eph. 1:11 after c. of his own will
Heb. 6:17 immutability of his c.

COUNSEL of God, or Lord.

Jud. 18:5 said, Ask c. of God
1 Sam. 14:37 Saul asked c. of G.
Ps. 33:11 c. of L. Prov. 19:21
Is. 19:17 bec. of the c. of Lord
Jer. 23:18 stood in c. of Lord
Luke 7:39 rejected c. of God
Acts 2:23 determinate c. of God

My COUNSEL.

Prov. 1:25 set at naught my c.
   30 they would none of my c.
Is. 46:10 my c. shall stand
Dan. 4:27 O king, let my c. be

Own COUNSEL.

Hos. 10:6 ashamed of his own c.

COUNSELLOR.

1 Chr. 26:14 Zechariah a wise c.
Is. 3:3 Lord taketh away c.
   9:6 be called Wonderful, C.

COUNSELLORS

Ezr. 4:5 hired c. against them

Job 3:14 at rest with c. of earth
Prov. 11:14 multitude of c. 24:6
Is. 1:26 restore thy c, as at begin.

COUNSELS.

Job 37:12 turned about by his c.
Ps. 5:10 fall by their own c.
Prov. 1:5 shall attain to wise c.
Is. 25:1 c. of old are faithful
Jer. 7:24 in c. of their evil heart
1 Cor. 4:5 manifest c. of heart

COUNT.

Acts 20:24 neither c. I my life
Phil. 3:8 I c. all loss, c. but dung
2 Thes. 1:11 c. you worthy
1 Tim. 6:1 c. masters worthy of
Phile. 17 if thou c. me a partner
Jam. 1:2 c. it joy when ye fall

COUNTED.

Gen. 15:6 c. it to him Ps. 103:31;
   Rom. 4:3; Gal. 3:6
Luke 21:36 c. worthy to escape
Acts 5:41 rejoic. were c. worthy
Rom. 2:26 uncir. be c. for circ.
Phil. 3:7 those I c. lost for Christ
2 Thes. 1:5 c. worthy of kingdom
1 Tim. 1:12 he c. me faithful
Heb. 3:3 c. worthy of more glory

COUNTENANCE.

Gen. 4:5 Cain was wroth c. fell
Jud. 13:6 his c. like c. of angel
2 K. 8:11 be settled his c. oh H.
Neh. 2:2 why is thy c. sad
   20:24 light of c. cast not down
Ps. 4:6 lift light of thy c. on us.
Prov. 15:13 maketh a cheerful c.
   25:23 so angry c. a backbiting
   27:17 so man sharpeneth c. of
Cant. 2:14 see c. thy c. is comely
Mat. 6:16 as hypocrites, of sad c.
Acts 2:28 full of joy with thy c.
Rev. 1:16 c. was as sun shineth

COUNTRY.

Jud. 11:21 Isr. possessed that c.
Ruth 1:2 came into c. of Moab
2 Sam. 15:23 all the c. wept
Mat. 9:31 his fame in all that c.
Mark 5:10 not send th. out of c.
   27:27 they drew near to some c.
Heb. 11:9 as in a strange c.

Far COUNTRY.

Jos. 9:6 we be come from f. c. 9

Mat. 21:33 householder went into
    far c. Mark 12:1
Luke 15:13 journey into a far c.

OWN country.
Lev. 16:29 one of own c. 24:22
1 K. 10:13 went to her o.c.
Mark 6:1 came into his own c.
John 4:44 proph. no honor in o.c.

Thy COUNTRY.
Num. 20:17 let us pass thro' t. c.
Jon. 1:8 what is thy c.?

COUNTRY Villages.
1 Sam. 6:18 both of c. villages

COUNTRYMEN.
2 Cor. 11:26 in perils by own c.
1 Thes. 2:14 like things of your c.

COUNTRIES.
Gen. 26:3 to thy seed these c. 4
Zec. 10:9 remember me in far c.
Luke 21:21 that are in c. enter

COUPLED.
1 Pet. 3:2 conversation c. with f.

COURAGE.
Jos. 2:11 nor any more c. in any
2 Chr. 15:8 took c. put away idols
Dan. 11:25 stir up c. ag. king
Acts 28:15 thanked God took c.

Good COURAGE.
Ps. 27:14 be of g. c. he shall stre.
    thy heart, 31:24

COURAGEOUS.
Acts 13:25 John fulfilled his c.
2 Thes. 3:1 may have fre c.
2 Tim. 4:7 I have finished my c.

COURT.
Amos 7:13 and it is the king's c.
Rev. 11:2 c. without the temple

COURTS.
2 K. 21:5 built altars for hosts of
Ps. 65:4 he may dwell in thy c.
100:4 enter his c. with praise
Is. 1:12 to tread my c.?
  62:9 drink it in c. of holiness
Ezek. 9:7 fill c. with the slain
Zec. 3:7 shalt also keep my c.
Luke 7:25 delicately in king's c.

COVENANT.
Gen. 9:12 tok. of c. 13, 17; 17:11
Lev. 26:15 that ye break my c.
Num. 25:12 my c. of peace
Deut. 4:13 dec. unto you his c.

Jud. 2:1 I will never break c.
1 Sam. 20:8 thy serv. in c. of L.
1 K. 19:10 Israel forsaken c. 14
2 K. 13:23 bec. of c. with Abrah.
1 Chr. 16:15 be mindful of his c.
2 Chr. 15:12 into c. to seek Lord
Neh. 13:29 defiled c. of priestho.
Ps. 25:14 will show them his c.
Prov. 2:17 forgetteth c. of her G.
Is. 28:18 c. with death be disan.
Jer. 11:2 hear ye words of c. 6
21 may c. be broken with Da.
Ezek. 16:8 into a c. with thee
Dan. 11:32 do wickedly against c.
Hos. 10:4 falsely in making a c.
Zec. 11:10 I might break my c.
Mal. 2:4 my c. be with Levi, 5
Rom. 1:31 c. breakers
Gal. 3:15 tho' it be but a m.'s c.
Heb. 8:6 mediator of a better c.

Book of the COVENANT.
2 K. 23:2 Josiah read all the w.
    of book of c. 2 Chr. 34:30

Establish COVENANT.
Gen. 6:18 establish my c. 9:9

Everlasting COVENANT.
Gen. 9:16 I may remember e. c.
  19 c. with Isaac for an ever. c.
2 Sam. 23:5 an ever, c. ordered
1 Chr. 16:17 confirmed to Israel
Is. 24:5 have broken everlast. c.
Ezek. 37:26 everlast. c. with them
Heb. 13:20 thro' blood of ever. c.
  29:9 keep words of this c. and do
  33:9 they have kept thy c.
1 K. 11:11 hast not k. c. Ps. 78:10
Ps. 25:10 to such as k. c. 103:18
Dan. 9:4 keep c. and mercy

Made COVENANT.
1 Chr. 11:3 David m. c. with eld.
Is. 28:15 m. a. c. with death

Make COVENANT.
Gen. 17:2 m. c. bet. me and thee

New COVENANT.
Jer. 31:31 n. c. with Is. Heb. 8:8
Heb. 8:13 a new c. the first old

Remember COVENANT.
Gen. 9:15 I will r. my c. Lev.
Amos 1:9 rem. not the broth. c.
Luke 1:72 and to rem. his holy c.

COVENANT of Salt.
Lev. 2:13 salt of c. to be lacking
COVENANTED.
Hag. 2:5 word I c. with you
COVENANTS.
Rom. 9:4 to whom pertaineth c.
COVER.
Ex. 33:22 c. thee while I pass
Jer. 46:8 I will c. the earth
Ezek. 7:18 horror shall c. them
Hos. 2:9 flax given to c. her
 10:8 mount, c. us. Luke 23:30
Mark 14:65 and c. his face
1 Cor. 11:7 man not to c. head
1 Pet. 4:8 charity c. mult. of sins
COVERED.
Gen. 7:19 mountains were c. 20
Ex. 14:28 waters c. chariots
Num. 4:20 when holy things c.
Deut. 32:15 art c. with fatness
Jud. 4:18 Jael c. Sisera, 19
1 Sam. 19:13 Mich. c. the image
1 K. 1:1 c. David with clothes
2 K. 19:1 Hezekiah c. himself
Job 23:17 c. dark from my face
Ps. 44:15 shame of face c. me
Lam. 2:1 c. dan. of Z. with clo.
 3:16 he hath c. me with ashes
Ezek. 1:11 two wings c. bod. 23
Hab. 3:3 his glory c. heavens
Mat. 8:24 was c. with waves
 10:26 nothing c. that shall not
1 Cor. 11:6 the woman be not c.
COVERED face.
Gen. 38:15 Tamar had c. her face
2 Sam. 19:4 but David c. his face
Est. 7:8 they c. Haman's face
Head COVERED.
2 Sam. 15:30 David had his h. c.
Est. 6:12 Haman, his head c.
COVERETH.
Num. 22:11 c. face of the earth
Job 9:24 he c. faces of judges
Ps. 73:6 violence c, as garment
Prov. 10:6 vio. c. the mouth 11
Jer. 3:25 our confusion c. us
Ezek. 28:14 art cherub that c.
Mal. 2:16 for one c. violence
Luke 8:16 candle c. it with ves.
COVERING, Substantive.
Gen. 20:16 thee a c. of the eyes

Ezek. 28:13 precious stone thy c.
1 Cor. 11:15 hair is given for c.
COVERT.
Job 38:40 when lions abide in c.
 40:21 behemoth lieth in c. of
Is. 4:6 a tabernacle for a c.
COVET.
Ex. 20:17 thou shalt not c. Deut.
COVETOUSNESS.
Ex. 18:21 men hating c.
Ps. 119:36 incline not heart to c.
Prov. 28:16 hateth c. sh. prolong
Jer. 6:13 given to c. 8:10
Ezek. 33:31 heart goeth after c.
Hab. 2:9 that coveteth an evil c.
Mark 7:22 out heart proceed. c.
Luke 12:15 he said, beware of c.
Rom. 1:29 filled with all c.
2 Cor. 9:5 as a matter not of c.
Eph. 5:3 c. let it not be named
Col. 3:5 mortify c. wh. is idola.
1 Thes. 2:5 nor used cloak of c.
Heb. 13:5 conver. be without c.
2 Pet. 2:3 through c. make mer.
COW.
Amos 4:3 every c. at that before
CRAFT.
Dan. 8:25 cause c. to prosper
Mark 14:1 take him by c.
Acts 18:3 he was of same c.
CRAFTINESS.
Luke 20:23 he perceived their c.
2 Cor. 4:2 not walking in c. nor
CRAFTY.
2 Cor. 12:16 being c. I caught
CRAFTSMEN.
2 K. 24:14 carried away c. 16
CREATE.
Ps. 51:10 c. in me a clean heart
CREATED.
Gen. 1:1 in the begin. God c. he.
Deut. 4:32 day God c. man
Ps. 89:12 north and south h. c.
Mal. 2:10 hath not one God c.
Mark 13:19 creation G. c.
1 Cor. 11:9 man c. for the wom.
Eph. 1:10 workmanship c. in C.
Col. 1:16 were all things c.
1 Tim. 4:3 G. c. to be received
Rev. 4:11 hast c. all things, for

CREATION.
Mark 10:6 from c. male and fe.
Rom. 1:20 from c. are clearly
Rev. 3:14 beginning of c. of God

CREATOR.
Ec. 12:1 remember c. in youth
Is. 40:28 c. of ends of the earth
43:15 I am the Lord, c. of Israel
Rom. 1:25 creature more than c.
1 Pet. 4:19 as to a faithful c.

CREATURE.
Gen. 1:20 bring forth moving c.
Lev. 11:46 this is law of every c.
Mark 16:15 gospel to every c.
Col. 1:23
Rom. 8:19 expectation of c.
2 Cor. 5:17 he is a new c.

Living CREATURES.
Ezek. 1:5 likeness of four liv. c.

CREDITOR, S.
Is. 50:1 to which of my c.
Luke 7:41 c. had two debtors

CREEP.
Lev. 11:31 unclean all that c.
Ps. 104:20 beasts of forest c.
2 Tim. 3:6 of this sort c. into

CREEPING thing, s.
Gen. 1:26 dominion over ev. c. t.
Hab. 1:14 men as c. things
Acts 10:12 P. saw c. things, 11:6
Rom. 1:23 like to c. things

CRIME.
Job 31:11 his is a heinous c.

CRIMSON.
Is. 1:18 your sins be like c.

CROOK-BACKED.
Lev. 21:20 c.-b. not approach

CROOKED.
Lam. 3:9 hath made my paths c.

CROSS.
Mat. 10:38 taketh not his c. is not
worthy of me, Luke 14:27
16:24 c. and follow me, Mark
8:34; 10:21; Luke 9:23
27:32 compelled to bear c. Mark
15:21; Luke 23:26
40 if S. of God come down from
the c. 42; Mark 15:30, 32
John 19:17 bearing c. went forth
19 wrote title, and put it on c.
25 stood by the c. his mother

1 Cor. 1:17 lest c. be of none ef.
18 preaching of c. foolishness
Gal. 5:11 offence of the c. ceased
6:12 suf. persecution for c. of C.
14 should glory, save in the c.

CROWN.
Ezek. 21:26 take off the c.
Zec. 9:16 as the stones of a c.
John 19:5 J. wearing c. of thorns
1 Cor. 9:25 a corruptible c.
Phil. 4:1 beloved, my joy and c.
1 Thes. 2:19 our c. of rejoicing
2 Tim. 4:8 c. of righteousness
Jam. 1:12 he shall rec. c. of life
1 Pet. 5:4 shall receive c. of glory
Rev. 2:10 give thee a c. of life

CROWN of gold.
Est. 8:15 Mordecai with c. of g.

CROWNED.
Ps. 8:5 hast c. him with glory
Prov. 14:18 c. with knowledge
Cant. 3:11 his mother c. him
Nah. 3:17 thy c. are as locusts
2 Tim. 2:5 not c. except he strive
Heb. 2:9 Jesus c. with glory

CROWNEDST.
Heb. 2:7 c. him with glory and

CROWNS.
Ezek. 23:42 beau. c. on their h.
Zec. 6:11 make c.; 14 c. to Helem
Rev. 4:4 elders had c. of gold

CRUCIFY.
Mat. 20:19 to Gentiles, to c. him
23:34 some of them ye shall c.
27:31 to c. him, Mark 15:20
Mark 15:13 cried again c. him, 14
Luke 23:21 c. him, c. John 19:6, 15
Heb. 6:6 c. Son of God afresh

CRUCIFIED.
Mat. 26:2 bet. to be c. Luke 24:7
27:22 said, Let him be c. 23
26 del. him to be c. John 19:16
35 c. him, John 19:23
38 thieves c. 44; Mark 15:32;
Luke 23:33; John 19:18
28:5 Jesus w. was c. Mark 16:6
John 19:20 where Jesus was c. 41
Acts 2:23 by wicked hands c.
36 made J. whom ye c. L. 4:10
Rom. 6:6 old man is c. with him
1 Cor. 1:13 was Paul c. for you?

23 preach Christ c. unto Jews
2:2 Jesus Christ and him c.
8 not have c. Lord of glory
2 Cor. 13:4 tho'c. through weak.
Gal. 2:20 I am c. with Christ
3:1 Chr. set forth, c. among you
5:24 are christ's have c. flesh
6:14 by whom the world is c.
Rev. 11:8 where Lord was c.

CRUEL.
Gen. 49:7 wrath, for it was c.
Prov. 5:9 thou give years to c.
Is. 13:9 day of Lord cometh c.
19:4 Egyptians give to c. lord
Jer. 6:23 they are c. 50:42
Heb. 11:36 trial of c. mockings

CRUMBS.
Mat. 15:27 eat of c. Mark 7:28
Luke 16:21 to be fed with the c.

CRUSH.
Amos 4:1 which c. the needy

CRUSHED.
Jer. 51:34 Nebuch. hath c. me

CRY, Substantive.
Gen. 18:21 accord, to c. come up
Ex. 2:23 their c. came up, 3:9
3:7 I have heard their c. I
Job 16:18 let my c. have no place
34:28 c. of poor to come to him,
Ps. 9:12 forget, not c. of humble
Prov. 21:13 at c. of poor
Ec. 9:17 more than c. of him
Is. 5:7 for right. behold a c.
Zep. 1:10 be a c. from fish-gate
Mat. 25:6 midnight was c. made

Great CRY.
Gen. 18:20 c. of S. is great, 19:13
27:34 Esau cried with a great c.

Hear CRY.
Ex. 22:23 I will hear their c.

CRIES.
Jam. 5:4 c. of them that reaped

CRY Verb.
Ps. 22:2 I c. in the daytime
27:7 O Lord, when I c. 28:2
Prov. 8:1 doth not wisdom c. and
21:13 shall c. but not be heard
Is. 8:4 before child c. My father
Jer. 2:2 go and c. in ears of Jer.
Lam. 3:8 when I c. he shutteth
Ezek. 9:4 c. for abominations

Hos. 8:2 Israel c. we know thee
Joel 1:19 Lord, to thee will I c.
Luke 18:7 avenge elect, which c.
Rom. 8:15 whereby we c. Abba

CRY aloud.
Job 19:7 I c. aloud but not judgm.
Ps. 55:17 at noon will I c. aloud
Is. 24:14 c. aloud from the sea
Mic. 4:9 why c. a.? is there no

CRY out.
1 Sam. 8:18 ye shall c. out
Mark 10:47 c. out, Have mercy
Luke 19:40 stones would c. out

CRIED.
Gen. 27:34 E. c. with bitter cry
Num. 11:2 c. to Moses
Deut. 22:24 dam. bec. she c. not
Jud. 5:28 mother c. through lat.
1 Sam. 17:8 G. c. to armies of Isr.
2 Sam. 20:16 then c. a wise w.
1 K. 13:2 c. against altar, 4, 32
2 K. 2:12 Elisha c. My father
Job 29:12 I delivered poor that c.
Ps. 18:6 in my distress I c. to G.
24 c.unto him, he heard
30:2 O Lord I c. to thee
34:6 this poor man c. and the L.
Is. 6:4 moved at voice of him c.
Dan. 6:20 he c. O Daniel
Hos. 7:14 not c. to me with heart
Zec. 7:13 as he c. and they would
Mat. 14:30 Peter c. Lord save me
Mark 9:26 spirit c. and rent him
John 7:37 Jesus c. if any thirst
Rev. 10:3 he c. seven thunders
Rev. 14:18 c. to him that had sic.

CRIED with a loud voice.
2 Sam. 19:4 D. c. w. l. v. O Absa.
Mat. 27:46 ninth hour J. c. w. l. v.
Acts 7:60 S. c. w. a loud voice
16:28 Paul c. with a loud voice
Rev. 6:10 c. w. a. l. v. How long

CRIED out.
Mat.8:29 spirits c. out, Luke 4:33
14:26 c. o. for fear, Mark 6:49
20:30 blind men c. out
Mark 1:23 unclean spirit c. out
Acts 19:28 c. out Great is D. 34

CRIEST, ETH.
Gen. 4:10 brother's blood c.
1 Sam. 26:14 that c. to the king?

52

Job 24:12 soul of wounded c.
Prov. 1:20 wisdom c. 8:3; 9:3
Is. 26:17 as a woman c. out
Jer. 12:8 my heritage c. ag. me
Mic. 6:9 Lord's voice c. to city
Rom. 9:27 Esa. as also c.

CRYING.
1 Sam. 4:14 Eli heard noise of c.
Mat. 3:3 c. in wilderness, Mark
  1:3; Luke 3:4; John 1:23
21:15 children c. in the temple
Acts 8:7 c. spirits came out
Gal. 4:6 c. Abba, Father
Heb. 5:7 prayers with strong c.
Rev. 21:4 no more death, nor c.

CRYSTAL.
Rev. 4:6 a sea of glass, like c.
21:11 light of city clear as c.
  22:1 a pure river, clear as c.

CUBITS.
Gen. 6:15 length of the ark 300 c.
1 K. 6:2 length of the house 60 c.
2 K. 14:13 brake wall of Jerusalem, 400 c. 2 Chr. 25:23
Ezek. 40:23 gate to gate 100 c.
Dan. 3:1 height of image 60 c.

CUCKOO.
Lev. 11:16 c. ab. Deut. 14:15

CUCUMBERS.
Num. 11:5 we remember the c.

CUMBRANCE.
Deut. 1:12 I alone bear your c.?

CUNNINGLY.
2 Pet. 1:16 c. devised fables

CUP
Prov. 23:31 giveth its color in c.
Zec. 12:2 Jerus. c. of trembling
Mat. 10:42 c. of c. wat. Mark 9:41
  20:22 to drink c. Mark 10:38
  23:25 make clean outside of c.
  Mark 14:23; Luke 22:17, 20;
  1 Cor. 11:25.
  39 let this c. pass from me,
  Mark 14:36; Luke 22:42
Luke 22:20 this c. is now testament.
John 18:11 c. Father hath given
1 Cor. 10:16 c. of blessing
  21 cannot drink c. of L. and c.
  11:27 drink c. of Lord unworthily
Rev. 14:10 without mixt. into c.

CUP-BEARER.
Neh. 1:11 I was the king's c.-b.

CUP-BEARERS.
1 K. 10:5 saw c.-b. 2 Chr. 2:4

CURE, ED.
Jer. 53:6 I will c. them, and
Hos. 5:13 could he not c. you
Mat. 17:16 disciples, not c. him
Luke 7:21 same hour he c. many
John 5:10 Jews said to him c.

CURSE, Substantive.
Lam. 3:65 give thy c. unto them
Dan. 9:11 the c. is poured upon
Zec. 5:3 this is c. that goeth
  8:13 ye were c. among heathen
Mal. 2:2 I will send c.
  3:9 ye are cursed with a c. ye
  4:6 lest I smite earth with a c.
Acts 23:12 bound under a c. 14
Gal. 3:10 of law, are under c.
  13 redeemed us from c. of law
Rev. 22:3 shall be no more c.

CURSE, Verb.
Job. 1:11 c. thee to thy face, 2:5
  2:9 said his wife, c. God and die
Ps. 62:4 but they c. inwardly
  100:28 let them c. but bless thou
Prov. 11:26 people shall c. him
  24:24 him shall the people c.
  30:10 accuse not serv. lest he c.
Ec. 7:21 hear servant c. thee
  10:20 c. not king, c. not the rich
Is. 8:21 c. their king, and God
Jer. 15:10 every one doth c. me
Mal. 2:2 I will c. your blessings
Mat. 5:44 bl. th. that c. Lu, 6:28
  26:74 began to c. Mark 14:71
Rom. 12:14 bless, and c. not
Jam. 3:9 therewith c. we men

CURSED.
Gen. 3:14 serpent c.; 17 ground
  4:11 Cain c.; 9:25 c. be Canaan
Jos. 6:26 c. be man bu. Jericho
Jud. 9:27 and c. Abimelech
Ec. 7:22 likewise hast c. other
Jer. 11:3 c. obeyeth not covenant
Mal. 1:14 but c. be the deceiver
Mat. 25:41 depart from me ye c.
John 7:49 know not law are c.
Gal. 3:10 c. that continueth not

CURSEDST.
Mark 11:21 fig-tree thou c. is
CURSETH.
Ex. 21:17 he that c. his father,
Lev. 24:15 whoso c. his God
Prov. 30:11 genera. c. their father
Mat. 15:4 c. his father or mother,
   let him die, Mark 7:10
CURSING.
Ps. 10:7 full of c. Rom. 3:14
   109:17 loved c. so let it come
Prov. 29:24 hear c. bewrayeth not
Heb. 6:8 thorns, is nigh to c.
Jam. 3:10 out of same mouth c.
CURTAINS.
Hab. 3:7 of Midian did tremble
CUSTOM.
Jud. 11:39 was a c. in Israel
Ezr. 3:4 accord. to c. Jer. 32:11
Mat. 9:9 saw Matthew at receipt
   17:25 whom do kings take c.?
Luke 1:9 ac. to c. of priest's office
Rom. 13:7 c. to whom c. is due
1 Cor. 11:16 we have no such c.
CUSTOMS.
Lev. 18:30 these abominable c.
Jer. 10:3 c. of this people
Acts 6:14 shall change c. of M.
CUT, Participle.
Acts 5:33 c. to the heart, 7:54
CUT, Verb.
Dan. 2:5 ye will not shall be c.
CUT asunder.
Ps. 129:4 c. a. cords of wicked
Jer. 50:23 hammer of earth c. a.
Zec. 11:10 Beauty and c. it a.
Mat. 24:51 c. him a. Luke 12:46
CUT down.
Ex. 34:13 c. down their groves,
Num. 13:23 c. down a. branch. 24
Ps. 37:2 shall soon be c. down
Is. 9:10 sycamores are c. down
Jer. 22:7 c. d. thy choice cedars
Nah. 1:12 thus shall be c. down
Zep. 1:11 merch. people c. down
Luke 13:7 c. it down
CUT off.
Gen. 9:11 nor all flesh be c. off
Lev. 17:10 will c. him off, 18:29;
Num. 4:18 c. not off tribe of K.
Deut. 12:29 G. shall c. off nations

Ruth 4:10 dead be not c. off
1 Sam. 2:31 I will c. off thy arm
   24:4 David c. off the skirt of, 5
   28:9 how Saul c. off wizards
   31:9 and they c. off Saul's head
2 Sam. 4:12 and c. off their hands
   20:22 c. off the head of Sheba
1 K. 9:7 will I c. off Is. out off
Prov. 2:22 wicked shall be c. off
Is. 9:14 will c. off head and tail
   10:7 to c. off nations not a few
   11:13 adversary of Jud. be c. off
   14:22 c. off from Babylon
   15:2 every beard c. off
Jer. 7:28 truth is c. off fr. mouth
Lam. 2:3 c. off in anger
Hab. 3:17 tho' the flock be c. off
Zep. 1:3 c. off man from land
Mal. 2:12 Lord will c. off man
Mat. 5:30 if right hand offered c.
   it off, 18:8; Mark 9:43, 45
Mark 14:47 c. off his ear, Luke
   22:50; John 18:10, 26
Rom. 11:22 shalt also be c. off
2 Cor. 11:12 I may c. off occasion
Gal. 5:12 I would they were c. off
CYMBAL.
1 Cor. 13:1 I am as tinkling c.
CYMBALS.
2 Sam. 6:5 play. on c. 1 Chr. 13:8
2 Chr. 5:13 lift up voice with c.
CYPRESS.
Is. 44:14 he taketh the c.
CYPRUS.
Acts 4:36 country of C. 11:20
CYRENE.
Mat. 27:32 found a man of C.
CYRUS.
2 Chr. 36:22 the first year of C.
D.

DAMASCUS,
Acts 9:2 desired letters to D. 10,
   19, 22, 27; 22:6, 10; 26:12
Gal. 1:17 I returned again to D.
DAMNABLE.
2 Pet. 2:1 who bring in d. heres.
DAMNATION.
Mat. 23:14 shall receive greater
Mark 3:29 in danger of eternal d.
Rom. 3:8 whose d. is just

DAMNED.
Mark 16:16 believeth not be d.
Rom. 14:23 doubteth is d.
DAN, a person
Gen. 30:6; 35:25; 49; 16,17
DAN, a place.
Gen. 14:14 pursued them unto D.
Tribe of DAN.
Num. 1:38 num. of D. 13:12; 34:22
DANCE, Verb.
Ec. 3:4 and a time to d.
DANCING.
Ps. 30:11 my mourning into d.
Luke 15:25 as he came heard d.
DANGER.
Mat. 5:21 in d. of judgment, 22
22 in d. of council, of hell-fire
DANIEL.
Ezek. 14:14 though Noah, D. and
DARK.
Joel 2:10 sun and moon be d.
Mic. 3:6 d. to you, day shall be d.
2 Pet. 1:19 shineth in a d. place
DARKENED.
Rev. 8:12 so as third part was d.
9:2 sun and the air were d.
DARKLY.
1 Cor. 13:12 we see thro' a glass d.
DARKNESS.
Gen. 1:2 d. was upon the deep
1 John 2:11 d. hath blinded
Jude 6 everlast, chains under d.
IN DARKNESS.
Ps. 82:5 they walk on in d.
Prov. 20:20 out in obscure d.
Ec. 2:14 fool walketh in d.
John 8:12 not walk in d.
1 John 1:6 and walk in d. we lie
DARKNESS, with light.
Gen. 1:4 G. divided light from d.
1 Pet. 2:9 out of d. into marv. l.
1 John 1:5 in Him is no d. at all
DARTS.
Eph. 6:16 to quench fiery d. of
DASH.
Ps. 2:9 d. in pieces like a pot.
91:12 lest thou d. foot against a
Mat. 4:6; Luke 4:11
DAUGHTER.
Mark 7:26 cast devil out of her d.
DAUGHTER-IN-LAW.

Ruth 4:15 d.-in-l. which lov. thee
MY DAUGHTER.
Mat. 9:18 my d. is even now d.
15:22 my d. is vexed
Mark 5:23 my d. at point of d.
DAVID.
Ruth 4:22 Jesse begat D. Mat.
1 Sam. 16:13 came upon D.
Ps. 72:20 prayers of D. son of J.
Mat. 9:27 son of D. 15:22; 20:30;
Rom. 1:3 C. seed of D. 2 Tim. 2:8
Rev. 3:7 key of D.; 5:5 root, 22:16
House of DAVID.
1 K. 12:19 fol. D. but J. 2 Chr.
10:19
Luke 1:27 Joseph, of h. of D. 69
DAVID, joined with king.
1 Sam. 21:11 this D. k. of land?
2 Sam. 2:4 anointed D. k. over J.
Servant DAVID.
2 Sam. 7:5 my servant D. 8, 26
DAY.
Gen. 1:5 God called the light d.
Dan. 6:10 petition 3 times a d.
Joel 2:2 a d. of darkness and
Mic. 3:6 d. be dark over them
Mat. 24:38 d. Noe ent. Luke 17:27
50 L. shall come in a d. when
25:13 know the d. nor the hour
Mark 1:35 great while before d.
Luke 1:20 d. these be performed
John 6:39 raise it ag. at last d.
Acts 1:2 until d. he was tak. up
2 Cor. 6:2 now is the d. of salv.
2 Pet. 1:19 till the d. dawn, and
All the DAY long.
Deut. 28:32 longings a. t. d. l.
Prov. 21:26 coveteth all the d. l.
Rom. 10:21 a. t. d. l. stret. my h.
First DAY.
Gen. 1:5 evening and morn. f. d.
Third DAY.
Hos. 6:2 third d. he will raise us
Mat. 10:21 be raised again the
third d. 17:23; Luke 9:22
Seventh DAY.
Gen. 2:3 G. bless. s. d. Ex. 20:11
31:17 on seventh d. God rested
Eighth DAY.
Lev. 12:3 on eighth d. be circum.

Great DAY.
John 7:37 great d. of feast
Rev. 6:17 g. d. of his wrath

DAY of Judgment.
Mat. 10:15 more tolerable for S.
11:22 Tyre and Sidon at d. of j.
12:36 account in the d. of ju.
2 Pet. 2:9 res. unjust to d. of ju.
1 John 4:17 boldness in d. of ju.

DAY of the Lord.
Is. 2:12 d. of L. be on every one
1 Cor. 5:5 saved in d. of Lord
2 Cor. 1:14 ye are on. in d. of L.
1 Thes. 5:2 as a thief. 2 Pet. 3:10
Rev. 1:10 the Spirit on Lord's d.

DAY, joined with Night.
Gen. 1:14 to divide d. from n.
Jos. 1:8 shalt meditate therein d.
1 Sam. 19:24 naked all d. and n.
1 K. 8:29 eyes be opened towards
Is. 4:5 sm. by d. fla. fire by n.
Luke 2:37 prayers night and d.
1 Thes. 2:9 laboring d. and n.
2 Tim. 1:3 in prayers n. and d.

One DAY.
2 Pet. 3:8 o. d. with L. as 1,000 yr.

Sabbath DAY.
Ex. 16:26 seventh d. is sa. 20:10
20:8 s. - d to keep it h. Deut. 5:12

This DAY.
Ex. 12:14 t. d. for a memorial
Jos. 14:11 I am as strong t. d.
24:15 choose this d. whom
serv.Mat. 6:11 give us this d. daily
b.
Luke 2:11 is born t. d. a Saviour

DAY of trouble.
2 K. 19:3 this is d. of t. Is. 37:3
Ps. 20:1 L. hear thee in d. of t.

DAYTIME.
Luke 21:37 in d. he was teaching

His DAYS.
Gen. 6:3 his d. shall be 120 years

In the DAYS.
Luke 1:25 L. dealt with me in d.
4:25 widows in d. of Elias
17:26 in the d. of Noe; 28 Lot

In those DAYS.
1 Sam. 3:1 precious in those d.
Jer. 33:16 in those d. J. be saved
Joel 2:29 in th. d. will I pour out

Latter DAYS.
Num. 24:14 peo. do to pe. in l.d.
Deut. 4:30 l. d. if thou turn to L.
Jer. 23:20 in lat. d. con. it, 30:24
Ezek. 38:16 ag. my people in l. d.
Dan. 2:28 what shall be in l. d.
Hos. 2:5 shall fear Lord in l. d.

Sabbath DAYS.
Mat. 12:15 on sab. d. priests prof.
10 lawful to heal on sab. d.?
12 lawful to do well on s. d.?

Thy DAYS.
Ex. 20:12 hon. thy father that t.
d. may be long. Deut. 25:15

Three DAYS.
Gen. 40:12 branches are three d.
26:61 destroy the temple, and to
build it in t. d. 27:40 ; Mark
Luke 2:46 after t. d. found in t.
Acts 9:9 S. th. d. without sight
Rev. 11:9 three d. and a half

Five DAYS.
Num. 11:19 nor five d. nor ten d.

Six DAYS.
Ex. 20:9 six, d. shalt thou labor,
John 12:1 J. six d. bef. passover

Seven DAYS.
Is. 30:26 light of sun as of a. d.

Ten DAYS.
Dan. 1:12 prove thy servant t. d.
Rev. 2:10 have tribulation ten d.

Forty DAYS.
Ex. 24:18 Moses in mount forty
d. 34:28; Deut. 9:9; 10:10
Num. 13:25 after forty d. 14:34
Deut. 9:25 I fell before L. f. d.
Ezek. 4:6 bear iniquity of J. f. d.

Your DAYS.
Deut. 11:21 y. d. may be multi.

DAILY.
Ps. 13:2 sorrow in my heart d.
42:10 d. to me, Wh. is thy God?
56:1 fighting d. oppresseth me
2 would d. swallow me up
61:8 I may d. perform my vows
68:19 Lord, who d. loadeth us
72:15 and d. shall he be praised
74:22 foolish reproach. thee d.
86:3 I cry d.; 88:9 I called d.
88:17 about me d. like water
Prov. 8:30 I was d. his delight

34 watching d. at my gates
Is. 58:2 yet they seek me d.
Luke 9:23 take up his cross d.
Acts 2:46 continuing d. with one
47 Lord added to church d.
1 Cor. 15:31 I die d.

DEACON.
1 Tim. 3:8 d. must be grave

DEAD.
2 Sam. 9:8 look on such d. dog
Ps. 31:12 forgotten as a d. man
Mat. 2:20 are d. son, child's life
8:22 let the d. bury their d.
32 God is not the God of the d.
Mark 12:27; Luke 20:38
23:27 full of d. men's bones
Luke 7:12 a d. man carried out
10:30 leaving him half d.
John 5:21 Father raiseth up d.
11:25 though d. yet shall live
Acts 2:29 patriarch David is d.
1 Cor. 15:15 if so be d. rise not
35 will say, How are d. raised
1 Thes. 4:16 d. in Chr. shall rise
Heb. 6:1 repent, from d. works
1 Pet. 2:24 we being d. to sin
Jude 12 twice d. plucked by
Rev. 1:5 J. first-begotten of d.

For the DEAD.
1 Cor. 15:29 are baptized for the
d. why baptized for d.?

From the DEAD.
Mat. 14:2 J. is risen from the d.

Is DEAD.
1 Tim. 5:6 is d. while she liveth.
Jam. 2:17 without works is d. 20

DEADLY.
Mark 16:18 drink d. thing
Jam. 3:8 tongue full of d. poison

DEAF.
Mat. 11:5 the d. hear, Luke 7:22
Mark 7:32 brought to him one d.

DEALT.
Luke 1:25 hath L. d. with me
Rom. 12:3 G. hath d. to ev. man

DEAR.
1 Thes. 2:8 bec. ye were d. to us

DEARLY beloved.
1 Cor. 10:14 my d. b. Phil. 4:1

DEATH.
Job. 27:15 remain be buried in d.

Ps. 6:5 in d. no remem. of thee
13:3 lest I sleep the sleep of d.
48:14 God be our guide unto d.
Cant. 8:6 for love is strong as d.
Is. 25:8 swallow up d. in victory
Jer. 8:3 d. chosen rather than life
Luke 2:26 not see d. bef. seen C.
22:33 to prison and d.
23:22 I found no cause of d.
John 4:47 he was at point of d.
Acts 2:24 loosed the pains of d.
Rom. 5:10 reconciled to God by
6:3 were baptized into his d.
23 for the wages of sin is d. but
1 Cor. 3:22 life or d. all are yours
54 d. is swallowed up in vict.
55 O d. where is thy sting?
56 the sting of d. is sin
2 Cor. 1:9 sentence of d.
10 del. us from so great a d.
7:10 sorrow of world worketh d.
Phil. 2:8 obedient to d. the d. of
cross
Heb. 2:9 suffering of d. crowned,
Jam. 1:15 sin, bringeth forth d.
1 John 3:14 not abideth in d.
Rev. 1:18 keys of hell and of d.

From DEATH.
Jam. 5:20 shall save a soul f. d.

Shadow of DEATH.
Ps. 23:4 valley of shad. of d.
Mat. 4:16 that sat in s. of d.
Luke 1:79 light to them in s. of d.

DEBORAH.
Gen. 35:8 D. died, was buried
Jud. 4:4 and D. judged Israel

DEBT,S.
2 K. 4:7 sell oil, pay thy d.
Prov. 22:26 are sureties for d.
Mat. 6:12 forgive us our d. as
30 into prison till he pay d.
Rom. 4:4 reward reckoned of d.

DEBTOR.
Mat. 23:16 swear by gold, is a d.
Rom. 1:14 I am d. to the Greeks
Gal. 5:3 a d. to do the whole law

DEBTORS.
Mat. 6:12 as we forgive our d.
Luke 7:41 a creditor had two d.

DECAPOLIS.
Mat. 4:25 followed him from D.

DECEIT, S.

Ps. 10:7 his mouth is full of d.
55:11 d. and guile depart not
Prov. 12:5 coun. of wicked are d.
   20 d. is in them that imag. ev.
Is. 30:10 speak smooth, proph. d.
Amos 8:5 falsify. balances by d.
Col. 2:8 spoil you thro, vain d.
1 Thes. 2:3 exhortation not of d.

DECEITFUL.

Ps. 5:6 Lord will abhor d. man
Prov. 11:18 worketh a d. work
2 Cor. 11:13 such are d. workers
Eph. 4:22 according to d. lusts

DECEITFULLY.

2 Cor. 4:2 handling word of G. d.

DECEITFULNESS.

Mat. 13:22 the d. of rich, choke
   the word, Mark 4:19

DECEIVED.

1 Tim. 2:14 Adam was not d. b ut
2 Tim. 3:13 deceiv. and being d.
Tit. 3:3 were foolish. d.

DECENTLY.

1 Cor. 14:40 done d. and in order

DECLARE.

1 Chr. 16:24 d. his glory among
   the heathen, Ps. 96:3
Job 12:8 fishes shall d. unto thee
Ps. 9:11 d. among people
   19:1 the heavens d. glory of G.
Jer. 5:20 d. this in house of Jac.
Mic. 3:8 d. to Jacob his transg.
Mat. 13:36 d. parable of tares
Acts 13:32 we d. glad tidings

DECLARED.

Col. 1:8 who d. to us your love1

DECREE, S.

Luke 2:1 a d. from C. Augustus
Acts 16:4 delivered d. to keep

DEDICATE.

2 Chr. 2:4 I build to d. it to God

DEED

Col. 3:17 ye do in word or d.

DEEP sleep.

Gen. 2:21 a d. sleep to fall on A.
1 Sam. 26:12 d. s. was on them
Prov. 19:15 sloth, casteth in d. s.
Is. 29:10 spirit of d. sleep

DEFENCE.

Phil. 1:7 and in d. of the gospel
   17 I am set for d. of gospel

DEFY.

Num. 23:7 curse me Jacob, d. Is.
1 Sam. 17:10 I d. armies of Israel

DEFILE.

Lev. 11:44 nor d. yours. 18:24
Dan. 1:8 not d. with king's meat
Mat. 15:18 d. the man, Mark 7:15
1 Cor. 3:17 if any d. temple
Jude 8 filthy dreamers d. flesh

DEFILED.

Ezek. 4:13 shall Isr. cat d. bread
   5:11 because d. my sanctuary
   18:6 nor d. neighbor's wife, 15
   22:4 d. thyself in idols, 23:7
   23:38 d. my sanctuary same day
   28:18 hast d. thy sanctuaries
   43:8 d. my holy name
Mark 7:2 disc. eat with d. hands
1 Cor. 8:7 conscience weak, is d.
Tit. 1:15 them that are d. their

DEFRAUD.

1 Thes. 4:6 no man d. his brother

DELICATE.

Is. 47:1 no more be called d.
Jer. 6:2 likened Zion to d. wom.

DELIGHT, Substantive.

Deut. 10:15 L. had d. in thy faith.
Ps. 1:2 his d. is in law of the L.
Prov. 8:30 I was daily his d.
Is. 58:2 take d. in app. to God
Jer. 6:10 no d. in word of Lord.

DELIGHT, Verb.

Num. 14:8 if Lord d. in us
Ps. 37:4 d, thyself also in Lord
Prov. 1:22 long will scorners d?

DELIGHTS.

2 Sam. 1:24 clothed you with d.
Ps. 119:92 law been my d.
Prov. 8:31 my d. with sons of m.
Ec. 2:8 I gat me the d. of men
Cant. 7:6 how pleasant for d.

DELIVER.

Ex. 23:31 I will d. the inhabit.
Num. 21:2 indeed d. this people
   32:39 neither any that can d. out
Jos. 2:13 d. our lives from death
Jud. 7:7 by the 300 will I d. M.
Ps. 6:4 d. my soul, 17:13; 22:20;

116:4; 120:2
Ps. 7:2 none to d. 50:22
23:14 shalt d. his soul rom hell
Ec. 8:8 wick. d. those given
Is. 5:29 none shall d. prey
47:14 not d. thems. from flame
50:2 have I no power to d.?
Jer. 15:9 residue will I d.
 18:21 d. their children to famine
Ezek. 13:21 I will d. my peo. 23
14:14 d. but their own souls
Dan. 3:29 no god d. after this
Amos 2:14 nor mighty d. himself
Mic. 5:8 teareth, and none can d.
Mat. 10:21 bro. d. bro. to death
Acts 25:16 to d. any man to die
1 Cor. 5:5 d. such a one to Satan
2 Cor. 1:10 death, and doth d.
2 Pet. 2:9 Lord know. how to d.
DELIVER him.
Ps. 2 not d. h. to will of enemies
71:11 for there is none to d. h.
Prov. 19:19 if d. him must do it
Mat. 20:19 d. him to G. Mark
    10:33; Luke 20:20; Acts 21:11
27:43 let him d. him now
DELIVER me.
Gen. 32:11 d. me from Esau
Job 6:23 d. me from enemies, Ps
    31:15 ; 59:1
Ps. 7:1 save me from them, d. m.
39:8 d. me from all my transg.
43:1 O d. me from the deceitful
59:2 d. me from workers of iniq.
69:14 d. me out of the mire
71:2 d. me in thy righteous. 31:1
140:1 d. me from the evil man
142:6 d. me from my persecutors
143:9 d. me from mine enemies
Is. 44:17 d. me, thou art my God
Acts 25:11 no man may d. me
Rom. 7:24 d. me from body of d.?
2 Tim. 4:18 d. me from evil work
DELIVER thee.
Job 5:19 d. t. in six troubles
Dan. 6:16 thy G. will d. thee
DELIVER them.
Acts 7:25 God by his hand d. t.
Heb. 2:15 d. t. who through fear
DELIVER us.
Mat. 6:13 d. us fr. evil, Luke 11:4

2 Cor. 1:10 he will yet d. us
Gal. 1:4 d. us from evil world
DELIVER you.
Mat. 10:17 d. you up, Mark 13:9
DELIVERANCE.
Luke 4:18 to preach d. to capt.
Heb. 11:35 not accepting d.
DELIVERED.
Ps. 22:5 they cried and were d.
Prov. 11:8 is d. out of trouble
Ec. 9:15 by wisdom he d. city
Is. 36:19 d. Samaria out
 38:17 d. it from pit of corrupt
Jer. 20:13 d. soul of the poor
Ezek. 3:19 d. thy soul, 33:9
 14:16 they only shall be d.
Dan. 3:28 d. serv. that trusted
Joel 2:32 call on L. shall be d.
Amos 9:1 shall not be d.
Mic. 4:10 go to Bab. there be d.
Hab. 2:9 d. from power of evil
Rom. 4:25 was d. for our offenc.
2 Cor. 4:11 are always d. to dea.
2 Thes. 3:2 d. from unreas. men
1 Tim 1:20 whom I ha. d. to S.
2 Tim. 4:17 I was d. out of the
    mouth of the lion
Heb. 11:11 by faith Sarah was d.
2 Pet. 2:7 and d. just Lot, vexed
Jude 3 faith once d. to the sain.
DELIVERED him.
Mat. 18:34 d. him to tormentors
27:2 d. him to P. Pilate, Mark
    15:1
 18 for envy d. him, Mark 15:10
 26 d.h. to be cruc. John 19:16
John 18:30 we, not d. h. to thee
Acts 7:10 d. h. out of afflictions
DELIVERED me.
Ex. 18:4 d. me fr. swo. of Pha.
Jud. 12:3 I saw ye d. me not
2 Sam. 22:18 he d. me from my
    strong enemy, Ps. 18:17
Job 10:11 d. me to the ungodly
Ps. 18:43 d. me from striv. of pe.
54:7 d. me out of all my trouble
John 19:11 d. me hath great, sin
2 Tim. 3:11 of them all L. d. me
DELIVERED up.
Acts 3:13 glorified Son ye a. up
Rom. 8:32 but d. him up for

1 Cor. 15:24 have d. up kingdom
DELIVERED you.
Rom. 6:17 obeyed doctrine d. y.
1 Cor. 11:23 that I d. y. 15:3
DELIVERER.
Jud. 3:9 L. raised up d. to Is. 15
Rom. 11:26 come out of Sion t.
DEN,S.
Jud. 6:2 Israel made them d.
Job 37:8 th. the beasts go into d.
Ps. 10:9 lieth as a lion in his d.
104:22 lay them down in d.
Jer. 7:11 house a d. of robbers
Dan. 6:16 cast him into d. of li.
Amos 3:4 y. lion cry out of d.?
Mat. 21:13 a d. of th. Mark 11:17
Heb. 11:38 they wandered in d.
Rev. 6:15 bond and free hid in d.
DENY.
Mat. 10:33 d. me, him will I d.
16:24 let him d. himself, Mark
8:34; Luke 9:23
26:34 d. me thrice, 75; Mark
14:30, 72
Luke 20:27 d. th. is any resur.
2 Tim. 2:12 d. him, he will d. us
Tit. 1:16 in works they d. him.
DEPART.
Phil. 1:23 d. and to be with Chr.
Jam. 2:16 d. in peace, be clothed
Not DEPART.
Ps. 55:11 guile d. not from str.
Prov. 3:21 not d. from eyes, 4:21
Is. 54:10 kindness shall not d.
59:21 my Spirit and wo. not d.
Jer. 32:40 shall not d. from me
Mat. 14:16 they need not d. give
Luke 4:42 that he should not d.
DEPARTED.
Rev. 6:14 heaven d. as a scroll
DEPTH.
Mat. 18:6 drowned in d. of sea
Mark 4:5 no d. of earth wither.
Rom. 8:39 nor d. sep. us fr. love
Eph. 3:18 d. of the love of Christ
DEPTHS.
Mic. 7:19 cast sins into d. of sea
DESCEND.
Ps. 49:17 glory not d. after him
Ezek. 26:20 that d. into pit, 31:16
Mark 15:32 let C. d. from cross

Acts 11:5 I saw a vision, ves. d.
Rom. 10:7 who d. into the deep
1 Thes. 4:16 L. sh. d. fr. heaven
DESCENDED.
Ex. 19:18 L. d. on Sinai in fire
DESCENT.
Heb. 7:3 Melchizedek without d.
DESERT, Wilderness.
Ex. 5:3 three days jour. into d.
John 6:31 did e. manna in the d.
DESERT land.
Deut. 32:10 found him in a d. l.
DESIRE, Verb.
Neh. 1:11 d. to fear thy name
Dan. 2:18 d. mercies of G. of h.
1 Cor. 14:1 d. spiritual gifts
Jam. 4:2 ye d. to have, not obt.
Rev. 9:6 men shall d. to die, and
DESIRED.
Ps. 19:10 more to be d. th. gold
Prov. 8:11 d. not to be compared
Ec. 2:10 what my eyes d. I kept
Is. 26:9 with my soul I d. thee
Acts 12:20 they d. peace
1 John 5:15 have petitions we d.
DESIRES.
Ps. 37:4 give thee d. of thy h.
DESOLATE.
Ps. 25:16 mercy, for I am d.
69:25 let their habitation be d.
Is. 1:7 your country is d.
Jer. 2:12 be ye very d. saith L.
Lam. 1:13 d. all day, 3:11
Hos. 13:16 Sam, shall become d.
Acts 1:20 let his habitation be d.
1 Tim. 5:5 a wid. indeed, and d.
Rev. 17:16 and make her d.
DESOLATION.
Ps. 73:19 how brought into d.
Prov. 1:27 fear cometh as d.
Is. 17:9 in that day shall be d.
Jer. 22:5 this house sh. bec. a d.
Mic. 6:16 should make thee d.
Mat. 12:25 ev. kingd. divided ag.
itself is br. to d. Luke 11:17
24:15 abom. of d. Mark 13:14
DESOLATIONS.
Dan. 9:2 70 years in d. of Jeru.
18 and behold our d.
26 to end of war d. determined

DESPERATE, LY.
Job 6:26 speeches of one that is d.
Is. 17:11 in the day of d. sorrow
Jer. 17:9 the heart is d. wicked
DESPISE.
Lev. 26:15 if ye d. my statutes
Job 5:17 d. not chast. Almighty.
  Prov. 3:11; Heb. 12:5
  9:21 I would d. my life
  10:3 sho. d. work of thy hands
  31:13 if d. cause of man-servant
Ps. 51:17 contrite h. wilt not d.
  73:20 thou shalt d. their image
  102:17 will not d. their prayer
Prov. 1:7 but fools d. wisdom
  6:30 men do not d. a thief, if
  23:9 a fool will d. the wisd. of
  22 d. not thy mother when old
1 Cor. 11:22 or d. ye church of G.
  16:11 let no man there, d. him
1 Thes. 5:20 d. not prophesyings
1 Tim. 4:12 let none d. thy youth
Tit. 2:15 let no man d. thee
2 Pet. 2:10 that d. government
DESPISED.
Gal. 4:14 my tempta. ye d. not
Jam. 2:6 but ye have d. the poor
DESTITUTE.
Jam. 2:15 if a bro. or sister be d.
DESTROY.
Gen. 18:23 d. right, wi. wicked?
Prov. 1:32 prosp. of fools d. th.
Dan. 8:25 by peace shall he d.
John 2:19 J. said, d. this temple
Acts 6:14 this Jesus d. this place
2 Thes. 2:8 shall d. with brightn.
1 John 3:8 might d. works of d.
Rev. 11:18 d. th. wh. d. the earth
I WILL, or WILL I DESTROY.
Gen. 6:7 I will d. man whom I
Ex. 23:27 I will d. the people
  30:13 saith Lord I will d. idols
Amos 9:8 I will d. sinf. kingdom
Mark 1:58 I will d. this temple
1 Cor. 1:19 I will d. wisd. of wise
not DESTROY.
Rom. 14:20 d. n. work of God
To DESTROY.
John 10:10 thief cometh to d.
Jam. 4:12 one lawgiver able to d.

DESTROYED.
Rom. 6:6 body of sin might be d.
Not DESTROYED.
Dan. 7:14 his kingdom not be d.
2 Cor. 4:9 cast down, but not d.
Shall be DESTROYED.
Gen. 34:30 I shall be d. I and
Est. 4:14 father's houses be d.
Utterly DESTROYED.
Is. 34:2 L. hath ut. d. all nations
DESTROYER.
Ex. 12:23 d. come into houses
Jud. 16:24 the d. of our country
Prov. 28:24 is companion of a d.
1 Cor. 10:10 were destroyed of d.
DESTROYING.
Ezek. 9:1 d. weapon in his hand
  20:17 eye spared from d. them
DESTRUCTION.
1 K. 20:42 appointed to utter d.
2 Chr. 22:4 counsellors to his d.
Est. 8:6 to see d. of my kindred
  103:4 redeemeth thy life fr. d.
Prov. 1:27 your d. as a whirlw.
  10:14 mouth of foolish near d.
Prov. 24:2 for their heart stu. d.
Is. 1:28 d. of transgr. together
  10:25 anger cease in their d.
Mat. 7:13 br. is way lead. to d.
Rom. 3:16 d. and mis. in ways
1 Cor. 5:5 Satan for d. of flesh
1 Thes. 5:3 then sud. d. cometh
DETERMINED.
Is. 19:17 counsel he hath d.
Dan. 9:24 seventy weeks are d.
1 Cor. 2:2 I d. not to know sa. J.
2 Cor. 2:1 d. this with myself
DEVICE.
2 Chr. 2:14 to find out every d.
Acts 17:29 graven by man's d.
DEVICES.
Prov. 1:31 be filled with own d.
Jer. 11:19 had devised d. ag. me
2 Cor. 2:11 not ignorant of his d.
Mat. 4:1 to be tempted of the d.
  9:32 man poss. with d. 12:22
  11:18 he hath a d. Luke 7:33
  17:18 Jesus rebuked the d.
Mark 5:15 poss. with d. 16, 18
Luke 4:2 forty days tempt. of d.
John 6:70 and one of you is a d.

8:44 ye are of your father the d.
10:20 many said, He hath a d.
13:2 d. having put into Judas
Acts 10:38 heal, all oppr. with d.
13:10 thou child of the d.
Eph. 4:27 neither give pla. to d.
6:11 to stand aga. wiles of d.
1 Tim. 3:6 fall into cond. of d.
7 lest he fall into snare of d.
2 Tim. 2:26 rec. out of sna. of d.
Heb. 2:14 p. of death, that is d.
Jam. 4:7 resist d. and he will fl.
1 Pet. 5:8 your adversary the d.
1 John 3:8 commit. sin is of d.
Jude 9 Mich. contend, with d.
Rev. 2:10 d. cast some into pris.
12 d is come down
20:2 old serpent which is the d.

DEVILS.

Lev. 17:7 no more of. sac. to d.
Deut. 32:17 they sacrificed to d.
Ps. 106:37 sacrificed sons to d.
Mat. 4:24 poss. with d. 8:16, 28,
33; Mark 1:32; Luke 8:36
8:31 the d. besought, Mark 5:12
Mark 9:38 saw one casting out
d. in thy name, Luke 9:49
16:17 in my name cast out d.
Luke 4:41 d. came out of many
8:2 out of whom went seven d.
9:1 authority over all d.
13:32 tell that fox, I cast out d.
1 Cor. 10:20 Gent. sacrifice to d. I
Jam. 2:19 d. believe and tremble
Rev. 9:20 should not worship d.

DEVISE.

Mic. 2:1 woe to them d. iniquity

DEVISED.

2 Pet. 1:16 cunningly d. fables

DEVOUR.

1 Pet. 5:8 seeking wh. he may d.
Rev. 12:4 to d. her child as soon

Fire DEVOUR.

Jud. 9:15 let fire d. the cedars
Ps. 21:9 the fire shall d. them
Is. 26:11 f. of enemies d. them
Ezek. 15:7 another fire d. them
Amos 5:6 break out like f. d. it
Nah. 3:13 fire may d. thy cedars

DEVOURED.

Zec. 9:4 shall be d. with fire

Mat. 13:4 fowls came d. them,
Mark 4:4; Luke 8:5
Luke 15:30 thy son d. living
Rev. 20:9 fire came and d. them

DEVOUT.

Luke 2:25 Sim. was just and d.
Acts 2:5 at Jerusal. Jews d. men

DIADEM.

Is. 28:5 and for a d. of beauty
62:3 a royal d. in hand of God.

DIE.

Job. 2:9 said, Curse God and d.
Prov. 10:21 fools d. for want of
Ec. 7:17 d. before thy time
Is. 22:18 large country, there d.
Zec. 11:9 that dieth, let it d.
Mat. 15:$ curs, father or mother
Luke 20:36 nei. can d. any more
Rom. 5:7 for a man will one d.
1 Cor. 15:22 as in Adam all d.

I DIE.

Prov. 30:7 deny me not bef. I d.
1 Cor. 15:31 I d. daily

NOT DIE.

2 Chr. 25:4 fath. n. d. for child.
Prov. 23:13 shall n. d. Ezek. 18:17,
21, 28; 33:15; John 21:23
Is. 51:14 he should not d.
Ezek. 13:19 souls should not d.
Heb. 1:12 we shall not d. Lord
John 6:50 eat thereof and not d.

Surely DIE.

2 K. 1:4 but shalt surely d. 6, 16

To DIE.

1 Cor. 9:15 better for me to d.
Phil. 1:21 to live is C. to d. is
Heb. 9:27 app. to men once to d.
Rev. 3:2 that are ready to d.

Ye DIE.

John 8:21 ye sh. d. in yo, sins, 24
Rom. 8:13 if live after flesh ye d.

DIETH.

Rom. 6:9 Christ d. no more
14:7 no man d. to himself

DYING.

Heb. 11:21 by faith Jac. when d.

DIG.

Job 3:21 d. for it more than for
6:27 ye d. a pit for your friend
11:18 thou shalt d. about thee
24:16 in dark d. thro' houses

Ezek. 8:8 d. now in the wall
DIGNITY, IES.
Ec. 10:6 folly is set in great d.
Hab. 1:7 d. proceed of themsel
2 Pet. 2:10 sp. evil of d. Jude 8
DILIGENCE.
Prov. 4:23 keep heart with all d.
Rom. 12:8 that ruleth, with d.
2 Cor. 8:7 as ye abound in all d.
3 Tim. 4:9 do thy d. to come, 21
Heb. 6:11 ev. one do sh. same d.
2 Pet. 1:5 giv. all d. add to faith
DILIGENT.
Prov. 10:4 hand of d. mak. rich
12:24 hand of d. shall bear rule
27 substance of d. is precious
22:29 seest a man d. in busi.
2 Cor. 8:22 whom we have ofter
2 Pet. 3:14 d. ye be fou. in peace
Heb. 11:6 rew. of them d. seek
12:15 looking d. lest any fail
1 Pet. 1:10 prophets searched d.
DINE.
John 21:12 J. saith, Come and d.
DINNER.
Prov. 15:17 better is a d. of herbs
DIP.
Luke 16:24 that he may d. finger
DIRECT.
Ps. 5:3 morning d. my prayer
Prov. 3:6 he shall d. thy paths
Is. 45:13 I will d. all his ways
2 Thes. 3:5 L. d. hearts into love
DISCERN.
Jos. 4:11 d. bet. right and left
Mat. 3:18 d. bet. right, and wick.
Mat. 16:3 can d. sky, Luke 12:56
Heb. 5:14 senses exer. to d. good
DISCERNED.
1 Cor. 2:14 because spiritually d.
DISCIPLE.
Mat. 10:24 d. is not above his
master, Luke 6:40
42 give cup of cold water to d.
27:57 Joseph also was Jesus' d.
Acts 21:16 old d. with whom lodge
My DISCIPLE.
Luke 14:26 not be my d.
27 hear cross cannot be my d.
33 fors. not all, not be my d.

DISCIPLES.
Mat. 9:14 then came d. of John
Mark 2:18 why d. of John and of
Pharisees fast, Luke 5:33
8:14 d. forgotten to take bread
Luke 19:37 d. began to rejoice
John 3:25 betw. John's d. and
4:1 Je. bap. more d. that John
9:28 but we are Moses' d.
13:5 began to wash the d. feet
18:17 art one of this man's d.?
20:18 told d, she had seen Lord
Acts 9:1 breath. slaughter ag. d.
26 Saul assayed to join the d.
19:1 Ephesus, finding certain d.
30 the d. suffered him not
20:7 d. came to break bread
30 to draw away d. after them
HIS DISCIPLES.
Mat. 8:25 his d. awoke him
28:7 tell his d. he is risen
13 say ye, h. d. came by night
Luke 5:30 murmur. against h. d.
6:20 lifted up his eyes on his d.
11:1 as John taught his d.
John 2:11 his d. believed on him
27 came his d. and marvelled
6:22 his d. were gone away
9:27 will ye also be his d.?
18:1 with his d. over Cedron
2 resorted thither with his d.
20:26 again his d. were within
Of his DISCIPLES.
Mat. 11:2 sent two of his d. Mark
11:1; 14:13; Luke 19:29
Mark 7:2 d. eat with unw. hands
John 6:66 many of his d. went
25 art not th. also one of h. d.
21:12 none of his d. durst ask
To his DISCIPLES.
Mat. 14:19 gave loaves to his d.
Mark 4:34 expounded all to h. d.
Luke 10:23 he turned to his d.
John 21:14 showed hims. to h. d.
My DISCIPLES.
Is. 8:16 seal law among my d.
Mat. 26:18 keep passover with
my d. Mark 14:14; Luke 22:11
John 8:31 my d. indeed, 13:35
15:8 so shall ye be my .d.

THY DISCIPLES.

Mat. 9:14 t. d. fast not, Mark 2:18
12:2 thy d. do what is not lawf.
15:2 t. d. transgress tradition?
17:16 d. they could not cure
Mark 7:5 walk not t. d. accor. to
9:18 t. d. to cast him, Luke 9:40
Luke 19:39 Master rebuke thy d.
John 7:3 t. d. see works thou

DISCORD.

Prov. 6:14 he soweth d.
19 soweth d. among brethren

DISCOURAGED.

Col. 3:21 children, lest they be d.

DISCREET.

Gen. 41:39 none so d and wise
Tit. 2:% teach yo. women to be d..

DISCRETION.

Prov. 1:4 to the young man d.
2:11 d. shall preserve thee
3:21 keep wisdom and d.
5:2 thou mayest regard d.
11:22 a fair woman without d.
19:11 d. deferreth his anger

DISEASE.

Ec. 6:2 this is vanity, an evil d.
Mat. 4:23 healing d. 9:35; 10:1
John 5:4 whole of whatsoever d.

DISEASES.

Ps. 103:3 who healeth all thy d.
Mat. 4:24 were taken with divers
d. Mark 1:34;; Luke 4:40
Luke 9:1 gave power to cure d.
Acts 19:12 d. departed from them

DISEASED.

Mat. 9:20 woman d. with issue
14:35 brought all d. Mark 1:32
John 6:2 miracles he did on d.

DISHONESTY.

2 Cor. 4:2 renounced things of d.

DISHONOR.

1 Cor. 15:43 sown in d. raised in
2 Cor. 6:8 by honor and d.
2 Tim. 2:20 are vess. some to d.

DISHONOR, ETH.

Mic. 7:6 the son d. the father
Rom. 1:24 to d. their own bodies
2:23 breaking law, d. God
1 Cor. 11:4 man d. head; 5 wom.

DISMAYED.

Ob. 9 mighty men shall be d.

DISOBEDIENCE.

Rom. 5:19 by one man's d.
2 Cor. 10:6 readiness to rev. d.
Eph. 2:2 worketh in child, of d.
5:6 on children of d. Col. 3:6

DISOBEDIENT.

1 K. 13:26 man of G. who was d.
Rom. 1:30 d. to par. 2 Tim. 3:2
10:21 forth my hands to d. peo.
1 Tim. 1:9 law was made for d.

DISORDERLY.

2 Thes. 3:6 withd. from broth. d.
2 Thes. 3:7 behaved not ours, d.
11 some walk among you d.

DISPENSATION.

1 Cor. 9:17 a d. of gospel
Eph. 1:10 d. of fulness of times
3:2 heard of d. of grace of God
Col. 1:25 minister acc. to d. of G.

DISPLEASED.

Dan. 6:14 king d. with himself
Jon. 4:1 it d. Jonah exceedingly
Zec. 1:2 L. been d. with fathers
15 sore d. with heathen at ease,
for I was but a little d.
Mat. 21:15 scribes saw, were d.

DISPUTE, ED.

Job 23:7 righteous might d.
Mark 9:34 d. who sh. be greatest
Acts 9:29 S. d. ag. the Grecians
17:17 Paul d. in the synagogue
Jude 9 Mich. d. about body of M.

DISPUTING, S.

Acts 6:9 d. with Stephen
15:7 been much d. Peter rose
19:8 d. and persuading, 9
24:12 they neither found me d.
Phil. 2:14 all things without d.
1 Tim. 6:5 perverse d.

DISSIMULATION.

Rom. 12:9 let love be without d.

DISTRESS, Substantive.

Prov. 1:27 mock when d. cometh
Is. 25:4 stre. to the needy in d.
Zep. 1:15 that day is a day of d.
17 I will bring d. upon men
Luke 21:23 great d. in land
25 on the earth d. of nations
Rom. 8:35 love of C.? shell d.
1 Thes. 3:7 comforted in your d.

DISTRESSED.

2 Cor. 4:8 troubled yet not d.

DISTRIBUTE.

Luke 18:22 sell all and d. to poor

1 Tim. 6:18 rich to be ready to d.

DIVERS,.

Mat. 4:24 sick with d. diseases.

Heb. 1:1 in d. manners spake

2:4 witness with d. miracles

9:10 d. washings; 13:9 d. doct.

Jam. 1:2 fall into d. temptations

DIVERSITIES.

1 Cor. 12:4 d. of gifts; 6 opera

28 set in church d. of tongues

DIVIDE.

Gen. 1:6 let firmanent d. water1 K.

3:25 d. living child, 26

DIVIDED.

Mat. 12:25 house d. not stand.

Mark 3:24; Luke 11:17

Luke 12:52 five in one house d.

53 father be divided aga. son.

DIVIDETH.

Mat. 25:32 d. his sheep fr. goats

DIVIDING.

2 Tim. 2:15 rightly d. the word

DIVINE Verb.

Mic. 3:6 that ye shall not d.

11 prophets d. for money

DIVINE, Adjective.

Heb. 9:1 ordinances of d. service

2 Pet. 1:3 d. power hath given

DIVISION, S.

Jud. 5:15 for d. of Reuben, 16

Luke 12:51 may but rather d.

John 7:43 there was a d. among

the people, 9:16; 10:19

Rom. 16:17 mark them wh. ca. d.

1 Cor. 1:10 be no d. among you

DIVORCE, ED.

Jer. 3:8 given her a bill of d.

Mat. 5:32 shall marry her d.

DIVORCEMENT.

Deut. 24:1 write her bill of d. 3

Mark 10:4 M. suffered bill of d.

DO.

1 Chr. 17:2 all in thy heart

23 and d. as thou hast said

21:8 d. away iniq. of thy serv.

2 Chr. 19:6 take heed what ye d.

Ps. 40:8 I delight to d. thy will

Prov. 3:27 power of hand to d.

Is. 10:3 d. in day of visitation?

Mic. 6:8 but to d. justly

Mat. 5:19 shall d. and teach

12:50 whosoever sh. d. the will

of my Father, Mark 3:35

21:27 author. I d. these things,

Mark 11:33; Luke 20:8

23:5 works they d.

John 2:5 whatsoever he saith d.

5:30 I can of myself d. nothing

7:17 if any man will d. his will

8:29 I d. those things please

9:33 of G. he could d. nothing

14:12 works I d. shall he d. also

14 ask in my name, I will d. it

Acts 1:1 of all Jesus began to d.

Rom. 1:32 not only d. the same

7:15 for what I d. I allow not,

but what I hate, that d. I

1 Cor. 7:36 let him d. what he

10:31 ye d. all to glory of God

Col. 3:17 whatsoe. ye d. in word

or deed, d. all in na. of L.J.

Heb. 4:13 whom we have to d.

1 John 3:22 and d. those things

Can, or canst, DO

Luke 12:4 no more they can d.

John 5:19 Son can d. nothing, 30

Phil. 4:13 I can d. all through C.

DO, with evil.

2 Cor. 13:7 I pray that ye d. no e.

1 Pet. 3:12 against them that d. e.

DO, joined with good.

Jud. 17:13 Lord will d. me good

1 Sam. 1:23 d. what seemeth g.

44:36, 40; 2 Sam, 19:27, 37

3:18 the Lord d. what seemeth

him good, 2 Sam. 10:12

What have I to DO.

1 K. 17:18 w. h. I to d. with thee?

2 K. 3:13; 2. Chr. 35:21; Mark

5:7; Luke 8:28; John 2:4

I shall, I will, will I, or]
shall I DO.

John 14:13 ask, that will I d.

14 ask in my name, I will d. it.

2 Cor. 11:12 what I do, I will d.

Must DO.

Acts 16:30 wh. m. I d. to be sav?

DO, joined with no or not.

Ex. 20:10 in it thou shalt not d.
  any work, Lev. 23:31
Lev. 16:29 d. no work, 23:3, 28;
Ezr. 7:26 whoso will not d. law
Ps. 119:3 also d. no iniquity
Ezek. 5:9 not d. any more

Shall we, or we shall DO.

Est. 1:15 what sh. we d. to V.?
Ps. 60:12 through God w. sh. d.
  valiantly, 108:13
Jon. 1:11 what shall we d.?
John 6:28 d. th. we might work?

DO, joined with so.

Mat. 7:12 sh. d. to you, so d. ye
18:35 so shall Father d. to you

DO well.

Is. 1:17 cease d. evil, lea. d. well
Jon. 4:9 I d. well to be angry
Mat. 12:12 to d. well on sabbath
John 11:12 he shall d. well
1 Pet. 2:14 them that d. w.
2 Pet. 1:19 ye d. w. that ye take
3 John 6 if bring shalt d. well

DOER.

Prov. 17:4 wicked d. giveth heed
Jam. 1:23 be not d. of word
  25 not a forgetful hearer, but d.
4:11 thou art not a d. of the law

DOERS.

Jam. 1:22 be ye d. of the word

DOEST.

Jam. 2:19 believest, thou d. well

DOETH.

Job. 5:9 d. great things, 9:10;
  37:5; Ps. 72:18; 136:$
Ps. 1:3 what, he d. shall prosper
Dan. 4:35 d. accord. to his will
  9:14 L. is righteous in all he d.
Mal. 2:12 L. cut off man d. this
Mat. 6:3 left know what right d.
Rom. 10:5 that d. these things
  shall live by them, Gal. 3:12
Eph. 6:8 good thing any man d.

DOCTOR, S.

Luke 2:46 J. in midst of the d.
Acts 5:34 Gamaliel a d. of law

DOCTRINE.

Is. 28:9 make to understand d.
Mat. 7:28 aston. at his d. 23:33;
  16:12 beware of d. of Pharisees
Mark 1:27 what new d. is this?

John 7:17 shall know of the d.
Acts 2:42 conti. in apostles' d.
  5:28 filled Jerus. with your d.
  18:12 being astonished at the d.
  17:19 what this new d. is?
Eph. 4:14 with every wind of d.
1 Tim. 1:3 teach no other d.
  4:13 give attendance to d.
  5:17 who labor in word and d.
  6:1 his d. be not blasphemed
2 Tim. 3:16 is profitable for d.
  4:2 exhort with long suf. and d.
Tit. 2:7 in d. showing incorrupt.
  10 adorn d. of God our Saviour
Heb. 6:1 principles of the d.
  2 of the d. of baptisms, and
2 John 9 abideth not in the d. of
  Christ; abideth in d.

Good DOCTRINE.

Prov. 4:2 I give you good d.
1 Tim. 4:6 in words of good d.

Sound DOCTRINE.

1 Tim. 1:10 contrary to sound d.
2 Tim. 4:3 not endure sound d.

DOCTRINES.

1 Tim. 4:1 heed to d. of devils
Heb. 13:9 not carried with str. d.

DOG.

Jud. 7:5 as a d. lappeth

DOGS.

Ex. 22:31 cast it to the d. Mat.
  15:26; Mark 7:27
Ps. 22:16 d. have compassed me
Mat. 7:6 which is holy unto d.
Luke 16:21 the d. licked his sores
Phil. 3:2 beware of d.

DOING.

Ex. 15:11 d. wonders
Mat. 24:46 find so d. Luke 12:$3
Acts 10:38 went about d. good
Rom. 12:20 in so d. shalt heap
Eph. 6:6 d. the will of God

Well-DOING.

Gal. 6:9 w. in w.-d. 2 Thes. 3:13

DOMINION.

Gen. 1:26 d. over the fish, 28
  27:40 thou shalt have the d.
  37:8 shalt thou have d. over us?
Ps. 8:6 to have d. over the works
Mat. 20:25 princes exercise d.
Rom. 6:9 death hath no more d.

14 sin not have d. over you
7:1 law hath d. over a man
2 Cor. 1:24 d. over your faith
1 Pet. 4:11 to whom be praise and
d. for ever, 5:11; Rev. 1:6
Jude 8 despise d.
25 to the only wise God be d.

DONE.
Ex. 18:9 goodness L. had d. to I.
Dan. 11:36 determined sh. be d.
Mat. 6:10 thy will be d. 26:42;
25:21 well d. good servant, 23
40 as ye have d. it to one of
27:54 things that were d. 28:11
Luke 1:49 hath d. great things
Rom. 9:11 d. any good or evil
1 Cor. 9:15 nor be so d. unto me
13:10 in part shall be d. away
14:26 let all be d. to edifying
40 be d. decently
Eph. 6:13 having d. all to stand
Phil. 2:3 nothing be d. through
strife
Col. 4:9 known all things d.
Rev. 16:17 saying, it is d. 21:6

He hath, or hath he DONE.
1 Chr. 16:12 rem. his works he
hath d. Ps. 78:4; 98:1; 105:5
Is. 12:5 he hath d. excel. things
Mark 7:37 he hath d. all things

Thou hast DONE.
Ps. 40:5 wonderful works t.h.d.
52:9 praise thee bec. t.h.d. it
109:27 know that thou h. d. it

DOOR.
Mark 1:33 city was gather. at d.
2:2 no room, no not about the d.
16:3 who roll us stone from d.?
John 10:1 entereth not by the d.
Acts 5:9 feet at d. to carry thee
12:13 as Peter knocked at the d.
1 Cor. 16:9 great d. and effectual
2 Cor. 2:12 a d. was opened to me
Col. 4:3 open a d. of utterance
Jam. 5:9 judge standeth bef. d.
Rev. 3:8 before thee an open d.

DOOR, with house.
Ezek. 8:14 to d. of Lord's h. 47:1

DOOR, with keeper, s.
Ps. 84:10 I had rather be a d.-k.

DOOR, with posts.
Ex. 12:7 blood on upper d.-p.

DOOR, with tabernacle.
Ex. 29:4 bring to d. of tab. 40:12;
Lev. 4:4; 8:3, 4; 12:6; Num.
6:10
Deut. 31:15 pillar of cloud ov. d.

DOORS.
Jud. 3:25 opened not d. of parlor
16:3 Samson took d. of the city
1 Sam. 3:15 Samuel opened t. d.
Job 31:32 opened d. to traveller
Mat. 24:33 at the d. Mark 13:29
Acts 5:19 angel opened prison d.

DOUBLE.
Is. 40:2 rec. d. for all her sins
Zec. 9:12 I will render d. to thee
1 Tim. 3:8 deacons not d.-tong.

DOUBLE-MINDED.
Jam. 1:8 a d.-m. man is unstable
4:8 purify your hearts, ye d.-m.

DOUBT, S.
Gal. 4:20 for I stand in d. of you
1 John 2:19 wo. no d. have come

DOUBTED.
Mat. 28:17 but some d.

DOUBTFUL.
Luke 12:29 nel. be ye of d. mind
Rom. 14:1 not to d. disputations

DOUBTING.
John 13:22 d. of whom he spake

DOVE.
Gen. 8:8 N. sent forth a d. 10,12

DOVES.
Nah. 2:7 lead as with voice of d.
Mat. 10:16 harmless as d.
John 2:14 those that sold d.

DRAGON.
Rev. 12:3 behold, a great red d.

DRANK.
John 4:12 Jacob d. thereof
1 Cor. 10:4 d. of that spirit, rock

DRAUGHT.
Luke 5:4 let down nets for a d.

DRAW.
John 6:44 except the Father d. him
12:32 I will d. all men unto me

DRAW near.
1 Sam. 14:36 let us d. near to G.
Ps. 73:28 good to d. n. to God
Heb. 10:22 d. n. with true heart

67

DRAW nigh.
Jam. 4:8 d. n. to G. he will d. n.
DRAWN.
Ezek. 21:5 Lord d. my sword, 28
Acts 11:10 d. up again to heaven
Jam. 1:14 d. away of his own
DRAWETH.
Luke 21:8 the time d. near
28 your redemption d. nigh
Jam. 5:8 coming of L. d. nigh
DREADFUL.
Mal. 1:14 name d. among heath.
4:5 great and d. day of the Lord
DREAM, Substantive.
1 K. 3:5 to Solomon in a d.
Is. 29:7 fight ag. Ariel be as a d.
Jer. 23:28 hath d. let him tell d.
Dan. 2:4 tell thy servants the d.
7:1 Daniel had a d. wrote d.
Joseph in a d. 2:13, 19
DREAM, Verb.
Joel 2:28 old men d. Acts 2:17
DREAMED.
Dan. 2:1 Nebuchadnezzar d.
DREAMS.
Gen. 37:8 hated him for his d.
42:9 Joseph remembered the d.
1 Sam. 28:6 answer, not by d. 15
Dan. 1:17 understand. in d. 5:12
Zec. 10:2 diviners told false d.
DREGS.
Ps. 75:8 d. wicked shall drink
DREW.
Gen. 24:20 Rebekah d. water, 45
37:28 they d up Joseph
Ex. 2:10 I d. him out of water
2 Sam. 22:17 he d. me out of
many waters, Ps. 18:16
Mat. 26:51 Peter d his sword,
DREW near, or nigh.
Zep. 3:2 d. not near to her God
Luke 15:25 elder son d. n. to ho.
Acts 7:17 time of promise d. n.
DRINK, Verb.
Ob. 16 the heathen d. continu-
ally, yea, they shall d.
Hag. 1:6 ye d. but are not filled
Zec. 9:15 d. and make a noise
Mat. 10:42 whoso giveth to d. to
20:22 are ye able to d. of the cup
I shall d. of? Mark 10:38

23 shall d. indeed, Mark 10:39
26:27 saying, d. ye all of it
29 not d. till that day I d. it,
27:34 gave him vinegar to d.
48 put it on a reed and gave
him to d. Mark 15:36
Mark 16:18 if d. any deadly th.
John 4:10 saith, Give me to d.
7:37 let him come to me and d.
18:11 shall I not d.?
1 Cor. 10:4 did all d. the same
21 d. cup of L. and of devils
11:25 this do, as oft as ye d. it
12:43 all to d. into one Spirit
DRINK, with wine.
Prov. 4:17 d. wine of violence
9:5 d. of wine I have mingled
31:4 it is not for kings to d. w.
DRINKETH.
John 4:13 d. this wa. shall thirst
14 d. of water I shall give him
6:54 d. my blood hath eter. life
56 d. my blood, dwelleth in me
1 Cor. 11:29 d. unworth. d. dam.
DRINKING.
Mat. 11:18 John came neither
eating nor d. Luke 7:33
DRIVE.
Ex. 6:1 with a strong hand d. out
23:28 hornets, which shall d.
DRIVEN.
Deut. 4:19 be c. to worship them
Ps. 40:14 let be d. backward
Prov. 14:32 wicked is d. away
Is. 8:22 shall be d. to darkness
Dan. 4:33 d. from men, 5:21
9:7 through all countries d.
Hos. 13:3 as chaff d. with whirl
Jam. 1:6 like wave d. with wind
DROPPED, ETH.
Jud. 5:4 heavens d. clouds d.
1 Sam. 14:26 the honey d.
2 Sam. 21:10 water d. on them
Job 29:22 my speech d. on them
Ps. 68:8 heavens d. at pres. of G.
Ec. 10:18 thr. idleness house d.
Cant. 5:5 hands d. with myrrh
DROUGHT.
Hos. 13:5 know thee in land of d.
Hag. 1:11 and I called for a d.

DROWNED.

Ex. 15:4 are d. in Red sea

DRUNK.

1 Sam. 1:15 I have d. nei. wine
2 Sam. 11:13 Dav. made Uriah d.
Cant. 5:1 d. my wine
Is. 51:17 hast d. cup of his fury
Jer. 46:10 be d. with their blood
Ob. 16 d. on my holy mountain
Luke 5:39 having d. old wine

DRUNKARD.

Is. 24:20 the earth reel like a d.

DRUNKEN.

Acts 2:15 not d. as ye suppose
1 Cor. 11:21 and another is d.

DRUNKENNESS.

Rom. 13:13 not in rioting and d.
Gal. 5:21 works of flesh are d.

DRIED.

Hos. 9:16 their root is d. up
  13:15 his fountain be d. up
Joel 1:10 the new wine is d. up

DUE.

1 Chr. 15:13 sought not after d.
  16:29 the glory d. to his name,
Rom. 13:7 to whom tribute is d.
1 Cor. 7:3 to the wife d. benevol.

DUE season.

Gal. 6:9 in d. s. we shall reap

DUE time.

1 Pet. 5:6 he may exalt you in d. t.

DULCIMER.

Dan. 3:5 d. and music, 10, 15

DULL.

Mat. 13:15 ears are d. Acts 28:27
Heb. 5:11 ye are d. of hearing

DUMB.

Ex. 4:11 or who maketh the d.
Ps. 38:13 I was as a d. man
Prov. 31:8 open thy mouth for d.
Is. 35:6 tongue of d. shall sing
Hab. 2:18 to make him d. idols
Mat. 9:32 bro. to him a d. man
  33 the d. spake, Luke 11:14
  12:22 and d. and he healed
Mark 9:25 thou d. spirit, come
Acts 8:32 lamb d. before shearer
2 Pet. 2:16 the d. ass speaking

DUNGEON.

Lam. 3:53 cut off my life in d.
  55 called on thy name out of d.

DUST.

Gen. 19 d. thou art, to d. shall ret.
Mat. 10:14 sha. off the d. of your
  feet, Mark 6:11; Luke 9:5

As the DUST.

Gen. 13:16 thy seed as the d. of
  the earth, 28:14; 2 Chr. 1:9

Of the DUST.

Gen. 2:7 L formed man of the d.

DWELL.

Ps. 15:1 who sh. d. in thy holy hill
Col. 1:19 in him sh. all fulness d.
  3:16 let word of C. d. in you
1 Pet. 3:7 husbands d. with them
1 John 4:13 we d. in him
Rev. 7:15 he on throne shall d.

DWELL with earth.

Dan. 4:1 languages that d. in all
  the earth, 6:25

DWELL, with house.

Prov. 21:9 better d. in the corner
  of a house, 25:24

DWELL safely.

Prov. 1:33 to me shall d. safely

DWELL in safety.

Lev. 25:18 ye shall d. in the land
  in safety, 19; Deut. 12:10
Deut. 33:12 beloved of the Lord
  shall d. in safety

DWELLEST.

Rev. 2:13 works where thou d.

DWELLETH.

Joel 3:21 I cleanse, for L. d. in Z.
Acts 7:48 d. not in temples made
  with hands, 17:24
Rom. 7:17 I, sin th. d. in me, 20
1 Cor. 3:16 Spirit of G. d. in you
Col. 2:9 d. the fulness of God
2 Tim. 1:14 H. G. d. in us
Jam. 4:5 spirit that d. in us.
1 John 3:17 how d. love of G.?
  24 that keepeth com. d. in him
  4:12 if we love, God d. in us
  15 J. is S. of G. God d. in him
1 John 4:16 he that d. in love, d.
2 John 2 which d. in us
Rev. 2:13 slain am, you, Satan d.

DWELLING, Substantive.

Mark 5:3 his d. among tombs

DWELLING.

1 K. 8:30 in heaven thy d. place

69

2 Chr. 30:27 prayer up to holy d.
Job 8:22 d. place of the wicked
Ps. 49:11 d. places to all genera.
Is. 4:5 create on every d. place
Joel 3:17 Lord your God in Z.
Acts 2:5 were d. at Jerusalem
DWELT.
John 1:14 W. made flesh and d.
E.

EACH.
Acts 2:3 tongues sat upon e. of
2 Thes. 1:3 charity toward e. oth.
EAGLES.
Is. 40:31 mount with wings as e.
EAR.
Mat. 10:27 what ye hear in the e./
26:51 smote off his e. Mark 14:47
Luke 12:3 ye have spoken in e.
22:51 touched his e. and healed
John 18:26 servant whose e. Pet.
1 Cor. 2:9 not seen, nor e. heard
12:16 if the e. shall say
Rev. 2:7 he that hath e. let hear,
  11, 17, 29; 3:6, 13, 22, 13:9
Incline EAR.
Ps. 17:6 in, thine e. to me, 71:2;
  88:2' Is. 37:17; Dan. 9:18
EARLY.
Prov. 1:28 they shall seek me e.
  8:17 seek me e. shall find me
Is. 26:9 will I seek thee e.
Hos. 5:15 they will seek me e.
  6:4 as e. dew it goeth, 13:3
Luke 24:22 woman e. at sepulch.
John 18:28 led J. and it was e.
  20:1 com. Mary Magdalene
Jam. 5:7 till he receive e. rain
EARS.
Prov. 23:9 speak not in the e. of a
fool 26:17 taketh a dog by the e.
Is. 11:3 the hearing of his e.
  32:3 the e. of them that hear
33:15 stoppeth e. from hearing
35:5 e. of deaf shall be unstop.
43:8 and deaf that have e.
Mark 7:33 put fingers into his e.
  35 his e. were opened
8:18 having e. hear ye not?
1 Pet. 3:12 and his e. are open to

EARS to hear.
Deut. 29:4 L. hath not g. e. to h.
Ezek. 12:2 they have e. to hear
Mat. 11:15 e. to h. 13:9, 43; Mark
  4:9, 23; 7:16; Luke 8:8; 14:35
Your EARS.
Luke 4:21 scripture fulfil, in y. e.
  9:44 let sayings sink in your e.
EARS of Corn.
Gen. 41:5 seven e. of com, 22
EARNESTLY.
Num. 22:37 did I not e. send
1 Cor. 12:31 covet e. the best gifts
2 Cor. 5:2 we groan e. desiring
Jude 3 should e. con. for faith
EARTH.
Gen. 1:2 the e. was without form
Ex. 9:29 e. is the Lord's Deut.
  10:14; Ps. 24:1; 1 Cor. 10:26
Neh. 9:6 thou made e. Is. 45:12
Ps. 2:8 uttermost parts of the e.
  12:6 silver tried in furnace of e.
25:13 his seed shall inherit the e.
33:5 e. is full of goodness of L.
46:2 though the e. be removed
Ps: 97:1 let the e. rejoice
102:25 laid the founda. of the e.
  104:5; Prov. 8:29; Is. 48:13
Prov. 3:19 L. founded e. Is. 24:1
  30:21 for three things e. disquiet.
Mal. 4:6 I smite e. with curse
Mat. 5:5 meek shall inherit e.
  35 sw. not by e. it is footstool
Jam. 5:7 precious fruit of the e.
2 Pet. 3:10 e. and works therein
Rev. 7:3 hurt not the e. nor sea
All the EARTH.
Luke 23:44 darkn. over all the e.
Rom. 10:18 sou. went into a. t. e.
In the EARTH.
Joel 2:30 show wonders in the e.
Mat. 25:18 digged in the e.
  25 hid thy talent in the e.
Mark 4:31 mustard seed sown in
  t.e. less than all seeds in t. e.
1 John 5:8 three that witn. i.t.e.
EARTHEN.
2 Cor. 4:7 treasure in e. vessels
EARTHLY.
John 3:12 if I told you e. things

70

EARTHQUAKES.

Mat. 24:7 famines and e. Mark
13:8; Luke 21:11

EASIER.

Ex. 18:22 be e. for thyself
Mat. 9:5 whether is e. to say.

EASILY.

1 Cor. 13:5 is not e. provoked
Heb. 12:1 sin which doth e. beset

EAST.

Gen. 3:24 e. of garden of Eden
Mat. 2:1 wise men from the e.
2 seen his star in the e. 9
8:11 come from e. Luke 13:29
Rev. 7:2 angels ascending from e.

EASTER.

Acts 12:4 after e. to bring him

EAST wind.

Hab. 1:9 faces sup. up as e. wind

EASY.

Jam. 3:17 wisdom from ab. is e.

EAT.

Gen. 2:16 of ev. tree thou may e.
3:5 day ye e eyes sh. be opened
6 Eve did e.; 12 I did e. 13
14 and dust shalt thou e.
16 in sorrow shalt thou e.
27:4 savory meat that I may e.
31:46 and they did e. there
40:17 the birds did e. them
43:32 Egyptians e. by themsel.
Ex. 10:5 the locusts shall e.
12:8 bitter herbs they shall e.
43 no str. sh. e.
Deut. 12:15 e. in gates, 21; 15:22
15 unc. and clean e. 22; 26:12
2 Sam. 9:11 e. at table, 1 K. 2:7
1 K. 14:11 him that dieth of J.
dogs e. 16:4; 21:23;
17:12 that we may e. and die
19:5 arise e. Acts 10:13; 11:7
Ec. 5:11 are increased that e. them
12 whether be e. little or much
10:16 princes e. in the morning
17 princes e. in due season
Cant. 4:16 come into gar. and e.
Is. 4:1 we will e. our own bread
7:15 butter and honey sh. he e.
22 not plant and another e.
Mat. 26:26 take e. this my body,
Mark

14:22; 1 Cor. 11:24
Mark 2:16 e. with publicans
6:44 that did e. were above 5,000
14:12 mayest e. the passover, 14;
Luke 22:8, 11; John 18:28
15:23 let us e. and be merry
24:43 he took it, and did e.
Rom. 14:2 believeth he may e. all
2 Thes. 3:10 work not, neither e.
2 Tim. 2:17 word will e. as cank.
Acts 9:9 did neither e. nor drink
1 Cor. 9:4 power to e. and to d.
27 e. and drink unworthily
28 so let him e. and drink

He did EAT.

Mark 1:6 John did e. locusts
Luke 4:2 days he did e. nothing

EAT not.

Gen. 2:17 shall not e. 3:1, 3
3:11 I commanded not to e. 17
9:4 blood not e. Lev. 19:26; Deut.
12:16, 23, 25; 15:23
Mark 7:3 exc. they wash e. not, 4
Luke 22:16 I will not e. thereof
1 Cor. 5:11 with such no not to e.
10:28 e. not for his sake

Shall ye EAT.

Lev. 10:14 wave-breast shall ye e.
11:3 cheweth the cud, that shall
yee. Deut. 14:4, 6

EATEN.

1 K. 13:28 lion not e. the carcass
Jer. 31:29 e. sour grapes, Ezek.
18:2 Joel 1:4 locust left c.w. e 25

EATETH.

John 6:54 whoso e. my flesh
56 that e. my flesh dwelleth in
57 so he that e. me shall live
58 he that e. of this bread

EDEN.

Gen. 2:15 man into garden of E.
Is. 51:3 her wilderness like E.
Ezek. 28:13; 31:9, 16, 18; 36:35
Joel 2:3 is as the garden of E.
Amos 1:5 cut off sceptre from E.

EDGE of the sword.

Jer. 21:7 smite them with e. of s.
Luke 21:24 Jews fall by e. of sw.
Heb. 11:34 thro' faith esca. e. of s.

EDGED.

Ps. 149:6 two-e. sword in hand

Prov. 5:4 sharp as a two- e. sword
Heb. 4:12 word of God sharper
than two e. sword
Rev. 1:16 mouth sharp two e. 6

EDIFICATION.
Rom. 15:2 please neighbor to e.
1 Cor. 14:3 speaketh to men to e.
2 Cor. 10:8 L. hath given us for e.
13:10 Lord hath given me to e.

EDIFIED.
Acts 9:31 churches had rest, e.
1 Cor. 14:17 the other is not e.

EDIFIETH.
1 Cor. 8:1 knowledge puffeth,
charity e.
14:4 he that speaks e. hims. he
that prophes. e. the church

EDIFY.
Rom. 14:19 one may e. another
1 Cor. 10:23 lawful but e. not
1 Thes. 5:11 e. one another.

EDIFYING.
1 Cor. 14:5 church may receive e.
12 that ye may excel to the e.
14:26 let all things be done to e.
2 Cor. 12:19 all thin, for your e.
Eph. 4:12 e. of body of Christ
16 the body to the e. of itself
29 good to the use of e.
1 Tim. 1:4 quest, rather than

EFFECT, Substantive.
Mat. 15:6 com. of G. of none e.
Mark 7:13 word of God of none e.
Rom. 3:3 unbelief make the faith
of God without e.
4:14 prom. of none e. Gal. 3:17
9:6 word hath taken none e.
1 Cor. 1:17 cr. of C. be of none e.
Gal 5:4 Chr. is become of no e.

EFFECTUAL.
Jam. 5:16 the e. prayer of right.

EFFEMINATE.
1 Cor. 6:9 nor e. shall inherit

IN and into EGYPT.
Gen. 46:4 go down with thee i. E.
Mat. 2:13 flee into E. 14

Land of EGYPT.
Gen. 13:10; 41:19, 54; 45:18; 47:6
Heb. 8:9 out of the land of E.
Jude 5 saved peo. out of L. of E.

Out of EGYPT.
Gen. 13:1 Abraham out of E.

EGYPTIAN, S.
Ex. 2:11 E. smiting Heb. 12, 19

EIGHT.
Gen. 17:12 he that is e. days old,
21:4; Luke 2:21

EIGHT hundred.
Gen. 5:4 Adam lived e. h. years

EITHER.
John 19:18 crucifi. on e. side one

ELDER.
Luke 15:25 his e. son was in field
1 Tim. 5:2 entreat the e. women
1 Pet. 5:5 younger, submit to e.

ELDER, for ruler.
1 Tim. 5:1 rebuke not an e.
19 against e. receive not accu.

ELDERS.
Lev. 4:15 e. of congr. lay hands
Num. 11:25 L. gave spirit to 70 e.
Deut. 29:10 before the L. your e.
31:28 gather to me all e.
2 K. 6:32 Elisha and e. sat
10:1 Jehu sent to e. of Jezreel
19:2 Hezekiah sent e. Is. 37:2
Ps. 107:32 in assembly of e.
Prov. 31:23 known among e.
Joel 1:14 gather the e. 2:16
Mat. 15:2 tradition of the e.?
16:21 suffer things of e. 27:12
26:59 e. sought false witness
Mark 7:3 tradition of the e.
8:31 rejected of the e. Luke 9:22
15:1 held a consultation with e.
Acts 4:5 e were gath. together
6:12 stirred up the peo. and e.
14:23 ordained e. in ev. church
. . . . les and e. came
. . . .
16:4 decrees ordained of the e.
1 Tim. 5:17 e. rule well
Jam. 5:14 call for e. of church
Rev. 4:4 I saw twenty-four e.
10:24 e. fall, 5:8; 14; 11:16; 19:4

ELECT.
Is. 41:1 mine e. in whom my
45:4 Israel mine e. I have called
Mat. 24:22 for the e. those days
shall be short. Mark 13:20
31 angels gather e. Mark 13:27

Luke 18:7 G. avenge his own e.?
Rom. 8:33 to charge of God's e.?
Col. 3:12 put on as e. of G. bow.
1 Tim. 5:21 before the e. angels
2 Tim. 2:10 endure for thee. sake
Tit. 1:1 to the faith of God's e.
2 John 1 the elder to the e. lady

ELECTION.

2 Pet. 1:10 your calling and e.

ELEVEN.

Gen. 32:22 Jacob took his e. sons
37:9 sun, moon, and e. stars
Mat. 28:16 e. disciples went to G.
Mark 16:14 he appeared to the e.
Luke 24:9 told to the e. and rest
33 found the e. gath. together

ELI.

1 Sam. 1:25 brou. the child to E.
2:12, 27; 3:5, 6, 8, 12, 14, 4:14
Mat. 27:46 cried, E. E. lama,
Mark 15:34

ELIJAH, or ELIAS.

1 K. 17:1 E. the Tishbite, 15, 22
23 E. took the child down
18:2 E. went to A. 7, 16, 40, 46
19:1 E. had done, 9:20; 21:20-
2 K. 1:8 is E. the Tishbite, 13, 17
2:1 E. into heaven, 8, 11, 14, 15
3:11 poured wa. on hands of E.
2 Chr. 21:12 came a writing fr. E.
Mal. 4:5 behold I will send you E.
Mat. 11:14 E. which was to come
16:14 say E. Mark 6:15; Lu. 9:8
17:3 app. E. Mark 9:4; Lu. 9:30
11 E. shall come, Mark 9:12
12 E. come already, Mark 9:13
27:47 calleth for E. Mark 15:35
49 E. will come, Mark 15:36
Luke 1:17 before in power of E.
9:54 fire to consume as E. did
John 1:21 art thou E.? art th. 25
Rom. 11:2 scripture saith of E.
Jam. 5:17 E. was a man subject

ELOQUENT.

Ex. 4:10 O my lord, I am not e.

EMBALM, ED.

Gen. 50:2 Jos. commanded physician to e. his father; physicians e. Israel
26 they e. Joseph in Egypt

EMBRACE.

Prov. 4:8 when thou dose e. her
5:20 why wilt thou e. bosom?
Cant. 2:6 hand doth e. me, 8:3
Acts 20:1 Paul e. disciples
Heb. 11:13 and e. the promises

EMBRACING.

Ec. 3:5 time to refrain from e.

EMMANUEL.

Is. 7:14 his name E. Mat. 1:23
8:8 breadth of thy land, O E.

EMPTY, Adjective.

Is. 24:1 Lord maketh earth e.
29:8 hungry man awak. soul e.
Luke 1:53 rich be sent e. away

EMPTY, Verb.

Lev. 14:36 that they e. the house
Ec. 11:3 Clouds e. themselves
Jer. 51:2 fanners shall e. her land
Hab. 1:17 shall they e. their net
Zec. 4:12 which e. the golden oil

ENCAMP.

Ps. 27:3 a host e. against me
Zec. 9:8 I will e. about my house

ENCAMPETH.

Ps. 34:7 angel of Lord e. round

END.

Gen. 6:13 e. of all flesh is come
2 K. 10:21 Baal full from e.
Ps. 7:9 wickedness come to an e.
38 e. of wicked shall be cut off
39:4 make me know mine e.
Prov. 5:4 e. bitter; 23:18 the. is e.
Is. 2:7 any e. of their treasures.
9:7 of his governm. sh. be no e.
13:5 come from the e. of heaven
45:17 world without e.
46:10 the e. from the beginning
Dan. 7:28 is the e. of the matter
8:17 time of e. shall be the vis.
19 at the time e. shall be, 11:27
9:26 the e. thereof be with flood
11:6 and in the e. of years
40 time of e. king of sou.
12:4 seal the book even to the e.
8 O Lord, what shall be the e.
9 words are clos. up, till the e.
13 go thy way till the e. be
Mat. 13:39 harvest is e. of world
24:3 sign of e. of the world?
14 then shall the e. come
31 gath. from one e. of heaven

26:58 Peter sat to see the e.
28:1 in the e. of the sabbath
Luke 1:33 his kingdom be no e.
18:1 a para. to them, to this e.
22:37 concern. me have an e.
John 18:37 to this e. was I born
Rom. 6:21 e. of those th. is death
22 the e. everlasting life
10:4 Christ is the e. of the law
14:9 to this e. Christ hath died
2 Cor. 11:15 e. according to works
Eph. 3:21 glory, world without e.
Phil. 3:19 whose e. is destruction
1 Tim. 1:5 e. of com. is charity
Heb. 6:8 whose e. is to be burned
Jam. 5:11 ye have seen e. of Lord
1 Pet. 1:9 receiv. e. of your faith
4:17 e. of them that obey not
Rev. 21:6 Alpha and Omega, the
beginning and the e. 22:13

TO THE END.
Ex. 8:22 to the e. thou mayest
kno. I am the L. Ezek. 20:26
Deut. 17:20 to the e. that he may
prolong his days.
Mat. 10:22 endur. to the e. shall
be saved, 24:13; Mark 13:13
1 Pet. 1:13 and hope to the e.

Unto the END.
Heb. 3:6 hold fast confidence u.e.
14 if hold begin, steadfast u. e.
6:11 assurance of hope unto e.

ENDLESS.
1 Tim. 1:4 heed to e. genealogies
Heb. 7:16 after power of an e. life

ENDEAVOR,.
2 Pet. 1:15 will e. ye may be able

ENDUED.
Luke 24:49 ye be e. with power
Jam. 3:13 e. with knowledge

ENDURE.
Ps. 9:7 the Lord shall e. for ever,
102:12, 26; 104:31
30:5 weeping may e. for a night
2 Thes. 1:4 tribulations that ye e.
2 Tim. 2:3 therefore e. hardness

ENDURED.
Rom. 9:22 God e. with long-suff.
2 Tim. 3:11 what persecut. I e.

ENDURETH.
John 6:27 meat which e. unto life

1 Cor. 13:7 charity e. all things
Jam. 1:12 bless, that e. tempta.

ENDURETH for ever.
1 Chr. 16:34 his mercy e. forever,
41:2 Chr. 5:13; 7:3, 6; 20:21;
Ezr. 3:11; Ps. 106:1; 107:1;
118:1-4; 136:1-3, etc.; 138:8;
Jer. 33:11
1 Pet. 1:25 word of the L. e.f.e.

ENEMY.
1 Cor. 15:26 the last e. is death
Jam. 4:4 friend of world e. of G.

Thine ENEMY.
Rom. 12:20 if th. e. hung. feed h.

ENEMIES.
Mic. 7:6 are of own house
Rom. 5:10 when e. we were rec.
11:28 as con. gospel, they are e.
1 Cor. 15:25 put all e. under feet
Phil. 3:18 e. of the cross of Chr.
Col. 1:21 e. in your mind

Mine ENEMIES.
Num. 23:11 curse mine e. 24:10
Deut. 32:41 vengeance to mine e.
1 Sam. 2:1 enlarged over m. e.
14:24 be avenged on mine e.
2 Sam. 5:20 L. hath broken forth
upon mine e. 1 Chr. 14:11
22:4 saved from m. e. Ps. 18:3
38 pursued mine e. Ps. 18:37
41 necks of m. e. Ps. 18:40
49 bringeth me forth fr. m. e.
1 Chr. 12:17 betray me to mine e.
Ps. 3:7 hast smitten all mine e.
5:8 lead me, O. L. bec. of m. e.
6:7 eye waxeth old bec. of m. e.
10 let all mine e. be ashamed
7:6 because of rage of mine. e.
9:3 m. e. are turned
18:48 he deliv. me from mine. e.
23:5 in presence of mine e.
25:2 let not m. e. triumph, 35:19
19 consider m. e. they are ma.
27:2 m. e. came to eat my flesh
6 he lifted up above mine e.
11 because of mine e.
12 deliv. me n. to will of m. e.
31:11 I was a reproach am. m. e.
15 from hand of mine e.

Your ENEMIES.
Mat. 5:44 love y. e. Luke 6:27, 35

74

ENMITY.
Gen. 3:15 I will put e. betw. thee
ENOCH.
Gen. 33:9 Esau said, I have e.
Gen. 45:28 it is e. Jos. is yet alive
Ex. 9:28 entreat Lord, for it is e.
2 Chr. 31:10 we have had e. to e.
Prov. 30:15 things say not, It is e.
ENTER.
Mat. 5:20 in no case e. into king.
6:6 prayest e. into thy closet
7:13 e. in at str. gate, Luke 13:24
21 that saith, Lord, shall e. in
10:11 city ye e. Luke 10:8, 10
12:29 e. str. man's h. Mark 3:27
45 e. in dwell there, Luke 11:26
18:8 it is better to e. into life
halt, 9; Mark 9:43, 45, 47
19:17 if thou wilt e. into life
24 rich man to e. into kingdom,
Mark 10:25; Luke 18:25
Luke 8:16 which e. in may see
13:24 many will seek to e. in
24:26 and to e. into his glory?
John 3:4 can he e. into womb
5 he cannot e. into king. of G.
Acts 14:22 through tribulation e.
20:29 grievous wolves shall e. in
Heb. 4:3 e. into rest, if e. rest, 5
11 let us labor to e. that rest
10:19 us. holiest by blood of Jes.
Rev. 15:8 no man able to e. tem.
21:27 in no wise e. that defileth
22:14 e. in thro. gates into city
ENTER not.
26:41 e. n. into temp. Luke 22:40
ENTERTAIN.
Heb. 13:2 not forgetful to e. stran.
ENTREAT.
Ruth 1:16 e. me not to leave thee
Phil. 4:3 I e. thee also, y.- fellow
1 Tim. 5:1 but e. him as a father
ENTREATETH.
Job 24:21 he evil e. the barren
ENVY, Substantive.
Prov. 14:30 e. is rotten. of bones
27:4 who able to stand bef. e.?
Ec. 9:6 hatred and e. is perished
Is. 11:13 e. of Ephraim shall dep.
26:11 be ashamed for their e.
Ezek. 35:11 according to thine e.

Mat. 27:18 for e. Mark 15:10
Acts 7:9 patriarchs mov. with e.
13:45 Jews filled with e. spake
17:5 the Jews moved with e.
Rom. 1:19 full of e. murder
Phil. 1:15 prea. Christ even of e.
1 Tim. 6:4 whereof cometh e.
Tit. 3:3 living in malice and e.
Jam. 4:5 spirit in us lusteth to e.
ENVY, Verb.
Prov. 3:31 e. not the oppressor
ENVYING.
Rom. 13:13 let us walk, not in e.
1 Cor. 3:3 for whereas there is e.
Gal. 5:26 e. one another
Jam. 3:14 but if ye have bitter e.
16 where e. is, is confusion
ENVYINGS.
2 Cor. 12:20 I fear lest there be e.
Gal. 5:21 wor. of the flesh are e.
ENVIOUS.
Ps. 37:1 e. aga. workers of iniq.
73:3 for I was e. at the foolish
Prov. 24:1 be not e. ag. evil men
EPHESUS.
Acts 18:19 P. came to E. 21; 19:17
Rev. 1:11 to E., 2:1 angel at E.
EQUAL.
Mat. 20:12 hast made them e.
John 5:18 himself e. with God
Phil. 2:6 not rob. to be e. with G.
Col. 4:1 gave servants what is e.
Rev. 21:16 breadth and height e.
ERR.
Mat. 22:29 ye do e. not know, the
scriptures, Mark. 12:24, 27
Heb. 3:10 e. in their hearts
Jam. 1:16 do not e. my beloved
5:10 if any e. from the truth
ERRED.
Ps. 119:110 I e. not from thy pre.
Is. 28:7 have e. thro' wine, priest
1 Tim. 6:10 have e. from the faith
21 some have e. concern. faith
2 Tim. 2:18 concern. tru. have e.
ERROR.
2 Sam. 6:7 smote Uzzah for his e.
Mat. 27:64 last e. worse than first
Jam. 5:20 from the e. of his way
2 Pet. 2:18 them who live in e.
1 John 4:6 know we spirit of e.

Jude 11 after the e. of Baalam
ESAU.
Gen. 25:25 his name E. 27, 29
27:11 E. is a hairy m. 21, 24, 42
Heb. 11:20 Isaac blessed E.
12:16 profane person as E.

ESCAPE, Verb.
Joel 2:3 nothing shall e. them
Ob. 14 cut of those that did e.
Mat. 23:33 e. damnati, of hell?
Rom. 2:3 shalt e. judg. of God?
1 Cor. 10:13 will make a way to e.
1 Thes. 5:3 and they shall not, e.
ESCAPED.
Jud. 3:29 e. not, 1 Sam. 30:17
21:17 inherit, for them that e.
1 Sam. 14:41 J. taken, but peo. e.
19:10 D. fled and e. that night
2 Sam. 1:3 out of the ca. am I e.
4:6 and Rachab and Baanah e.
Job 1:15 I only am e. 16, 17, 19
19:20 e. with the sk. of my teeth
Ezek. 24:27 opened to him e.
33:21 one that had e. came
John 10:39 e. out of their hands
Acts 27:44 so they e. all safe
28:4 tho' he e. the sea. yet ven.
2 Cor. 11:33 I was let down and e.
Heb. 11:34 through faith e.
12:25 if e. not who refused him
2 Pet. 1:4 e. corruption in world
2:18 those that were clean e.
20 e. the pollutions of world
ESPECIALLY.
Gal. 6:10 e. the househ. of faith
1 Tim. 4:10 e. of tho, that believe
5:8 prov. s. for them of his own
17 e. they who labor in word
2 Tim. 4:13 but e. the parchments
Phile. 16 a brother beloved s.
ESPOUSED.
Mat. 1:18 when Mary was e. to J.
ESTABLISH.
Rom. 3:31 yea, we e. the law
10:3 going about to e. own
16:25 power to e. you
1 Thes. 3:2 sent Tim. to e. you
13 s. your hearts unblameable
2 Thes. 2:17 s. you in ev. g. word
3:3 Lord shall s. you, and keep

Heb. 10:9 that he may e. second
Jam. 5:8 patient, s. your hearts
1 Pet. 5:10 the God of all grace s.
ESTABLISHED.
Gen. 9:17 token of covenant I e.
1 K. 2:12 king, was e. greatly
2 Chr. 1:9 L. let thy promise be e.
Job 21:8 seed is e. in their sight
Prov. 3:19 L. hath e. the heavens
4:26 let all thy ways be e.
ESTATE.
Luke 1:48 low e. of his handm.
Rom. 12:16 con. to men of low e.
Phil. 2:19 when I know your s.
20 naturally care for your s.
4:11 whatso, s. I am to be cont.
ESTEEMED.
Prov. 17:28 e. a man of underst.
Is. 29:16 be e. as potter's clay
Luke 16:15 e. among men is abo.
ETERNAL.
Deut. 33:27 e. God is thy refuge
Mark 3:29 in danger of e. damn.
Rom. 1:20 e. power and Godhead
2 Cor. 4:17 an e. weight of glory
Eph. 3:11 ac. to e. purpose in C.
2 Tim. 2:10 obt. salv. with e. glo.
Heb. 5:9 author of e. salvation
6:2 the doctrine of e. judgment
Jude 7 suff. vengeance of e. fire
ETERNAL life.
Mark 10:17 that I may inherit e.
John 3:15 believe sh. have e. l.
6:54 drink, my blood, hath e. l.
10:28 give unto my sheep e. life
12:25 hateth life, keep it to e. l.
17:2 give e. life to as many
Ro.6:23 but the gift of God is e.l.
1 Tim. 6:12 lay hold on e. life, 19
Tit. 1:2 in hope of e.l. which G.
3:7 accord. to hope of e. life
1 John 1:2 e.l. which was with F.
20 the true God, and e. life
Jude 21 for mercy of L. to e. life
ETERNITY.
Is. 57:15 lofty One that inhab. e.
ETHIOPIA.
Est. 1:1 from India to E. 8:9
Acts 8:27 a man of E. an eunuch
ETHIOPIAN.
Num. 12:1 because of E. woman

EUPHRATES.
Gen. 2:14 the fourth river is E.
EVANGELIST, S.
Acts 21:8 house of Philip the e.
Eph. 4:11 he gave some e.
2 Tim. 4:5 do the work of an e.
EVEN. or EVENING-TIDE
Gen. 24:63 to meditate at e. tide
Is. 7:14 behold, at e. t. trouble
EVER.
John 4:29 told me all e. I did
8:35 but the Son abideth e.
1 Thes. 4:17 so e. be with the L.
5:15 e. follow that wh. is good
2 Tim. 3:7 e. learning, never able
Heb. 7:24 this man continueth e.
FOR EVER.
Jos. 4:24 ye might fear L. for e.
2 Chr. 7:16 name be there for e.
33:4 Jerusalem name be for e.
Ps. 89:1 sing of mercies of L.for e.
105:8 remembered covenant f. e.
Dan. 2:44 his kingdom stand f. e.
4:34 praised him that liveth f. e.
Joel 3:20 Judah shall dwell for e.
Ob. 10 shalt be cut off for e.
Mic. 2:9 tak. away my glory f. e.
Rom. 1:25 Creator, blessed for e.
Heb. 10:12 for e. sat down
14 perfected f. e. them sancti.
1 Pet. 1:23 which liveth for e.
25 word of Lord endureth f. e.
2 John 2 be with us for e.
Live for EVER.
Gen. 3:22 tree of life and l. for e.
Ps. 22:26 heart shall live for e.
John 6:51 if any man eat of this
bread, he shall l. for e. 58
For EVER and EVER.
Jer. 7:7 land I gave for e and e.
25:% to you and fathers for e. a.
Dan. 7:18 pos. kingdom f. e. a. e.
12:3 as the stars for e. and e.
Mic. 4:5 in name of God f. e. a. e.
Gal. 1:5 glory for e. and e. Phil.
4:20; 1 Tim. 1:17; 2 Tim.
4:18; Heb. 13:21
Heb. 1:8 throne O G. is for e. a. e.
Rev. 4:9 who liveth for e. a. e. 10;
5:14; 10:6; 15:7
5:13 honor be to L. for e. and e.

7:12 power be to our G. f.e.a.e.
11:15 C. shall reign for e. and e.
20:10 be tormented for e. and e.
EVERLASTING.
Gen. 17:18 an e. posession, 48:4
31:33 the e. God, Is. 40:28; Rom.
16:26
Is. 9:6 Be called, the e. Father
Mat. 18:8 cast into e. fire, 25:41
Luke 16:9 into e. habitations
2 Thes. 1:9 pun. with e. destruc.
2:16 hath given us e. consolation
1 Tim. 6:16 be honor and pow. e.
Rev. 14:6 the e. gospel to preach
From EVERLASTING.
Mic. 5:2 whose goings forth f. e.
EVERLASTING life.
Dan. 12:2 awake, some to e. life
Mat. 19:29 shall inherit e. life
John 6:47 believeth on me hath e.
life Gal. 6:8 shall of the Sp.reap l.e.
EVERMORE.
1 Thes. 5:16 rejoice e.
Rev. 1:18 behold, I am alive for e.
EVERY.
Is. 45:23 e. knee, Rom. 14:11
Mat. 4:4 by e. word that proc.
1 Cor. 4:17 as I teach e. wh. in e.
Eph. 1:21 abo. e. name, Phil 2:9
Heb. 12:1 lay aside e. weight
Jam. 1:17 e. good and perf. gift
EVIDENCE.
Heb. 11:1 e. of things not seen
EVIL.
Gen. 19:19 some e. take me, I die
Ex. 5:23 done e. to this people
32:14 the L. repented of the e.
2 Sam. 24:16; 1 Chr. 21:15
Ps. 7:4 if I rewarded e. to him
21:11 intended e. against thee
23:4 I will fear no e. for thou art
Prov. 1:16 feet run to e. Is. 59:7
33 shall be quiet from fear of e.
3:29 devise not e. ag. neighbor
Ec. 2:21 is vanity, and a great e.
Is. 3:9 rewarded e. to themselves
Jer. 1:14 out of north an e. 6:1
4:4 because of e. of your doings,
23:2; 26:3; 44:22
Mal. 1:8 ye of. sick, is it not e.
2:17 every one that doeth e.

Mat. 5:11 all manner of e.
6:34 sufficient to the d. is the e.
9:4 why th. ye e. in your hearts?
27:23 What e. hath he done?
Mark 15:14; Luke 23:22
Mark 9:39 lightly speak e. of
John 3:20 doeth e. hateth light
Rom. 2:9 every soul that doeth e.
7:19 e. I would not, that I do
17 recomp. to no man e. for e.
1 Cor. 13:5 charity thinketh no e.
1 Thes. 5:15 none render e. for e.
22 abstain from appear. of e.
1 Tim. 6:10 money root of all e.
Tit. 3:2 speak e. of no man
Jam. 3:8 tongue is an unruly e.
1 Pet. 3:9 not rendering e. for e.
3 John 11 doeth e. not seen
evil joined with good.
Gen. 2:9 tree of kno. g. and e. 17
44:4 wheref. rewarded e. for g.?
Deut. 1:39 no kno. bet. g. and e.
1 Sam. 25:21 requit. me e. for g.
Ps. 35:12 rew. me e. for g. 109:5
Prov. 15:3 behold. e. and the g.
31:12 will do him good, not e.
Is. 5:20 woe to th. call e. g. g. e.
Mic. 3:2 hate good and love e.
Rom. 7:21 do g. e. is present
Heb. 5:14 exerc. to disc. g. and e.
3 John 11 follow not e. but good
From EVIL.
Ps. 34:13 keep thy tongue f. e.
14 dep. f. e. 37:27; Prov. 3:7
121:7 preserve thee f. all e.
EVIL, Adjective.
Gen. 6:5 thoughts only e. 8:21
Ezek. 5:16 e. arrows of famine
38:10 shalt think an e. thought
Hab. 2:9 coveteth an e. covetous.
Mat. 5:45 sun to rise on the e.
7:11 if being e. Luke 11:13
18 cannot bring forth, e. fruit
12:34 how can ye being e. speak
39 an e. generation, Luke 11:29
15:19 out of the heart proceed
e. thoughts, Mark 7:21
24:48 if e. servant say in heart
John 3:19 because deeds were e.
Acts 24:20 found e. doing in me
1 Cor. 15:33 e. communications

Gal. 1:4 deliver us from e. world
Eph. 4:31 e. speaking be put aw.
Phil. 3:2 beware of evil workers
Col. 3:5 mortify e. concupiscence
1 Tim. 6:4 cometh e. surmisings
Tit. 1:12 Cretians are e. beasts
Heb. 10:22 sprinkled from e.
Jam. 2:4 judges of e. thoughts
4:16 all such rejoicing is e.
1 Pet. 2:1 laying aside e. speak.
Rev. 2:2 canst not bear them e.
EVIL day or days.
Eph. 5:16 because days are e.
6:13 able to withstand in e. day
EVIL, doer or doers.
Job 8:20 neither will he help e. d.
Ps. 26:5 hated congrega. of e. d.
2 Tim. 2:9 I suffer troub. as e. d.
1 Pet 2:12 speak ag. you as e. d.
EVIL man or men.
Prov. 2:12 deli. from way of e. m.
Prov. 28:5 e. m. unders. not judg.
29:6 in transg. of e. m. is snare
Mat. 12:35 e. m. out of e. trea-
sure, bring, e. th. Luke 6:45
EVIL spirit or spirits.
Jud. 9:23 e. s. betw. Abimelech
1 Sam. 16:14 e. s. troub. him, 15
16 when e. spirit is upon thee
23 e. spirit departed from him
18:10 e. spirit came on S. 19:9
Luke 7:21 cured many of e. s.
8:2 a woman healed of e. spirits
Acts 19:12 e. s. went out of them
15 e. s. said, Jesus, I know, Pa.
EVIL things.
Rom. 1:30 inventors of e. things
1 Cor. 10:6 not lust after e. t.
EVIL way.
Jer. 18:11 return ye from e. w.
25:5; 26:3; 35:15; 36:3, 7
23:22 turned them from e. way
Jon. 3:8 turn ev. one from e. w.
10 saw they turned from e. w.
EVIL work or works
2 Tim. 4:18 deliver me from e. w.
Jam. 3:16 and every e. w.
1 John 3:12 his own w. were e.
EVIL, Adverb.
Rom. 14:16 not good be e. spoken
1 Cor. 10:30 am I e. spoken of

Jam. 4:11 sp. not e. he that spe.
e. of brother, speaks e. of law
1 Pet. 3:16 whereas they speak e.
17 than suffer for e. doing
4:4 speaking e. of you
14 on their part e. spoken of
2 Pet. 2:2 way of truth e. spok. of
10 speak e. of dignities, Jude 8
12 speak e. of things they understand not, Jude 10

EVILS.

Deut. 31:17 e. shall befall them,
will say, Are not these e.
Ps. 40:12 innumer. e. comp. me
Jer. 2:13 have committed two e.
Ezek. 6:9 loathe themselves for e.
20:43 loathe yourselves for all e.
Luke 3:19 for all e. II. had done

EWE or EWES.

Gen. 21:28 Abraham set seven e.
Lev. 14:10 take one e. lamb

EXALT.

2 Dor. 11:20 if a man e. himself

EXALTED.

Num. 24:7 kingdom shall be e.
2 Sam. 5:12 he had e. kingdom
22:47 e. be the God of the rock
of my salvation, Ps. 18:46
12:4 mention that his name is e.
ꜱꜱꜱ ꜱ ꜱ ꜱ ꜱ
Mat. 11:23 e. to heav. Luke 10:15
23:12 humble himself shall be
e. Luke 14:11; 18:14
Luke 1:52 e. them of low degree

EXALTEST, ETH.

2 Cor. 10:5 every thing that e.
2 Thes. 2:4 e. him above all

EXAMPLE, S.

Mat. 1:19 make her a public e.
John 13:15 have given you an e.
1 Cor. 10:6 were our e.
1 Tim. 4:12 e. of believers
Heb. 4:11 fall after same e.
Jam. 5:10 prophets for e. suffer.

EXCEED.

Deut. 25:3 forty stripes and not

EXCEEDING.

Gen. 15:1 thy e. great reward
Dan. 3:22 the furnace was e. hot
Mat. 2:10 rej. with e. great joy
5:12 rejoice and be e. glad

Rom. 7:13 sin become e. sinful
2 Cor. 4:17 work. e. weight glory
9:14 for e. grace of God in you
1 Tim. 1:14 grace of L. e. abund.
1 Pet. 4:13 be glad al. with e. joy
2 Pet. 1:4 e. great promises
Jude 24 you faultless with e. joy

EXCEEDINGLY.

1 Thes. 3:10 praying e..

EXCELLENT.

Job. 37:23 Almighty is e. in power
Ps. 8:1 how e. thy name1 9
36:7 how e. is thy loving-kind.
Prov. 8:6 will speak of e. things
12:26 righte, more e. th. neigh.
Dan. 2:31 whose brightn. was e.
5:12 e. spirit found in d. 6:3
1 Cor. 12:31 show I a more e. way
Heb. 1:4 obtained a more e. name
8:6 obtained a more e. ministry
11:4 A. offered more e. sacrifice
2 Pet. 1:17 voice from the e. glo.

EXCEPT.

Ps. 127:1 e. L. build, e. L. keep
Amos 3:3 two walk e. agreed?
Mat. 5:20 e. righteousness exc.
18:3 I say to you e. ye be conv.
24:22 e. day be short, Mark 13:20
Luke 13:2 e. ye repent, ye shall
per.5
John 3:2 e. G. be with him
3 e. a man be born again
3:5 e. a man be born again
3:5 e. a man be born of water
27 nothing e. it be given
4:48 e. ye see signs and wonders
6:44 e. the Father draw him
53 e. ye eat fle. of the S. of m.
15:4 ye cannot bear fruit e. ye
20:25 e. I see print of the nails
Rom. 10:15 how preach e. they be
sent
2 Cor. 12:13 e. I was not burden.
2 Thes. 2:3 e. come a falling aw.

EXCESS.

Mat. 23:25 within are full of e.
Eph. 5:18 wine, wherein is e.
1 Pet. 4:3 lusts, and e. of wine
4 ye run not to the same e.

EXCUSE.

Luke 14:18 began to make e.

Rom. 1:20 so they are without e.
EXCUSE, Verb.
2 Cor. 12:19 think you we e. our.
EXERCISE.
1 Tim. 4:8 bodily e. profit. little
EXHORTATION.
Luke 3:18 many things in e.
Acts 13:15 ye have word of e. say
  20:2 when P. had given much e.
Rom. 12:8 exhort. let wait on e.
1 Cor. 14:3 speak, unto men to e.
2 Cor. 8:17 he accepted the e.
1 Thes. 2:3 e. was not of deceit
1 Tim. 4:13 give attendance to e.
Heb. 12:5 ye have forgot, the e.
  13:22 suffer the word of e.
EXORCISTS.
Acts 19:13 vagabond Jews, e.
EXPECTATION.
Ps. 9:18 e. of poor shall not per.
  62:5 wait on G. my e. from him
EXPEDIENT.
1 Cor. 6:12 all things not e. 10:23
2 Cor. 8:10 e. for you who begun
  12:1 it is not e. for me to glory
EXPERIENCE.
Gen. 30:27 by e. the Lord blessed
Ec. 1:16 my heart had e. of wis.
Rom. 5:4 worketh e. and e.
EXPRESS.
Heb. 1:3 being e. image of person
EXTORTION, ER, ERS.
1 Cor. 5:10 not altogether with e.
  11 if any be drunkard, an e.
  6:10 nor e. inherit kingd. of G.
EYE.
Ex. 21:24 e. for e. Lev. 24:20;
  Deut. 19:21; Mat. 5:38
Is. 52:8 for they shall see e. to e.
  64:4 nei. hath e. seen, 1 Cor. 2:9
Mat. 7:3 mote in brother's e.beam.
  in thine own e. Luke 6:41,42
  18:9 if e. offend thee pluck out
  19:24 camel go thro' e. of needle.
  Mark 10:25; Luke 18:25
1 Cor. 12:16 bec. I am not the e.
  15:52 in twinkling of an e.
Rev. 1:7 every e. shall see him
EYE-SERVICE.
Eph. 6:6 not with e.-s. Col. 3:22
EYES.

Ps. 15:4 in whose e. vile person
John 9:6 anoint. e. of blind man
  32 opened e. of one born blind
  10:21 can devil open e. of blind
Rom. 11:8 given e. should not see
Eph. 1:18 e. of your understand.
1 John 2:16 lust of the e. and pri.
Our EYES.
Mat. 20:33 that our e. be opened
1 John 1:1 have seen with our e.
Own EYES.
Num. 15:39 seek not after own e.
Deut. 12:8 what is right in his
  own e. Jud. 17:6; 21:25
Neh. 6:16 ene. cast down in o. e.
Job. 32:1 because righteous in o. e.
Ps. 36:2 he flattereth him, in o. e.
Prov. 3:7 be not wise in own e.
Is. 5:21 woe to them wise in o.e.
Gal. 4:15 would have plucked o.e.
Their EYES.
Gen. 42:24 bound S. before t. e.
Is. 6:10 shut t. e. lest see with t.
  e. Mat. 13:15; Acts 28:27
Luke 24:16 their e. were holden
  31 their e. were opened
John 12:40 he hath blinded, t. e.
Rom. 3:18 no fear of G. bef. t. e.
Rev. 7:17 all tears from t. e. 21:4
Thine EYES.
Lam. 2:18 let not apple of t. e.
Your EYES.
Is. 29:10 Lord hath closed y. e.
  40:26 lift up y. e. Jer. 13:20
Ezek. 24:21 the desire of your e.
Mal. 1:5 your e. shall see, the L.
Mat. 13:16 blessed are your e.
F.

FABLES.
1 Tim. 1:4 nor give heed to f.
FACE.
Gen. 3:19 in sweat of f. shall eat
  16:8 I flee from f. of mistress
  24:47 I put ear-rings upon her f.
Ex. 2:15 Moses fled f. of Pharaoh
  14:25 let us flee from f. of Israel
  34:29 skin of his f. shone, 30, 35
Nah. 2:1 dasheth come before f.
Mat. 6:17 anoint head, wash f.
2 Cor. 3:7 could not behold f.

11:20 if man smite you on f.
Gal. 1:22 unkn. by f. to churches
FACE of the deep.
Gen. 1:2 darkness upon f. of t. d.
FACE to FACE.
Gen. 32:30 I have seen G. f. to f.
Deut. 5:4 talked with you f. to f.
34:10 M. whom L. knew f. to f.
Acts 2516 have accusers f. to f.
1 Cor. 13:12 a glass, but f. to f
3 John 14 and speak f. to f.
Fell on FACE, or FACES.
Dan. 2:46 Nebuch. f. upon his f.
Mat. 17:6 disci.; 26:39 J. f. on f
Luke 5:12 leper; 17:16 S. f. on f.
Rev. 11:16 24 elders f. on their f.
FACE of the Lord.
Ps. 34:16 f. of the Lord against
   them that do evil, 1 Pet. 3:12
Lam. 2:19 heart before f. of L.
Luke 1:76 go before f. of Lord
Seek FACE.
2 Chr. 7:14 if my people s. my f.
Set FACE.
Dan. 9:3 I set my f. to Lord God
FACE shine.
Num. 6:25 L. make f. to s. on thee
Ps. 31:16 make thy f. to shine on
   thy servant, 119:135
Ec. 8:1 maketh his f. to shine
Mat. 17:2 his f. did shine as sun
FACES.
Is. 3:15 that ye grind f. of poor
13:8 their f. shall be as flames
25:8 will wipe tears from all f.
Jer. 1:8 be not afraid of their f.
30:6 all f. turned into paleness
42:15 set f. to enter, 17:44; 12
Lam. 5:12 f. of elders not hon.
Ezek. 1:6 ev. one four f. 10, 11, 15
Dan. 9:7 unto us confusion of f.
Mat. 6:16 hypocrites disfigure f.
FADETH.
Is. 1:30 as an oak, whose leaf f.
40:7 grass withereth, flower f. 8
1 Pet. 1:4 inheritance f. not away
5:4 cro. of glory that f. not aw.
FAIL, Verb.
Deut. 28:32 eyes f. with longing
31:6 he will not f. thee, 8; Jos.
   1:5; 1 Chr. 28:20

Prov. 22:8 rod of his anger sh. f.
FAINT, Verb.
Deut. 20:3 let not your hearts f.
Is. 40:30 shall f. Amos 8:13
   31 walk and not f.

FAITH.
Mat. 6:30 O ye of little f. 8:26
   14:31; 16:8; Luke 12:28
8:10 great f. no not. Luke 7:9
17:20 f. as grain of mustard seed
23:23 judgment, mercy, and f.
Mark 4:40 ye have no f.?
Luke 17:5 Lord increase our f.
18:8 wh. S. of man com. fl. f.?
Acts 6:5 Ste. a man full of f. 8
14:9 that he had f. to be healed
22 exhorting to continue in f.
27 opened door of f. to Genti.
16:5 churches established in f.
20:21 f. toward our L. Jesus C.
24:24 Felix heard P. concern. f.
Rom. 1:5 obedience to f.
17 righte. of G. rev. fr. f. to f.
4:5 f. counted for righteous, 9
16 f. of. of the f. of Abraham
9:30 righte, which is of f. 10:6
10:8 word of F. which we prea.
17 so then f. cometh by hear.
23 eat. not of f. not of f. is sin
16:26 for the obedience of f.
1 Cor. 12:9 another f. by same S.
13 now abideth f. hope, chari.
Gal.1:23 f. which once destroy.
3:2 or by the hearing of f. 5
12 law is not of f. but man
23 before f. came; 25 f. is co.
5:6 f. which worketh by love
22 fruit of Sp. is love, joy, f.
Eph. 4:5 one L. one f. one bapt.
13 come in the unity of the f.
Phil. 1:25 further, and joy of f.
1 Thes. 1:3 rememb. work of f.
2 Thes. 1:11 work of f. with pow.
1 Tim. 3:9 holding the mystery of f.
5:8 he hath denied the f. and is
6:10 have erred from the f. 21
11 follow f.; 3:8 reprobate f.
3:10 thou hast fully known f.
Tit. 1:1 the f. of God's elect
4 T. mine own son aft. com. f.

F

81

10:22 in full assurance of f.
23 hold fast profession of f.
11:1 f. is substance of things
    f. impossi. to pl. G.
12:2 and finisher of our f.
13:7 whose f. follow, consider.
Jam. 17 f. with. works is
dead.20,26
    18 hast f. and I have works
    22 f. wrought with works, and
    by works was f. made perf.
5:15 prayer of f. shall save sick
1 John 5:4 overcome. wor. our f.
Jude 3 earnestly contend for f.

By FAITH.
Hab. 2:4 shall live by f. Rom.
    1:17; Gal. 3:11; Heb. 10:38
Rom. 3:22 righteous. of G. by f.
    28 justi. b. f. 5:1; Gal. 2:16; 3:24
2 Cor. 5:7 walk by f. not by sight
Gal. 2:20 I live by f. of S. of God
    26 child. of G. by f. in Chr. J.
5:5 hope of righteousness by f.
Eph. 3:12 we have access by f.
Phil. 3:9 righteousn. of G. by f.
Heb. 11:4 by f. Abel; 5 by f. En.
    7 by f. Noah; 8 by f. Ara. 9, 17
    20 by f. Isaac; 21 Jac.; 22 Jos.
    23 by f. Moses, 24:27; 31 Rah.
    29 by f. passed through Red s.
    30 by f. walls of Jer. fell down

In FAITH.
Rom. 4:19 being not weak in f.
    20 but was strong in f.
14:1 him weak in f. receive you
1 Cor. 16:13 stand fast in f.
2 Cor. 13:5 exam. wh. ye be in f.
Col. 1:23 if ye continue in the f.
1 Tim. 1:2 Tim. my own son i. f.
    4 godly edifying which is in f.
3:13 they purchase boldn. in f.
Heb. 11:13 these all died in f.
Jam. 1:6 but let them ask in f.
2:5 poor of this world, rich in f.
1 Pet. 5:9 resist, steadfast in f.

Through FAITH.
Acts 3:16 through f. in his name
Rom. 3:25 propitiation t. f.
    30 justify uncircumcision t. f.
Gal. 3:8 God justify heathen t. f.
Eph. 2:8 are ye saved t. f.

Phil. 3:9 righteousu. wh. is t. f.
Col. 2:12 risen t. f. of ope. of G.
Heb. 6:12 t. f. inherit promises
    11:3 t. f. we und. worlds framed
Thy FAITH.
Mat. 9:22 t. f. hath made thee
    whole, Mark 5:24; 10:52;
    Luke 8:48; 17:19
Your FAITH.
Mat. 9:29 according to y. f. be it
Luke 8:25 where is your f.?
2 Cor. 1:24 dominion over y. f.
    10:15 when your f. is increased
Phil. 2:17 offer, on service of y. f.
1 Thes. 1:8 your f. to God-ward
2 Thes. 1:3 y. f. groweth exceed.
Jam. 1:3 trying of y. f. worketh
1 Pet. 1:7 trial of y. f. precious
    21 that y. f. might be in God
2 Pet. 1:5 add to your f. virtue
2 Sam. 20:19 f. in Israel
Ps. 12:1 the f. fail from am. men
Is. 1:21 how is f. city become
Hos. 11:12 Ju. is f. with saints
Mat. 24:45 who then is f.
    25:21 well done, good and f. se.
Luke 12:42 who is f. and wise?
    16:10 f. in least is f. in much
Acts 16:15 ye have judged me f.
1 Cor. 1:9 God is f. 10:13
Eph. 1:1 to saints and f. in C. J.
1 Thes. 5:24 f. is he that calleth
2 Thes. 3:3 L. is f. who stablish
1 Tim. 1:12 Christ he counted f.
    15 a f. saying, 4:9; Tit. 3:8
1 John 1:9 he is f. to forgive us
FAITHFULNESS.
Lam. 3:23 great thy f.
FAITHLESS.
Mat. 17:17 O f. generation, Mark
    9:19; Luke 9:41
FALL, Verb.
2 Sam. 1:15 f. on h. 1 h. 2:29, 31
    24:14 f. in hand of G. not f. into
    hand of man, 1 Chr. 21:13
Prov. 10:8 a prating fool sh. f. 10
    11:5 wicked shall f.
Ec. 4:10 if they f. one lift fellow
Is. 10:4 they sh. f. under slain
Mic. 7:8 mine enemy, when I f.
Mat. 10:29 not one sparrow f.

Acts 27:17 lest they f. into quic.
1 Cor. 10:12 take heed lest he f.
1 Tim. 3:6 f. into condemnation
Heb. 4:11 lest any f. after same
 10:31 fearful to f. into hands
Jam. 1:2 ye f. into temptations
Jam. 5:12 swear not, lest ye f.

FALL, joined with sword.
Joel 2:8 they f. on the sword
Luke 21:24 shall f. by edge of s.
Phile 1:12 f. out to fur. of gospel

Are FALLEN.
1 Cor. 15:6 some are f. asleep, 18
Gal. 5:4 law, ye are f. from grace
Rev. 17:10 seven kings, five a. f.

Is FALLEN.
Is.21:9 B. is f. Rev. 14:8; 18:2
 59:14 truth is f. in the streets
 Jer. 51:8 Babylon is suddenly f.

FALLING.
1 Cor. 14:25 f. he will worsh. G.
2 Thes. 2:3 except come a f. aw.
Jude 24 is able to keep from f.

FALSE.
Ex. 23:1 shalt not raise f. report
Prov. 11:1 f. balance is abomina-
tion

FALSE prophets.
Mat. 7:15 f. p. in sheep's cloth.
 21:11 many f. p. shall rise, 24
Mark 13:22 f. p. rise show signs
Luke 6:26 did fathers to the f. p.
1 John 4:1 f. p. gone out

FALSE witness, es.
Ex. 20:16 thou shalt not bear f.
 wit. Deut. 5:20; Mat. 19:18
Prov. 6:19 a f. w. speaketh lies
 12:17 a f. w. show. deceit, 14:5

FALSELY.
Lev. 6:3 lost, and sweareth f.
 19:11 neither deal f. nor lie
Mat. 5:11 say evil against you f.
1 Tim. 6:20 opop. of science f.
1 Pet. 3:16 f. accuse good conv.

FALSIFYING.
Amos 8:5 f. balances by deceit

FAMINE.
Job. 5:22 at destruc. f. thou sh. la.
 30:3 want and f. were solitary
Ps. 33:19 keep them alive in f.
 37:19 in days of f.

105:16 he called for a f.
Is. 14:30 I will kill root with f.
 51:19 destruction, f. and sword
Amos 8:11 I will send f.
Luke 4:25 great f. through land

FAMINES.
Mat. 24:7 shall be f. pestilences,
 Mark 13:8; Luke 21:11

FAST, Verb.
2 Sam. 12:23 child dead, why f.?
Is. 58:4 ye f. for strife, sh. not f.
Jer. 14:12 when f. I will not hear
Zec. 7:5 did ye at all f. unto me?
Mat. 6:16 ye f. be not of sad
 counten. that may ap. to f.
 9:14 disc. f. not? Mark 2:18
 15 then f. Mark 2:20; Lu. 5:35
Mark 2:18 disc. of J. used to f.
 19 children of bridechamber f.
Luke 5:33 discip. of J. f. ofter?

FASTED, EST.
Mat. 4:2 Jesus f. forty days
 6:17 when thou f. anoint head
Acts 13:3 f. laid hands on them

FASTING, S.
Ps. 35:13 humbled soul with f.
 69:10 chast. my soul with f.
109:24 knees weak through f.
Joel 2:12 turn ye with f.
Mat. 17:21 but by f. Mark 9:29
Acts 10:30 four days ago I was f.
 14:23 and had prayed with f.
 27:33 fourteenth day ye cont. f.
1 Cor. 7:5 give yourselves to f.
2 Cor. 6:5 approv. ourselves in f.
 11:27 f. often, in cold and nak.

FATHER.
Ps. 68:5 a f. of fatherless is God
103:13 as a f. pitieth children
Prov. 3:12 correcteth, as f. son
 4:1 hear the instruction of a f.
 10:1 maketh a glad f. 15:20
 17:21 f. of a fool hath no joy
 23:24 f. of righteous sh. rejoice
Is. 9:6 called everlasting F.
Mal. 2:10 have we not all one f.?
Mat. 11:25 Jesus said, I th. thee, F.
 26 so F. Lu. 10:21; John 11:41
 27 knoweth the Son but the F.
 15:4 that curseth f. Mark 7:10

83

29 that hath forsaken f. for my
name's sake, Mark 10:29
28:19 baptizing in name of F.
Mark 13:32 knoweth no man but F.
14:36 Abba, F. all th. possible
Luke 10:22 who the F. is, but S.
22:42 F. if willing, remove cup
23:34 F. forgive them, they
46 F. into thy hands I com.
John 1:14 only begotten of F.
18 Son who is in bosom of F.
3:35 F. loveth the Son, 5:20
23 shall worship F. in spirit
5:19 do noth. but what F. do
22 the F. judgeth no man, but
23 honor the Son even as F.
26 the F. hath life in himself
36 works F. hath giv. me bear
witness F. hath sent me
37 F. which hath sent, 8:16;
12:49; 14:24; 1 John 4:14
5:45 will ac. you to the F.
6:37 all the F. giveth me, shall
39 F. will that I lose nothing
42 Jesus whose f. we know?
John 6:44 exc. the F. draw him
45 learned of F. cometh to me
46 not any hath seen the F. he
57 se. me, and I live by the F.
8:16 am not alone, but I and F.
18 F. beareth witness of me
27 unders. not he spake of F.
29 F. hath not left me alone
41 we have one F. even God
44 devil is liar, and the f. of it
10:15 F. know. me, so I the F.
38 F. save me from this hour
12:27 F. save me from this hour
28 F. glorify thy name, then
13:1 should depart unto the F.
3 that F. had given all things
14:6 com. to the F. but by me
8 Lord, show us the F.
9 seen me, hath seen the F.
11 I in F. and F. in me, 17:21
13 F. may be glorified in Son
16 pray the F. for you, 16:26
31 I love the F. as F. gave co.
15:9 as the F. hath love me, so
16 whatsoever ye ask F. 10:26
26 I will send Comfor. from F.

16:3 not known the F. nor me
15 all things F. hath, are mine
16 because I go to the F. 17
25 show you plainly of the F.
27 the F. loveth you, because
28 I came from F. and go to F.
32 am not alone, F. is with me
17:1 F. hour is come, glorify S.
5 O F. glorify thou me with
11 holy F. keep th. given me
24 F. I will they be where I am
25 O right, F. world hath not
Acts 1:4 wait for promise of F.
7 F. put in his own power
2:33 received of F. the promise
Rom. 4:11 be f. of them believe
6:4 as Christ was raised by F.
8:15 whereby we cry, Abba, F.
11:28 are belov. for the F. sake
15:6 F. of our L.J.C. 2 cor. 1:3;
11:31; Eph. 1:3; 1 Pet. 1:3
1 Cor. 8:6 is but one God, the F.
15:24 deliv. up kingdom to F.
2 Cor. 1:3 F. of mercies
6:18 I will be a F. unto you
Gal. 1:3 peace from F. 2 Tim.
1:2; Tit. 1:4
4 ac. to will of God and our F.
4:2 until time appointed of F.
6 Spirit crying, Abba, F.
Eph. 1:17 G. of Jesus F. of glory
2:18 access by one Spirit to F.
3:14 bow my knees unto the F.
4:6 one God and F. aol
Phil. 2:11 is Lord, to glory of F.
Col. 1:19 it plea. F. that all fuln.
2:2 acknowl. of mystery of F.
1 Thes. 1:1 church in God the F.
Heb. 1:5 I will be to him a F. he
12:7 what son F. chasten. not?
9 in subjection to F. of spirits
Jam. 1:17 com. from F. of lights
3:9 bless we God, even the F.
1 Pet. 1:2 foreknowl. of the F.
17 call on F. who judgeth
2 Pet. 1:17 receiv. from F. honor
1 John 1:2 life wh. was with F.
3 our fellow, is with F.
2:1 an advocate with the F.J.
13 because ye have known F.
15 love of the F. is not in him

84

16 pride of life is not of the F.
22 antichrist deni. F. and Son
23 whoso deni. S. hath not F.
24 continue in the S. and in F.
3:1 what manner of love the F.
5:7 three bear record, the F.
2 John 3 mercy and peace fr. F.
4 we received a com. from F.
9 abideth in Christ hath F.
Jude 1 sanctified by God the F.

His FATHER.
Gen. 2:24 shall a man leave his f.
Mark 10:7; Eph. 5:31

MY FATHER.
Mat. 20:23 it is prepared of my F.
24:36 that day know. but my F.
42 my F. thy will be done
Luke 2:49 about my F. business
John 6:32 my F. giv. you true bread
65 except it be given of my F.
10:29 my F. is greater than all
30 I and my F. are one
32 good works from my F.
15:1 my F. is the husbandman
8 herein is my F. glorified

Thy FATHER.
Prov. 1:8 instruct. of thy f. 23:22
6:20 keep thy f. commandment
23:25 t. f. and mother sh. be gl.
27:10 thy f. friend forsake not
Mat. 6:4 t. F. who seeth in sec.
6 pray to t. F. who is in secret

Your FATHER.
Mat. 5:16 glorify your F. in hea.
45 may be children of your F.
48 as y. F. in heaven is perfect
6:1 otherwise no reward of y. F.
8 y. F. knoweth what things ye
have need of, 32; Luke 12:30
14 if ye forgive, y. F. will for.
15 nei. will y. F. forgive your
trespasses, Mark 11:25, 26
10:29 sparrow fall without y. F.
18:14 not will of y. F. one perish
23:9 call no man y. f. on earth.
for one is your F. in heaven
Luke 6:36 as your F. is merciful
12:32 y. F. pleas. to give kingd.
John 8:38 that seen with your F.
41 ye do the deeds of your f.
42 J. said, if god were your F.

44 ye are of y. f. the devil, and
the lusts of y. f. ye will do

FATHERS.
Heb. 12:9 we had f. who corrected

FAULT, S.
1 Sam. 29:3 I found no f. in him
Ps. 19:12 cleanse from secret f.
Luke 23:4 I find no f. in th. man,
14; John 18:38; 19:4, 6
1 Cor. 6:7 utterly a f. among you
Gal. 6:1 man be overtaken in f.
Heb. 8:8 finding f. with them
Jam. 5:16 conf. f. one to another
1 Pet. 2:20 if when buffeted for f.
Rev. 14:5 without f. bef. throne

FAULTLESS.
Heb. 8:7 if first cov. had been f.
Jude 24 is able to present you f.

FAVOR.
Job 10:12 granted me life and f.
Ps. 5:12 with f. compass him
30:5 in his f. is life,
7 by f. made mountain to sta.
44:3 because hadst a f. to them
106:4 remember me with f. thou
112:5 a good man showeth f.
119:58 I entreated thy f.
Prov. 11:27 seek, good procur. f.
13:15 good understand. giv. f.
14:9 among righteous there is f.
35 king's f. toward wise serv.
16:15 his f. is as a cloud of rain
19:6 many entreat f. of prince
12 king's f. is as dew up. grass
21:10 his neighbor findeth no f.
22:1 lov. f. rather to be chosen
29:26 many seek the ruler's f.
31:30 f. is deceitful
Is. 26:10 f. be showed to wicked
27:11 formed show them no f.
60:10 but in my f. I had mercy
Dan. 1:9 brought Daniel into f.
Luke 2:52 Jesus increased in f.

Find or found FAVOR.
1 Sam. 16:22 David hath f. f.
Prov. 3:4 so f. f. in sight of God
28:23 find more f. than he flat.

FEAR, Substantive.
Gen. 9:2 f. of you be on ev. beast
Ex. 15:16 f. sh. fall upon them
Est. 9:3 f. of Mordecai fell on them

Ps. 5:7, in thy f. will I worship
119:38 thy serv. devot. to thy f.
Prov. 1:26 mock when f. cometh
27 when your f. cometh as d.
Prov. 1:33 be quiet from f. of evil
3:25 be not afraid of sudden f.
10:24 f. of wicked come on him
20:2 f. of king as roaring of lion
29:25 f. of man bringeth a snare
Is. 14:3 shall give thee rest from f.
Mal. 1:6 where is my f.?
Luke 1:12 Z. saw him, f. fell on
Rom. 13:7 f. to whom f. is due
2 Tim. 1:7 not giv. us spirit of f.
Heb. 12:28 reverence and godly f.
1 Pet. 1:17 pass time of soj. in f.
1 John 4:18 no f. in l. cast out f.

For FEAR.

Is. 31:9 to his strong-hold f. f.
Jer. 46:5 f. f. was round about
Luke 21:26 hearts failing for f.

Fear of the LORD.

1 Sam. 11:7 f. of L. 2 Chr. 17:10
Job 28:28 f. of the L. is wisdom
Ps. 19:9 f. of the Lord is clean
111:10 f. of L. begin. of wisdom
Is. 11:2 spirit of know, and f. of L.
Acts 9:31 walking in f. of the L.

With FEAR.

Ps. 2:11 serve the Lord with f.
Mat. 28:8 with f. and great joy
Eph. 6:5 obedience w. f. and tr.
Phil. 2:12 work out salva. w. f.

FEARS.

Ps. 34:4 delivered me fr. all my f.

FEAR, Verb.

Luke 12:5 whom ye shall f.
Rom. 8:15 spirit of bondage to f.
2 Cor. 12:20 I f. lest not find you
1 Tim. 5:20 others also may f.
Heb. 4:1 let us f. lest a promise
Rev. 2:10 f. none of those things

FEAR God.

Is. 29:23 they sh. f. G. of Israel
Luke 23:40 dost not thou f. G.?
Acts 13:16 f. God, give audience
1 Pet. 2:17 f. God, honor the k.
Rev. 14:7 f. God, and give glory

Fear the LORD.

Deut. 6:2 mightest f. t. L. thy G.
13 shalt f. L. 10:20; 2 K. 17:39

24 to f. L. for our good always
10:12 f. the L. walk in his ways
14:23 to f. L. 17:19, 31:12, 13
1 Sam. 12:14 if ye will f. the L.
24 f. L. serve him in truth
Ps. 33:8 let all the earth f. the Lord
135:20 ye that f. L. bless the L.
Prov. 3:7 f. L. depart from evil
24:21 f. the Lord, and the king
Jer. 5:24 nor say th. Let us f. L.

FEAR not.

Deut. 20:3 f. not your enemies
31:8 L. doth go before thee, f.
not, Jos. 8:1; 1 Chr. 28:20
Is. 43:1 f. n. I have redeemed thee
54:4 f. n. thou shalt not be ash.
Mat.10:28 f. not them who kill
body
28:5 angel said to women, f. not
Rev. 1:17 f. not, I am the first

Not FEAR.

Ex. 9:30 ye will n. yet f. the L.
Luke 23:40 dost not thou f. God?
Heb. 13:6 not f. what man do

FEARED God.

Job. 1:1 Job was one that f. God
Acts 10:2 Cornelius was one f. G.

FEARED greatly.

Ps. 89:7 God is g. to be f.

FEARED the Lord.

Mal. 3:16 that f. spake oft, a
book of remem. for th. f. L.

FEARFUL.

Mat. 8:26 f. O ye of little faith?
Rev. 21:8 f. have part in the lake

FEARFULLY.

Ps. 139:14 f. and wonderf. made

FEAST.

Gen. 19:3 L. made f. ; 21:8 Abr.
26:30 Isaac; 29:22 Laban
Ezek. 45:23 seven days of f. pre.
Mat. 27:15 at that f. wont to release a prisoner, Mark 15:6
Luke 2:42 after custom of f.
14:13 makest a f. call the poor
John 2:8 bear to governor of f.
4:45 Galileans hav. seen all he
did at f. for they went to f.

FEAST day or days.

Hos. 2:11 cause her f. d. to cease
Mat. 26:5 now on f. d. Mark 14:2

FEAST of the passover.
Mat. 26:2 f. of pass. Mark 14:1
Solemn FEAST.
Deut. 16:15 seven days keep s. f.
FEAST of tabernacles.
Lev. 23:34 shall be the f. of tab.
Deut. 16:16 in f. 31:10; 2 Chr.
  8:13
John 7:2 Jews' f. was at hand
FEAST of unleavened bread.
Ex. 12:17 ob. f. 23:15; 34:18
Lev. 23:6 on the 15th day is f.
Mat. 26:17 f. of un. discip. came
Mark 14:1 was the f. Luke 22:1
FEAST of weeks.
Ex. 34:22 ob. f. - Deut. 16:10
Appointed FEASTS.
Is. 1:14 ap. f. my soul hateth
FED.
1 Cor. 3:2 have f. you with milk
FEET.
Ex. 3:5 shoes off thy f. Acts 7:33
2 Sam. 22:34 maketh my f. like
  hinds'
Dan. 2:33 his f. part of iron, 42
10:6 f. like br. Rev. 1:15; 2:18
Nah. 1:15 f. of him bringeth good
Mat. 10:14 shake off the dust of
  your f. Mark 6:11; Luke 9:5
Acts 3:7 his f. received strength
4:35 laid at apostles' f. 37; 5:2
13:25 shoes of his f. not worthy
51 shook off dust of their f.
Rom. 3:15 f. swift to shed blood
10:15 f. of them preach gospel
Eph. 6:15 f. shod with prepara.
Heb. 12:13 stra. paths for your f.
Rev. 3:9 worship before thy f.
13:2 his f. as the f. of a bear
At his FEET.
Jud. 4:10 with 10,000 at his f.
Hab. 3:5 burning coals at his f.
Acts 5:10 Sapphira fell at his f.
Rev. 1:17 I fell at his f. as dead
Under FEET.
Ps. 8:6 put all things under his
  f. 1 Cor. 15:27; Eph. 1:22
Lam. 3:34 u. his f. all prisoners
Mat. 7:6 trample u. their f.
Rom. 16:20 bruise Sat. u. your f.
1 Cor. 15:25 all enemies u. his f.

FEET, with wash, ed.
Ex. 30:19 A. and his sons shall
  wash their f. 21; 40:31
2 Sam. 11:8 Uriah, go w. thy f.
Ps. 58:10 w. f. in blood of wick.
Cant. 5:3 I have washed my f.
Luke 7:38 wash his f. with tears
John 13:5 wash the disciples' f.
  6 Lord, dost thou wash my f.?
  14 if I your L. have w. your f.
1 Tim. 5:10 she ha. w. saints' f.
FELL.
Jos. 22:20 wrath f. on congrega.
Jud. 7:13 smote tent that it f.
  8:10 there f. 120,000 men
  16:30 the house f. on the lords
1 Sam. 4:18 Eli f. from seat
2 Sam. 4:4 Mephibosheth f.
  20:8 Joab's sword f. out, as he
  21:9 they f. all seven together
1 K. 2:25 Benaiah f. on Adonijah
2 K. 2:13 mantle that f. from Elijah
  6:5 axe head f. into the water
FELL down.
Jos. 6:20 shouted, the wall f. d.
Jud. 5:27 he bowed, he f. d.
1 Sam. 31:1 f. d. in Gil. 1 Chr. 10:1
Dan. 3:7 all nations f. d. and w.
  23 these three f. d. in furnace
Mat. 2:11 wise men f. d. and wo.
Luke 5:8 P. f. d. at Jesus' knees
  8:28 man which had devils f. d.
Acts 5:5 Ananias f. d.; 10 Sapp.
  10:25 Cornelius; 16:29 jailer
Heb. 11:30 by faith the walls f. d.
  22:8 John f. d. before the angel
FELLOW-WORKERS.
Col. 4:11 these only are my f.-w.
FELLOWSHIP.
Ps. 94:20 iniq. have f. wi. thee?
1 Cor. 1:9 called to f. of his Son
  10:20 sh. have f. with devils
2 Cor. 6:14 what f. hath righte.
  8:4 f. of ministering to saints
Gal. 2:9 the right hand of f.
Eph. 3:9 is f. of the mystery
  5:11 no f. with works of darkn.
Phil. 1:5 your f. in the gospel
1 John 1:3 have f. with us, our f.
FEMALE.
Gen. 1:27 male and f. created, 5:2

Gal. 3:28 in Christ male nor f.

FERVENT, LY.

1 Pet. 1:22 ye love one another f.
4:8 above all th. have f. charity
2 Pet. 3:10 melt with f. heat, 12

FEW.

Job 14:1 man is of f. days
Ec. 5:2 let thy words be f.
Mat. 7:14 f. there be that find it
9:37 laborers are f. Luke 10:2
29:16 call, but f. chosen, 22:14

FIELD.

Mat. 13:44 is like unto treas.hid in
a f. 27:7 bought the potter's f. 10
27:8 the f. of blood, Acts 1:19
Acts 1:18 this man purchas. a f.

In the FIELD.

Luke 2:8 sheph. abiding in the f.

Of the FIELD.

Joel 1:11 harv. of the f. is perish.
Mat. 6:28 consider lilies of the f.
30 if G. so clothe grass of t. f.

FIFTIETH.

Lev. 25:10 shall hallow f. year
11 a jubilee shall that f. year be

FIGHT, Substantive.

1 Tim. 6:12 fight the good f.
2 Tim. 4:7 I have fought a good f.

FIGHT, Verb.

Jer. 51:30 men forbome to f.
Zec. 14:14 Judah shall f. at Jerusa.
John 18:36 then would my ser. f.
1 Cor. 9:26 f. I not as beateth air
Jam. 4:2 ye kill, ye f. and war

FILL, Verb.

Job 18:21 f. mouth with laughing
15:2 sh. wise man f. his belly?
Prov. 1:13 we shall f. our houses
8:21 I will f. their treasures
Is. 8:8 sh. f. breadth of thy land
Hag. 2:7 will f. house with glory
Rom. 15:13 God of hope f. you

FILLED.

Gen. 6:13 earth is f. with viol.
Acts 2:2 mighty wind f. house
4:8 Peter f. with the Holy Ghost
5:3 why hath Satan f. thy heart
9:17 be f. with the Holy Ghost
13:9 Paul f. with Holy Ghost
Rom. 1:29 f. with all unright.
15:14 f. with all knowledge

24 I be somewhat f. with
2 Cor. 7:4 I am f. with comfort
Eph. 3:19 be f. with all fulness
5:18 with wine, but f. with Sp.
Phil. 1:11 f. with fruits of right.
Col. 1:9 be f. with knowledge
2 Tim. 1:4 I may be f. with joy
Jam. 2:16 be ye warmed and f.

Shall be FILLED.

Luke 1:15 J. s. be f. with Holy G.
3:5 every valley shall be f.
6:21 blessed hunger, ye sh. be f.

Was FILLED.

Gen. 6:11 earth was f. with viol.
Luke 1:41 Elis. w. f. with H. G.
67 Zacharias was f. with H. G.
Acts 19:29 city w. f. with confu.
Rev. 15:8 temple w. f. with smoke

Were FILLED.

Hos. 13:6 were f. and their heart
Luke 4:28 they w. f. with wrath
6:11 they were f. with madness
8:23 they were f. with water
Acts 2:4 w. all f. with H. G. 4:31
3:10 they were f. with wonder
5:17 were f. with indignation
13:45 Jews were f. with envy

FILTH.

1 Pet. 3:21 not put away f. of flesh

FILTHINESS.

Jam. 1:21 wheref. lay apart all f.
Rev. 17:4 full of abomin. and f.

FILTHY.

1 Tim. 3:3 not greedy of f. lucre, 8
Tit. 1:7 not given to f. lucre
11 teaching for f. in. 1 Pet. 5:2

FIND.

Prov. 2:5 shalt f. knowl. of God
Ec. 7:27 one by one f. out acc.
12:10 to f. out acceptable words
Luke 6:7 might f. accusation
12:38 f. them so, blessed serv.
13:7 seeking fruit and f. none
15:4 that wh. is lost till he f. it
8 seek diligently till she f. it?
Rom. 9:19 doth he yet f. fault?
2 Cor. 9:4 and f. you unprepared
2 Tim. 1:18 f. mercy of Lord

I FIND.

Luke 23:4 I f. no fault in this
man, John 18:38; 19.-4, 6

Shall, or shalt FIND.

Prov. 8:17 they that seek me
early s. f. me Jer. 29:13

FINDETH.

Prov. 3:13 happy man f. wisdom
8:35 whoso f. me f. life.
Ec. 9:10 whats, thy hand f. to do.
Mat. 7:8 seeketh f. Luke 11:10
10:39 that f. his life shall lose it

FINE gold.

2 Chr. 3:5 overlaid with f. gold
Is. 13:12 more preci. than f. g.

FINE linen.

Ex. 25:4 ye shall take f. linen
26:1 curtains of f. twined linen
31 v. of f. l. 36:35; 2 Chr. 3:14
36 f. twined linen 27:9, 16, 18;
36:37; 38:9, 16, 18
35:35 all manner of work and f.
linen, 38:23; 2 Chr. 2:14
36:8 curtains of f. linen
1 Chr. 15:27 clothed wi. robe f. l.
Ezek. 27:7 f. linen from Egypt
Luke 16:19 man in pur. and f. l.
Rev. 19:8 granted to be arrayed f.l.

FINISH.

Acts 20:24 I might f. my course
Rom. 9:28 he will f. the work
2 Cor. 8:6 would also f. in you

FINISHER.

Heb. 12:2 J. author and f. of faith

FIRE.

Ex. 40:38 f. was on tabernacle by
night, Num. 9:16; Deut. 1:33
1 Chr. 21:26 ans. fr. heaven by f.
Prov. 6:27 take f. in bosom?
Is. 9:5 burning and fuel of f.
44:16 burneth part in the f. and
saith, Aba. I have seen f.
Dan. 3:27 upon bod. f. had no p.
Mat. 3:10 ev. tree that bringeth
not good fruit is cast into f.
7:19; Luke 3:9; John 15:6
11 baptize with Holy Ghost
and f. Luke 3:16
13:42 cast into furnace of f. 50
17:15 he falleth into f. Mar. 9:22
18:8 he cast into everlasting
f.Mark 9:43, 46
25:41 cursed, into everlasting f.
Acts 3:3 cloven tong. like as of f.

1 Cor. 3:13 sh. be reveal. by f. 15
2 Thes. 1:8 in flamin. f. taking
Jam. 3:5 great mat. little f. kin.
1 Pet. 1:7 though tried with f.
Rev. 8:5 angel filled censer with f.
7 there followed hail and f.
15:2 sea of glass mingled w. f.
20:9 f. came down from God
14 dea. and hell cast lake of f.
21:8 in lake wh. burneth with f.

Pillar of FIRE.

Ex. 14:24 L. looked thro' p. of f.

Set FIRE.

Jam. 3:6 tongue s. on f. course
of nature, is set on f. of hell

FIRMAMENT.

Gen. 1:6 f. in midst of waters
Dan. 12:3 shine as bright, of f.

FIRST.

Jam. 3:17 wisd. from above is f.
1 John 4:19 love him bec. he f.
Rev. 2:4 thou hast left thy f. love

FIRST-BORN.

Gen. 19:31 f.-b, said to youn. 34
Heb. 11:28 he that destroyed f.-b.
12:23 are come to church of f.-b.

FIRST-FRUIT, S.

Ex. 22:29 to offer the f. ripe fr.
Prov. 3:9 honor L. with f.-fruits
Mic. 7:1 my soul desired f. fruit
Rom. 8:23 have f.-f. of Spirit
1 Cor. 15:20 C. f.-f. of them th. 23
Jam. 1:18 kind of f.-fr. of creat.
Rev. 14:4 being the f.-f unto God

FISH.

Gen. 1:26 dom. over f. of sea. 28
Jon. 1:17 Lord prepared great f.
Mat. 7:10 if he ask f. will he give

FITLY.

Prov. 25:11 word f. spok. appl. of

FIVE.

John 4:18 hast had f. husbands
5:2 a pool having f. porches
1 Cor. 14:19 I rath, speak f. wor.
2 Cor. 11:24 f. times rec. 40 strip.

FLAME.

Jud. 13:20 f. w. up, angel in f.
Ps. 29:7 voice of L. div. f. of fire
Is. 10:17 Holy One shall be for a f.
43:2 nei. sh. f. kindle upon thee
Ezek. 20:47 f. sh. not be quench.

Dan. 7:9 throne was like fiery f.
Ob. 18 house of Jos shall be a f.
Luke 16:24 tormented in this f.

FLATTER, ETH.

Ps. 5:9 they f. with their tongue
Prov. 2:16 stranger who f. 7:5

FLATTERING.

1 Thes. 2:5 neither used f. words

FLATTERY, IES.

Job. 17:5 speaketh f. to friends
Prov. 6:24 f. of strange woman

FLEECE.

Jud. 6:37 f. of wool in flo. 38, 39

FLEE.

Jam. 4:7 res. the devil, he will f.

FLESH.

Gen. 24 and they shall be one f.
Ps. 56:4 not fear wht f. can do
Mat. 16:17 f. and blood not rev.
 19:5 sh. be one f. 6; Mark 10:8;
 1 Cor. 6:16; Eph. 5:31
John 1:14 the WORD was made f.
 6:63 the f. profiteth nothing
Acts 2:30 seed of David accord-
 ing to f. Rom. 1:3
Rom. 3:29 shall no f. be justified
Jude 8 filthy dream, defile the f.
 23 even garments spotted by f.
Rev. 19:18 f. of capt. f. of might.
 21 all fowls were filled with f.

All FLESH.

Gen. 6:12 a. f. had corrupt. way
Ps. 65:2 to thee shall all f. come
Is. 40:5 all f. sh. see it together
 66:16 will L. plead with all f.
 23 all f. shall come to worship
 24 they sh. be abhorr. to all f.
Jer. 25:31 will plead with all f.
 32:27 I am the Lord God of a. f.
Joel 2:28 pour S. on a. f. Acts 2:17
Zec. 2:13 silent all f. before Lord
Luke 3:6 a. f. sh. see salv. of G.
John 17:2 given power over a. f.
1 cor. 15:39 a. f. is not same fl.

In the FLESH, or in FLESH.

1 Tim. 3:16 G. was manif. in t. f.
Rom. 7:18 in my f. dwel. no good
Col. 1:24 afflict. of Ch. in my f.

Of the FLESH.

John 1:13 not of will of the f.
 3:6 which is born of t. f. is flesh

Rom. 8:5 mind the things of t. f.
Col. 2:11 the body of sins of t. f.
Heb. 9:13 the purifying of the f.
1 Pet. 3:21 put away filth of t. f.
1 John 2:16 lust of t. f.

FLESHLY.

2 Cor. 1:12 not with f. wisdom
 3:3 but in f. tables of the heart
Col. 2:18 puff. up by his f. mind
1 Pet. 2:11 abstain from f. lusts

FLIES.

Ex. 8:21 send swarms of f. 31

FLOCK.

Hab. 3:17 the f. shall be cut off
Zec. 9:16 save them as f. of peo.
 11:4 will feed f. of slaughter, 7
Mal. 1:14 deceiver wh. hath in f.
Mat. 26:31 sheep of f. sh. be scat.
Luke 2:8 keeping watch over f.
Acts 20:29 griev wolves not
 sparing f.
1 Pet. 5:2 feed f. of God am, you
 3 being ensamples to the f.

FLOCKS, with herds.

Gen. 13:5 Lot also had f. and h.

FLOOD.

Gen. 6:17 bring a f. of water
Gen. 7:17 f. was forty d. on earth
Is. 59:19 enemy come in like f.
Amos 8:8 rise up wholly as f. 9:5
Nah. 1:8 an overrunning f.

FLOW.

Job 20:28 his goods shall f. away
Ps. 147:18 wind blow, waters f.
Cant. 4:16 the spices may f. out
Is. 2:2 nations shall f, unto it
 48:21 waters to f. out of rock
John 7:38 out of belly sh. f.l.w.

FLOWETH.

Lev. 20:24 f. with milk and hon.
 Num. 13:27; 14:8; 16:13, 14;
 Deut. 6:3; 11:9; 26:15; 27:3;
 31:20; Jos. 5:6

FLOWING.

Ex. 3:8 f. with milk and honey,
 17; 13:5; 33:3; Jer. 11:5;
 32:22; Ezek. 20:6, 15
Prov. 18:4 well-sp. of wis. as f.

FLOWER.

Is. 18:5 sour grape is rip. in f.
 40:7 f. fadeth, 8; Neh. 1:4; Jam.

1:10, 11; 1 Pet. 1:24

FLY, Verb.
Hab. 1:8 they shall f. as eagle

FOLD, Substantive.
John 10:16 sheep wh. not of this
f. one f. and one shepherd

FOLLOW.
1 Cor. 14:1 f. after charity, desire
Phil. 3:12 I f. after, if that I may
1 Thes. 5:15 f. that which is good
2 Thes. 3:9 ensample to you to f.
1 Tim. 5:24 men they f. after
6:11 man of God f. 2 Tim. 2:22
Heb. 12:14 f. peace with all men
2 Pet. 2:2 shall f. pernicious way
3 John 11 f. not that which is evil
Rev. 14:4 they that f. the Lamb

FOLLOW me.
Mat. 4:19 Jes. saith, f. me, 8:22;
9:9; Mark 2:14; Luke 5:27
16:24 take up cross f. me, Mark
8:34; 10:21; Luke 9:23
19:21 sell that thou hast, f. me,
Luke 18:22

FOLLOWED.
Num. 32:12 f. Lord, Deut. 1:36
Jos. 6:8 ark of covenant f. them
Amos. 7:15 L. took me as I f. flock
Mat. 27:55 many wom. wh. f. J.
Mark 10:28 we left all and f. thee,
Luke 22:54 and Peter f. afar off
Acts 13:43 relig. proselytes f. P.
Rom. 9:30 Gent. who f. not righ.
31 who f. after law of righteo.
1 Cor. 10:4 drank of rock that f.
1 Tim. 5:10 f. every good work
2 Pet. 1:16 not f. cun. dev. fables
Rev. 6:8 Death, hell f. with him

FOLLOWED him.
Mat. 4:20 they left their nets and
f. him, Mark 1:18
22 left the ship and f. him
25 f. him great multitude, 8:1;
12:15; 19:2; 20:29; Mark 2:15;
5:24; Luke 23:27; John 6:2
8:23 disciples f. him, Luke 22:39
9:27 two blind men f. him
26:58 Peter f. him, Mark 14:54

FOLLOWERS.
1 Cor. 4:16 f. of me, 11:1; Phil 3:17
Eph. 5:1 be ye f. of God

1 Thes. 1:6 f. of us and of the L.
2:14 ye became f. of churches
Heb. 6:12 f. of them who thro' fa.
1 Pet. 3:13 be f. of that is good

FOLLOWETH.
John 8:12 f. me not walk in dar.

FOLLOWING.
Jos. 22:16 from f. Lord, 18, 23, 29;
1 Sam. 12:20; 2 K. 17:21;
2 Chr. 25:27; 34:33
Jud. 2:19 in f. other gods
2 Sam. 2:19 Asahel turned not
from f. Abner, 26, 30

FOLLY.
Prov. 5:23 in his f. he sh. go ast.
13:16 a fool layeth open his f.
26:11 so a fool returneth to his f.
Ec. 1:17 to know wisdom and f.
10:1 so a little f. him in reput.
Is. 9:17 every mouth speaketh f.
Jer. 23:13 seen f. in the prophets
2 Cor. 11:1 hear with me in my f.
2 Tim. 3:9 f. be made manifest

FOOD.
Gen. 2:9 every tree good for f.
1 Tim. 6:8 hav. f. and raiment
Jam. 2:15 be destitute of daily f.

FOOL.
1 Sam. 26:21 have played the f.
Ps. 14:1 f. said in heart, 53:1
Prov. 15:5 f. despiseth father's instr.
17:7 excel. speech becom. not f.
Mat. 5:22 wh. shall say, Thou f.
Luke 12:20 f. this night thy soul
1 Cor. 3:18 f. that he may be wise
15:36 thou f. that thou sowest
2 Cor. 11:16 no man think me a f.
12:6 to glory, I shall not be a f.
11 am become a f. in glorying

As a FOOL.
2 Sam. 3:33 died Abner as a f.?

Of a FOOL.
Prov. 12:15 way of a f. is right
17:21 father of a f. hath no joy
Ec. 7:6 so is laughter of the f.

FOOLISH.
Deut. 32:6 requite L. f. people?
21 provoke them to anger with
a f. nation, Rom. 10:19
Job 5:2 for wrath killeth the f. man
Ps. 5:5 f. not stand in thy sight

73:3 for I was envious at the f.
22 so f. was I and ignorant
Prov. 9:6 forsake the f. and live
13 a f. woman is clamorous
10:1 f. son heaviness of mother
Is. 44:25 maketh knowledge f.
Jer. 4:22 for my people is f.
Mat. 7:26 be likened to a f. man
25:2 five were wise and five f.
Rom. 1:21 f. heart was darkened
2:20 an instructor of the f.
1 Cor. 1:20 f. wis. of this world
Gal. 3:1 O f. Galatians
3 are ye so f.? having begun
Eph. 5:4 filthiness, nor f. talking
1 Tim. 6:9 rich, fall into f. lusts
2 Tim. 2:23 f. questions, Tit. 3:9
Tit. 3:3 we were sometimes f.
1 Pet. 2:15 silence ignorance of f.

FOOLISHNESS.
Ps. 69:5 O G. thou knowest my f.
Prov. 12:23 heart of fools pro. f.
Mark 7:22 f. come from within
1 Cor. 1:18 to them that perish f.
21 by f. of preaching to save
25 f. of God is wiser than men
3:19 wisdom of this world is f.

FOOT.
Ps. 91:12 lest thou dash f. against a
stone, Mat. 4:6; Luke 4:11
Dan. 8:13 to be trodden under f.
Amos 2:15 swift of f. not deliver
John 11:44 bound hand nd f.
Acts 7:5 so much as to set his f.

Right FOOT, left FOOT.
Rev. 10:2 he set his r. f. upon the
sea, and his l.f. on the earth

FORBEAR, ING.
Eph. 4:2 f. in love, Col. 3:13
1 Thes. 3:1 could no longer f.

God FORBID.
Gen. 44:7 God f. 17; Jos. 22:29;
24:16; 1 Sam. 12:23; 14:45;
20:2; Job 27:5; Luke 20:16;
Rom. 3:4, 6, 31;' 6:2, 15; 7:7,
13:9; 14; 11:1, 11; 1 Cor. 6:15;
Gal. 2:17; 3:21; 6:14

FOREFRONT.
2 Sam. 11:15 Uriah in f. of battle

FOREHEAD.
1 Sam. 17:49 stone sunk in his f.

FOREHEADS.
Rev. 7:3 sealed serv. of God in f.
9:4 not seal of God in their f.
13:16 all to receive a mark in f.
14:1 Father's name in their f.
20:4 nor received his mark on f.
22:4 his name sh. be in their f.

FOREKNOWLEDGE.
Acts 2:23 delivered by f. of God
1 Pet. 1:2 according to f. of God

FORGAVE, EST.
Mat. 18:27 and f. him the debt
32 O wicked servant, I f. all
2 Cor. 2:10 if I f. any thing; for
your sakes f. I it
Col. 3:13 as Christ f. you

FORGET.
Hos. 4:6 also f. thy children
Heb. 6:10 G. not unrighte. to f.
13:16 to communicate f. not

FORGIVE.
Gen. 50:17 f. trespass of brethren
Ex. 10:17 f. my sin this once
Mat. 6:12 f. us as we f. Luke 11:4
14 if ye f. men their trespasses
15 ye f. not, neither will your
9:6 hath power on earth to f.
sins, Mark 2:10; Luke 5:24
18:21 how oft sin, and I f. him?
35 if ye from your hearts f. not
Mark 2:7 can f. sins, Luke 5:21
11:25 praying, f. that your
26 it not f. your F. will not f.
Luke 6:37 f. ye shall be forgiven
17:3 brother repent, f. him, 4
23:34 Father f. them
2 Cor. 2:7 ye ought rather to f.
10 to whom ye f. any, I f. also
12:13 to you, f. me this wrong
1 John 1:9 to f. us our sins

FORGIVEN.
Lev. 4:20 it sh. be f. 26, 31, 35;
5:10, 13, 16, 18, 6:7; 19:22;
Num. 15:25, 26, 28; Deut. 21:8
Mark 4:12 sin should be f. them
Luke 6:37 forgive and ye sh. be f.
7:47 her sins which are many
are f. to whom little is f.
Eph. 4:32 for Christ's sake f. you
Col. 2:13 having f. all trespasses
Jam. 5:15 com. sins they sh. be f.

1 John 2:12 bec. your sins are f.
FORGIVENESS, ES.
Ps. 130:4 there is f. with thee
Dan. 9:9 the L. our G. belong f.
Mark 3:29 nev. f. but in danger
Acts 5:31 him G. exalt. to give f.
13:38 through him is preached f.
26:18 they may receive f. of sins
Eph. 1:7 have f. of sins, Col. 1:14
FORGOTTEN.
Ezek. 22:12 hast f. me, saith L.
23:35 because thou hast f. me
Hos. 4:6 seeing thou hast f. law
8:14 Israel hath f. his Maker
13:6 therefore have they f. me
FORM, Substantive.
Rom. 2:20 hast f. of knowledge
Phil. 2:6 who being in f. of God
2 Tim. 3:5 having a f. of godliness
FORMED.
Gen. 2:7 God f. man of the dust
Prov. 26:10 great God that f. all
Is. 27:11 f. them show no favor
54:17 no weapon f. against thee
Jer. 1:5 before I f. thee in belly
33:2 the L. that f. it to establish
Amos 7:1 he f. grasshoppers
Gal. 4:19 till Christ be f. in you
1 Tim. 2:13 Adam first f. then E.
FORMER.
Ec. 1:11 no rem. of f. things
Jer. 5:24 giveth f. and latter rain
Hos. 6:3; Joel 2:23
Mal. 3:4 pleasant as in f. years
Eph. 4:22 concern. f. conversa.
Rev. 21:4 f. things passed away
FORNICATION.
Mat. 5:32 saving for f. 19:9
John 8:41 we be not born of f.
Acts 15:20 abstain fr. f. 29; 21:25
1 Cor. 5:1 f. among you, such f.
6:13 the body is not for f. but
Gal. 5:19 works of the flesh. f.
Eph. 5:3 f. let it not be named
1 Thes. 4:3 should abstain fr f.
Rev. 9:21 nor repent of their f.
Rev. 19:2 corrupt earth with her f.
FORNICATIONS.
Ezek. 16:15 poured out thy f.
FORNICATOR, S.
1 cor. 5:9 not to com. with f.

Heb. 12:16 lest there be any f. or
FORSAKE.
2 Chr. 7:19 if ye f. my statutes
Ezr. 8:22 wrath ag. them f. him
Ps. 27:10 father and mother f.
Prov. 9:6 f. the foolish, and live
**Have, hast, hath FOR-
SAKEN.**
Ps. 22:1 why hast thou f. me?
Mat. 27:46; Mark 15:34
71:11 saying, God hath f. him
Ezek. 8:12 Lord hath f. earth, 9:9
Mat. 19:27 we have f. all
2 Pet. 2:15 which h. f. right way
Not FORSAKEN.
2 chr. 13:10 the Lord is our God,
we have not f. him
Ezr. 9:9 n. f. us in our bondage
Is.62:12 be called a city not f.
2 Cor. 4:9 persecuted, but not f.
FORSAKING.
Heb..10:25 not f. the assembling
FORSWEAR.
Mat. 5:33 thou sh. not f. thyself
FORTY stripes.
Deut. 25:3 f. str. he may give
2 Cor. 11:24 of the Jews rec. f. s.
FORTY years.
Ex. 16:35 man. f. y. Neh. 9:21
Num. 14:33 wander f. y. 32:13
FORTRESS, ES.
Dan. 11:7 f. of king of the north
10 be stirred up even to his f.
Hos. 10:14 thy f. shall be spoiled
FOUGHT.
Jos. 10:14 L. f. for Isr. 42: 23:3
2 Tim. 4:7 I have f. a good fight
Rev. 12:7 Michael f. ag. dragon
FOUND.
1 Sam. 13:22 no sword f. in hand
25:28 evil not been f. with thee
29:3 I have f. no fault in him
2 Sam. 7:27 f. in his heart to
pray this prayer, 1 Chr. 17:25
Dan. 5:27 art weighed and f.
wanting 11 these men f. Daniel
praying
Hos. 9:10 I f. Israel like grapes
12:4 he f. him in Beth-el and
8 I have f. me out substance
Mic. 1:13 transg. of Is. f. in thee

Mat. 2:8 have f. him bring word
8:10 not f. so gr. faith, Luke 7:9
Luke 2:16 f. babe ly. in a manger
46 after three days f. him
4:17 f. place where it was writ.
7:10 they f. the servant whole

Be FOUND.
Hos. 10:2 sh. they be f. faulty
Zep. 3:13 nor deceit, tongue be f.
Zec. 10:10 place not be f.
Acts 5:39 lest be f. to fight ag. G.
1 Cor. 4:2 a steward be f. faithful

FOUND grace.
Gen. 6:8 Noah f. g. in eyes of L.
33:4 Joseph f. grace in his sight
Ex. 33:12 thou hast also f. g. 17
Jer. 31:2 people f. g. in wildern.

Is FOUND.
Luke 15:24 was lost and is f. 32

Was FOUND.
Gen. 44:12 cup w. f. in B. sack
1 Sam. 13:22 with S. and J. w. f.
1 Pet. 2:22 nor w. guile f. in mon.
Rev. 5:4 was f. worthy to open
Rev. 14:5 in th. mo. w. f. no guile

Was not FOUND.
Mal. 2:6 iniq. w. n. f. in his lips
Heb. 11:5 Enoch was not f.

FOUNDATION.
Hab. 3:13 discovering f. to neck
Hag. 2:18 day the f. was laid
Zec. 12:1 which lay f.of the earth
Rom. 15:20 bui. on ano. man's f.
1 Cor. 3:10 master-build, laid f.
11 for other f. can no man lay
12 if any build on this f. gold
Eph. 2:20 on f. of the prophets
1 Tim. 6:19 laying up a good f.
2 Tim. 2:19 f. of G. standeth sure
Heb. 1:10 laid f. of the earth

FOUNDATION of the World.
Rev. 13:8 L. slain from f. of w.
17:8 names not writ. fr. f. of w.

FOUNDATIONS.
2 Sam. 22:8 f. of heaven moved
16 f. were discov. Ps. 18:7, 15
Job 38:4 when I laid f. of earth?
Is. 51:13 Lord that laid f. of earth
Ezek. 30:4 Egypt's f. brok. down
Mic. 1:6 will discover f. thereof
Acts 16:26 f. of prison were shak.

Heb. 11:10 for a city that hath f.

FOUNTAIN.
Prov. 14:27 fear of Lord is a f. of
life Ec. 12:6 pitcher be broken at f.
Jer. 2:13 f. of living wat. 17:13
Rev. 21:6 I will give of f. of life

FOUR.
Gen. 2:10 river became f. heads
Prov. 30:15 f. say not. It is eno.
18 be f. things wh. I know not
24 be f. things little on earth
29 f. things are comely
Dan. 3:25 lo, I see f. men loose
17 these f. beasts are f. kings
22 f. kingdoms shall stand
Amos 1:3 for f. w. not turn away
Zec. 1:18 and behold f. horns
Mat. 24:31 gather his elect from
the f. winds, Mark 13:27

FOURFOLD.
2 Sam. 12:6 restore the lamb f.
Luke 19:8 any thing, I restore f.

FOURSQUARE.
Rev. 21:16 the city lieth f.

FOURTEEN.
Gen. 31:41 serv. f. years for dan
Mat. 1:17 from Dav. to carrying
away f. to Ch. f. generations

FOWL.
Gen. 1:26 dominion over f. 28

FOWLS.
Mat. 6:26 the f. they sow not
13:4 f. dev. Mark 4:4; Lu. 8:5

FOX, ES.
Jud. 15:4 Samson caught 300 f.
Ezek. 13:4 thy proph. are like f.
Mat. 8:29 f. ha. holes, Luke 9:58
Luke 13:32 go tell f. I cast out

FRANKINCENSE.
Ex. 30:34 spices with pure f.

FRECKLED.
Lev. 13:39 it is a f. spot groweth

FREE.
Ex. 21:2 in sev. year go out f.
Deut. 15:12; Jer. 34:9, 14
John 8:32 truth sh. make you f.
36 if Son make you f. f. indeed
Acts 22:28 but I was f. born
Rom. 5:15 not as offence, so f.
16 f. gift is of many offences
18 f. gift came upon all men

94

6:18 being made f. from sin, 22
20 were f. from righteousness
1 Cor. 7:21 if mayest be made f.
19 though I be f. from all men
Gal. 3:28 bond nor f. Col. 3:11
5:1 liberty where. C. made us f.
Eph. 6:8 receive of L. bond or f.
1 Pet. 2:16 as f. not using liberty

FREED.
Rom. 6:7 he dead, is f. from sin

FREELY.
Hos. 14:4 I will love them f.
Mat. 10:8 f. received, f. give
Rom. 3:24 justified f. by grace
2 Cor. 11:7 preach, gospel of G. f.
Rev. 21:6 of fountain of life f.

FREEWILL-OFFERING.
Deut. 12:6 thither bring f. offer.
Ps. 119:108 accept f. - offerings

FREE-WOMAN.
Gal. 4:22 had two sons by f.-w.
23 but he of f. was by promise
31 not child. of bondw. of f.-w.

FRET.
Lev. 13:55 burn it in fire, it is f.

FRIEND.
Ex. 33:11 G. spake as man to f.
Deut. 13:6 if thy f. entice thee
Jud. 14:20 he used as his f.
Is. 41:8 art seed of Abra. my f.
Mic. 7:5 trust ye not in a f.
Mat. 11:19 f. of public. Luke 7:34
20:13 f. I do thee no wrong
Luke 11:5 shall have a f. and
John 11:11 our f. Lazarus sleepeth
Jam. 2:23 Abraham call. f. of G.
4:4 f. of world, is enemy of G.

FRIENDS.
Prov. 14:20 the rich hath many f.
Prov. 18:24 hath f. show him friend
Jer. 20:4 thee a terror to thy f.
6 buried there, thou and thy f.
38:22 thy f. have set thee on
Lam. 1:2 her f. have dealt treac.
Zec. 13:6 wounded in house of f.
Mark 3:21 when his f. heard of it
5:19 J. saith, Go home to thy f.
Luke 7:6 centurion sent f. to him
12:4 my f. be not afraid of them
14:12 a dinner, call not thy f.
15:6 he calleth together his f.

21:16 ye shall be betrayed by f.
23:12 Pilate and Herod made f.
John 15:13 down his life for his f.

FRIENDSHIP.
Prov. 22:24 no f. with angry man
Jam.4:4 f. of world is enmity

To and FRO.
Gen. 8:7 a raven, went to and f.
2 K. 4:35 Elisha walked to and f.
Eph. 4:14 no more tossed to a f.

FROGS.
Ex. 8:2 all thy borders with f.

FROWARD.
Deut. 32:20 a very f. generation
2 Sam. 22:27 with f. wilt show
thyself f. Ps. 18:26
Ps. 101:4 a f. heart shall depart
Prov. 2:12 man speaketh f. thin.
3:32 f. is abomination to Lord
4:24 put away fr. thee f. mouth
6:12 walketh with a f. mouth
13 and the f. mouth do I hate
10:31 f. tongue shall be cut out
11:20 of a f. heart, are abomin.
30 shut. eyes to devise f. things
17:20 f. heart, findeth no good
21:8 the way of a man is f.
22:5 thorns are in way of the f.
1 Pet. 2:18 serv. be subject to f.

FRUIT.
Gen. 1:29 every tree wherein is f.
4:3 Cain brought of the f.
2 Sam. 16:2 summer f. for young
Ps. 21:10 their f. shalt destroy
105:35 locusts devoured the f.
127:3 f. of womb is his reward
Is. 4:2 f. of earth shall be excellent
Ezek. 17:9 cut off the f. thereof
Hos. 10:13 have eaten f. of lies
Amos 2:9 destroyed f. from ab.
Mat. 12:33 and his f. good, for the
tree is known by his f.
21:19 let no f. grow on thee
26:29 I will not drink of f. of the
vine, Mark 14:25
Luke 1:42 bles. is f. of thy womb
13:6 sought f. and found none
7 I come seeking f. on fig-tree
20:10 should give him of the f.
John 4:36 gather. f. to life eter.
Rom. 1:13 I might have some f.

Gal. 5:22 f. of Spirit is love
Eph. 5:9 f. of Sp. is in all good
Phil. 1:22 this is f. of my labor
FRUITFUL.
Gen. 1:22 be f. 28:8;17; 9:7; 35:11
17:6 I will make thee exceed. f.
20 Ishmael f.; 48:4 Jacob f.
Ps. 107:34 f. land into barrenness
148:9 f. trees, praise the Lord
Is. 5:1 hath vineyard in a f. hill
32:12 shall lament for f. vine
Jer. 4:26 f. place was a wildern.
Col. 1:10 f. in every good work
FRUITS.
Gen. 43:11 take of the best f.
2 Cor. 9:10 increase f. of righte.
Phil. 1:11 filled with f. of right
Jam. 3:17 wisdom full of good f.
FULFIL.
Phil. 2:2 f. ye my joy, that ye be
FULFILLED.
Mat. 1:22 that it might be f. 2:15
23; 8:17; 12:17; 13:35; 21:4
27:35; John 12:38; 15:25; 17:12
18:9, 32, 19:24, 28
2:17 was f. that poken, 27:9
5:18 in no wise pass till all be f.
13:14 is f. prophecy of Esaias
24:34 shall not pass till all be f.
John 3:29 my joy therefore is f.
Rom. 13:8 loveth another hath f.
law
Gal. 5:14 law is f. in one word
FULFILLING.
Rom. 13:10 love is the f. of law
Eph. 2:3 f. desires of flesh
FULL.
Job 14:1 few days f. of trouble
Mic. 3:8 f. of power by spirit
Hab. 3:3 earth f. of his praise
Zec. 8:5 st. f. of boys and girls
Mat. 6:22 f. of light, Luke 11:36
14:20 of fragments twelve bask.
f. Mark 6:43
23:27 f. of dead men's bones, 28
Luke 1:57 now Eliz. f. time came
4:1 Jesus being f. of Holy Gh.
16:20 L. laid at gate f. of sores
John 1:14 among us f. of grace
7:8 my time is not yet f. come
15:11 your joy might be f. 16:24

Acts 2:13 men f. of new wine
6:3 look out men f. of Holy G. 5
9:36 Dorcas f. of good works
13:10 said, O f. of all subtilty
Rom. 1:29 f. of envy, murder
1 Cor. 4:8 now ye are f. now rich
Phil. 4:12 instructed to be f.
18 and abound. I am f.
Jam. 3:8 tongue f. of deadly poi.
1 Pet. 1:8 joy unspeak. f. of glo.
2 Pet. 2:14 eyes f. of adultery
1 John 1:4 your joy may be f.
Is FULL.
Nah. 3:1 is all f. of lies and rob.
Luke 11:34 body is f. of light, is f.
39 inward part is f. of ravening
FULLNESS.
Col. 1:19 in him sho, all f. dwell
2:9 in him dwelleth f. of God.
FURNACE, S.
Dan. 3:6 into midst of fiery f. 11
Mat. 13:42 cast into f. of fire, 50
FURTHERANCE.
Phil. 1:12 rather to f. of gospel
G

GABRIEL. Dan. 8:16; 9:21;
Luke 1:19, 26
GAD.
Gen. 30:11 she called his name G.
Tribe of GAD.
Num. 1:25 of t. of G. 45,650, 2:14
Rev. 7:5 tribe of G. sealed 12,000
GAIN Substantive.
Prov. 1:19 every one greedy of g.
3:14 g. is better than fine gold
Mic. 4:13 I will consec. g. to L.
1 Tim. 6:5 supposing g. is godli.
6 godliness with content, is g.
GAIN, Verb.
Mat. 16:26 g. who. wor. and lose
soul, Mark 8:36; Luke 9:25
GAIUS.
1 Cor. 1:14 I baptiz. none but G.
3 John 1 un. the well-beloved G.
GALILEE.
Jos. 20:7 G. for a city of refuge
Luke 4:14, 44; 23:5, 55; John
7:41, 52
GALILEAN, S.
Luke 13:1 told him of the G.

23:6 asked whe. man were a G.
GALLOWS.
Est. 6:4 to hang Mordecai on g.
GAMALIEL.
Acts 5:34 P. named G.; 23:3 feet
GAP.
Ezek. 22:30 that should stand in g.
GARDEN.
Gen. 2:15 and put him in the g.
Ezek. 28:13 in Eden the g. of G.
36:35 desolate land like as g. of E.
Joel 2:3 land as g. of Eden before
GARMENT.
1 K. 11:29 Jero. clad with new g.
Ezr. 9:5 rent g. and mantle
Is. 61:3 g. of praise for spirit
Dan. 7:9 g. was white as snow
Mic. 2:8 pull off robe with the g.
Hag. 2:12 holy flesh in skirt of g.
Mat. 9:16 new cloth to old g.
  Mark 2:21; Luke 5:36
 20 touched hem of g. 21; 14:36;
  Mark 5:27; Luke 8:44
22:11 had not wedding g. 12
GARMENTS.
Num. 15:38 fringes in bord. of g.
Ezr. 2:69 gave 100 priests' g.
Ec. 9:8 let thy g. be alw. white
Cant. 4:11 smell of g. smell of L.
Is. 9:5 battle is g. rolled in blood
52:1 put on beautiful g. O Jer.
Zec. 3:3 J. clothed wi. filthy g. 4
Mat. 21:8 spread g. Mark 11:8
 27:35 parted his g. Mark 15:24
Luke 24:4 two men in shining g.
Acts 9:39 coats and g. Dor. made
Rev. 3:4 few names not defiled g.
 16:15 blessed that keepeth his g.
GATE.
Mat. 7:13 enter in at straight g.
 wide is g. broad is way, 14;
Luke 13:24
His GATE.
Acts 3:2 daily at g. of temple
 10 sat for alms at beautiful g.
Water GATE.
Neh. 3:26 Nethin. dwelt ag. w. g.
GATES
Deut. 12:12 rejoice with your g.
Jos. 6:26 in youngest son set up
 g. 1 K. 16:34

Jud. 5:8 new gods, war in g.
 11 people of Lord shall go to g.
2 Chr. 31:2 A. app. to pra. in g.
Neh. 1:3 g. burnt, 2:3 13, 17
 12:30 priests and Lev. purifi. g. 9
Ps. 9:14 thy praise in the g.
 24:7 lift up your heads, O ye g.
87:2 Lord loveth the g. of Zion
100:4 enter into g. with thanks.
Prov. 31:23 husband is known in g.
Mat. 16:18 g. of hell not prevail
Rev. 21:12 city had twelve g. at
GATHER.
Is. 31:15 owl g. under shadow
49:11 shall g. lambs with arms
43:5 will g. thee from the west
62:10 highway, g. out the stones
66:18 will g. all nations
GATHERED.
Mic. 7:1 when g. sum. of fruits
Mat. 13:40 as tares are g.
 47 net cast and g. of every king
GATHERED together.
Acts 4:26 rulers g. to. against L.
 12:12 many g. together praying
1 Cor. 5:4 g. t. and my spirit
Rev. 16:16 g. t. into pl. Armaged.
 19:19 beast and army g. t.
GATHERETH.
Prov. 6:8 ant g. food in harvest
10:5 that g. in summer is wise
Is. 10:14 one g. eggs th. are left
Mat. 12:30 g. not scat. Luke 11:23
 23:37 as a hen g. her chickens
John 4:36 he that reapeth g. fruit
GAVE.
Gen. 14:20 g. tithes of all, Heb. 7:2
4
Job 1:21 L. g. Lord hath taken
Is. 43:3 I g. Egypt for ransom
Gal. 1:4 g. him. for sins, Tit. 2:14
 2:20 loved me, g. himself for me
Eph. 1:22 g. him to be head over
 4:8 captive and g. gifts
 11 he g. some apostles, some
 5:25 loved church g. hims, for
1 Tim. 2:6 g. himself ransom
Rev. 13:2 dragon g. him power
GENERATION.
Deut. 23:2 not enter to tenth g.
 3 Am. to tenth g. not enter

Dan. 4:3 his. dom. f. g. to g. 34
Mat. 1:1 book of g. of Jesus Ch.
23:36 things come on this g.
24:34 this g. not pass, Mark
13:30: Luke 21:32
1 Pet. 2:9 ye are a chosen g.
GENERATIONS.
Gen. 2:4 these are g. of heavens
5:1 g. of Ad.; 6:9 g. of N. 10:1
6:9 Noah was perfect in his g.
Ex. 3:15 memorial to all g.
Mat. 1:17 g. fr. Abr. to Dav. 14 g.
GENTILE.
Rom. 2:9 Jew first, also of g. 10
GENTILES.
Is. 42:6 light to g. 49:6; Luke
2:32; Acts 13:47
Mat. 20:19 shall deliver him to the
g.
Rev. 11:2 the court is given to g.
GENTLE.
2 Tim. 2:24 ser. of L. must be g.
1 Pet. 2:18 subject not only to g.
GENTLENESS.
Gal 5:22 fruit of the Spirit is g.
GENTLY.
2 Sam. 18:5 deal g. with Absalom
GET thee.
Mat. 4:10 J. saith, g. t. hence, S.
16:23 said to Peter, g. t. behind
me, S. Mark 8:33; Luke 4:8
GETHSEMANE.
Mat. 26:36 called G. Mark 14:32
GIANT.
2 Sam. 21:16 of g. 18; 1 Chr. 20:4
1 Chr. 20:6 son of g.; 8 born to g.
GIANTS.
Gen. 6:4 there were g. in earth
Num. 13:33 we saw g. sons of A.
Jos. 15:8 lot of J. at valley of g.
GIFTS.
Mat. 7:11 to gi. good g. Lu. 11:13
1 Cor. 12:1 concerning spirit. g.
4 there are diversities of g.
9 another g. of healing, 28; 30
31 covet earnestly the best g.
14:1 and desire spiritual g.
Eph. 4:8 and gave g. to men
Heb. 2:4 God witness with g.
GIVE.
Gen. 15:2 what wilt g. me?

Deut. 16:17 every man g. as he is
able, Ezek. 46:5, 11
25:3 forty stripes he may g.
John 4:14 water I shall g. him
6:27 meat Son of man shall g.
52 can this man g. his flesh?
10:28 I g. to them eternal life
12:22 what thou ask G. will g.
13:29 that he should g. to poor
14:16 he shall g. you Comforter
27 my peace I g. I unto you
Acts 3:6 such as I have g. I thee
6:4 will g. ourselves to prayer
20:35 more blessed to g. than r.
Rom. 8:32 him also freely g.
Rev. 13:15 power to g. life to im.
22:12 g. every man ac. to work
I will GIVE.
Rev. 2:10 I will g. thee a crown
23 I w. g. ev. one ac. to works
28 I will g. him the morn. star
11:3 I will g. power to my two
Lord GIVE.
Ex. 12:25 to land which L. will
g. you, Lev. 14:34; 23:10, 25:2
Num. 15:2
16:8 Lord shall g. flesh to eat
Num. 22:13 Lord refuseth to g.
36:2 L. com. to g. land by lot
Deut. 1:25 land the Lord doth g.
28:65 L. shall g. tremb. heart
Jos. 17:4 L. com. to g. inherit.
1 K. 15:4 L. his God did g. lamp
2 Chr. 25:9 L. is able to g. much
Ps. 29:11 L. g. strength to peo.
84:11 L. will g. grace and glory
85:12 L. shall g. which is good
Is. 7:14 L. hims. shall g. a sign
14:3 the Lord shall g. thee rest
30:20 Lord g. you bread of adv.
Zec. 10:1 L. g. showers of rain
Luke 1:32 L. shall g. him throne
2 Tim. 1:16 L. g. mercy to house
GIVE thanks.
Ps. 18:49
1 Chr. 16:8 g. t. to the L.
Ps. 6:5 in grave who shall g. t.
30:4 g. th. at the remembrance
of his holiness, 97:12
12 O Lord, I will g. t. for ever
35:18 I will g. t. in congregation

98

75:1 to thee, O God, do we g. t.
79:13 so we thy people will g. t.
92:1 good thing to g. t. to Lord
106:47 to g. t. to holy name
119:62 at midnight I will g. t.
122:4 tribes go up to g. thanks
136:2 g. t. to God of gods, 26
140:13 right, g. t. to thy name
Eph. 1:16 I cease not to g. t. for
Col. 1:3 we g. t. to G. and Father
1 Thes. 1:2 we g. thanks to God
5:18 in everything g. thanks
2 Thes. 2:13 we are bound to g. t.
Rev. 11:17 we g. thee t. L. G. A.

GIVEN.

Mat. 13:11 g. you to know mys.
of king. Mark 4:11; Lu. 8:10
19:11 save they to whom it is g.
Mark 4:24 that hear more be g.
Luke 12:48 much g. much req.
John 3:27 nothing, except it be g.
5:26 g. to the Son to have life
6:39 of all he hath g. me
65 no man come except g. him
Acts 4:12 none other name g.
Rom. 5:5 H. Ghost which is g.
1 Cor. 2:12 things freely g. of G.
Eph. 5:2 C. loved and g. hims. for
us
Phil. 1:29 you g, in behalf of C.
2:9 g. him a name above ev. n.
1 John 3:24 Sp. wh. he hath g. us

I have, or have I GIVEN.

Is. 55:4 I h. g. him for witness
John 13:15 I h. g. an example
17:8 I h. g. words thou gave, 14
22 glory gavest me, I h. g. th.

GIVER.

2 Cor. 9:7 G. loveth a cheerful g.

GIVETH.

1 Pet. 21:26 right, g. spareth not,
22:9 28:27 that g. to poor sh. not
lack Ec. 2:26 God g. to good man
wisdom, to sinner g. travail
John 3:34 God g. not Spirit
6:32 Father g. you true bread
John 6:33 who g. life to the world
37 all the Father g. me
10:11 good shepherd g. his life
14:27 not as the world g. give I
Acts 17:25 he g. to all life

Rom. 12:8 g. with simplicity
1 Cor. 3:7 G. that g. the increase
15:57 thanks to G. who g. victory
2 Cor. 3:6 letter killeth, sp. g. life
1 Tim. 6:17 g. richly all things
Jam. 1:5 ask of God that g. to all
4:6 g. more grace, God g. grace
1 Pet. 4:11 of ability that God g.
Rev. 22:5 L. God g. them light

GIVING.

1 Pet. 3:7 g. honor to the wife
2 Pet. 1:5 g. all diligence

GLAD.

Ps. 34:2 hear and be g. 69:32
45:8 have made thee g.
104:34 be g. in Lord;
107:30 are they g. bec. quiet
122:1 g. when said, Let us go
126:3 things, whereof are g.
Prov. 10:1 a g. father, 15:20
12:25 father and mother be g.
24:17 heart not be g.
27:11 make my heart g.
Luke 15:32 we make merry, be g.

GLADNESS.

2 Chr. 29:30 sang praises with g.
30:21 Israel kept feast with g.
23 kept other seven days w. g.
Est. 8:16 had light, and g. 17
Ps. 4:7 thou put g. in my heart
30:11 thou girded me with g.
45:7 anoi. with oil of g. Heb. 1:9
15 with g. shall they be brou.
51:8 make me to hear joy and g.
97:11 g. is sown for the upright
100:2 serve the Lord with g.
105:43 brought chosen with g.
106:5 that I may rejoice in g.
Is. 30:29 have song and g. of heart
35:10 obtain joy and g. 51:11
51:3 joy and g. found therein
Jer. 7:34 voice of mirth and g.
16:9; 25:10
31:7 sing with g. for Jacob
33:11 heard voice of joy and g.
48:33 joy and g. taken fr. field
Joel 1:16 joy and g. from h. of G.
Zec. 8:19 h. of Jud. joy and g.
Mark 4:16 who receive it with g.
Luke 1:14 shalt have joy and g.
Acts 2:46 eat meat w. g. of heart

12:14 she opened not gate for g.
14:17 fill, hea. with food and g.
Phil. 2:29 receive him with all g.

GLORIFY.

Ps. 22:23 seed of Jacob g. him
50:15 and thou shalt g. me
86:9 nations shall come and g.
12 and I will g. thy name
Is. 24:15 g. ye Lord in the fires
25:3 the strong people g. thee
Jer. 30:19 I will also g. them
Mat. 5:16 g. Father in heaven
John 12:28 F. g. thy name
13:32 God sh. g. him in himself
16:14 he shall g. me
17:1 g. thy son, that thy Son g.
5 g. me with own self
21:19 what death he sho. g. G.
Rom. 15:6 mind and mouth g. G.
9 that Gentiles might g. God
1 Cor. 6:20 g. God in body and s.
2 Cor. 9:13 g. God for your subj
1 Pet. 2:12 g. God in day of visi.
4:16 g. God on this behalf
Rev. 15:4 and g. thy name

GLORIFIED.

Lev. 10:3 bef. all peo. I will be g.
Is. 26:15 increased nation, art g.
44:23 L. hath g. himself in Is.
49:3 O Is, in whom I will be g.
55:5 Holy One of Is. hath g. 60:9
60:21 that I may be g.
61:3 planting of L. that he be g.
Is. 66:5 said, Let the Lord be g.
Ezek. 28:22 I will be g. in midst
39:13 the day that I shall be g.
Dan. 5:23 God hast thou not g.
Mat. 9:8 marvelled, and g. God,
Mark 2:12; Luke 5:26
15:31 they g. the God of Israel
Luke 4:15 synagogues, being g.
7:16 and they g. God
13:13 made straight, and g. G.
17:15 leper g. G.; 23:47 centur.
John 7:39 because Jes. not yet g.
11:4 Son of God might be g.
12:16 but when Jesus was g.
23 the Son of men should be g.
28 I have g. it, will glorify it
13:31 Son of man g. God is g.
32 if G. be g. in him G. sh. gl.

14:13 Father may be g. in Son
15:8 my Father g. ye bear fruit
17:4 I have g. thee on earth
10 and I am g. in them
Acts 3:13 G. of fathers hath g. S.
4:21 men g. God
11:18 held peace, and g. God
13:48 Gentiles g. word of Lord
21:20 they of Jerusalem g. Lord
Rom. 1:21 they g. him not as G.
8:17 that we may be also g.
30 wh. he justified, them he g.
Gal. 1:24 and they g. God in me
2 Thes. 1:10 wh. become to be g.
12 name of Jesus may be g.
3:1 that word of Lord may be g.
Heb. 5:5 so Christ g. not himself
1 Pet. 4:11 G. in all things be g.
14 but on your part he is g.
Rev. 18:7 how much g. herself

GLORIFIETH, ING.

Ps. 50:23 whoso, offer, praise g.
Luke 2:20 sheph. returned, g. G.
5:25 departed to own ho. g. God
18:43 blind man followed, g. G.

GLORY, Substantive.

1 Chr. 29:11 thine is greatness,
power and g. Mat. 6:13
Est. 5:11 H. told g. of riches
Prov. 3:35 wise shall inherit g.
17:6 g. of children are fathers
20:29 g. of young men is stren.
25:27 to search own g. is not g.
23:12 righteous rej. there is g.
Is. 4:5 the g. shall be a defence
5:14 g. and pomp desc. unto it
10:3 where will ye leave g.?
Luke 2:14 g. to G. in high, 19:38
Acts 7:2 G. of g. appeared
12:23 because he gave not G. g.
Rom. 8:18 not wor. be com. with g.
1 Cor. 11:7 woman is the g. of the
man 15 wo. ha. long hair, is g.to h.
2 Cor. 3:18 all are changed from g.
to g. 4:17 work,eternal wgt of g.
8:23 messengers, and g. of Christ
Eph. 1:6 praise of g. of his grace
17 Father of g. give you Spirit
18 know what is riches of g.
3:13 tribulations, wh. is your g.
21 g. in the church by Chr. J.

Phil. 1:11 fruits, by Christ to g.
4:19 according to his rich. in g.
20 God and our F. be g. forev.
Heb. 3:3 man counted worthy mo. g.
1 Pet. 21:24 g. of man as flower of grass
Jude 25 only G. our Savio. be g.
Rev. 4:11 worthy to rec. g. 5:12
7:12 blessing and g. to our God.

GLORY of God.

Ps. 19:1 heavens declare g. of G.
Prov. 25:2 g. of God to conceal
Rom. 3:23 short of g. of God

GNAT.

Mat. 23:24 strain at g. sw. camel

GOATS.

Gen. 30:32 spotted and speck, am. g.
Mat. 25:32 divid. sheep from g.
33 set the g. on his left hand

Other GOD.

Ex. 34:14 shalt worship no o. g.

GOD.

2 Sam. 22:32 who is G. save the Lord? Ps. 18:31
Is. 45:22 I am G. there is none else
Mat. 19:17 there is none good but one, that is G. Mark 10:18; Luke 18:19
Mark 12:32 there is one G.
John 1:1 the Word was with G.
3:2 do miracles, ex. G. with him
2 Cor.4:4 g. of this world blinded
Tit. 1:16 profess they know G.
Rev. 21:3 G. hims. be with them
4 G. shall wipe away all tears
7 I will be his G. he be my son

Against GOD.

Rom. 8:7 carnal mind en. a. G.

Before GOD.

Gen. 6:11 earth was corrupt b. G.
Ps. 61:7 he shll abide b.G. for ever
68:3 let righteous rejoice b. G.
Rev. 20:12 I saw dead stand b. G.

HOLY GOD.

Jos. 24:19 he is a holy G. jealous

GOD is.

Ps. 46:1 G. is refuge and str. 62:8
54:4 Behold, G. is my helper
Acts 10:34 G. is no resp. of per.

1 Cor. 33 G. is not author of confus.
1 John 1:5 G. is light; 4:8 is love,16
3:20 G. is greater th. our heart

Living GOD.

Mat. 16:16 art Christ, Son of living G. John 6:69
Rom. 9:26 be called chil. of l. G.
2 Cor. 3:3 with the Spirit of l.G.
6:16 ye are the temple of l.G.
1 Tim. 3:15 church of the l. G.
4:10 we trust in the l.G. 6:17
Heb. 3:12 evil heart dep. fr. l.G.

My GOD.

Gen. 28:21 then sh. L. be my G.
Ruth 1:16 people, thy G. my G.
Ps. 22:10 my G. fr. my mother's belly 38:21 O my G. be not far,
71:12 89:26 thou art my Fath.my G. 104:33 praise to my G. 146:2
118:28 my G. I will praise thee
145:1 I will extol thee, my G.
Prov. 30:9 name of my G. in vain
Phil. 4:19 my G. supply need
Rev. 3:12 write name of my G.

No GOD.

Is. 44:6 besides me there is no G. 8;
45, 5, 14, 21

Of GOD.

Rom. 13:1 powers that be ord.of G.

Our GOD.

Ps. 40:3 a new song, pr. to o. G.
67:6 G. our G. shall bless us
68:20 our G. is the G. of salvat.
77:13 so great a G. as our G.?

Thy GOD.

Dan. 6:20 is thy G. able to deliver?
10:12 chasten thyself bef. t.G.
Mic. 6:8 walk humbly with t. G.

To, or unto GOD.

Ps.73:28 good to draw near to G.
Jam. 4:7 submit yourselves to G.

Your GOD.

Ex. 8:25 go ye, sacrifice to y. G.
Num. 26:12 I will be your God, ye my people, Jer. 7:23; 11:4;
30:22; Ezek. 36:28

GODLY.

Ps. 4:3 L. set apart him that is g.
12:1 help, for the g. man ceas.
32:6 for this every one g. pray
Mal. 2:15 he might seek g. seed

2 Cor. 1:12 in g. sincer. our con.

7:9 sorry after a g. manner, 11

10 for g. sorrow worketh rep.

11:2 jeal. over you with g. jeal.

2 Tim. 3:12 all that live g. in C.

Tit. 2:12 that ye should live g.

Heb. 12:28 serve G. with g. fear

2 Pet. 2:9 how to deliver the g.

3 John 6 bring for after g. sort

GODLINESS.

1 Tim. 2:2 may lead a life in g.

10 becometh women profes. g.

4:7 exer. thyself rather unto g.

8 g. is profit. unto all things

6:3 the doctrine according to g.

5 supposing that gain is g.

6 g. with contentment is gain

11 follow righteousness, g. fai.

2 Tim. 3:5 having a form of g.

Tit. 1:1 truth which is after g.

2 Pet. 1:3 things pertain to g.

6 add to g. brotherly kind. 7.

3:11 persons ought to be in g.

GODS.

Gen. 3:5 ye shall be as g.

Deut. 12:31 have done abomina. to

their g. sons and dan. in fire to g.

Jer. 5:7 swom by th. that are no g.

10:11 g. have not made heaven

Acts 19:26 be no g. made with

hands

Among the GODS.

Ex. 15:11 am. t. g. who like th.?

Ps. 86:8 a. t. g. none like thee

Other GODS.

Ex. 20:3 no other g. before me,

Deut. 5:7

GOLD.

Ex. 25:12 shalt cast four rings of g.

for ark, 26; 26:29; 28:23, 26,

27; 37:3, 13

13 stav. of shittim-wood, over-

lay with g. 28; 26:29, 37;

30:5 ;37:4, 15, 28

18 two cherubim of g. 37:7

26:8 fifty taches of g. 36:13

32 hooks sh. be of g. 37; 36:38

28:6 ephod g.; 8 girdle; 15 b.p.

11 ouches of g. 13; 39:6 , 13, 16

24 chains of g.; 33 bells of g.

32:24 who hath g. let him br. it

39:3 beat g. into thin plates

40:5 set altar of g. before ark

Num. 7:14 ten shekels of g. 20

84 at dedication 11 spoons of g.

86 g. of spoons 120 shekels

31:50 captains' obla. g. chains

2 Chr. 10:2 queen of Sh.came with

g. 14 wt. of g. in year, 2 Chr.9:13

16 made 200 targ. of beaten g.

17 made 300 shields of g.

18 overlaid throne with best g.

Ps. 19:10 more to be des. than g.

Prov. 16:16 better to get wis.than g.

20:15 g. and a multi. of rubies

Zec. 13:9 I will try th. as g. is tried

1 Pet 1:7 faith more pre. than g.

Pure GOLD

Rev. 21:18 city p. g.; 21 street

GOLD, with silver.

Ps. 119:72 law better than g. and s.

Prov. 8:10 not silver receive

knowledge rather than g.

22:1 favor rather than s. or g.

25:11 apples of g. in pict. of s.

GOLIATH.

1 Sam. 17:4 G. of G. went out. 23

GOMORRAH.

Mat. 10:15 toler. for G. Mark 6:11

GONE out.

Mat. 12:43 when unclean spirit

is g. out, Luke 11:24

GOOD, Substantive

1 Sam. 24:17 rewarded me g. for

evil

Prov. 3:27 with not g. from th.

11:17 doeth g. to his own soul

27 he that diligently seek. g.

12:44 a man satisfied with g.

13:2 eat g. by fruit of his mouth

21 to righteous g. sh. be repaid

14:22 truth to them that dev. g.

16:20 hand. matter wisely f. g.

17:20 froward heart find. no g.

22 a merry heart doeth g.

Is. 52:7 bringeth good tidings of g.

GOOD, Adjective.

Ps. 37:23 steps of g. man ord. by L.

112:5 a g. man showeth favor

119:39 thy judgments are g.

66 teach g. judg. and knowl.

Prov. 2:9 shalt unders. ev. g. pa.

102

20 walk in way of g. men
12:25 g. word mak. heart glad
14:19 the evil bow before the g.
15:23 word in season, how g.
30 g. report maketh bones fat
20:18 with g. advice make war
25:1 name rather than riches
Luke 6:38 g. measure, pressed down
1 Pet. 3:10 love life, and see g. days

Is GOOD.
Ps. 34:8 and see the Lord is g.
Mark 9:50 salt is g. Luke 14:34
Luke 18:19 none is g. save one

It is GOOD.
Ps. 52:9 name, for it is g. 54:6
73:28 it is g. to draw near to G.
92:1 it is a g. thing to give than.
119:71 it is I have been afflic.
147:1 it is g. to sing praises
Prov. 24:13 eat honey, be. it is g.

Not GOOD.
Gen. 2:18 not g. man be alone

GOOD, with thing.
Ps. 84:11 no g. th. will he withhold
92:1 it is g. t. to give thanks
Prov. 18:22 a wife, findeth g. th.

GOOD things.
Prov. 28:10 upright sh. have g. t.
Jer. 5:25 sins have withh. g. t.
Tit. 2:3 women teachers of g. t.
3:8 these t. are g. and profitable

GOOD tidings.
Luke 2:10 I bring you g. t.

GOOD understanding.
Prov. 3:4 find favor and g. und.
13:15 g. understan. giveth favor

GOOD works.
Mat. 5:16 may see your g. w.

GOODLY.
Gen. 39:6 Joseph was a g. person

GOODS.
Mat. 12:29 enter str. man's hou.
and take g.? Mark 3:27

GOSPEL.
Rom. 1:16 not ashamed of g. of Christ
Gal. 1:7 would pervert g. of Chr.
Phil. 1:27 let your conversation be as beco. g. striv. for faith of g.
1 Thes. 2:2 bold to speak the g. of

God
2 Thes. 1:8 on them that obey not the g. 1 Pet. 4:17
2:14 whereunto called you by g.
1 Tim. 1:11 according to g. of G.
Rom. 10:15 beautiful feet that p. g.

GOVERNMENT, S.
Is. 9:6 g. shall be upon shoulder
7 of inc. of his g. sh. be no end

GOVERNORS.
Mat. 10:18 sh. be brought bef. g.
1 Pet. 2:14 submit yoursel. to g.

GRACE.
Est. 2:17 E. obtained g. in sight
Ps. 45:2 g. poured into lips
84:11 Lord is a sun. will give g.
Prov. 1:9 an ornament of g.
3:22 so shall they be life and g.
34 giveth g. to lowly, Jam. 4:6
4:9 to head ornament of g.
Zec. 4:7 shoutings, crying, g. g.
12:10 will pour the Spirit of g.
John 1:14 begotten of F. full of g.
16 have all received g. for g.
17 g. and truth came by J. C.
Acts 4:33 great g. was on them
14:3 testimony to word of his g.
18:27 which believed thro' g.
20:32 com. you to word of g.
Rom. 1:5 by wh. we received g.
7 g. and peace from G. our F.
1 Cor. 1:3; 2 cor. 1:2; Gal
1:3; Eph. 1:2; Phil. 1:2; Col.
1:2; 1 Thes. 1:1; 2 Thes. 1:2;
Phile. 3
3:24 justified freely by his g.
4:4 reward is not reckoned of g.
16 that it might be by g.
5:2 we have access into this g.
17 receive abundance of g.
20 sin abounded, g. more
21 g. reign thro' righteousness
6:1 con. in sin, that g. abound?
14 under g.; 15 bec. under g.?
11:5 according to election of g.
6 if by g. no more of works
12:3 through g. given unto me
6 gifts differing according to g.
1 Cor. 10:30 if I by g. be partak.
15:10 g. bestowed not in vain
2 Cor. 4:15 g. red. to glory of G.

8:6 finish in you the same g.
7 see that ye abound in this g.
9:8 G. is able to make g. abound
12:9 my g. is sufficient for thee
Gal. 1:6 who called you to g.
15 G. who called me by his g.
2:9 when James perceived g.
5:4 justi. by law, fallen from g.
Eph. 1:6 praise of the glory of g.
7 according to riches of g.
2:5 by g. saved through faith, 8
7 might show the riches of g.
3:8 to me is this g. given
4:7 to ev. one of us is given g.
29 may minister g. to hearers
6:24 g. with all that love L. J.
Phil. 1:7 are all partakers of g.
Col. 3:16 sing. with g. in hearts
4:6 let speech be alway with g.
18 g. be with you, 2 Tim. 4:22;
Tit. 3:15; Heb. 13:25
2 Thes. 2:16 hope through g.
1 Tim. 1:2 g. mercy. and peace
from G. our Father, 2 Tim.
1:2; Tit. 1:4; 2 John 3
1:14 g. of Lord abundant
6:21 g. be with thee. Amen
2 Tim. 1:9 called us accord. to g.
2:1 be strong in the g. in Christ
Tit. 3:7 justified by g.
Heb. 4:16 boldly to throne of g.
10:29 despite to the Spirit of g.
12:28 let us have g. to serve G.
13:9 the heart be estab. with g.
Jam. 1:11 g. of fashion perisheth
4:6 giveth more g. g. to humble
1 Pet. 1:2 g. be multi. 2 Pet. 1:2
10 prophesied of g. to come
13 hope for g. 3:7 heirs of g.
5:5 God giveth g. to humble
10 G. of g. called us to glory
2 Pet. 3:18 grow in g. and in Ch.
Rev. 1:4 g. from him

GRACE of God.
Luke 2:40 g. of God upon him
Acts 11:23 he had seen g. of God
13:43 persua. to con. in g. of G.
14:26 recom. to g. of G. 15:40
20:24 the gospel of g. of God
Rom. 5:15 g. of G. hath abound.
1 Cor. 1:4 g. of G. given by J. C.

15:10 by g. of God I am what I
am, yet not I, but g. of God
Gal. 2:21 not frustrate g. of G.
Tit. 2:11 g. of G. bringeth salv.
Heb. 2:9 by g. of G. taste death
12:15 any man fail of g. of G.
1 Pet. 4:10 stewards of g. of G.

GRACIOUS.
Prov. 11:16 g. wo. retain. honor

GRACIOUSLY.
Gen. 33:11 G. hath dealt g. with

GRAFTED.
Rom. 11:19 that I might be g. in

GRAIN.
Mat. 13:31 kingdom of heaven is
like a g. of mustard-seed,
Mark 4:31; Luke 13:19
17:20 faith as a g. of mustard-s.
ye shall say to this mount.
remove, Luke 17:6

GRANTED.
Job 10:12 hast g. life and favor
Prov. 10:24 desire of right. be g.
Acts 11:18 G. g. Gen. repentance

GRAPE.
Lev. 19:10 not gather g. of wine
Deut. 32:14 drink blood of g.

GRASS.
Gen. 1:11 earth bring forth g.
Deut. 11:15 send g. for thy cattle
38:2 distil as showers upon g.
2 Sam. 23:4 the g. springing out
1 K. 18:5 find g. to save horses
2 K. 19:26 as g. of the field, as g.
Prov. 19:12 as dew on g.
27:25 tender g. showeth itself
Mat. 6:30 clothe g. Luke 12:28
Rev. 8:7 all green g. burnt up
9:4 should not hurt g. of earth

GRAVE, Substantive.
Ps. 6:5 in g. who give thanks?
John 12:17 called Lazarus out of g.
1 Cor. 15:55 g. wh. is thy victory?
Ex. 29:36 pl. of pure gold, g. on
2 Chr. 2:7 send a man that can g.
14 sent a cunning man to g.

GRAVEN image.
Ex. 20:4 sh. not make unto thee

GRAVES.
Mat. 27:52 the g. were opened
53 bod. of saints came out of g.

104

GREAT.

2 Sam. 22:56 thy gentleness hath made me g. Ps. 18:35
Ps. 25:11 pardon iniquity, it is g.
Lam. 3:23 g. is thy faithfulness
Ezek. 17:3 g. eagle g. wings, 7
Mat. 5:12 be glad, g. is reward in heaven, Luke 6:23, 35
22:38 first and g. commandment
Luke 9:48 least among you shall be g.

GREAT, power.

Jer. 27:5 made the earth, man, and beast by my g. p. 32:17
Acts 4:33 with g. p. gave apostles

GREAT thing, s.

Mark 3:8 heard what g. t. he did
Luke 8:39 published g. t. J. had done
Acts 9:16 g. t. he must suffer

GREATEST.

Mat. 18:4 humble as child, same is g.
1 Cor. 13:13 g. of these is charity

GREATLY.

1 Chr. 16:25 the L. is g. to be praised, Ps. 48:1; 96:4; 145:3

GREEDILY.

Prov. 21:26 coveteth g. all day

GREEN.

Ps. 23:2 lie down in g. pastures

GRIEF, S.

Ps. 6:7 my eye is consumed because of g. 31:9
31:10 my life is spent with g.
69:26 to g. of those wounded
Prov. 17:25 fool. son g. to father
Ec. 1:18 in much wisd. much g.
2:23 days are sorrows, travail g.
Is. 17:11 harv. a heap in day of G.
53:3 a man acquainted with g.
4 borne our g. carried sorrows
10 pleased Lord put him to g.
Heb. 13:17 do it with joy, not g.
1 Pet. 2:19 consc. to. G. endure g.

GRIEVE.

1 Sam. 2:23 man to g. thy heart
1 Chr. 4:10 keep from evil, not g.
Ps. 78:40 oft did they g. him
Lam. 3:33 not willingly g. men
Eph. 4:30 g. not H. Spirit of God

GRIEVED.

Gen. 45:5 be not g. that ye sold me
Est. 4:4 queen exceedingly g.
Job 30:25 my soul g. for the poor?
Ps. 73:21 heart g. I was pricked
95:10 forty years was I g.
Is. 54:6 L. called as a woman g.
Dan. 7:15 I Daniel was g.
11:30 he shall be g. and return
Amos 6:6 not g. for affliction
Mark 10:22 he went away g.
John 21:17 Peter was g.
Rom. 14:15 if brother g.
2 Cor. 2:4 not that ye be g.
5 he hath not g. me.
Heb. 3:10 I was g. with generati.
17 with whom g. forty years?

GRIEVOUS.

Prov. 15:1 g. words stir up anger
10 correct, g. to him that fors.

GROANING, S.

John 11:38 Jesus g. in himself
Rom. 8:26 g. that cannot be ut.

GROUND.

Gen. 2:5 not a man to till g.
7 God formed man of dust of g.
4:2 Cain was a tiller of the g.
Mat. 13:8 into good g. Luke 8:8

GUIDE.

Ps. 25:9 meek will g. in judgm.
31:3 for thy name's sake g. me
32:8 I will teach and g. thee
73:24 shalt g. me with counsel
112:5 g. his affairs with discre.
Prov. 11:3 integrity of upright g.
Is. 51:18 there is none to g. her
58:11 L. shall g. thee continual
Luke 1:79 g. feet into way of p.
John 16:13 he will g. you
1 Tim. 5:14 you. women g. hous

GUILE.

Ps. 32:2 in whose spirit is no g.
34:13 lips from g. 1 Pet. 3:10
1 Pet. 2:1 lay aside malice and g.
22 nor was g. found in his mo.
Rev. 14:5 in mo. was found no g.

GUILTY.

Gen. 42:21 we are verily g.
Prov. 30:10 lest curse, thou be g.

GUILTLESS.

Mat. 12:7 not have condemned g.

H.

HABITATION.
Job 5:3 but suddenly I cursed h.
24 shalt visit h. and sh. not sin
8:6 h. of righteousness prosper.
Ps. 26:8 loved h. of thy house
71:3 be thou my strong h.
89:14 the h. of thy throne, 97:2
91:9 made the Most High thy h.

HAGGAI.
Ezr. 5:1 H. prophesied to J. 6:14

HAIL.
Ex. 9:18 cau. to rain grievous h.

HAIR.
2 Sam. 14:26 bec. h. was heavy
Mat. 5:36 not make one h. wh. or
bl.
1 Cor. 11:14 if a man have long h.

HAIRS.
Mat. 10:30 the h. of your head
are numbered, Luke 12:7
Luke 7:38 wipe with h. of h. 44

HAIRY.
Gen. 27:11 Esau h. man; 23 hands
h.
2 K. 1:8 Elijah was a h. man
Ps. 68:21 h. scalp of such a one

HALF.
1 K. 3:25 h. child to one, h. oth.

HALLOWED.
Ex. 20:11 bless. sabbath and h. it

HAND.
Ex. 14:16 stretch out h. over the sea
Ps. 123:2 serv. look to h. of masters
127:4 in h. of mighty man
Prov. 6:3 come into h. of friend
10:4 poor dealeth slack h. but
h. of diligent maketh rich
12:24 h. of diligent bear rule
17:16 in h. of fool get wisdom?

HAND of God.
1 Sam. 5:11 h. of G. heavy
2 Chr. 30:12 h. of G. give heart
Ezr. 8:18 by good h. of God upon
us 22 h. of G. is upon them
Job 2:10 re. good at the h. of G.?
19:21 h. of God touched me
Ec. 2:24 from the h. of God
9:1 wise are in the h. of God
Mark 16:19 and sat on right h. of

G. Rom. 8:34; Col. 3:1; Heb.
10:12; 1 Pet 3:22
Acts 2:33 by right h. of God
7:55 stand. on right h. of G. 56
1 Pet. 5:6 under the h. of God

His HAND.
Prov. 19:24 a slothful man hideth
his h. 26:15
7:32 bes. to put h. h. upon him
John 3:35 given all th. into h. h.
18:22 struck with palm of his h.
Acts 28:3 a viper fastened on his h.

Mighty HAND.
Ex. 3:19 let go, not with m. h.
Deut. 4:34 take him a nation by m.
h. 5:15 God bro. out of Eg. by
a mighty h. 6:21; 7:8, 19, 9:26;
11:2; 26:8; 34:12
2 Chr. 6:32 is come for thy m. h.
Ezek. 20:33 with a m. h. I rule
Dan. 9:15 out of Eg. with m. h.
1 Pet. 5:6 hum. under m. h. of G.

Right HAND.
Ps. 16:8 he is at my right h.
11 at thy r. h. are pleasures
Mat. 5:30 if thy r. h. offend thee
6:3 let not left know r. h. doeth

Thy HAND.
Gen. 22:12 lay not thy h. upon the
lad
24:2 thy h. under my thigh, 47:29
Acts 4:30 stretch. forth thy h. to
heal

HANDMAID.
Gen. 16:1 Sarai had a h. Hagar
29:24 Zilpah to be L.'s h. 35:26
29 Bil. Rachel's h. 30:4; 35:25

HANDS.
Ps. 134:2 lift up h. in the sanctuary
Prov. 6:10 folding of h. 24:33
17 hate the h. shed inno. blo.
Acts 5:12 h. of apostles wonders
wr.
1 Tim. 2:8 lifting up holy h.

His HANDS.
Job 1:10 blessed work of his h.

My HANDS.
Gen. 20:5 in innocency of my h.
Ps. 22:16 pierced my h. and my feet
26:6 wash my h. in innocency
63:4 lift my h. in thy name

73:13 I have washed my h.
119:48 my h. will I lift
Thy HANDS.
Luke 23:46 to thy h. I com. my
John 21:18 shalt stretch thy h.
HANGED.
Mat. 18:6 bet. millst. were h. ab.
his neck, Mark 9:42; Lu. 17:2
27:5 Judas went and h. himself
Acts 5:30 and h. on tree, 10:39
HANGETH.
Job 26:7 h. earth upon nothing
HAPPY.
Ps. 127:5 h. man hath quiver full
137:8 h. he who reward. thee, 9
144:15 h. people in such a case,
h. peo. whose God is the L.
146:5 h. is he that hath G. of J.
Prov. 3:13 h. man find. wisdom
14:21 h. he hath mercy on poor
16:20 whoso trust. in L. h. is he
28:14 h. is man that fear. alway
29:18 that keepeth law, h. is he
1 Pet. 3:14 suffer for righte. h. ye
4:14 reproached for Ch. h. ye
HARDEN.
Ex. 4:21 I will h. Pharaoh's
heart, 7:3; 14:4
HARDENED.
Ex. 7:13 L. h. Phar.'s heart, 9:12
HARDENETH.
Prov. 21:29 wicked man h. face
28:14 h. heart fall into mischief
HARLOT.
Jos. 2:1 spies came to h.'s home
6:17 only Rahab the h. shall live.
Prov. 7:10 woman wi. attire of h.
HARM.
Lev. 5:16 amends for h. done
HARMLESS.
Mat. 10:16 serp, and h. as doves
Phil. 2:15 may be h. sons of G.
Heb. 7:26 holy, h. and undefiled
HARP.
Ps. 33:2 praise L. with h. 150:3
43:4 on the h. will I praise thee
71:22 I will sing with h. 92:3;
98:5; 147:7; 149:3
HARPERS.
Rev. 14:2 I heard the voice of h.
18:22 voice of h. heard no more

HARVEST.
Mat. 13:30 grow together until h.
39 the h. is end of the world
Mark 4:29 put in sickle, h. come
Luke 10:2 said, The h. is great
John 4:35 fields are white to h.
Rev. 14:15 the h. of earth is ripe
HATE.
Lev. 19:17 shalt not h. brother
Ps. 97:10 ye that love Lord h. evil
Prov. 1:22 fools. will ye h. know.
6:16 these six doth the Lord h.
8:13 fear of the Lord is to h. evil
Amos 5:15 h. the evil, love the
good
Mat. 5:44 good to th. h. y. Luke
6:27
Luke 6:22 blessed are ye when men
h.
HATED.
Prov. 1:29 they h. knowledge
5:12 how have I h. instruction?
14:17 man of wicked dev. is h.
HATETH.
Ps. 11:5 loveth viol. his soul h.
Prov. 12:1 he that h. reproof is
brutish
13:5 a righteous man h. lying
24 he that spareth rod h. son
15:10 that h. reproof shall die
27 he that h. gifts shall live
HATRED.
Gal. 5:20 witchcraft, h. variance
HAUGHTY.
Prov. 16:18 h. spirit before a fall
18:12 before destruction heart h.
21:24 h. scorner is his name
HEAD.
Jud. 13:5 no razor come on h.
1 Sam. 17:57 Goliath's h. in hand
Ps. 3:3 the lifter up of my h.
Amos 8:10 bring baldness on every
h.
Mat. 5:36 neither swear by thy h.
27:30 sm. him on h. Mark 15:19
Mark 6:24 h. of John the Baptist
John 13:9 also my hands and h.
1 Cor. 11:4 h. cov. dishonereth
10 ought to ha. power on her h.
12:21 the h. to the feet
Eph. 1:22 gave him h. to church,

H

107

4:15; Col. 1:8

HEAD, for ruler, governor.

1 Cor. 11:3 h. of man is Ch. h. of woman man, h. of Ch. is G.

Eph. 5:23 husband is h. of wife. even as Christ is h. of church

HEAL.

Deut. 32:39 I kill, I wound, I h.

Jer. 3:22 I will h. your backslid.

17:14 h. me, O Lord

30:17 I will h. thee of wounds

Hos. 6:1 ha. torn, and will h. us

14:4 I will heal their backslidings

Mat. 8:7 I will come and h. him

10:8 h. the sick, Luke 9:2; 10:9

12:10 h. on sab.-day Luke 14:3

13:15 be converted and I sho. h. them, John 12:40; Acts 28:27

Mark 3:2 h. on sabbath, Luke 6:7

Luke 4:18 to h. broken-hearted

23 Physician, h. thyself

John 4:17 come down and h.

Acts 4:30 stretching hand to h.

HEALED.

Ps. 107:20 sent his word and h. th.

Is. 6:10 and convert, and be h.

53:5 with his stripes we are h.

Mat. 4:24 palsy, and he h. them

8:8 my serv. shall be h. Lu. 7:7

12:15 follow, he h. them, 14:14

Luke 8:43 nor could be h. of any

17:15 saw he was h. turned ba.

22:51 touch. his ear and h. him

John 5:13 h. wist not who it was

Acts 4:14 beh. man who was h.

14:9 that he had faith to be h.

Heb. 12:13 but let it rather be h.

1 Pet. 2:24 wh. stri. ye were h.

Rev. 13:3 deadly wo. was h. 12

HEALING, Substantive.

1 Cor. 12:9 another gift of h. 28

30 have all the gifts of h.?

HEAR.

Gen. 21:6 all that h. laugh

Ex. 32:18 them that sing do I h.

Num. 23:18 ri. up, Balak, and h.

30:4 h. her vow and her bond

Deut. 1:16 h. causes betw. breth.

4:10 make them h. my words

5:1 h. Is. the statutes, 6:3; 9:1; 20:3; Is. 48:1; Mark 12:29

27 h. all the L. our G. doth say

12:28 h. these words, I com.

13:12 shall h. say in one of cit.

30:12 bring it that we may h.

31:12 h. and fear L. 13; Jer. 6:10

Jos. 3:9 h. the words of the L.

Jud. 5:3 h. O ye kings, give ear

1 Sam. 2:23 h. your evil dealings

15:14 low. of oxen which I h.

16:2 if Saul h. it, he will kill me

2 Sam. 20:16 cr. out of city, h. h.

1 K. 4:34 h. wisdom of Solomon,

Ps. 4:1 h. my prayer, O G. 39:12; 54:2; 84:8; 102:1; 143:1

20:1 L. h. thee in day of troub.

Prov. 1:8 h. instruction of father

Ex. 7:5 better to h. rebuke of wise

Jer. 18:2 cause thee to h. my words

Mark 4:18 are such as h. the word, 20; Luke 8:12, 13

Luke 8:21 wh h. word and do it, 11:28

John 10:3 sheep h. voice

12:47 if man h. words, bel. not

Shall HEAR.

Job 22:27 prayer to him, he s. h.

Ps. 34:2 humble shall h. thereof

55:17 cry, and he s. h. my voice

HEARD.

Ps. 34:4 I sought the L. he h. me

Jon. 2:2 I cried to L. and he h.

1 Cor. 2:9 eye not seen. nor ear h.

Phil. 4:9 ye have h. and seen

HEARETH.

John 9:31 God h. not sinners

HEARING.

Rom. 10:17 faith cometh by h.

HEART, Noun.

Prov. 22:15 foolish. bound in h. of child

Mat. 4:6 the h. of fathers, h. of child.

2 Cor. 3:3 written in fleshly tables of h.

Eph. 6:6 doing will of G. from h.

Col. 3:22 in singl. of h. fear. God.

HEART, with all.

Deut. 13:3 love the Lord with all your h. 30:6; Mat. 22:37; Mark 12:30, 33; Luke 10:27

26:16; do them with all thy h.

108

Perfect HEART.
1 K. 8:61 h. be p. with the Lord
11:4 h. not p. with Lord. 15:3
Pure HEART.
1 Pet. 1:22 love one an. with p. h.
Tender HEARTED.
Eph. 4:32 kind one to ano. t.-h.
HEARTS.
Jos. 7:5 h. of the people melted
Among the HEATHEN.
1 Chr. 16:24 declare his glory
  am. the h. Ps. 96:3
Ps. 46:10 I will be exalted a. t. h.
96:10 say a. t. h. Lord reigneth
110:6 he shall judge am. the h.
126:2 a. h. L. ha. done great
HEAVEN.
Ps. 69:34 h. and earth praise him
Is. 60:1 h. is my throne, Acts 7:49
Luke 16:17 easier for h. and earth
John 1:51 ye shall see h. open
Rev. 21:1 I saw a new h. and earth
From HEAVEN.
Is. 14:12 how art thou fal. f. h.
Dan. 4:31 a voice f. h. Mat. 3:17;
  Luke 3:22; John 12:28
In HEAVEN.
Mat. 6:20 but lay up treasures in h.
Luke 15:7 joy in h. over one sinner
Into HEAVEN.
Acts 1:11 gazing i. h. taken i. h.
7:55 Stephen looked up into h.
HEAVENS.
Prov. 3:19 he established the h.
Is. 65:17 behold, I create new h.
66:22 new h. which I will make
HEAVIER.
Prov. 27:3 a fool's wrath is h.
HEAVINESS.
Is. 61:3 garm. of praise for h.
Phil. 2:26 brother was full of h.
HEDGE, S.
Job 1:10 not made a h. ab. him?
HEIGHT.
Rom. 8:39 nor h. nor depth
HEIR, S.
Gen. 15:3 born in my house is h.
21:10 Ishmael shall not be h.
Prov. 30:23 handmaid h. to mis.
Jer. 49:1 hath Is. no sons? no h.?
Mat. 21:38 this is the h. Mark

12:7; Luke 20:14
Rom. 4:13 should be h. of world
8:17 h. of G. joint h. with Ch.
Gal. 3:29 h. according to promise
4:1 h. as long as he is a child
7 an h. of God through Christ
30 son of bond-w. sh. not be h.
Eph. 3:6 Gent. sh. be fellow-h
Tit. 3:7 h. according to the hope
Heb. 1:2 whom he appointed h.
14 who shall be h. of salvation
11:7 became h. of righteousness
HELD.
Ex. 17:11 wh. Moses h. up hand
Est. 5:2 king h. out golden scep.
HELL.
Deut. 32:22 fire burn unto low. h.
2 Sam. 22:6 sorrows of h. compassed me, Ps. 18:5; 86:13
Job 11:8 deeper than h.
26:6 h. is naked before him
Ps. 9:17 wicked turned into h.
16:10 not le. soul in h. Acts 2:27
55:15 go down quick to h.
116:3 pains of h. gat hold on me
169:8 bed in h. thou art there
Prov. 5:5 steps take hold on h.
7:27 house way to h. going do.
15:11 h. and destruction bef. L.
24 he may depart from h.
23:14 deliver his soul from h.
Jon. 2:2 out of belly of h.
Hab. 2:5 enlargeth desire as h.
Mat. 5:22 in danger of h. fire
29 body be cast in h. 30
10:28 body in h. Luke 12:5
16:18 gates of h. sh. not prevail
18:9 having two eyes to be cast
  into h. Mark 9:47
23:33 can ye escape damna. of h.?
Luke 16:23 in h. lifted up his eyes
Acts 2:31 soul was not left in h.
Jam. 3:6 tong. is set on fire of h.
2 Pet. 2:4 cast angels down to h.
Rev. 1:18 keys of h. and death
6:8 name Death, h. followed
20:13 death and h. del. up dead
14 death and h. cast in lake
HELMET.
Is. 59:17 h. of salvation on head
Eph. 6:17 the h. of salvation

1 Thes. 5:8 h. hope of salvation

HELP, Verb.

2 Chr. 19:2 should. thou h. the ungodly

20:9 thou wilt hear and h.

25:8 for God hath power to h.

26:13 power to h. the king

28:23 h. them that they may h.

32:8 with us is the L. to h. us

Job 8:20 nei. will he h. evil-doers

Ps. 12:1 h. L.; 22:11 none to h.

22:19 haste thee to h. 38:22;
40:13; 70:1

37:40 L. h. them; 46:5 G. h. her

119:86 h. me; 173 thy hand h.

175 let thy judgments h. me

Ec. 4:10 hath not another to h.

Is. 41:10 will h. thee, 13, 14: 44:2

50:7 the Lord God will h. me, 9

Lam. 1:7 people fell, none did h.

Ezek. 32:21 speak out of hell with them that h. him

Dan. 11:45 come to end, none h.

Mat. 15:25 saying, Lord, h. me

Mark 9:22 have compass. h. us

24 L. I believe, h. mine unbel.

Luke 5:7 they sh. come and h.

10:40 bid her therefore h. me

Acts 21:28 crying out, M. of Israel, h.

Phil. 4:3 h. women wh. labored

Heb. 4:16 to h. in time of need

HELPED.

2 Chr. 26:15 was marvellously h.

Job 26:2 how hast thou h. him

Ps. 28:7 I am h.; 118:13 L. h. me

116:6 brought low, he h. me

Is. 41:6 h. ev. one his neighbor

49:8 in day of salvation h. thee

Rev. 12:16 earth h. the woman

HELPER.

2 K. 14:26 nor any h. for Israel

Job 30:13 mar my path, no h.

Ps. 10:14 art h. of fatherless

30:10 L. my h.; 54:4 G. my h.

Heb. 13:6 Lord is my h.

HELPERS.

1 Chr. 12:18 peace be to thy h.

2 Cor. 1:24 but are h. of your joy

3 John 8 be fellow-h. to the truth

HELPETH.

1 Chr. 12:18 for thy God h. thee

Is. 31:3 both he that h. shall fall

Rom. 8:26 Sp. also h. infirmities

1 Cor. 16:16 sub. to. ev. one h. us

HELPING.

Ps. 22:1 why art so far from h.

2 cor. 1:11 h. together by prayer

HEN.

Mat. 23:37 h. gath. ch. Lu. 13:34

HERBS.

Mat. 13:22 is greatest among all
h. Mark 4:32

Rom. 14:2 who is weak, eat. h.

HERD, S.

Lev. 27:32 concerning tithe of h.

Deut. 12:21 shalt kill of thy h.

Joel 1:18 h. of cattle perplexed

Jon. 3:7 let not h. taste any thing

Hab. 3:17 shall be no h. in stalls

Mat. 8:30 a h. of swine feeding

HERITAGE.

Ex. 6:8 I will give it you for h.

Ps. 127:3 children are a h. of the L.

HEROD.

Luke 3:1 H. tetrarch of Galil. 19

9:7 H. heard of Jesus, 13:31

23:7 sent J. to H. 8, 11, 12, 15

HERODIAS.

Mat. 14:3 John in prison for H. 6

Luke 3:19 H. reprov. by J. for H.

HID.

Gen. 3:8 Adam and his wife h.

Ex. 2:2 h. Moses three months

Jos. 2:4 Rahab h. the spies, 6

Ps. 119:11 word I h. in my heart

Mat. 11:25 h. fr. wise, Lu. 10:21

13:33 h. in three meas. Lu. 13:21

25:18 and h. his lord's money

25 and h. thy talent in earth

Luke 1:24 Elizabeth h. herself

John 8:59 but Jesus h. himself

HIDDEN.

Prov. 28:12 wicked rise, man h.

Is. 45:3 give thee h. riches

1 Cor. 2:7 h. wisdom G. ordained

4:5 bring to light h. things

Rev. 2:17 give to eat of h. manna

HIDE.

Gen. 18:17 shall I h. from Abra.?

Ps. 17:8 h. me under thy wings

Prov. 2:1 h. my com. with thee
Ezek. 28:3 no secret they can h.

HIGH.

Ps. 131:1 things too h. for me
Prov. 24:7 wisdom is too h. for a fool
John 19:31 sabbath was a h. day
2 Cor. 10:5 cast. down ev. h. th.
Phil. 3:14 prize of the h. calling

Most HIGH.

Num. 24:16 knowledge of M. H.
2 Sam. 22:14 M. H. ut. his voice
Ps. 7:17 sing praise to name of the Lord the M. H. 9:2; 92:1
47:2 the Lord M. H. is terrible
50:14 pay thy vows to the M. H.
56:2 fight aga. thee, O M. H.
57:2 I will cry unto God M. H.
Lam. 3:35 before face of M. H.
38 out of M. H. proc. not evil
Dan. 4:17 M. H. ruleth in kingd.
24 the decre of the M. H.

HIGHER.

Ps. 61:2 lead to Rock that is h.
Is. 55:9 as hea. are h. than earth, so my ways h. th. your ways

HIGHEST.

Mat. 21:9 hosan. in h. Mark 11:10
Luke 1:32 called Son of the H.
2:14 glory to G. in H. 19:38
6:35 ye shall be chil. of the H.

HIGHLY.

Luke 1:28 Thou art h. favored

HIGH-MINDED.

Rom. 11:20 not h.-m. 1 Tim. 6:1

HILL.

Mat. 5:14 city that is set on a h.
Luke 3:5 ev. h. be brought low

HOLY HILL.

Ps. 43:3 bring me to thy h.h.?

HILL, with top.

Ex. 17:9 will stand on top of h.
Num. 14:44 pres. to go to h. t.
Jud. 16:3 S. carried to top of h.
2 K. 1:9 Elijah sat on top of a h.

HILLS.

Ps. 50:10 cattle on thousand h.
121:1 will lift mine eyes to h.
Is. 54:10 mount. depart, h. remov.
Hos. 10:8 say to h. Fall on us
Joel 3:18 h. shall flow with milk

HINDER, Verb.

Acts 8:36 what h. me to be bap.?
1 Cor. 9:12 lest we sho. h. gospel
Gal. 5:7 who did h. you?

HINGES.

Prov. 26:14 door turneth upon h.

HIP.

Jud. 15:8 sm. them h. and thigh.

HIRE, Substantive.

Mic. 3:11 priests thereof teach for h.
Mat. 20:8 give them their h.
Luke 10:7 labor, worthy of his h.

HIRED.

Gen. 30:16 h. with son's mandr.
Lev. 19:13 wages of him h.
Mat. 20:7 bec. no man hath h. us

HIRED servants.

Deut. 24:14 thou sh. not oppress h.-s.

HITTITE.

Gen. 25:9 in field of Eph. the H.

HOLD.

1 K. 2:9 now h. him not guiltless
Est. 4:11 h. out golden sceptre
Job 9:28 wilt not h. me innocent
13:19 if I h. my tongue
Is. 41:14 L. h. thy right hand
42:6 and I will h. thy hand

HOLD peace.

Jer. 4:19 cannot h. peace
Zep. 1:7 h. thy p. at pres. of L.
Mat. 20:31 reb. them bec. they sh. h. p. Mark 10:48; Luke 18:39
Mark 1:25 h. thy p. Luke 4:35
Luke 19:40 if they h. p. the sto.
Acts 12:17 beckoning to h. th. p.
18:9 be not afraid, h. not thy p.
1 Cor. 14:30 let the first h. his p.

HOLINESS.

Ex. 15:11 who like thee, in h.?
1 Chr. 16:29 worship L. in beauty of h. Ps. 29:2; 96:9
Luke 1:75 might serve him in h.
Acts 3:12 by h. made man walk
Rom. 1:4 according to spirit of h.
6:22 ye have your fruit unto h.
2 Cor. 7:1 perfect. h. in fear of G.
Eph. 4:24 new man created in h.
1 Thes. 3:13 stablish hearts in h.

4:7 not to uncleanness, but to h.
1 Tim. 2:15 conti. in faith and h.
Tit. 2:3 in behavior as becom. h.
Heb. 12:10 be partakers of his h.
  14 peace with men, and h.

HOLLOW.
Gen. 32:25 h. of thigh, 32

HOLY.
Ex. 3:5 pl. th. standest h. ground
30:25 an oil of h. ointment
  32 it is h. and sh. be h. unto y.
Lev. 10:10 difference bet. h. and
unh.
  19:2 I the L. your G. am h. 21:8
  20:7 be ye h.; 21:7 he is h.
27:30 tithe of the land is h. to L.
Num. 15:40 remember and be h. to
G.
  16:3 all the congregation are h.
  5 show who are his, who is h.
1 Sam. 2:2 none h. as the Lord
2 K. 4:9 this is a h. man of God
2 Chr. 23:6 for they are h.
Ps. 20:6 hear from his h. heaven
  22:3 but thou art h. O thou that
  28:2 lift hands tow. thy h. orac.
  86:2 pres. my soul, for I am h.
  98:1 his h. arm hath gotten vic.
  99:5 worship at footst. he is h.
Ps. 105:42 remembered h. prom.
  145:17 L. is h. in all his works
Prov. 9:10 knowl. of h. is under
  30:3 nor have I knowl. of the h.
Is. 6:3 h. h. h is the Lord of Hosts
27:13 worship in h. mountain
52:10 L. made bare his h. arm
58:13 call sabbath, h. of the l.
64:11 h. and beaut. house is burnt
Ezek. 44:23 differ. betw. h. and
profane
Mark 6:20 he was just and h.
  8:38 with h. angels, Luke 9:26
Luke 1:70 by the mouth of h.
prophets, Acts 3:21
John 17:11 h. Father keep those
Acts 4:27 against thy h. child J.
  7:32 place thou standest is h.
Rom. 1:2 prom. in h. scriptures
  7:12 commandment is h. just
  12:1 bodies h. sacrifice to G.
  16:16 salute with h. kiss, 1 Cor.

16:20; 2 Cor. 13:12; 1 Thes.
5:26; 1 Pet. 5:14
1 Cor. 3:17 temple of God is h.
Eph. 1:4 be h. with. blame, 5:27
Col. 1:22 present h. and unblam.
  3:12 elect of G. h. and beloved
1 Thes. 5:27 to all h. brethren
1 Tim. 2:8 up h. hands
2 Tim. 1:9 called us with h. call.
  3:15 hast known h. scriptures
Tit. 1:8 bishop be sober, h. tem.
Heb. 7:26 high-pr. beca. us who is
h.
1 Pet. 1:15 h. in conversation, 16
  2:5 h. priesth. offer up sacrifices
  3:5 h. women who trusted in G.
2 Pet. 1:18 with him in h. mount
  21 h. men spake mov. by H. G.
  3:2 spoken before by h. prophe.
  11 persons to be in all h. conv.
Rev. 3:7 saith he that is h.
  4:8 h. h. h. L. God almighty
  6:10 how long, O L. h. and true
  20:6 h. who ha. part in first res.
  22:6 Lord G. of the h. prophets
  11 he th. is h. let him be h. st.

HOLY Ghost.
Mat. 1:18 with child of H. G. 20
  3:11 with H. G. Mark 1:8; Luke
  3:16; John 1:33; Acts 1:5
  12:31 blasph. ag. H. G. not forgiven, Mark 3:29; Luke 12:10
  32 whoso. speak. against H. G.
  28:19 baptize in name of H. G.
Mark 12:36 David said by the H.
  Ghost, Acts 1:16
  13:11 not ye speak, but H. G.
Luke 1:15 John filled with H. G.
  35 H. G. shall come upon thee
  41 Elizabeth filled with H. G.
  67 Zacharias filled with H. G.
Luke 2:25 Sim. H. G. upon him
  26 revealed unto him by H. G.
  3:22 H. G. desc. in bodily shape
  4:1 Jesus being full of H. G.
  12:12 H. G. shall teach you
John 7:39 H. G. not yet given
  14:26 Comforter, who is H. G.
  20:22 receive ye H. G. Acts 2:38
Acts 1:2 he thro. H. G. had given
  8 the H. G. is come on you

112

2:4 all filled with H. G. 4:31
33 promise of the H. G.
4:8 filled with the H. Ghost
5:3 S. filled he. to lie to H. G.?
32 are witnesses, so is H. G.
6:3 men full of the H. Ghost
5 Stephen, man full of H. G.
7:51 stiff-n. alw. resist H. G.
55 Stephen full of H. Ghost
8:15 prayed th. might re. H. G.
17 hands on th. received H. G.
18 when S. saw H. G. was giv.
19 hands, they receive H. G.
9:17 might. be filled with H. G.
31 walking in comfort of H. G.
10:38 G. anoint. J. with H. G.
44 H. G. fell on all who heard
45 on Gentiles was pou. H. G.
47 received H. G. as well as we
11:15 H. G. fell on them
16 shall be baptized with H. G.
24 Barnabas, full of H. G.
13:4 being sent forth by H. G.
9 filled with H. Ghost
52 disciples filled with H. G.
15:8 giving H. G. as he did
28 it seemed good to the H. G.
16:6 forbidden of H. G. to prea.
19:2 received H. G.? we have
not heard there be H. G.
6 hands on them, H. G. came
20:23 save that the H. G. witn.
28 H. G. made you overseers
21:11 thus saith the H. Ghost
28:25 spake H. G. by Esaias
Rom. 5:5 shed in hearts by H. G.
9:1 consci. bear, wit. in H. G.
14:17 kingd. of G. joy in H. G.
15:13 through power of H. G.
16 being sancti. by the H. G.
1 Cor. 2:13 words wh. H. G. tea.
6:19 body is temple of H. G.
12:3 Jesus is Lord, but by H. G.
2 Cor. 6:6 by the H. G. by love
13:14 communion of H. G.
1 Thes. 1:5 gospel came in H. G.
6 rec. word with joy of H. G.
2 Tim. 1:14 good k. by H. G.
Tit. 3:5 by renewing of H. G.
Heb. 2:4 with gifts of H. G.
3:7 H. G. saith, To-day if ye h.

6:4 made partakers of H. G.
9:8 H. Ghost this signifying
10:15 whereof H. G. is a witness
1 Pet. 1:12 H. G. sent fr. heaven
2 Pet. 1:21 as moved by H. G.
1 John 5:7 Fat. Word, and H. G.
Jude 20 beloved, pray. in H. G.

HOLY name.
Ps. 103:1 L. bless his h. n. 145:21

HOLY One.
Ps. 16:10 nor suffer H. O. to see
corruption, Acts 2:27; 13:35
Mark 1:24 I know th. who th. a.
the H. O. of G. Luke 4:34
Acts 3:14 ye denied the H. One

HOLY place.
Lev. 16:24 shall wash his flesh in h.
p.
Heb. 9:12 Christ entered h. p.
25 priest entered ev. year h. p.

HOLY places.
2 Chr. 8:11 bec. the places are h.
Ps. 68:35 terrible out of thy h. p.
Ezek. 21:2 drop thy word to. h. p.
Heb. 9:24 Ch. is not entered h. p.

Shall be HOLY.
Lev. 27:32 the tenth s. be h. unto
the L.
Deut. 23:14 theref. s. camp be h.
Ezek. 45:1 portion s. be h.
Joel 3:17 then s. Jerusalem be h.

HOLY Spirit.
Ps. 51:11 take not H. S. fr. me
Is. 63:10 rebel. and vexed H. S.
11 put his H. S. within him?
Luke 11:13 heav. Fa. give H. S.
Eph. 1:13 sealed wi. H. S. of pro.
4:30 grieve not the H. S. of God
1 Thes. 4:8 given us his H. S.

HOME.
1 Chr. 13:12 bring ark of G. h. 13
John 20:10 disc. went to their own
h.
1 Cor. 11:34 hunger, eat at h.
14:35 ask husbands at h.
2 Cor. 5:6 we are at h. in body
1 Tim. 5:4 to show piety at h.
Tit. 2:5 be discreet, keepers at h.

HONEST.
Luke 8:15 an h. and good heart
Acts 6:3 seven of h. report

Rom. 12:17 h. in sight of all
2 Cor. 8:21 h. th. in sight of L.
13:7 do that which is h.
Phil. 4:8 whatso. things are h.
1 Pet. 2:12 having conversat. h.

HONESTLY.
Rom. 13:13 walk h. as in the day
1 Thes. 4:12 walk h. toward them
Heb. 13:18 in all things to live h.

HONESTY.
1 Tim. 2:2 lead life god. and h.

HONEY.
Deut. 8:8 a land of oil-olive and
h. 2 K. 18:32
Job 20:17 sh. not see brooks of h.
Ps. 19:10 judgment sweeter than
h. 119:103
Prov. 24:13 eat h. is good, 25:16
25:27 not good to eat much h.
Cant. 4:11 h. and milk and ton.
5:1 honey-comb with my h.
Is. 7:15 butter and h. sh. he eat
22 butter and h. sh. ev. one eat
Rev. 10:9 thy mouth sweet as h.
10 in my mouth sweet as h.

HONEY-COMB.
Ps. 19:10 sweeter than h.-c.
Prov. 5:3 lips of str. wo. as h.-c.
16:24 pleasant words are as h.-c.
24:13 eat h.-c. sweet to thy taste
27:7 full soul loatheth a h. -c.
Luke 24:42 gave piece of h.-c.

HONOR, S.
Est 1:20 wives shall give to husb. h.
Ps. 8:5 crowned with h. Heb. 2:7, 9
21:5 h. and maj. thou laid on him
26:8 where thine h. dwelleth
49:20 in h. and understandeth
66:2 sing forth h. of his name
71:8 mouth filled with thy h.
Prov. 3:16 left hand riches and h.
4:8 she shall bring thee to h.
8:18 riches and h. are with me
11:16 gracious woman retain. h.
15:33 bef. h. is humility, 18:12
20:3 an h. to cease from strife
21:21 follow. mercy, findeth h.
22:4 fear of L. are riches and h.
25:2 h. of kings to search
26:1 h. is not seemly for a fool
8 so is he that giv. h. to a fool

29:23 h. shall uphold humble
31:25 and h. are her clothing
Ec. 6:2 to wh. G. hath given h.
10:1 that is in reputation for h.
Dan. 5:18 G. gave father glory and
h.
Mal. 1:6 where is mine h.?
Mat. 13:57 prophet not without
h. Mark 6:4; John 4:44
John 5:41 I rec. not h. from men
44 receive h. one of another
8:54 honor myself, h. is nothing
Acts 28:10 hon. us with many h.
rom. 2:7 seek glory and h.
10 h. to ev. man worketh good
9:21 of same lump ma. ves. to h.
12:10 in h. prefer. one another
13:7 render h. to wh. h. is due
1 Cor. 12:23 bestown abund. h. 24
2 Cor. 6:8 by h. and dishonor
Col 2:23 not in h. to satis. flesh
1 Thes. 4:4 to possess vessel in h.
1 Tim. 1:17 to G. be h. and glory
5:17 elders worthy of double h.
6:1 count masters worthy of h.
16 to whom be h. and power
2 Tim. 2:20 some to h. 21
Heb. 3:3 more h. than house
5:4 no man taketh h. to himself
1 Pet. 1:7 to praise. h. glory
3:7 h. to wife as weaker vessel
2 Pet. 1:17 from G. the Father h.
Rev. 4:9 beasts give glory and h.
11 to receive glory and h. 5:12
5:13 h. power, and might, be to
him, 7:12; 19:1
19:7 let us rejoice, give h.
21:24 glory and h. to it, 26

HONOR, Verb.
Ex. 20:12 h. thy father and thy
mother, Deut. 5:16; Mat.
15:4; 19:19; Mark 7:10; 10:19;
Luke 18:20; Eph. 6:2
Prov. 3:9 h. L. with thy substa.
Is. 29:13 with lips do h. me

HONORABLE.
2 Sam. 23:23 was more h. than the
thirty
Mark 15:43 Jos. an h. counsellor
Luke 14:8 lest more h. man be
Acts 13:50 J. stirred up h. wom.

17:12 h. women not few believ.
1 Cor. 4:10 ye are stro. ye are h.
12:23 members we think less h.
Heb. 13:4 marriage h. bed unde.

HOPE.

Ps. 78:7 might set their h. in G:
146:5 happy he whose h. is in L.
Prov. 10:28 h. of right. gladness
11:7 h. of unjust men perisheth
13:12 h. defer. mak. heart sick
14:32 the right. hath h. in death
19:18 chast. son wh. there is h.
26:12 h. of fool than him, 29:20
Ec. 9:4 joined to liv. there is h.
Jer. 17:7 blessed man whose h. L. is
31:17 there is h. in end, saith L.
Lam. 3:21 therefore have I h.
Joel 3:16 L. will be h. of his peo.
Zec. 9:12 turn, ye prisoners of h.
Acts 16:19 h. of gains was gone
23:6 h. and resurrection of dead
24:15 h. tow. G. which th. allow
26:6 judged for h. of the prom.
27:20 all h. we should be saved
28:20 for h. of Israel I am bound
Rom. 5:4 patience, experien. h.
5 h. maketh not ashamed
8:24 sa. by h. but h. seen is not h.
1 Cor. 9:10 be partaker of his h.
13:13 faith, h. charity , th. three
15:19 in this life only we ha. h.
2 Cor. 1:7 our h. of you is stead.
3:12 seeing that we have such h.
10:15 h. when faith is increased
Gal. 5:5 the Spirit wait for h.
Eph. 1:18 h. of his calling
2:12 no h. with. G. in world
4:4 as ye are called in one h.
Col. 1:5 h. laid up for you in hea.
23 not moved from h. of gospel
27 Christ in you, h. of glory
1 Thes. 1:3 patience of h. in Jes.
2:19 for what is our h. or joy?
4:13 as others who have no h.
1 Tim. 1:1 Lord Jesus, is our h.
Tit. 2:13 for that blessed h.
3:7 accord. to h. of eternal life
Heb. 3:6 rejoic. of h. firm to end
6:11 full assurance of h. to end
7:19 bringing in of a better h.
1 Pet. 1:3 begot. us to a lively h.

21 faith and h. might be in G.
3:15 reason of h. that is in you
1 John 3:3 man that hath this h.

In HOPE.

Ps. 16:9 rest in h. Acts 2:26
Rom. 4:18 ag. hope believ. in h.
5:2 rejoice in h. of glory of God
15:13 that ye may abound in h.
Tit. 1:2 in h. of eternal life

My HOPE.

Job 17::15 where is now my h.?
19:10 my h. hath he removed
31:24 if I have made gold my h.
Ps. 39:7 my h. is in thee
71:5 thou art my h. Jer. 17:17
119:116 asha. of my h. Phil. 1:20

HOPE, Verb.

Job 6:11 stren. that I should h.
Ps. 22:9 didst make me h.
38:15 L. do I h. thou wilt hear
42:5 h. thou in God, 11; 43:5
71:14 but I will h. continually
119:49 hast caused me to h.
81 h. in thy word, 114; 130:5
130:7 let Israel h. in L. 131:3
Lam. 3:24 there. will I h. in him
26 that man both h. and wait
Luke 6:34 them of whom ye h.
Acts 26:7 our tribes h. to come
Rom. 8:24 why doth he h. for?
25 if we h. for that we see not
Phil. 2:23 him I h. to send pres.
1 Pet. 1:13 be sober, and h.to end

HOSANNA.

Mat. 21:9 h. to the Son of D. 15
Mark 11:9 h. bles. is he that com.
h. in highest, 10; John 12:13

HOSPITALITY.

Rom. 12:13 giv. to h. 1 Tim. 3:2
Tit. 1:8 but a lover of h.
1 Pet. 4:9 use h. one to another

HOST.

Luke 2:13 heavenly h. prais. G.

HOSTAGES.

2 K. 14:14 Jehoash took h. and
returned to Sam. 2 Chr. 25:24

HOUR.

Mat. 9:22 whole from that h.
15:28 dau. whole from that h.
17:18 ch. was cured from that h.
20:3 went out about the third h.

12 these have wro. but one h.

24:44 such an h. as ye think not, 50; Luke 12:40, 46

25:13 know neither day nor h.

Mat. 27:46 ninth h. Jesus cried, Mark 15:34

Mark 13:11 given you in that h.

14:35 it pos. the h. might pass

15:25 third h. they cruci. him

Luke 10:21 in that h. J. rejoiced

12:39 what h. thief would come

John 4:52 them inq. he the h. he began to amend, at sev. h. fev. left

5:25 the h. is coming, 28; 16:32

7:30 h. was not yet come, 8:20

12:23 h. is come, Son be gl. 17:1

27 Fa. save me from this h. for this cause came I to this h.

13:1 Jes. knew his h. was come

Same HOUR.

Mat. 8:13 serv. was healed s. h.

10:19 given you s. h. Luke 12:12

Luke 7:21 same h. cured many

20:19 s. h. sou. to lay ha. on him

Acts 16:33 took them s. h. of the night

Rev. 11:13 s. h. was earthquake

HOUSE.

Jud. 16:30 the h. fell upon the lords

1 Sam. 25:28 L. make my lord sure h.

2 Sam. 5:8 lame and blind not co. to h.

Prov. 12:7 h. of righteous shall stand

Mat. 7:25 and beat upon that h. 27; Luke 6:48

12:25 every h. divided ag. itself

20 strong man's h. Mark 3:27

Mark 10:29 hath left h. or brethren

HOUSE, with father.

Est. 4:14 and f.'s h. be destroyed

John 2:16 make not my F.'s h. a house of merchandise

14:2 in F.'s h. are many mans.

HOUSE of God.

Gen. 28:17 none oth. but h. of G.

Ps. 84:10 door-keeper in h. of G.

HOUSE, with Lord.

1 Sam. 1:7 she went to h. of L.

24 Hannah bro. him unto the

h. of the L. 2 K. 12:4, 9, 13; 22:4; 2 Chr. 34:14

Ps. 23:6 dw. in h. of L. for ever

27:4 dwell in h. of L. all my life

92:13 be planted in h. of Lord

MY HOUSE.

1 K. 20:15 all things that are in my h. Is. 39:4

Job 17:13 the grave is my h.

Ps. 101:2 in my h. wi. perf. heart.

Is. 3:7 in my h. is neither bread

Own HOUSE.

1 Tim. 3:4 ruleth well his o. h.

5 know not how to rule o. h.

5:8 especially for those of o. h.

Heb. 3:6 Ch. as a Son over o.h.

HOUSES.

Ex. 12:7 upper door-posts of the h.

1 Tim. 3:12 deacons rul. h. well

HOUSEHOLD.

Prov. 31:27 look well to ways of her h.

Acts 16:15 baptized and her h.

1 Cor. 1:16 baptized h. of Steph.

Gal. 6:10 are of the h. of faith

HUMBLE.

Job 22:29 he shall save h. person

Ps. 9:12 forgetteth not cry of h.

10:12 O Lord, forget not the h.

17 L. hast heard desire of h.

34:2 the h. shall hear thereof

69:32 h. shall hear this and be

Prov. 16:19 better be of h. spirit

29:23 honor shall uphold the h.

Is. 57:15 with him of h. spirit, to revive spirit of h.

Jam. 4:6 giv. gra. to h. 1 Pet. 5:5

HUMBLE, Verb.

Mat. 18:4 h. himself, 23:12

2 Cor. 12:21 my God will h. me

Jam. 4:10 h. your. in sight of L.

1 Pet. 5:6 h. yourselves under G.

HUMILITY.

Prov. 15:33 bef. honor is h. 18:12

22:4 by h. are riches and honor

Acts 20:19 serving L. with h.

Col. 2:18 no man begu. you in h.

23 in will-worship and h.

1 Pet. 5:5 and be clothed with h.

HUNGER, Verb.

Mat. 5:6 blessed are they that h.

after righteous. Luke 6:21
Luke 6:25 woe to full, ye shall h.
John 6:35 com. to me sh. never h.
Rom. 12:20 if enemy h. feed him
1 Cor. 4:11 we both h. and thirst
11:34 if any man h. let him eat
Rev. 7:16 they shall h. no more

HUNGERED.

Mat. 4:2 afterwards a h. Luke 4:2
12:3 what David did when he was
a h. Mark 2:25; Luke 6:3
25:35 I h. and ye gave me meat

HUNGRY.

Ps. 107:9 filleth h. soul with
goodness
36 there he maketh h. to dwell
146:7 Lord giveth food to the h.
Prov. 6:30 to satis. soul when h.
25:21 if enemy be h. give bread
Is. 8:21 hardly bestead and h.
when h. shall fret themselv.
9:20 snatch on right hand, be h.

HUSBAND.

Ex. 4:25 bloody h. art thou, 26
Rom. 7:2 h. dead she is loosed, 3
1 Cor. 7:3 h. render to wife due
benevolence, like. wife to h.
4 h. hath not power of own
11 let not h. put away his wife
14 unbeliev. h. is sanctified by
wife, and wife sancti. by h.
2 Cor. 11:2 espoused to one h.
Gal. 4:27 more chil. than hath h.
Eph. 5:23 the h. is head of wife
1 Tim. 3:2 h. of one wi. Tit. 1:6

Her HUSBAND.

2 Sam. 11:26 wife of U. heard h.
h. was dead, she mo. for h. h.
Prov. 12:4 virt. wife cro. to h. h.
31:11 heart of h. h. trust in her
23 her h. is known in the gates
28 h. h. riseth up and prai. her
Ezek. 16:45 loatheth her h. and
children
Mat. 1:19 Jos. her h. being just
Luke 16:18 mar. her aw. fr. h. h.
Rom. 7:2 bound by law to h. h.
1 Cor. 7:2 woman have h. own h.
10 let not wife depart fr. her h.
11 be reconciled to her h.
34 how she may please her h.

39 bound as long as her h.
Eph. 5:33 wife reverence her h.
Rev. 21:2 bride adorned for her h.

My HUSBAND.

Gen. 29:32 my h. will love me
34 will my h. be joined to me
30:18 given maiden to my h.
Deut. 25:7 my h. brother refuseth
2 Sam. 14:5 I am a widow, my h.
dead, 2 K. 4:1
Hos. 2:7 and return to my first h.

Thy HUSBAND.

Gen. 3:16 desire shall be to t. h.
Num. 5:19 anoth. inst. of t. h. 20
2 K. 4:26 is it well with thy h.
Is. 54:5 thy Maker is thy h.
Acts 5:9 that have buried t. h.
1 Cor. 7:16 thou shalt save thy h.

HUSBANDS.

1 Cor. 14:35 ask their h. at home
Eph. 5:22 wives submit to h. 24
25 h. love your wives, Col. 3:19
Col. 3:18 wives, submit to own h.
1 Tim. 3:12 deac. h. of one wife
Tit. 2:4 teach women to love h.
5 be obedient to their own h.
1 Pet. 3:1 in subjection to own h.
7 ye h. dwell with them accor.

HYMN, S.

Eph. 5:19 spea. in psalms and h.
Col. 3:16 admo. in psalms and h.

HYPOCRISY, IES.

Mat. 23:28 within are full of h.
Mark 12:15 he knowing their h.
Luke 12:1 leaven of Pharisees h.
1 Tim. 4:2 speaking lies in h.
1 Pet. 2:1 aside all malice and h.
Jam. 3:17 wisdom pure witho. h.

HYPOCRITE.

Job 8:13 the h. hope shall perish
17:8 innocent stir up against h.
20:5 joy of h. but for a moment
27:8 what is the hope of the h.?
34:30 that the h. reign not, lest
Prov. 11:9 h. with mouth destroy
Is. 9:17 for every one is a h.
Mat. 7:5 h. first cast out beam
Luke 6:42 thou h. cast beam out
13:15 h. doth not each loose ox?

HYPOCRITES.

Mat. 6:2 not sound trump. as h.

5 thou shalt not be as h.
16 when ye fast. be not as h.
15:7 ye h. well did Esaias pro-
phesy, Mark 7:6
16:3 O h. ye discern face of sky,
Luke 12:56
22:18 Why tempt ye me, ye h.
23:13 Phari. h. ye shut kingd.
ag. men, 14, 15, 23, 25, 26, 29
24:51 ap. him portion with h.
Luke 11:44 scribes and Phari. h.

I.

IDLE.
Ex. 5:8 be i. therefore they cry
Prov. 19:15 i. soul suffer hunger
Mat. 12:36 ev. i. word men speak
1 Tim. 5:13 they learn to be i.
IDLENESS.
Prov. 31:27 eateth not bread of i.
IDOLATER, S.
1 Cor. 5:10 with the covet. or i.
6:9 i. not inherit kingdom of G.
10:7 neither be i. as some were
Eph. 5:5 who is i. hath any inh.
Rev. 21:8 i. have part in the lake
22:15 murderers and i. and liars
IDOLATRY, IES.
Acts 17:16 city wholly given to i.
1 Cor. 10:14 beloved, flee from i.
Gal. 5:20 the works of the flesh i.
Col. 3:5 covetousness, which is i.
1 Pet. 4:3 walked in abomina. i.
IDOL.
2 Chr. 33:7 set i. in house of God
Acts 7:41 offered sacrifice to i.
1 Cor. 8:4 i. noth. in world, 10:19
IDOLS.
Lev. 19:4 turn not to i.; 26 no i.
26:30 cast your carcasses on i.
Ezek. 6:6 your i, may be broken
1 Cor. 8:1 touching th. offered to
i. 4, 10; 10:19, 28; Rev. 2:14, 20
12:2 Gentiles carried to dumb i.
2 Cor. 6:16 agree. of G. with i.?
1 Thes. 1:9 turned to God from i.
1 John 5:21 keep yoursel. from i.
Rev. 9:20 not wor. devils and i.
IGNORANCE.
Is. 56:10 all i. they are all dumb
63:16 though Abram be i. of us

Acts 4:13 perceived they were i.
Rom. 1:13 I would not have you
i. brethren, 1 Cor. 10:1; 12:1;
2 Cor. 1:8; 1 Thes. 4:13
10:3 being i. of God's righteous.
11:25 sh. be i. of this mystery
1 Cor. 14:38 man i. let him be i.
2 Cor. 2:11 not i. of Satan's devi.
Heb. 5:2 have compassion on i.
2 Pet. 3:5 they willingly are i.
8 be not i. of this one thing
IMAGE.
Gen. 1:26 let us make man in our
i. 27; 9:6
Lev. 26:1 nor rear up a standing
i. Deut. 16:22
2 Cor. 3:18 changed into same i.
4:4 Christ is i. of God, Col. 1:15
Col. 3:10 i. of him that created
Heb. 1:3 express i. of his person
10:1 not the very i. of things
Rev. 13:14 make i. to the beast
15 give life to the i. of beast
14:9 if any man worship i.
11 have no rest, who worsh. i.
Molten IMAGE.
Deut. 9:12 made them a m. i.
IMAGINATION, S.
Gen. 6:5 i. of his heart was evil
Deut. 29:19 though I walk in i.
1 Chr. 28:9 understands all the i.
29:18 keep this in i. of heart
Prov. 6:18 heart th. devis. wic. i.
Jer. 23:17 ev. one walketh after i.
Luke 1:51 scattered proud in i.
Rom. 1:21 became vain in th. i.
2 Cor. 10:5 casting down i.
IMAGINE.
Zec. 7:10 let none i. evil, 8:17
Zcts 4:25 do peo. i. vain things?
IMMEDIATELY.
Mat. 26:74 i. the cock crew, Luke
22:60; John 18:27
Mark 1:31 i. the fever left her
4:15 Satan cometh i. and taketh
Lu. 6:49 i. fell; 8:44 i. stanched
19:11 kingdom of God i. appear
John 5:9 and i. man was whole
Acts 12:23 i. angel of L. smote
16:26 i. all doors were opened
Gal. 1:16 i. conferred not

Rev. 4:2 and i. was in the Spirit

IMMORTAL.
1 Tim. 1:17 K. eternal, i. invis.

IMMORTALITY.
Rom. 2:7 to them who seek for i.
1 Cor. 15:53 mortal must put on i.
54 mortal shall have put on i.
1 Tim. 6:16 i. dwelling in light
2 Tim. 1:10 brought i. to light

IMPOSSIBLE.
Mat. 17:20 nothing i. unto you
19:26 with men is i. Mark 10:27;
Luke 18:27
Luke 1:37 with G. noth. i. 18:27
Heb. 6:4 i. for those enlightened
18 it was i. for G. to lie
11:6 without faith i. to please G.

IMPUTE, ED.
Rom. 4:8 Lord will not i. sin
11 righteous. mi. be i. to them
22 therefore it was i. to him for
righteousness, 23; Jam. 2:23
24 to whom it shall be i.
5:13 sin not i. wh. th. is no law

IMPUTETH, ING.
Rom. 4:6 to whom G. i. righte.
2 Cor. 5:19 not i. tresp. to them

INCENSE.
Ex. 30:8 shall burn perpetual i.
Mal. 1:11 ev. place i. be offered
Luke 1:10 without at time of i.
Rev. 8:3 given to him much i.
4 smoke of i. ascended bef. G.

Sweet INCENSE.
Ex. 25:6 spices for sweet i. 35:8,
28; Num. 4:16
31:11 oil and s. i. for holy place
39:38 brought oil and s. i. to M.

INCORRUPTIBLE.
Rom. 1:23 changed glory of i. G.
1 Cor. 9:25 to obtain an i. crown
15:52 the dead shall be raised i.
1 Pet. 1:4 an inheri. i. undefiled
23 born of i. seed by word of G.

INCREASE, Substantive.
1 Cor. 3:6 I planted, G. gave i. 7
Eph. 4:16 maketh i. of the body
Col. 2:19 body incr. wi. i. of G.

INCREASE, Verb.
Dan. 11:39 he shall i. with glory
Luke 17:5 said, Lord, i. our faith

John 3:30 must i. I must decrea.
2 Cor. 9:10 i. fruits of righteous.
1 Thes. 3:12 L. make y. i. in love
2 Tim. 2:16 i. to more ungodli.

INCREASED.
Acts 6:7 and the word of God i.
16:5 churches i. in number daily
2 Cor. 10:15 hope when faith is i.
Rev. 3:17 rich, and i. with goods

INDEED.
Mat. 3:11 I i. baptize, Mark 1:8;
Luke 3:16
Mark 11:32 he was a prophet i.
Luke 23:41 i. just.; 24:34 risen i.
Rom. 8:7 law, neither i. can be
1 Tim. 5:3 hon. widows are wi. i.
5 that is widow i. desolate, 16

INDIGNATION.
2 K. 3:27 great i. against Israel
Rev. 14:10 poured out cup of i.

INFALLIBLE.
Acts 1:3 showed hims. by i. proo.

INFANT, S.
1 Sam. 15:3 slay man, wo. and i.
Job 3:16 as i. wh. never saw light
Is. 65:20 no more an i. of days
Hos. 13:16 i. be dashed in pieces
Luke 18:15 they bro. i. to him

INFIDEL.
2 Cor. 6:15 that believ. with i.?
1 Tim. 5:8 is worse than an i.

INFIRMITIES.
2 Cor. 11:30 things conc. mine i.
12:5 I gl. not, but in mine i. 9
10 I take pleasure in mine i.
1 Tim. 5:23 use wine for thine i.
Heb. 4:15 touched with feel. of i.

INGATHERING.
Ex. 23:16 feast of i. end of year

INHABITED.
Ex. 16:35 till th. came to land i.
Lev. 16:22 iniqu. to a land not i.
Ezek. 12:10 cities i. be laid waste

INHABITERS.
Rev. 8:13 woe, woe, to i. of earth
12:12 woe to i. of earth and sea

INHERIT.
Gen. 15:8 sh. I kn. th. I sh. i. it?
Num. 18:24 given it to LEv. to i.
Deut. 1:38 shall cause Is. to i. it
Jud. 11:2 not i. in fa.'s house

I

1 Sam. 2:8 i. the throne of glory
Ps. 25:13 his seed. sh. i. the earth
Prov. 3:35 the wise shall i. glory
  8:21 those who love me, i. sub.
Mat. 19:29 sh. i. everlasting life
  25:34 come i. the kingdom pre.
Mark 10:17 that I may i. eternal
  life, Luke 10:25; 18:18
1 Cor. 6:9 unrigh. not i. king. G.
  10 nei. extortion. i. Gal. 5:21
  15:50 flesh and blood cannot i.
  kingd. of G. nor cor. i. inc.
Heb. 6:12 thro' faith i. promises
1 Pet. 3:9 ye should i. blessing
Rev. 21:7 he overcom. i. things

INHERITANCE.
Ex. 15:17 plant th. in thine i.
Jer. 10:16 Is. rod of his i. 51:19
Ezek 46:18 not take people's i.
Mat. 21:38 let us seize on his i.
Eph. 1:11 in whom obtained i.
Col. 1:12 partakers of i. of saints
  3:24 ye shall rec. the rew. of i.
Heb. 1:4 he hath by i. obtained
  9:15 promise- of eternal i.
1 Pet. 1:4 begot. i. incorruptible

INIQUITY.
1 Sam. 20:8 if th. be in me i. slay
me
2 Sam. 24:10 to take away i. of thy
servant, 1 Chr. 21:8
2 Chr. 6:30 is there i. in my tongue?
11:6 G. exact. less th. i. deserv.
  14 if i. be in thy hand
  15:5 thy mouth uttereth thine i.
  16 filthy is man wh. drink. i.
  22:23 put away i. from thy tab.
  31:11 i. to be punished, 28
  33:9 nor is there i. in me
  34:32 if I have done i.
Ps. 7:3 if be i. in my hands
  32:2 to whom L. imputeth not i.
  5 thou forgavest i. of my sin
  36:3 words of his mouth are i.
  39:11 dost correct man for i.
  66:18 if I regard i. in my heart
  85::2 forgiven i. of thy people
  119:133 let not i. have dominion
Prov. 16:6 by truth i. is purged
  22:8 soweth i. shall reap vanity
Is. 40:2 her i. is pardoned

Jer. 2:22 thine i. is marked before
me
13:22 greatn. of i. are thy skirts
14:20 acknowledge i. of fathers
16:10 our i. 17 i. hid from eyes
30:14 multi. of i. 15; Hos. 9:7
32:18 recompensest i. of fathers
Lam. 2:14 not discovered thine i.
Ezek. 28:15 till i. found in thee
Hos. 12:8 they shall find no i. in me
13:12 i. of Ephraim bound up
14:1 thou hast fallen by thine i.
Mal. 2:6 i not found in his lips
1 Cor. 13:6 rejoiceth not in i. but
Tit. 2:14 might redeem us fr. i.
Heb. 1:9 and thou hast hated i.

Mine INIQUITY.
1 Sam. 20:1 what is mine i.?
2 Sam. 22:24 I kept myself from
  mine i. Ps. 18:23
Job 7:21 not take away m. i.
10:6 thou inquirest after m. i.
  14 not acquit me from mine i.
  14:17 thou sewest up m. i.
  31:33 hiding m. i. in my bosom
Ps. 25:11 pardon m. i. it is great
  31:10 stre. faileth beca. of m. i.
  32:5 mine i. have I not hid
  51:2 wash me thoro. fr. m. i.

INN.
Luke 2:7 no room for them in i.

INNOCENCY.
Gen. 20:5 in the i. of my hands
Ps. 26:6 wash my hands in i.
  73:13 I washed hands in i.
Da. 6:22 i. was found in me

INSTRUCT.
Deut. 4:36 hear, th. he mi. i. thee
Neh. 9:20 gavest thy S. to i. th.
Ps. 16:7 my reins also i. me
  32:8 I will i. thee and teach th.
Is. 28:26 God doth i. him
1 Cor. 2:16 that he may i. him

INSTRUCTED.
Prov. 21:11 the wise is i. he
receiveth
Is. 8:11 L. spake thus and i. me
  40:14 i. him and taught him
Mat. 14:8 being bef. i. of her
mother
Acts 18:25 was i. in way of Lord

Rom. 2:18 being i. out of law
Phil. 4:12 in all things, I am i.
INSTRUCTION.
Ps. 50:17 seeing thou hatest i.
Prov. 1:2 to know wisdom and i.
3 to receive the i. of wisdom
7 fools des. wisdom and i. 15:5
8 son, hear i. of thy father, 4:1
4:13 take hold of i.
8:10 receive my i.; 33 hear i.
9:9 give i. to a wise man
10:17 in way of life that keep. i.
12:1 loveth i. loveth knowledge
13:1 wise son heareth father's i.
18 shame to him that refus. i.
15:32 refus. i. despiseth his soul
33 fear of L. is the i. of wisd.
16:22 but the i. of fools is folly
19:20 hear counsel and rec. i.
27 cease to hear i.
23:12 apply thy heart to i.
23 buy also i. and understand.
Jer. 17:23 not hear nor rec. i.
32:33 not hearkened to rec. i.
Ezek. 5:15 a repro. a taunt, an i.
Zep. 3:7 surely thou wilt rec. i.
2 Tim. 3:16 scrip. is profitable i.
INSTRUMENT.
Ps. 33:2 wi. i. of ten strings, 92:3
144:9 sing new song, O G. on i.
Is. 28:27 not thr. with thresh. i.
41:15 make th. sharp thresh. i.
Ezek. 33:2 song of one play on i.
INSTRUMENTS.
Ps. 68:25 players on i. followed
150:4 with stringed i.
Ec. 2:8 musical i. of all sorts
Is. 38:20 sing song to stringed i.
Hab. 3:19 singing on stringed i.
INSURRECTION.
Ps. 64:2 i. of workers of iniquity
Mark 15:7 bound th. th. made i.
who had commit. mur. in i.
INTEGRITY.
Gen. 20:5 i. of my heart, 6
Job 2:3 still he holdeth fast his i.
Ps. 7:8 according to my i. in me
25:21 i. and uprightn. preserve
26:1 I have walked in mine i.
11 as for me, I will walk in i.
41:12 thou uphold. me in my i.

78:72 fed accord. to i. of heart
Prov. 11:3 i. of upright guide th.
19:1 poor that walketh in i.
20:7 just man walketh in his i.
INTENT, S.
1 Cor. 10:6 i. we should not lust
Eph. 3:10 i. that now to princi.
Heb. 4:12 discerner of i. of heart
INTERCESSION, S.
Is. 53:12 i. for transgressors
Jer. 7:16 ne. lift cry, nor make i.
27:18 let th. now make i. to L.
Rom. 8:26 Sp. maketh i. 27, 34
11:2 maketh i. to G. ag. Israel
Heb. 7:25 liveth to make i.
1 Tim. 2:1 prayers and i. be ma.
INTERMISSION.
Lam. 3:49 ceaseth not without i.
INTERPRET.
Gen. 41:8 none could i. to Phar.
12 accord. to dream he did i.
1 Cor. 12:30 do all i.; 14:5 exc. i.
14:13 he may i.; 27 let one i.
INTERPRETATION.
Gen. 40:5 i. of dream, 41:11
12 Joseph said, This is the i.
of it, 18; Dan. 4:24; 5:26
Prov. 1:6 unders. proverb and i.
Dan. 2:45 dream is certain, and i.
sure
4:19 i. thereof be to thine ene.
1 Cor. 12:10 another i. of tongues
14:26 everyone of you ha. an i.
Heb. 7:2 by i. king of righteous.
2 Pet. 1:20 no prophecy of pri. i.
INTERPRETATIONS.
Gen. 40:8 do not i. belong to G.?
INTERPRETED.
Mat. 1:23 being i. is, G. with us
Mark 5:41 wh. is, being i. damsel
15:22 being i. place of a skull
34 i. my God, my God
John 1:38 i. master; 41 i. Christ
Acts 4:36 i. son of consolation
INTERPRETER, S.
Gen. 42:23 Joseph spake to th. by i.
1 Cor. 14:28 if there be no i. keep
INTERPRETING.
Dan. 5:12 i. of dreams found in
INVENTIONS.
Ps. 99:8 tookest veng. of their i.

106:29 prov. him to anger wi. i.
INVISIBLE.
Rom. 1:20 i. things clearly seen
Col. 1:15 image of the i. God
16 heaven and earth, vi. and i.
1 Tim. 1:17 to King immortal, i.
Heb. 11:27 seeing him who is i.
INVITED.
Est. 5:12 to-morrow am I i.
IRON, Substantive.
Deut. 4:20 L. brought you out of
the i. furnace, 1 K. 8:51; Jer. 11:4
1 Sam. 17:7 spear's head weighed
609 shekels of i.
Ps. 2:9 break them with rod of i.
Prov. 27:17 i. sharpeneth i.
Is. 60:17 for i. I will bring silver
ISAAC.
Gen. 17:19 his name I. 21:3, 12
22:2 take thine only son I. 9
21:4 take a wife for I. 14
23:1 I called Jacob, blessed h.
31:42 fear of I. had been with
48:15 God before wh. I walked
Heb. 11:20 I. blessed Jacob, Jam.
2:21
ISAIAH, or ESAIS.
2 K. 20:1 I. came to him, Is. 38:1
2 Chr. 26:22 acts did I. wr. 32:32
Is. 20:3 my serv. I hath walked
ISHMAEL.
Gen. 16:11 call name I. 15, 16
17:18 O that I. mi. live, 20, 25
28:9 then went Esau unto I.
ISHMAELITES.
Gen. 37:27 let us sell him to I.
ISLAND.
Acts 27:26 must be cast on certain
i.
28:1 knew i. was called Melita
7 possess. of Chief man of i.
ISLANDS.
Is. 11:11 receive people from i.
ISLE.
Rev. 1:9 was in i. called Patmos
ISRAEL.
Gen. 32:28 na. no more J. but I.
35:10 I sh. be name, 1 K. 18:31
47:31 I. bowed him. on bed's h.
Ps. 25:22 redeem I. out of all troub.
Jer. 50:20 iniquity of I. sought, 51:5

Rom. 10:19 did not I. know?
11:2 intercession ag. I. 7, 26
ISRAELITE.
Rom. 11:1 I also am an I.
ISSACHAR.
Gen. 30:18 L. called his name I.
ISSUES.
Ps. 68:20 to God belong the i.
Prov. 4:23 out of heart are i.
IVORY.
Rev. 18:12 no man buy. ves. of i.
J.

JACOB.
Gen. 25:26 he was called J. 27
Num. 23:7 curse me, J. and defy
Ps. 20:1 God of J. 46:7; 75:9; 76:6
81:1; 84:8; 94:7; 114:7; 132:2;
146:5
87:2 Z. more than dwell. of J.
135:4 L. chos. J. Is. 10:21; 14:1
Is. 2:3 of J. 41:21; Mic. 4:2; Mat.
22:32; Mark 12:26; Luke 20:37;
Acts 3:13; 7:32, 46
27:9 iniq. of J. purged, 48:20
41:5 call himself by name J. 23
58:14 feed with heritage of J.
Amos 7:2 by whom sh. J. arise? 5
Mal. 1:2 J. yet I loved J. Ro. 9:13
John 4:6 J.'s well was there
Rom. 11:26 turn ungodl. from J.
Heb. 11:20 by faith Is. bles. J. 21
JAILER.
Acts 16:23 charging j. to keep
JAIRUS.
Mark 5:22 J. a ruler, Luke 8:41
JAMES.
Mat. 4:21 J. and John, Mark 1:19
10:2 J. son of Zeb. Mark 3:17
3 J. son, Mark 3:18; Acts 1:13
13:55 J. and Joses, Mark 6:3;
15:40; 16:1; Luke 24:10
17:1 Peter, J. and John, Mark
5:37; 9:2; 13:3; 14:33; Luke
8:51; Acts 1:13
Mark 10:41 displ. wi. J. Lu. 5:10
Acts 12:2 Herod killed J. wi. sw.
17 show to I. 15:13; 21:18
1 Cor. 15:7 after that seen of J.
Gal. 1:19 save J. Lord's brother
2:12 certain came from J. 9

JASPER.
Rev. 4:3 to look upon like a j.
21:18 build. of wall of city was j.

JAVELIN.
1 Sam. 18:10 j. in S. hand, 19:9

JAWBONE.
Jud. 15:15 Samson found j. of ass

JEALOUS.
Ex. 20:5 I the Lord thy G. am a
j. God, 34:14; Deut. 4:24;
5:9; 6:15; Jos. 24:19
2 Cor. 11:2 for I am j. over you

JEALOUSY.
2 Cor. 11:2 jealous with godly j.

JEHOASH, or JOASH.
2 K. 11:21 J. seven years old

JEHOIAKIM.
2 K. 23:34 name to J. 2 Chr. 36:4

JEHOSHAPHAT.
1 K. 4:3, 17; 15:24' 1 Chr. 18:15
22:2 J. came to Ahab. 2 K. 3:14

JEHOSHUA.
Num. 13:16 Oshea J. 1 Chr. 7:27

JEHOVAH.
Ex. 6:3 by J. was I not known
Ps. 83:18 wh. name alone is J.
Is. 12:2 Lord J. is my strength
26:4 the Lord J. is everlasting

JEHU.
Hos. 1:4 blood of Jezreel on J.

JEREMIAH.
2 K. 23:31; 24:18; Jer. 52:1
2 Chr. 35:25 J. lamented for Jos.
36:12 humb. bef. J. 22; Ezr. 1:1
Neh. 10:2 J. sealed, 12:1, 12, 34
Jer. 1:1 words of J. son of Hilk.
51:64 thus far are words of J.
Mat. 2:17 was spoken by J. 27:9
16:14 others say thou art J.

JERICHO.
Jos. 2:1 view J. 3:16; 6:1; 24:11
Heb. 11:30 walls of J. fell

JEROBOAM.
1 K. 11:28 J. mighty man of valor

JEROBOAM, with Nebat.
1 K. 11: 26; 12:15; 16:3, 26, 31;
21:22; 22:52; 2 K. 3:3; 9:9;
10:29; 13:2, 11; 14:24; 15:9,
18, 24, 28; 2 Chr. 10:15

JERUSALEM.
Jos. 18:28 wh. is J. Jud. 19:10

2 Sam. 24:16 on J. 1 Chr. 21:15
1 K. 3:1 end of build. wall of J.
11:13 J. I have chosen, 2 K.
23:27; 2 Chr. 6:6
Ps. 51:18 build walls of J. 79:1, 3;
147:2
122:3 J. is builded as a city
6 pray for peace of J. 128:5
125:2 as mount. round about J.
137:6 pref. not J. abo. ch. joy, 7
Is. 31:5 defend J. 33:20
40:2 sp. comfortably to J. 52:9
62:1 for J.'s sake not rest till, 7
Jer. 39:8 walls of J. 44:2, 6
Joel 3:1 bring captivi. of J. 20;
Zec. 1:17 choose J. 2:12; 8:3
Mal. 3:4 offering of J. sh. be pie.
Mat. 3:5 out to him J. Mark 1:5
16:21 how he must go to J.
Luke 2:22 parents bro. him to J.
13:4 abo. all dwelt in J.,?
33 prophet perish out of J.
John 4:20 in J. men ou. to wors.
12:12 heard Jesus coming to J.
Acts 9:2 bound unto J. 20:22
21:31 all J. in uproar, 22:18
Rom. 15:31 service for J. accept.
1 Cor. 16:3
Gal. 4:25 J. wh. now is; 26 J. ab.
Rev. 3:12 the new J. 21:2,,10

O JERUSALEM.
Mat. 23:37 O J. J. Luke 13:34

JESSE.
Ruth 4:17 O, fath. of J. Mat. 1:5
Acts 13:22 found David son of J.

JESUS.
Mat. 1:21 shalt call his name J.

JESUS, for Joshua.
Acts 7:45 brought in with J. into
Heb. 4:8 if J. had given th. rest

JEW.
Est. 3:4 told them he was a J.
Rom. 1:16 to J. first, 2:9, 10
Gal. 2:14 a J. livest as Gentiles

King of the JEWS.
Mat. 2:2 born K. of the J.?
27:11 art thou K. of t. J.? Mar.
15:;2 Luke 23:3; John 18:33
29 hail, K. of the J. Mar. 15:18;
John 19:3
37 this is K. of the J. Mark

J

123

15:26; Luke 23:38; Jo. 19:19
Mark 15:9 K. of the J. John 18:39
12 whom ye call K. of the J.
Luke 23:37 if thou be K. of the J.
John 19:21 I am K. of the J.

JEZEBEL.

1 K. 16:31 took to wife J. 18:4
Rev. 2:20 sufferest that wom. J.

JEZREEL.

2 Sam. 2:9 Ish-bosh, king over J.
Hos. 1:4 avenge blood of J.

JOAB.

2 Sam. 2:18 of Zeruiah, J. 22, 24

JOB.

Job 1:1 man whose name was J.
Jam. 5:11 heard of patience of J.

JOEL.

Joel 1:1 the word came to J.
Acts 2:16 spok. by the proph. J.

JOHN, son of Zacharias.

Mat. 3:4 J. had raim. Mark 1:6
Mat. 3:14 J. came, but J. for him
14:10 behe. J. Mark 6:16; Lu. 9:9
21:26 hol. J. Mat. 11:32; Lu. 20:6
Luke 1:13 call his name J. 60
9:7 J. was risen from the dead
John 1:6 a man sent from God, J.
Acts 13:24 when J. first preached

JOHN, the Apostle.

Mat. 4:21 James and J. he called
th. 10:2; Mark 1:19; 3:17
Luke 22:8 Pet. and J. to prepare
Acts 3:1 Peter and J. went
12:2 Herod killed brother of J.
Rev. 1:1 signifi. it to serv. J. 4, 9
21:2 J. saw the new Jerusalem

JOINTS.

Col. 2:19 body by j. knit togeth.
Heb. 4:12 divid. of j. and marrow

JOINT-HEIRS.

Rom. 8:17 and j.-h. with Christ

JONAH.

2 K. 14:25 spake by his servant J.
Jon. 1:3 J. rose up, 7, 15, 17
4:6 the gourd to come over J.
Mat. 12:39, 41; 16:4; Lu. 11:29, 30

JONATHAN.

Jud. 18:30 J. and his sons were
1 Sam. 13:2 men were with J. 22
14:13 J. climbed on hands
20:13 the Lord do so to J. 16, 37

2 Sam. 1:4 S. and J. are dead, 26
4:4 J. had a son was lame, 9:3
Jer. 40:8 J. came to Gedal. to M.

JORDAN.

Gen. 13:11 Lot chose plain of J.
Jos. 3:15 J. overfloweth banks
4:3 stones out of midst of J.
22:25 made J. a border betw. us
Jud. 3:28 fords of J. 7:24; 12:5
2 Sam. 19:15 king returned to J.
2 K. 2:13 Elisha stood by J.
5:10 saying, Wash in J. seven
Job-40:23 trust. can draw up J.
Ps. 42:6 remember fr. land of J.
114:3 J. was driven back, 5
Jer. 12:5 do in swelling of J.?
49:19 from swelling of J. 50:44
Zec. 11:3 pride of J. is spoiled
Mat. 3:6 in J. Mark 1:5, 9

JOSEPH.

Gen. 30:24 she called his name J.
37:5 J. dreamed a dream
39:5 Egypt.'s house for J.'s sake
40:9 butler told his dream to J.
49:22 J. is a fruitful bough, 26
50:7 J. went up to bury father
Deut. 33:13 J. blessed be his land
1 Chr. 5:2 the birthright was J.
Ps. 80:1 leadest J. like a flock
105:17 J. who was sold for a ser.
Ezek. 37:16 for J. stick of Ephr.
47:13 J. shall have two portions
48:32 one gate of J. gate of B.
Amos 6:6 grieved for afflict. of J.
Acts 7:9 patriarchs sold J. 13, 14
Heb. 11:21 J. blessed sons of J. 22

JOSEPH, husband of Mary.

Mat. 1:16; 2:13; Luke 2:4; 3:23;
4:22: John 1:45; 6:42

JOSEPH, name of divers men.

Num. 13:7 of Igal, son of J.
Mat. 27:57 J. of Arim. 59; Mark
15:43; 45; Lu. 23:50; Jo. 19:38
Luke 3:24 was son of J. 26, 30
Acts 1:23 two, J. called Barsabas

**JOSHUA, JEHOSHUA,
OSHEA.**

Ex. 17:13 J. discomfited Amalek
24:13 Moses and his minister J.
Jos. 1:10 J. commanded officers,
2:1 to 24:31

124

1 Sam. 6:14 into field of J. 18
1 K. 16:34 wh. he spake by J.
Hag. 1:1 J. son of Josed. 12, 14
Zec. 3:1 showed me J. h.-priest
6:11 set crowns on head of J.

JOURNEYED.
Gen. 12:9 Ab. j. going south, 20:1
13:11 Lot j. east; 33:17 Jacob j.
35:5 Israel j. toward Beth-el
Ex. 40:37 th. j. not, Num. 9:21
Num. 9:17 children of Israel j. 18
Acts 9:3 as S. j. he came near Da.
7 men j. with him stood, 26:13

JOY Substantive.
1 Chr. 12:40 there was j. in Israel
Ezr. 3:13 not discern shout of j.
Neh. 8:10 j. of L. is your strength
Est. 8:16 light, j. and honor
Job 8:19 this is the j. of his way
Ps. 16:11 presence fulness of j.
27:6 offer in tabem. sacrifi. of j.
39:5 j. cometh in the morning
43:4 I go to G. my exceeding j.
51:12 restore to me j. of salva.
67:4 be glad and sing for j.
105:43 bro. forth people with j.
126:5 sow in tears sh. reap in j.
Prov. 12:20 counsel. of peace is j.
14:10 stranger not intermed. j.
17:21 father of a fool hath no j.
23:24 beget, wise child have j.
Ec. 2:10 with, not heart from j.
26 God giveth knowled. and j.
Is. 9:3 increased j. accord. to j.
17 L. sh. have no j. in yo. men
12:3 with j. shall ye draw water
16:10 j. taken out plentiful field
24:8 j. harp ceas.; 11 j. is dark.
29:19 meek sh. incre. th. j. in L.
35:2 rej. even with j. and sing.
10 everl. j. on their heads, 51:11
60:15 a j. of many generations
61:3 give them oil of j.
7 everlasting j. sh. be to them
65:14 servants shall sing for j.
18 beho. I create her peo. a j.
66:5 he shall appear to your j.
Jer. 15:16 word was j. of my hea.
31:13 turn th. mourning into j.
38:9 it sh. be to me a name of j.
11 there sh. be heard voice of j.

Jer. 48:33 j. is tak. fr. plen. field
Lam. 5:15 the j. of our heart is
ceased
Ezek. 24:25 take fr. them j. of gl.
36:5 with the j. of all th. heart
Hos. 9:1 rejoice not, O Is. for j.
Joel 1:12 j. is withered from men
Zep. 3:17 rejo. over thee with j.
Mat. 13:20 anon with j. receiveth
it, Luke 8:13
44 for j. thereof goeth and sell.
25:21 enter into j. of thy L. 23
Lu. 1:44 babe leaped in wo. for j.
6:23 rej. in that day, leap for j.
10:17 seventy returned with j.
15:7 j. in heav. over one sinner
10 there is j. in pres. of angels
24:41 they yet believed not for j.
John 3:29 my j. therefo. is fulfil.
15:11 that my j. might remain in
you, th. your j. might be full
16:20 sorrow be turned to j.
21 for j. that a man is born
22 your j. no man tak. fr. you
24 that your j. be full
17:13 j. fulfilled in themselves
Acts 2:28 make me full of j.
13:52 discip. were filled with j.
20:24 finish my course with j.
Rom. 14:17 kingdom of God is j.
15:13 God filled you with j.
32 co. to you wi. j. by will of G.
2 Cor. 1:24 are helpers of your j.
2:3 that my j. is j. of you all
7:13 more joyed we for j. of T.
8:2 their j. abounded to riches
Gal. 5:22 Spirit is love, j. peace
Phil. 1:4 making request with j.
25 furtherance and j. of faith
2:2 my j. 4:1 j. and crown
1 Thes. 1:6 received word with j.
2:19 what is our hope or j.?
20 for ye are our glory and j.
3:9 j. wherewith we j. before G.
2 Tim. 1:4 I may be filled with j.
Phile. 20 let me have j. of thee
Heb. 12:2 for j. that was bef. him
13:17 do it with j. not with grief
Jam. 1:2 count it j. when ye fall
4:9 j. be turned into heaviness
1 Pet. 1:8 rej. with j. unspeakab.

125

4:13 glad also with exceeding j.
1 John 1:4 j. be full, 2 John 12
3 John 4 no greater j. than to h.
Jude 24 faultless with exceed. j.

Shout, or Shouted for JOY.

Ezr. 3:12 shouted aloud for j.
Job 38:7 sons of God shouted f. j.
Ps. 5:11 let them sh. f. j. 35:27
  32:11 s. f. j. all th. are upright
  65:13 the valleys shout for j.
  132:9 let thy saints s. for j. 16

JOY, Verb.

Ps. 21:1 shall j. in thy strength
Is. 9:3 j. bef. thee accord. to joy
  65:19 I rejoice and j. in my peo.
Zep. 3:17 j. over thee with sing.
Rom. 5:11 but we also j. in God
Phil. 2:17 j. and rejoice wi. you
1 Thes. 3:9 joy wherewith ye j.

JOYFUL.

Is. 61:10 soul shall be j. in my G.
2 Cor. 7:4 j. in all our tribulat.

JUDAH.

Gen. 29:35 she called his name J.

JUDAS.

Mat. 13:55 brethren Sim. and J.
  26:47 J. one of twelve, Mark
  14:43; Lu. 22:47; John 18:3, 5
  27:3 J. repented, bro. 30 pieces
John 13:29 because J. had bag
  14:22 J. saith, How is it

JUDGE, Substantive.

Gen. 18:25 J. of all the earth
Ps. 50:6 for God is j. himself
Luke 12:14 who made me j.?
Acts 10:42 j. of quick and dead
  18:15 j. of no such matters
2 Tim. 4:8 Lord the righteous j.
Heb. 12:23 G. the J. of all
Jam. 5:9 J. standeth before the door

**JUDGE, Verb, applied to God
and Christ.**

Deut. 32:36 L. sh. j. his people,
  Ps. 50:4; 135:14; Heb. 10:30
1 Sam. 2:10 L. j. ends of earth
1 K. 8:32 j. servants, 2 Chr. 6:23
1 Chr. 16:33 cometh to j. the
  earth, Ps. 96:13; 98:9
2 Chr. 20:12 wilt thou not j.?
Ps. 7:8 the L. sh. j. the people
  righteously, 9:8; 50:4; 96:10

10:18 j. fatherless and oppressed
26:1 j. me, O Lord, 7:8; 35:24;
  43:1; 54:1; Lam. 3:59
82:8 arise, O God, j. the earth
96:13 j. the world with righteousness, 98:9; Acts 17:31
110:6 shall j. among the heathen
Ec. 3:17 God shall j. righteous
Is. 2:4 shall j. among nations
  3:13 Lord standeth to j. people
  11:3 not j. after sight of eyes, 4
  51:5 mine arm shall j. people
Ezek. 7:3 will j. accord. to ways
Joel 3:12 will I sit to j. heathen
Mic. 4:3 shall j. among people
John 5:30 I j. my judg. is just
  8:15 I j. no man; 16 yet if I j.
  26 things to say and to j.
  12:47 I came not to j. world
Rom. 2:16 G. j. secrets of men
  3:6 how sh. G. j. the world?
2 Tim. 4:1 j. quick and dead,
  1 Pet. 4:5
Heb. 13:4 adulterers God will j.
Rev. 6:10 dost thou not j.
  19:11 in righteousnes he doth j.

**JUDGE, applied to MAN, or
other things.**

Ex. 18:13 Moses sat to j. people
  16 I j. one and another
John 7:24 j. not accord. to appearance, but j. right. judg.
  8:15 j. after flesh; 12:48 same j.
  18:31 j. him accord. to your law
Acts 4:19 j. ye; 13:46 j. yoursel.
  23:3 sittest thou to j. me?
Rom. 14:13 let us not j. one anoth.
1 Cor. 5:12 what have I to do to j.
  wi. do ye not j. them within?
  6:2 do not know saints j. world?
  3 know ye not we sh. j. angels?
2 Cor. 5:14 because we thus j.
Col. 2:16 let no man therefore j.
Jam. 4:11 but if thou j. the law

JUDGED.

Ps. 9:19 let heathen be j.
  109:7 wh. j. let him be condem.
Rom. 2:12 j. by law, Jam. 2:12
  3:7 am I also j. as a sinner?
1 Cor. 2:15 he himself j. no man
  6:2 if the world sh. be j. by you

126

10:29 for why is my liberty j. of
11:31 judge we should not be j.
32 we are j. we are chastened
14:24 convinced; he is j. of all
Heb. 11:11 she j. him faithful
1 Pet. 4:6 be j. according to men
Rev. 11:18 that they should be j.
16:5 righteous bec. thou j. thus
19:2 he hath j. the great whore
20:12 dead j. out of those things
13 j. ev. man accord. to works

JUDGEST.
Rom. 2:1 whoso. thou art that j.
3 O man, that j. them
14:4 that j. another man's ser.?
Jam. 4:12 who art thou j. ano.?

JUDGETH.
Job 21:22 j. those that were high
Ps. 7:11 God j. the righteous
58:11 a God that j. in earth
Prov. 29:14 that faithfully j.
John 5:22 the Father j. no man
8:50 one that seeketh and j.
12:48 hath one that j. him
1 Cor. 2:15 he that is spirit. j. all
4:4 he that j. me is the Lord
5:13 th. that are without, G. j.
Jam. 4:11 that j. his brot. j. law
1 Pet. 1:17 with. respect of pe. j.
2:23 com. himself to him that j.
Rev. 18:8 strong is the L. that j.

JUDGMENT.
Est. 1:13 that knew law and j.
Job 8:3 doth God pervert j.?
Ps. 7:6 awake for me to the j.
9:7 prepared his throne for j.
8 minister j. to people in righ.
16 L. known by j. he execut.
33:5 loveth right, and j. 37:28
72:2 shall judge thy poor with j.
76:3 j. to be heard from heaven
9 G. arose to j. save the meek
89:14 justice and j. are hab. 97:2
94:15 j. sh. return to righteous.
119:66 teach me j. and knowle.
121 I have done j. and justice
149 quicken me accord. to j.
122:5 there are set thrones of j.
140:9 exec. on them j. written
Prov. 1:3 instr. of wisdom and j.
2:8 he keep, the paths of j.

8:20 in the midst of paths of j.
13:23 destroyed for want of j.
17:23 tak. gift to perv. ways j.
19:28 ungodly witnes scom. j.
20:8 that sitteth in throne j.
28:5 evil men understand not j.
29:4 king by j. establish. land
26 ev. man's j. cometh from L.
31:5 nor perv. j. of the afflicted
Ec. 8:5 wise man disce. time and j.
6 to ev. purp. th. is time and j.
Is. 1:17 seek j. 21 full of j.
Mal. 2:17 say, Where is G. of j.
Mat. 5:21 in danger of the j. 22
7:2 with what j. ye judged
12:18 show j. to the Gentiles
20 he send forth j. unto victo.
23:23 have omitted j. mercy
Luke 11:42 pass over j. love of G.
John 5:22 committed all j. to S.
27 given him authori. to ex. j.
7:24 but judge righteous j.
9:39 for j. I am come into world
12:31 now is the j. of this world
16:8 reprove the world of j. 11
Acts 8:33 his j. was taken away
24:25 as he reasoned of j. Felix
Rom. 1:32 knowing the j. of God
2:2 j. of G. is according to truth
3 think. thou sh. escape j. of
5 revelation of righteous j. of
5:16 j. by one to condemnation
18 j. came to all to condemna.
1 Cor. 1:10 joined together in j.
4:3 I sh. be judged of man's j.
2 Thes. 1:5 token of the j. of G.
1 Tim. 5:24 open, going before
to j.
Heb. 6:2 eternal j.; 9:27 after
this the j.
10:27 certain fearful look. for j.
Jam. 2:13 have j. without mercy, rejoiceth against j.
1 Pet. 4:17 j. begin at ho. of G.
2 Pet. 2:3 whose j. lingereth not
4 chains of darkness, reser. j.
Jude 6 to j. of the great day
15 to execute j. upon all
Rev. 14:7 hour of his j. is come
17:1 show j. of the great-whore
Rev. 18:10 in one hour thy j. co.

20:4 and j. was given to them
In JUDGMENT.
Deut. 1:17 not respect per. in j.
Job 9:32 come together in j.
JUST.
Gen. 6:9 Noah was j. man
Job 9:2 should man be j. with God
12:4 j. man is laughed to scorn
Prov. 3:33 bless. habitation of j.
4:18 path of j. as shining light
9:9 teach a j. man, he will incr.
10:6 blessing upon he. of the j.
20 tongue of j. is as choice sil.
31 mouth of j. bringeth wisd.
11:1 a j. weight is his delight
Prov. 17:26 to punish the j. is
18:17 first in own cause seem. j.
20:7 j. man walketh in integrity
24:16 j. man falleth seven times
29:10 hate upright, j. seek soul
Is. 26:7 way of j. is uprightness,
dost weigh path of j.
29:21 j. for thing of naught
45:21 a j. God, and a Saviour
Lam. 4:13 shed blood of j. in her
Ezek. 18:5 man be j. and do right
9 he is j. he shall surely live
Hos. 14:9 j. shall walk in thm
Amos 5:12 they afflict the j.
Hab. 2:4 j. sh. live by faith, Rom.
1:17; Gal. 3:11; Heb. 10:38
Zep. 3:5 the j. Lord is in midst
Zec. 9:9 he is j. and hav. salva.
Mat. 1:19 Joseph being a j. man
5:45 send. rain on j. and unjust
13:49 sever wicked from am j.
27:19 nothing to do with j. man
24 innocent of blood of j. per.
Mark 6:20 know. he was j. man
Phil. 4:8 whatsoev. things are j.
Col. 4:1 give servants which is j.
Heb. 2:2 received j. recompense
12:23 sp. of j. men made perfect
Jam. 5:6 condemned and kill. j.
1 Pet. 3:18 the j. for the unjust
2 Pet. 2:7 delivered j. Lot
1 John 1:9 he is j. to forgive sins
Rev. 15:3 j. and tr. are thy ways
JUSTIFICATION.
Rom. 4:25 raised again for our j.
5:16 givt of many offences to j.

18 free gift ca. on all men to j.
JUSTIFIED.
Gal. 5:1 j. by faith we have peace
9 j. by his blood, we shall be
8:30 whom he j. he also glorifi.
1 Cor. 4:4 yet am I not hereby j.
6:11 ye are j. in name of L. J.
Gal. 2:16 not j. by law, 3:11
5:4 whosoever are j. by law
1 Tim. 3:16 j. in spirit
Jam. 2:21 was not Abraham j.?
24 see how by works man is j.
JUSTUS.
Acts 1:23 who was surnamed J.
Col. 4:11 Jesus who is called J.
K.

KEEP.
Ex. 23:7 k. thee from false matter
Num. 6:24 L. bless thee and k.
1 Chr.4:10 k. me from evil
Ps. 17:8 k. me as apple of eye
19:13 k. from presumptuous sins
25:20 O k. my soul, and deliver
34:13 k. thy tongue from evil
37:34 k. his way; 39:1 k. mouth
89:28 my mercy wi. I k. for him
103:9 nor will k. anger for ever
106:3 blessed are they k. judg.
113:9 barren women to k. house
119:2 blessed they th. k. his tes.
100 because I k. thy precepts
106 will k. thy righteous judg.
146 I shall k. thy testimonies
127:1 except Lord k. city
140:4 k. me fr. hands of wicked
141:3 O L. k. the door of my lips
Prov. 2:11 underst. shall k. thee
20 mayest k. paths of righteous
3:21 my son, k. sound wisdom
26 L. shall k. thy foot fr. being
4:6 love wisdom. she sh. k. thee
13 k. instructi. let her not go
7:1 my son, k. my words
5 k. thee from strange woman
8:32 blessed they th. k. my ways
22:5 he that doth k. his soul, 18
28:4 such as k. the law contend
Ec. 3:6 time to k. and cast away
John 14:23 man love me k. my
words

Rom. 2:25 profiteth, if th. k. law
26 k. the righteousness of law
Phil. 4:7 peace of G. k. y. hearts
1 Tim. 5:22 k. thyself pure
2 Tim 1:14 commit. to thee k. by H. G.
Jam. 1:27 to k. himself unspot.
1 John 5:21 k. yourselves fr. idols
Jude 21 k. yoursel. in love of G.
Jude 24 him that is ab. to k. you
Rev. 1:3 blessed th. that k. thin.
 3:10 k. thee from hour of temp.
 22:9 who k. sayings of this book

KEEP commandments.

Ex. 16:28 refuse ye to k. my c.
 20:6 mercy to th. that k. my c.
Deut. 5:10; 7:9; Dan. 9:4
Lev. 22:31 sh. ye k. my c. and do
 them, Deut. 4:40; 6:17; 7:11
 26:3 k. my com. Deut. 11:22;
 19:9; 28:9; 30:10; 1 K. 3:14
Deut. 5:29 fear me and k. my c.
 8:2 know whet. th. would. k. c.
 26:17 avouched Lord to k. his c.
 18 that thou shouldest k. c.
Jos. 22:5 take heed to k. com.
1 K. 2:3 charge of Lord to k. c.
 6:12 k. my comman. 2 K. 17:13;
 Prov. 4:4; 7:2
 8:58 incline hearts to k. his c.
 61 heart be perfect to k. his c.
 9:6 not k. com. I will cut off Is.
1 Chr. 29:19 Sol. perf. hea. to k. c.
Ps. 78:7 works of G. but k. his c.
 119:60 delayed not to k. thy c.
 115 dep. evil-doers, I will k. c.
Prov. 3:1 let thy heart k. my c.
 6:20 my son, k. thy father's c.
Ec. 8:2 coun. thee to k. king's c.
 12:13 fear God and k. his com.
Mat. 19:17 enter life, k. the c.
John 14:15 if ye love me, k. my c.
1 Tim. 6:14 k. this c. witho. spot
1 John 2:3 we kn. him if we k. c.
 3:22 ask we receive, bec. we k. c.
 5:2 we love God and k. his com.
 3 love of God that we k. his c.
Rev. 12:17 war with seed wh. k. c.
 14:12 they which k. the c. of G.

KEEP silence.

1 Cor. 14:28 let him k. s. in chur.

34 let women k. sil. in church.

KEEPER.

Gen. 4:2 Abe; was a k. of sheep
 9 am I my brother's k.?
Ps. 121:5 Lord thy k.
Acts 16:27 k. of prison awaking

KILL.

Ex. 20:13 thou shalt not k. Deut.
 5:17; Mat. 5:21; Rom. 13:9
1 Sam. 19:2 Saul seeketh to k. thee,
 17.
Mark 3:4 to save life, or to k.?
Acts 10:13 rise, Peter, k. and eat

KILLED.

Gen. 37:31 Joseph's coat, k. kid
Mat. 16:21 k. and raised again,
 Mark 8:31; 9:31
Rom. 8:36 for thy sake we are k.
2 Cor. 6:9 chastened and not k.

KILLETH.

Lev. 24:17 he that k. any man sh.
 be put to dea. Num. 35:30

KINDS.

Gen. 8:19 creepeth after their k.
2 Chr. 16:14 with divers k. spices
Jer. 15:3 appoint over th. four k.
1 Cor. 12:10 divers k. of tongues
 14:10 are so many k. of voices

KINDLY.

Gen. 50:21 Joseph spake k. to
 breth.
Jos. 2:14 deal k. and truly
Ruth 1:8 the L. deal k. with you
1 Sam. 20:8 deal k. with thy ser.
Rom. 12:10 be k. one to another

KINDNESS.

Ruth 2:20 not left off k. to living
 3:10 show. more k. in latter end
1 Sam. 20:14 show me the k. of the
 L.
2 Sam. 2:5 showed k. to your lord
 6 I also will requite you this k.
 9:3 that I may show k. to him
 16:17 is this thy k. to friend?
1 K. 3:6 kept for David this great k
Neh. 9:17 G. gracious, of great k.
Est. 2:9 maiden obt. k. of him
Ps. 31:21 showed me marvel. k.
 119:76 merciful k. be my comf.
 141:5 right. smite, it sh. be a k.
Prov. 19:22 desire of man is his k.

K

129

31:26 in her tongue is law of k.
Is. 54:8 with k. will I have mercy
  10 k. shall not depart from thee
Jer. 2:2 I remem k. of thy youth
Joel 2:13 he is of gr. k. Jon. 4:2
2 Cor. 6:6 by long-suffering by k.
Eph. 2:7 in his k. toward us
Col. 3:12 on k. humblen. of mind
Tit. 3:4 after the k. of G. our

Loving-KINDNESS.
Ps. 17:7 show thy l.-k. 92:2
26:3 thy l.-k. is before mine eyes
36:7 how excellent is thy l.-k.
  10 O continue thy l.-k. to them
42:8 Lord will command l.-k.
48:9 we thought of thy l.-k. O G.
51:1 have mercy accord. to l.-k.
63:3 thy l.-k. is better than life
88:11 sh. l.-k. be dec. in grave?
89:33 l.-k. will i not take fr. him
107:43 understand l.-k. of the L.
119:88 quicken me after l.-k. 159

Loving-KINDNESSES.
Ps. 25:6 remem. mercies and l.-k.
89:49 where are thy former l.-k.
Is. 63:7 mention l.-k. of the Lord

KING.
Gen. 14:18 M. k. of Sal. Heb. 7:1
Ex. 1:8 arose new k. over Egypt
Num. 23:21 shout of a k. am. th.
  24:7 his k. be higher than Agag
Deut. 17:14 I will set k. over me
  33:5 and he was k. in Jeshurun
Jud. 8:18 resem. child. of a k.
  9:8 trees went to anoint a k.
  17:6 in those days no k. in Isr.
  18:1; 19:1; 21:25
1 Sam. 2:10 L. give strength to k.
  8:5 go make us a k. to judge us
  6 gi. a k. 9 show man. of k. 11
  10 have a k. 22 make th. a k.
  20 that our k. may judge us
  10:19 nay, but set a k. over us
2 Sam. 5:12 estab. him k. over I.
  12:7 I anointed thee k. over Is.
1 K. 1:35 Solomon k. in my stead
Ps. 5:2 my k. and my God, 84:3
  10:16 Lord is k. for ever, 29:10
  18:50 deliverance giveth he to k.
Ps. 21:1 k. shall joy in thy stren.
  24:7 k. of glory shall come in, 9

8 who is k. of glory? the Lord
33:16 no k. saved by multitude
45:1 things I made touc. the k.
  11 so shall the k. greatly desi.
  14 brought to the k. in raim.
47:6 praises to k. 7 God is k.
61:6 prolong k. life and years
72:1 give the k. thy judgments
74:12 God is my k. of old
89:18 H. One of israel is our k.
98:6 make a noise bef. L. the k.
99:4 k. also loveth judgment
149:2 children of Z. joyful in k.
Prov. 14:28 people is the k. hon.
  35 k. favor toward wise serv.
  20:28 mercy and truth pres. k.
  22:11 the k. shall be his friend
  24:21 fear the Lord and the k.
  25:5 take wicked from bef. k.
Ec. 2:12 man do cometh after k.
  10:20 curse not the k. in thought
Is. 6:5 mine eyes ha. seen the k.
  23:15 according to days of one k.
Jer. 10:10 true God, everlasting k.
Ezek. 26:7 I will bring a k. of kings
  37:22 one k. be k. to them all, 24
Dan. 4:37 I honor k. of heaven
  11:3 a mighty k. shall stand up
Hos. 3:4 Is. sh. abide without k.
Zec. 14:9 L. shall be k. over all
  earth 16 go up to worship k. 17
Luke 14:31 what k. goeth to war
  19:38 blessed be k. that cometh
  23:2 that he himself is Ch. a k.
John 6:15 to make him k.
  12:15 behold thy k. com. on ass
  13:37 Pil. said, Art thou a k.?
Acts 7:18 till another k. arose
1 Tim. 1:17 now to the k. etem.
  6:15 K. of kings, and L. of lords
Heb. 11:23 not afraid of k. com.
1 Pet. 2:13 whe. to k. as supreme
  17 fear God, honor the k.
Rev. 9:11 they had a k. over th.
  15:3 just are thy ways, K. of sai.
  17:14 L. of lords, K. of ki. 19:16

KINGDOM.
Est. 5:3 be given to half of k. 6; 7:2
Dan. 2:44 sh. G. of heaven set up a
k.
Acts 1:6 restore k. again to Isr.?

Heb. 12:28 k. th. cannot be mov.
Jam. 2:5 heirs of k. he promised
2 Pet. 1:11 entrance into everl. k.

KINGDOM of God.

Mat. 6:33 but seek ye first the k.
   of God, Luke 12:31
12:28 k. of God is come unto
   you, Luke 10:9, 11:20
19:24 than for a rich man to enter into k. of G. Mark 10:23;
   4:11 to know the mystery of k.
   of God, Luke 8:10
9:1 till they have seen k. of G.
   47 better to enter into k. of G.
10:14 such is k. of G. Luke 18:16
   15 whoso not receive k. of G.
   24 hard for th. trust in riches
   to enter k. of G. 25; Lu. 18:25
12:34 art not far from k. of God
14:25 I drink it new in k. of G.
15:43 which waited for the k. of
   God, Luke 23:51
Luke 4:43 I must preach k. of G.
6:20 for yours is the k. of God
7:28 least in k. of G. greater th.
9:2 sent th. to preach k. of G. 60
   27 not taste de. till see k. of G.
   62 lo. back, not fit for k. of G.
13:28 see prophets in k. of God
John 3:3 bo. ag. can see k. of G.
   5 cannot enter into k. of God
Acts 1:3 things pertaining to k.
   of God, 8:12; 19:8
14:22 thro' tribul. enter k. of G.
28:23 expou. and testi. k. of G.
Rom. 14:17 k. of G. is not meat
1 Cor. 4:20 k. of God is not in w.
6:9 unright. not inherit k. of G.
   10 nor extortioners inhe. k. of
   God, Gal. 5:21; Eph. 5:5
15:50 flesh can. in. k. of G.
2 Thes. 1:5 worthy k. of God
Rev. 12:10 is come k. of our God

KINGDOM of heaven.

Mat. 3:2 repent, for k. of heaven
   is at hand, 4:17; 10:7
5:3 theirs is k. of heaven, 10
   19 least in k. of h. g. in k. of h.
   20 in no case ent. k. of h. 18:3
7:21 saith, Lord, sh. ent. k. of h.
8:11 sit with Abrah. in k. of h.

11:11 least in k. of h. gre. th. he
   12 k. of heaven suffer. violence
13:11 know mysteries of k. of h.
16:19 give thee keys of k. of h.
18:1 who is great. in k. of h.? 4
23:13 shut up k. of h. aga. men

His KINGDOM.

Ps. 103:19 h. k. ruleth over all
145:12 glorious majesty of h. k.
Is. 9:7 h. k. to order and establi.
Dan. 4:3 his k. is an everl. king.
   34 h. k. fr. generat. 6:26; 7:14
   11:4 h. k. broken and pluck. up
Mat. 12:26 h. k. stand? Lu. 11:18
   13:41 gather out of his k. all th.
16:28 S. of man coming in h. k.
Luke 1:33 of h. k. sh. be no end
1 Thes. 2:12 called you to h. k.

My KINGDOM.

John 18:36 my k. not of th. world

Thy KINGDOM.

Ps. 145:11 speak of glory of thy k.
   13 thy k. is everlasting kingd.
Dan. 4:26 t. k. shall be sure
   5:11 man in t. k. 26 numb. t. k.
   28 t. k. divided to Med. and P.
Mat. 6:10 t. k. come, Luke 11:2
20:21 the other on left in t. k.
Luke 23:42 thou comest to t. k.

KISS, ES.

Prov. 27:6 k. of an enemy deceit.
Cant. 1:2 k. me with k. of mouth
Luke 7:45 thou gavest me no k.
   22:48 betra. Son of man wi. k.?
Rom. 16:16 salute with a holy k.
1 Cor. 16:20 gr. wi. k. 2 Cor. 13:12
1 Thes. 5:26 greet breth. w. h. k.
1 Pet. 5:14 greet with k. of chari.

KISS, Verb.

Gen. 27:26 come near and k. me
   31:28 not suffered to k. my sons
1 K. 19:20 k. my father and mot.
Ps. 2:12 k. Son, lest he be angry
Luke 7:45 not ceased k. my feet
22:47 Judas drew near to J. to k.

KISSED.

Gen. 27:27 Ja. came and k. him
   29:11 Jacob k. Rachel and wept
48:10 J. k. Joseph's sons
   50:1 Jos. fell on fa.'s face k. him
Ex. 4:27 met Moses and k. him

131

1 Sam. 20:41 Jonathan and David k
Ps. 85:10 and peace k. each other
Prov. 7:13 caught him k. him
Mat. 26:49 said, Hail, Master,
  and k. him, Mark 14:45
Luke 7:38 M. k. feet and anointed
  15:20 fell on his neck and k. him
Acts 20:37 fell on P.'s neck k. h.

KNEE.

Gen. 41:43 they cried, Bow the k.
Is. 45:23 unto me every k. sh.
  bow, Rom. 14:11; Phil. 2:10
Mat. 27:29 bowed the k. bef. him
Rom. 11:4 bowed the k. to Baal

KNEEL, ED.

Gen. 24:11 ma his camels k. do.
2 Chr. 6:13 Solomon k. on knees
Ps. 95:6 let us k. before the L.
Dan. 6:10 D. k. three times a day
Luke 22:41 and Jesus k. down
Acts 7:60 Stephen k. and cried
  9:40 Peter k. prayed; 20:36 P.
  21:5 we k. down on the shore

KNEELING.

1 K. 8:54 Solomon rose from k.

KNEES.

Gen. 30:3 maid sh. bear on my k.
Deut. 28:35 Lord smite thee in k.
1 K. 8:54 arose fr. kneeling on k.
  18:42 Elijah put face bet. his k.
  19:18 k. have not bowed to Baal
2 K. 1:13 fell on k. before Elijah
  4:20 sat on mother's k. till noon
2 Chr. 6:13 Sol. kneeled on his k.
Ezr. 9:5 I fell on my k.
Job 3:12 why did k. prevent me
Ezek. 7:17 k. weak as water, 21:7
  47:4 the waters were to the k.
Dan. 6:10 kneeled on k. three times
Mark 15:19 bowing k. worship.
Luke 5:8 PEter fell at Jesus' k.
Eph. 8:14 bow my k. to Father

KNEW.

Mat. 7:23 profess I never k. you
  12:25 J. k. thoughts, Luke 6:8
  25:24 I k. thee, thou art hard m.
Mark 1:34 because they k. him
Luke 4:41 they k. he was Christ
  12:47 servant k. his lord's will
  24:31 eyes opened, they k. him
John 2:24 because he k. all men

25 for he k. what was in man
  6:64 Jesus k. from the beginning
  11:42 I k. that thou hearest me
  57 if any man k. where he we
  13:1 Jesus k. his hour was co.
  11 he k. who should betray h.
  28 no man at the table k. for
  18:2 Judas k. the place
Acts 12:14 Rhoda k. Peter's voi.
  22:29 k. that he was a Roman
Rom. 1:21 bec. when they k. G.
1 Cor. 2:8 no. of princes of wo. k.
2 Cor. 5:21 sin, who k. no sin
  12:2 I k. a man in Christ, 3
Col. 1:6 since ye k. grace of God
  2:1 k. what great conflict I have
Jude 5 though ye once k. this
Rev. 19:12 name writ. no man k.

KNIT.

1 Sam. 18:1 Jonathan k. to Da.
1 Chr. 12:17 my heart be k. to y.
Col. 2:2 hearts k. together in lo.

KNOCK.

Mat. 7:7 k. it sh. be op. Lu. 11:9
Rev. 3:20 I stand at door and k.

KNOW.

Ps. 46:10 still, and k. that I am G.
  59:13 let them k. that G. ruleth
  103:16 place shall k. it no more
  139:23 k. my heart, k. my thou.
  142:4 no man would k. me
  143:8 k. way wherein I should
Prov. 1:2 k. wisd. and instruct
  4:1 attend to k. understanding
  10:32 righteous k. wh. is accept.
  27:23 dilig. to k. state of flocks
Ec. 1:17 gave heart to k. wisd.
  7:25 applied heart to k. wisdom
  8:17 tho. a wise man think to k.
  9:5 the living k. they shall die
  11:9 k. that G. will bring to ju.
Is. 7:16 before the child shall k.
  41:20 that they may see and k.
  49:26 all flesh shall k. I am
  52:6 my people sh. k. my name
  58:2 and delight to k. my ways
Jer. 2:19 k. it is evil to forsake
Jer. 15:15 k. that for thy sake I suf.
  16:21 cause them to k. my hand,
  and they sh. k. my name is
  17:9 heart deceit. who can k. it?

24:7 give them a heart to k. me
31:34 k. the Lord, for they shall
all k. me, Heb. 8:11
36:19 let no man k. where ye be
Ezek. 2:5 k. ha. been a pro. 33:33
Dan. 2:21 know, to them who k.
4:25 k. that M. High ruleth, 32
7:16 made me k. interpretation
Hos. 14:9 prudent, and he sh. k. th.
Zec. 2:11 k. the L. sent me, 4:9
Mal. 2:4 ye sh. k. I have sent th.
Mat. 6:3 let not thy left hand k.
7:11 k. how to give, Luke 11:13
9:30 see no man k. it. Mark
5:43; 7:24; 9:30
13:11 it is given to you to k.
Mark 4:11; Luke 8:10
Rev. 3:9 make them k. I have loved

KNOWLEDGE.

Gen. 2:9 tree of k. good and ev. 17
2 Chr. 1:12 wisdom and k. is grant.
Ps. 19:2 night to night show. k.
73:11 is there k. in Most High?
94:10 he that teacheth man k.
119:66 teach me judgm. and k.
139:6 such k. too wonder. for me
144:3 what is man thou takest
k. of?
Prov. 1:7 fear of Lord begi. of k.
22 fools take k. 2:3 cri. after k.
29 they hated k. did not choose
2:6 out of his mouth cometh k.
10 k. is pleasant to thy soul
3:20 by k. depths are broken up
5:2 that thy lips may keep k.
8:10 k. rather than choice gold
12 and find out k. of inventions
9:10 k. of Holy is understanding
10:14 wise men lay up k.
11:9 thro' k. sh. just be deliver.
12:23 a prud. man concealeth k.
13:16 ev. prud. man deal. wi. k.
14:6 k. easy to him that unders.
7 perceiv. not in him lips of k.
18 prudent are crowned with k.
15:2 tongue of wise useth k.
Ec. 1:18 increaseth k. increaseth
sor.
2:26 God giveth a man k. and joy
7:12 excellency of k. is wisdom
Eph. 1:17 wisdom in k. of him

3:19 love of G. which passeth k.
4:13 unity of faith and k. of S.

KNOWLEDGE of God.

Prov. 2:5 thou shalt find k. of G.
2 Pet. 1:2 peace, thro' k. of God

KNOWLEDGE of the Lord.

2 Chr. 30:22 taught good k. of L.
Is. 11:9 earth full of k. of the L.
2 Pet. 2:20 escaped thro' k. of L.

No KNOWLEDGE.

Deut. 1:39 child. that day no k.
Is. 5:13 because they have no k.

L.

LABAN.

Gen. 30:36 Jac. fed rest of L.'s
flocks

LABOR, Substantive.

Gen. 31:42 G. seen l. of my hands
Neh. 5:13 God sha. ev. man fr. l.
Ps. 90:10 their strength l. sorrow
104:23 man goeth to l. till even.
105:44 inherited l. of the people
107:12 bro. down heart with l.
109:11 let stranger spoil his l.
128:2 sh. eat the l. of thy hands
Prov. 10:16 l. tendeth to life
13:11 gathereth by l. shall incr.
Ec. 1:3 wh. profit hath man of l.
2:19 shall he rule over all my l.
21 man whose l. is in wisdom
22 what hath man of all his l.?
Rom. 16:6 bestow. much l. on us
1 Cor. 3:8 man rec. accord. to l.
15:58 know your l. is not in vain
Gal. 4:11 lest I bestow. l. in vain
Phil. 1:22 this is fruit of my l.
1 Thes. 1:3 remember. l. of love
2 Thes. 3:8 but wrought with l.
Heb. 6:10 not forget your l. of lo.
Rev. 2:2 I kn. thy l. and patience

LABOR, Verb.

Ex. 20:9 six days l. Deut. 5:13
Prov. 21:25 his hands refuse to l.
23:4 l. not to be rich, cease from
Mat. 11:28 co. to me all ye th. l.
Heb. 4:11 l. to enter into that rest

LABORED.

Rev. 2:3 for my name's sake l.

LABORER, S.

Mat. 9:37 harvest plenteous, but

133

l. few, 38; Luke 10:2
20:1 went out early to hire l.
Luke 10:7 l. is worthy of his hire
1 Cor. 3:9 l. together with God
1 Tim. 5:18 l. is worthy of rewa.
Jam. 5:4 behold the hire of the l.

LABORETH.

Prov. 16:26 he that l. l. for hims.
Ec. 3:9 wh. profit in that he l.?
1 Cor. 16:16 sub. to ev. one that l.
2 Tim. 2:6 the husbandm. that l.

LACK, Substantive.

Hos. 4:6 peo. destroyed for l. kn.
1 Thes. 4:12 that ye l. of nothing

LACK, Verb.

Prov. 28:27 giv. to poor sh. not l.
Mat. 19:20 I kept, wh. l. I yet?
Jam. 1:5 any l. wisd. ask of God

LACKEST.

Mark 10:21 but one thing thou l.
Luke 18:22

LADEN.

Mat. 11:28 all that are heavy l.
2 Tim. 3:6 women, l. with sins

LAKE.

Luke 5:1 Jesus stood by l. of G.
2 two ships standing by the l.
8:23 a storm of wind on the l.
33 herd ran violently into l.
Rev. 20:10 devil cast into l. of fire
14 death and hell cast in l.
15 not in bo. of life. cast into l.

LAMB.

Gen. 22:8 God will provide himself
a l.
Ex. 12:3 they shall take a l. 21
29:39 one l. th. sh. offer in morn.
other l. at even. 41; Nu. 28:4
Lev. 23:12 sh. offer a l. with.
blemish
Num. 15:5 with the sacrifice for
one l.
Is. 11:6 wolf shall dwell with l.
16:1 send ye l. to ruler of land
53:7 he was brought as a l. to
the slaughter. Jer. 11:19
65:25 wolf and l. sh. feed toget.
Ezek. 45:15 one l. out of a flock
Hos. 4:16 L. will feed them as l.
John 1:29 behold the L. of G. 36
Acts 8:32 a l. dumb bef. shearer

1 Pet. 1:19 as a l. without blem.
Rev. 5:6 midst of eld. stood a L.
12 worthy the L. that was slain
6:16 hide us from wrath of L.
7:10 salvation to our G. and L.
14 made white in blood of L.
17 L. shall feed and lead
12:11 overc. him by blood of L.
14:1 L. stood on the mount Si.
4 these are they that follow L.
10 tormented in presence of L.
17:14 war with L. and L. overc.
19:7 for marriage of L. is come
21:9 show thee bride, L. wife
14 twelve apostles of L.
22 God Alm. and L. are temple
27 writ. in the L. book of life
22:1 out of thr. of God and L. 3

LAME.

Mat. 11:5 the l. walk, 15:31; 21:14;
Luke 7:22
Luke 14:13 call poor, l. and blind
Acts 3:2 a man, l. fr. womb, car.

LAMENT.

John 16:20 Ye shall weep and l.
Rev. 18:9 kings of earth shall l.

LAMP.

Ps. 119:105 thy word is l. to feet
132:17 ordained l. for mine ano.
Prov. 6:23 commandment is a l.
13:9 l. of wicked sh. be put out
20:20 curs. father, l. be put out
Is. 62:1 salva. as l. that burneth
Rev. 8:10 burning as it were l.

LANDS.

Mat. 19:29 hath forsaken houses,
l. Mark 10:29

LASCIVIOUSNESS.

Mark 7:22 out of heart proceed l.
2 Cor. 12:21 not repented of the l.
Gal. 5:19 works of flesh manif. l.
Eph. 4:19 given themselves to l.
1 Pet. 4:8 when we walked in l.

LAST.

2 Sam. 23:1 l. words of David
Prov. 5:11 thou mourn at the l.
Mat. 12:45 l. state of that man is
worse than first. Luke 11:26
19:30 first shall be l. and l. first,
20:16; Mark 10:31; Luke 13:30
27:64 l. error worse than the fi.

Mark 9:35 first, same sh. be l.
Luke 12:59 till th. hast paid l. m.

LAST day, s.
John 11:24 he shall rise again at l.d
Heb. 1:2 spoken in l. d. by his S.
Jam. 5:3 heaped treasure for l. d.
2 Pet. 3:3 come in l. d. scoffers

LAST, time, s.
1 Pet. 1:5 to be revealed in l. t.
20 manifest in these l. times
1 John 2:18 children, it is the l. t.
Jude 18 should be mockers in l. t.

LATCHET.
Mark 1:7 l. of wh. shoes, Lu. 3:16

LATTER.
Deut. 11:14 give first and l. rain
Job 19:25 Redeemer, st. at l. day
29:23 open. mouth, as for l. rain
Prov. 16:15 as cloud of l. rain
19:20 mayest be wise in l. end
Jer. 3:3 there ha. been no l. rain
5:24 form. and l. rain in season
Dan. 8:23 l. time of their kingd.
Hos. 6:3 as l. and former rain
Joel 2:23 l. rain in first month
Amos 7:1 in beginning of l. grow.
Hag. 2:9 glory of l. house greater
Zec. 10:1 rain in time of l. rain
1 Tim. 4:1 in l. times some dep.

LAUGH.
Gen. 18:13 wheref. did Sarah l.?
21:6 G. made me to l. all will l.
Ec. 3:4 time to weep, time to l.
Luke 6:21 ye that weep, ye sh. l.

LAUGHTER.
Ps. 126:2 mouth filled with l.
Prov. 14:13 in l. heart sorrowful
Ec. 2:2 I said of l. It is mad
7:3 sorrow is better than l.
Jam. 4:9 l. turned to mourning

LAW.
Ps. 1:2 in his l. he meditates
37:31 l. of his G. is in his heart
78:5 for he appointed a l. in Is.
Prov. 1:8 forsake not the l. of thy
mother, 6:20
29:18 that keep. l. happy is he
Jer. 44:23 not obey. nor walk. in l.
Lam. 2:9 the l. is no more
Ezek. 7:26 l. perish from priests
Hos. 4:6 has forgotten l. of God

Mal. 2:6 l. of truth was in mouth
7 sh. seek the l. at his mouth
9 have been partial in the l.
Mat. 5:17 not to come to dest. l.
18 sh. in no wise pass fr. the l.
40 if any man sue th. at the l.
22:36 great commandment in l.
40 on two command. hang l.
23:23 omitted weigh. mat. of l.
Luke 2:27 do after custom of l.
5:17 were doctors of l. sitting
16:17 one tittle of the l. to fail
John 1:17 l. was given by Moses
7:19 did not Moses give you l.?
John 18:31 judge him according to
l. 19:7 by our l. he ought to die
Acts 6:13 blasphe. words aga. l.
7:53 have received l. by angels
13:15 reading of l. and prophets
39 not justified by l. of Moses,
15:5 command to keep l. of Mo.
24 circumcised and keep the l.
18:15 a question of l. look to it
19:38 l. is open; 21:20 zeal. of l.
22:12 devout man accord. to l.
23:3 sittest thou to jud. after l.
25:8 nor against l. of the Jews
28:23 persua. them out of the l.
Rom. 2:12 sin. in l. judged by l.
13 not hearers of the l. are just
14 Gentiles have not l. to do
things contained in l. these
hav. not l. are a l. unto the
20 the form of truth in the l.
23 that makest thy boast of
the l. through break. the l.
3:20 by deeds of l. no flesh be
justified, for by the l. is
knowl. of sin 28; Gal. 2:16
21 righ. of God witnessed by l.
27 by what l. excluded? by l.
31 do we make void the l.?
7:1 speak to them wh. know l.
2 wo. bound by l. to husband
4 ye also become dead to the l.
7 is l. sin, I had not kno. sin,
but by l. for lust, ex. l. said
8 without l. sin was dead
12 the l. is holy, and comman.
14 know th. the l. is spiritual
16 l. that is good 1 Tim. 1:8

22 I delight in the l. of God
23 I see another l. warring ag.
the l. of my mind, to l. of
25 with mind I serve l. of God
8:2 the L. of life made me free
3 for what the l. could not do
4 righteousness of the l. fulfil.
7 carnal mind not subject to l.
9:31 Israel followed l. of righte.
10:4 Christ is the end of the l.
13:8 loveth another. fulfilled l.
10 love is the fulfilli. of the l.
1 Cor. 6:1 dare any of you to l.?
6 brother goeth to l. with bro.
7:39 wife is bound by the l.
15:56 strength of sin is the l.
Gal. 2:16 not just. by works of l.
19 I thro' the l. am de. to the l.
21 if righteousness come by l.
3:2 received ye Spirit by the l.?
5 miracles, doeth he it by l.?
11 no man is justified by the l.
12 and the l. is not of faith
13 C. redeem. us fr. curse of l.
19 wheref. then serveth the l.?
21 is the l. aga. the promises?
righteous. had been by the l.
24 l. was our schoolmaster
5:3 is a debtor to do the who. l.
14 all the l. is fulfil. in one w.
6:2 so fulfil the l. of Christ, 13
Phil. 3:6 touching righ. in the l.
9 mine own righteou. of the l.
1 Tim. 1:7 to be teache. of the l.
9 l. is not made for right. man
Tit. 3:9 avoid content. about l.
Heb. 7:5 take tithes accord. to l.
10:28 he that desp. Moses' l. died
Jam. 1:25 looketh into perfect l.
2:8 fulfil the royal ye do well
12 they th. be judged by the l.
1 John 3:4 whosoever commit.
teth sin transgres, also the l.

LAW of the Lord.
Ex. 13:9 L's l. lie in thy mouth
Ps. 1:2 delight is in l. of the L.
19:7 the l. of the L. is perfect
119:1 blessed th. walk in l. of L.

My LAW.
Ex. 16:4 whether walk in my l.
2 Chr. 6:16 childr. walk in my l.

Prov. 3:1 my son, forg. not my l.
Under the LAW.
Rom. 6:14 ye are not under t. l.
15 sho. we sin bec. not u. l.?
Gal 5:18 led by Sp. are not u. t. l.

LAY hands.
Mark 5:23 come l. thy h. on her
16:18 l. h. on sick, they recover
Luke 21:12 they shall l. h. on you
1 Tim. 5:22 l. h. suddenly on no
LAY hold.
Prov. 3:18 tree of life to th. l. h.
1 Tim. 6:12 l. h. on eter. life, 19
Heb. 6:18 l. h. on hope set be. us
LAY up.
Prov. 7:11 l. up my commandm.
10:14 wise men l. up knowledge
Mat. 6:19 l. not up for you treas.
20 l. up treasures in heaven
2 Cor. 12:14 children not to l. up

LAID.
Gen. 22:6 wood, and l. it on Isa.
30:41 Jacob l. rods before cattle
1 K. 3:20 l. it in her bosom, and
l. her dead child in my bos.
Mat. 27:60 l. it in his own new
tomb
Mark 7:30 her daughter l. on bed
16:6 behold where they l. him
Luke 2:7 first-born l. in manger
16:20 Lazarus was l. at his gate
23:53 wherein never man before
was l. John 19:41
John 11:34 wh. have ye l. him?
20:2 know not wh. th. l. him, 13
Acts 3:2 l. at gate of temple
LAID hands.
Mat. 18:28 l. h. took him by thr.
Mark 6:5 l. h. on a few sick folk
Luke 4:40 l. h. on ev. one of th.
13:13 he l. his h. on her
John 7:30 but no man l. hands
on him, 44; 8:20
Acts 4:3 l. h. on apostles, 5:18
6:6 they l. h. on the deacons
19:6 Paul l. his h. on them
LAZARUS.
Luke 16:20 beggar named L.
John 11:2 Mary whose broth. L.
LEAD.
Ex. 13:21 pillar of cloud l. them

32:34 l. the people to the place
Deut. 32:12 Lord alone did l. hi.
Ps. 61:2 l. to rock higher than I
Prov. 8:20 l. in way of righteou.
Is. 11:6 a little child shall l. them
Mat. 6:13 l. us not into temptat.
Luke 11:4
15:14 if blind l. blind, Lu. 6:39
1 Tim. 2:2 we may l. a quiet life
Rev. 7:17 Lamb feed and l. them

LEAH.

Gen. 29:16 daughter was L. 30:19
Ruth 4:11 L. make wom. like L.

LEAN.

Prov. 3:5 l. not to own underst.
Mic. 3:11 yet they l. on the Lord
John 21:20 l. on his breast at su.

LEAP.

Luke 6:23 rejoice ye, l. for joy

LEAPED.

2 Sam. 22:30 l. over wa. Ps. 18:29
Luke 1:41 babe l. in womb, 44
Acts 14:10 and he l. and walked

LEAPING.

2 Sam. 6:16 Michal saw David l.
Acts 3:8 and he l. up and walked

LEARN.

Deut. 4:10 may l. to fear, 14:23
5:1 may l. and keep, and do th.
34:13 children may l. to fe. the L.
Ps. 119:71 might l. statutes, 73
Prov. 22:25 lest thou l. his ways
Is. 1:17 l. to do well, seek judg.
26:9 inhabitants l. righteousne.
10 will not wicked l. righteou.
29:24 that murmured l. doctrine.
Jer. 12:16 diligently l. ways of peop.
Mat. 9:13 go l. what th. meaneth
11:29 l. of me, for I am meek
1 Cor. 14:35 l. anythi. let th. ask
1 Tim. 2:11 let wom. l. in silence
5:4 l. first to sh. piety at home
Tit. 3:14 l. to maint. good works

LEARNED.

Prov. 30:3 I neith. l. wisdom nor
John 6:45 man that hath l. of F.
Acts 7:22 Moses l. wisdom of E.
Eph. 4:20 ye have not so l. Chr.
Phil. 4:11 l. in ev. state to be co.
2 Tim. 3:14 contin. in thing thou

l. knowing of wh. th. l. th.
Heb. 5:8 yet l. he obedience

LEARNING.

Prov. 1:5 wise man will incre. l.
9:9 just man, he will incre. in l.
Dan. 1:17 G. gave them skill in l.

LEAST.

Gen. 32:10 not worthy l. of merc.
Mat. 2:6 not l. among the princ.
11:11 l. in kingdom of heaven
is greater than he, Luke 7:28

LEAVE.

Gen. 2:24 l. father and mother,
Mat. 19:5; Mark 10:7; Eph.
5:31
44:22 the lad cannot l. his fath.
Luke 19:44 not l. in th. one stone
John 14:27 my peace I l. wi. you
16:28 I l. world and go to Fath.
32 l. me alone, yet I am not al.
Acts 6:2 we should l. the word
1 Cor. 7:13 let her not l. him.
Heb. 13:5 I will never l. thee

I will not LEAVE.

2 K. 2:2 I will not l. thee, 4:30
John 14:18 I w. n. l. you comfort.

LEAVEN.

Mat. 13:33 kingdom of heaven is
like l. Luke 13:21
16:6 beware of the l. Phar. and Sad.
11; Mark 8:15; Luke 12:1
12 th. not beware of l. of bread
1 Cor. 5:6 little l. leaveneth wh.
lump, Gal. 5:9

LEAVENED.

Mat. 13:33 till whole was l. Luke
13:21

LEAVENETH.

1 Cor. 5:6 little leaven l. lump,
Gal. 5:9

LEAVING.

Rom 1:27 l. natural use of wom.
Heb. 6:1 l. principles of Christ
1 Pet. 2:21 suffered, l. an examp.

LED.

Ex. 13:18 God l. them through
wilde.
Prov. 4:11 l. thee in right paths
Mat. 4:1 Jes. l. of Spirit, Lu. 4:1
Luke 4:29 l. Jesus to brow of hill

LEG, S.

Prov. 26:7 l. of lame not equal
Dan. 2:33 his l. of iron
John 19:33 they brake not his l.
LEGION.
Mark 5:9 name is L. Luke 8:30
LEND.
Ex. 22:25 if thou l. money
Deut. 28:12 l. to many nations
Luke 6:35 love enemies, do good
and l.
LENT.
1 Sam. 1:28 I l. him to the Lord
LEPER.
Lev. 14:3 if leprosy be healed in l.
Mat. 8:2 th. came a l. Mark 1:40
26:6 house of Sim. l. Mark 14:3
LEPERS.
Mat. 10:8 cleanse l. raise dead
11:5 l. are cleansed, Luke 7:22
Luke 4:27 many l. were in Israel
17:12 ten men that were l.
LEPROSY.
Mat. 8:3 his l. was cleansed,
Mark 1:42; Luke 5:13
Luke 5:12 man full of l. besought
LEPROUS.
Ex. 4:6 hand was l. as snow
Num. 12:10 Miriam became l.
LETTERS.
Est. 1:22 Ahasuerus sent l.
9:20 Mordecai sent l. to Jews, 30
Tribe of LEVI.
Num. 1:49 not num. t. of L. 3:6
LEVITICAL.
Heb. 7:11 were by l. priesthood
LEWDNESS.
Jud. 20:6 th. have committed l.
Hos. 2:10 will I discover her l.
Acts 18:14 matter of wrong or l.
LIAR.
Job 24:25 who will make me a l.?
Prov. 19:22 poor man better than a
l.
Rom. 3:4 God true, ev. man a l.
1 John 5:10 believ. not G. made
him l.
LIARS.
Rev. 21:8 all l. have th. part in lake
LIBERAL, LY.
Prov. 11:25 l. soul sh. be made fat
Jam. 1:5 God giveth all men l.

LIBERTY.
Acts 26:32 man might been set at l.
Rom. 8:21 from bondage into l.
10:29 my l. judged of another
2 Cor. 3:17 Sp. of L. is, there is l.
Gal. 5:1 stand fast in the l. wherew.
13 ye have been called to l.
Jam. 1:25 whoso look. to law of l.
2:12 be judged by the law of l.
1 Pet. 2:16 not using l. for a cloak
2 Pet. 2:19 they promise them l.
LICE.
Ex. 8:16 dust became l. 17, 18
Ps. 105:31 l. in all their coasts
LIE, falsehood.
Ps. 62:9 men of hi. degree are a l.
2 Thes. 2:11 they sh. believe a l.
LIES.
Prov. 14:5 a false witness will utter
l.
25 deceitful witness speak. l.
19:5 speaketh l. shall not escape
9 he that speaketh l. sh. perish
Ezek. 22:28 divining l. unto them
LIE, Verb.
Lev. 6:2 if a soul l. to his neigh.
19:11 steal, nor l. one to another
Prov. 14:5 faith, witn. will not l.
Is. 63:8 my peo. that will not l.
Acts 5:3 hath S. filled heart to l.?
Rom. 9:1 I say truth in Christ, I
l. not, 1 Tim. 2:7
2 Cor. 11:31 L. knoweth. I l. not
Col. 3:9 l. not one to another
Tit. 1:2 life, God that cannot l.
promised, Heb. 6:18
Jam. 3:14 l. not against the truth
1 John 1:6 we l. and do not truth
LIFE.
Gen. 2:7 G. breathed the breath of
l.
9 tree of l. in garden, 3:22
Deut. 12:23 blood is l. not eat l.
Ps. 16:11 wilt show me path of l.
21:4 asked l. of thee, thou gav.
Prov. 3:18 she is a tree of l. to them
4:23 out of heart are issues of l.
6:23 reproofs are the way of l.
Mat. 18:9 better to enter into l. with
one eye, Mark 9:45
John 5:40 will not come to me that

might have l. 10:10
6:33 giveth l. unto the world
35 I am the bread of l. 48
53 blood, ye have no l. in you
63 words I speak to you, are l.
8:12 shall have the light of l.
29:31 believing ye might have l.
Acts 2:28 known to me ways of l.
17:25 seeing he giveth to all l.
Jam. 1:12 sh. receive crown of l.
Rev. 2:7 I give to eat of tree of l.
16 I will give thee a crown of l.

His LIFE.

Mat. 10:39 he that find. h. l. sh.
lose it; he that loseth his l.
sh. find it, 16:25; Mark 8:35:
Luke 9:24; 17:33; John 12:25
20:28 to give his l. a ransom for
many, Mark 10:45
Luke 14:26 hate not his own l.
John 10:11 good Shep. give. h. l.
15:13 lay down h. l. for friends

My life.

John 13:37 lay do. my l. for thy
sake
Acts 20:24 nor count I my l. dear

LIFT hand, s.

Gen. 14:22 l. up my h. to Lord
Deut. 32:40 I l. up my h. and say
Ps. 10:12 l. up thy h. forget not
63:4 I l. up my h. in thy name
134:2 l. up hands in sanctuary
Is. 49:22 l. up my h. to Gentiles
Lam. 2:19 l. up h. towards him

LIFT voice.

Job 38:34 canst l. up voice to
clouds?
Ezek. 21:22 l. up v. with shout.

LIFTER.

Ps. 3:3 the l. up of my head

LIFTETH.

Ps. 113:7 he l. needy out of
dunghill
147:6 the lord l. up the meek

LIFTING.

1 Chr. 15:16 l. up voice with joy
Neh. 8:6 amen, with l. up hands
Ps. 141:2 l. up of my hands
Prov. 30:32 foolishly in l. up. th.
1 Tim. 2:8 pray, l. up holy hands

LIGHT.

Mat. 11:30 yoke easy, burden l.

LIGHT, Substantive.

Mat. 5:14 l. of world; 15 it giveth l.
16 let your l. so shine be. men
6:22 the l. of the body is the
eye, Luke 11:34, 36
Luke 16:8 wiser than children of l.
John 1:4 life was the l. of men
7 came to bear witness of l. 8
9 true l. wh. lighteth every m.
3:19 l. is come into the world
8:12 I am l. of world, he that
fol. me sh. have l. of life, 9:5
11:9 because he seeth the l.
Acts 12:7 a l. shined in the prison
Rom. 2:19 l. of them are in dark.
13:12 put on the armor of l.
1 Cor. 4:5 bring to l. hid, things
2 Cor. 4:4 lest l. of gospel shine
6 commanded l. to shine out
Eph. 5:8 are l. walk as chil. of l.
13 all things made mani, by l.
whatso. doth manifest is l.
1 Thes. 5:5 are all children of l.
1 Pet. 2:9 called you to marvel. l.
1 John 1:5 G. is l. in him no da.
Rev. 21:23 the Lamb is the l.
thereof

Give LIGHT.

Mat. 5:15 g. l. to all, Luke 11:36
2 Cor. 4:6 g. l. of knowle. of G.
Eph. 5:14 Christ shall g. thee l.

LIGHTING.

Mat. 3:16 a dove, and l. on him

LIGHTNING.

Mat. 24:27 as l. cometh out of
the east, Luke 17:24

LIKENESS.

Gen. 1:26 make man after l. 5:1
Rom. 6:5 in l. of his death, we
shall be in l. of resurrection

LILY.

Cant. 2:1 I am the l. of the va.
Hos. 14:5 Is. shall grow as the l.

LILIES.

Mat. 6:28 consider the l. how
they grow, Luke 12:27

LION.

Num. 24:9 Israel lay down as a l.
Deut. 33:20 Gad dwelleth as a l.
Jud. 14:8 turned to see carc. of l.

bees and honey in care. of l.
1 Sam. 17:34 ca. a l. and took la.
2 Sam. 17:10 heart as hea. of a l.
23:20 slew l. in pit, 1 Chr. 11:22
1 K. 13:24 a l. met him by way
    and slew him, l. also stood
20:36 a l. sh. slay thee; a l. fou.
Job 4:10 roaring of l. voice of l.
10:16 huntest me as a fierce l.
28:8 nor the fierce l. passed by
38:39 wilt th. hunt prey for l.?
Ps. 7:2 lest tear my soul like l.
10:9 lieth in wait secretly as a l.
17:12 like a l. greedy of his prey
22:13 they gaped on me as a l.
91:13 thou shalt tread on the l.
Prov. 19:12 king's wra. is as a l.
20:2 fear of king is as roar. of l.
22:13 saith, There is a l. in way
26:13 l. in way, a l. in the street
30:30 a l. strongest am. beasts
Ec. 9:4 liv. dog better th. dead l.
Is. 35:9 no l. there. nor ravenous
1 Pet. 5:8 devil as a l. walk. abo.

LIONS.
Dan. 6:27 D. from power of l.

LIPS.
Ps. 12:2 flat l. do they speak
31:18 lying l. be put to silence
63:5 praise thee with joyful l.
120:2 deli. my soul from lying l.
Prov. 10:21 l. of righteous feed
    many
32 l. of righteous know
15:7 l. of wise disperse knowl.
Mat. 15:8 that honoreth me with
Rom. 3:13 poison is under th. l.
Heb. 13:15 fruit of l. giv. thanks

His LIPS.
Prov. 10:19 refrain his l. is wise

LITTLE.
1 K. 18:44 l. cloud like a man's
    hand
Ps. 8:5 made him a l. lower than
    the angels, Heb. 2:7
Prov. 6:10 a l. sleep, l. slumber,
    a l. folding, 24:33
15:16 better is l. with fear of L.
16:8 better is l. with righteous
Mark 5:23 my l. daughter lieth
Luke 7:47 to whom l. is forgiven

Jam. 3:5 tongue is a l. member

LITTLE one, s.
Mat. 10:42 dri. to one of th. l. o.
18:6 offend one of these l. ones,
    Mark 9:42; Luke 17:2
10 despise not one of th. l. o.
14 one of these l. o. sho. perish

LIVE.
Gen. 3:2 tree of life l. for ever
Ezek. 16:6 when thou wast in blood
    l.
Hab. 2:4 just sh. l. by his faith,
John 11:25 tho' he were de. yet sh. l
Acts 17:28 in him we l. and move
Rom. 8:13 if ye l. after flesh. ye sh.
    die, 12:18 l. peaceably with all
    men
Tit. 2:12 we should l. soberly

LIVES.
1 John 3:16 lay down l. for breth.

LOAVES.
1 Sam. 25:18 Abigail took 200 l.
Mat. 14:17 we have here but 5 l.
19 and he took five l. Mark
    6:38; Luke 9:13
15:34 how many l. have ye?
36 took the seven l. Mark 8:6
16:9 nor remem. five l. of 5,000
10 nor the seven l. of the 4,000
Mark 6:44 eat of l. were 5,000
52 consider. not miracles of l.

LOCUSTS.
Ex. 10:4 to-morrow I will bri. l.
Deut. 28:38 l. shall consume it
Mat. 3:4 his meat was l. and wild
    honey, Mark 1:6

LOINS.
Heb. 7:5 came out of l. of Abrah.
10 he was yet in . of his father
1 Pet. 1:13 wheref. gird l. of mind

LONGING.
Ps. 107:9 he satisfieth the l. soul
119:20 soul break. for l. it hath

LONG-SUFFERING.
Ex. 34:6 Lo. G. l.-s. Num. 14:18'
    Ps. 86:15; 2 PEt. 3:9
Jer. 15:15 me not aw. in thy l.-s.
Rom. 2:4 despi. riches of his l.-s.
9:22 endured with much l.-s.
2 Cor. 6:6 by l.-s. by kindness
Gal. 5:22 fruit of Sp. is love, l.-s.

140

Eph. 4:2 with l.-s. forbearing
Col. 1:11 strengthened to all .-s.
 3:12 elect of G. meekness, l.-s.
1 Tim. 1:16 Ch. might show l.-s.
2 Tim. 3:10 kno. my faith, l.-s.
 4:2 with all l.-s and doctrine
2 Pet. 3:15 l.-s. of L. is salvation
LOOK.
Prov. 27:23 and l. well to herds
Cant. 4:8 l. from top of Amana
Is. 5:30 if one l. unto the land
 8:21 curse king, and l. upward
 22 they shall l. unto the earth
 17:7 shall a man l. to his maker
 22:4 l. away fr. me, I will weep
 31:1 they l. not to H. One of Is.
 42:18 l. ye blind, th. ye may see
 45:22 l. unto me, and be saved
 51:1 l. to rock whence are hewn
 56:11 all l. to their own way
 69:11 l. for judgment, but none
 66:2 but to this man will I l.
Jer. 13:16 while ye l. for light
 39:12 take and l. well to him
 40:4 and I will l. well to thee
 46:5 mighty fled, and l. not back
 47:3 fathers not l. back to chil.
Hos. 3:1 who l. to other gods
Jon. 2:$ l. toward holy temple
Mic. 7:7 therefore I l. to the Lord
Nah. 2:8 but none shall l. back
Mat. 11:3 l, for ano.? Luke 7:19,
 20
Mark 8:25 and made him l. up
Luke 21:28 thi, begin, then l. up
John 7:52 l. for out of Galilee
Acts 6:3 l. ye out seven men
2 Cor. 3:13 steadfastly l. to end
Phil. 3:20 we l. for the Saviour
1 Pet. 1:12 angels desire to l. in.
2 Pet. 3:14 seeing ye l. for such thi.
2 John 8 l. to yourselves
Rev. 5:3 no man able to l. there
LOOK on, or upon.
Ex. 3:6 Moses afraid to l. on G.
Lev. 13:3 priest l. u. the plague
Num. 15:39 that ye may l. u. it
2 Sam. 9:8 l. u. such a dead dog
 16:12 L. will l. u. my affliction
2 Chrs. 24:22 L. l. u. and require
Job 6:28 be content, l. upon me

40:12 l. u. ev. one that is proud
Ps. 22:17 bones stare and l. upon
 25:18 l. upon mine affliction
 35:17 how long wilt thou l. u.?
 84:9 l. u. face of thine anointed
 119:132 l. u. me, and be merciful
Prov. 4:25 let th. eyes l. right on
 23:31 l. not on wine wh. it is red
Cant. 1:6 l. not on me
 6:13 that we may l. upon thee
Is. 33:20 l. upon Zion, the city
 51:6 l. upon the earth beneath
Mic. 4:11 let our eye l. u. Zion
Nah. 3:7 that l. u. thee, shall flee
Hab. 1:13 purer eyes l. u. iniq.
 2:15 mayest l. u. their nakedn.
Zec. 12:10 l. u. me they pierced
Luke 9:38 master, l. u. my son
John 4:35 lift eyes, l. upon fields
 19:37 l. u. him they have pierced
Acts 3:4 P. and J. said. l. u. us, 12
LOOKED.
Gen. 19:26 his wife l. back fr.
behind
LOOSED.
Mat. 16:19 be l. in heaven, 18:18
 18:27 compassion, and l. him
Mark 7:35 string of his tongue
 was l. Luke 1:64
Luke 13:12 woman art l. fr. infir.
 16 ought not daughter to be l.
Acts 2:24 having l. pains of death
Rom. 7:2 husb. be dead, she is l.
1 Cor. 7:27 art thou l. fr. wife?
LORD.
1 Sam. 2:2 th. is none holy as L.
Mat. 22:43 how doth D. call him
 L.? 45; Mark 12:37; Luke 20:44
Luke 6:46 call me L. L. and do not
Phil. 2:11 confess Jesus C. is L.
Rev. 17:14 for he is L. of lords,
 19:16
Before the LORD.
Gen. 18:22 Abra. stood b. the L.
Lev. 10:2 they died b. L. Num. 3:4
Ps. 109:15 be b. the L. continually
2 Pet. 2:11 no railing accus. b.L.
LORD God.
Hab. 3:19 L. G. is my strength
LORD my God.
Dan. 9:4 prayed unto L. m. G. 20

LORD thy God.

Deut. 4:31 L. t. G. is a merciful G.
8:5 so L. thy G. chasteneth thee
Is. 42:3 I am the L. thy God
Mat. 4:7 thou shalt not tempt
the L. thy God, Luke 4:12

I the LORD.

Is. 45:19 I the L. speak righteousn.
Ezek 34:24 I the L. will be their G.

In the LORD.

1 Sam. 2:1 heart rejoiceth in t. L.
Ps. 4:5 put your trust in the L.
11:1 in the L. put I my trust,
26:1; 31:6; 73:28
31:24 all ye that hope in the L.
32:11 be glad in the L. and rej.
34:2 my soul shall boast in t. L.
35:9 my soul be joy. in the L.
37:4 delight thyself in the L.
Is. 58:14
7 rest in the L. and wait
56:10 in t. L. will I praise his
64:10 the righteous shall be gl.
in the L. 104:34
Prov. 3:5 trust in the L. wi. hea.
Is. 26:4 in t. L. Jehovah is ever.
45:24 in the L. have I righteous.
25 in the L. seed of Is. justifi.
Zep. 3:2 trusted not in the L.
Acts 9:42 many believed in t. L.
14:3 speaking boldly in the L.
Rom. 16:2 ye receive her in t. L.
12 who labored much in t. L.
1 Cor. 1:31 glorieth, let him glo.
in the L. 2 Cor. 10:17
4:17 faith. in L. 7:22 call. in L.
7:39 be married, only in the L.
9:1 my work in the L.?
2 apostleship are ye in t. L.
Eph. 2:21 a holy temple in t. L.
4:17 therefore, testify in the L.
5:8 now are ye light in the L.
6:1 obey your parents in the L.
10 brethren, be strong in t. L.
Phil. 4:1 sta. fast in t. L. 1 Thes. 3:8
2 be of the same mind in t. L.
Col. 3:18 submit to husb. in t. L.
1 Thes. 5:12 th. over you in t. L.
2 Thes. 3:4 have confidence in L.
Phile. 16 the flesh and in t. L.
20 let me have joy of thee in

t. L. refr. my bowels in t. L.
Rev. 14:13 bless. are dead in t. L.

LORD is.

Ex. 9:27 the L. is righteous, I
wicked, 2 Chr. 12:6
15:2 the L. is my strength
Num. 14:9 the L. is with us
18 the L. is long-suffering, of
great, Nah. 1:3
Ps. 34:8 O taste and see L. is good
89:18 L. is our defence and king
92:15 show that L. is upright
113:4 L. is high ab. all nations
118:6 the L. is on my side
121:5 L. is keeper, L. is shade
125:2 the L. is round about
129:4 L. is righteous, 145:17;
Lam. 1:18; Dan. 9:14
145:18 L. is nigh to all that call
Prov. 16:29 L. is far from wicked
Is. 30:18 L. is God of judgment
Luke 24:34 the L. is risen indeed
2 Cor. 3:17 the L. is that Spirit
Phil. 4:5 the L. is at hand
Heb. 13:6 the L. is my helper
1 Pet. 2:3 tasted the L. is graci.

Serve the LORD.

Ps. 2:11 s. L. wi. fear, rejoice
100:2 serve t. L. with gladness

LOSE, ETH

Mat. 10:39 he that findeth his
life shall l. it, 16:25; Mark
8:35; Luke 9:24
39 he that l. his life for my sa.
42 no wise l. reward, Mark 9:41
16:26 and l. his own soul, Mark
8:36; Luke 9:25
Luke 15:4 if he l. one sheep

LOST, passively.

Mat. 15:24 not sent but to l. sheep
18:11 Son is come to save what
was l. Luke 19:10
Luke 15:4 go after that wh. is l.
6 I found my sheep which is l.
24 son was l. 32 brother was l.

LOST, actively.

Mat. 5:13 if salt l. savor, Mark
9:50; Luke 14:34
John 18:9 gav. me, I have l. none

LOT.

Gen. 11:27 Haran begat L. 31

13:5 L. had flocks, 7, 11; 14:12
19:1 L. sat in gate of Sod. 10, 36
Luke 17:32 remember L. wife

LOT.
Acts 1:26 the l. fell on Matthias

LOTS.
1 Sam. 14:42 cat l. bet. me and
Mat. 27:35 casting l. Mark 15:24

LOUD.
Ps. 33:3 play skillf. wi. l. noise
98:4 make a l. noise and rejoice
150:5 praise him on l. cymbals

LOUD, with voice.
Prov. 27:14 bles. friend with l. v.
Acts 14:10 said with a l. v. Stand

LOVE.
2 Sam. 13:15 hatred greater than l.
Prov. 10:12 up strifes, l. covereth sins
  15:17 a dinner of herbs wh. l. is
  17:9 covereth transg. seeketh l.
  27:5 rebuke better than secret l.
  7 many waters cannot quen. l.
Jer. 2:33 why trim. way to seek l.?
John 15:13 greater l. hath no man
Rom. 8:35 separate from l. of C.?
2 Cor. 13:11 G. of l. shall be with y
Gal 5:13 by l. serve one another
  22 the fruit of the Spirit is l.
Eph. 3:19 to know the l. of Christ
1 Thes. 4:9 as touching brotherly l.
  5:8 on breastpla. of faith and l.
1 Tim. 6:10 l. of money is root of all e.
1 John 2:15 l. of F. is not in him
  3:4 behold what l. Father ha.
  4:7 love one another, l. is of G.
Rev. 2:4 thou hast left thy first l.

LOVE of God.
Rom. 8:39 to separa. us fr. the l. of G.

In LOVE.
Eph. 3:17 rooted and grounded in l.
  4:2 forbearing one another in l.
  15 but speaking the truth in l.

LOVE, Verb.
Lev. 19:18 thou shalt l. thy neighbor as thyself, 34; Mat. 19:19; 22:39; Mark 12:31
Deut. 6:5 thou shalt l. the L. thy G. with all thy heart, 10:12;

11:1, 13, 22; 19:9; 30:6
Mat. 5:44 but I say, l. your enemies, Luke 6:27, 32, 35
  46 if ye l. them which l. you
  6:24 hate one l. other, Luke 16:13
John 14:23 if a man l. me, Fath. l. him
  15:12 that ye l. one another, 17
Eph. 5:25 husb. l. your wives as C. loved ch. 28, 33; Col. 3:19
Tit. 2:4 young women to l. hus.
1 John 4:19 l. him bec. he first loved us 20 can he l. G. hath not seen

I LOVE.
Rev. 3:19 as many as I l. I rebuke

LOVE not.
Prov. 20:13 l. not sleep
1 John 2:15 l. not the world
  3:18 n. l. in word nor tongue

LOVED.
1 K. 3:3 Solomon l. the Lord
  11:1 Solomon l. many women
1 John 4:11 if God so l. us
  19 love him, bec. he first l. us
Rev. 1:5 to him that l. us

LOVELY.
Phil. 4:8 whatsoev. things are l.

LOVETH.
Prov. 3:12 whom L. l. he correct.
  12:1 l. instruction, l. knowledge
  13:24 that l. him, chasten. him
Luke 7:47 little is forgiven, l. little
John 3:35 Father l. Son, 5:20
  12:25 that l. his life sh. lose it
  14:21 hath com. he it is l. me, he that l. me be loved of Fa.
  24 l. me not, keep, not sayings
Rom. 13:8 that l. another
Eph. 5:28 that l. wife l. himself
Heb. 12:6 whom L. l. he chasten.
1 John 2:10 he that l. his brother
  3:10 he that l. not his brother
  4:7 ev. one that l. is born of G.
  21 he who l. God. l. his brother

LOW.
Ps. 136:23 remember. us in l. estate
Prov. 29:23 man's pride br. him l.
Luke 1:48 he regardeth l. estate
  52 exalted them of l. degree
Rom. 12:16 to men of l. estate

Jam. 1:9 brother of l. degree
10 rich in that he is made l.

LOWER.

Eph. 4:9 descended into l. parts

LOWEST.

Deut. 32:22 shall burn to l. hell
Ps. 86:13 deliv. soul from l. hell
88:6 thou hast laid me in l. pit
Luke 14:9 begin to take l. room
10 and sit down in the l. room

LOWLY.

Prov 3:34 he giveth grace to l.
11:2 but with l. is wisdom
16:19 be of humble spirit wi. l.
Zec. 9:9 l. and riding on an ass
Mat. 11:29 for I am meek and l.

LUKEWARM.

Rev. 3:16 because thou art l.

LUST.

Jam. 1:15 when l. hath conceived
1 John 2:16 l. of flesh, l. of eye

LUST, Verb.

Mat. 5:28 look. on woman to l.
1 Cor. 10:6 not l. after evil things
Jam. 4:2 ye l. and have not

LUSTS.

Rom. 13:14 no provision, to fulfil l.
Gal. 5:24 crucified flesh with l.
Eph. 2:3 conversa. in l. of flesh
4:22 corrupt accord. to deceit. l.
1 Tim. 6:9 foolish and hurtful l.
2 Tim. 2:22 flee youthful l.
4:3 after own l. heap teachers
Tit. 2:12 that denying worldly l.
3:3 divers l. and pleasures
Jam. 4:1 hence, even of your l.?
3 may consume it on your l.
1 Pet. 1:14 according to former l.
2:11 you abstain fr. freshly l.
2 Pet. 2:18 allure thro' l. of flesh
Jude 16 complain. walk. after l.
18 walk after their ungodly l.

LYING, spirit.

1 K. 22:22 a l. spi. in the mouth
of prophets, 2 Chr. 18:21
23 Lord hath put a l. spirit in
prophets, 2 Chr. 18:22.

M.

MADNESS.

Deut. 28:28 smite thee with m.

Ec. 1:17 to know wisd. and m.
7:25 wickednes of folly and m.
Luke 6:11 they were filled w. m.

MAGICIAN, S.

Gen. 41:8 Pharaoh called for m.
Ex. 7:11 the m. of Egypt did so
in like manner, 22; 8:7, 18
9:11 m. could not stand bef. M.

MAGISTRATE, S.

Luke 12:11 they bring you to m.
58 when thou goest to the m.
Acts 16:20 Paul and Silas to m.

MAGNIFY.

Ps. 34:3 O m. the Lord with me
Luke 1:46 my soul doth m. the L.
Acts 10:46 sp. wi. tongues, m. G.
Rom. 11:13 apostle, I m. office

MAID.

Ex. 2:8 m. went and called mother
Mat. 9:24 m. is not dead
26:71 another m. saw him, Mark
14:69; Luke 22:56
Luke 8:54 called, saying, m. arise

MAIDENS.

Ps. 78:63 m. not giv. to marri.
148:12 y. men and m. praise L.
Luke 12:45 ser. begin to beat m.

MAJESTY.

1 Chr. 29:11 thine, O Lord, is m.
Est. 1:4 showed honor of his m.
Job 37:22 with G. is terrible m.
Ps. 21:5 honor and m. hast thou
29:4 voice of the L. is full of m.
45:3 glory and m. 4 in m. ride
93:1 Lord is clothed with m.
96:6 honor and m. are bef. him
104:1 thou art clothed with m.
145:5 speak of honor of thy m.
12 glorious m. of his kingdom
Is. 2:10 glory of his m. 19, 21
24:14 shall sing for m. of the L.
26:10 not behold the m. of Lord
Dan. 4:30 built for honor of m.
36 excellent m. added to me
Mic. 5:4 feed in m. of name of L.
Heb. 1:3 on right hand of m. 8:1
2 Pet. 1:16 eye-witnes, of his m.
Jude 25 to God be glory and m.

MALICE.

1 Cor. 5:8 not with leaven of m.
14:20 howbeit in m. be ye chil.

144

Eph. 4:31 put away fr. you all m.
Col. 3:8 also put off all these, m.
Tit. 3:3 sometimes living in m.
1 Pet. 2:1 laying aside all m.

MAN.

1 K. 2:9 Solomon was a wise m.
1 Chr. 27:32 D.'s uncle a w. m.
Prov. 1:5 a w. m. hear and iner.
9:8 rebuke w. m. he will love
9 give instruction to wise m.
14:16 w. m. feareth, and depart.
16:14 a w. m. pacify wr. of king
17:10 reproof enter. into a w. m.
21:22 wise m. scaleth the city
26:12 m. w. in own conceit?
29:9 if w. m. contend. w. foolish
11 but a wise m. keepeth it in
Ec. 8:5 a wise m.'s heart discerneth
17 tho' a w. m. think to know
9:15 found in it a poor wise m.
10:2 w. m.'s heart at right hand
12 words of a wise m. gracious
Jer. 9:12 w. m. they may unde.?
23 let not wise m. gl. in wisd.
Mat. 7:24 liken him to a w. m.
1 Cor. 6:5 not a w. m. am. you
Jam. 3:13 who is a w. m. endued

MANGER.

Luke 2:7 and laid him in a m.

MANIFEST.

Phil. 1:13 bonds in Christ are m.
Col. 4:4 that I may make it m.
1 Tim. 3:16 God was m. in flesh

MANIFESTATION.

1 Cor. 12:7 m. of S. giv. to man
2 Cor. 4:2 m. of truth commend.

MANIFESTED.

Mark 4:22 hid wh. sh. not be m.
John 2:11 and m. forth his glory
17:6 m. thy name unto men
Rom. 3:21 righteous. of G. is m.
Tit. 1:3 in due time m. his word
1 John 3:5 m. to take away our sins
8 for this purp. was S. of G. m.
4:9 in this was m. love of God

MANIFOLD.

Neh. 9:19 in m. mercies forsook,
27 m. mercies gavest them
Ps. 104:24 how m. are works
Amos 5:12 I kn. your m. transg.
Luke 18:30 not receive m. more

Eph. 3:10 known m. wisd. of G.
1 Pet. 1:6 through m. temptatio.
4:10 stewards of m. grave of G.

MANKIND.

1 Tim. 1:10 law of them defile m.

MANNA.

Ex. 16:15 they said, It is m.
35 Israel did eat m. 40 years
Heb. 9:4 golden pot that had m.
Rev. 2:17 to eat of hidden m.

MANNER.

Luke 1:66 what m. of child sh.th.be
7:39 what m. of woman this
9:55 know not wh. m. of spirit
24:17 what m. of communicat.?
John 19:40 as m. of J. is to bury
Acts 17:2 Paul, as his m. was
20:18 know wh. m. I have been
22:3 according to perfect m.
26:4 my m. of life from youth
2 Cor. 7:9 sorry after godly m.
1 Thes. 1:5 ye kn. what m. of m.
9 what m. of entering in we
Heb. 10:25 as the m. of some is
Jam. 1:24 forge. what m. of man
1 Pet. 1:11 wh. m. of time the S.
15 holy in all m. of conversa.
2 Pet. 3:11 what m. of persons
1 John 3:1 behold what m. of love
Rev. 11:5 in this m. be killed

After this MANNER.

Mat. 6:9 after this m. pray ye
1 Cor. 7:7 one a. this m. and an.

MANNERS.

Lev. 20:23 not walk in m. of nat.
1 Cor. 15:33 ev. com. co. good m.
Heb. 1:1 God in divers m. spake

MANSIONS.

John 14:2 in Fa.'s ho. many m.

MANTLE, S.

1 K. 19:13 Elijah wrapped in m.
19 El. cast his m. upon Elisha
2 K. 2:13 Elisha took Elijah's m. 14

MARRED.

Mark 2:22 the bottles will be m.

MARK, Substantive.

Gen. 4:15 L. set a m. upon Cain
Phil. 3:14 press tow. m. for prize
Rev. 13:16 caused all to rec. a m.

MARKET.

Mat. 11:16 children sitting in m.

M

145

Luke 11:43; 20:46
Mark 7:4 when they come fr. m.
Luke 7:32 child. sitting in m.-pl.
John 5:2 a pool by the sheep-m.
Acts 16:19 drew them into m.-p.
17:17 disputed in the m. daily.

MARRIAGE.
Ex. 21:10 duty of m. sh. he not
Mat. 22:2 king made m. for son
9 all ye find, bid to the m.
30 in resurrection not given in
   m. Mark 12:25; Luke 20:35
24:38 given in m. until day N.
25:10 ready went wi. him to m.
Luke 17:27 given in m. 20:34
1 Cor. 7:38 giveth her in m.
Heb. 13:4 m. is honorable in all
Rev. 19:7 m. of Lamb is come
9 called to m. supper of Lamb

MARRY.
Gen. 38:8 go to bro. wife, m. her
Deut. 25:5 wife of dead sh. not m.
Is. 62:5 so shall thy sons m.
Mat. 5:32 m. her that is divorced
   19:9; Mark 10:11
19:10 be so, it is not good to m.
22:24 brother shall m. his wife
30 nei. m. nor given in marri.
   Mark 12:25; Luke 20:35
1 Cor. 7:9 cannot cont. let them
   m. better to m. than to burn
36 he sinneth not, let them m.
1 Tim. 4:3 forbidding to m. and
   5:14 younger wom. m. bear chil.

MARRIED.
Jer. 3:14 turn, for I am m. to you
Mal. 2:11 m. dau. of strange god
Mat. 22:25 first when he had m.
Mark 6:17 for he had m. her
Luke 14:20 m. a wife, can. come
17:27 they drank, they m. wives
Rom. 7:3 husband liv. she be m.
1 Cor. 7:10 to the m. I command
33 but he that is m. careth for
34 she that is m. car. for thin.
39 to be m. to whom she will

MARROW.
Ps. 63:5 soul satisfied as wi. m.
Prov. 3:8 health and m. to bones

MARTYR, S.
Acts 22:20 blood of thy m. Step,

Rev. 2:13 Anti. was faithful m.
17:6 drunken with blood of m.

MARVEL.
Mark 5:20 and all men did m.
John 5:20 that ye may m.
7:21 done one work, and ye m.
Acts 3:12 Is. why m. ye at this?

MARVELLED.
Mat. 8:10 Jesus heard it. he m.
Luke 7:9 when J. heard, he m. at
   him
John 4:27 m. he talked wi. wom.
7:15 Jews m. how knoweth this

MARVELLOUS.
Ps. 98:1 he hath done m. things
118:23 it is m. in our eyes, Mat.
   21:42; Mark 12:11
1 Pet. 2:9 called you into m. light

MARY.
Mat. 1:16 Joseph husband of M.
Luke 1:27 virgin's name was M.
John 12:3 M. took pound of oint.
19:25 M. stood by cross, 20:16
Acts 1:14 conti. in prayer. wi. M.

MARY Magdalene.
Mat. 27:56 amo. wh. were M. M.
   61; Mark 15:40; John 19:25
Mark 16:1 M. M. brought spices,
   Luke 24:10
John 20:18 M. M. told disciples

MASTER.
Jud. 19:22 spake to m. of house
Mat. 8:19 m. I will follow thee
9:11 why eat. your m. wi. pub.?
10:25 if they have called m. Be.
17:24 doth not your m. pay tri.?
22:16 m. we know that thou art
   true, Mark 12:14
Mark 5:35 why troubl. thou m.?
10:17 good m. what shall I do?
   Luke 10:25
13:35 ye know not wh. m. com.
Luke 7:40 m. say; 8:24 perish
   8:49 daugh. dead, troub. not m.
   13:25 when m. of house is risen
John 3:10 art thou a m. of Isr.?
11:28 m. is come and call. for th.
13:13 ye call me m. ye say well
14 I your m. washed your feet
Acts 27:11 centurion believed m.
Eph. 6:9 m. is in heaven, Col. 4:1

146

Thy MASTER.

1 Sam. 29:10 rise early wi. t. m.
2 Sam. 9:9 I give t. m. all that S.
  12:8 t. m. house, t. m. wives
  16:3 where is thy m. son?

MASTER-BUILDER.

1 Cor. 3:10 as wise m.-b. I have

MASTERS.

Ex. 21:4 children sh. be her m.
Ps. 123:2 eyes of serv. look to m.
Prov. 25:13 refresheth soul of m.
Amos 4:1 say to m. let us drink
Mat. 6:24 no man can serve two
  m. Luke 16:13
  23:10 neither be ye called m.
Eph. 6:5 be obedient to m. Col.
  3:22. Tit. 2:9; 1 Pet. 2:18
  9 ye, m. do the same things
  unto them, Col. 4:1
1 Tim. 6:1 count their m. worthy
  2 believ. m. let th. not despise

MATTER.

2 Chr. 8:15 departed not from
  any m.
Neh. 6:13 have m. for evil report
Est. 2:23 inquisition made of m.
Prov. 11:13 spirit concealeth m.
  16:20 that handleth a m. wisely
  17:9 repeat. m. separateth frien.
  18:13 answereth m. bef. heareth
Ec. 10:20 hath wings tell m.
Acts 15:6 elders consider this m.
  18:14 said, If it were m. of wro.

MEAL-TIME.

Ruth 2:14 at m.-t. come hither

MEANS.

Luke 5:18 sought m. to bring

MEANT.

Gen. 50:20 God m. it unto good

MEASURE.

Is. 5:14 hell opened without m.
Mat. 7:2 with what m. you mete,
  Mark 4:24; Luke 6:38
  23:32 fill ye up m. of your fath.
Mark 6:51 amazed beyond m.
Luke 6:38 good m. pressed down
John 3:34 G. giveth not Sp. by m.
2 Cor. 1:8 were pressed out of m.
  11:23 in stripes above m.
Eph. 4:7 according to m. of Ch.
  16 working in m. of every part

MEASURED.

Jer. 31:37 heaven ab. can be m.
  33:22 sand of sea cannot be m.

MEAT.

1 K. 10:5 she saw the m. of his
  table, 2 Chr. 9:4
Prov. 6:8 ant provideth her m.
Lam. 1:19 elders dies whi. they
  sou. m.
Ezek. 16:19 my m. which I gave
  thee 29:5 I have given thee for m.
  to beasts, 34:5, 8
Mat. 3:4 and his m. was locusts
  6:25 life more th. m.? Lu. 12:23
  9:10 as Jesus sat at m. in house,
    26:7; Mark 2:15; 14:3; 16:14;
    Luke 24:30
Mat. 25:42 hungered, gave me no
  m.
Luke 8:55 commanded to give her
  m
John 4:32 I have m. to eat ye know
  34 my m. is to do will of him
  6:27 labor not for the m. which
  perisheth, but for that m.
Acts 2:46 eat their m. with glad.
  27:33 besou. them to take m. 34
Rom. 14:15 grie. wi. thy m. dest.
  not with m. for wh. C. died
  17 kingdom of God not m.
1 Cor. 3:2 with milk, not wi. m.
  8:8 m. commend. us not to G.
  13 if m. make brother offend
  10:3 did eat same spiritual m.
Heb. 5:12 milk. not strong m.
  12:16 for m. sold his birthright

MEDDLE.

Prov. 20:19 m. not with him
  24:21 m. not th. given to change

MEDDLING.

2 Chr. 35:21 forbear fr. m. with G.
Prov. 20:3 every fool will be m.

MEDIATOR.

Gal. 3:19 angels in hand of m.
  20 a m. is not a m. of one
1 Tim. 2:5 is but one m. Jesus
Heb. 8:6 m. of a better covenant
  9:15 he is m. of New Testament
  12:24 J. m. of the new covenant

MEDICINE, S.

Prov. 17:22 doeth good like a m.

Jer. 30:18 thou hast no heal. m.
46:11 in vain thou use many m.
Ezek. 47:12 the leaf sh. be for m.

MEDITATE.

Gen. 24:63 Isaac went out to m.
Jos. 1:8 m. therein day and nig.
Ps. 1:2 doth m. day and night
63:6 m. on th. in night watches
77:12 I will m. of all thy work
119:15 I m. in thy precepts, 78
23 serv. m. in thy statutes. 48
148 I might m. in thy word
143:5 I m. on all thy works
Is. 33:18 thy heart sh. m. terror
Luke 21:14 settle it not to m.
1 Tim. 4:15 m. upon these things

MEDITATION.

Ps. 5:1 give ear, consider my m.
19:14 let m. of heart be accept.
49:3 m. of heart sh. be of under.
104:34 m. of him shall be sweet
119:97 love thy law, it is my m.
99 thy testimonies are my m.

MEEK.

Num. 12:3 Moses was very m.
Ps. 22:26 m. sh. eat and be satis.
25:9 m. will he guide in judgm.
37:11 m. shall inherit the earth
76:9 God arose to save all m.
147:6 the Lord lifted up the m.
149:4 beautify m. with salvation
Is. 11:4 for the m. of earth
29:19 m. shall increase their joy
61:1 good tidings to the m.
Amos 2:7 turn aside way of m.
Zep. 2:3 seek L. ye m. of earth
Mat. 5:5 blessed are the m.
11:29 for I am m. and lowly
21:5 thy king cometh to thee m.
1 Pet. 3:4 ornament of a m. spirit

MEEKNESS.

Ps. 45:4 because of truth and m.
Zep. 2:3 seek m. ye shall be hid
1 Cor. 4:21 sh. I come in sp. of m.?
2 Cor. 10:1 beseech by m. of Chr.
Gal. 5:23 fruit of the Spirit is m.
6:1 restore in the spirit of m.
Eph. 4:2 with lowliness and m.
Col. 3:12 put on m. long-suffer.
1 Tim. 6:11 love, patience, m.
2 Tim. 2:25 in m. instruct. those

Tit. 3:2 showing m. to all men
Jam. 1:21 receive with m. word
3:13 works with m. of wisdom
1 Pet. 3:15 reason of hope wi. m.

MEET, Verb.

Amos 4:12 prepare to m. thy G.
Zec. 2:3 angel went out to m.
Mat. 25:1 went forth to m. bridegro
Mark 14:13 there shall m. you a
man, Luke 22:10
Luke 14:31 ten thou. to m. him
Acts 28:15 came to m. us as far
1 Thes. 4:17 in clouds to m. Lord

MELCHISEDEK.

Ps. 110:4 order of M. Heb. 5:10

MELODY.

Is. 23:16 make sweet m. sing
51:3 found therein, voice of m.
Amos 5:23 not hear m. of viols
Eph. 5:19 making m. to Lord

MELTED.

Jos. 5:1 heard that th. hearts m.
7:5 the hearts of the people m.
Ps. 22:14 heart m. in midst
107:26 soul m. bec. of trouble

MELTETH.

Ps. 119:28 my soul m. for
heaviness

MEMBER.

1 Cor. 12:14 body is not one m.
19 all one m. where were bo.?
26 one m. suffer, one m. honor.
Jam. 3:5 the tongue is a little m.

MEMBERS.

Rom. 13:5 every one m. one of
another
1 Cor. 6:15 your bodies m. of C.
12:12 the body hath many m.
Eph. 4:25 are m. one of another
5:30 we are m. of his body
Col. 3:5 mortify your m. on ear.
Jam. 3:6 tongue one of our m.
4:1 lusts that war in your m.

MEMORY.

Ps. 109:15 cut off m. of them
Prov. 10:7 m. of the just blessed
Ec. 9:5 m. of them is forgotten
1 Cor. 15:2 keep in m. I preach.

MEN-PLEASERS.

Eph. 6:6 eye-servants as m.-p.
Col. 3:22

Wise MEN.

Deut. 1:13 take ye wise m. and
Job 15:18 which w. m. have told
  34:2 hear my words, O ye w. m.
Ps. 49:10 seeth that wise m. die
Prov. 10:14 w. m. lay up knowl.
  13:20 walketh with w. m.
  29:8 w. m. turn away wrath
Ec. 9:17 words of w. m. heard
Is. 19:12 where are thy wise m.
  29:14 wisd. of w.m. shall perish
  44:25 turneth w. m. backward
Jer. 8:9 the wise m. are ashamed
  10:7 the wise m. of the nations
  51:57 make drunken her w. m.
Ezek. 27:8 thy wise m. O Tyrus
Dan. 2:12 to destroy all wise m.
  4:6 decree to bring in all w. m.
Ob. 8 destroy w. m. out of Edom
Mat. 2:1 came w. m. from east
1 Cor. 1:26 not many wise m.
  10:15 I speak as to w. m.

MENSTRUOUS.

Is. 30:22 cast away as m. cloth
Lam. 1:17 Jeru. is as m. woman

MENTION, Substantive.

Ex. 23:13 make no m. of other
  gods, Jos. 23:7
1 Sam. 4:18 made m. of ark of G.
Ps. 71:16 make m. of thy righte.
Rom. 1:9 m. you alw. in my pra.
  Eph. 1:16; 1 Thes. 1:2
Phile. 4 m. of thee in my praye.

MERCHANDISE.

Mat. 22:5 farm, another to m.
John 2:16 F.'s house hou. of m.

MERCY.

Gen. 24:27 destitute master of m.
  43:14 God give you m. before
Ex. 34:7 keeping m. for thousands, Dan. 9:4
Num. 14:18 the Lord is of great
  m. Ps. 103:11; 145:3
Deut. 7:9 keep coven. and m. 12
2 Sam. 7:15 m. not depart from
  him, 1 Chr. 17:13; Ps. 89:24
  15:20 m. and truth be with thee
1 Chr. 16:34 his m. endureth for
  ever, 41; 2 Chr. 5:13; 7:3, 6;
  20:21; Ezr. 3:11; Ps. 106:1;
  107:1; 118:1; 136:1-26; Jer.

  33:11
Ezr. 7:28 extended m. to me
  9:9 extend. m. to us in sight of
Neh. 1:11 m. in sight of man
Ps. 21:7 thro' m. of Most High
  23:6 goodness and m. follow me
  25:10 paths of the Lord are m.
  32:10 m. shall comp. him about
  33:18 them that hope in his m.
  52:8 I trust in the m. of God
  57:3 send forth m. and truth
  59:10 God of m. sh. prev. me, 17
  61:7 O prepare m. and truth
  62:12 unto thee belongeth m.
  66:20 not turned m. from me
  77:8 is his m. cl. gone for ever?
  85:10 m. and truth m. together
  86:5 plenteous in m. 15; 103:8
  80:2 m. sh. be built up for ever
  14 m. and truth go be. thy face
  28 my m. will I keep for him
  98:3 remembered m. toward Is.
Prov. 3:3 let not m. forsake thee
  14:21 he that hath m. on poor
  22 m. and truth sh. be to them
Is. 49:10 that hath m. on them
  54:10 Lord that hath m. on thee
  60:10 my favor had m. on thee
Hos. 6:6 I desired m. and not sacrif.
  10:12 reap in m. 12:6 keep m.
  14:3 in thee the fatherl. find m.
Jon. 2:8 forsake their own m.
Mic. 6:8 do justly, and love m.
  7:18 because he delight. in m.
  20 wilt perform m. to Abraham
Hab. 3:2 L. in wrath remem. m.
Mat. 5:7 merciful, sh. obtain m.
  23:23 omitted judgment and m.
Luke 1:50 m. on them fear him
  54 Is. in remembran. of his m.
  72 to perform the m. promised
  78 through tender m. of God
Rom. 9:23 glory on vessels of m.
  11:30 obtained m. thro' unbelief
  31 your m. th. also may ob. m.
  15:9 might glorify God for m.
1 Cor. 7:25 obtai. m. to be faith.
2 Cor. 4:1 as we have received m.
Gal. 6:16 peace and m. on Israel
Eph. 2:4 God who is rich in m.
Phil. 2:27 God had m. on him

1 Tim. 1:2 m. and peace fr. G.

2 Tim. 1:2; Tit. 1:4; 2 John 3

13 I obtained m. because, 16

2 Tim. 1:16 Lord give m. to hou.

18 he may find m. of the Lord

Tit. 3:5 according to m. he saved

Heb. 4:16 that we may obtain m.

10:28 desp. law died without m.

Jam. 2:13 judgm. without m. th.

showed no m. m. rejoiceth

3:17 wisd. from above full of m.

5:11 pitiful and of tender m.

1 Pet. 1:3 according to abund. m.

2:10 m. now have obtained m.

Jude 2:21 looking for m. of Lord J.

Have MERCY.

Zec. 10:6 for I have m. upon them

Mat. 9:13 I will have m. 12:7

27 thou son of David, h. m. on

me, 15:22; 20:30, 31; Mark

10:47, 48; Luke 18:38, 39

Luke 16:24 Abraham, h. m. on m.

17:13 Jesus, Master, h. m. on us

Rom. 9:15 I will have m. on wh.

I will have m. 18

11:32 that he might h. m. on all

MERCY, with show, ed, eth.

Gen. 39:21 Lord was with Josep.

and showed him m.

1 K. 3:6 hast showed to d. my

father, great m. 2 Chr. 1:8

2 Chr. 6:14 s. m. to thy servants

Ps. 37:21 the righteous s. m.

85:7 s. us thy m. O Lord

Luke 1:58 L. s. great m. on her

10:37 that showed m. on him

Rom. 9:16 but of God that s. m.

Jam. 2:13 that hath s. no m.

Tender MERCIES.

Ps. 25:6 remem. thy t. m. 51:1

40:11 withhold not thy ten. m.

77:9 in anger shut up his t. m.

79:8 thy tender m. prevent us

103:4 L. crown. thee with t. m.

119:77 thy t. m. come unto me

156 great are thy ten. m. O L.

145:9 t. m. over all his works

MERCIFUL.

Ps. 26:11 redeem me, and be m.

to me, 41:4, 10; 56:1; 57:1

86:3; 119:58, 132

59:5 be not m. to any wicked

67:1 G. be m. to us, and bl. us

Prov. 11:17 m. man doeth good

Is. 57:1 m. men are taken away

Jer. 3:12 I am m. saith the Lord

Joel 2:13 he is gracious and m.

Jon. 4:2 knew thou art a m. G.

Mat. 5:7 m. shall obtain mercy

Luke 6:36 be m. as your F. is m.

18:13 God be m. to me a sinner

Heb. 2:17 be a m. high-priest

8:12 be m. to their unrigh1.

MERRY.

Jud. 16:25 their hearts were m.

19:6 and let thy heart be m.

Ruth 3:7 Boaz's heart was m.

1 Sam. 25:36 Nabal's heart m.

2 Sam. 13:28 when Amnon is m.

1 K. 4:20 Judah and Isr. were m.

21:7 and let thy heart be m.

2 Chr. 7:10 sent people away m.

Est. 1:10 heart of king was m.

Prov. 15:13 m. heart ma. cheerf.

15 m. heart ha. continual feast

17:22 a m. heart doeth good

Ec. 8:15 better to eat and be m.

9:7 drink wine with a m. heart

10:19 laughter, wine maketh m.

Is. 24:7 the m. hearted do sigh

Jer. 30:19 voi. of th. th. make m.

31:4 dances of th. that make m.

Luke 12:19 ease, eat and be m.

15:23 and be m. 24; 29 I might

32 it was meet we should be m.

Jam. 5:13 is any m.? sing psal.

Rev. 11:10 rejoice and make m.

MERRILY.

Est. 5:14 go in m. with king

MESSAGE.

Jud. 3:20 I have m. from God

Prov. 26:6 sendeth m. by fool

Hag. 1:13 spake liag. in L.'s m.

Luke 19:14 citiz. sent m.aft. him

1 John 1:5 m. we ha. heard, 3:11

MESSENGER.

Gen. 50:16 sent a m. to Joseph

Prov. 25:13 faithful m. to them

Is. 42:19 as my m. that I sent?

Hag. 1:13 Haggai, the Lord's m.

Mal. 2:7 he is m. of L. of hosts

3:1 send m. of covenant, Mat.

11:10; Mark 1:2; Luke 7:27
2 Cor. 12:7 m. of Satan to buffet
Phil. 2:25 companion, your m.

MESSENGERS.

Gen. 32:3 Jacob sent m. to Esau
Jos. 6:17 Rahab hid the m. 25
1 Sam. 19:11 Saul sent m. to
   David, 14, 15, 20, 21
   25:14 David sent m. to salute
2 Sam. 3:12 sent m. to D. on his
   behalf
   11:4 Dav. sent m. to Bathsheba
   12:27 Joab sent m. to David
2 K. 1:3 meet the m. of Ahaziah
   19:23 m. th. hast reproached L.
Jer. 27:3 send by hand of the m.
Nah. 2:13 voice of m. no more
Luke 7:24 m. of John were gone
   9:52 and sent m. before his face
2 Cor. 8:23 m. of the churches
Jam. 2:25 Rahab had receiv. m.

MESSIAH.

Dan. 9:25 from commandment
   to build Jerus. unto the M.
   the Prince shall be 7 weeks
   26 after 62 weeks M. be cut off
John 1:41 found M. wh. is Christ
   4:25 I know that M. cometh

METHUSELAH.

Gen. 5:27 days of M. 969 years
1 Chr. 1:3 M. Lamech, Luke 3:27

MICHAEL.

Dan. 10:13 M. ch. prince, 21; 12:1
Jude 9 M. contending with dev.
Rev. 12:7 M. fought ag. dragon

MICHAL.

1 Sam. 14:49 S.'s yr. daughter M.

MIDNIGHT.

Ex. 11:4 m. I will go into Egypt
   12:29 at m. L. smote first-born
Jud. 16:3 Samson lay till m.
Ruth 3:8 at m. man was afraid
1 K. 3:20 she arose at m. and
Ps. 119:62 at m. I will give than.
Mat. 25:6 at m. there was a cry
Mark 13:35 come at even or m.
Luke 11:5 shall go to him at m.
Acts 16:25 at m. Paul prayed
   20:7 P. continued speech till m.

MIDST.

Luke 4:30 passing thro' m. of th.

John 7:14 about the m. of feast
   8:59 going through m. of them
Rev. 8:13 flying thro' m. of heav.

MIDWIFE.

Gen. 35:17 m. said unto Rachel

MIGHT, Substantive.

Deut. 6:5 love thy God with all thy
m.
2 Sam. 6:14 D. danced with all m.
Est. 10:2 Ahasue. power and m.
Ps. 76:5 none of the men of m.
   145:6 speak of m. of thy acts
Ec. 9:10 find. do it with thy m.
Is. 33:13 ye that acknow. my m.
Dan. 2:20 wisdom and m. are his
   23 O G. who hast given me m.
   4:30 build by m. of my power
Mic. 7:16 nations confound. at th.
m.
Zec. 4:6 not by m. nor by power
Eph. 1:21 far above all m. power
   3:16 to be strengthened with m.
   Col. 1:11
   6:10 L. and in power of his m.
2 Pet. 2:11 angels greater in m.
Rev. 7:12 glo. and m. be unto G.

MIGHTY.

Gen. 18:18 Abraham bec. a m.
nation
   23:6 thou art a m. prince
Job 9:4 wise in heart, m. in streng.
Ps. 82:1 God in congrega. of the m.
Mat. 13:58 he did not many m.
works there, Mark 6:5
Eph. 1:19 working of m. power

MILE.

Mat. 5:41 compel thee to go a m.

MILK, Substantive.

Joel 3:18 hills shall flow with m.
1 Cor. 3:2 I have fed you with m.
   9:7 who eateth not of the m.?
Heb. 5:12 as have need of m.?
   13 ev. one useth m. is a babe
1 Pet. 2:2 new-born babes des. m.

MILLSTONE.

Mat. 18:6 a m. hanged about his
   neck, Mark 9:42; Luke 17:2

MIND, Substantive.

1 Chr. 28:9 serve with willing m.
Mark 5:15 his right m. Luke 8:35
Luke 12:29 nei. be of doubtful m.

Acts 17:11 all readiness of m.
20:19 serv. L. with humi. of m.
Rom. 1:28 ga. up to reprobate m.
7:25 with m. I serve law of God
8:7 carnal m. enmity against G.
27 knoweth what is m. of Sp.
11:34 who hath kno. m. of L.?
1 Cor. 1:10 joined in the same m.
2 Cor. 8:12 if a willing m. it is
accept. 13:11 brethr. be of one m.
Phil. 1:27; 2:2
Eph. 2:3 desires of flesh and m.
Phil. 2:3 in lowli. of m. let each
5 let this m. be in you wh. was
4:2 be of the same m. in the L.
Col. 2:18 puffed up by fleshly m.
3:12 humbleness of m. meekn.
2 Thes. 2:2 not soon shaken in m.
2 Tim. 1:7 spirit of sound m.
Tit. 1:15 m. and conscience defi.
3:1 put them in m. to be subj.
Heb. 8:10 my laws into th. m.
1 Pet. 3:8 be ye all of same m.
4:1 arm yours. like. wi. one m.
Rev. 17:9 m. which hath wisdom
13 these have one m. and shall

MINDED.

Ruth 1:18 she was steadfastly m.
2 Chr. 24:4 m. to repair house
Ezr. 7:13 m. of th. own free will
Rom. 8:6 to be cam. m. is death,
to be spiritually m. is life
11:20 be not high-m. but fear
15:5 grant you to be like-m.
Phil. 2:2 that ye be like-m.
20 no man like-m. will care
3:15 as many as be perf. be thus
m. if ye be otherwise m.
1 Thes. 5:14 comf. the feeble-m.
1 Tim. 6:17 rich be not high-m.
2 Tim. 3:4 men heady, high-m.
Tit. 2:6 exhort to be sober-m.
Jam. 1:8 double-m. man unstab.
4:8 purify hearts ye double-m.

MINDFUL.

Ps. 8:4 what is man, that thou
art m. of him? Heb. 2:6
111:5 ever be m. of covenant
Is. 17:10 not been m. of rock
2 Tim. 1:4 being m. of thy tears
2 Pet. 3:2 be m. of words spoken

MINDS.

Phil. 4:7 peace of G. keep yo. m.
Heb. 10:16 in m. will I write
12:3 wear. and faint in your m.
2 Pet. 3:1 I stir up your pure m.

MINISTER.

Mat. 20:26 your m. Mark 10:43
Acts 26:16 make th. a m. and witn.
Rom. 15:16 be m. of Jesus to Gent.
Gal. 2:17 is Ch. the m. of sin?
Eph. 3:7 whereof I was made a
m. Col. 1:23, 25
1 Thes. 3:2 brother and m. of G.
1 Tim. 4:6 a good m. of Christ
Heb. 8:2 a m. of the sanctuary

MINISTER, Verb.

Ex. 28:1 that he may m. to me in
the priest's office, 3, 4, 41;
29:1, 44; 30:30: 31:10; 35:19;
39:41; 40:13, 15
1 Sam. 2:11 child did m. to Lord
1 K. 8:11 priest could not stand
to m. 2 Chr. 5:14
Heb. 1:14 m. to heirs of salvation
1 Pet. 4:11 if any man m. let do it

MINISTERED.

1 K. 19:21 Elijah, and m. to him
Mat. 4:11 angels came and m. to
him, Mark 1:13
Acts 13:2 as they m. and fasted
20:34 have m. to my necessities
2 Cor. 3:3 epistle of Ch. m. by us
Phil. 2:25 that m. to my wants
Col. 2:19 having nourishment m.
2 Tim. 1:18 many th. m. unto me
Heb. 6:10 have m. to the saints
2 Pet. 1:11 entrance be m. to you

MINISTRY.

2 Chr. 7:6 D. praised by their m.
Acts 1:25 that he may take part of
m.
1 Cor. 16:15 addicted to m. of sa.
2 Cor. 4:1 seeing we have this m.
5:18 giv. us m. of reconciliation
6:3 that the m. be not blamed
Eph. 4:12 work of m. for edifyi.
Col. 4:17 take heed to the m.
Tim. 1:12 putting me into m.

MIRACLE

Ex. 7:9 P. sh. speak, Show a m.
Mark 9:39 no man which shall do

m.
Acts 4:16 a notable m. been done
  22 on wh. this m. was wroug.

MIRACLES.
Num. 14:22 which have seen m.
Deut. 11:3 have not seen his m.
  29:3 th. eyes have seen those m.
Jud. 6:13 where be all his m.
John 2:11 beginning of m. did J.
  23 many beli. wh. they saw m.
  3:2 no man can do th. m. ex. G.
  6:26 not because ye saw the m.
  7:31 will he do more m. th. this
  9:16 can a sinner do such m.?
  11:47 this man doeth many m.
  12:37 he had done so many m.
Acts 2:22 approved of God by m.
  6:8 Stephen did great m.
  8:6 hearing and seeing the m.
  13 wondered, beholding the m.
  15:12 what m. G. had wrought
  19:11 G. wrought spec. m. by P.
1 Cor. 12:10 to the working of m.
  28 teachers; after that m.
  29 are all workers of m.?
Gal. 3:5 he that worketh m.
Heb. 2:4 G. bearing witn. wi. m.
Rev. 13:14 decei. by means of m.
  16:14 spirits of devils work. m.
  19:20 false prophet th. wro. m.

MIRY.
Ps. 40:2 bro. me out of m. clay

MIRIAM.
Neh. 8:12 peo. went to make m.
Ps. 137:3 that wasted us des. m.
Prov. 14:13 end of m. heaviness
Ec. 2:1 I will prove th. with m.
  7:4 heart of fools is in ho. of m.
  8:15 then I commended m.
Is. 24:8 m. of tabrets
  11 the m. of the land is gone

MISCARRYING.
Hos. 9:14 give them a m. womb

MISCHIEFS.
Ps. 52:2 thy tongue deviseth m.
  140:2 imagine m. in their heart

MISERABLE.
1 Cor. 15:19 are of all most m.

MISERY, IES.
Ec. 8:6 the m. of a man is great
Lam. 3:19 re. mine affliction and

m.
Jam. 5:1 howl for your m.

MISTRESS.
Gen. 16:8 flee fr. my m. S. 9 return
to
Is. 24:2 as with maid so with m.
Nah. 3:4 the m. of witchcrafts

MISUSED.
2 Chr. 36:16 they m. his prophe.

MITE, S.
Mark 12:42 a certain poor widow
  threw in two m. Luke 21:2
Luke 12:59 thou hast paid last m.

MOCKED.
Num. 22:29 bec. thou hast m. me
Jud. 16:10 m. me, 13, 15
1 K. 18:27 at noon, Elijah m. th.
2 K. 2:23 little child. m. Elisha
2 Chr. 36:16 m. the messengers of
God
Neh. 4:1 Sanballat m. the Jews
Job 12:4 one m. of his neighbor
Mat. 2:16 H. saw that he was m.
  27:29 they bowed the knee and
  m. 31; Mark 15:20
Luke 18:32 m. spitef. entreated
  22:63 men that held J. m. him
  23:11 Herod m. 36 soldiers m.
Acts 17:32 resurrection, some m.
Gal. 6:7 not deceiv. G. is not m.

MOCKER, S.
Job 17:2 are th. not m. with me?
Ps. 35:16 hypocrit. m. in feasts
Prov. 20:1 wine is a m. st. drink
Is. 28:22 be not m. lest bands be
Jer. 15:17 sat not in assem. of m.
Jude 18 sh. be m. latter times

MOCKEST, ETH.
Job 11:3 when thou m. sh. no m.
  13:9 as one m. anoth. do ye so
  39:22 m. at fear, not affrighted
Prov. 17:5 m. poor repro. Maker
  30:17 that m. at his father

MOCKING.
Gen. 21:9 saw son of Hagar m.

MODERATION.
Phil. 4:5 let your m. be known

MODERATELY.
Joel 2:23 gi. you former rain m.

MODEST.
1 Tim. 2:9 adom in m. apparel

MONEY.

Gen. 28:13 I will give thee m. for field 47:15 m. faileth; 18 our m. spent
Jud. 16:18 lords bro. m. to Delilah
Jer. 32:44 men shall buy fields for m.
Mat. 17:24 received trib. m. ca.
  27 thou shalt find a piece of m.
  22:19 show me the tribute m.
  25:18 earth, hid his lord's m.
  27 m. to exchang. Luke 19:23
  28:12 large m. to soldiers, 15
Mark 6:8 they took no m. in their purse, Luke 9:3
  12:41 people cast m. into treas.
  14:11 and promised to give him m. Luke 22:5
Acts 4:37 brought m. and laid it
  8:18 Simon offered them m.
  20 P. said, m. perish with thee
  24:26 hoped m. sho. been given
1 Tim. 6:10 love of m. root of all

MONEY-CHANGERS.

Mat. 21:12 Jesus overthrew tables of m.-c. Mark 11:15
John 2:14 found in temple m.-c.

MONTHS.

Rev. 9:5 be tormented five m. 10
  11:2 tread under foot 42 m.
  13:5 power given to con. 42 m.

MOON.

Ec. 12:2 while sun, m. or stars

MORDECAI.

Ezr. 2:2 M. came up, Neh. 7:7
Est. 2:5 a Jew, name was M.
  10:3 M. was next to Abasuerus.

MORNING.

Job. 7:21 thou shalt seek me in m.
Ps. 5:3 my voice shalt thou hear in the m. O Lord, in the m.
  30:5 but joy cometh in the m.
Is. 14:12 O Lucifer, son of m.
Mat. 16:3 in the m. it will be fo.
  27:1 when the m. was come
Mark 11:20 in m. as they passed
  13:35 at cock-crowing, or in m.

Early in the MORNING.

Gen. 19:27 Abraham gat up e. in the m. 21:14; 22:3
  28:18 Jacob rose up e. in the m.

  31:55 Laban rose e. in the m.
Ex. 8:20 said, Rise e. in m. 9:13
  24:4 Moses rose early in m. 34:1
Jos. 3:1 Joshua rose early in the m. 6:12; 7:16; 8:10
1 Sam. 1:19 they rose up e. in t. m. 29:11; 2 K. 3:22; 19:35;
  2 Chr. 20:20; Is. 37:36
  15:12 Sa. rose e. in m. 17:20 D.
  29:10 wherefore rise e. in the m.
Job 1:5 Job rose up e. in the m.
Prov. 27:14 rising early in the m.
Mat. 20:1 went early in the m.
Mark 16:2 early in the m. came to sepulchre, Luke 24:1
Acts 5:21 entered temple e. in m.

Every MORNING.

Ex. 16:21 gath. manna every m.

MORNING star.

Job 38:7 wh. m. s. sang together
Rev. 22:16 I, Jesus, am bright m. s.

MORROW.

Prov. 3:28 to- m. shall be as this day
Mat. 6:30 to-m. is cast into the oven, Luke 12:28
  34 take no thought for m. for m. sh. take thought for itself
Luke 13:32 to-day, and to-m.
  33 walk to-day and to-m.
Acts 20:7 P. rea. to depart on m.
  25:22 to-m. thou shalt hear him
Jam. 4:13 to-day or to-m. will go

MORSEL.

Prov. 17:1 bet. dry m. and quiet
Heb. 12:16 E. for m. sold birthri.

MORTAL.

Job 4:17 m. man mo. just th. G.?
Rom. 6:12 sin reign in m. body
  8:11 quicken m. bodies by Spi.
1 Cor. 15:53 m. on immortal. 54
2 Cor. 4:11 J. manifest, in m. fle.

MOSES.

Ex. 2:10 called his name M.
Jos. 1:5 as I was with M. 3:7
Ps. 103:7 made kn. ways to M.
Is. 63:12 by right hand of M.
Jer. 15:1 though M. stood be. me
Mal. 4:4 remember law of M.
Mat. 17:3 there appeared M. and
  19:7 why did M. command.?

23:2 Pharisees sit in M.'s seat
Mark 10:3 what did M. com.?
Mark 12:19 M. wrote, Luke 20:28
Luke 16:29 M. and prophets
20:37 M. showed at the bush

MOTE.

Mat. 7:3 m. in brother's eye,
Luke 6:41
4 let me pull m. out of th. eye
5 then th. see clear. to cast m.
out of broth.'s eye, Luke 6:42

MOTH.

Ps. 39:11 beauty consu. like m.
Is. 50:9 m. shall eat them, 51:8

MOTHER.

Gen. 3:20 was m. of all living
Ruth 1:8 ret. each to m.'s house
Jer. 50:12 m. be sore confounded
Hos. 2:2 plead with your m.
Mic. 7:6 daughter riseth up ag.
her m. Mat. 10:35; Lu. 12:53
Mat. 8:14 P.'s wife's m. Lu. 4:38
14:8 before instructed of her m.
19:12 so born from m.'s womb
20:20 m. of Zebedee's children
Luke 1:43 m. of L. come to me?
John 2:1 m. of J. there, Acts 1:14
Acts 12:12 hou. of Mary, m. of J.
Gal. 4:26 Jerusalem m. of us all
Rev. 17:5 the m. of harlots and

His MOTHER.

Prov. 10:1 son is heavi. of h. m.
15:20 foolish man despis. h. m.
29:15 left bringeth h.m. to sh.
Acts 3:2 lame fr. h. m. wo. 14:8

MOTHER-IN-LAW.

Ruth 1:14 Or. kissed her m.-i.-l.
2:23 R. dwelt with her m.-i.-l.
Mic. 7:6 dau.-in-law ag. m.-i.-l.
Mat. 10:35; Luke 12:53

My MOTHER.

Mat. 12:48 Jesus said, Who is
my m.? Mark 3:33
49 behold my m. and brethren,
Mark 3:34; Luke 8:21

Thy MOTHER.

Prov. 1:8 the law of thy m. 6:20
23:22 and despise not thy m.

MOTHERS.

1 Tim. 5:2 entreat elder women as
m.

MOUNT of Olives.

Mat. 21:1 they were come to the
m. of Olives, Luke 19:29
24:3 upon m. of O. Mark 13:3
26:30 they went out into m. of
O. Mark 14:26; Luke 22:39
Luke 19:37 at descent of m. of O.
21:37 and abode in m. of O.
Acts 1:12 returned fr. m. of O.

MOUNTAIN.

Gen. 14:10 they th. re. fled to m.
19:17 escape to m. 19 not escape
Ex. 3:1 came to the m. of G.
Mat. 5:1 he went up into a m.
14:23; 15:29; Mark 3:13; 6:46;
Luke 6:12; 9:28; John 6:3, 15
17:1 bringeth them into high m.
9 and as they came down from
the m. Mark 9:9
20 have faith, say to this m.
Remove, 21:21; Mark 11:23
28:16 m. where Jesus appointed
Luke 8:32 swine feeding on m.
Heb. 12:20 much as beast tou. m.
Rev. 6:14 every m. and isl. rem.
8:8 a great m. burning with fire

MOUNTAINS.

Gen. 8:4 the ark rested upon the m.
1 K. 19:11 a strong wind rent m.
Ps. 148:9 m. and hills praise the L.

MOURN.

Gen. 23:2 Ab. came to m. Sarah
Ec. 3:4 time to m. time to dance
Mat. 5:4 blessed are they that m.
9:15 child. of bride-chamb. m.?
24:30 all the tribes of earth m.
Luke 6:25 laugh, for ye sh. m.
Jam. 4:9 afflicted, m. and weep

MOURNED.

2 Sam. 11:26 Bath-sheba m. for
Uriah
13:27 David m. for his son Abs.
14:2 one that had m. for ead
Zec. 7:5 when ye m. and fasted
Mat. 11:17 we have m. unto you,
Luke 7:32
Mark 16:10 as they m. and wept

MOURNING.

Ps. 30:11 turned m. to dancing
Is. 60:20 days of m. shall be ended
Mat. 2:18 great m. Rachel weep.

2 Cor. 7:7 he told us your m.
Jam. 4:9 laugh. be turned to m.
Rev. 18:8 one day death and m.

MOURNING.

Gen. 37:35 go down to grave m.
2 Sam. 11:2 put on m. apparel
Est. 6:12 H. hasted to house m.
Job. 30:28 I went m. without sun
Ps. 38:6 I go m. all day long
  42:9 why go I m. because of op-
  pression of enemy? 43:2
Jer. 9:17 call for the m. women
  16:7 m. to comf. them for dead
Ezek. 7:16 m. for their iniquities
Dan. 10:2 D. was m. three weeks

MOUTH.

Ps. 8:2 out of m. of babes
  32:9 m. must be held with brid.
1 Cor. 9:9 not muzzle m. of ox

My MOUTH.

Ps. 34:1 praise continual. in my m.
  49:3 my m. shall speak of wisd.
  51:15 my m. sh. forth thy praise
  71:8 my m. be filled with praise
  78:1 incl. ears to wor. of my m.
  2 I will open my m. in a para.
  89:1 with my m. will I make kn.
  109:30 praise the L. with my m.
  145:21 my m. sh. speak praise
Mat. 13:35 open my m. in parab.
Rev. 3:16 spew thee out of my m.

MOUTH, with opened.

Num. 22:28 Lord opened m. of the
ass

Thy MOUTH.

Rom. 10:9 confess with thy m.
Your MOUTH.
Eph. 4:29 no corrupt communication out of your m. Col. 3:8

MOUTHS.

Dan. 6:22 G. hath shut lions' m.

MOVE.

Acts 17:28 live, m. ha. our being

MOVED.

Gen. 1:2 Sp. of God m. on waters
2 Sam. 24:1 he m. David against
them
Est. 5:9 Mord. m. not for him
Ps. 121:3 not suffer thy foot to be
m.
Prov. 12:3 root of the righteous

shall not be m.
Mat. 9:36 he was m. with com-
  passion on them, 14:14; 18:27;
  Mark 1:41; 6:34
  20:24 were ,m. with indignation
Acts 2:25 that I sho. not be m.
Col. 1:23 be not m. from gospel
1 Thes. 3:3 no man be m. by th.
Heb. 11:7 Noah, m. with fear
  11:28 kingd. wh. cannot be m.
2 Pet. 1:21 as m. by the H. Ghost
Rev. 6:14 mount. and island m.

MULE.

2 Sam. 13:29 every man upon m.
  18:9 Absalom rode upon a m.
1 K. 1:33 to ride on my m. 38:44
Ps. 32:9 be not as horse or m.

MULES.

Gen. 36:24 found m. in wildern.
2 K. 5:17 given to sorv. two m.
1 Chr. 12:40 on camels and m.
Ezr. 2:66 their m. were 245, Neh.
  7:68.
Est. 8:10 sent letters by m. 14
Is. 66:20 bring your breth. on m.

MULTIPLY.

Gen. 1:22 be fruitful and m. 28;
  8:17; 9:7; 35:11
  16:10 I will m. Hag. seed, 17:20
  22:17 in multiplying I will m.
  thy seed, 26:4, 24; Heb. 6:14
  28:3 G. Almighty bless and m.
Ex. 1:10 deal wisely, lest th. m.

MULTIPLIED.

Deut. 1:10 L. your G. ha. m. you
Acts 12:24 word of G. grew and m.

MULTITUDE.

Gen. 16:10 it shall not be numb.
  for m. 32:12; 1 K. 3:8
Est. 5:11 Haman told of the m.
  10:3 Mordecai accepted of m.
Ps. 60:13 O God, in m. of mercy
Prov. 11:14 m. of counsellors, 24:6
Luke 2:13 th. was wi. angel a m.
  20:47 while he yet sp. behold m.
John 5:13 a m. being in that pl.
  21:6 not able for m. of fishes
Acts 4:32 the m. that believed
  6:5 saying pleased whole m.
  21:22 m. must come together
Jam. 5:20 sh. save a soul fr. dea.

and shall hide a m. of sins
1 Pet. 4:8 charity cov. m. of sins

MULTITUDES.
Mat. 21:9 m. cried, saying,
Hosanna

MURDER, S.
Mat. 15:19 out of the heart pro-
ceed m. Mark 7:21
19:18 said, Thou shalt do no m.
Mark 15:7 Barab. committed m.
Luke 23:19 for m. cast in pri. 25
Rom. 1:29 envy, m. debate
gal. 5:21 flesh are envyings, m.
Rev. 9:21 nor repented of th. m.

MURDERERS.
Rev. 21:8 m. shall have part

MURMUR.
Num. 14:36 made congrega. m.
17:5 whereby they m. ag. you
John 6:43 m. not am. yourselves
1 Cor. 10:10 neither m. as some

MURMURED.
Ex. 16:2 whole congregation of Isr.
m. Num. 14:2; 16:41
Deut. 1:27 ye m. in your tents
Ps. 106:25 but m. in their tents
Mark 14:5 they m. against hor
Luke 15:2 they m. saying, This
man
19:7 m. that he was going to be
John 6:61 he knew his disciples m.
1 Cor. 10:10 as some of them m.

MURMURERS.
Jude 16 these are m. complainers

MURMURING, S.
Ex. 16:7 he heareth your m. 8, 9,
12; Num. 14:27
Num. 17:5 make to cease m. of L.
10 take away their m. fr. me
John 7:12 much m. among peo.
Acts 6:1 a m. against Hebrews
Phil. 2:14 do all thi. without m.

MUSIC.
1 Sam. 18:6 meet Saul with m.
2 Chr. 5:13; 23:13; 34:12
2 Chr. 7:6 wi. instruments of m.
Ec. 12:4 dau. of m. bro. low
Lam. 3:63 rising; I am their m.
Dan. 3:5 kinds of m. 7:10, 15
6:18 instruments of m. brought
Amos 6:5 inv. instruments of m.

Luke 15:25 elder son heard m.

MUSICAL.
1 Chr. 16:42 m. instrum. of God
Neh. 12:36 m. instru. of David
Ec. 2:8 as m. instruments.

MYRRH.
Est. 2:12 6 months wi. oil of m.
Prov. 7:17 perf. my bed with m.
Cant. 3:6 perf. with m. and
frankinc.
Mat. 2:11 presented gold and m.

MYSTERY.
Mark 4:11 given to know m.
Eph. 1:9 made known to us m.
3:3 made known to me the m.
4 knowledge in the m. of Ch.
5:32 this is a great m.
6:19 to make known m. of the
gospel. Col. 1:26, 27; 4:3
2 Thes. 2:7 m. of iniq. doth work
1 Tim. 3:9 holding m. of faith
16 great is the m. of godliness

MYSTERIES.
Mat. 13:11 m. of the kingdom, to
them not given, Luke 8:10
1 Cor. 4:1 stewards of m. of God
13:2 tho' I understand all m.
14:2 in the Sp. he speaketh m.

N.

NAAMAN.
2 K. 5:1 N. was leper, 11, 20, 27
Luke 4:27 none cleansed, sav. N.

NAILS.
Deut. 21:12 sh. head, pare her n.

NAILING.
Col. 2:14 he n. it to his cross

NAKED.
Gen. 2:25 were n. not ashamed
3:7 knew they were n. 10, 11
Job 1:21 n. came I out of womb,
and n. shall I return thither
Mat. 25:36 n. and ye clothed me
38 when saw we thee n.? 44
Mark 14:51 cloth ab. his n. body
52 and fled from them n.
John 21:7 Peter was n. and cast

NAKEDNESS.
Rom. 8:35 shall n. separate us?
2 Cor. 11:27 in cold and n.
Rev. 3:18 shame of n. not appear

NAME.

Ps. 69:30 I will praise the n. of G.
82:18 whose n. alone is Jehovah
99:3 let th. praise thy great n.
113:3 the L.'s n. is to be praised
Prov. 10:7 n. of wicked shall rot
22:1 good n. rather than riches
30:9 lest I take n. of G. in vain
Ec. 7:1 good n. bet. than ointm.
Dan. 2:20 blessed be the n. of G.
Mat. 28:19 baptizing them in n. of F.
John 5:43 am come in my Fath.'s n.
10:25 I do in my Father's n.
Acts 4:7 by wh. n. ha. ye done this
12 none other n. under heaven
30 wonders done by n. of Jes.
1 Cor. 6:11 justified in the n. of L.J.
Phil. 2:10 at n. of J. ev. knee shall b.
Col. 3:17 do all in the n. of L. J.
1 Tim. 6:1 n. of G. be not blas.

BY, or by the NAME.

John 10:3 calleth his sheep by n.
Acts 4:10 by the n. of J. this man
1 Cor. 1:10 I bes. you by n. of L.

His NAME.

Ps. 135:3 praises to h. n. it is pleas
148:13 praise his n. for his n.
149:3 praise his n. in the dance
Is. 7:14 his n. Imman. Mat. 1:23
9:6 his n. be called Wonderful
12:4 that his n. is exalted
47:4 the Lord of hosts is his n.
48:2; 51:15; 54:5; Jer. 10:16;
31:35; 32:18; 50:34; 51:19
Mat. 1:23 sh. call h. n. Emman.
25 h. n. Jesus, Luke 1:31; 2:21
12:21 in h. n. shall Gent. trust
Mark 6:14 h. n. was spread ab.
Luke 1:13 thou sh. call his n. J.
24:47 remission of sins in h. n.
John 1:12 that believe on his n.
2:23 many believed in his n.
20:31 might have life thro' h. n.
Acts 3:16 h. n. thro' faith in h. n.
5:41 worthy to suffer for his n.
10:43 thro' his n. remis. of sins
15:14 take out a peo. for his n.
Rom. 1:5 am. all nations for h. n.
Heb. 6:10 love ye show. to. h. n.

13:15 giving thanks to h. n.
Rev. 3:5 not blot out his n.

NAME.

1 Sam. 16:3 anoi. to me him I n.
28:8 bring him up wh. I shall n.
Is. 62:2 mouth of Lord shall n.

NAMED, ETH.

Gen. 27:36 is he not rightly n. Jac.?
Rom. 15:20 not where Ch. was h.
1 Cor. 5:1 forni. not n. am. Gen.
Eph. 1:21 ab. ev. name that is n.
3:15 fam. in heav. and earth n.
5:3 covetousn. let it not be n.
2 Tim. 2:19 every one that n. G.

NAMES.

Gen. 2:20 Adam gave n. to cattle
Luke 10:20 n. written in heaven
Acts 1:15 number of n. were 120
Phil. 4:3 wh. n. are in book of li.
Rev. 13:8 whose n. not written, 17:8
21:12 n. written, n. of 12 tribes
14 in them the n. of 12 apostl.

NAOMI.

Ruth 1:2 Elimelech's wife, N. 20
4:5 buy, field of hand of N. 9, 17

NAPKIN.

Luke 19:20 I have kept in n.
John 11:44 face bound with a n.
20:7 n. that was about his head

NATIVITY.

Ruth 2:11 hast left land of n.
Jer. 46:16 let us go to land of n.

NATURE.

Rom. 1:26 change th. against n.
2:14 do by n. things in the law
11:24 olive-tr. wh. is wild by n.
were grafted contrary to n.
1 Cor. 11:14 doth not n. tea. you?
Gal. 2:15 Jews by n. not sinners
Eph. 2:3 by n. children of wrath
Heb. 2:16 took not n. of angels
Jam. 3:6 set. on fire course of n.
2 Pet. 1:4 partakers of divine n.

NATURAL.

Deut. 34:7 nor his n. force aba.
Rom. 1:26 women change n. use
27 men leaving n. use of wom.
31 without n. affec. 2 Tim. 3:3
11:21 G. spared not n. bran. 23
1 Cor. 2:14 n. man rece. not Sp.

15:44 sown n. body, is n. body
46 that which is n. was first
Jam. 1:23 a man behold. n. face
2 Pet. 2:12 th. as n. brute beasts

NAUGHT.

Gen. 29:15 sho. serve me for n.?
Job 1:9 doth Job fear G. for n.?
Ps. 33:10 counsel of heath. to n.
Prov. 1:25 set at n. all counsel
Is. 52:3 sold yourselves for n.
Jer. 13:14 vision, a thing of n.
Amos 6:13 which rejoice in thing
of n.

Acts 4:11 this is stone set at n.
5:36 scattered and brought to n.
38 if work of men, come to n.
19:27 craft in danger set at n.
Rom. 14:10 set at n. thy broth.?
1 Cor. 1:28 to bring to n. things
2:6 wisd. of th. world com. to n.
2 Thes. 3:8 man's bread for n.
Rev. 18:17 riches come to n.

NAUGHTINESS.

1 Sam. 17:28 the n. of thy heart
Prov. 11:6 taken in their own n.

NAVEL.

Prov. 3:8 sh. be health to thy n.
Cant. 7:2 thy n. is like a goblet
Ezek. 16:4 thy n. was not cut

NAVY.

1 K. 9:26 Solo. made n. of ships
27 Hir. sent in n. his servants
10:11 the n. of hiram bro. gold
22 Solomon had at sea a n.

NAY.

Mat. 5:37 let your communicati.
be yea, yea, n. n. Jam. 5:12
Acts 16:37 n. verily, but let th.
Rom. 3:37 n. but by law of faith
2 Cor. 1:17 be yea, yea, n. n.
18 word was not yea and n.
29 Jesus christ was not yea
and n.

NAZARETH.

Mat. 2:23 dw. in a city called N.
21:11 Jesus of N. Mark 1:24;
10:47; Lu. 4:34; 18:37; 24:19
Luke 1:26 Gabriel was sent to N.
John 1:45 J. of N. 18, 5, 7; 19:19;
Acts 2:22; 4:10; 6:14; 22:8
Acts 3:6 in name of Jesus of N.

10:38 God anointed Jesus of N.
26:9 contra. to name of Jesus
of N.

NAZARITE.

Num. 6:2 a vow of a N. to separate themselves, 18, 19, 20
Jud. 13:5 shall be a N. 7; 16:17

NEAR.

Is. 55:6 call upon L. while he is n.
Mat. 24:33 it is n. even at doors

NEBUCHADNEZZAR, NE-
BUCHADREZZAR.

Ezek. 26:7 I will br. on Tyrus N.
Dan. 2:1 N. dreamed 4:37
5:18 high G. gave N. a kingdom

NECESSARY.

Acts 13:46 n. the word be spoken
1 Cor. 12:22 memb. feeble are n.
2 Cor. 9:5 thought it n. to exhort
Phil. 2:25 supposed it n. to send
Tit. 3:14 good works for n. uses

NECESSITY.

Luke 23:17 of n. he must release
Rom. 12:13 distr. to n. of saints
1 Cor. 7:37 having no n. and ha.
9:16 for n. is laid upon me
2 Cor. 9:7 give not grud. or of n.
Phil. 4:16 once and ag. to my n.
Phile. 14 not be as it were of n.
Heb. 7:12 there is of n. a change
8:3 it is of n. this man have
9:16 there must of n. be death

NECESSITIES.

2 Cor. 6:4 as ministers of G. in n.
12:10 I take pleasure in n.

NECK.

Gen. 33:4 E. fell on his n. and
kissed
41:42 gold chain ab. Joseph's n.
Ps. 75:5 speak not with a stiff n.
Prov. 1:9 sh. be chains ab. thy n.
Cant. 4:4 thy n. is like the tow. of
D.
Jer. 17:23 they made their n. stiff
Mat. 18:6 a millstone hanged ab.
his n. Mark 9:42; Luke 17:2
Luke 15:20 father fell on his n.
Acts 15:10 yoke on n. of disciples
20:37 fell on P.'s n. kissed him

NECKS.

Jos. 10:24 feet on n. of th. kings

Jud. 8:21 ornaments on camels n.26
Neh. 3:5 put not n. to the work
Lam. 5:5 n. under persecution
Mic. 2:3 shall not remove your n.
Rom. 16:4 laid down th. own n.

NEED.

1 Sam. 21:15 ha. I n. of madmen
2 Chr. 2:16 as much as shalt n.
  29:17 shall not n. to fight in bat.
Ezr. 6:9 let wh. they n. be given
Prov. 31:11 sh. have no n. of sp.
Mat. 3:14 I have n. to be baptiz.
  6:8 your F. knoweth what thin.
  ye have n. of, 32; Lu. 12:30
  9:12 that be whole in. not a physician, Mark 2:17; Luke 5:31
  14:16 they n. not depart, give
  21:3 the L. hath n. of th. Mark
  11:3; Luke 19:31, 34
  26:65 what further n. have we?
  Mark 14:63; Luke 22:71
Mark 2:25 D. did when he had n.
Luke 9:11 healed th. that had n.
  15:7 just persons n. no repent.
John 13:29 things we have n. of
Acts 2:45 as ev. man had n. 4:35
Rom. 16:2 assist in what she n.
1 Cor.7:36 n. so require, let him
  12:21 not say, I have no n.
  24 our comely parts have no n.
Phil. 4:12 I kn. how to suffer n.
  19 God sh. supply all your n.
1 Thes. 4:9 brotherly love, n. not
write
  5:1 of the times ye have no n.
Heb. 4:16 to help in time of n.
  5:12 n. one teach you; n. milk
  7:11 what n. th. another priest
  10:36 ye have n. of patience
1 Pet. 1:6 n. be, ye are in heavi.
1 John 2:27 n. not any man teach
  3:17 see his brother have n.
Rev. 3:17 I have n. of nothing
  21:23 city no n. of sun or moon
  22:5 n. no candle, nor light

NEEDEST, ETH.

2 Tim. 2:15 workm. n. not to be
Heb. 7:27 who n. not offer sacrif.

NEEDLE.

Mat. 19:24 to go thro' eye of a n.
  Mark 10:25; Luke 18:25

NEEDY.

Deut. 15:11 open thy hand to n.
  24:14 servant that is poor and n.
Job 24:4 they turn n. out of way
  14 murderer kill. poor and n.
Ps. 9:18 n. not alway be forgot.
  12:5 the sighing of n. will arise
  35:10 del. poor and n. 72:4, 13
  37:14 bent bow to cast down n.
  40:17 I am poor and n. 70:5
  72:12 he sh. deliver the n. 82:4
  13 he sh. spare the poor and n.
  74:21 poor and n. praise thy na.
  82:3 justice to afflicted and n.
  4 del. poor and n. from wicked
  86:1 I am poor and n. 109:22
  113:7 lifteth n. out of dunghill
Prov. 30:14 de. n. from am. men
Is. 14:30 n. shall lie down in safety
  25:4 been a strength to the n.
  26:6 steps of n. shall tread it do.
  32:7 even when the n. speaketh
  41:17 poor and n. seek water
Jer. 5:28 right of n. do they not
  22:16 judg. cause of poor and n.
Ezek. 16:49 strength, hands of n.
  18:12 oppressed the poor and n.
  22:29 people vexed poor and n.
Amos 8:6 buy the n. for a pair of
shoes

NEGLECT.

Mat. 18:17 if he shall n. to hear
  them; n. to hear the church
1 Tim. 4:14 n. not gift in thee
Heb. 2:3 how escape, if n. salv.?

NEGLIGENT.

2 Chr. 29:11 be not n. for the L.
2 Pet. 1:12 not be n. to put you

NEIGHBOR.

Ex. 3:22 wom. borrow of n. 11:2
1 Sam. 15:28 hath given it to a n.
Prov. 27:10 better is a n. that is
Jer. 6:21 n. and friends sh. peri.
  9:20 and teach every one her n.
Luke 10:36 n. to him am. thieves

His NEIGHBOR.

Ps. 15:3 nor doeth evil to his n.
  101:5 whoso slandereth his n.
  25:18 bear false witn. ag. his n.
  26:19 man that deceiveth his n.
  29:5 flattereth h. n. spreadeth

Jer. 34:15 proclaiming li. to h. n. 17
Zec. 8:16 speak ev. man truth to
h.n. 17 let none imag. evil ag. h.n.
Mark 12:23 love h. n. as himself
Acts 7:27 he that did his n. wro.
Rom. 13:10 work. no evil to h. n.
15:2 let every one please his n.
Eph. 4:25 speak truth with h. n.

My NEIGHBOR.
Luke 10:29 to Je. Who is my n.?

Thy NEIGHBOR.
Ex. 20:16 thou sh. not bear false
witness ag. thy n. Deut. 5:20
Lev. 19:15 in righte. shalt judge thy
n. 17 in any wise rebuke thy n.
18 thou sh. love t. n. as thyself
Prov. 3:28 say not to thy n. Go
29 devise not evil against t. n.
24:28 be not witness ag. thy n.
25:9 debate thy cause with t. n.
Mat. 5:43 shalt love thy n. 19:19;
22:39 Mark 12:31; Luke
10:27 Rom. 13:9; Gal. 5:14;
Jam. 2:8

NEIGHBORS.
Ps. 28:3 speak peace to their n.

NET.
Mat. 4:18 cast n. into, Mark 1:16
Luke 5:6 multitude of fishes, n.
brake
John 21:6 cast n. on right side

NEW.
Is. 42:9 things I declare, 48:6
Mat. 9:16 cloth to an old gar.
26:28 is my blood of n. testament, Mark 14:24; Lu. 22:20;
1 Cor. 11:25
Mark 16:17 speak with n. tongues
John 13:34 n. com. I give you
Gal. 6:15 but a n. creature
1 John 2:7 write no n. comman.
8 n. commandment I write
Rev. 21:1 I saw n. heaven and n.
ear.

NICODEMUS.
John 3:1 N. a ruler of the Jews
7:50 N. came to Jesus, 19:39

NIGHT.
2 K. 19:35 th. n. the angel smote
2 Chr. 1:7 that n. did G. ap. to S.
Job 3:3 let n. perish in which

7 let that n. be solitary
4:13 the visions of the n.
Prov. 31:15 ariseth while it is yet n.
Is. 21:4 n. of pleas. turn. into fear
Dan. 6:18 king passed the n. fasting
Joel. 1:13 lie all n. in sackcloth
Mat. 26:31 sh. be offended beca.
of me this n. Mark 14:27
34 this n. thou shalt deny me.

BY night.
Gen. 31:24 G. ca. to La. in dre. by
n- 39 whet. stolen by day or by n.
40 drou. consu. me, frost by n.
Ex. 12:31 called M. and A. by n.
13:21 by n. in pillar of fire, 22;
14:20; 40:38; Neh. 9:12
Num. 9:16 appear. of fire by n.
21 taken up by day or by n.
Deut. 1:33 fire by n. to show way
23:10 unclean. chanceth by n.
1 Sam. 14:36 go after Phili. by n.
28:8 Saul came to woman by n.
2 Sam. 21:10 nor the beasts by n.
1 K. 3:5 Lord appeared to Solomon by n. 2 Chr. 7:12
2 K. 6:14 came by n. compassed
25:4 fled by n. Jer. 52:7
Ps. 91:5 sh. not be afraid by n.
121:6 nor moon smite thee by n.
134:1 by n. stand in house of L.
136:9 moon rule by n. Jer. 31:35
Prov. 31:18 goeth not out by n.
Cant. 3:1 by n. I sought him
Is. 4:5 shining of a fire by n.
Jer. 6:5 let us go by n. destroy
39:4 went forth out of city by n.
Dan. 7:2 I saw in my vision by n.

In the NIGHT.
1 Thes. 5:2 day cometh as thief
in the n. 2 Pet. 3:10

NIMROD.
Gen. 10:8 C. begat N. 1 Chr. 1:10

NINEVEH.
Jon. 1:2 go to N. 3:2, 3; 4:11

NOAH, NOE.
Gen. 6:8 N. found grace in eyes of
L.
9 gen. of N. 10:1, 32; 1 Cor. 1:4

NOISE.
Ps. 66:1 make a joyful n. to God,
all ye lands, 81:1; 95:1, 2;

98:4, 6; 100:1

NOISED.
Jos. 6:27 Joshua, fame was n.

NOON.
Ps. 55:17 at n. will I pray
Jer. 6:4 arise, let us go up at n.
Acts 22:6 about n. th. shone lig.

NORTH.
Gen. 28:14 thou sh. spread to n.
Dan. 11:6 come to king of the n.

From the NORTH.
Ps. 107:3 gathered from the n.
 and the south, Is. 49:12; Jer.
 16:15; 23:8
Is. 14:31 come f. t. n. a smoke
 41:25 I raised up one from t. n.
Jer. 4:6 I will bring evil f. the n.
 6:22; 10:22; 50:9, 41; 51:48
Ezek. 26:7 king of kings f. t. n.
 39:2 will cause th. to come f. n.
Amos 8:12 wander f. t. n. to east
Zec. 2:6 flee f. the land of t. n.
Luke 13:29 come f. t. n. sit down

NOTHING.
Jer. 10:24 lest th. bring me to n.
 38:14 ask a thing, hide n. fr. me
Jam. 1:4 and entire, wanting n.
 6 him ask in faith, n. wavering

Is NOTHING.
Prov. 8:8 there is n. froward or
1 Cor. 7:19 circumcision is n.

Of NOTHING.
1 Thes. 4:12 may have lack of n.

NOURISH.
Gen. 45:11 will I n. thee, 50:21

NOURISHED.
Acts 7:21 Pharaoh's daughter n him
1 Tim. 4:6 n. up in words of fai.
Jam. 5:5 have n. your hearts as

NUMBERED.
Mat. 10:30 hairs of your head are
 all n. Luke 12:7

NURTURE.
Eph. 6:4 bring th. up in n. of L.

O.

OATH.
Num. 30:2 if a man swear an o. 10
1 Chr. 16:16 mindful of o. to Isa.
Jam. 5:12 sw. not by any oth. o.

OBADIAH.

1 K. 18:3 Ahab called O. 4, 7, 16

OBED.
Ruth 4:17 called his name O.

OBEDIENCE.
Rom. 1:5 o. to faith among all
 5:19 by o. of one many be made
 6:16 or of o. unto righteousness
 16:19 your o. is come abroad
 26 made known for o. to faith
1 Cor. 14:34 women to be und. o.
2 Cor. 7:15 remembereth o. of all
 10:5 ev. thought to o. of Christ
 6 disobed. when o. is fulfilled
Phile. 21 confidence in thy o.
Heb. 5:8 learned o. by things suf.
1 Pet. 1:2 sanctifica. of Sp. to o.

OBEDIENT.
Ex. 24:7 Lord hath said, Be o.
Prov. 25:12 reprover on o. ear good
Is. 1:19 if o. ye shall eat good
 42:24 nei. were th. o. to his law
Acts 6:7 priests were o. to faith
Rom. 15:18 make Ge. o. by word
2 Cor. 2:9 know whether ye be o.
Eph. 6:5 servants be o. Tit. 2:9
Phil. 2:8 Ch. became o. to death
Tit. 2:5 wives, be o. to husbands
1 Pet. 1:14 be as o. children

OBEY.
Gen. 27:8 son, o. my voice, 13, 43
Deut. 11:27 a blessing if ye o. L.
 13:4 o. his voice,
Jos. 24:24 L.'s voice will we o.
1 Sam. 8:19 peo. refused to o. S.
 15:22 to o. is bet. than sacrifice
Neh. 9:17 and refused to o.
Job 36:11 if they o. and serve
Ps. 18:44 as th. hear, they sh. o.
Prov. 30:17 despis. to o. mother
Jer. 7:23 o. my voice, 11:4, 7
 26:13 amend your ways, o. voice
 of the Lord your God, 38:20;
 Zec. 6:15
 42:6 we will o. the voice of the
 L. our God, that it may be
 well with us wh. we o. the L.
Dan. 7:27 shall serve and o. him
Mat. 8:27 winds and sea o. him.?
 Mark 4:41; Luke 8:25
Mark 1:27 unclean spirits o. him
Luke 17:6 plucked up, it shall o.

162

Acts 5:29 o. G. rather than men
32 God hath given to them o.
Rom. 2:8 them that o. unright.
6:12 that ye sho. o. it in lusts
16 servants to o. his servants
ye are to whom ye o.
Eph. 6:1 o. parents. Col. 3:20
Col. 3:22 servants o. masters
Tit. 3:1 put them in mind to o.
Heb. 5:9 salvation to all that o.
13:17 o. them that have the rule
Jam. 3:3 put bits that th. may o.

Not OBEY, OBEY not.
Deut. 11:28 curse, if ye will not
21:18 not o. voice of his father
. 1 Sam. 15:19 wh. didst thou n. o.?
Jer. 42:13 we will not o. the L.
Dan. 9:11 might n. o. thy voice
Acts 7:39 our fathers would n. o.
Rom. 2:8 and do not o. the truth
Gal. 3:1 who bewitched you, th.
you should not o.? 5:7
2 Thes. 1:8 ven. on th. that o. n.
3:14 if any man o. n. our word
1 Pet. 3:1 if any man o. not word
4:17 them that o. not gospel?

OBEYED.
Heb. 11:8 by faith Abraham o.
1 Pet. 3:6 Sarah o. Abraham

OBSERVE.
Mat. 28:20 teaching them to o.
Gal. 4:10 ye o. days, and months
1 Tim. 5:21 then o. these things

OBSTINATE.
Is. 48:4 I knew that thou art o.

OBTAIN.
Gen. 16:2 may be I may o. chil.
Prov. 8:35 o. favor of the Lord
Is. 35:10 they shall o. joy, 51:11
Dan. 11:21 shall o. the kingdom
Luke 20:35 worthy to o. th. world
Rom. 11:31 thro' mercy o. mercy
1 Cor. 9:24 so run, that ye may .o.
9:25 do it to o. corrutp, cro.
1 Thes. 5:9 to o. salvation by L.
2 Tim. 2:10 o. salvation in C. J.
Heb. 4:16 that we may o. mercy
11:35 might o. bet. resurrection
Jam. 4:2 ye kill and cannot o.

OFFENCE.
Mat. 18:7 woe to man by who o.

com.
Acts 24:16 a conscience void of o.
Rom. 5:15 not as o. so is free gift,
for thro' o. of one m. des. 18
17 by one man's o. death reig.
Rom. 5:20 that the o. might abo.
9:33 stumbling-stone, rock of o.
14:20 man who eateth with o.
1 Cor. 10:32 give no. o. 2 Cor. 6:3
2 Cor. 11:7 have I committed o.
Gal. 5:11 o. of cross ceased
Phil. 1:10 with. o. till day of Ch.
1 Pet. 2:8 o. to them wh. stumble

OFFENCES.
Mat. 18:7 beca. of o. for it must
needs be that o. Luke 17:1
Rom. 4:25 was deliver. for our o.
5:16 the free gift of many o.
16:17 mark them which cause o.

OFFEND.
Job 34:31 I will not o. any more
Jer. 2:3 that devour him shall o.
Mat. 5:29 if thy right eye o. thee
30 if thy right hand o. thee,
18:8, 9; Mark 9:43, 45, 47
13:41 gather all things that o.
17:27 lest we should o. them
18:6 whoso o. one of these,
Mark 9:42; Luke 17:2
John 6:61 said, Doth this o. you?
1 Cor. 8:13 brother o. lest he o.
Jam. 2:10 yet o. in one point
3:2 in many things we o. all

OFFENDED.
Gen. 40:1 butler and baker had o.
Mat. 11:6 blessed is he who shall
not be o. Luke 7:23

OFFER.
Ex. 22:29 o. the first-fruits
Deut. 33:19 shall o. sacrifices of
righteousness, Ps. 4:5
1 Sam. 2:19 with her husb. to o.
sacri.
28 him my priest, to o. on alt.
2 Sam. 24:12 o. thee three things,
1 Chr. 21:10
1 Chr. 29:14 to o. so willingly, 17
Ezek. 20:31 when ye o. your gifts
Amos 4:5 o. sacrifice of thanksg.
Mal. 1:7 ye o. polluted bread
Mat. 5:24 then come and o. gift

O

Luke 6:29 cheek, o. also other
11:12 will he o. him scorpion?
Heb. 5:1 o. gifts and sacrifices
3 ought for hims. to. o. for sins
7:27 needeth not to o. sacrifice
8:3 h.-priest ordained to o. this
man ha. somewhat also to o.
9:25 he should o. himself often
13:15 by him let us o. sacrifice
1 Pet. 2:5 by J. C. to o. sacrifice
Rev. 8:3 should o. with prayers

OFFERED.

Jud. 5:2 willingly o. themselv. 9
Ezr. 1:6 that was willingly o.
2:68 some of fathers o. freely
Ezek. 20:28 o. there th. sacrifices
Amos 5:25 have ye o. me sacri.?
Jon. 1:16 and o. sacrifice to Lord
Mal. 1:11 inc. be o. to my name
Acts 8:18 Simon o. them money
15:29 meats o. to idols, 21:25
Heb. 5:7 he had o. up prayers
7:27 when he o. up himself
9:7 blood, wh. he o. for himself
9 o. gifts; 14 o. himself to G.
28 C. o. to bear sins of many
11:4 by faith Abel o. to God
17 Ab. when tried, o. up Isaac
Jam. 2:21 A. justified when he o.

OFFICE.

Rom. 12:4 all mem. have not same
o.
1 Tim. 3:1 if a man desire o.
10 let them use o. of deacon, 13
Heb. 7:5 receive o. of priesthood

OFFICER.

Mat. 5:25 deliv. thee to o. and o.
cast into prison, 12:58

OFFICERS.

Gen. 40:2 Pha. wroth with two o.
1 K. 4:7 Solomon had 12 o. over
Isr.
Is. 60:17 I will make th. o. peace
John 7:46 o. answ. Never man spak
18:3 Judas having received o.
12 o. took Je. 22 o. struck Jes.
Acts 5:22 the o. found them not

OFFSPRING.

Job 5:25 thy o. as grass of earth
Is. 22:24 sh. hang on him, the o.
44:3 pour blessing on thine o.

48:19 o. of bowels like gravel
61:9 their o. shall be known
65:23 seed of the blessed, and o.
Acts 17:28 we are also his o. 29
Rev. 22:16 I am the o. of David

OIL.

Gen. 28:18 Jacob poured o. on the
top of it, 35:14
Ex. 30:25 make it o. for holy ointm.
Lev. 2:1 shall pour o. upon it, 6
Lev. 14:16 priest dip right finger in
o.
2 K. 4:2 nothing in house save o.
Ps. 23:5 anoint my head with o.
55:21 words were softer than o.
104:15 o. to make face to shine
109:118 come like o. into bones
141:5 be a kindness, an excel. o.
Prov. 5:3 mouth smoother th. o.
21:20 o. in dwelling of the wise
Is. 61:3 give o. of joy for moum.
Mat. 25:3 the foolish took no o.
Luke 7:46 with o. didst not ano.

OINTMENT.

Ex. 30:25 make oil of holy o.
Mat. 26:7 box of precious o.
Mark 14:3; Luke 7:37
John 11:2 M. anoin. the L. wi. o
12:3 Mary took pound of o.
house was filled with o. of the o.

OMNIPOTENT.

Rev. 19:6 Lord God o. reigneth

ONCE.

Heb. 7:27 for this he did o. when
1 Pet. 3:18 Ch. suffered o. for sins

ONE.

Gen. 2:24 shall be o. flesh, Mat.
John 10:30 I and my Fa. are o.

Not ONE.

Rom. 3:10 is none right. not o.

There is ONE.

Mark 12:32 the truth; th. is o. G.
1 Tim. 2:5; Jam. 2:19

ONE thing.

Job 9:22 this is o. t. theref. I said
Luke 10:42 o. thing is needful

OPEN, Adjective.

Jer. 32:19 th. eyes o. on ways of
men

OPEN.

Jer. 50:26 o. her storehouses, cast

164

Ezek. 37:12 I will o. your graves
Luke 12:36 when knock. may o.

OPENED.

Heb. 4:13 all things are o. to him
Rev. 4:1 a door was o. in heaven

OPENEST.

Ps. 104:28 thou o. thy hand

OPENLY.

Mat. 6:4 F. reward thee o. 6, 18
Mark 8:32 spake that saying o.
John 7:4 seeketh to be known o.
11:54 Jesus walked no more o.
Acts 10:40 God showed him o.

OPPORTUNITY.

Mat. 26:16 o. to bet. Luke 22:6
Gal. 6:10 as we have o. do good
Phil. 4:10 careful, ye lacked o.
Heb. 11:15 o. to have returned

OPPOSITIONS.

1 Tim. 6:20 avoiding o. of science

OPPRESS.

Ex. 3:9 the Egyptians o. them
Deut. 23:16 shalt not o. servant

OPPRESSETH.

Prov. 14:31 he that o. poor, 22:16
28:3 a poor man that o. the poor

OPPRESSION.

2 K. 13:4 Lord saw o. of Israel
Ps. 12:5 for o. of poor will I arise
Ezek 46:18 sh. not take inherit. by
o.

OPPRESSIONS.

Is. 33:15 despiseth the gain of o.

OPPRESSOR.

Job 3:18 they hear not voice of o.
Ps. 72:4 shall break in pieces o.
Prov. 3:31 envy not o. cho. none

ORDAIN.

1 Chr. 17:9 I will o. a place for my
pe.
Is. 26:12 L. that wilt o. peace
1 Cor. 7:17 so o. I in all churches
Tit. 1:5 thou shouldest o. elders

ORDAINED.

Ps. 8:2 out of mouth of babes o.
3 moon and stars thou hast o.
Mark 3:14 Jesus o. 12 to be with
1 Tim. 2:7 I am o. preacher to G.
Heb. 5:1 ev. high-priest is o. 8:3
9:6 when these things were o.

ORDER.

1 Cor. 16:1 have gi. o. to church.

In ORDER.

2 Sam. 17:23 put his house in o.
2 K. 20:1 set house in o. Is. 38:1
1 Cor. 15:23 ev. man shall rise in
his o.
Tit. 1:5 I left thee to set in o.

ORDERED.

Ps. 37:23 steps of good man are o.

ORGAN, S.

Ps. 150:4 praised him with o.

ORION.

Job 38:31 loose the bands of O.?

ORNAMENT.

1 Pet. 3:4 o. of meek, quiet spirit

ORNAMENTS.

Ex. 33:4 no man put on him o.
Is. 61:10 decketh himself with o.
Jer. 2:32 can a maid forget her o.

ORPAH.

Ruth 1:4 name of one O. other R.

OTHER.

Gen. 28:17 none o. but ho. of G.
John 15:24 works no. o. man did
Acts 4:12 nei. is salva. in any o.

OTHERS.

Mat. 5:47 wh. do ye more th. o.?
Mark 15:31 saved o. Luke 23:35

OTHERWISE.

Gal. 5:10 will be none o. minded
1 Tim. 6:3 if any man teach o.

OUGHT, or rather AUGHT.

Mat. 5:23 brother hath o. ag. th.
Mark 11:25 forgive, if ye have o. ag
John 4:33 brought him o. to eat?

OUGHT.

Rom. 8:26 to pray for as we o.

OUTER.

Ezek. 46:21 broug. me to o. court
Mat. 8:12 o. darkn. 22:13; 25:30

OUTSIDE.

1 K. 7:9 o. towards great court
Ezek. 40:5 beho. a wall on the o.
Mat. 23:25 o. of cup, Luke 11:39
26 that o. of them be clean also

OUTSTRETCHED.

Deut. 26:8 us out with an o. arm
Jer. 21:5 fight you with o. arm
27:5 made earth by my o. arm

OUTWARD.

1 Sam. 16:7 looketh on o. appear.

Mat. 23:27 appear beautiful o.
Rom. 2:28 which is o. in flesh
2 Cor. 4:16 tho' our o. man perish
    10:7 things after o. appearance?
1 Pet. 3:3 not that o. adorning

OUTWARDLY.

Mat. 23:28 o. appear righteous
Rom. 2:28 not a Jew wh. is one o.

OVERCAME.

Acts 19:16 evil spi. was, o. them
Rev. 3:21 even as I also o.
    12:11 o. him by blood of Lamb

OVERCOME.

Jer. 23:9 man whom wine hath o.
Luke 11:22 stronger shall o. him
John 16:33 I have o. the world
Rom. 3:4 o. wh. thou art judged
    12:21 be not o. of evil, o. evil
1 John 2:13 o. wicked one, 14
    4:4 are of God, have o. them
Rev. 11:7 beast sh. o. witnesses
    13:7 war with saints, o. them
    17:14 and Lamb shall o. them

OVERCOMETH.

1 John 5:4 born of God o. world,
    victory o. world, 5

OVERFLOW.

Deut. 11:4 water of Red sea o.

OVERSEER.

Prov. 6:7 the ant having no o.

OVERSHADOW, ED.

Mat. 17:5 bright cloud o. them,
    Mark 9:7; Luke 9:34
Luke 1:35 power of High. o. thee

OVERTAKE.

Hos. 10:9 the battle did not o. them
1 Thes. 5:4 should o. you as thief

OVERTHREW.

Gen. 19:25 God o. these cities, 29
Ex. 14:27 L. o. Eg. Ps. 136:15
Deut. 29:23 which L. o. in anger
Is. 13:19 when G. o. Sodom and
    Gomo. Jer. 50:40; Amos 4:11
Jer. 20:16 be as cities the Lord o.
Mat. 21:12 J. o. tables of money-
    chang. Mark 11:15; John 2:15

OVERTHROW.

Prov. 18:5 not good to o. righte.
Acts 5:39 if it be of G. ye can. o.
2 Tim. 2:18 o. the faith of some

OVERTOOK.

Jud. 20:42 battle o. men of
Benjamin

OWE.

Rom. 13:8 o. no man any thing

OWED.

Mat. 18:24 one o. him 10,000 tal.
    28 one which o. him a 100 pen.

OWEST, ETH.

Mat. 18:28 pay me that thou o.
Luke 16:5 how much o. thou? 7
Phile. 18 thee, or o. thee aught
    19 o. to me even thine own

OWN.

1 Cor. 6:19 ye are not your o.
    10:24 let no man seek his o.
    13:5 charity seeketh not her o.
1 Tim. 5:8 provide not for his o.

OX.

Deut. 25:4 not muzzle o. treadeth
out

OXEN.

1 K. 19:20 Elisha left o. ran after
Elij.
Jer. 51:23 I break husb. and o.
Dan. 4:25 eat gr. as o. 33; 5:21

P.

PAIN.

Ps. 25:18 mine affliction and p.
    48:6 p. as a woman in travail,
    Is. 13:8; 26:17
Ezek 30:16 Sin shall have great p.
Mic. 4:10 p. and labor to bring
Rom. 8:22 creation travail. in p.
Rev. 16:10 gnawed tongues for p.
    21:4 nor shall th. be any more p.

PAINS.

1 Sam. 4:19 p. came upon her
Acts 2:24 hav. loosed p. of death

PAINTED, ST.

2 K. 9:30 Jezebel p. her face
Ezek. 23:40 thou p. thy eyes

PALACE.

1 Chr. 23:19 perfect heart to build
the p.
Ps. 45:15 enter into king's p.
Is. 25:2 made p. of srangers
Dan. 4:4 flourishing in my p.

PALM.

Lev. 14:15 pour into p. 26
John 18:22 struck Jesus with p.

PALM branches.
Neh. 8:15 to mount and fet. p. b.

PALMS.
1 Sam. 5:4 p. of hands cut off
2 K. 9:35 they found skull and p.
Is. 49:16 grav. thee on p. of han.
Mat. 26:67 others smote him wi.
    p. of their hands, Mark 14:65
Rev. 7:9 white robes, p. in han.

PALSY, IES.
Mat. 4:24 he healed them,
    Mark 2:3; Luke 5:18
8:6 ser. lieth at home sick of p.
9:2 Je. said to sick of p. S. thy
    sins be forgiven, Mark 2:5
Mark 2:10 sick of p. Luke 5:24
Acts 8:7 many taken with p. and

PANGS.
Is. 13:8 p. sh. take hold of them
21:3 p. take hold me as p. of w.
26:17 wom. crieth out in her p.
Jer. 48:41 heart of wom. in p. 49:22
50:43 p. as of a wom. Mic. 4:9

PARABLE.
Ps. 49:4 I will incline ear to a p.
Mat. 13:18 hear p. of the sower
24 ano. p. put he, 31, 33; 21:33
34 with. p. sp. not, Mark 4:34
24:32 learn a p. of the fig-tree,
    Mark 13:28; Luke 21:29
Luke 5:36 he spake a p. to them,
    6:39; 8:4; 12:16; 13:6; 14:7;
    15:3; 18:1, 9; 19:11; 20:9;
    21:29; John 10:6

PARABLES.
Mat. 13:3 spake many things to
    them in p. 13:34; 22:1; Mark
    3:23; 4:2, 13, 33; 12:1
Mark 4:13 how will ye kn. all p.?
Luke 8:10 p. seeing might not see

PARADISE.
Luke 23:43 to-day with me in p.
Rev. 2:7 in the midst of p. of G.

PARCHED.
Is. 35:7 p. ground become pool
Jer. 17:6 shall inhabit p. places

PARDON.
Ex. 34:9 p. our iniq. Num. 14:19
2 K. 24:4 which Lord would not p.
2 Chr. 30:18 good L. p. ev. one
Neh. 9:17 G. ready to p. gracious

Job 7:21 why not p. my transg.?
Ps. 25:11 for name's sake p. ini.
Is. 55:7 he will abundantly p.
Jer. 5:1 I will p. it; 7 shall I p.
33:8 I will p. all their iniquities
50:20 I will p. whom I reserve

PARDONED, ETH.
Num. 14:20 I have p. ac. to word
Is. 40:2 tell her that iniq. is p.
Lam. 3:42 thou hast not p.
Mic. 7:18 G. like thee, P. iniq.?

PARENTS.
Mat. 10:21 children shall rise up
    against their p. Mark 13:12
Luke 2:27 brought in child Je.
8:56 her p. were astonished, but
18:29 is no man that hath left p.
21:16 ye shall be betrayed by p.
John 9:2 who did sin, man or p.?
22 these words spake p. 23
Rom. 1:30 diso. to p. 2 Tim. 3:2
2 Cor. 12:14 chi. not lay up for p.
Eph. 6:1 chil. obey. Col. 3:20
1 Tim. 5:4 learn to requite th. p.
Heb. 11:23 Mo. was hid of his p.

PART.
Neh. 1:9 cast out to uttermost p.
1 Cor. 16:17 was lacking on your p.
Rev. 21:8 liars sh. have p. in lake
22:19 G. shall take away his p.

PARTS.
Ezek. 31:16 comforted in the nether
    p. of earth, 32:18, 24
Eph. 4:9 descended into low. p.

PARTED.
Mat. 27:35 p. his garmen. Mark
    5:24; Luke 23:34; John 19:24

PARTAKER.
Ps. 50:18 been p. with adulterers
1 Cor. 9:10 sho. be p. of his hope
23 I be p. thereof with you
1 Tim. 5:22 p. of oth. men's sins
2 Tim. 1:8 be thou p. of afflicti
2:6 husbandman be p. of fruits
1 Pet. 5:1 I am also p. of the gl.
2 John 11 biddeth G. speed is p.

PARTAKERS.
Mat. 23:30 not been p. in blood
Rom. 15:27 if Gentiles have been
    p. of their spiritual things
1 Cor. 9:13 are p. with the altar

10:17 we are all p. of that bread
18 are not they which eat p.?
21 cannot be p. of Lord's table
2 Cor. 1:7 you are p. of sufferings
Eph. 3:6 p. of his promise in Ch.
Phil. 1:7 all are p. of my grace
Col. 1:12 to be p. of inheritance
1 Tim. 6:2 they are p. of benefit
Heb. 2:14 children p. of flesh
  and blood
  3:1 p. of the heavenly calling
  14 for we are made p. of christ
  6:4 made p. of the Holy Ghost
  12:10 that we be p. of his holiness
1 Pet. 4:13 p. of Christ's suffer.
2 Pet. 1:4 p. of the divine nature
Rev. 18:4 that ye be not p. of her

PARTIES.

Ex. 22:9 both p. come bef. judg.

PASS.

Mat. 26:39 cup p. fr. me, Mark
14:35

Not PASS.

Mat. 24:35 heaven and earth shall
pass away, but my word sh. n. p.
away, Mark 13:31; Lu. 21:33

PASS through.

Gen. 30:32 p. t. thy flock to-day
Lam. 3:44 prayers sho. not p. t.

PASSED.

Job 4:15 spirit p. before my face
John 5:24 but is p. from death to
  life, 1 John 3:14
Rom. 5:12 death p. on all men
Heb. 4:14 High-pri. p. into heav.
Rev. 21:1 first earth were p. aw.
  4 former things are p. away

PASSED by.

1 K. 19:11 Lord p. by; 19 Elijah p.
by
Mat. 20:30 heard that Jesus p. by

PASSED over.

Gen. 32:10 with staff I p. over
Jordan

PASSED through.

Heb.11:29 they p. thro' Red sea

PASSETH.

Eph. 3:19 love of C. p. knowled.
Phil. 4:7 peace of G. p. underst.

PASSIONS.

Acts 14:15 we are men of like p.

Jam. 5:17 Elias subject to like p.

PASSOVER.

Ex. 12:11 it is L.'s p. ye sh. eat,
  27; Lev. 23:5;
  43 this is the ordinance of p.
Mat. 26:17 wh. wilt we eat p.?
  Mark 14:12; Luke 22:8, 11
John 18:28 that they might eat p.
  19:14 it was preparation of p.

PAST.

2 Cor. 5:17 old things p. away

PASTURE.

Ps. 95:7 we are peo. of his p. 100:3

PATH.

Job 30:13 mar my p. set forward
Ps. 16:11 show me the p. of life
119:105 thy word a light to my p.
Prov. 4:26 ponder the p. of thy feet.
Joel 2:8 walk, every one in his p.

PATHS.

Ps. 17:4 kept me fr. p. of destroyer
  23:3 leadeth me in p. of righte.
Prov. 2:8 keep. p. of judgment
Prov. 2:13 leave p. of uprightn.
  19 nei. take hold of p. of life
  20 keep p. of the righteous
  8:6 direct p. 17 p. are peace
  4:11 I have led thee in right p.
  7:25 go not astray in her p.
  8:2 standeth in places of p.
  20 I lead in p. of judgment
Heb. 12:13 made strai. p. for feet

PATIENCE.

Mat. 18:26 have p. with me, and
  I will pay thee all, 29
Luke 24:19 in p. possess ye your
souls
Rom. 5:3 tribulation worketh p.
  4 p. experience, experi. hope
  8:25 do we with p. wait for it
2 Cor. 6:4 ministers of God in p.
  12:12 signs we. am. you in all p.
Col. 1:11 strengthened to all p.
1 Thes. 1:3 remem. your p. in J.
2 Thes. 1:4 gl. in you for your p.
1 Tim. 6:11 follow after love, p.
2 Tim. 3:10 hast known my p.
Tit. 2:2 be found in faith, p.
Heb. 6:12 thro' p. inh. promises
  10:36 ye have need of p.
  12:1 run with p. race before us

Jam. 1:3 trying of faith work. p.

4 let p. have her perfect work

5:7 husbandman hath long p.

10 an example of p. 11 p. of J.

2 Pet. 1:6 add to temper. p. to p.

Rev. 1:9 compan. in p. of Jesus

2:2 I know thy p. 19; 3 hast p.

3:10 hast kept word of my p.

13:10 here is p. of saints, 14:12

PATIENT.

Ec. 7:8 p. in sp. better than pro.

Rom. 2:7 p. continu. in well-do.

12:12 in hope, p. in tribulation

1 Thes. 5:14 be p. toward all men

2 Thes. 3:5 p. waiting for Christ

1 Tim. 3:3 inc. but p. 2 Tim. 2:24

Jam. 5:7 be p. breth. 8 ye also p.

PATIENTLY.

Ps. 37:7 rest in L. and wait p.

40:1 I waited p. for the Lord

Heb. 6:15 after he had p. endured

1 Pet. 2:20 if ye be buff. take it p.

PATRIARCH, S.

Acts 2:29 freely speak of p. Dav.

7:8 Jacob begat the twelve p.

9 p. sold Joseph into Egypt

Heb. 7:4 p. Abraham paid tithes

PATTERN, S.

Ex. 25:9 p. of all instruments

Heb. 8:5 accord. to p. I showed

9:23 necessary that p. of things

PAUL.

Acts 13:9 then Saul, called P.

28:16 but P. was suffered to

PAY.

Prov.19:17 giv. will he p. again

22:27 if hast nothing to p.

Ec. 5:4 defer not to p. it, p. that

5 not vow, than vow and not p.

Jon. 2:9 I will p. that I vowed

Mat. 17:24 doth not mas. p. tri.?

18:25 had not to p. Luke 7:42

26 p. thee all; 28 p. th. owest

30 cast into prison, till he p.

34 till he p. all that was due

23:23 ye p. tithe of mint, anise

Rom. 13:6 for this cause p. trib.

PEACE.

Mark 4:39 said to sea, p. be still

PEACE.

Gen. 41:16 G. give P. answ. of p.

1 K. 4:24 Solom. had p. on all side

2 K. 9:22 what p. so long as witchc.

1 Chr. 22:9 I will give p. to Isr.

Ezr 9:12 not seek their p. or wealth

Est. 9:30 Mord. sent words of w.

Is. 9:6 Prince of p. 7 increase p.

48:22 th. is no p. to wicked, 57:21

53:5 chastisem. of our p. on him

54:13 great shall be p. of thy chil.

Jer. 16:5 I have taken away my p.

Ezek. 34:25 make a covena. of p.

37:26

Dan. 8:25 by p. he shall destroy

Zec. 8:16 execute judgment and p.

19 therefore love truth and p.

Mal. 2:5 covenant of life and p.

Mat. 10:13 worthy, let p. come

34 th. not I am come to send p.

Mark 9:50 have p. one with ano.

Luke 1:79 guide feet to way of p.

2:14 on earth p. good will tow.

10:6 if son of p. th. your p. rest

12:51 I am come to give p.?

19:38 p. in heaven. gl. in highe.

42 things belong to thy p.

John 14:27 p. I lea. you, p. I give

16:33 in me you might have p.

Acts 10:36 preaching p. by Jesus

Rom. 1:7 p. from God the Fath.

1 Cor. 1:3; 2 Cor. 1:2; Gal.

1:3; Eph. 1:2; Phil. 1:2

2:10 p. to every man work. good

5:1 justified, we have p. with G.

8:6 to be spiritually mind. is p.

10:15 that preach gospel of p.

14:17 the kingdom of God is p.

19 fol things that make for p.

15:13 fill you with all joy and p.

1 Cor. 7:15 G. hath call. us to p.

14:33 author of p. as in church.

Gal. 5:22 Spirit is love, joy, p.

Eph. 2:14 is our p. 15 making p.

17 Christ came and preach. p.

4:3 unity of Spirit in bond of p.

6:15 preparation of gospel of p.

Phil. 4:7 p. of God passeth und.

Col. 1:2 grace and p. from G. our

Father, 1 Thes. 1:1; 2 Thes.

1:2; 1 Tim. 1:2; 2 Tim. 1:2;

Tit. 1:4; Phile. 3; 2 John 3

3:15 p. of God rule in your hea.

1 Thes. 5:3 when they sh. say p.
13 be at p. among yourselves
2 Thes. 3:16 L. of p. give you p.
2 Tim. 2:22 follow p. Heb. 12:14
Jam. 3:18 p. of them th. ma. p.?
Rev. 1:4 p. from him that is, was
6:4 power giv. to him to take p.
In PEACE.
Gen. 26:29 sent thee away in p.
1 K. 22:27 in prison, until I come in
p.
Job 5:24 thy taber. shall be in p.
Ps. 4:8 I will lay me down in p.
55:18 he delivered my soul in p.
Is. 26:3 wilt keep him in perf. p.
Jer. 29:7 in p. sh. ye have peace
34:5 but thou shalt die in p.
Mal. 2:6 walked with me in p.
Luke 2:29 let. serv. depart in p.
1 Cor. 16:11 cond. him forth in p.
2 Cor. 13:11 one mind, live in p.
Jam. 2:16 depart in p. be warm,
3:48 righteousness is sown in p.
2 Pet. 3:14 be found of him in p.
PEACEABLE.
Gen. 34:21 these men p. with us
2 Sam. 20:19 one of them th. p.
1 Chr. 4:40 land was wi. and p.
Is. 32:18 peo. dwell in p. habita.
1 Tim. 2:2 lead a quiet and p. li.
Heb. 12:11 yieldeth the p. fruit
Jam. 3:17 wisd. is pure, p. gent.
PEACEABLY.
Gen. 37:4 could not speak p.
1 Sam. 16:4 said, Comest thou p.
Jer. 9:8 speaketh p. to neighbor
Rom. 12:18 live p. with all men
PEACEMAKERS.
Mat. 5:9 blessed are the p.

Mat. 13:46 found p. of great price
PEARLS.
Mat. 7:6 neither cast p. bef. sw.
13:45 like merchant seeking p.
1 Tim. 2:9 not with p. or costly
PECULIAR.
Ex. 19:5 sh. be p. treasure to me
Deut. 14:2 be a p. people unto
himself, 26:18; 1 Pet. 2:9
Ps. 135:4 chosen Is. for p. treas.
Ec. 2:8 I gath. p. treas. of kings

Tit. 2:14 purify to himself p.
people
PENKNIFE.
Jer. 36:23 Jehu. cut roll with p.
PENNY.
Mat. 20:2 ag. with laborers for p.
PENTECOST.
Acts 2:1 wh. day of P. was come
1 Cor. 16:8 tarry at Eph. until P.
PENURY.
Prov. 14:23 talk of lips ten. to p.
Luke 21:4 she of her p. cast all
PEOPLE.
Gen. 27:29 let p. serve thee
His PEOPLE.
Ps. 14:7 captivity of his p. 53:6
29:1 strength to his p. L. will
bl. his p. with peace. 68:35
50:4 that he may judge his p.
Rev. 21:3 and they shall be h. p.
My PEOPLE.
Is. 52:6 my p. shall know my name
Hos. 4:6 my p. are destroyed for
lack
2 Cor. 6:16 they shall be my p.
To, or unto the PEOPLE.
Ps. 72:3 shall bring peace to the p.
PERADVENTURE.
Gen. 18:24 p. there be 50 righte.
PERCEIVE.
Deut. 29:4 not given heart to p.
2 K. 4:9 I p. this is a holy man
Mat. 13:14 shallsee. and sh. not
p. Mark 4:12; Acts 28:26
Mark 8:17 p. ye not, neither unders.
John 4:19 I p. thou art a prophet
Acts 10:34 p. G. is no respect. of
per.
PERCEIVED.
Mat. 22:18 Jesus p. their wickedn.
Mark 2:8 Jesus p. they reasoned
Luke 1:22 p. he had seen vision
5:22 when Jesus p. th. thoughts
20:23 but he p. their craftiness
John 6:15 J. p. would make him
Acts 4:13 p. they were unlearned
23:6 Paul p. part were Pharise.
Gal. 2:9 James p. grace giv. me
PERDITION.
2 Thes. 2:3 be revealed, son of p.
Heb. 10:39 who draw back to p.

2 Pet. 3:7 and p. of ungodly men
PERFECT, Adjective.
Job 8:20 G. not cast away a p. man
Ps. 37:37 p. man, end is peace
101:2 behave myself in a p. way
   6 he that walketh in a p. way
Prov. 2:21 p. shall remain in it
Acts 24:22 having more p.
knowledge
Rom. 12:2 what is p. will of God
2 Cor. 12:9 strength p. in weakn.
Gal. 3:3 are ye made p. by flesh?
Eph. 4:13 till we come to p. man
Phil. 3:12 not as tho' already p.
   15 as many as be p.
Col. 1:28 present every man p. in
   4:12 stand p. in will of God
1 Thes. 3:10 p. which is lacking
2 Tim. 3:17 man of G. may be p.
Heb. 2:10 Captain of salvation p.
   5:9 being made p. beca. Author
   7:19 for law made nothing p.
   9:9 not make him did service p.
   10:1 law never make comers p.
   11:40 without us not made p.
   12:23 spirits of just men made p.
   13:21 G. make you p. in every
Jam. 1:4 let patience have her p.
   work, that ye may be p.
   17 every p. gift is from above
   25 looketh into p. law of liber.
   2:22 by works was faith ma. p.
   3:2 offend not, same is p. man
1 Pet. 5:10 after suffer. make p.
1 John 4:17 herein is love made p.
   18 p. love casteth out fear, he
   that feareth is not p. in love
Is PERFECT.
Deut. 32:4 his work is p.
Job 36:4 he that is p. in kn. 37:16
Ps. 19:7 law of L. is p. convert.
Mat. 5:48 as Father in heaven
Luke 6:40 every one that is p.
1 Cor. 13:10 that wh. is p. is co.
PERFECTED.
Mat. 21:16 thou hast p. praise
Luke 13:32 third day I shall be p.
Heb. 10:14 by one offer he ha. p.
1 John 2:5 in him is love of G. p.
   4:12 love one ano. his love is p.
PERFECTING.

2 Cor. 7:1 p. holin. in fear of G.
Eph. 4:12 for p. of the saints
PERFECTION.
Job 11:7 find Almighty to p.?
Ps. 119:96 I have seen an end of p.
Heb. 6:1 let us go on to p.
PERFORM.
Jer. 29:10 I will p. good word,
   33:14
Phil. 1:6 p. it until day of J. Ch.
PERFUMED.
Prov. 7:17 p. bed with myrrh
Cant. 3:6 who is this cometh p.?
PERIL.
Rom. 8:35 shall p. separate us?
PERILOUS.
2 Tim. 3:1 p. times shall come
PERISH.
Gen. 41:36 p. not thro' famine
Ex. 19:21 and many of them p.
Num. 17:12 die, we p. we all p.
Est. 3:13 cause to p. all J. 7:4
Prov. 11:10 wh. wicked p. 28:28
   29:18 there is no vision, peo. p.
Mat. 5:29 one of thy mem. p. 30
   8:25 L. save us, we p. Luke 8:24
   9:17 wine runneth out, bot. p.
   18:14 one of little ones sho. p.
Mark 4:28 carest th. not we p.?
2 Cor. 4:16 tho' outward man p.
   inwa.
2 Thes. 2:10 unrig. in th. that p.
2 Pet. 3:9 not willing any sho. p.
Shall PERISH.
Ps. 1:6 way of ungodly shall p.
   37:20 wick. s. p. 92:9 enemies p.
   102:26 they s. p. thou endure
Prov. 19:9 he that speaketh lies s.p.
   21:28 a false witness shall p.
Is. 29:14 wisd. of wise men s. p.
   41:11 that strive with thee s.p.
   60:12 king. not serve thee s. p.
Jer. 4:9 heart of the king s.p.
   6:21 neighbor and friend s. p.
   10:11 the gods s. p. 15; 51:18
Ezek. 7:26 law s. p. from priest
John 10:28 the sheep s. never p. 5
Rom. 2:12 sinned with. law, s.p.
1 Cor. 8:11 shall weak brother p.
Heb. 1:11 they s. p. thou remai.
2 Pet. 2:12 shall p. in their cor.

Jos. 22:20 that man p. not alone
2 Sam. 1:27 weapons of war p.1
PERISHETH.
Prov. 11:7 hope of unjust men p.
Ec. 7:15 th. is a just man that p.
PERPETUAL.
Gen. 9:12 cov. for p. generations
Jer. 8:5 slid. back by p. backsliding?
15:18 why is my pain p. and my
23:40 bring upon you p. shame
PERSECUTE.
Job 19:22 why do ye p. me as G.
Mat. 5:11 bles. when men p. you
44 pray for them which p. you
10:23 when they p. you in one
Luke 11:49 they shall p. 21:12
John 15:20 they will also p. you
Rom. 12:14 bless them which p.
PERSECUTED.
Mat. 5:10 blessed which are p.
12 so p. they prophets bef. you
John 15:20 if they have p. me
Acts 22:4 I p. this way unto death
1 Cor. 4:12 being p. we suffer it
2 Cor. 4:9 we are p. not forsaken
Gal. 1:23 p. us in times past
1 Thes. 2:15 killed L. and p. us
PERSECUTEST, ING.
Acts 9:4 Saul, Saul, why p. thou me? 22:7; 26:14
5 I am Jesus, whom thou p. 22:8; 26:15
Phil. 3:6 concern. zeal, p. church.
PERSECUTION.
Lam. 5:5 under p. have no rest
Mat. 13:21 wh. p. ari. Mark 4:17
Acts 8:1 great p. against church
11:19 were scatter. abroad on p.
Rom. 8:35 sh. p. sep. us fr. C.?
Gal. 5:11 why do I yet suffer p.?
2 Tim. 3:12 godly shall suffer p.
PERSECUTIONS.
Mark 10:30 have lands with p.
2 Cor. 12:10 I take pleasure in p.
2 Thes. 1:4 faith in all your p.
2 Tim. 3:11 kn. my p. at Antioch
PERSEVERANCE.
Eph. 6:18 watching with all p.
PERSON.
2 Sam. 4:11 have slain a righ. p.

14:14 nei. doth G. respect any p.
Job 22:29 shall save humble p.
Ps. 15:4 a vile p. is contemned
49:10 fool and brutish p. perish
101:4 I will not kn. a wicked p.
105:37 feeble am. their tribes
Prov. 28:17 to the blood of any p.
Is. 32:5 vile p. shall be no more
PERSUADE.
1 K. 22:21 I will p. him; 22 thou sh. p.
2 Chr. 32:11 doth not Hezek. p.
Mat. 28:14 we will p. him, and
2 Cor. 5:11 terrors of L. p. men
Gal. 1:10 do I now p. men?
PERSUADED.
2 Chr. 18:2 Ahab p. Jehosaphat
Prov 25:15 forbea. is a prince p.
Luke 16:31 will not be p. of one
20:6 be p. John was a prophet
Acts 13:43 p. them to continue
14:19 who p. the people
16:4 Paul p. Jews and Greeks
19:26 Paul hath p. much people
21:14 when he would not be p.
26:26 I am p. none of th. things
Rom. 4:21 p. that what he had
8:38 I am p. that nothing can
14:5 let every man be fully p.
14 I know and am p.
15:14 I myself also am p. of you
2 Tim. 1:5 I am p. that in thee
12 I am p. he is able to keep
Heb. 6:9 are p. bet. things of you
11:13 hav. seen afar off, were p.
PERSUADETH, EST.
2 K. 18:32 when Hezekiah p. you
Acts 18:13 P. p. men to worship
26:28 almost thou p. me to be
PERSUASION.
Gal. 5:8 p. cometh not of him
PERTAIN.
1 Sam. 25:22 all that p. to him
Rom. 15:17 things which p. to G.
1 Cor. 6:3 things p. to this life
2 Pet. 1:8 all things that p. to life
PERTAINED.
Jud. 6:11 under oak that p. to J.
1 Sam. 25:21 of all that p. to N.
PERVERSE.
Num. 22:32 thy way is p. bef. me

Deut. 32:5 they are a p. generat.
Job 6:30 cannot disc. p. things?
9:20 my mouth sh. prove me p.
Prov. 4:24 p. lips put from thee
Prov. 8:8 noth. fro. or p. in them
12:8 he of a p. heart sh. be desp.
14:2 he that is p. despiseth him
17:20 hath a p. tongue falleth
19:1 he that is p. in his lips
23:33 heart shall utter p. things
28:6 he that is p. in his ways
18 he that is p. in ways sh. fall
Is. 19:14 L. mingled a p. spirit
Mat. 17:17 O p. genera. Luke 9:41
Acts 20:30 men arise speaking p.
Phil. 2:15 blameless in p. nation
1 Tim. 6:5 p. disputings of men

PERVERT.

Deut. 16:19 a givt doth p. words
24:17 thou shalt not p. judgm.
Job 8:3 doth God p. judgment or
34:12 nor will the Al. p. judgm.
Prov. 17:23 to p. ways of judgm.
31:5 and p. the judgment of any
Mic. 3:9 hear this, ye that p. eq.
Acts 13:10 not cease to p. right
Gal. 1:7 would p. the gos. of C.

PERVERTED.

Job 33:27 have p. what was right
Is. 47:10 thy wisdom, it hath p.
Jer. 3:21 they have p. their way
23:36 ye have p. the words of G.

PERVERTETH.

Deut. 27:19 cursed be he that p.
Prov. 10:9 he that p. his ways
19:3 foolishness of a man p. way
Luke 23:14 man that p. people

PESTILENCE.

Ex. 5:3 lest he fall on us wi. p.
9:15 I may smite thee with p.
Num. 14:12 will sm. th. with p.
Ezek 6:11 by sword, famine, and p.
12
12:16 I will leave a few from p.

PESTILENCES.

Mat. 24:7 shall be p. Luke 21:11

PETER.

John 18:26 ear P, cut off, 21:17
Acts 3:3 see. P. and John, 4:8, 13
10:13 P. kill and eat, 44; 11:7
Gal. 1:18 went to see P. 2:7, 8, 14

Simon PETER.

Mat. 4:18 Jesus saw S. called P.

PETITION, S.

1 K. 2:16 ask one p. deny me not
20 I desire one small p. of thee
Est. 5:8 if it please king to grant p.
Ps. 20:5 Lord fulfil all thy p.
Dan. 6:13 maketh p. three times a
day

PHARAOH.

Gen. 12:17 the Lord plagued P.
1 K. 7:8 Solo. made a house for P.
HEb. 11:24 to be called son of P.

PHARISEE.

Mat. 23:26 thou blind P. cleanse
Luke 18:10 went to pray, one a P.
Acts 23:6 I am a P. son of a P.
Phil. 3:5 touching the law a P.

PHARISEES.

Mat. 9:14 why do P. fast? Mark
2:18
16:6 beware of leaven of the P.
11; Mark 8:15; Luke 12:1
23:2 scribes and P. sit in M. seat
Luke 5:30 P. murmured, 15:2
John 3:1 a man of the P. named
Nic.

PHILIP.

Mat. 10:3 P. and Barthol. Mark

PHILISTINE.

2 Sam. 21:17 Abishai smo. the P

PHILISTINES.

Gen. 21:34 Abraham in P. land
23:14 Isaac had flocks, P. euv.
15 P. stopped wells Abrah. 18
Zep. 2:5 land of P. I will destroy

PHYSICIAN.

Mat. 9:12 th. that be wh. need
not a p. Mark 2:17; Luke 5:31
Luke 4:23 proverb, p. heal thys.
Col. 4:14 Luke, the beloved p.

PHYSICIANS.

Gen. 50:2 Joseph com. p. to embalm father; p. embalm. Is.

PICTURES.

Prov. 25:11 apples of gold in p.

PIECE.

Jer. 37:21 give him daily p. bre.

PIERCE.

Num. 24:8 p. them with arrows
2 K. 18:21 hand, p. it, Is. 36:6

PIERCED.

Job 30:17 my bones are p.
Ps. 22:16 p. my hands and feet
Zec. 12:10 they sh. look on me wh. they have p. John 19:37
John 19:34 one of soldiers p. side
1 Tim. 6:10 p. th. with sorrows
Rev. 1:7 they also which p. him

PIETY.

1 Tim. 5:4 learn to show p.

PILATE.

Mat. 27:2 they delivered him to Pontius P. 24; Mark 15:1
Mark 15:5 so that P. marvel. 44
John 18:33 P. entered judg. hall

PILGRIMS.

Heb. 11:13 we. strangers and p.
1 Pet. 2:11 as p. abs. from lusts

PILLAR.

Gen. 19:26 became a p. of salt
35:20 Jacob set p. on R.'s grave

PITCHED.

Gen. 12:8 Abram p. his tent. and
1 Chr. 15:1 David prepared place for ark. p. tent, 16:1; 2 Chr. 1:4

PITY, Substantive.

Deut. 7:16 eye shall have no p.
Mat. 18:33 as I had p. on thee

PITY, Verb.

Deut. 13:8 nor shall thine eye p. him, 19:13, 21
Prov. 28:8 him that will p. poor
Joel 2:18 then the Lord will p.
Zec. 11:5 th. sheph. p. them not

PITIETH.

Ps. 103:13 as a father p. his chil. so L. p. them th. fear him

PITIFUL.

1 Pet. 3:8 love as brethren, be p.

PLACE, Substantive.

Neh. 2:3 p. of my father's sepul.
Mat. 28:6 see the p. where the Lord lay, Mark 16:6
1 Cor. 11:20 come together into one p.

PLAGUE, Substantive.

Ex. 11:1 bri. one p. on Pharaoh
Lev. 13:3 hair in p. turned wh. 17
Num. 11:33 L. smote people with a p.

Mark 5:29 she was healed of p.
34 and be whole of p.

PLAGUES.

Gen. 12:17 L. plagued Ph. wi. p.
Ex. 9:14 I will send all my p.
Mark 3:10 as many as had p.
Luke 7:21 cured many of their p.

PLAIN, Adjective.

Ps. 27:11 lead me in a p. path
Prov. 8:9 th. are p. to him that
15:19 the way of righteous is p.
Is. 40:4 and rough places made p.
Jer. 48:21 judgment come on p.
Mark 7:35 loosed, he spake p.

PLAIN, Substantive.

Jer. 17:26 shall come from the p.
Ezek. 8:4 the vision that I saw in p.

PLAINS.

2 K. 25:5 Chaldees overtook him in the p. Jer. 39:5; 52:8
2 Chr. 9:27 cedar in lower p.

PLAINLY.

Is. 32:4 stammerer sh. speak p.
John 10:24 if thou be C. tell us p.
11:14 Jesus said to them p.
16:25 I shall show you p.
29 now speakest thou p. and
Heb. 11:14 such things declare p.

PLAITING.

1 Pet. 3:3 let it not be p. of hair

PLANTS.

1 Chr. 4:23 that dwell among p.
Ps. 128:3 thy children like p.
Ezek. 31:4 riv. run. about his p.

PLANT, Verb.

Jer. 18:9 a kingdom, to build to p.
24:6 p. and not pluck, 42:10
35:7 nor shall you sow, nor p.

PLANTED.

Gen. 2:8 God p. a garden eastw.
9:20 Noah p. vine; 21:33 A. p.
Num. 24:6 trees which L. hath p.
Ec. 3:2 pluck up that which is p.
Mat. 15:13 heavenly Fath. not p.
21:33 householder p. Mark 12:1;

PLATTED.

Mat. 27:29 p. crown of thorns. Mark 15:17; John 19:2

PLAY.

1 Sam. 16:16 that he shall p. wi.
17 now a man that can p. well

Is. 11:8 sucking child shall p.
Ezek. 33:32 and can p. well on

PLEAD.

Is. 1:17 judgment, p. for widow

PLEASANT.

Gen. 2:9 ev. tree grow that is p.
3:6 p. to the eyes and a tree
Prov. 2:10 knowledge is p.
Lam 1:11 have given their p. things
Dan. 10:3 I ate no p. bread

PLEASANTNESS.

Prov. 3:17 her ways are w. of p.

PLEASE.

Is. 2:6 p. themselves in children
55:11 accomplish that wh. I p.
Rom. 8:8 they in flesh cannot p.
15:1 bear and not p. ourselves
2 let every one p. his neighbor
Cor. 7:32 car. how he may p. L.
33 p. his wife; 34 she may p.
10:33 even as I p. all men
Gal. 1:10 do I seek to p. men?
1 Thes. 2:15 they p. not G.
4:1 ought to walk and to p. G.
2 Tim. 2:4 that ye may p. him
Tit. 2:9 to p. them well in all
Heb. 11:6 with. faith impos. p. G.

PLEASED.

Gen. 45:16 it p. Pharaoh well
Jud. 13:23 if the Lord were p.
14:7 and she p. Samson well
1 K. 3:10 Solomon's speech p. L.
Est. 2:9 the maiden p. the king
5:14 the thing p. Haman, he
Is. 53:10 it p. the Lord to bruise
Mal. 1:8 will he be p. with thee?
Acts 6:5 saying p. the multitude
12:3 bec. Herod saw it p. Jews
Rom. 15:3 for even Christ p. not
26 for it hath p. them of, 27
1 Cor. 1:21 it p. G. by foolishness
7:12 she p. to dwell with him
12:18 God set members as it p.
15:38 G. giveth it a body as it p.
Gal. 1:10 for if I yet p. men, I
15 it p. God to reveal his Son
Col. 1:19 p. Father that in him
Heb. 11:5 had testimony he p. G.

Well PLEASED.

Mat. 3:17 in whom I am well p.
12:18; 17:5; Mark 1:11; Luke

3:22; 2 Pet. 1:17
1 Cor. 10:5 God was not well p.
Heb. 13:16 such sacri. G. is w. p.

PLEASETH.

Gen. 16:6 do to her as it p. thee
Jud. 14:3 get her for me, she p.
Ec. 7:26 whoso p. G. sh. escape
8:3 he doeth whatsoever p. him

PLEASING.

Est. 8:5 if I be p. in his eyes
Hos. 9:4 neither shall they be p.
Col. 1:10 worthy of L. to all p.
1 Thes. 2:4 so we speak, not as p.
1 John 3:22 do things that are p.

Well-PLEASING.

Phil. 4:18 acceptable, well-p. to G.
Col. 3:20 for this is well-p. to L.
Heb. 13:21 work. what is well-p.

PLEASURE.

Is. 58:3 in day of your fast find p.
Mal. 1:10 I have no p. in you
Luke 12:32 Father's good p. to
1 Tim. 5:6 that liv. in p. is dead
Heb. 10:6 in sac. thou ha. no p. 8
38 my soul shall have no p. in
12:10 chastened us after own p.

PLENTIFUL.

Ps. 68:9 thou didst send p. rain
Is. 16:10 joy is taken out of p.
Jer. 2:7 and I brought you to p.
48:33 gladness is taken from p.

PLENTY.

Prov. 3:10 barns be filled with p.
28:49 he that tilleth shall ha. p.
Joel 2:26 sh. eat in p. and praise

PLOUGHSHARES.

Is. 2:4 beat sw. into p. Mic. 4:3
Joel 3:10 beat your p. into swo.

PLUCK.

Mat. 5:29 if right eye offend thee
p. it out, 18:9; Mark 9:47
John 10:29 no man is able to p. th.

PLUCKED.

Ezr. 9:3 p. off hair of my head
Neh. 13:25 and p. off their hair
Jer. 12:15 after I have p. them out
Luke 17:6 be thou p. up by the root
Gal. 4:15 p. out your own eyes

POISON.

Rom. 3:13 p. of asps under lips
Jam. 3:8 tongue is evil, full of p.

POLLUTED.

Lam. 4:14 p. themselves with blood
Ezek. 16:6 I saw thee p. in own bl. 22
20:13 sabbaths greatly p. 16, 21, 24

PONDERED.

Prov. 4:26 p. the path of thy feet
 5:6 lest thou p. the path of life
Luke 2:19 Mary p. them in her heart

POOL.

2 Sam. 2:13 on one side of the p.
John 5:2 there is at Jerusal. a p.
 7 no man to put me into p.

POOR.

1 Sam. 2:7 L. make. p. and rich
Job 20:10 chil, sh. seek to please p.
Ps. 9:18 expecta. of p. not perish
Prov. 10:4 becometh p. dealeth
 15 destruction of p. is poverty
13:7 mak. himself p. hath riches
 8 the p. heareth not rebuke
 23 much food is in tillage of p.
14:20 p. is hated of neighbor
 21 hath mercy on p. happy
21:13 stoppeth ears at cry of p.
 22:2 rich and p. meet together
 7 the rich ruleth over the p.
Mat. 5:3 blessed are p. in spirit
26:11 ye have the p. always,
 Mark 14:7; John 12:8
Mark 12:43 p. widow, Luke 21:3
Luke 6:20 blessed be ye p. yours
Jam. 13:16 he causeth rich and p. to

Is POOR.

Ec. 4:13 better is a p. and wise

PORTION.

Deut. 21:17 giv. him double p.
 32:9 the Lord's p. is his people
1 Sam. 1:5 to Hannah he gave p.
Ezr. 4:16 shalt have no p.
Neh. 2:20 no p. nor right in Jer.
Ps. 16:5 L. is the p. of mine inher.
 17:14 who have p. in this life
73:26 God is my p. for ever
119:57 thou art my p. 142:5
Lam. 3:24 the Lord is my p.
Mat. 24:51 appoint him his p.
Luke 12:42 to give them their p.
 46 his p. with unbelievers
 15:12 give me the p. of goods

PORTIONS.

1 Sam. 1:4 gave her daughters p.

POSSESS.

Ezek. 35:10 be mine, we will p.
 36:12 I will cause Is. to p. thee
Dan. 7:18 the saints shall p. the
Luke 18:12 give tithe of all I p.
 21:19 in patience p. your souls

POSSESS, with land.

Is. 57:13 put. trust in me, shall p.l.
Amos 2:10 I bro. you to p. land

POSSESSED.

Ps. 139:13 thou hast p. my reins
Dan. 7:22 saints p. the kingdom
Luke 8:36 he that was p. cured
Acts 16:16 a damsel p. with a spirit

POSSESSION.

Gen. 17:8 I will give land of Can.
 for everlasting p. 48:4
 47:11 gave them p. in land of E.
Deut. 32:49 which I gave Israel for p.
Jos. 12:6 Moses gave it for a p.
Acts 5:1 An. with Sap. sold a p.
 7:5 would give it to him for a p.
 45 with Jesus into p. of Gent.
Eph. 1:14 redemption of the p.

POSSESSIONS.

Gen. 34:10 and get you p. therein
 47:27 and Israel had p. therein
Num. 32:30 they shall have p.
Jos. 22:4 get to land of your p.
1 Sam. 25:2 whose p. were in C.
1 Chr. 9:2 inhabitants dw. in p.
2 Chr. 11:14 Levites left their p.
 32:29 Hezeki. prov. p. of flocks
Ec. 2:7 I had great p. of great
Ob. 17 Jacob shall pos. their p.
Mat. 19:22 had p. Mark 10:22
Acts 2:45 sold p. and part. them
 28:7 same quart. were p. of P.

POSSESSOR, S.

Gen. 14:19 high G. p. heaven, 22
Zec. 11:5 whose p. slay them
Acts 4:34 many as were p. lands

POSSIBLE.

Mat. 19:26 G. all p. Mark 10:27
24:24 if p. dec. elect, Mar. 13:22
26:39 if p. let this cup pass fr. me, Mark 14:35
Mark 9:23 all things p. to him

14:36 all things p. Luke 18:27
Acts 2:24 not p. he sho. be hold.
20:16 if p. at Jerusal. day of P.
Rom. 12:18 if p. live peaceably
Gal. 4:15 if p. ye would have
Heb. 10:4 not p. blood of bulls

POST,S.

2 Chr. 30:6 p. went with letters,
 Est. 3:13, 15; 8:10
Est. 8:14 p. rode on mules
Job 9:25 days are swifter than p.
Jer. 51:31 one p. run to meet an.

POST.

1 Sam. 1:9 E. sat on seat by a p.
Ezek. 40:16 on each p. palm-trees

POSTS.

Jud. 16:3 Samson took two p.

Side-POSTS.

Ex. 12:7 stri. blood on 2 s.-p. 22

POSTERITY.

Ps. 109:13 let his p. be cut off
Dan. 11:4 not be divid. to his p.

POT.

Ex. 16:33 take a p. put manna
Heb. 9:4 golden p. with manna

POTTAGE.

Gen. 25:30 feed me w. p. 34 J. gave

POTTER.

Mat. 27:10 gave th. for p.'s field

POURED.

Gen. 28:18 Jacob p. oil on stone
Lev. 8:12 Mo. p. oil on Aaron's
head
21:10 on whose head oil was p.
1 Sam. 10:1 Samuel p. oil on S.'s
head
Ps. 142:2 I p. out my complaint

POURING.

Luke 10:34 his wounds, p. in oil

POVERTY.

Prov. 6:11 p. co. as armed, 24:34
10:15 destruction of p. is th. p.
11:24 withhold. but tend. to p.
13:18 p. be to him that refuseth
20:13 not sleep, lest come to p.
23:21 drun. and glut. come to p.
2 Cor. 8:2 their deep p. abounded
 9 ye thro' his p. might be rich
Rev. 2:9 I kn. thy works and p.

POWDERS.

Ex. 32:20 Moses burnt calf to p.

Deut. 28:24 make rain of land p.
2 K. 23:6 stamped the grove to p.
 15 stamp. alt. to p. 2 Chr. 34:7
Cant. 3:6 perfumed wi. all the p.

POWER.

Gen. 49:3 dignity, excellency of p.
Ec. 8:4 word of a king is, there is p.
 8 no man hath p. over spirit
Dan. 6:27 delivered D. fr. p. of lion
Mic. 3:8 I am full of p. by Spirit
Zec. 4:6 nor by p. but my Spirit
Mat. 9:6 hath p. to forgive sins,
Mark 2:10; Luke 5:24
 8 had given such p. to men
10:1 p. ag. uncl. spir. Luke 9:1
24:30 clouds with p. Luke 21:27
26:64 ri. hand of p. Mark 14:62
28:18 all p. is given me in heav.
Mark 3:15 p. to heal sickness.
9:1 kingd. of God come with p.
Luke 1:35 p. of Highest oversha.
4:6 said All this p. will I give
 32 for his word was with p.
 36 with p. he command. spirits
5:17 p. of the Lord was present
10:19 I give you p. to tread on
serp. and over p. of enemy
12:5 fear him that ha. p. to cast
20:20 deli. him to p. of governor
22:53 this is the p. of darkness
24:49 until ye be endued with p.
John 1:12 to them gave he p.
10:18 p. to lay it down, and p.
17:2 given him p. over all flesh
10:10 p. to crucify, p. to release
Acts 1:7 Fa. hath put in own p.
 8 receive p. after Holy Ghost
4:7 by what p. ha. ye done this?
5:4 was it not in thine own p.?
6:8 Stephen full of faith and p.
10:38 anointed Jesus with p.
Rom. 9:21 hath not pot. p. over cla
13:2 whosoever resisteth the p.
 3 wilt thou not be afraid of p.?
15:13 through p. of Holy Ghost
 19 by the p. of the Spi. of God
16:25 now to him that is of p.
1 Cor. 2:4 in demonstration of p.
4:19 not kn. speech, but the p.
5:4 with p. of our L. J. Christ
6:12 not be bro. under p. of any

14 raise us up by his own p.
7:4 wife and husb. have not p.
9:4 ha. we not p. to eat and dr.?
5 have not we p. to lead wife?
12 if oth. be partak. of this p.
over you, we ha. not used p.
11:10 wom. ought to have p.
15:24 put down author. and p.
2 Cor. 4:7 excel. of p. be of God
8:3 to p. yea, beyond their p.
12:9 that the p. of Ch. may rest
13:10 according to p. G. given
Eph. 1:19 exceeding greatness of
his p. work. of his mighty p.
21 above princi. p. and might
2:2 accord. to prince of p. of air
3:7 the effectual work of his p.
20 accord. to p. that worketh
Phil. 3:10 know the p. of resur.
Col 1:13 deliv. us from p. of darkn.
2:10 head of all princi. and p.
2 Thes. 1:9 pun. fr. glory of his p.
11 fulfil work of faith with p.
2:9 working of Satan wi. all p.
3:9 not because we have not p.
1 Tim. 6:16 wh. be honor and p.
2 Tim. 1:7 G. hath giv. sp. of p.
3:5 hav. godliness, denying p.
Heb. 1:3 by word of his p.
2:14 destroy him that had p.
2 Pet. 1:3 p. given all things
16 made known p. of our Lord
Rev. 5:13 honor and p. be to him
IN POWER.
Prov. 3:27 it is in p. of thy hand
18:21 and life in p. of tongue
Is. 40:26 that he is strong in p.
Nah. 1:3 slow to anger, gr. in p.
Luke 4:14 J. returned in p. of Sp.
1 Cor. 4:20 not in word, but in p.
15:43 sown in weakn. rai. in p.
Eph. 6:10 strong in Lord and p.
1 Thes. 1:5 in word and in p.
2 Pet. 2:11 angels greater in p.
My POWER.
Rom. 9:17 I might show my p.
1 Cor. 9:18 I abuse not my p.
No POWER.
Is. 50:2 have I no p. to deliver?
Dan. 8:7 there was no p. in th ram
John 19:11 ha. no p. against me

Rom. 13:1 th. is no p. but of God
Rev. 20:6 second death hath no p.
POWERFUL.
Ps. 29:4 the voice of the L. is p.
2 Cor. 10:10 for his letters are p.
Heb. 4:12 word of G. is quick, p.
POWERS.
Rom. 8:38 nor p. can sepa. fr. G.
13:1 p. that be ordained of God
Eph. 3:10 p. in hevenly places
6:12 against principalit. and p.
PRAISE, Substantive.
Deut. 26:19 to make thee high in p.
Jud. 5:3 I will sing p. to the L.
God of Israel, Ps. 7:17; 9:2;
57:7; 61:8; 104:33
1 Chr. 16:35 may glory in thy p.
2 Chr. 23:13 taught to sing p.
Neh. 9:5 who is exalted above p.
12:46 days of D. we, songs of p.
Ps. 9:14 I may show all thy p.
22:25 my p. shall be of thee
30:12 glory may sing p. to thee
33:1 for p. is comely for upright
34:1 his p. shall be in my mou.
35:28 shall speak of thy p.
48:10 thy p. to ends of earth
50:23 whoso offereth p. glorifie.
51:15 my mouth sh. show thy p.
65:1 p. waiteth for thee, O God
66:2 and make his p. glorious
8 make voice of his p. be hea.
71:6 my p. shall be continually
8 mouth be filled with thy p.
100:4 enter his courts with p.
106:2 who can show all his p.?
108:1 I will sing, and give p.
119:171 my lips shall utter p.
138:1 before gods will I sing p.
145:21 mouth sh. speak p. of L.
147:1 p. is comely; 7 sing p. on
148:14 exalteth the p. of saints
149:1 sing his p. in congregati.
Is. 42:10 sing his p. from end of
ear.
12 declare his p. in the islands
43:21 they sh. show forth my p.
48:9 and for my p. will I refrain
60:18 th9u shalt call thy gat. P.
61:3 garment of p. for heaviness
11 L. will cause p. to sp. forth

Jer. 13:11 might be to me a p.
17:26 bring. sacrifices of p. 33:11
33:9 shall be to me a joy, a p.
51:41 how is p. of earth surpr.?
Hab. 3:3 earth was full of his p.
Zep. 3:20 make you a p. am. all peo
Mat. 21:16 thou hast perfect. p.
Luke 18:43 they saw it, gave p.
John 9:24 give G. the p.
12:43 p. of men more than p. G.
Rom. 2:29 whose . is not of m.
13:3 thou shalt have p. of same
1 Cor. 4:5 ev. man have p. of G.
2 Cor. 8:18 whose p. is in gospel
Eph. 1:6 predestinat. to p. of gl.
 12 p. of gl. who trusted in C. 14
Phil. 1:11 J. C. to p. and gl. of G.
4:8 if any p. think on th. things
Heb. 2:12 in church will I sing p.
13:15 let us offer sacrifice of p.
1 Pet. 1:7 might be found to p.
2:14 for p. of them that do well
4:11 to whom be p. for ever

PRAISE, Verb.

Ps. 21:13 so will we sing and p.
22:23 ye that fear Lord p. him
30:9 shall the dust p. thee?
42:5 I shall yet p. him, 11; 43:5
44:8 in G. we boast, p. name
45:17 there. shall people p. thee
49:18 men p. thee, wh. doest w.
63:3 lips sh. p. thee; 5 mou. p.
67:3 let peop. praise th. 5 pe. p.
69:34 heaven and earth p. him
71:14 I will yet p. thee more
74:21 poor and needy p. name
76:10 wrath of man sh. p. thee
88:10 sh. dead arise and p. th.?
89:5 heavens sh. p. thy wonders
99:3 let them p. thy great name
107:32 p. him in assem. of elders
113:1 p. him, O serv. of L. 135:1
115:17 dead p. not the Lord
Ps. 142:7 br. out of pris. that I p.
145:4 genera. sh. p. thy works
 10 thy works shall p. thee, O
147:12 p. L. Jeru. p. G. O Zion
148:1 p. ye L. p. him in heights
2 p. him, angels, p. him, host
3 p. sun and moon, p. ye stars
4 p. him, ye heaven of heavens

149:3 let them p. name in dance
150:1 p. G. in sanctu. p. him in
2 p. him for his acts, p. him
3 p. with trump; 4 p. timbrel
5 p. him on sounding cymbals
Prov. 27:2 let anot. man p. thee
28:4 forsake the law p. wicked
31:31 let her own works p. her
Is. 38:18 grave cannot p. thee
 19 the living her shall p. thee
Jer. 31:7 p. ye and say, O Lord
Dan. 2:23 I thank and p. thee
4:37 I p. and extol K. of heaven
Joel 2:26 p. the name of the Lord

PRAISES.

2 Chr. 29:30 commanded Lev. to
 sing p. to Lord, they sang p.
Ps. 9:11 sing p. to the Lord in Z.
22:3 O thou that inhabitest p.
Ps. 27:6 yea, I will sing p. to G.
 47:6; 68:32; 75:9; 108:3
47:7 sing p. with understanding
56:12 render p. to thee, 144:9
68:4 sing to G. p. to his name
78:4 to genera. to come p. of L.
146:2 I will sing p. to my God
147:1 good to sing p. to our G.
149:3 sing p. to him with timb.
Is. 63:7 I will mention p. of Lord
Acts 16:25 Paul and Silas sang p.
1 Pet. 2:9 show forth p. of him

PRAISETH.

Prov. 31:28 her husb. also, p. her

PRAISING.

Luke 2:13 heavenly host p. God
 20 shepherds returned p. God
Acts 2:47 eat with gladn. p. G.
3:8 and leaping, and p. God, 9

PRATING.

Prov. 10:8 a p. fool shall fall. 10

PRAY.

1 Sam. 12:23 I should sin in
ceasing to p.
2 Sam. 7:27 in his heart to p.
1 K. 8:30 when they p. 35, 42, 44,,
 48; 2 Chr. 6:26, 34, 38
13:6 p. th. my hand be restored
2 Chr. 6:24 p. make supplica. 32
7:14 if my people shall p.
Ps. 5:2 my God, to thee will I p.
55:17 morn, and noon will I p.

179

I. 16:12 come to sanctuary to p.
45:20 p. to a god cannot save
Jer. 29:12 p. to me, and I will heark
37:3 p. now to the L. 42:2, 20
Zec. 7:2 sent men to p. before L.
8:21 speedily p. before Lord, 22
Mat. 5:44 p. for them which de-
spitefully use, Luke 16:27
6:5 for they love to p. standing
6 p. to Father which is in sec.
9 after this manner p. ye
9:38 p. L. of harvest, Luke 10:2
14:23 he went to a mount. to p.
Mark 6:46; Luke 6:12; 9:28
19:13 put hands on them and p.
24:20 p. your fight be not in
winter, Mark 13:18
26:36 go p. yonder, Mark 14:32
41 watch and p. Mark 13:33,
Mark 11:24 what ye desire when ye
p.
Luke 11:1 Lord, teach us to p.
2 he said to them. When ye p.
18:1 men ought always to p.
John 14:16 I will p. Fath. 16:26
17:9 I p. for th. p. not for world
15 I p. not that thou take them
20 nor p. I for these alone
Acts 8:22 p. God if perh. thought
24 Simon said, p. ye to the L.
10:9 P. went on house-top to p.
Rom. 8:26 kn. not what we p. for
1 Cor. 11:13 wom. p. uncovered?
14:3 let him p. that he interpr.
14 if I p. in unknown tongue
15 p. with sp. p. with underst.
Jam. 5:13 any afflicted? let hi. p.
14 and let them p. over him
16 confess your faults, and p.
1 John 5:16 I do not say he sh. p.

PRAYED.
1 Sam. 1:10 Hannah p. to L. 21
27 for this child I p. 8:6 Sam.
2 K. 4:33 Elisha p. L. 6:17, 18
19:15 Hezekiah p. before Lord
20:2; 2 Chr. 30:18; 32:24
2 Chr. 32:20 Isaiah p. 33:13 Ma.
Jer. 32:16 Jeremiah p. unto L.
Dan. 6:10 D. p. 3 ti. a day, 9:4
Jon. 2:1 Jonah p. to L. 4:2
Mat. 26:39 Je. fell and p. 42:44;

Mark 14:35, 39; Luke 22:41
Mark 1:35 solitary place and p.
Luke 5:3 Jesus p. him he would
16 withdrew into wilde. and p.
9:29 as he p. countenance alter.
18:11 the Pharisee stood and p.
22:32 I p. that thy faith fail not
44 agony he p. more earnestly
John 4:31 his disciples p. him
Acts 1:24 the disciples p. and sa.
4:31 when they had p. the place
10:48 then they p. him to tarry
13:3 had fasted and p. 14:23
16:9 p. him, saying, Come to M.
25 at midnight Paul and S. p.
20:36 Paul kneeled on shore and p.
22:17 while I p. in the temple
28:8 to whom P. entered and p.
Jam. 5:17 E. p. it mi. not rain, 18

PRAYER.
2 Sam. 7:27 pray this p. to thee
1 K. 8:28 respect p. of thy serv.
Mat. 17:21 not out but by p. and
fasting, Mark 9:29
Luke 1:13 Zacharias, thy p. hea.
Acts 3:1 temple at hour of p.
12:5 p. made without ceasing
16:13 p. was wont be made
1 Cor. 7:5 give yourselves to p.
2 Cor. 1:11 helping by p. for us
9:14 by their p. for you, which
Eph. 6:18 praying with all p.
Phil. 1:4 in every p. of mine
19 turn to my salvat. thro' p.
4:6 by p. let requests be known
1 Tim. 4:5 it is sanctified by p.
Jam. 5:15 p. of faith shall save
16 p. of a righteous man avail.
1 Pet. 4:7 be sober, watch un. v.

My PRAYER.
Ps. 4:1 have mercy, hear my p.
17:1; 39:12; 54:2
5:3 in morn, will I direct my p.
6:9 the Lord will receive my p.
35:13 my p. returned to bosom
42:8 my p. to God of my life
55:1 give ear unto my p. O God
61:1 attend to my p. 64:1; 84:8;
86:6; 102:1; 143:1
66:19 attended to voice of my p.
20 God hath not turned my p.

180

69:13 my p. is to thee
88:2 let my p. come before th.
13 in morn. sh. my p. prev. th.
141:2 let my p. be set bef. thee
5 my p. shall be in their calam.
Lam. 3:8 he shutteth out my p.
Jon. 2:7 my p. came to thee
Rom. 10:1 my p. to G. for Is. is

PRAYERS.

Ps. 72:20 p. of David are ended
Is. 1:15 when ye make manyp.
Mat. 23:14 for pretence making
long p. Mark 12:40; Luke
20:47
Luke 2:37 Anna continued in p.
5:33 disciples of John make p.?
Acts 2:42 breaking bread, and p.
10:4 thy p. are come up bef. G.
Rom. 1:9 I make mention of you
in my p. Eph. 1:16; 1 Thes.
15:30 strive with me in your p.
1 Tim. 2:1 I exh. that p. be made
5:5 widow indeed continu. in p.
Phile. 22 thro' your p. be given
Heb. 5:7 when he had offered p.
1 Pet. 3:7 that your p. be not
12 his ear is open to their p.
Rev. 5:8 which are p. of saints
8:3 offer it with p. of saints, 4

PRAYEST.

Mat. 6:5 when thou p. be not, 6.

PRAYETH, ING.

1 Sam. 1:12 as Hannah contin. p.
1 K. 8:28 hearken to prayer wh.
thy servant p. 2 Chr. 6:19, 20
Is. 44:17 he worshippeth it, p.
Dan. 9:20 I was speaking, and p.
Mark 11:25 when ye stand p.
Luke 1:10 people were p. with.
3:21 Jes. p. the heaven opened
9:18 as he was alone p.
11:1 he was p. in certain place
Acts 9:11 beh. he p. 11:5 I was p.
12:12 many were together p.
1 Cor. 11:4 every man p. with his
14:14 my spirit p. but my und.
2 Cor. 8:4 p. us to rec. the gift
Eph. 6:18 p. always in the Spirit
Col. 1:3 p. for you; 4:3 p. for us
1 Thes. 3:10 night and day p.
Jude 20 ye p. in the Holy Ghost

PREACH.

Neh. 6:7 appoint. prophets to p.
Is. 61:1 hath anointed me to p.
Jon. 3:2 p. to it preaching I bid
Mat. 4:17 fr. that Je. began to p.
10:27 what ye hear, that p. upon
11:1 he departed thence to p.
Mark 1:4 John did p. baptism
3:14 send th. forth to p. Luke 9:2
Luke 4:18 to p. deliverance, 19
9:60 go and p. kingdom of God
Acts 5:42 ceased not to p. J. C.
10:42 he commanded us to p.
15:21 in every city them that p.
16:6 forbidden by H. Ghost to p.
17:3 Je. whom I p. to you is C.
Rom. 10:8 word of faith wh. we p.
15 how shall they p. exc. sent?
1 Cor. 1:23 we p. Christ crucified
9:16 tho' I p. the gospel, I have
noth. to glory, woe if I p. not
15:11 so we p. so ye believed
2 Cor. 4:5 we p. not ourselves
Gal. 2:2 the gospel which I p.
5:11 breth. if I yet p. circumci.
Eph. 3:8 I should p. am. Gent.
Phil. 1:15 some indeed p. Christ
16 one p. Christ of contention
Col. 1:28 we p. warning every
2 Tim. 4:2 p. the word, be inst.

PREACHED.

Mark 1:39 he p. in their synagogues
2:2 he p. the word to them
6:12 p. that men should repent
16:20 went and p. every where
Luke 3:18 many others thi. p. he
16:16 the kingdom of God is p.
Acts 3:20 J. C. who before was p.
4:2 p. thro' J. the resurrection
8:5 p. C. to Samaria; 35 p. Jes.
25 p. the word of L. p. gospel
40 philip p. in all cities till he
9:20 Saul p. C. in synagogues
10:37 baptism which John p.
13:5 they p. the word of God
24 when John had first p. bef.
38 p. to you forgiveness of sins
42 that th. words might be p.
15:36 let us visit wh. we ha. p.
17:13 word of G. was p. of Paul
18 he p. J. and the resurrect.

20:7 Paul p. ready to depart
1 Cor. 9:27 lest wh. I p. to others
15:2 keep in memory what I p.
12 if C. be p. that he rose
2 Cor. 1:19 J. who was p. am. you
11:4 Jes. whom we have not p.
Gal. 1:8 oth. gospel th. we ha. p.
Eph. 2:17 and p. peace to you
Phil. 1:18 Christ p. and I rejoice
Col. 1:23 was p. to every creature
1 Tim. 3:1 p. unto the Gentiles
Heb. 4:2 word p. did not profit
6 they to whom it was first p.
1 Pet. 3:19 p. to spirits in prison

PREACHER.
Ec. 1:1 words of p. son of David
12 I the p. was king over Isr.
12:9 because p. was wise
10 the p. sought to find words
Rom. 10:14 hear without a p.?
1 Tim. 2:7 ord. a p. 2 Tim. 1:11
2 Pet. 2:5 Noah, p. of righteous.

PREACHEST, ETH, ING.
Jon. 3:2 preach to it the p. I bid
Mat. 3:1 came John p. Luke 3:3
12:41 at p. of Jonas, Luke 11:32
Luke 8:1 p. and showing tidings
9:6 through towns p. the gospel
Acts 8:4 went every where p.
12 p. concern. kingdom of G.
10:36 p. peace by Jesus Christ
11:19 p. word to none but Jews
19:13 by Jesus, whom Paul p.
20:9 as P. was long p. Eutychus
25 among wh. I have gone p.
28:31 p. the kingdom of God
Rom. 2:21 p. a man sho. not steal
16:25 according to p. of Jesus
1 Cor. 1:18 p. of cross is foolish.
21 by foolishness of p. to save
2:4 my p. was not with enticing
2 Cor. 10:14 come to you p. gos.
11:4 cometh p. another Jesus

PRECEPT.
Is. 28:10 p. upon p. p. on p. 13

PRECIOUS.
Ps. 139:17 how p. thy thoughts
Prov. 1:13 sh. find p. substance
3:15 wis. is more p. than rubies
Is. 13:12 man more p. than gold
Dan. 11:8 carry away th. p. ves.

43 power over all p. things
Jam. 5:7 waiteth for the p. fruit
1 Pet. 1:7 more p. than gold
19 but with p. blood of Christ

PREDESTINATE, ED.
Rom. 8:29 did foreknow. did p.
30 wh. he did p. them he call.
Eph. 1:5 hav. p. us to adoption
11 p. according to purpose

PREMEDITATE.
Mark 13:11 neither p. whatsoev.

PREPARATION.
Prov. 16:1 p. of heart of man
Mat. 27:62 day that followed the
day of p. Mark 15:42; Luke
23:54; John 19:14, 31, 42
Eph. 6:15 shod with p. of gospel

PREPARE.
Mat. 11:10 shall p. way bef. thee
26:17 where wilt thou th. we p.
Mark 14:12; Luke 22:8, 9
Luke 3:4 p. ye way of L. 7:27
John 14:2 I go to p. place, 3

PREPARED.
2 Cor. 19:3 Jeboshaphat p. his heart
Est. 6:4 Mordecai on gallow p.7:10
Zep. 1:7 Lord hath p. a sacrifice
Mat. 20:23 it sh. be given to the
for whom it is p. Mark 10:40
25:34 kingdom p. 41 into fire p.
Mark 14:15 a large upp. room p.
Luke 1:17 people p. for the Lord
2:31 p. before face of all people
12:47 knew L.'s will, but p. not
1 Cor. 2:9 things God p. for them
2 Tim. 2:21 p. to ev. good work
Heb. 10:5 a body hast thou p. me
11:7 Noah p. ark to the saving
16 he hath p. for them a city

PREPAREST, ETH.
2 Chr. 30:19 p. heart to seek G.
Ps. 23:5 p. a table before me

PRESENCE.
Gen. 3:8 hid from p. of the Lord
4:16 Cain went from p. of Lord
45:3 Joseph, s bret. troub. at p.
2 Sam. 16:19 in thy father's p. so
will I be in thy p.
Est. 7:6 Haman was afraid at p.
Ps. 51:11 cast me not away fr. thy p.
95:2 come bef. p. with thanks,

100:2 come bef. p. with singing
114:7 tremble at p. of the Lord
140:13 upright sh. dw. in thy p.
Zep. 1:7 hold peace at p. of Lord
In the PRESENCE.
Gen. 25:18 Ish. died in t. p. of
breth.
2 Sam. 16:19 I not serve in the p.
1 K. 8:22 Solomon stood in the p.
1 Chr. 24:31 cast lots in t. p. of D.
Ps. 23:5 a table in t. p. of enem.
116:14 in the p. of all his peo. 18
Prov. 17:18 in the p. of friend
25:6 put not thyself in the p.
Jer. 28:1 Hanan. spake in the p.
Luke 1:19 stand in the p. of God
 14:10 worship in the p. of them
15:10 joy in the p. of ang. of G.
John 20:30 signs did J. in the p.
Acts 3:13 deni. him in t. p. of P.
 16 given him soundness in p.
27:35 gave thanks to G. in t. p.
1 Thes. 2:19 are not ye in the p.
Heb. 9:24 appear in the p. of G.
Rev. 14:10 in p. of ang. in p. of L.
PRESENT, substantive.
1 K. 9:16 for a p. to his daughter
PRESENT, Adjective.
Ps. 46:1 G. is p. help in trouble
1 Cor. 3:22 things p. or to come
Gal. 1:4 deliver us fr. p. world
4:18 not only when I am p.
2 Tim. 4:10 hav. loved p. world
Tit. 2:12 live godly in p. world
PRESENT, ED.
1 Sam. 17:16 Goliath the Phil. p.
hims.
2:1 Satan came to p. himself
Jer. 36:7 will p. their supplicat.
Ezek. 20:28 they p. provocation
Dan. 9:18 we do not p. supplica.
Mat. 2:11 they p. to him gifts
Luke 2:22 bro. him to p. to Lord
Acts 9:41 call. saints, p. her alive
Rom. 12:1 that ye p. your bodies
2 Cor. 4:14 raise by Jesus, p. us
11:2 that I may p. you to Christ
Eph. 5:27 might p. it to himself
Col. 1:22 p. you holy unblamable
 28 ye may p. ev. man perfect
PRESERVE.

Gen. 19:32 we may p. seed, 34
Ps. 61:7 prepare truth which may p.
64:1 hear me, p. my life fr. fear
79:11 p. th. those th. are to die
86:2 p. my soul, for I am holy
121:7 L. p. thee, he sh. p. soul
 8 Lord shall p. thy going out
140:1 O L. p. me fr. vio. man, 4
Prov. 2:11 discretion shall p. th.
Luke 17:33 lose his life sh. p. it.
1 Sam. 30:23 Lord who hath p.
2 Sam. 8:6 L. p. D. 1 Ch. 18:6, 13
Job 10:12 visitation p. my spirit
Ps. 31:23 the Lord p. the faithful
37:28 his saints are p. forever
116:6 the Lord p. the simple
145:20 L. p. them that love him
Prov. 2:8 he p. way of his saints
 16:17 keep. his way p. his soul
1 Thes. 5:23 sp. soul, and body p.
PRESS, ED.
Jud. 16:16 Delilah p. wi. words
Mark 3:10 p. on to touch him
Luke 6:38 good measure p. down
8:45 multit. throng and p. thee
2 Cor. 1:8 were p. above measure
Phil. 3:14 I p. toward the mark
PRETENCE.
Mat. 23:14 for a p. make long
 prayers, Mark 12:40
PREVAIL.
Mat. 16:18 gates of hell sh. not p.
PREVAILED.
Gen. 7:18 waters p. and inc. 19
Acts 19:16 in whom evil spirit p.
Rev. 5:5 root of David hath p.
PREVENT.
Job 3:12 why did knees p. me?
Ps. 59:10 G. of mercy shall p. me
79:8 let thy tender mercies p.
88:13 in morn. sh. my prayer p.
Amos 9:10 evil shall not p. us
1 Thes. 4:15 shall not p. them
PREVENTED, EST.
Ps. 21:3 p. him with blessings
119:147 I p. dawning of morn.
Mat. 17:25 Jesus p. him, saying,
PREY.
Ezek 22:27 princes like wol. raven.
PRICE, S.
Job 28:18 p. of wisdom is above

rubi.

Prov. 17:16 p. in hand of fool?

31:10 her p. is far above rubies

Mat. 13:46 found one pearl of p.

Acts 4:34 brought p. of the thin.

5:2 kept back part of the p. 3

1 Cor. 6:20 bought with a p. 7:23

1 Pet. 3:4 meek spirit of great p.

PRICKED, ING.

Ps. 73:21 I was p. in my reins

Acts 2:37 th. were p. in th. heart

PRICKS.

Acts 9:5 kick against the p. 26:14

PRIDE.

1 Sam. 17:28 p. and naughtiness

2 Chr. 32:26 Hez. humbled for p.

Prov. 8:13 p. I hate; 11:2 p. com.

13:10 by p. cometh contention

14:3 mouth of fool, is rod of p.

16:18 p. goeth before destructi.

29:23 a man's p. bring him low

Ezek. 30:6 p. of power sh. come do.

Mark 7:22 out of heart proce. p.

1 Tim. 3:6 being lifted up wi. p.

1 John 2:16 p. of life, not of Fa.

PRIEST.

Lev. 1:9 p. shall make atonement for them, 15:15, 30; 61:30; 19:22

1 Sam. 2:35 raise me up a faithf. p.

Lam. 2:6 despis. the king and p.

Heb. 7:15 after Melchizedek aris. a p.

High-PRIEST.

Lev. 21:10 h.- p. not uncover head

John 18:15 disciple was kn. to h.-p.

Acts 4:6 were of kindred of h.-p.

9:1 Saul went to the h.-p.

22:5 also the h.-p. doth witness

23:4 revilest thou God's h.-p.?

Heb. 2:17 be a faithful h.-p.

3:1 consider apostle h.-p. of

4:14 have great h.-p. in heaven

15 h.-p. wh. cannot be touched

5:1 h.-p. taken from amo. men

5 C. glo. not himself to be h.-p.

10 called a h.-p. after Me. 6:20

7:26 such a h.-p. became us

8:1 we have such a h.-p. on thr.

9:7 second, went h.-p. alone

25 the h.-p. entereth holy place

13:11 bro. into sanctu. by h.-p

PRIESTS.

Neh. 9:34 we nor our p. kept thy law

Ps. 99:6 Moses and Aaron among p.

132:9 let thy p. be clothed with

16 clothe her p. with salvation

Mal. 2:1 p. this command. is for you

Mat. 12:4 lawf. only for p. to eat

5 p. profane sabbath, Mark 2:26; Luke 6:4

Mark 2:26 is not lawful but for p.

Rev. 1:6 made us p. to God. 5:10

20:6 sh. be p. of God and christ

High- PRIESTS.

Heb. 7:28 the law maketh men h.-p.

PRIESTHOOD.

1 Pet. 2:5 a holy p. 9 a royal p.

PRINCE.

Is. 9:6 called the P. of peace

Jer. 51:59 Seraiah was a quiet p.

34:24 my servant David, a p.

37:25 David sh. be th. p. for ev.

38:2 the p. of Meshech, 3; 39:1

Dan. 1:9 Daniel in favor with prin.

9:25 build unto Messiah the P.

Mat. 9:34 casteth out dev. by p. of devils, 12:24; Mark 3:22

John 12:31 the p. of this world

16:11 p. of this world is judged

Acts 3:15 killed the P. of life

5:31 him God exalted to be a P.

Rev. 1:5 Jesus Christ P. of kings

PRINCESS, ES.

1 K. 11:3 Solom. had 700 wiv. p.

PRINCIPALITY, IES.

Rom. 8:38 p. nor powers able

Eph. 1:21 far above all p. power

6:12 wrestle ag. p. and power

Col. 1:16 p. were created by him

2:10 head of all p. and power

Tit. 3:1 mind to be subject to p.

PRINCIPLES.

Heb. 5:12 one teach you first p.

6:1 p. of the doctrine of Chr.

PRINT.

John 20:25 exc. I see p. of nails, and put my finger into p.

PRISON.

Is. 42:7 bring out prisoners from p.

22 all of them hid in p.
53:8 he was taken from p.
61:1 proclaim opening of the p.
Jer. 33:1 word came to Jerem. while
 in p. 37:21; 38:6, 28; 39:15
39:14 took Jeremiah out of p.
52:11 put Zedekiah in p.
Mat. 4:12 John was cast into p.
18:30 he cast him into p.
25:36 I was in p. ye came to me
 39 when saw we thee in p.? 44
Mark 1:14 after J. was put in p.
6:17 Her. had bound John in p.
Luke 3:20 he shut up John in p.
22:33 go with thee both into p.
23:19 for murder cast in p. 25
John 3:24 John not yet cast in p.
Acts 5:18 put apostles in com. p.
 19 angel by night op. p. doors
8:3 men and women, com. to p.
12:4 Peter in p. 5 kept in p.
 7 light in p. 17 L. br.. out of p.
16:23 Paul and Silas cast in p.
 24 inner p. 27 p. doors open
26:10 saints did I shut in p.
1 Pet. 3:19 preach. to spirits in p.
Rev. 2:10 shall cast some into p.
20:7 S. shall be loosed out his p.

PRISONER.
Ps. 79:11 let sighing of p. come
Mat. 27:15 release to people a p.
Acts 23:18 P. p. called me to him
25:27 unreasonable to send a p.
28:17 yet was I delivered p.
Eph. 3:1 1 P. the p. of Jesus,
2 Tim. 1:8 not ashamed of his p.

PRISONERS.
Gen. 39:20 where king's p. were
Ps. 69:33 L. despiseth not his p.
146:7 the Lord looseth the p.
Is. 24:22 be gathered togeth. as p.
42:7 bring out p. from prison
49:9 mayest say to p. Go forth
Lam. 3:34 crush under feet the p.
Zec. 9:12 turn to str.-hold, p. of hope
Acts 16:25 praises, p. heard them
 27 supposing p. had been fled
27:1 delivered Paul and other p.

PRISONS.

Luke 21:12 delivering you in. p.
Acts 22:4 del. in p. men and wo.

PRIZE.
1 Cor. 9:24 but one receiveth p.
Phil. 3:14 I press toward the p.

PRIZED.
Zec. 11:13 price that I was p. at

Jos. 6:10 word p. out of mouth
Job 40:5 but I will p. no further
Is. 51:4 for a law shall p. from me
Jer. 9:3 they p. from evil to evil
Mat. 15:18 p. out of mouth defile
 19 heart p. murders, Mark 7:21
Eph. 4:29 no corrupt commu. p.

PROCEEDED.
Luke 4:22 gracious words wh. p.
John 8:42 for I p. forth from God
Acts 12:3 he p. to take Peter also
Rev. 19:21 sword p. out of mouth

PROCEEDETH, ING.
Gen. 24:50 thing p. from the L.
Deut. 8:3 by every word that p.
 out of mouth of G. Mat. 4:4
Rev. 11:5 fire p. out of th. mouth
22:1 water of life p. out of thr

PROCLAIM.
Ex. 33:19 I will p. name of Lord
Lev. 25:10 p. lib. Deut. 20:10 p. peace
Jud. 7:3 to p in ears of people
1 K. 21:9 p. a fast, set Naboth on
Is. 61:2 p. the acceptable year of L
Jer. 84:17 I p. a liberty for you to
 sw. Amos 4:5 p. the free-offerings

PROCLAIMED.
Ex. 34:5 p. name of Lord, 6
1 K. 21:12 they p. a fast, set
2 K. 10:20 solemn assem. and p.
2 Chr. 20:3 Jehoshaphat p. a fast
Ezr. 8:21 I p. a fast at Ahava
Est. 6:11 Haman p. before him
Is. 62:11 hath p. Thy salvation
Jer. 36:9 they p. a fast before L.
Jon. 3:5 p. a fast, put on sackc.
Luke 12:3 be p. on house-tops

PROCURETH.
Prov. 11:27 seek, good p. favor

PRODUCE.
Is. 41:21 p. your cause, saith L.

PROFANE, Adjective.

1 Tim. 1:9 law is made for p.
4:7 ref. p. and old wives' fables
6:20 avoid p. babbi. 2 Tim. 2:16

PROFANE, Verb.
Lev. 18:15 shall not p. holy things
Amos 2:7 to p. my holy name
Mat. 12:5 priests in temple p.
Acts 24:6 gone about to p. temp.

PROFANED.
Lev. 19:8 he p. hallowed things

PROFESS.
Deut. 26:3 I p. this day to the L.
Mat. 7:23 I p. I never knew you
Tit. 1:16 they p. they know God

PROFESSED, ING.
Rom. 1:22 p. themsel. to be wise
2 Cor. 9:13 glori. God for your p.
1 Tim. 2:10 becometh women p.
6:12 hast p. a good profession

PROFESSION.
Heb. 3:1 the High-priest of our p.

PROFIT, Substantive.
Job 21:15 what p. if we pray
35:3 what p. if I be cleansed
Prov. 14:23 in all labor th. is p.
2:11 there was no p. under sun
7:11 by wisdom there is p. to
Jer. 16:19 things where. is no p.

PROFIT, Verb.
Is. 57:12 works, shall not p. thee
Jer. 23:32 they sh. not p. this peo.
Mark 8:36 what p. if gain world
1 Cor. 12:7 ev. man to p. withal
14:6 what shall I p. you?
Gal. 5:2 Ch. shall p. you nothing
Heb. 4:2 word preach, did not p.
Jam. 2:14 what doth it p. breth.

PROFITABLE.
Job 22:2 can a man be p. to God?
Ec. 10:10 wisdom is p. to direct
Mat. 5:29 p. members perish, 30
Acts 20:20 I kept noth. p. to you
1 Tim. 4:8 godliness is p. to all
2 Tim. 3:16 all Scripture is p.
4:11 M. is p. to me for ministry
Tit. 3:8 th. things are p. to men
Phile. 11 but now p. to thee

PROFITED, ETH.
Hab. 2:18 what p. graven image
Mat. 15:5 it is a gift whatever
thou might. be p. Mark 7:11

16:26 what is man p. if he gain
John 6:63 quicken. flesh p. noth.
Rom. 2:25 circumcision p. if th.
1 Cor. 13:3 not char. it p. noth
1 Tim. 4:8 bodily exerci. p. little
Heb. 13:9 not p. them that occu.

PROLONG, ED.
Deut. 4:26 not p. your days, 30:18
40 that thou mayest p. days on
earth,
32:47 ye shall p. your days
Job 6:11 that I should p. life?
Ps. 61:6 thou will p. king's life
Prov. 28:2 by knowl. shall be p.
16 he that hateth covet. sh. p.
Ec. 8:12 a sinner's days be p.
Ezek 12:28 none of my words be p.
more
Dan. 7:12 their lives were p. for

PROLONGETH.
Prov. 10:27 fear of Lord p. days

PROMISE, Substantive.
1 K. 8:56 not failed of good p.
2 Chr. 1:9 let p. to David be esta.
Neh. 5:12 do according to this p.
13 perform, not p. accor. to p.
Ps. 77:8 doth p. fail evermore?
105:42 remembered his holy p.
Luke 24:49 send p. of my Fath.
Acts 1:4 wait for p. of the Father
2:33 received p. of Holy Ghost
39 the p. is to you and children
7:17 time of the p. drew nigh
13:23 his p. ha. raised a Saviour
32 p. made to fathers
23:21 looking for a p. from thee
26:6 hope of the p. made of G. 7
Rom. 4:13 p. that he sh. be heir
14 the p. is made of none effect
16 the p. might be sure to seed
20 he staggered not at the p.
9:8 chil. of p. counted for seed
9 this is word of p. I will come
Gal. 3:14 receive p. of the Spirit
17 sho, make p. of none effect
18 it is no more of p. but God
gave it to Abraham by p.
19 to whom the p. was made
22 that the p. by faith of J. C.
29 ye are heirs according to p.
4:23 he of free woman was by p.

186

28 we, as Isaac, children of p.
Eph. 1:13 with Holy Spirit of p.
2:12 strangers from coven. of p.
3:6 partakers of his p. in Christ
6:2 first commandment with p.
1 Tim. 4:8 hav. the p. of the life
2 Tim. 1:1 according to p. of life
Heb. 4:1 fear, lest a p. being left
6:13 God made p. to Abraham
15 after he endured he obtai. p.
17 will. to show to heirs of p.
9:15 p. of eternal life, 10:36
11:9 sojourned in land of p.
heirs wi. him of the same p.
39 these all received not the p.
2 Pet. 3:4 wh. is p. of his coming
9 Lord not slack concer. his p.
13 according to his p. we look
1 John 2:25 this is the p. he hath

PROMISE, Verb.

2 Pet. 2:19 while they p. liberty,
they servants of corruption

PROMISED.

Num. 14:40 go to place Lord p.
Deut. 1:11 L. bless as he p. 15:6
1 K. 2:24 made me house he p.
5:12 L. gave S. wisdom as he p.
Rom. 1:2 gospel wh. he had p.
4:21 what he p. he was able
Tit. 1:2 p. before world began
Heb. 10:23 he is faithful that p.
11:11 him faithful that had p.
12:26 hath p. saying, Yet once
Jam. 1:12 L. p. to them love, 2:5
1 John 2:25 hath p. us eter. life

PROMISEDST.

1 K. 8:24 David that thou p. 25
Neh. 9:15 p. they sho. go to land

PROMISES.

Rom. 9:4 to whom pertain p.
15:8 to confirm p. made to fath.
2 Cor. 1:20 all p. of God in him
7:1 having therefore these p.
Gal. 3:16 to Abra. were p. made
21 is law against p. of God?
Heb. 6:12 thro' faith inherit p.
8:6 established upon better p.
11:13 not having received p.
17 he that received p. off. son
33 through faith obtained p.
2 Pet. 1:4 given to us precious .p.

PROOF, S.

Acts 1:3 hims. alive by many p.
2 cor. 2:9 might know the p.
8:24 show to them the p. of love
13:3 since ye seek a p. of christ
Phil. 2:22 ye know the p. of him
2 Tim. 4:5 p. of thy ministry

PROPER.

1 Chr. 29:3 mine own p. good
Acts 1:19 in p. tongue, Aceldama
1 Cor. 7:7 every man hath p. gift
Heb. 11:23 saw he was a p. child

PROPHECY.

2 Chr. 15:8 when Asa heard p. of
Oded
Neh. 6:12 he pronounced this p.
Prov. 31:1 p. that his mother tau.
him
Mat. 13:14 fulfilled p. of Esaias
1 Cor. 12:10 ano. p. by same Sp.
13:2 though I have the gift of p.
1 Tim. 4:14 gift given thee by p.
2 Pet. 1:19 a more sure word of p.
20 no p. of script. is of private
21 p. came not by will of man
Rev. 1:3 bless, they that hear p.
11:6 rain not in da. of th. p.
19:10 testimony of J. is sp. of p.
22:7 blessed that keepeth th. p.
10 seal not the say, of the p.
19 if any man take from this p.

PROPHESY, Verb.

Jer. 14:14 prophets p. lies, p. false
Mat. 15:7 well did Es. p. of you
26:68 p. unto us, thou Ch. Mark
14:65; Luke 22:64
Acts 21:9 had virgins wh. did p.
1 Cor. 13:9 part. and p. in part
14:1 rather p. 39 covet to p.
24 if all p. 31 we may all p.
Rev. 10:11 thou must p. before

PROPHESIED.

Acts 19:6 sp. with tongues and p.
1 Cor. 14:5 I would rather ye p.
Jude 14 Enoch p. of these things

PROPHESIETH.

1 Cor. 11:5 p. with head uncov.
14:3 he that p. speak. unto men
4 he that p. edifieth church
5 greater he that p. than he

PROPHESYING, S.

1 Cor. 11:4 p. having head cover.
14:6 exce. I speak to you by p.
22 but p. serveth not for them
1 Thes. 5:20 desp. not p. prove all

A PROPHET.

Mat. 11:9 what went ye to see? a p.
13:57 a p. is not without honor,

False PROPHET.

Acts 13:6 f. p. a Jew named Bar.

PROPHETS.

Rom. 11:3 L. they have killed p.
1 Cor. 12:28 secondarily. p. thir.

False PROPHETS.

Mat. 7:15 beware of false p.
24:11 many false p. shall rise,
24; Mark 13:22
Luke 6:26 so did th. fath. to f. p.
2 Pet. 2:1 were f. p. among them
1 John 4:1 many f. p. gone out

PROPHETESS.

Ex. 15:20 Miriam p. took timb.

PROPORTION.

1 K. 7:36 to the p. of every one
Rom. 12:6 accord. to p. of faith

PROSPECT.

Ezek. 40:44 p. was to the south
46 p. north; 42:15 p. east, 43:4

PROSPER.

Gen. 24:40 G. send angel, p. thee
42 if now thou do p. my way
39:3 Lord made Joseph to p. 23
Num. 14:41 transgress. not p.
Deut. 28:29 sh. not p. in thy wa.
29:9 that ye may p. in all ye do.
1 Chr. 22:11 my son, L. p. thee
13 shalt p. if thou takest heed
2 Chr. 20:20 believe proph. so sh.
ye p.
26:5 Lord God made him to p.
Neh. 1:11 p. I pray thee, thy ser.
2:20 G. of heaven, he will p. us
Ps. 1:3 what. he doeth shall p.
73:12 ungodly p. in the world
122:6 they sh. p. that love thee
Prov. 28:13 cover. his sins not p.
Ezek. 17:15 shall he p.? sh. he
escape?
Dan. 8:24 he sh. destroy and p.
25 he shall cause craft to p.
3 John 2 I wish th. thou may p.

PROSPERED, ETH.

Gen. 24:56 seeing L. p. my way
Jud. 4:24 hand of Is. p. ag. Jab.
2 Sam. 11:7 deman, how war p.
2 K. 18:7 Hezek. p. 2 Chr. 31:21;
32:30; 2 Chr. 14:7 Asa p.
1 Chr. 29:23 Solomon p.
Ezr. 5:8 work p. in their hands
6:14 p. thro' prophesying of H.
Ps. 37:7 because of him that p..
Prov. 17:8 whi, it turneth it p.
Dan. 6:28 Dan. p. in reign of D.
8:12 cast down truth. and it p.
1 Cor. 16:2 as God hath p. him
3 John 2 in health, ev. as soul p.

PROSPERITY.

Ps. 73:3 I saw the p. of the wicked

PROSPEROUS, LY.

Jos. 1:8 thou make thy way p.
Jud. 18:5 way we go sh. be p.
2 Chr. 7:11 Solomon p. effected
Ps. 45:4 in thy majesty ride p.
Job 8:6 habitation of righte. p.
Zec. 8:12 the seed shall be p.

PROTECTION.

Deut. 32:38 rise up and be yo. p.

PROTEST, ED, ING.

1 Sam. 8:9 p. solemnly unto th.
1 K. 2:42 and I p. unto thee
Jer. 11:7 I p. to your fathers, ris.
early and p. saying, Obey
Zec. 3:6 the angel of the L. p.
1 Cor. 15:31 I p. by rejoic. in C.

PROUD.

Job 26:12 smiteth through the p.
Ps. 12:3 tongue speak p. things
31:23 and rewardeth the p. doer
86:14 p. are risen against me
94:2 render a reward to the p.
101:5 him that hath a p. heart
119:21 thou hast rebuked the p.
51 p. have had me in derision
122 let not the p. oppress me
140:5 p. have hid a snare for me
Prov. 6:17 Lord hateth a p. look
15:25 L. will destroy house of p.
16:5 p. in heart abomina. to L.
19 to divide spoil with the p.
21:4 a p. heart is sin
24 p. scorner, deals in p. wra.
28:25 p. heart stirreth up strife
Ec. 7:8 better than p. in spirit

188

Jer. 50:29 hath been p. 31 O most p.
32 most p. sh. stumble and fa.
Hab. 2:5 he is a p. man, neither
Mat. 3:15 p. happy; 4:1 p. stub.
Luke 1:51 hath scattered the p.
Rom. 1:30 unrighte. p. boasters
1 Tim. 6:4 he is p. know. noth.
2 Tim. 3:2 lov. of themselves, p.
Jam. 4:6 G. resisteth p. 1 Pet. 5:5

PROVETH, ING.

Deut. 13:3 Lord your G. p. you
Acts 9:22 Saul p. that this is Ch.
Eph. 5:10 p. what is accept. to L.

PROVERB.

Prov. 1:6 to understand a p. and
Jer. 24:9 to be a p. and a curse
Ezek. 14:8 make him a sign and p.
Hab. 2:6 take up a p. ag. him
John 16:29 spea. plain. and no p.
2 Pet. 2:22 happ. according to p.

PROVERBS.

Prov. 1:1 p. of Solo. 10:1; 25:1
Ec. 12:9 preacher set in orer p.
Ezek. 16:44 ev. one that useth p.
John 16:25 sp. in p. no more in p.

PROVIDE.

Gen. 28:8 G. will p. hims. lamb
30:30 shall I p. for own house?
Ex. 18:21 thou sh. p. able men
2 Chr. 2:7 men whom Da. did p.
Rom. 12:17 p. things honest
1 Tim. 5:8 any p. not for house

PROVIDED.

Deut. 33:21 p. first part himself
1 Sam. 16:1 I have p. me a king
2 Sam. 19:32 p. king of susten.
1 K. 4:7 p. victuals for king, 27
Ps. 65:9 when thou hast p.
Luke 12:20 things th. hast p.?
Heb. 11:40 having p. bet. things

PROVISION.

Gen. 42:25 give them p. for way
Ps. 132:15 I will bless her p.
Rom. 13:14 ma. not p. for flesh

PROVOCATION.

Ps. 95:8 harden not your hearts
as in p. Heb. 3:8, 15

PROVOKE.

Jer. 7:19 they p. me to anger?
44:8 in that ye p. me to wrath
1 Cor. 10:22 do we p. L. to jeal.?

Eph. 6:4 p. not your chil. to wr.
Heb. 3:16 wh. they heard. did p.
10:24 p. to love and good works

PROVOKED.

Num. 14:23 nor sh. any that p.
1 Chr. 21:1 Satan p. David
Ps. 106:33 they p. spirit of Moses,
1 Cor. 13:5 char. is not easily p.
2 Cor. 9:2 your zeal p. very many

PROVOKING.

1 K. 14:15 made groves, p. Lord
Ps. 78:17 by p. the Most H.
Gal. 5:26 vain glory, p. one ano.

PRUDENCE.

2 Chr. 2:12 son endued with p.
Prov. 8:12 I wisd. dwell with p.
Eph. 1:8 abound. in wisd. and p.

PRUDENT.

1 Sam. 16:18 Dav. p. in matters
Prov. 12:16 p. man cover. shame
23 a p. man conceal. knowl.
13:16 every p. man dealeth with
14:8 wisdom of p. to understand
15 the p. looketh to his goings
18 p. are crowned with knowl.
15:5 he that regar. p. repr. is p.
16:21 the wise shall be called p.
19:14 a p. wife is from the Lord
22:3 a p. man forese. evil, 27:12
Is. 10:13 I have done it, for I am p.
29:14 understanding of p. men
Hos. 14:9 who is p. and he shall?
Amos 5:13 p. shall keep silence
Mat. 11:25 hid these things from
the wise and p. Luke 10:21
1 Cor. 1:19 understanding of p.

PRUDENTLY.

Is. 52:13 my servant sh. deal p.

PRUNE, ED.

Lev. 25:3 six years shalt thou p.
Is. 5:6 it shall not be p.

PRUNING.

Is. 2:4 beat spears into p. hooks
Joel 3:10 beat p. hooks into spe.
Mic. 4:3 beat spears into p. hoo.

PSALM.

1 Cor. 14:26 every one hath a p.?

PSALMIST.

2 Sam. 23:1 David sweet p. of Is

PSALMS.

1 Chr. 16:9 sing p. Ps. 105:2

189

Ps. 95:2 joyful noise with p.
Luke 20:42 D. saith in book of p.
24:44 which were written in p.
Acts 1:20 written in book of P.
Eph. 5:19 speak. to yours. in p.
Col. 3:16 admonish. other in p.
Jam. 5:13 is any merry? sing p.

PSALTERY.

1 Sam. 10:5 meet prop. with a p.
Ps. 33:2 sing with the p. 144:9
57:8 awake p. and harp, 108:2
71:22 I will praise with p. 92:3
81:2 bring hither harp with p.
150:3 praise him with p. harp
Dan. 3:5 sound of p. 7, 10, 15

PUBLIC, LY.

Mat. 1:19 make her a p. example
Acts 18:28 p. convinced the Jews
20:20 but have taught you p.

PUBLICAN, S.

Mat. 5:46 do not p. same? 47
9:10 many p. sat with him,
  Mark 2:15; Luke 5:29
11 why eat, your master wi. p.
10:3 Thomas, and Matthew p.
Mat. 11:19 a friend of p. Lu. 7:34
18:17 let him be as hea. and p.
21:31 p. go into kingdom of G.
Luke 3:12 came p. to be baptized
5:27 he saw a p. named LEvi
7:29 justi. G. being baptized
15:1 then drew near to him p.
18:10 the one Pharisee, other p.
11 God, I thank thee, not as p.
13 p. standing afar off, said

PUBLISH.

Deut. 32:3 I will p. name of L.
Amos 4:5 proclaim and p. fr. offer.

PUBLISHED.

Est. 3:14 Haman's decree p. 8:13
Ps. 68:11 great company p. it
Jon. 3:7 he caused it to be p.
Mark 7:36 more a gre. deal th. p.
13:10 the gospel must first be p.
Luke 8:39 p. through whole city
Acts 10:37 that word wh. was p.
13:49 word of the Lord was p.

PUBLISHETH.

Is. 52:7 that p. peace, p. salvat.
Nah. 1:15 feet of him p. peace

PUFFED up.

1 Cor. 4:6 no one of you be p. up
18 some are p. up, as though I
19 not speech of th. are p. up
13:4 charity is not p. up
Col. 2:18 vainly p. up

PULL, ED.

Mic. 2:8 p. off robe with garm.
Mat. 7:4 p. out mote, Luke 6:42
Luke 14:5 not p. him out on sab.?

PUNISH.

Lev. 26:18 p. you sev. times, 24
Prov. 17:26 to p. just not good
Is. 13:11 I will p. world for evil
Jer. 9:25 p. them are circumcised
Zep. 1:12 p. men that are settled
Zec. 8:14 as I thoug. to p. them
Acts 4:21 how th. might p. them

PUNISHED.

Ex. 21:20 shall surely be p. 22
21 not be p. he is his money
Ezr. 9:13 p. less than iniq. des.
Job 31:11 it is iniq. to be p. 28
Prov. 21:11 when scorner is p.
22:3 simple are p. 27:12
Jer. 44:13 as I have p. Jerusa.
50:18 punish as I have p. king
Zep. 3:7 not cut off, how I p.
Zec. 10:3 shepherds, I p. goats
Acts 22:5 br. them bou. to be p.
26:11 I p. them in every synag.
2 Thes. 1:9 p. with destruction
2 Pet. 2:9 day of judgm. to be p.

PUNISHMENT.

Gen. 4:13 p. great. th. I can bear
Lev. 26:41 accept p. of iniq. 43
1 Sam. 28:10 no p. shall hap. th.
Job 31:3 a strange p. to workers
Prov. 19:19 man of wrath suf. p.
Lam. 3:39 for p. of his sins
4:6 p. of my people is greater
  than the p. of Sodom
22 p. of thine iniq. is accomp.
Ezek. 14:10 bear p. of their iniq.
Amos 1:3 I will not turn away p.
  thereof, 6, 9, 11, 13; 2:1, 4, 6
Zec. 14:19 this shall be p. of Eg.
Mat. 25:46 go into everlasting p.
2 Cor. 2:6 such a man is this p.
Heb. 10:29 how much sorer p.
1 Pet. 2:14 for p. of evil-doers.

PUNISHMENTS.

Job 19:29 bringeth p. of sword
Ps. 149:7 execute p. upon people
PURCHASE, ED.
Acts 20:28 p. with his own blood
Eph. 1:14 redemption of p. pos.
PURE.
Ps. 12:6 words of the Lord are p.
 19:8 commandment of L. is p.
119:140 thy word is very p.
Prov. 15:26 words of p. are plea.
20:9 who can say, I am p. fr. sin?
Phil. 4:8 whatsoev. things are p.
Heb. 10:22 bodies washed with p.
Jam. 1:27 p. relig. and undefiled
3:17 wisdom fr. above is first p.
2 Pet. 3:1 I stir up your p. minds
1 John 3:3 purifieth as he is p.
Rev. 15:6 ang. clothed in p. linen
22:1 showed a p. river of water
PURELY.
Is. 1:25 I will p. purge away
PURENESS.
Job 22:30 deliv. by p. of hands
Prov. 22:11 he loved p. of heart
2 Cor. 6:6 appro. ourselves by p.
PURER.
Lam. 4:7 Nazarites p. than snow
Hab. 1:13 thou art of p. eyes
PURGE, ETH.
Dan. 11:35 sonme of th. p. them
Mal. 3:3 p. as gold and silver
Mat. 3:12 p. his floor, Luke 3:17
John 15:2 branch that bea. he p.
1 Cor. 5:7 p. out the old leaven
2 Tim. 2:21 if a man p. himself
Heb. 9:14 p. your conscience
PURGED.
1 Sam. 3:14 Eli's house not be p.
2 Chr. 34:8 when he had p. land
Prov. 16:6 by mercy iniq. is p.
Is. 4:4 b. blood of Jerusalem
6:7 iniq. taken away, sin is p.
22:14 this iniq. shall not be p.
27:9 by this iniq. of Jacob be p.
Ezek. 24:13 beca. I have p. thee,
 and thou was not p.
Heb. 1:3 when he had p. our sins
9:22 almost all thi. are by law p.
10:2 bec. worshippers once p.
2 Pet. 1:9 forgotten he was p.

PURGING.
Mark 7:19 the draught, p. meats
PURIFICATION.
Est. 2:12 so were the days of their
p.
Luke 2:22 days of her p.
Acts 21:26 accomp. of days of p.
PURIFY.
Mal. 3:3 he shall p. sons of Levi
John 11:55 went to Jerus. to p.
Acts 21:24 take and p. thyself
Tit. 2:14 p. a peculiar people
Jam. 4:8 p. your hearts
PURIFIED, ETH.
Num. 31:23 p. with water of
separat.
2 Sam. 11:4 Bathsheba was p.
Ps. 12:6 pure words, as silver p.
Dan. 12:10 many shall be p.
Acts 24:18 certain J. found me p.
Heb. 9:23 things in heavens p.
1 Pet. 1:22 ye p. your souls
1 John 3:3 this hope p. himself
PURIFIER.
Mal. 2:3 he shall sit as a p.
PURIFYING.
Lev. 12:4 continue in blood of p.
Num. 8:7 sprinkle water of p.
Est. 2:12 things for p. of women
John 2:6 manner of p. of Jews
3:25 th. arose question about p.
Acts 15:9 p. their hearts by faith
Heb. 9:13 sanctifi. to p. of flesh
PURITY.
1 Tim. 4:12 exam. in faith, in p.
5:2 rebuke younger with all p.
PURPLE.
Mark 15:17 clothed him with p.
 20 they took off the p. fr. him
Luke 16:19 a rich man clo. in p.
PURPOSE.
Prov. 20:18 ev. p. is established
Ec. 3:1 time to ev. p. 17; 8:6
Jer. 49:30 Nebu. conceived a p.
51:29 ev. p. of L. be performed
Dan. 6:17 that p. be not chang.
Acts 11:23 that with p. of heart
27:13 suppos. obtained their p.
 43 centurion kept them fr. p.
Rom. 8:28 called according to p.
9:11 that the p. of God stand

191

17 for this p. I raised thee up
Eph. 1:11 according to p. of him
3:11 accord. to eternal p. in C.
6:22 for same p. Col. 4:8
2 Tim. 1:9 called us accor. to p.
3:10 hast fully known my p.
1 John 3:8 for this p. Son of God

PURPOSE, ED.

Ps. 17:3 p. mouth sh. not trans.
140:4 who have p. to overthrow
Is. 14:24 I ha. p. so sh. it stand
26 the purpose p. on earth
23:9 Lord hath p. to stain pride
46:11 I have p. it, will do it
Jer. 4:28 I p. it, will not repent
26:3 repent me of evil wh. I p.
36:3 will hear all evil wh. I p.
49:20 purposes that he p. 50:45
Lam. 2:8 Lord p. to destroy wall
Dan. 1:8 Daniel p. not to defile
Acts 19:21 Paul p. to go to Jeru.
20:3 Paul p. to return thro' M.
Rom. 1:13 oftent. I p. to come
2 Cor. 1:17 I p. accord. to flesh?
Eph. 1:9 his will wh. he hath p.
3:11 purp. which he p. in C. J.

PURPOSETH, ING.

Gen. 27:42 Esau p. to kill thee
2 Cor. 9:7 as he p. in heart

PURSE, S.

Mat. 10:9 silver nor brass in p.
Mark 6:8 no money in their p.
Luke 10:4 neither p. nor scrip
22:25 I sent you without p.

PURSUE.

Gen. 35:5 did not p. sons of J.
Ps. 34:14 seek peace, and p. it

PURSUED.

Gen. 14:14 Abram p. to Dan, 15
31:23 and Laban p. Jacob, 36
Ex. 14:8 Pharaoh p. Israel, 9, 23;
Jud. 7:23 Gideon p. Mid. 25; 8:12
1 Sam. 7:11 Israel p. Phil. 17:52
2 Sam. 22:38 I p. enemies, Ps.
18:37

PURSUETH, ING..

Prov. 13:21 evil p. sinners, to right.

PUT.

Gen. 3:15 I will p. enmity bet. thee
Prov. 25:10 heareth it p. thee to
shame

Is. 42:1 I have p. my Spirit upon
him.
Jer. 31:33 p. my law in inward parts
Ezek. 11:19 I will put a new spirit
within you, 36:26, 27; 37:14
1 Cor. 15:24 p. down authority
Heb. 8:10 I will p. my laws in mind
10:16 p. my laws into th. hearts

PUT away.

1 Sam. 1:14 Eli said, p. a. wine
Mark 10:2 lawful to p. a. wife?
12 if a woman p. a. her husb.
1 Cor. 7:11 let not husb. p. a. wife,
12

PUT forth.

Jud. 15:15 Samson p. f. took

PUT on.

Mat. 6:25 nor what ye shall p. on,
Luke 12:22
Mark 6:9 not p. on two coats
Rom. 13:14 p. ye on the L.J.C.
Gal. 3:27 baptized, have p. on C.
Eph. 4:24 p. on new m. Col. 3:10
Col. 3:12 p. on bowels of mercies
14 p. on charity, which is bo.

PUT out.

Gen. 38:28 one p. out his hand

PUT trust.

1 Chr. 5:20 they p. th. t. in him
Ps. 4:5 p. your trust in the Lord
9:10 know thy name, p. trust
in them

PUTREFYING.

Is. 1:6 wounds, bruises, p. sores

Q.

QUAILS.

Ex. 16:13 at even q. came up.
Num. 11:31 a wind fr. L. bro q.
32 the people stood, gather. q.
Ps. 105:40 asked, he brought q.

QUARTER.

Mark 1:45 came to him fr. ev. q.

QUEEN.

1 K. 10:1 q. of Sheba heard of
fame of Solomon,
Est. 1:9 Vashti q. made feast

QUENCH.

1 Thes. 5:19 q. not the Spirit

QUENCHED.

Mark 9:43 fire never be q. 45

QUESTION, Substantive.

Mat. 22:35 lawyer asked him q.
Mark 11:29 I ask one q. ans. me
John 3:25 arose q. bet disciples

QUESTIONS.

1 K. 10:1 queen came to prove q.
3 Sol. told her q. 2 Chr. 9:1, 2
Mat. 22:46 nei. ask him more q.
Luke 2:46 hearing and asking q.
Acts 23:29 accused of q. of law,
25:19 certain q. against him
26:3 kn. thee to be expert in q.
2 Tim. 2:23 unlearned q. Tit. 3:9

QUICK.

1 Pet. 4:5 to judge q. and dead

QUICKEN.

Ps. 71:20 thou shalt q. me again
80:18 q. us, we will call on name
149:37 q. me in thy way
Ps. 119:40 q. me in thy righteou.
149 q. me accord. to judgment
143:11 q. me. L. for name's sake
Rom. 8:11 shall q. mortal bodies

QUICKENED.

Eph. 2:1 you he q. who were de.
5 q. us toge. with C. Col. 2:13
1 Pet. 3:18 death in flesh, q. by S.

QUICKENETH.

John 5:21 Father q. them, Son q.
6:63 Sp. q. flesh profit. nothing
Rom. 4:17 God, who q. dead
1 Tim. 6:13 God, who q. all thi.

QUICKENING.

1 Cor. 15:45 Adam made q. spir.

QUICKLY.

Ex. 32:8 turned q. out of way,
Deut. 9:12, 16; Jud. 2:17
1 Sam. 20:19 thou sh. go down q.
2 Sam 17:18 went both of them away q.
21 arise, pass q. over the wat.
2 K. 1:11 said, Come down q.
Ec. 4:12 thereof. cord not q. bro.
Mat. 5:25 agree with adversa. q.
28:7 go q. tell discip. he is risen
8 they departed q. Mark 16:8
Luke 16:6 sit down q. write fifty
John 18:27 J. That thou doest do q.
Acts 12:7 saying, Arise up q. P.
Rev. 2:5 repent, else I come q. 16
8:11 behold, I come q. 22; 7, 12

22:20 I come q. even so come

QUIET.

Job 21:23 dieth, being at ease, q.
Ps. 35:20 devise ag. q. in land
107:30 glad, because they be q.
Prov. 1:33 whoso hearken. be q.
Ec. 9:17 wor. of wise heard in q.
Is. 7:4 take heed, and be g. fear
14:7 the earth is at rest, and q.
Jer. 47:7 be q. seeing L. given charge
49:23 sorrow on sea, can. be g.
51:59 Seraiah was a q. prince
Ezek. 16:42 fury rest, I will be q.
Nah. 1:12 though q. be cut down
Acts 19:36 ye ought to be q.
1 Thes. 4:11 that ye stu. to be q.
1 Tim. 2:2 we may lead a q. life
1 Pet. 3:4 ornament of a q. spirit

QUIETED, ETH.

Ps. 131:2 q. myself as a child
Zec. 6:8 q. my spirit in north

QUIETLY.

Lam. 3:26 q. wait for salva. of L.

QUIETNESS.

Jud. 8:28 the country was in q.
1 Chr. 22:9 I will give q. to Isr.
Job 20:20 sh. not feel q. in belly
34:29 q. who can make trouble?
Prov. 17:1 bet. dry morsel and q.
Ec. 4:6 better is handful with q.
Is. 30:15 in q. be your strength
32:17 righte. q. and assurance
Acts 24:2 we enjoy great q.
2 Thes. 3:12 we ex. that with q.

QUIVER.

Gen. 27:3 take thy q. and bow
Ps. 127:5 man that hath q. full

R.

RABBI.

Mat. 23:7 called of men, r. r.
8 be not ye called r. for one is
John 1:38 R. wh. dwellest thou?
49 R. thou art the Son of God
3:2 R. we know thou art teach.
26 R. he that was with thee
6:25 R. when cam. thou hither?

RACE.

Ps. 19:5 strong man to run a r.
1 Cor. 9:24 they wh. run in a r.

Q
R

Heb. 12:1 run with patience r.

RACHEL.

Gen. 29:12 Jacob told R. that he
30:1 R. bare no chil. R. 2, 22
35:19 R. died, 24; 46:22; 48:7
Ruth 4:11 make woman like R.
Jer. 31:15 R. weeping, Mat. 2:18

RAGED, ETH.

Prov. 14:16 fool r. is confident

RAGING.

Ps. 89:9 thou rulest r. of sea
Prov. 20:1 strong drink r.
Luke 8:24 rebuked r. of water

RAHAB.

Jos. 2:1 house of R. 6:17, 25
Heb. 11:31 by faith harlot R
Jam. 2:25 was not R. justified?
Mark 15:29 that passed r. on J.
Luke 23:39 one of malefactors r.

RAILER.

1 Cor. 5:11 keep not com. wi. r.

RAILING.

1 Tim. 6:4 whereof co. strife, r.
1 Pet. 3:9 not rendering r. for r.
2 Pet. 2:11 angels br. not r. accu.
Jude 9 durst not bring r. accus.

RAIMENT.

Gen. 24:53 serv. gave r. to Reb.
27:15 Rebekah took goodly r.
1 Tim. 6:8 having food and r.
Jam. 2:2 1 poor man in vile r.
Rev. 3:5 be clothed in white r.
18 buy white r. that thou ma.
4:4 I saw 24 elders in white r.

RAIN, Substantive.

Gen. 7:12 r. was upon earth
8:2 r. from heaven was restrain.
Ex. 9:33 the r. was not poured
34 Pharaoh saw the r. ceased
Lev. 26:4 will give you r. in due
season, Deut. 11:14; 28:12
Deut. 11 drink. of r. of heaven
1 Sam. 12:17 call on L. to send r.
1 K. 18:1 I will send r. upon earth
41 a sound of abundance of r.
Job 5:10 giveth r. upon the earth
Ps. 68:9 didst send plentiful r.
147:8 I. prepareth r. for earth
Prov. 25:14 like clouds with r.
26:1 snow in summer, and. r. in
28:3 oppresseth poor is like a r.

Ec. 11:3 if clouds be full of r.
12:2 nor clouds return after r.
Mat. 5:45 he sendeth r. on just
7:25 and the r. descended, 27
Acts 14:17 did good, and gave r.
28:2 because of the present r.
Heb. 6:7 earth drinketh in the r.
Jam. 5:18 and the heav. gave r.

RAIN, Verb.

Gen. 2:5 L. not caused it to r.
7:4 cause to r. 40 days and nights
Hos. 10:12 come and r. righteou.
Jam. 5:17 E. pray it mig. not r.

RAINBOW.

Rev. 4:3 th. was a r. round about
10:1 and a r. was upon his head

RAINED.

Gen. 19:24 L. r. upon S. and G.
Ex. 9:23 the L. r. hail on Egypt
Ps. 78:24 r. down manna, 27
Luke 17:29 it r. fire from heaven
Jam. 5:17 it r. not for 3 y.'s 6 m.

RAISE.

Gen. 38:8 r. up seed to brother?
Ex. 23:1 shalt not r. false report
Deut. 18:15 L. thy God r. up r.
prophet, 18; Acts 3:22; 7:37
25:7 refuseth to r. up to brother
Jos. 8:29 r. ther. a heap stones
Ruth 4:5 r. up name of dead, 10
Mat. 3:9 r. children to A. Lu. 3:8
22:24 r. up seed to his brother,
Mark 12:19; Luke 20:28
John 2:19 three days I will r. it
6:39 r. it at last day, 0, 44, 54
Acts 2:30 he r. C. to sit on thro.
26:8 why incredible G. r. dead?
1 Cor. 6:14 sh. r. up us by power
2 Cor. 4:14 sh. r. up us by Jesus
Heb. 11:19 God able to r. him.
Jam. 5:15 L. shall r. him up

RAISED.

Ex. 9:16 I r. thee up to show my
power, Rom. 9:17
Is. 14:9 it r. up kings of nations
23:13 Assyrians r. palaces of C.
41:2 r. righteous man from eat
25 I r. up one from the north
45:13 I r. him up in righteous.
Jer. 6:22 great nation r. fr. earth
29:15 L. r. proph. in Babylon

50:41 kings shall be r. fr. earth
51:11 L. r. spirit of kings of M.
Dan. 7:5 bear r. up on one side
Amos 2:11 I r. up sons for prop.
Zec. 2:13 r. out of holy habitati.
  9:13 when I r. thy sons, O Zion
Mat. 11:5 dead r. up, Luke 7:22
16:21 r. again, 17:23; Luke 9:22
Luke 1:69 r. up horn of salvation
20:37 dead are r. Moses showed
John 12:1 Laz. whom he r. 9, 17
Acts 2:24 whom God hath r. up,
  32; 3:15, 26; 4:10; 5:30; 10:40;
  13:30, 33, 34; 17:31; Rom.
  10:9; 1 Cor. 6:14; 2 Cor.
  4:14; Gal. 1:1; Eph. 1:20
12:7 angel r. Peter; 13:22 r. Da.
13:23 G. r. Israel a Saviour J.
Rom. 4:24 bel. on him that r. J.
  25 r. again for our justification
6:4 C. was r. fr. dead by Father
9 Ch. r. fr. dead, dieth no mo.
7:4 to him who is r. from dead
8:11 if Sp. of him that r. Jesus
1 Cor. 15:15 r. up C. wh. he r. n.
  16 dead rise not, C. is not r.
  17 if C. be not r. faith is vain
  35 men say, How are dead r.?
  42 sown in cor. r. in incorru. 52
  43 it is r. in glory, r. in power
  44 sown natu. body, r. spirit.
Eph. 2:6 r. us together in Ch. J.
Col. 2:12 through G. who r. him
1 Thes. 1:10 Son, he r. from dea.
2 Tim. 2:8 Je. seed of Da. was r.
HEb. 11:35 wom. received dead r.
1 Pet. 1:21 bel. in G. that r. him

RAISINS.
1 Sam. 25:18 Ab. took 100 clus. r.

RAM.
Gen. 15:9 take a r. 3 years old
22:13 a r. caught in a thicket
Ex. 29:15 take one r. 16 slay r.
  22 r. of conse. 27, 31; Lev. 8:22
Lev. 9:2 take r. for burnt-offeri.
  4 r. peace-offer. 19:21 trespass
Num. 5:8 besi. r. for atonement
  Ezr. 10:19 they offered r.
Ezek. 43:23 they sh. offer a r. 25
45:24 ephah for a r. 46:5, 7, 11
46:6 in day of new moon a r.

Dan. 8:3 I saw r. had two horns
  4 I saw r. pushing westward
  6 goat ran to r. had two horns
  7 no power in r. to deliver r.

RAMS.
Ezek. 27:21 Kedar occupied in r.
  34:17 judge betw. r. and goats
Ezek. 39:18 ye sh. dr. blood of r.
Mic. 6:7 L. be pleased with r.?

RAMS' horns.
Jos. 6:4 seven priests shall bear
  before ark r. horns, 5, 6, 8, 13

RAMS' skins.
Ex. 25:5 r. sk. dyed red, 26:14;
  35:7; 36:19; 39:34

RAMAH, RAMA.
Jos. 18:25 R. a city of tribe of
Jud. 4:5 Deborah dwelt betw. R.

RAMOTH-GILEAD.
Deut. 4:43; Jos. 20:8; 21:38

RAN.
Gen. 18:2 Abr. r. from tent-door
  7 r. to herd; 24:17 r. meet R.
24:20 Rebek. r. to well to draw
29:12 Rachel r. and told father
33:4 Esau r. and embraced him
Ex. 9:23 fire r. along the ground
Num. 11:27 r. man and told Mo.
16:47 Aaron r. into congregat.
Jos. 7:22 messen. r. to A.'s tent
Jude 11 r. after error of Balaam

RANKS.
Joel 2:7 shall not break their r.
Mark 6:40 sat down in r. by
  hundreds.

RANSOM, Substantive.
Prov. 6:35 will not regard any r.
13:8 r. of man's life are riches
21:18 wicked be r. for righteous
Is. 43:3 I gave Egypt for thy r.
Mat. 20:28 even as the Son of
  man ga. life a r. Mark 10:45
1 Tim. 2:6 who gave himself r.

RATHER.
Mat. 25:9 go ye r. to th. th. sell
Mark 5:26 but r. grew worse
1 Cor. 7:21 be made free, use it r.
Gal. 4:9 or r. known of God
Heb. 13:19 I beseech you r. do

RAVEN, S.
Gen. 8:7 Noah sent forth a r.

195

Lev. 11:15 r. unclean, Deut. 14:14
1 K. 17:4 comma. r. to feed thee
6 the r. brought Elijah bread
Job 38:41 prov. r. food. Ps. 147:9
Luke 12:24 consider r. nei. sow

RAVENING.

Mat. 7:15 they are r. wolves

RAVISHED

Prov. 5:19 be thou r. with love

RAZOR.

Num. 6:5 nor r. upon head. Jud.
13:5; 16:17; 1 Sam. 1:11
Ps. 52:2 tongue like a sharp r.
Is. 7:20 Lord shave with a r.

REACH.

John 20:27 r. hither thy finger
Gen. 28:12 ladder's top r. to hea.

REACHETH.

Jer. 4:10 the sword r. to the soul
18 because it r. to thy heart
51:9 Bab.'s judgm. r. to heaven
Dan. 4:22 thy greatness r. heav.

READ (short e).

Mat. 12:3 have ye not r.? 19:4;
21:16; 22:31; Mark 2:25;
12:10, 26; Luke 6:3
John 19:20 this r. many of Jews
Acts 8:28 eunuch r. Esaias prop.
32 place of scripture wh. he r.
13:27 prophets r. ev. sab. 15:21
23:34 Governor had r. the letter
2 Cor. 3:2 epistle known and r.
15 when M. is r. the veil is on
Col. 4:16 when this epistle is r.
1 Thes. 5:27 that this epistle be r.

READ (long e).

Rev. 5:4 none worthy to r. book

READING.

Acts 13:15 after the r. of the law
2 Cor. 3:14 untaken away in r.
1 Tim. 4:13 give attendance to r.

READY.

Num. 32:17 we will go r. armed
Deut. 26:5 a Syrian r. to perish
2 Sam. 15:15 thy servants are r.
18:22 hast no tidings r.?
Ezr. 7:6 Ezra was a r. scribe
Neh. 9:17 art a God r. to pardon
Est. 3:14 they should be r. 8:13
Prov. 24:11 those r. to be slain
31:6 stro. drink to him r. to pe.

Ec. 5:1 r. to hear th. give sacrif.
Is. 27:13 who were r. to perish
38:20 the L. was r. to save me
Dan. 3:15 if ye be r. to worship
Tit. 3:1 be r. to every good work
Heb. 8:13 is r. to vanish away
1 Pet. 1:5 r. to be revealed
3:15 be r. always to give answer
4:5 give account to him th. is r.
5:2 not for lucre, of a r. mind
Rev. 3:2 things that are r. to die
12:4 wo. was r. to be delivered

REAP.

Jer. 12:13 sown wheat, r. thorns
Hos. 8:7 sown wind, r. whirlwind
10:12 sow in righte. r. in mercy
Mic. 6:15 th. sh. sow, but not r.
Mat. 6:26 fowls of the air r. not
25:26 I r. where I sowed not
John 4:38 to r. whereon no labor
1 Cor. 9:11 if we r. carnal things
2 Cor. 9:6 sow. sparingly r. spar.
Gal. 6:7 man sow, that sh. he r.
8 soweth to flesh shall r. cor.
9 we shall r. if faint not
Rev. 14:15 thrust in sickle and r.

REAPED.

Hos. 10:13 wickedness r. iniquity
Jam. 5:4 laborers which r. fields
Rev. 44:16 his sickle, ear. was r.

REAPER, S.

Amos 9:13 ploughm. overtake r.
Mat. 13:30 say to r. gather tares
39 enemy is devil, r. are angels

REAPETH.

Is. 17:5 the harvest-man r. ears
John 4:36 he that r. recei. wages
37 one soweth, another r.

REAPING.

1 Sam. 6:13 Beth-shem. were r.
Mat. 25:24 man, r. Luke 19:22

REASON.

1 Pet. 3:15 ask, you a r. of hope

By REASON.

Ps. 78:65 man shout. by r. wine
90:10 if by r. of str. be fourscore
Is. 49:19 too nar. by r. of inhabi.
Ezek. 19:10 branches by r. of wa.
Dan. 8:12 given by r. of transgr.
Jon. 2:2 I cried by r. of affliction
John 12:11 by r. many beli. on J.

Rom. 8:20 by r. of him who subj.
Heb. 5:3 by r. hereof, off. for sins
7:23 not continue by r. death
2 Pet. 2:2 by r. of whom truth

REASON.

Job 9:14 ch. words to r. with you
Is. 1:18 now, let us r. together
Mat. 16:8 J. said, Why r. among
yourselves, Mark 2:8; 8:17
Luke 5:21 scr. and Pha. began r.
22 what r. ye in your hearts?

REASONABLE.

Rom. 12:1 sacrifice, your r. serv.

REASONED.

Mat. 16:7 r. am. themselv. 21:15;
Mark 8:16; 11:31; Luke 20:5
Mark 2:8 J. perceived they so r.

REASONING.

Mark 2:6 scribes r. in th. hearts
12:28 having heard them r. tog.

REBEKAH.

Gen. 22:23 Bethuel begat R.
24:15 R. ca. out, 51, 59, 60, 67
25:28 R. loved Jacob, 20
26:7 should kill me for R. 35
27:42 words of Es. were told R.
29:12 that he was R. son, 35:8
49:31 they buried Isaac and R.
Rom. 9:10 when R. conceived

REBEL.

Num. 14:9 only r. not aga. Lord
Jos. 1:18 whosoever r. shall die
22:16 builded altar ye might r.
19 r. not agai. L. r. not ag. us
1 Sam. 12:14 ye obey and not r.
15 if ye will not obey L. but r.

REBELLED.

Gen. 14:4 thirteenth year they r.
Num. 20:24 because ye r. ag. my
word at Meribah, 27:14;
Deut. 1:26, 43; 9:23
1 K. 12:19 Rehobo, fled, so Is. r.
ag. house of Da. 2 Chr. 10:19
2 K. 1:1 Moab r. ag. Israel, 3, 5, 7
18:7 Hezek. r. ag. Assyria
2 Chr. 13:6 Jerob. r. ag. his lord
Neh. 9:26 disobe. and r. ag. thee
Ps. 5:10 for they r. against thee
105:28 they r. not against word
107:11 they r. ag. words of God
Is. 1:2 nourish. children, they r.

63:10 r. and vexed Holy Spirit
Dan. 9:5 r. by departing fr. thee
9 to God mercy, though we
have r.
Hos. 13:16 Samaria r. against G.

REBELLION.

Deut. 31:27 know thy r. and stiff
1 Sam. 15:23 r. is as witchcraft
Neh. 9:17 in r. appointed a capt.

REBELLIOUS.

Is. 1:23 princes r. companions
30:1 woe to r. chil. saith Lord
9 a r. people; 50:5 I was not r.
Jer. 4:17 she ha. been r. saith L.
5:23 this people hath a r. heart
Ezek. 2:3 send thee to a r. nation
5 they are a r. house, 6, 7; 3:9,
26, 27; 12:2, 3
8 be not r. like that r. house
12:2 dwell. in midst of r. house
17:12 say to r. house, 44:6

REBUKE, substantive.

Phil. 2:15 without r. in per. nat.

REBUKE, Verb.

1 Chr. 12:17 God look thereon, r.
Prov. 9:8 r. wise man
Is. 2:4 shall r. nations, Mic. 4:3
Zec. 3:2 Lord r. thee, even Lord
that hath chosen Jer. r. thee
Mal. 3:11 r. devo. for your sakes
Mat. 16:22 P. r. him, Mark 8:32
Luke 17:3 if brot. trespass r. him
19:39 said, MAster, r. thy disc.
1 Tim. 5:1 r. not elder, entreat
20 them that sin, r. before all
2 Tim. 4:2 r. with long-suffering
Tit. 1:13 wheref. r. sharply, 2:15
Jude 9 Mich. said, The L. r. thee
Rev. 3:19 as many as I love I r.

REBUKED.

Ps. 9:5 hast r. the heathen, hast
106:9 he r. Red sea, it was dry
149:21 thou hast r. the proud
Mat. 8:26 he r. the wind and the
sea, Mark 4:39 stood, and r. the
fever
9:55 J. turned, r. James and J.
18:39 went before, r. blind man
23:40 thief answering, r. him
Heb. 12:5 nor faint wh. r. of him
2 Pet. 2:16 Balaam was r. for ini.

RECEIVE.

Ps. 6:9 Lord will r. my prayer
Prov. 2:1 if th. wilt r. my words
Dan. 2:6 ye shall r. of me gifts
Mic. 1:11 shall r. of you standing
Zep. 3:7 thou wilt r. instruction
Mat. 10:41 r. a prophet's reward
  11:5 the blind r. their sight.
Mark 4:16 r. the word with glad-
  ness, Luke 8:13
John 5:43 own name, him ye r.
  7:39 they that believe, r. H. G.
  16:24 ask and ye shall r.
Acts 1:8 but ye shall r. power
  2:38 ye shall r. gift of Holy G.
  8:15 pray, they might r. H. G.
  19 on who. I lay hands may r.
  9:12 that he might r. his sight
  10:43 believeth, r. remis. of sins
  26:18 may r. forgiveness of sins
Rom. 5:17 r. abundance of grace
2 Cor. 5:10 every one r. things
Gal. 3:14 might r. promise of S.
Eph. 6:8 same shall he r. of L.
Col. 3:24 shall r. reward of inh.
Heb. 7:8 men that die r. tithes
  9:15 might r. promise, 10:36
Jam. 1:7 think he r. any thing
1 Pet. 5:4 shall r. crown of glory
1 John 3:22 whatso. we ask we r.
2 John 8 that we r. a full reward
Rev. 14:9 if any man r. mark

RECEIVE, infinitively.

Luke 6:34 of whom ye hope to r.
Acts 8:27 ex. disciples to r. him
  20:35 more bles. to give than r.
3 John 8 we ought to r. such
Rev. 4:11 thou worthy to r. glo.
  5:12 worthy is L. to r. power
  13:16 causeth to r. mark in ha.

RECEIVED.

Gen. 26:12 Isaac r. hundred-fold
Ex. 32:4 Aaron r. at th. hand
Num. 12:14 let Miriam be r. in
  23:20 I r. commandm. to bless
Jos. 13:8 Gadites r. inheritance
1 Sam. 12:3 of wh. hand ha. I r.
2 K. 19:14 Hezekiah r. the letter,
  Is. 37:14
1 Chr. 12:18 David r. them
Job 4:12 mine ear r. little thereof

Ps. 68:18 hast r. gifts for men
Prov. 24:32 I looked and r. inst.
Is. 40:2 she hath r. of L.'s hand
Ezek. 18:17 hath not r. usury nor
Zep. 3:2 she r. not correction
Mat. 10:8 freely ye r. freely give
  13:20 r. into stony gr. 22 thorns
  23 r. seed into good ground
  20:9 r. every man a penny, 10
  84 immedi. their eyes r. sight
Mark 7:4 many things they r.
  10:52 he immediately r. sight,
  Luke 18:43; Acts 9:18
  16:19 was r. into heav. Acts 1:9
Luke 6:24 ye have r. consolation
  8:40 the people gladly r. him
  9:11 r. them, spake of kingdom
  51 time come he sho. be r. up
  10:38 Martha r. him into house
  15:27 r. him safe and sound
  19:6 Zaccheus r. him joyfully
  15 returned, having r. kingd.
John 1:11 ca. to his own, own r.
  12 as many as r. him he gave
  9:15 Pharis. asked how r. sight
Rom. 1:5 by whom we r. grace
  5:11 by whom we r. atonement
  8:15 have not r. spirit of bond.
  14:3 him that eateth, G. r. him
  15:7 rec. one another as C. r. us
2 Thes. 2:10 they r. not the truth
1 Tim. 3:16 believed, r. into gl.
Heb. 7:11 under it people r. law
  10:26 if sin after r. knowledge
  39 these r. not the promise
1 Pet. 4:10 every one hath r. gift
2 Pet. 1:17 he r. from God honor
2 John 4 we have r. a command
Rev. 2:27 power, as r. of Father
  19:20 that had r. mark of beast
  20:4 nor r. mark reigned wi. C.

RECEIVETH.

Jer. 7:28 nation r. not correction
Mal. 2:13 r. offer, with good-will
Mat. 7:8 that asketh r. Luke 11:10
Mark 9:37 r. not me, but him
  that sent me, Luke 9:48
Heb. 6:7 earth r. blessing fr. God
  7:9 L. who r. tithes, paid tithes

RECKONED.

Rom. 4:4 reward is not r. of gra.

198

9 r. to Abra. 10-how was it r.?

RECOMPENSE.

Joel 3:4 will ye render me r.?
7 I will return r. on your head
2 Cor. 6:13 for a r. in the same
Heb. 2:2 trangr. received a r.
10:35 hath great r. of reward
11:26 he had respect to the r.

RECOMPENSE, Verb.

Rom. 12:17 r. no man evil for evil
2 Thes. 1:6 r. tribulation to them
Heb. 10:30 hath said, I will r.

RECOMPENSED.

Luke 14:14 be r. at resurrection
Rom. 11:35 it shall be r. to him

RECONCILE.

Col. 1:20 to r. all things to him.

RECONCILED.

Mat. 5:24 first be r. to brother
Rom. 5:10 when enem. r. to God

RECONCILIATION.

2 Cor. 5:18 given us minist. of r.

RECORD, Substantive.

3 John 12 we bear r. our r. is true
Rev. 1:2 who bare r. of word of G.

RECOVER.

Jud. 11:26 did ye not r. them
Mark 16:18 hands on sick, th. r.

RED.

Gen. 25:25 came out r. all over
Ex. 25:5 rams skins dyed r.
  26:14; 35:7; 36:19; 39:34
  35:23 wi. wh. was found r. skins
Rev. 6:4 anot. horse that was r.
12:3 great r. dragon, sev. heads

RED sea.

Ex. 10:19 cast locusts into R. s.
  13:18 G. led them by the R. sea
  15:4 captains drowned in R. s.
  22 Moses bro. Israel from R. s.
Heb. 11:29 by faith passed R. s.

REDEEM.

Is. 50:2 short. that it cannot r.?
Gal. 4:5 r them were under law
Tit. 2:14 he might r. us fr. iniq.

REDEEMED.

Is. 1:27 Zion be r. with judgm.
43:1 fear not, I have r. thee
Luke 1:68 visited and r. his peo.
  24:21 who should have r. Israel
Gal. 3:13 Christ r. us from curse'

1 Pet. 1:18 not r. with corrupti.
Rev. 5:9 thou hast r. us to God
14:3 the 144,000 which were r.
4 these were r. from am. men

REDEEMER.

Job 19:25 I know that my R. liv.
Ps. 19:14 O L. my stren. and R.
78:35 the high G. was their R.
Prov. 23:11 their R. is mighty
Is. 41:14 thy R. Holy One, 54:5
43:14 saith L. your R. H. one
44:6 saith L. his R. L. of hosts
  24 sai. thy R. 48:17; 49:7; 54:8
47:4 as for our R. Lord of hosts
49:26 I the L. am thy R. 60:16
59:20 the R. shall come to Zion
63:16 art our Father, our R.
Jer. 50:34 their R. is strong

REDEMPTION.

Rom. 3:24 justified thro' r. in C.
8:23 for adoption, r. of our body
1 Cor. 1:30 Chr. is made to us r.
Eph. 1:7 in whom we have r.
  thro' his blood. Col. 1:14
Eph. 1:14 r. of purchased poss.
  4:30 sealed unto the day of r.
Heb. 9:12 obtain. eternal r. for us
  15 the r. of the transgressions

REFRAIN.

Prov. 1:15 r. thy foot from path
1 Pet. 3:10 r. his tong. from evil

REFUGE.

Ps. 9:9 L. be a r. for oppressed
  14:6 because the Lord is his r.
46:1 G. is r. 7, 11; 48:3 G. know
  57:1 thy wings will make my r.
59:16 my r. in day of trouble
62:7 my r. is God; 8 God is r.
71:7 thou art strong r. 142:5
91:2 is my r. 9; 94:22 G. is my
104:18 hills r. for wild goats
142:4 r. failed; 5 thou art my r.

REFUSE, Verb.

Acts 25:11 if offen. I r. not to die
1 Tim. 4:7 but r. profane fables
  5:11 but the younger widows r.
Heb. 12:25 r. not him that speak.

REGARD, Verb.

1 Sam. 25:25 r. not man of Belial
Hab. 1:5 r. wonder marvellously
Mal. 1:9 will he r. yo. persons?

Luke 18:4 fear not God nor r. man
Rom. 14:6 Lord he doth not r.
Luke 1:48 he r. his handmaid
18:2 feared not G. nei. r. man
Heb. 8:9 I r. them not, saith L.

REGARDETH.
Rom. 14:6 that r. day, r. it to L.

REGENERATION.
Mat. 19:28 wh. followed me in r.
Tit. 3:5 saved us by wash. of r.

REHOBOAM.
1 K. 11:43 R. son of Solo. 14:21

REIGN, Verb.
Luke 1:33 he shall r. over Jacob
Rom. 5:17 sh. r. in life by J. C.
Rev. 5:10 we shall r. on earth
11:15 he shall r. for ever

REIGNETH.
Is. 52:7 saith unto Z. Thy G. r.
Rev. 17:18 r. over kings of earth
19:6 Lord God omnipotent r.

REJECTED.
Mat. 21:42 stone which builders r. Mark 12:10; Luke 20:17
Mark 8:31 and he shall be r. of the elders, Luke 9:22

REJOICE.
Job. 20:18 he shall not r. therein
Ps. 2:11 serve L. r. with tremb.
5:11 all that put trust in thee r.
9:14 I will r. in thy salvation
13:4 those that trouble me r.
5 my heart shall r. in thy salv.
14:7 Ja shall r. and Is. be glad
20:5 we will r. in thy salvation
21:1 in thy salvation shall he r.
30:1 made foes to r. over me
32:21 our heart shall r. in him
35:9 my soul sh. r. in his salva.
19 let not mine enemies r. ov.
24 O Lord, let them not r. over
26 let them be ashamed that r.
38:16 lest they sho. r. over me
48:11 let Zion r. let Jud. be glad
51:8 bones th. hast brok. may r.
58:10 righteous r. wh. he seeth
60:6 G. ha. spok. I will r. 108:7
63:7 in shad. of thy wings I r.
11 but the king shall r. in God
65:12 hills r. 66:6 did we r.

68:3 let righteous r. exceed. r.
4 r. bef. him; 71:23 lips sh. r.
85:6 that thy people may r.
86:4 r. the soul of thy servant
89:12 Tabor and Hermon sh. r.
16 in thy name shall they r.
42 hast made enemies to r.
96:11 let heavens r. 12 trees r.
97:1 let earth r. isles be glad
98:4 make noise, r. sing praise
104:31 L. shall r. in his works
106:5 that I may r. in gladness
107:42 righte. shall see it and r.
109:28 be ashamed, let serva. r.
119:162 I r. at thy word
149:2 let Is. r. in him that made
Prov. 2:14 who r. to do evil
5:18 r. wife of thy youth
Luke 1:14 shall r. at his birth
6:23 r. ye in that day. and leap
10:20 in this r. not, rather r.
John 4:36 he that reapeth may r.
Acts 2:26 theref. did my heart r.
Rom. 5:2 r. in hope of gl. of God
12:15 r. with them that do r.
15:10 he saith, r. ye Gentiles

REJOICE before the Lord.
Lev. 23:40 r. bef. t. Lord 7 days
Deut. 12:12 r. bef. t. Lord your God
18 and thou shalt r. before the L. thy God, 16:11; 27:7

REJOICE in the Lord.
Ps. 33:1 r. in the L. righte. 97:12
Is. 41:16 r. in L. glory in H. One
61:10 I will greatly r. in the L.
Joel 2:23 chil. of Zion. r. in t. L.
Hab. 3:18 I will r. in the Lord
Zec. 10:7 heart shall r. in the L.
Phil. 3:1 brethren r. in the Lord
4:4 r. in the Lord alway

REJOICING.
1 Thes. 2:19 wh. our crown of r.?
Heb. 3:6 r. of hope firm to end
Jam. 4:16 boastings, such r. evil

RELIGION.
Jam. 1:26 this man's r. is vain
27 pure r. and undefiled bef. G.

RELIGIOUS.
Acts 13:43 r. proselytes follow. P.
Jam. 1:26 if any am. you seem r.

REMAIN.

John 6:12 gather fragm. that r.
15:11 my joy might r. in you
16 chosen that your fruit sh. r.
19:31 bodies sho. not r. on cross
1 Thes. 4:15 r. till coming of L.
Heb. 12:27 cannot be shaken r.
1 John 2:24 that ye have heard r.

REMAINETH.

Heb. 4:6 it r. some must enter in
9 there r. a rest to peop. of G.
10:26 there r. no sacrifice for sin

REMAINING.

John 1:33 on wh. shall see Sp. r.
Ex. 20:8 r. sab.- day to keep holy
Ps. 20:3 r. thy offerings, accept
7 we will r. name of the Lord
Prov. 31:7 r. misery no more
Ec. 5:20 he sh. not r. days of life
Is. 43:18 r. not former th.? 46:9
Jam. 3:16 neither shall they r. it.
14:10 he will now r. their iniq.
2 Tim. 2:8 r. that J. Ch. raised

I REMEMBER.

Jer. 2:2 I r. thee, the kindness

I will REMEMBER.

3 John 10 I will r. deeds he doeth

REMEMBER me.

Luke 23:42 L. r. me when comest

REMEMBERED.

Est. 9:28 days of Pur. sho. be r.
Job. 24:20 sin. shall be no more r.
Ec. 9:15 no man r. poor man
Is. 23:16 thou mayest be r.
Mal. 26:75 Peter r. the words of
Jesus, Luke 22:61

REMEMBRANCE.

Luke 1:54 hath holpen Is. in r.
22:19 do in r. of me. 1 Cor. 11:2

REMISSION.

Mat. 26:28 blo. shed for r. of sins
Mark 1:4 baptism of repentance
for r. Luke 3:3
Luke 1:77 salvation by r. of sins
24:47 that r. should be preached
Acts 2:38 baptized for r. of sins
10:43 whoso belie. sh. receive r.
Rom. 3:25 r. of sins th. are past
Heb. 9:22 without shed bl. no r.
10:18 where r. is, th. is no offe.

REMNANT.

Lev. 2:3 the r. of meat-offering

Hag. 1:12 r. of people obeyed L.
14 Lord stirred up spirit of r.
Rom. 9:27 Es. crieth, r. be saved

REMOVE.

Prov. 4:27 r. thy foot from evil
Mat. 17:20 say, r. hence, sh. be r.
Luke 22:42 if willing, r. this cup

REND.

Mat. 7:6 lest they turn and r.

RENDER.

1 Thes. 3:9 what thanks can we r.
5:15 see that none r. evil for ev.

RENDEREST.

1 Pet. 3:9 not r. evil for evil

RENEW.

Ps. 51:10 r. right sp. within me

REPAY.

Rom. 12:19 I will r. saith the L.
Phile. 19 I Paul, will r. it

REPENT.

Ezek. 14:6 r. and turn yourselves,
18:30
24:14 neither spare, nei. will r.
Joel 2:14 if he will return and r.
Jon. 3:9
Mark 1:15 r. ye, and believe
6:12 preach. that men should r.
Luke 13:3 except ye r. perish, 5
16:30 if one we. fr. dead will r.
17:3 if thy brother r. forgive, 4
Acts 2:38 r. and be baptized ev.
3:19 r. ye theref. be converted
8:22 r. of this thy wickedness
17:30 commandeth all men to r.
26:20 they should r. turn to G.
2 Cor. 7:8 I do not r. tho' I did r.
Rev. 2:5 and r. except thou r.
16 r. else I will come unto th.
21 I gave her space to r. of her
3:3 how thou hast rec. and r.
19 be zealous therefore and r.

REPENTANCE.

Mat. 3:8 fru. meet for r. Luke 3:8
11 I indeed bapti. you unto r.
Mat. 9:13 to call sinners to r.
Mark 2:17; Luke 5:32
Mark 1:4 John did prea. bap. of
r. Luke 3:3; Acts 13:24; 19:4
Luke 15:7 ninety-nine need no r.
2 Pet. 3:9 perish, all come to r.

REPLENISH.

Gen. 1:28 mult. and r. earth, 9:1
REPROACH.
2 Cor. 11:21 I speak concern. r.
1 Tim. 3:7 report, lest fall into r.
4:10 we both labor and suffer r.
Heb. 11:26 esteeming r. of Christ
13:13 without camp, bearing r.
My REPROACH.
Luke 1:25 my r. among men
REPROACH, Verb.
Luke 6:22 r. you for my sake
REPROACHFULLY.
Job 16:10 smitten me on cheek r.
1 Tim. 5:14 none occa. to spe. r.
REPROBATE.
Rom. 1:28 G. gave them to r.
2 Tim. 3:8 men r. concern. faith
Tit. 1:16 to every good work r.
REPROBATES.
2 Cor. 13:5 Chri. is in you, ex. r.
REPROOF.
Job 26:11 they are astonish. at r.
Prov. 1:23 turn you at my r.
2 Tim. 3:16 scri. profitable for r.
REPROVE.
John 16:8 he will r. world of sin
Eph. 5:11 no fellowship, rather r.
REPUTATION.
Gal. 2:2 privately to them of r.
Phil. 2:7 made himself of no r.
29 receive him, hold such in r.
REQUEST.
Phil. 1:4 in ev. prayer making r.
4:6 let your r. be known to God
REQUIRE.
1 Cor. 1:22 for the Jews r. a sign
7:36 r. let him do what he will
REQUIRED.
Prov. 30:7 two things have I r.
REQUITE.
1 Tim. 5:4 learn to r. th. parents
RESERVED.
Acts 25:21 Paul appealed to be r.
Rom. 11:4 I have r. 7,000 men
1 Pet. 1:4 inheritance r. in heav.
2 Pet. 2:4 deliv. to be r. to judg.
Jude 6 he hath r. in chains
RESIST.
Jam. 4:7 r. devil and he will flee
5:6 killed just, doth not r. you
1 Pet. 5:9 wh. r. steadfast in fai.

RESOLVED
Luke 16:4 I am r. what to do
RESPECT.
Is. 17:7 sh. have r. to Holy One
Phil. 4:11 I speak in r. of want
1 Pet. 1:17 without r. of persons
REST, Substantive.
Mat. 11:28 co. unto me, I give r.
29 ye sh. find r. to your souls
12:43 seek r. Luke 11:24
26:45 take your r. Mark 14:41
REST, Adjective.
Luke 12:26 why take tho. for r.?
24:9 told eleven and all the r.
Acts 2:37 to Pet. and r. of apost.
REST, Verb.
Heb. 4:4 God did r. seventh day
Rev. 4:8 r. not day and night
RESTED.
Gen. 2:2 he r. on seventh day,
3; Ex. 20:11; 31:17
RESTETH.
1 Pet. 4:14 Sp. of G. r. upon you
RESTITUTION.
Ex. 22:3 make full r. 5, 6, 12
RESTORE.
Ps. 51:12 r. to me joy of salvati.
Prov. 6:31 he shall r. sevenfold
Gal. 6:1 r. such a one in meek.
RESTORED.
Mark 8:25 sight r. saw clearly
Heb. 13:19 that I may be r.
RESURRECTION.
Mat. 22:23 th. is no r. Mark 12:18;
Acts 23:8; 1 Cor. 15:12
28 in r. whose wife sh. she be?
Mark 12:23; Luke 20:33
30 in r. they neither marry, 31
27:53 came out of graves aft. r.
Luke 14:14 be recompensed at r.
20:27 deny any r. 36 child. of r.
John 5:29 done good, to r. of life,
none evil, to r. of damnati.
11:25 J. said, I am the r. and life
Acts 1:22 witn. with us of his r.
2:31 David spake of r. of Christ
4:2 they preached thro' Jesus r.
33 witness of r. of Lord Jesus
17:18 preached Jesus and the r.
32 when they heard of the r.
23:6 of hope and r. I am called

24:15 there shall be a r. of dead
21 touching r. of the dead
Rom. 1:4 by r. from the dead
6:5 shall be in likeness of his r.
1 Cor. 15:13 but if there be no r.
21- by man came r. 42 so is r.
Phil. 3:10 know power of his r.
11 might attain to r. of dead
2 Tim. 2:18 r. is past already
Heb. 6:2 of r. from the dead
11:35 might obtain a better r.
1 Pet. 1:3 by r. of Jesus fr. dead
3:21 save us, by r. of Je. Christ
Rev. 20:5 this is the first r.
6 hath part in first r.

RETURN, Verb.

Gen. 3:19 dust th. art, to dust r.
Mat. 10:13 let your peace r.
12:44 r. into house, Luke 11:24
24:18 nor let him in field r.
Luke 8:39 r. to thine own house

RETURNED.

Luke 2:20 sheph. r. glorifying G.
4:14 Jesus r. in power of Spirit

REUBEN.

Gen. 29:32 called his name R.

Tribe of REUBEN.

Rev. 7:5 tribe of R. sealed 12,000

REVEAL.

Phil. 3:15 God sh. r. this unto y.

REVEALED.

Is. 22:14 r. in mine ears by L.
23:1 fr. Chittim it is r. to them
40:5 glory of the Lord sh. be r.
Mat. 10:26 nothing covered that
Rom. 1:17 therein right. of G. r.
Eph. 3:5 now r. to holy apostles
2 Thes. 1:7 when L. J. shall be r.
1 Pet. 1:5 to be r. in last time

REVELATION.

Rom. 2:5 r. of judgment of God
Rev. 1:1 r. of J. C. wh. God gave

REVERENCE, Verb.

Lev. 19:30 r. sanct. I am L. 26:2
Est. 3:2 king's serv. r. Haman
Mat. 21:37 they will r. my son,
Mark 12:6; Luke 20:13
Eph. 5:33 wife that she r. husb.

REVERENCE.

2 Sam. 9:6 Mephibosh. did r. Da.
1 K. 1:31 Bathsheba did r. king

Est. 3:2 Mord. did him not r. 5
Ps. 89:7 to be had in r. of all
Heb. 12:9 and we gave them r.
28 we may serve God with r.

REVIVED.

Rom. 7:9 command. came, sin r.
14:9 Ch. both died, rose, and r.

REWARD, Substantive.

Is. 3:11 the r. of hands be given
5:23 which justify wicked for r.
40:10 his r. is with him, 62:11
45:13 go my captives, not for r.
Luke 6:35 your r. shall be great
23:41 we receive due r. of deeds
Acts 1:18 field with r. of iniqui.
Rom. 4:4 to him that work. is r.
1 Cor. 3:8 man sh. receive his r.
14 abide, he shall receive a r.
9:17 if willingly, I have a r. 18
Col. 2:18 no man beg. you of r.
3:24 ye sh. receive r. of inherit.
1 Tim. 5:18 laborer worthy of r.
Heb. 2:2 recei. just recomp. of r.
10:35 great recompense of r.
11:26 he had respect to the r.
2 Pet. 2:13 shall receive the r. of
2 John 8 that we receive a full r.
Jude 11 after error of Bal. for r.
Rev. 11:18 thou shouldest give r.
22:12 I come quickly, my r. is

REWARD, Verb.

Deut. 32:41 and I will r. them

RHODA.

Acts 12:13 to hearken named R.

RIBS.

Gen. 2:21 God took one of his r.

RICH.

Luke 1:53 the r. he sent away
6:24 woe unto you that are r.
12:21 that is not r. toward God
14:12 call not thy r. neighbors
18:23 sorrowful, he was very r.
Rom. 10:12 same Lord is r. to all
1 Cor. 4:8 are full, now ye are r.
2 Cor. 6:10 yet making many r.
8:9 r. yet poor, ye might be r.
Eph. 2:4 God who is r. in mercy
1 Tim. 6:9 they th. will be r. fall
17 charge th. that are r. in this
18 and be r. in good works
Jam. 1:10 let the r. rejoice in th.

2:5 G. chosen poor, r. in faith?
Rev. 2:9 I know pov. thou art r.
RICH man, or men.
Mat. 19:23 r. m. sh. hardly enter
24 than a r. m. to enter kingd.
of God, Mark 10:25; Lu. 18:25
27:57 a r. man of Arimathea
Luke 12:16 ground of r. man bro.
16:1 a certain r. m. had a stew.
19 a r. man was clo. in purple
21:1 and saw the r. man casting
RICHES.
Ps. 37:16 bet. than r. of wicked
Prov. 3:16 in her left hand r.
Mat. 13:22 deceitful, of r. choke
word, Mark 4:19; Luke 8:14
Mark 10:23 hardly th. that ha. r.
24 them that trust in r. to en-
ter, Luke 18:24
Luke 16:11 who will commit r.?
Rom. 2:4 or despiseth thou r.?
9:23 make kn. r. of his glory
11:12 if fall of them be the r.
33 O the r. of the wisd. of God
2 Cor. 8:2 to r. of their liberality
Eph. 1:7 redemption accor. to r.
RIDER.
Ex. 15:1 horse and r. thrown, 21
RIGHT, Adjective.
Mark 5:15 his r. mind, Luke 8:35
Acts 4:19 whe. r. in sight of God
Is RIGHT.
Eph. 6:1 obey par. in L. this is r.
RIGHTEOUS.
Gen. 7:1 thee ha. I seen r. be. me
18:23 wilt destroy r. with wic.?
24 if th. be 50 r. wilt thou? 26
25 be far from thee to slay r.
20:4 L. wilt thou slay a r. nati.
38:26 said, She more r. than I
Ex. 23:7 innocent and r. sl. not
Num. 23:10 let me die death of r.
Deut. 4:8 nation ha. judg. so r.
25 I shall justify r. 2 Chr. 6:23
Jud. 5:11 r. acts, 1 Sam. 12:7
1 Sam. 24:17 thou more r. than I
2 Sam. 4:11 wick, slain r. person
1 K. 2:32 fell on two men more r.
8:32 justifying r. to give him
2 K. 10:9 Jehu said to peo. Be r.
Ezr. 9:15 G. of Israel r. Neh. 9:8

Job 4:7 where were r. cut off?
9:15 tho' I we. r. would not an.
10:15 if I be r. not lift up head
15:14 what is man, he be r.?
17:9 r. also sh. hold on his w.
23:3 is it pleas. to A. th. art r.
19 r. see it, glad, Ps. 107:49
23:7 r. might dispute with him
32:1 he was r. in his own eyes
Job 34:5 Job hath said, I am r.
35:7 if thou be r. what giv. thou
36:7 wit. not eyes fr. r. Ps. 34:15
40:8 cond. me that thou be r.
Ps. 1:5 nor sinners in cong. of r.
6 Lord knoweth way of the r.
5:12 wilt bless r. with favor
7:9 r. G. trieth hearts and reins
11 G. jud. r. angry wi. wicked
11:3 what can r. do? 5 L. tri. r.
14:5 God is in generation of r.
19:9 judgments of L. are true
and r. 119:7, 62, 106, 160, 164
31:18 lips speak against the r.
32:11 be glad in Lord, rej. ye r.
33:1 rejoice in L. O ye r. 97:12
34:17 r. cry, L. heareth them
19 ma. are the afflictions of r.
21 that hate r. sh. be desolate
35:27 glad that favor r. cause
37:17 but Lord upholdeth the r.
21 but the r. showeth mercy
25 have I not seen r. forsaken
30 mouth of r. speaketh wisd.
32 wicked watch r. to slay him
39 salvation of the r. is of Lor.
52:6 r. also shall see, fear, laugh
55:22 never suff. r. to be moved
58:10 r. rejoice, he seeth veng.
11 there is a reward for the r.
64:10 r. shall be glad in the L.
68:3 let r. be glad, let them rej.
69:28 let them not be wri. wi. r.
72:7 in his days sh. r. flourish
94:21 gather against soul of r.
112:4 L. full of compas. r. 116:5
6 r. be in everl. remembrance
118:15 rejoicing in tabem. of r.
20 gate, into which r. sh. ent.
119:106 keep thy r. judgments
137 r. art thou, O. Lo. Jer. 12:1
138 thy testimonials are r.

125:3 rod of wicked sh. not rest
on r. lest r. put forth hands
140:13 r. give thanks to thy na.
141:5 let r. smite, kindness
142:7 r. shall compass me about
145:17 Lord r. in all his ways
146:8 Lord loveth r. preserveth
Prov. 2:7 layeth up wisd. for r.
20 mayest keep paths of r.
10:3 will not suffer r. to famish
16 labor of r. tendeth to life
21 the lips of the r. feed many
24 desire of r. shall be granted
25 r. is an everlasting founda.
28 hope of r. sh. be gladness
30 r. shall never be removed
32 lips of r. kn. what is accep.
11:8 r. is deliv. out of trouble
10 well with r. city rejoiceth
21 seed of r. shall be delivered
23 desire of the r. is only good
28 r. shall flourish as a branch
31 r. be recompensed in earth
12:3 root of r. sh. not be moved
5 thoughts of the r. are right
7 house of the r. shall stand
12 root of the r. yieldeth fruit
26 r. is more excel. than neigh.
13:9 light of the r. rejoiceth
21 to r. good shall be repaid
25 r. eat. to satisfying of soul
14:9 among the r. there is favor
32 the r. hath hope in his dea.
15:6 in house of r.. is much tre.
19 way of the r. is made plain
28 heart of r. studieth to ans.
29 he heareth the prayer of r.
18:5 not good to overthrow r.
10 r. runneth into it, is safe
21:18 shall be ransom for r.
26 r. giveth and spareth not
23:24 fath. of r. greatly rejoice
24:15 lay not wait ag. dwe. of r.
24 saith to wicked, Thou art r.
28:1 wicked flee, but r. bold
10 causeth r. to go astray
28 when wicked perish, r. inc.
29:2 r. in authority peo. rejoice
6 the r. doth sing and rejoice
7 r. considereth cause of poor
16 the r. shall see their fall

Ec. 3:17 G. judge r. and wicked
7:16 be not r. overmuch
9:1 r. and wise in hand of God
2 one event to r. and wicked
Is. 3:10 say to r. it be well
24:16 heard songs, glory to r.
26:2 open ye, that r. may enter
41:26 declared, we say, He is r.
53:11 r. serv. shall justify many
57:1 r. peri. r. taken from evil
60:21 people also shall be all r.
Jer. 12:1 r. art thou, O L. I plead
20:12 O Lord of hosts triest r.
Ezek. 13:22 with lies made r. sad
21:3 cut off r. and wicked, 4
Ezek. 21:13 wh. I say to r. he sh.
Amos 2:6 they sold r. for silver
Hab. 1:4 wicked comp. about r.
13 wicked devou. him more r.
Mal. 3:18 discern between r. and
Mat. 9:13 not come to call the r.
  Mark 2:17; Luke 5:32
13:43 r. shine forth as sun
23:28 outwardly ap. r. to men
25:46 r. sh. go into life eternal
Luke 1:6 they were both r. bef. G.
18:9 trusted they were r.
John 7:24 judge not by ap. but r.
17:25 O r. F. world not known
Rom. 2:5 revel. of r. judg. of G.
3:10 there is none r. no not one
5:19 obed. of one, many made r.
2 Tim. 4:8 r. Judge shall give
Heb. 11:4 obt. witness he was r.
1 Pet. 3:12 eyes of L. are over r.
4:18 if r. scarcely be saved
2 Pet. 2:8 Lot vexed his r. soul
1 John 2:29 if ye know he is r.
3:7 doeth right. is r. as he is r.
12 his works evil, brother's r.
Rev. 16:5 angel say, Thou r.
7 O L. true and r. thy judgm.
22:11 that is r. let him be r. still
RIGHTEOUS man, or men.
Ps. 37:16 lit. r. m. hath is better
Prov. 10:11 mo. of r. m. is a well
13:5 a r. man hateth lying
21:12 r. m. wisely consi. house
25:26 a r. m. falling bef. wicked
28:12 when r. m. rejoice, glory
Is. 41:2 raised r. m. from east

Ezek. 3:20 r. m. doth turn, 18:26
23:45 r. m. they sh. judge them
Mat. 10:41 that receiveth a r. m.
in name of r. m. rec. r. m.'s
13:17 r. men desi. to see things
Luke 23:47 cert. this was a r. m.
Rom. 5:7 for r. m. will one die
1 Tim. 1:9 law not made for r. m.
2 Pet. 2:8 r. m. dwelling am. th.

RIGHTEOUSLY.

Deut. 1:16 judge r. Prov. 31:9
Ps. 67:4 sh. judge peo. r. 96:10
Is. 33:15 walk, r. sh. dwell high
Jer. 11:20 O Lord that judgest r.
Tit. 2:12 should live soberly, r.
1 Pet. 2:23 to him that judgeth r.

RIGHTEOUSNESS.

Deut. 6:25 it shall be our r.
24:13 shall be r. to thee bef. L.
33:19 shall offer sacrifices of r.
Job 29:14 I put on r. clothed me
36:3 ascribe r. to my Maker
Ps. 4:5 offer the sacrifices of r.
11:7 right. Lord loveth r. 33:5
15:2 worketh r. never be moved
23:3 leadeth me in paths of r.
24:5 r. fr. God of his salvation
40:9 I preached r. in congrega.
45:4 bec. of truth, meekness, r.
7 lovest r. hatest, Heb. 1:9
48:10 r. hand, O G. is full of r.
51:19 pleased with sacrifi. of r.
52:3 lying, rather than speak r.
58:1 speak r. O congregation?
72:2 shall judge people with r.
3 moun. bring peace, hills r.
85:10 r. and peace kis. each oth.
13 r. go before him
94:15 judgment shall ret. unto r.
96:13 he judge world wi. r. 98:9
97:2 r. habitation of his throne
99:4 executest r. J. 103:6
106:3 blessed is he that doeth r.
118:19 open to me gates of r.
119:144 r. of thy testimonies
172 all thy commandm. are r.
132:9 priests be clothed with r.
Prov. 2:9 sh. thou understand r.
8:18 durable riches, r. with me
20 I lead in the way of r.
10:2 r. deliver. from death, 11:4

11:5 r. of perfect direct his way
6 r. of upright shall del. them
18 to him that soweth r. rew.
19 as r. tend. to life, so he that
12:17 speaketh truth, show. r.
28 the way of r. life, in path.
13:6 r. keepeth him that is upr.
14:34 r. exalteth a nation, sin
15:9 he loveth him that fol. r.
16:8 bet. is a little with r. than
12 throne is established by r.
31 glory, if found in way of r.
21:21 followeth r. find. life, r.
Ec. 3:16 place of r. iniq. there
Is. 1:21 r. lodged in it
26 city of r. 27 converts wi. r.
5:23 take away r. of righteous
10:22 consum. overflow with r.
11:4 with r. shall he judge poor
Is. 11:5 r. be the girdle of his lo.
16:5 judgment, and hasting r.
26:9 inhab. of world will learn r.
10 showed, he will not learn r.
28:17 r. will I lay to plummet
32:16 r. shall remain in fruitful
17 work of r. peace; or r. quie.
33:5 the Lord filled Zion with r.
45:8 skies pour r. let r. spring
19 I the L. speak r. I declare
24 in the Lord have I r.
46:12 ye that are far from r.
51:1 follow r. 7 ye that know r.
54:17 their r. is of me, saith L.
58:2 seek me as a nation did r.
59:17 he put on r. as breastpl.
60:17 officers peace, exactors r.
61:3 might be called trees of r.
10 covered me with robe of r.
11 Lord will cause r. and pra.
63:1 until the r. thereof go forth
64:5 rejoiceth and worketh r.
Jer. 9:24 I Lord wh. exercise r.
22:3 execute ye judgm. and r.
23:6 name, Lord our r. 33:16
33:15 branch of r. to execute r.
51:10 Lord brought forth our r.
Ezek. 14:14 deliver souls by r. 20
18:20 r. of the righteous sh. be
33:12 r. of right. sh. not deliver
Dan. 4:17 break off thy sins by r.
9:7 O Lord r. belongeth to thee

24 bring in everlasting r.

12:3 they that turn many to r.

Hos. 10:12 he come and rain r.

Amos 5:7 who will leave off r. in

24 let r. run down as a stream

6:12 have turned fruit of r. to

Mic. 6:5 may know the r. of L.

Zep. 2:3 meek of earth seek r.

Mal. 4:2 shall Sun of r. arise

Mat. 3:15 becometh us to fulfil r.

5:6 hunger and thirst after r.

20 except r. exc. r. of scribes

21:32 John came in way of r.

Luke 1:75 in r. bef. him all days

John 16:8 rep. world of sin and r.

Acts 10:35 he that worketh r. is

13:10 enemy of all r. wilt th.?

24:25 reasoned of r. and judgm.

Rom. 1:17 therein is the r. of G.

2:26 uncircum. keep r. of law

3:5 unright. commend r. of G.

21 r. of God without the law

22 even the r. of God which is

4:6 to whom God imputed r.

11 seal of r. of the faith, that

r. might be imputed to them

13 promise was thro' r. to eter.

6:13 instruments of r. to God

16 sin to death, obed. unto r.

18 ye became the servants of r.

19 yield memb. servants to r.

20 were serv. of sin. free fr. r.

8:4 r. of law might be fulfilled

10 Spirit is life because of r.

9:30 have attained to r. even r.

31 Israel followed after r. hath

not attained to the law of r.

10:3 establish their own r. have

not submitted to the r. of G.

5 Moses desc. the r. of law

6 r. which is of faith speaketh

10 with heart man believ. to r.

14:17 not meat and drink, r.

1 Cor. 1:30 of God who is made r.

15:34 awake to r. and sin not

2 Cor. 3:9 much more minis. of r.

5:21 might be made r. of God

6:7 armor of r. on right hand

14 what fellowship hath r. wi.

9:10 increase fruits of your r.

11:15 transformed as mini. of r.

Gal. 2:21 if r. come by law, Ch.

3:21 r. should have been by law

5:5 we thro' Spirit wait for r.

Eph. 5:9 fruit of Sp. is r. and tr.

6:14 having the breastplate of r.

Phil. 1:11 filled with fruits of r.

3:6 touching r. which is in law

9 the r. which is of G. by faith

1 Tim. 6:11 fol. aft. r. 2 Tim. 2:22

2 Tim. 4:8 laid up a crown of r.

Tit. 3:5 not by works of r.

Heb. 1:8 sceptre of r. is sceptre

5:13 is unskilful in word of r.

7:2 by interpretation king of r.

11:7 became heir of r. by faith

33 subdued kingd. wrought r.

12:11 yieldeth peace. fruit of r.

Jam. 1:20 worketh not r. of God

3:18 fruit of r. is sown in peace

1 Pet. 2:24 dead to sin live to r.

2 Pet. 1:1 faith through r. of God

2:5 save Noe a preacher of r.

2 Pet. 2:21 bet. not kn. way of r.

3:13 new earth, wherein dw. r.

1 John 2:29 doeth r. born of God

3:7 he that doeth r. is righteous

10 doeth not r. is not of God

Rev. 19:8 fine linen r. of saints

For RIGHTEOUSNESS.

Gen. 15:6 Ab. believ. L. counted

to him f. r. Ps. 106:31; Rom. 4:3

Ps. 143:11 for thy r. sake bring

Is. 5:7 looked for r. but behold

Mat. 5:10 wh. are persecuted f. r.

Rom. 4:5 counted f. r. Gal. 3:6

9 reckoned to Abraham for r.

22 imp. to him f. r. Jam. 2:23

10:4 Ch. is the end of law f. r.

1 Pet. 3:14 if ye suffer for r. sake

His RIGHTEOUSNESS.

1 Sam. 26:23 L. render ev. his r.

1 K. 8:32 acc. to h. r. 2 Chr. 6:23

Job 33:26 will render man his r.

Ps. 7:17 praise L. acc. to his r.

22:31 they shall declare his r.

50:6 the heav. declare his r. 97:6

98:2 his r. hath openly showed

103:17 h. r. to children's child.

111:3 h. r. end. for ever, 112:3, 9

Ec. 7:15 just man perish in his r.

Is. 42:21 pleased for his r. sake

59:16 and his r. sustained him
Ezek. 3:20 turn fr. h. r. 18:24, 28
18:22 his r. that he hath done
33:12 not able to live for his r.
13 if he trust his own r. and
commit iniq. his r. not rem.
Mic. 7:9 and I shall behold his r.
Mat. 6:33 seek king. of G. h. r.
Rom. 3:25 to declare his r. 26
2 Cor. 9:9 given to poor his r.

In RIGHTEOUSNESS.

Lev. 19:15 in r. shalt thou judge
1 K. 3:6 walk. in truth and in r.
Ps. 9:8 he shall judge world in r.
17:15 I will beh. thy face in r.
65:5 terrible things in r. wilt
Prov. 8:8 words of mouth in r.
25:5 throne shall be estab. in r.
Is. 5:16 G. shall be sanct. in r.
32:1 a king shall reign in r.
42:6 I the L. called thee in r.
45:13 I have raised him in r.
23 word gone out of mou. in r.
48:1 mention G. of Isr. not in r.
54:14 in r. shalt thou be estab.
68:1 speak in r. mighty to save
Jer. 4:2 the Lord liveth in r.
Hos. 2:19 I will betroth thee in r.
10:12 sow in r. reap in mercy
Zec. 8:8 I will be their God in r.
Mal. 3:3 offer an offering in r.
Acts 17:31 will judge world in r.
Rom. 9:28 will cut it short in r.
Eph. 4:24 God is created in r.
2 Tim. 3:16 scrip. for instr. in r.
Rev. 19:11 in r. he doth judge

My RIGHTEOUSNESS.

Gen. 30:33 my r. answer for me
Deut. 9:4 for my r. Lord bro. me
2 Sam. 22:21 reward me accord.
to my r. 25; Ps. 18:20, 24
Job 6:29 return ag. my r. is in it
27:6 my r. I hold fast
35:2 my r. more than God's
Ps. 4:1 I call, O God of my r.
7:8 judge me, O L. ac. to my r.
Is. 41:10 uph. with hand my r.
46:13 I bring my r. 51:5 my r. is
51:6 my r. sh. not be abolished
8 but my r. shall be for ever
56:1 come, my r. to be revealed

Phil. 3:9 not having mine own r.

Thy RIGHTEOUSNESS.

Deut. 9:5 for thy r. or upright. 6
Job 8:6 habi. of t. r. prosperous
35:8 thy r. may profit son of
Ps. 5:8 lead me, O Lord, in t. r.
31:1 deliver me in thy r. 71:2
35:24 judge me, O L. ac. to t. r.
37:6 he shall bring forth thy r.
40:10 I have not hid thy r.
51:14 tongue shall sing of thy r.
69:27 let th. not come into t. r.
71:15 my mouth sh. show thy r.
16 I will make ment. of thy r.
19 thy r. O God, is very high
72:1 give thy r. unto king's son
88:12 thy r. be known in land
89:16 in t. r. sh. they be exalted
119:40 quicken t. r. 123 thy r.
143:1 answer me, and in thy r.
11 for t. r. sake bring my soul
Ps. 145:7 they sh. sing of thy r.
Is. 48:18 thy r. as waves of sea
57:12 I will declare thy r.
58:8 thy r. shall go before thee
62:2 the Gentiles shall see t. r.
Dan. 9:16 O Lord, accord. to t. r.

RIGHTEOUSNESSES.

Is. 64:6 our r. are as filthy rags
Ezek. 33:13 his r. sh. not be rem.
Dan. 9:18 not for our r. but thy

ROCK.

Mat. 7:24 built house upon r.
16:18 upon th. r. I built church
27:60 new tomb wh. he had
hewn out in the r. Mar. 15:46
Luke 8:6 some fell on r. 13 ou r.
Rom. 9:33 I lay in Si. a stumb.-
stone, r. of offence, 1 Pet. 2:8
1 Cor. 10:4 drank of spiritual r.

ROSE, Substantive.

Cant. 2:1 I am r. of Sharon
Is. 35:1 desert sh. blossom as r.

ROSE, Verb.

Luke 5:28 r. up and followed him
16:31 not be persua. tho' one r.
22:45 when he r. from prayer
Acts 5:36 bef. th. days r. Theud.
10:41 drink with him after he r.
Rom. 14:9 Christ bo. died and r.

ROTTENNESS.

Prov. 12:4 maketh asha. is as r.
14:30 envy is r. of the bones
RULE, Substantive.
Heb. 13:7 that have r. over you
17 obey them that have r. 24
RULE, Verb.
Col. 3:15 peace of G. r. in hearts
1 Tim. 3:5 kn. not how to r. ho.
5:17 elders that r. well, worthy
Rev. 2:27 r. with a rod of iron,
12:5; 19:15

RULERS.
Eph. 6:12 against r. of darkness
RULETH.
Hos. 11:12 Judah yet r. with G.
Rom. 12:8 he that r. with dilig.
1 Tim. 3:4 one that r. his house
RUNNETH.
Ps. 23:5 anoi. head, cup r. over
147:15 his word r. very swiftly
Prov. 18:18 righteous r. into it
Lam. 1:16 eyes r. do. wat. 3:48
RUNNING.
Luke 6:38 good meas. and r. ov.
Rev. 9:9 sound of char. r. to bat.
S.

SABBATH.
Ex. 16:23 to-morrow is holy s.
25 to-day is a s. to the Lord
20:10 sev. day is s. of L. 31:15;
35:2; LEv. 23:3; Deut. 5:14
31:14 ye shall keep the s. 16
Lev. 16:31 s. of rest, 23:3, 32
John 5:18 he not only had bro. s.
Acts 13:42 preached to th. next s.
16:13 on s. we went out of city
SACKCLOTH.
1 K. 20:31 put s. on loins, 32
2 K. 6:30 looked, had s. within
1 Chr. 21:16 D. and elders clo. s.
Est. 4:2 none enter cloth. with s.
Job 16:15 sewed s. upon my skin
Ps. 30:11 put off s. girded with
35:13 sick, my clothing was s.
69:11 I made s. also my garm.
Is. 3:24 stomacher, girding of s.
15:3 in street gir. them. with s.
20:2 loose s. from off thy loins
22:12 day did L. call to girding s.
SACRIFICE.

Hos. 3:4 Is. sh. abide witho. a s.
6:6 I desired mercy and not s.
Mat. 9:13; 12:7
Amos 4:5 offer a s. of thanksgiv.
Jon. 1:16 men offered a s. to L.
Zep. 1:7 L. hath prepared a s. 8
Mal. 1:8 if ye offer blind for s.
Mark 9:49 every s. sh. be salted
Luke 2:24 offer a s. accor. to law
Acts 7:41 in those days off. s. to
14:13 would have done s. with
Rom. 12:1 present your bodies s.
1 Cor. 8:4 off. in s. idols, 10:19, 28
Eph. 5:2 s. to G. for sweet savor
Phil. 2:17 off. on s. of your faith
4:18 s. accep. well-pleas. to God
Heb. 7:27 daily as those to offer s.
9:26 put away sin by s. of him
10:5 s. and off. thou wou. not, 8
12 had offered one s. for sins
26 remain. no more s. for sins
11:4 Abel offered more excel. s.
13:15 let us offer s. of praise
SACRIFICE, Verb.
Ex. 3:18 go. s. to L. 5:3, 8; 8:27;
10:25; 8:25 go ye s.
8:26 s. abomina. of Egyptians?
13:15 I s. to L. openeth matrix
20:24 thou shalt s. burnt-offer.
Deut. 15:21 blem. not s. it, 17:1
1 Sam. 1:3 Elkan. went up to s.
15:15 peo. spared best to s. to L.
16:2 I am come to s. to Lord. 5.
2 K. 14:4 as yet the people did s.
2 Chr. 33:17
17:35 nor shall s. to other gods
2 Chr. 11:16 came to J. to s. to L.
Ezr. 4:2 seek your God and do s.
Neh. 4:2 will they s.?
Ps. 54:6 I will freely s. to thee.
Ps. 107:22 s. sacrifices of thanks.
Ezek. 39:17 gath. to my s. I do s.
Hos. 4:13 s. on tops of mountains
14 they s. with harlots, there.
8:13 th. s. but L. accepteth not
12:11 they s. bullocks in Gilgal
13:2 let men that s. kiss calves
Jon. 2:9 I will s. with thanksgi.
Hab. 1:16 they s. unto their net
Zec. 14:21 they that s. sh. seethe
1 Cor. 10:20 Gentiles s. to devils

SACRIFICED.

Ex. 32:8 made calf, s. thereunto
Deut. 32:17 s. to devils, not to G.
Jos. 8:31 s. thereon peace-offer.
Jud. 2:5 they s. there unto Lord
1 Sam. 11:15 pe. went to G. to s.
2 Sam. 6:13 Dav. s. ox. and fatl.
1 K. 3:2 only the people s. in the
   high places, 3; 2 K. 12:3;
   15:4, 35; 16:4; 2 Chr. 28:4
  11:8 strange wives, s. to th. go.
2 K. 17:32 lowest priests wh. s.
1 Chr. 21:28 L. answ. then he s.
2 Chr. 5:6 asse. be. ark, s. sheep
  28:23 A. s. to gods of Damascus
Ps. 106:37 they s. sons to devils.
  38 they s. to idols of Canaan
Ezek. 39:19 sacri. which I have s.
Hos. 11:2 they s. to Baalim
1 Cor. 5:7 Ch. our Pass. is s. for
Rev. 2:14 things s. to idols, 20

SACRIFICEDST.

Deut. 16:4 flesh s. rem. all night

SACRIFICES.

Gen. 46:1 Is. at Beer-sheba off. s.
Ex. 10:25 thou must give us s.
  18:12 Jethro took s. for God
Lev. 10:13 s. of L. made by fire
  17:7 sh. no more offer s. to dev.
Num. 25:2 called people to s.
  28:2 s. observe to offer in season
Deut. 12:6 thither bring your s.
  33:19 offer s. of righteousness
Jos. 13:14 s. of L. their inherita.
  22:28 altar not for s. 29
1 Sam. 6:15 sacrificed s. to the L.
  15:22 hath L. as great del. in s.
1 Chr. 29:21 sacrificed s. in abu.
2 Chr. 7:1 fire came and cons. s.
  29:31 bring s. they brought in s.
Ezr. 6:3 place where he offer. s.
  10 may offer s. to G. of heaven
Neh. 12:43 that day th. offered s.
Ps. 4:5 offer s. of righteousness
  27:6 theref. will I offer s. of joy
  51:17 s. of God are a broken sp.
Prov. 17:1 house full of s.
Is. 1:11 to what purpose your s.?
  29:1 year to year, let th. kill s.
  56:7 their s. shall be accepted
Jer. 6:20 nor are your s. sweet

  7:21 burnt offerings to your s.
  17:26 bringing s. of praise to L.
Ezek. 20:28 saw hill, and offer. s.
Hos. 4:19 be ashamed, bec. of s.
  9:4 s. be as bread of mourners
Amos 4:4 bring your s. ev. mom.
  5:25 have ye offer. unto me s.?
Mark 12:33 love L. is more th. s.
Luke 13:1 blood Pi. mingl. wi. s.
Acts 7:42 offered s. forty years?
1 Cor. 10:18 eat s. partak. of altar
Heb. 5:1 offer gifts, s. for sins
  8:3 high-pri. ordained to offer s.
  9:9 were offered both gif. and s.
  23 heav. things with better s.
  10:3 in th. s. is a remembrance
  11 off. same s. that never can
  13:16 wi. such s. G. is well pie.
1 Pet. 2:5 priesthood to off. up s.

SACRIFICETH.

Ex. 22:20 he that s. to any good
Ec. 9:2 that s. him that s. not
Is. 65:3 peo. that s. in gardens
  66:3 he that s. a lamb
Mal. 1:14 and s. a corrupt thing

SACRIFICING.

1 K. 8:5 I. were wi. him s. sheep
  12:32 s. to calves he had made

SAINTS.

Heb. 6:10 ye have minis. to s.
Jude 3 faith once delivered to s.
  14 L. com. with 10,000 of his s.

SALVATION.

Ex. 14:13 and see the s. of the
  Lord, 2 Chr. 20:17
Deut. 32:15 esteemed rock of s.
1 Sam. 11:13 L. wrought s. in Is.
  14:45 Jona. who wro. great s.
  19:5 L. wrought great s. for Is.
2 Sam. 22:51 tower of s. for king
1 Chr. 16:23 show fr. day to d. s.
  35 save us, O God of our s.
2 Chr. 6:41 priests be clo. with s.
Ps. 3:8 s. belongeth to the Lord
  14:7 O th. s. of Is. we. come, 53:6
  24:5 righteous. from G. of his s.
  35:9 soul shall rejoice in his s.
  37:39 s. of the righteous is of L.
  50:23 to him will I show s. of G.
  68:19 blessed be L. G. of our s.
  20 he that is our G. is G. of s.

74:12 work, s. in midst of earth
78:22 they trusted not in his s.
79:9 help us, O God of our s.
85:4 turn us, O God of our s.
9 his s. nigh them th. fear him
95:1 joyf. noise to rock of our s.
96:2 show his s. fr. day to day
98:2 Lord hath made kn. his s.
3 ends of earth seen s. of God
116:13 I will take cup of s.
118:15 voice of s. in tabernacle
119:155 s. is far from wicked
132:16 clothe her priests with s.
144:10 he that giv. s. unto kings
149:4 will beautify meek with s.
Is. 12:3 water out wells of s.
25:9 be glad and rejoice in his s.
26:1 s. will G. appoint for walls
33:2 our s. in time of trouble
6 knowledge, and stren. of s.
45:8 earth open, let th. bring s.
17 Is. be sved with everlas. s.
46:13 place s. in Zion, for Israel
49:8 in a day of s. I helped thee
52:7 feet of him that publish. s.
10 ends of earth sh. see s. of G.
59:11 we look for s. far from us
16 therefore his arm bro. s.
17 put on helmet of s. on head
61:10 clo. me wi. garments of s.
62:1 s. thereof as lamp burneth
Jer. 3:23 in vain is s. hoped for fr.
hills, truly in L. is s. of Isr.
Lam. 3:26 wait for s. of Lord
Jon 2:9 that I vowed, s. of Lord
Hab. 3:8 didst ride on char. of s.
13 wentest for s. of thy people
even for s. with th. anointed
Zec. 9:9 Kings, just, having s.
Luke 1:69 raised up horn of s.
77 to give knowl. of s. to peo.
3:6 all flesh shall see s. of God
19:9 s. is come to this house
John 4:22 worship, s. is of Jews
Acts 4:12 nei. is s. in any other
13:26 to you is word of s. sent
47 be for s. to ends of the earth
16:17 th. men show us way of s.
28:28 s. of G. is sent to Gentiles
Rom. 1:16 power of God to s.
10:10 confession is made to s.

11:11 s. is come to Gentiles
13:11 s. nearer th. wh. we beli.
2 Cor. 1:6 comfort. is for your s.
6:2 in day of s. I succored thee;
now accepted time, day of s.
7:10 sorrow work. repent. to s.
Eph. 1:13 heard gospel of your s.
6:17 helmet of s. sword of Spirit
Phil. 1:28 evident token of s.
2:12 work out your s. with fear
1 Thes. 5:8 for a helm. hope of s.
9 appoi. us to obtain s. by L.
2 Thes. 2:13 G. chosen you to s.
2 Tim. 2:10 may obtain s. Christ
3:15 able to make wise to s.
Tit. 2:11 grace of G. bringeth s.
Heb. 1:14 who shall be heirs of s.
2:3 escape, if we neg. so great s.
10 Captain of their s. perfect
5:9 became Author of s. to all
6:9 things that accompany s.
9:28 sh. ap. without sin to s.
1 Pet. 1:5 kept thro' faith unto s.
9 your faith s. of your souls
10 of wh. s. prophets have inq.
2 Pet. 3:15 long-suffer, of L. is s.
Jude 3 to write to you of com. s.
Rev. 7:10 s. to G. 19:1 s. to Lord
12:10 now is come s. and stren.
My SALVATION.
Ex. 15:2 L. my song, bec. my s.
2 Sam. 23:3 shield, horn of my s.
47 be rock of my s. Ps. 18:46
23:5 all my s. all my desire
Job 13:16 he also shall be my s.
Ps. 25:5 thou art God of my s.
27:1 the Lord is my light and
my s. 62:6; Is. 12:2
9 O God of my s. 51:14; 88:1
38:22 O L. my s. 62:2 is my s. 6
62:1 God, from him com. my s.
7 G. my s. 89:26 rock of my s.
91:16 and show him my s.
118:14 L. ec. my s. 21; Is. 12:2
140:7 Lord the strength of my s.
Is. 12:2 G. is my s. is bec. my s.
46:13 my s. shall not tarry
49:6 my s. to end of the earth
51:5 my s. gone for. 6 for ever
8 my s. fr. generation to gene.
56:1 my s. is near to come

211

Mic. 7:7 wait for God of my s.
Heb. 3:18 joy in God of my s.
Phil. 1:19 I kn. this turn to my s.
Thy SALVATION.
Gen. 49:18 I waited for thy s.
1 Sam. 2:1 bec. I rejoice in t. s.
2 Sam. 22:36 hast also given me
  the shield of thy s. Ps. 18:35
Ps. 9:14 I will rejoice in thy s.
  13:5 my heart shall rej. in thy s.
  20:5 we will rejoice in thy s.
  21:1 in t. s. how shall he rej. 1
  5 his glory is great in thy s.
  35:3 say unto soul, I am thy s.
  40:10 declared faithful, and t. s.
  16 let such as love thy s. say
  51:12 rest. to me joy of t. s. 70:4
  71:15 mouth sh. show forth t. s.
  85:7 O Lord, grant us thy s.
  106:4 remember me with thy s.
  119:41 let t. s. come ac. to word
  81 my soul fainteth for thy s.
  123 mine eyes fail for thy s.
  166 Lord, I have hoped for t. s.
  174 I have longed for t. s. O L.
Is. 17:10 hast forgot. God of t. s.
  62:11 say to Zion, t. s. cometh
Luke 2:30 mine eyes ha. seen t. s.
SAMARITAN.
Luke 10:33 a certain S. came
SAMSON.
Jud. 13:24 his name S. 16:29
SAMUEL.
1 Sam. 1:20 son, called him S.
SANCTIFICATION.
1 Cor. 1:30 of G. is made to us s.
1 Thes. 4:3 will of G. even yo. s.
  4 kn. how to possess ves. in s.
2 Thes. 2:13 s. of Sp. 1 Pet. 1:2
SANCTIFY.
Joel 1:14 s. ye a fast, 2:15
  2:16 s. congregation, assemble
John 17:17 s. them thro' thy tru.
  19 for their sakes I s. myself
Eph. 5:26 s. and cleanse church
1 Thes. 5:23 God of peace s. you
Heb. 13:12 that he might s. peo.
1 Pet. 3:15 but s. the Lord God
SANCTIFIED.
John 10:36 him, whom the Fa. s.
  17:19 that they also might be s.

Acts 20:32 an inheritance among
  them which are s. 26:18
Rom. 15:16 being s. by H. Ghost
1 Cor. 7:14 husband is s. wife is s.
1 Tim. 4:5 it is s. by word of G.
2 Tim. 2:21 vessel s. for Master's
Heb. 2:11 they who are s. are all
  10:10 by which will we are s.
  14 he perfect. them that are s.
  29 coven. wherewith he was s.
Jude 1 to them that are s. by G.
SANCTUARY.
Ps. 20:2 L. send thee help fr. s.
  63:2 I have seen thee in the s.
Is. 8:14 L. of hosts, sh. be for s.
SAND.
Gen. 22:17 multi. seed as s. 32:12
  41:49 Joseph gathered corn as s.
Mat. 7:26 man built house on s.
Heb. 11:12 spr. of one many as s.
Rev. 13:1 I stood upon s. of sea
  20:8 number of whom is as s.
SANG.
Ex. 15:1 then s. Moses this song
Num. 21:17 Isr. s. Spring O well
Acts 16:25 Pa. and Sil. s. praises
SAPPHIRA.
Acts 5:1 Ananias, with S. wife
SAPPHIRE.
Rev. 21:19 founda. of wall was s.
SARAH.
Gen. 17:15 not Sar. but S. shall
  18:9 where is S. 11, 12, 13, 14
  20:2 Abraham said of S. She is
Heb. 11:11 thro' faith S. receiv.
1 Pet. 3:6 as S. obeyed Abraham
SARAI.
Gen. 11:29 Ab.'s wife S. 30; 16:1
  12:17 plagu. Pharaoh bec. of S.
  16:6 S. dealt hardly with Ha. 8
SAT.
John 4:6 Je. wearied, s. on well
Acts 3:10 s. for alms at beau. gate
Rev. 4:3 he that s. on throne
  14:14 one s. like Son of man
  19:11 s. upon him called Faith.
  19 war with him s. on horse
SATAN.
1 Chr. 21:1 S. provoked David to
Job 1:6 S. came among them, 2:1
  12 S. went from presence of L.

Ps. 109:6 S. stand at his hand
Zec. 3:1 S. stand. at right hand
2 L. said to S. L. reb. thee, O S.
Mat. 4:10 Get thee hence, 8.
12:26 if S. cast out S. Mark 3:23,
26; Luke 11:18
16:23 get thee behind me S.
Mark 8:33; Luke 4:8
Mark 4:15 S. taketh away word
Luke 10:18 beheld S. as lightning
13:16 S. hath bound eight, years
22:3 then entered S. into Ju. Is.
31 Simon, S. desired to ha. you
John 13:27 S. entered him
Acts 5:3 hath S. filled thy heart
26:18 turn fr. power of S. to God
Rom. 16:20 G. bruise S. und. feet
1 Cor. 5:5 deli. such an one to S.
7:5 S. tempt not for incontin.
2 Cor. 2:11 lest S. get advantage
11:14 S. transf. into angel of li.
12:7 messeng. of S. to buffet me
1 Thes. 2:18 come, but S. hinder.
2 Thes. 2:9 com. after work. of S.
1 Tim. 1:20 whom I deliv. to S.
5:15 some already turned aft. S.
Rev. 2:9 not Jl but synag. of S.
13 Satan's seat where S. dwel.
24 have not kno. depths of S.
3:9 make th. of synagogue of S.
12:9 dragon cast out, called S.
20:2 laid hold on drag. wh. is S.
7 S. shall be loosed out of pris.

SATISFY.
Ezek. 7:19 shall not s. their souls

SAUL.
1 Sam. 9:2 name was S. 14:51
17 when Samuel saw S. 18
10:11 is S. also among, 12; 19:24
21:11 S. hath sl. his thousands
Is. 10:29 Gibeah of S. is fled
Acts 7:58 man's feet name was S.
8:1 and S. was consenting to, 3
9:4 S. why perse. 22:7; 26:14
11 and inquire for one call. S.
17 s. the Lord hath sent, 22:13
22 but S. increased in strength
24 laying wait was kno. of S.
26 when S. was come to Jeru.
11:25 went to Tarsus to seek S.
30 by hands of Barnab. and s.

13:1 prophets brought up wi. S.
2 separate me Barnabas and S.
7 called for Barnabas and S.
9 S. set his eyes on him
21 G. gave unto th. S. son of C.

SAVE.
Mat. 1:21 Je. shall s. his people
16:25 whosoever will s. his life,
Mark 8:35; Luke 9:24; 17:33
18:11 Son of man come to s. th.
wh. was lost, Luke 19:10
27:42 saved others, himself he
cannot s. Mark 15:31
49 whether E. will come to s.
Mark 3:4 is it lawful to s. or
kill? Luke 6:9
Luke 9:56 not to destroy, but s.
23:35 s. himself, if he be Christ
37 s. thyself; 39 if Ch. s. thys.
John 12:47 not to judge, to s.
Acts 2:40 s. yourselves fr. gener.
27:43 centurion, willing to s. P.
Rom. 11:14 if I might s. some of
them, 1 Cor. 9:22
1 Cor. 1:21 preaching to s. them
7:16 shalt s. husband, s. wife
1 Tim. 1:15 Ch. came to s. sinn.
Heb. 5:7 him that was able to s.
Jam. 1:21 able to s. your souls
2:14 can faith s. him
4:12 able to s. and destroy
5:15 prayer of faith shall s. sick

SAVED.
1 Pet. 3:20 wherein 8 souls we. s.
4:18 if righteous scarcely be s.

SAVIOUR.
2 Sam. 22:3 my refuge, my S.
2 K. 13:5 the L. gave Israel a s.
Ps. 106:21 forgat God their S.
Is. 19:20 shall send them a S.
43:3 I am H. O. of Is. thy S.
11 I am L. beside th. is no S.
45:15 hidest thyself, O God, S.
21 a just G. and a S. th. is no.
60:16 know I the L. am thy S.
63:8 my peo. so he was their S.
Jer. 14:8 S. of Israel in trouble
Hos. 13:4 th. is no S. beside me
Luke 1:47 sp. rejoic. in G. my S.
2:11 born in city of Da. a. S.
John 4:42 this is Ch. S. of world

213

Acts 5:31 God exalted to be S.
13:23 God raised to Israel a S.
Eph. 5:23 Chr. is S. of the body
Phil. 3:20 whence we look for S.
1 Tim. 1:1 comm. of G. our S.
2:3 accept. in sight of G. our S.
4:10 trust in God who is S.
2 Tim. 1:10 appearing of our S.
Tit. 1:3 according to God our S.
4 peace from L. Jes. C. our S.
13 glorious appearing of our S.
3:4 after kind. of G. S. appear.
6 shed on us through C. our S.
2 Pet. 1:1 righteous, of G. our S.
11 kingdom of our Lord and S.
2:20 knowledge of our L. and S.
2:2 apostles of the Lord and S.
18 grow in knowledge of our S.
1 John 4:14 Fa. sent Son to be S.
Jude 25 to only wise God our S.

SAYINGS.
Acts 14:18 s. scarce restrained.

SCARLET.
Gen. 38:28 bound a s. thread, 30
Mat. 27:28 put on Jes. a s. robe

SCIENCE.
Dan. 1:4 in wisd. understand. s.
1 Tim. 6:20 avoi. babblings of s.

SCORNFUL.
Ps. 1:1 nor sitteth in seat of s.

SCORNING.
Prov. 1:22 scorners delight in s.

SCORPION.
Rev. 9:5 torment was as of s.

SCORPIONS.
Luke 10:19 power to tread on s.
Rev. 9:3 power, as s. have power
10 had tails like s. and stings

SCOURGE, Verb.
Mat. 10:17 they will s. in th. syn.
20:19 shall s. him, Mark 10:34;
Luke 18:33
23:24 some of them ye shall s.
Acts 22:25 is it lawful to s. Ro.?

SCRIPTURE.
2 Tim. 3:16 s. is by inspi. of G.
Jam. 4:5 think s. saith in vain?
1 Pet. 2:6 it is contained in s.
2 Pet. 1:20 no s. is of priv. inter.

SCRIPTURES.
Mat. 21:42 ha. ye nev. read in s.

22:29 not know. s. Mark 12:24
26:54 how shall s. be fulfilled?
Mark 14:49 s. must be fulfilled
Luke 24:27 he expounded in all s.
32 while he opened to us the s.
45 that they mi. understand s.

SEA.
Ex. 14:16 stretch hand over s. 27
21 Lord caused the s. to go
back, made the s. dry
20:11 L. made the s. Ps. 95:5;
Jon. 1:9; Acts 4:24; 14:15
Mat. 8:26 he arose and rebuk. s.
27 s. obey him, Mark 4:39, 41
23:15 ye compass s. and land
Luke 21:25 s. and waves roaring
Acts 27:40 commit. themsel. to s.
28:4 tho' he hath escaped the s.
1 Cor. 10:1 fathers passed thro' s.
Rev. 4:6 before throne was s. of
7:2 given to hurt earth and s.
10:6 created s. things therein
14:7 worship him that made s.
15:2 I saw a s. of glass, mingled
20:13 the s. gave up the dead.
21:1 and there was no more s.

In, and into the SEA.
Jon. 1:4 a mighty tempest in t. s.
12 and cast me into the s. 15
Mat. 8:24 arose a temp. in the s.
13:47 kingdom of heaven is like
a net cast into the s.
Mat. 21:21 cast into the s. Mark
11:23
Mark 9:42 we, cast i.s. Lu. 17:2
Luke 17:6 be thou plant. in t. s.
John 21:7 Pe. cast himself i.t.s.
Acts 27:38 cast out wheat i.t.s.
43 cast themselves into the s.
2 Cor. 11:26 in perils in the s.
Jam. 3:7 beasts and thi. in the s.
Rev. 5:13 ev. creature in the s.
16:3 ev. living soul died in t. s.
18:19 all that had ships in t. s.

Of the SEA.
Gen. 1:26 have dominion over
the fish of the s. 28; Ps. 8:8

SEAL, Substantive.
2 Tim. 2:19 hav. this s. the Lord
Rev. 6:3 the sec. s. 5 the third s.
7 the fourth s. 9 the fifth s.

12 when he opened the sixth s.
7:2 having s. of the living God
8:1 when he opened seventh s.
9:4 hurt those that have not s.
20:3 shut him up, set a s. upon

SEALS.
Rev. 5:1 book sealed with 7 s.
5 lion of J. prevail. to loose s.
9 thou art worthy to open s.
6:1 the Lamb opened one of s.

SEALED.
John 6:27 him hath G. the Fa. s.
Rom. 15:28 when I have s. to th.
2 Cor. 1:22 who hath s. and giv.
Eph. 1:13 ye were s. with H. Sp.
4:30 whereby ye are s. to-day

SEARCH, Verb.
John 5:39 s. scrip. they testify
7:52 s. out of G. aris. no proph.

SEASON, Substantive.
2 Cor. 7:8 though but for a s.
2 Tim. 4:2 instant in s. out of s.
Heb.11:25 pleas. of sin for a s.

SEASON, ED.
Lev. 2:13 shalt thou s. with salt
Mark 9:50 wherew. will s. it?
Luke 14:34 wherew. sh. it be s.?
Col. 4:6 speech be with grace, s.

SEATS.
Rev. 4:4 four and twenty s. upon
the s. twenty-four elders

SECRET, Substantive.
Mat. 6:4 alms may be in s. thy
Father who seeth in s. 6, 18
John 7:4 doeth any thing in s.
Eph. 5:12 thi, done of them in s.

SECRET, Adjective.
1 Sam. 19:2 abide in s. place
Mat. 13:35 kept s. from foundation of world, Rom. 16:25

SEDUCE, ED.
1 John 2:26 concern. them that s.
Rev. 2:20 Jezebel to s. my serv.

SEDUCERS.
2 Tim. 3:13 s. shall wax worse

SEE.
Gen. 2:19 to s. what he wou. call
11:5 Lord came down to s. city
44:23 shall s. my face no more
45:12 your eyes s. the eyes of
Ex. 3:3 s. this great sight, 4

5:19 officers s. th. were in evil
6:1 shalt s. what I will do to P.
Ps. 34:8 O taste and s. Lord is good
Mat. 5:8 pure in heart, sh. s. G.
John 1:39 come and s. 46; 11:34;
Rev. 6:1 , 3, 5, 7
50 thou shalt s. greater things
1 Pet. 3:10 that will s. good days
1 John 5:16 if any man s. brother
Rev. 1:7 every eye shall s. him

SEE not, or not SEE.
Mark 8:18 hav. eyes. s. ye not ?
Luke 2:26 n. s. dea. bef. seen C.
8:10 seeing, they might not s.
1 Pet. 1:8 tho' now ye s. him not
2 Pet. 1:9 blind, can not s. a far

SEEING.
Mat. 13:13 beca. they s. see not
14 s. ye shall see and shall not
perc. Mark 4:12; Acts 28:26
John 9:7 washed and came s.
2 Pet. 2:8 s. and hearing, vexed

SEED.
Mat. 13:19 s. by way-side, 20, 22
24 man sowed good s. in field
37 soweth good s. is S. of man
38 good s. are the children of
Luke 8:11 s. is the word of God
1 Pet. 1:23 born, not of corrup. s.
1 John 3:9 his s. remain, in him

HIS SEED.
Ps. 25:13 his s. sh. inherit earth
37:25 nor seen his s. beg. bread

Thy SEED.
Gen. 3:15 enmi. bet. t. s. and her
Gal. 3:16 to t. s. which is Christ

SEEK.
Ezr. 4:2 we s. your God as ye do
Ps. 4:2 vanity. s. after leasing
Mat. 6:32 th. things do Gent. s.
33 s. ye first the kingdom of
God, Luke 12:31
7:7 s. and ye sh. find, Lu. 11:9
Mark 1:37 All men s. for thee
3:32 thy brethren s. for thee
Luke 12:30 these thi. nations s.
Acts 10:19 behold, 3 men s. thee
21 P. said, I am he whom ye s.
Rom. 2:7 to th. who s. for glory
11:3 I am alone, they s. my life
1 Cor. 10:24 let no man s. his own

215

Gal. 1:10 do I s. to please men?
Phil. 2:21 all s. their own things
Col. 3:1 s. those thi. that are ab.
Heb. 11:14 that they s. a country
13:14 have no city, we s. one
Rev. 9:6 in th. days men s. death

SEEKEST.

John 4:27 said, What s. thou?
20:15 saith, Woman, whom s. thou?

SEEKETH.

Rom. 3:11 none that s. after God
Rom. 11:7 Isr. not obt. that he s.
1 Cor. 13:5 charity s. not her own

SEEKING.

1 Pet. 5:8 s. whom he may dev.

SEEMETH.

Prov. 14:12 which s. right, 16:25
18:17 first in own cause s. just.

SEEN.

Num. 14:22 have s. my glory
Ezek. 8:12 s. what ancients do
15 hast thou s. this? 17; 47:6
13:7 have ye not s. vain vision
Mat. 13:17 proph. desired to see
th. thi. not s. them, Lu. 10:24
21:32 ye had s. it, repented not
Luke 1:22 that he had s. a vision
2:20 praising G. for thi. had s.
1 Tim. 6:16 wh. no man hath s.
1 John 1:1 we have s. with eyes
3 have s. declare we unto you
3:6 whoso, sin. hath not s. him
4:14 we have s. and do testify
20 brot. whom he hath s. how
can he love G. he ha. not s.?

SEEN, passively.

1 Pet. 1:8 having not s. ye love

SEEST.

Luke 7:44 Simon s. thou wom.?
Jam. 2:22 s. thou how faith wro.

SEETH.

Ex. 4:14 wh. he s. thee, be glad
1 Sam. 16:7 L. s. not as man s.
Ps. 37:13 he s. his day is coming
40:10 he s. that wise men die
Ec. 8:16 day nor night s. sleep
Is. 28:4 that looked upon it, s. it
29:15 who s. us? 47:10 none s.
Ezek. 8:12 the Lord s. us not. 9:9

SELAH.

Ps. 3:2 no help for him in God, s.
See Ps. 4:2, 4; 7:5; 9:16, 20; 20:3;
21:2; 24:6, 10; 32:4, 7; 39:5, 11;
44:8; 46:3, 7, 11; 47:4; 48:8;
49:13, 15; 50:6; 52:3, 5; 54:3;
55:7, 19; 57:3, 6; 59:5, 13; 60:4;
61:4; 62:4, 8; 66:4, 7, 15; 67:1,
4; 68:7, 19, 32; 75:3; 76:3, 9;
77:3, 9, 15; 81:7; 82:2; 83:8;
84:4, 8; 85:2; 87:3, 6; 88:7, 10;
89:4, 37, 45, 48; 140:3, 5, 8;
143:6; Hab. 3:3, 9, 13

SELL.

Jam. 4:13 we will buy and s.
Rev. 13:17 no man mi. buy or s.

SEND.

Gen. 24:7 G. shall s. angel bef. 40
Jud. 13:8 man of God didst s.
Luke 16:24 s. Laz. 27 s. to house
John 14:26 Fa. will s. in name
Acts 3:20 he shall s. Jesus Christ
7:35 same did G. s. to be a ruler
10:5 s. men to Joppa, 32: 11:13

SENT forth.

Mat. 10:5 these twelve Jesus s. f.
22:3 s. forth his servants to call

SENT out.

Jam. 2:25 Rahab had s. them out

SENT, passive.

John 1:6 a man s. from God
8 John was s. to bear witness
1 Pet. 1:12 H. Ghost s. fr. heaven

SEPARATE, Verb.

Rom. 8:35 who sh. s. us fr. Ch.?
39 noth. be able to s. us fr. G.

SEPARATED.

Prov. 18:1 a man hav. s. himself
19:4 poor is s. from his neighb.

SEPULCHRE.

Is. 22:16 hewed out a s. here, as
he that he. out a s. on high
Mat. 27:60 rol. stone to door of s.
64 that the s. be made sure, 66
28:1 other Mary came to see s.
Mark 15:46 laid him in a s. and
rolled a stone to door of the
s. Luke 23:53; Acts 13:29
16:2 came to s. at rising of sun
3 who sh. roll st. fr. door of s.?
5 entering s. 8 fled from s.
Luke 23:55 wom. also beheld s.

216

24:1 in morning they came to s.
2 stone rolled fr. s. John 20:1
9 returned fr. s. 12 Peter ran
22 women were early at the s.
John 19:41 in garden th. was a s.
42 for the s. was nigh at hand
20:1 com. Mary when dark to s.
2 taken away L. out of the s.
3 that disciple came to s. 4, 8
6 cometh Peter, went into s.
11 Mary stood at s. weeping
Acts 2:29 s. wi. us unto this day
7:16 Jacob laid in s. Abraham

SERAPHIM.
Is. 6:2 above it stood the s. each
6 one of the s. hav. a live coal

SERPENT.
Gen. 3:1 the s. was more subtle
13 s. beguiled me, 2 Cor. 11:3
49:17 Dan shall be a s. by way
Num. 21:8 said, Make thee a s.
9 Moses made a s. of brass
2 K. 18:4 Hezek. brake brazen s.
Ps. 58:4 th. poison like pois. of s.
Prov. 23:32 at last it bit, like a s.
Mat. 7:10 will he give him a s.?
Luke 11:11
John 3:14 as Moses lifted up s.
Rev. 12:9 old s. called devil, 20:2

SERVANT.
Prov. 11:20 fool sh. be s. to wise
12:9 that is despi. and hath a s.
22:7 the borrower is s. to lender
29:19 a s. not correct. with wor.
30:10 accuse not s. to master
22 not bear s. when reigneth
Mat. 10:25 enough for s. to be as
his lo.
18:27 lord of that s. was moved
32 O thou wicked s. I forg. th.
20:27 be chief, let him be your
s. 23:11; Mark 10:44
24:45 is a faithful and wise s.
48 evil s. shall say, Luke 12:45
50 lord of s. sh. come, Luke 12:46
25:21 well done, th. good and
faithful s. 23; Luke 19:17
26 thou wicked and slothful s.
Luke 19:22
30 cast unprofit. s. into darkn.
26:51 P. struck s. of high-priest,

Mark 14:47; John 18:10
Mark 12:2 sent to husband. a s.
Luke 12:47 s. knew lord's will
14:21 so that s. showed his lord
17:7 which having a s. plowing
9 doth thank th. s.? I trow not
20:10 at season he sent a s. 11
John 8:34 commit. sin. s. of sin
35 the s. abideth not in house
13:16 s. is not greater, 15:20
15:15 s. knoweth not what lord
Rom. 1:1 Paul a s. of Je. Christ
14:4 who judgest ano. man's s.?
16:1 Phebe. a s. of the church
1 Cor. 7:21 art called being a s.?
22 being a s. is L.'s freeman
9:19 I made myself a s.
Gal. 1:10 I sho. not be s. of Chr.
4:1 child differeth noth. from s.
7 art no more a s. but a son
Phil. 2:7 he took the form of a s.

SERVANT, S. of God.
Gen. 50:17 forgive s. of God
1 Chr. 6:49 Moses the s. of God
2 Chr. 24:9 Moses s. of God laid
Neh. 10:29 by Moses s. of God
Dan. 6:20 O Daniel s. of liv. God
9:11 in law of Mo. the s. of God
Tit. 1:1 P. a s. of God, an apost.
Jam. 1:1 Ja. a s. of G. and of L.
1 Pet. 2:16 liberty, as a s. of G.
Rev. 7:3 sealed the s. of our God
15:3 song of Moses the s. of G.

SERVANTS.
Rom. 6:16 yield yoursel. s. to ob.
17 that ye were the s. of sin
18 became s. of righteousness
19 yielded your mem. s. to sin
20 s. of sin, were free fr. right
22 free from sin, bec. s. to God
1 Cor. 7:23 be not ye s. of men
2 Cor. 4:5 oursel. your s. for Jes.
Eph. 6:5 s. obedi. to mast. Col.
3:22; Tit. 2:9; 1 Pet 2:18
6 eye-service, but as s. of Chr.
Phil. 1:1 Paul and Tim, s. of Ch.
Col. 4:1 give your s. what is just
1 Tim. 6:1 as many s. as are un.
1 Pet. 2:16 liberty, but as s. of G.
2 Pet. 2:10 themselves are s. of c.
Rev. 7:3 we have sealed s. of G.

SERVE.

Zep. 3:9 s. him with consent
Mal. 3:14 it is in vain to s. God
Mat. 4:10 him only s. Luke 4:8
Mat. 6:24 no man can s. 2 mas.
  cannot s. G. and M. Lu. 10:13
Gal. 5:13 by love s. one another
Col. 3:24 reward, ye s. Lord Ch.
1 Thes. 1:9 turned fr. id. to s. G.

SERVED.

Deut. 17:3 hath gone, s. other
  gods, 29:26; Jos. 23:16
Jos. 24:2 faith. s. other gods, 15
  31 Israel s. the Lord all the days
  of Joshua, Jud. 2:7
Luke 2:37 Anna s. G. in temple
John 12:2 ma. supper, Martha s.
Acts 13:36 Da. had s. generation
Rom. 1:25 worship. s. creature

SERVICE.

2 Chr. 8:14 courses of priests to s.
  12:8 know my s. and s. of kingd.
  31:2 ev. man according to his s.
  35:2 encouraged them to s. of L.
  10 so s. of L. was prepared, 16
Ezr. 6:18 in courses for s. 7:19
Gal. 4:8 did s. to th. are no gods
Eph. 6:7 good-will doing s. to L.

SERVING.

Rom. 12:11 fervent in spirit, s. L.
Tit. 3:3 sometimes fool. s. lusts

SET.

Gen. 4:15 L. s. mark upon Cain

SET, passive.

Gal. 3:1 Ch. had been s. forth
Heb. 6:18 lay hold on hope s. bef.
  8:1 is s. on right hand, 12:2
  12:1 run the race s. before us
  2 joy that was s. before him

SETH.

Gen. 5:3 and called him S.
  6 S. begat Enos, 1 Chr. 1:1;
  Luke 3:28

SEVEN.

Gen. 46:25 Bil. all souls were s.
Lev. 23:15 s. sab. shall be com.
Jos. 6:4 s. priests bearing s.
  trumpets, 6, 8, 13
1 Sam. 2:5 barren hath born s.
2 Sam. 21:9 they fell all s. toge.
Job 5:19 in s. troubles no evil

Prov. 9:1 wisd. hath hewn s. pil.
  26:25 th. are s. abominations
Ec. 11:2 portion to s. also to S.
Is. 4:1 s. women take hold of 1
  11:15 L. shall smite in s. strea.
Ezek. 39:12 s. months be burying
Mic. 5:5 against him s. sheph.
Mark. 12:22 and s. had her, 23;
  Luke 20:31, 33
Rev. 1:4 John to s. churches in A.
  10:3 when he cried, s. thunders
  12:3 dragon, having s. heads
  and s. crowns. 13:1; 17:3, 7
  15:1 I saw s. angels having the
  s. last plagues, 6
  7 to s. angels s. golden vials
  17:1 one of the s. angels which
  had the s. vials, 21:9
  9 s. heads are s. mountains
  11 beast is of the s. and goeth

SEVENFOLD.

Gen. 4:15 venge. sh. be taken s.
  24 if Cain shall be avenged s.
  Lamech seventy and s.
Ps. 79:12 render s. into bosom
Prov. 6:31 he shall restore s.
Is. 30:26 light of sun shall be s.

SEVEN men.

2 Sam. 21:6 let s. men of his sons
Prov. 26:16 that s. m. that can
Jer. 52:25 s. m. that were near
Acts 6:3 look out s. m. of honest

SEVEN SONS.

Ruth 4:15 dau. better than s. s.
Job 1:2 were born unto him s. s.
  42:13 had s. s. and three daugh.
Acts 19:14 s. s. of Sceva a Jew

SEVEN spirits.

Mat. 2:45 then goeth he, and
  taketh s. s. Luke 11:26
Rev. 1:4 s. s. bef. throne of God
  4:5 lamps, wh. are s. s. of God
  5:6 seven eyes, are s. s. of God

SEVEN stars.

Amos 5:8 him that maketh s. s.
Rev. 1:16 in ri. hand s. s. 2:1; 3:1
  20 myst. of s. s. thou sawest;
  s.s. are angels of s. churches

SEVEN times.

Gen. 33:3 Ja. bowed bef. Es. s. t.
Lev. 4:6 priests shall sprinkle of

218

the blood s. t. 17; 8:11; 14:7;
16:14, 19; Num. 19:4
14:16 sprink. oil wi. flu. s. t. 27
51 sprinkle house s. t.
25:8 number s. t. seven years
Lev. 20:18 pu. s. t. more, 21, 24, 28
Ps. 119:164 s. t. a day do I praise
Prov. 24:16 a just man fall, s. t.
Dan. 4:16 s. t. pass, 23, 25, 32
Mat. 18:21 sh. I forgive? till s. t.
Luke 17:4 if brother tresp. s. t. a
day, and s. times a day turn

SEVEN years.

Gen. 29:18 serve s. y. for Rachel
20 Jac. served s. y. for Rachel
27 shalt serve me other s. y. 30
41:26 seven good kine are s. y.
the seven good ears are s. y.
29 2 y. of plenty, 34, 47, 48
53 the s. y. of plenteousness

SEVENTH.

Ex. 21:2 in s. he sh. go out free
31:15 the s. is sabbath of rest
Lev. 23:16 morrow after s. sab.

SEVENTY.

Luke 10:1 L. appointed other s.
17 the s. returned ag. with joy

SHADOW.

Ps. 17:8 hide me un. s. of wings
36:7 under s. of wings, 57:1
63:7 in s. of wings will I rejoice
Jon 4:5 and sat under in s.
6 it might be s. over his head
Mark. 4:32 fowls lodge under s.
Col. 2:17 a s. of things to come
Heb. 8:5 serve unto s. of heaven
10:1 having a s. of good things
Jam. 1:17 with whom no s. of tu.

SHAKE.

Mat. 10:14 s. off dust of your feet,
Mark 6:11; Luke 9:5

SHAME.

Jud. 18:7 none to put them to s.
1 Sam. 20:34 father had done s.
2 Sam. 13:13 sh. I cause s. to go?
Prov. 3:25 s. sh. be the promot.
9:7 reproveth scorner, getteth s.
10:5 is a son that causeth s.
1 Cor. 6:5 speak to your s. 15:34
11:6 if it be a s. for a woman
14 man have long hair, is a s.

14:35 s. for wo. to sp. in church
Eph. 5:12 a s. to speak of things

SHARP.

Ex. 4:25 Zippor. took a s. stone
Jos. 5:2 make thee s. knives
1 Sam. 14:4 bet. passa. a s. rock
Job 41:30 s. stones are under him,
he spread. s. pointed things
Ps. 45:5 arrow s. in the heart
57:4 their tongue s. sword
Prov. 5:4 s. as two-edged sword
25:18 man bears false witn. is s.
Is. 5:28 whose arrows are s.
49:2 made my mouth like s. sw.
Acts 15:39 contention was so s.
Rev. 1:16 out of his mouth went
a s. two-edged sword, 19:15
41:14 in his hand a s. sickle, 17
18 ang. cried to him had s. sic.

SHEBA, SHEBAH.

1 K. 10:1 when queen of S. heard
of Solomon, 2 Chr. 9:1

SHEEP.

Gen. 4:2 Abel was a keeper of s.
2 Sam. 7:8 took from follow, s.
24:17 but the..e s. what have
they done? 1 Chr. 21:17
1 K. 4:23 Sol.'s provision 100 s.

As SHEEP.

Acts 8:32 led as s. to slaughter
1 Pet. 2:25 as s. going astray

SHEPHERD.

Heb. 13:20 L. J. great s. of sheep

SHIELD.

2 Sam. 1:21 the s. of mighty, s. of
Saul as though not anoint.
22:3 he is my s. Ps. 3:3; 28:7;
119:114; 144:2
36 given me the s. of salvation, Ps. 18:35
1 K. 10:17 3 poun. of gold to 1 s.
Ps. 5:12 compass him as with s.
33:20 Lord is our s. 59:11; 84:9
35:2 take hold of s. and buckler
76:3 brake arrows of bow, the s.
Prov. 30:5 s. to them that trust
Is. 22:6 Kir uncovered the s.
Jer. 46:3 order buckler and s.

SHILOH.

Jos. 18:1 assemb. together at S.

SHINE.

219

Mat. 5:16 let your light s.
13:43 righteous s. forth as sun
17:2 his face did s. as sun
2 Cor. 4:4 lest light of Ch. sho. s.
6 G. commanded light to s.
Phil. 2:15 among whom ye s. as
Rev. 18:23 candle sh. s. no more
21:23 no need of sun or moon s.

SHINED.
Acts 9:3 suddenly there s. about
12:7 and a light s. in the prison
2 Cor. 4:6 G. hath s. in our hearts

SHOES.
Mark 1:7 latchet of whose s.
Luke 3:16; Acts 13:25

SHOW-BREAD.
Ex. 25:30 set upon a table s.-b.
1 Sam. 21:6 no bread but s.-b.
Mat. 12:4 David entered and did
eat s.-b. Mark 2:26; Luke 6:4

SHOW.
Mat. 8:4 s. thys. to priest. Mark
1:44; Luke 5:14; 17:14
11:4 s. John the things ye hear
14:2 mighty works s. Mark 6:14
1 Tim. 6:15 in his times he sh. s.
2 Tim. 2:15 s. thyself appr. to G.
Heb. 6:11 that every one's, dilig.
Jam. 2:18 s. me thy faith witho.
3:13 s. works out of good conv.
1 Pet. 2:9 s. forth praises of him
1 John 1:2 s. unto you etern. life
Rev. 1:1 angel to s. servants, 22:6

God, or Lord SHOWED.
Mic. 6:8 he hath s. thee, O man
Rom. 1:19 G. hath s. it to them
2 Pet. 1:14 L. Jesus hath s. me

SICK.
Mat. 4:24 brou. to him s. people
8:14 Pet.'s wife's moth. s. of fe.
16 healed all th. were s. 14:14
9:12 but they that are s. Mark
2:17; Luke 5:31
10:8 heal the s. cleanse the lepers, Luke 9:2; 10:9
25:36 I was s. and ye visited me
Mark 6:5 laid hands on a few s.
13 anoint. many that were s.
56 laid s. in streets, Acts 5:15
16:18 lay hands on the s.
Luke 7:2 centurion's serv. was s.

10 serv. whole that had been s.
John 4:46 a nobleman's son s.
11:1 Laz. of Bethany was s. 2
3 L. he whom thou lovest is s.
Acts 9:37 Dorcas was s. and died
19:12 brou. the s. handkerchiefs
28:8 father of Publius lay s.
Phil. 2:26 heard he had been s.
2 Tim. 4:20 Tro. I left at Mil. s.
Jam. 5:14 s. let him call elders

SICKNESS.
John 11:4 s. is not unto death

SICKNESSES.
Mat. 8:17 sa. Himself bare our s.

SIGHT.
Mat. 11:5 the blind receive their
s. 20:34; Luke 7:21
Luke 4:18 preach s. to the blind
23:48 came to s. smote breasts
24:31 he vanished out of their s.
John 9:11 washed and I recei. s.
Acts 1:9 received him out of s.

SIGHT of God.
1 Tim. 2:3 acceptable in s. of G.

Thy SIGHT.
Mat. 11:26 so it seemed good in
thy s. Luke 10:21
Luke 15:21 sin. ag. heav. in t. s.
18:42 Jesus said, Receive thy s.

SIGHTS.
Luke 21:11 fearful s. sh. there be

SIGNS.
Rom. 15:19 through mighty s.
and wonders, 2 Cor. 12:12
2 Thes. 2:9 work. of Satan. wi. s.
Heb. 2:4 G. bearing wit. with s.

SILENCE.
1 Tim. 2:11 let wom. learn in s.
12 nor to usurp but to be in s.
1 Pet. 2:15 may put to s. ignore
Rev. 8:1 there was s. in heaven

Tribe of SIMEON.
Num. 1:23 t. of S. numb. 59,300

SIMON.
Mat. 10:4 S. Canaan. Mark 3:18
13:55 James, Jos. S. Mark 6:3
Acts 8:9 man S. who beforetime
13 then S. himself believed also
9:43 Peter tarried many days at
Joppa wi. one S. 10:6, 17, 32

SIN.

Ex. 16:1 I came to wildern. of S.
17:1 journey. fr. S. Num. 33:12
Ezek. 30:15 pour my fury up. S.
16 S. shall have great pain

SIN.

Gen. 4:7 not well, s. lie, at door
Ex. 34:7 forgiv. iniquity, and s.
Lev. 4:3 if priest s. accord. to s.
14 wh. s. is known, cong. offer
6:26 priest offereth it for s. 9:15
19:17 not suffer s. on neighbor
Num. 5:6 when man or wom. s.
12:11 I beseech, lay not s. upon
19:9 it is a purification for s. 17
27:3 father died in his own s.
Deut. 15:9 cry to L. it be s. 24:15
19:15 witness sh. not rise for s.
21:22 if a man have com. s.
22:26 in damsel no s. wor. death
23:21 it would be s. in thee
24:16 put to death for his own s.
2 K. 14:6; 2 Chr. 25:4
1 Sam. 15:23 rebel. as s. of witch.
1 K. 8:34 forgive s. of thy people
36 forgive the s. of thy servants,
2 Chr. 6:25, 27
12:30 this thing bec. a s. 13:34
2 K. 8:34 forgive s. of thy people
36 forgive the s. of thy servants,
2 Chr. 6:25, 27
12:30 this thing bec. a s. 13:34
2 K. 12:16 s. money was priests'
Job 20:11 his bones are full of s.
Ps. 32:1 blessed whose s. cover.
51:5 in s. did mother con. me
109:7 let his prayer become s.
14 let not s. of mother be blot.
Prov. 10:16 wicked tendeth to s.
19 in words there want. not s.
14:9 fools make a mock at s.
34 s. is a reproach to any peo.
21:4 plowing of wicked is s.
24:9 thought of foolishness is s.
Is. 5:18 woe to th. who draw s.
30:1 that they may add s. to s.
31:7 idols your hands ma. for s.
53:10 make soul an offer. for s.
12 he bare s. of many
Jer. 17:1 s. of Ju. writ. with pen
3 I will give high place for s.
51:5 th. land was filled with s.

Lam. 4:6 punishm. of s. of Sod.
Hos. 4:8 eat up s. of people
10:8 s. of Is. shall be destroyed
12:8 no iniq. in me that were s.
Amos 8:14 sw. by s. of Samaria
Mic. 1:13 beginning of s. to Zion
6:7 fruit of body for s. of soul
Zec. 13:1 a fount. opened for s.
Mat. 12:31 all s. sh. be forgiven
John 1:29 tak. away s. of world
8:7 that is without s. am. you
34 whoso commit. s. serv. of s.
9:41 if blind, should have no s.
15:22 not come, had not s. 24
16:8 Comfor. will reprove of s. 9
19:11 deliv. me hath greater s.
Acts 7:60 lay not s. to th. charge
Rom. 3:9 J. and Gentil. under s.
20 by law is knowledge of s.
4:7 blessed whose s. is covered
5:12 s. ent. world, death by s.
13 till the law s. was in world
20 where s. abounded, grace
21 as s. reigned unto death
6:1 shall we continue in s.?
2 sh. we th. are dead to s. live?
7 he that is dead is freed fr. s.
10 he died, he died to s. once
11 reck. yourselves dead to s.
12 let not s. reign in yo. body
13 nor yield your memb. to s.
14 s. shall not have dominion
16 serv. ye are, whether of s.
17 G. thanked, were serv. of s.
18 being made free from s. 22
20 wh. ye were servants of s.
23 for the wages of s. is death
7:7 is law s.? G. forbid; kn. s.
8 s. tak. occasion wro. in me;
without law s. is dead
9 commandm. came, s. revived
11 s. by commandm. slew me
17 s. that dwelleth in me, 20
23 bring. me into captiv. to s.
25 but with flesh, the law of s.
8:3 s. condemned s. in the flesh
10 body dead because of s.
14:23 whats. is not of faith is s.
1 Cor. 6:18 every s. a man doeth
15:56 the sting of death is s. and
the strength of s. is the law

2 Cor. 5:21 made him be s. for us
Gal. 2:17 Ch. the minister of s.?
3:22 scrip. conclu. all under s.
2 Thes. 2:3 man of s. be revealed
Heb. 3:13 be hardened through s.
4:15 tempted, yet without s.
9:26 he appeared to put away s.
28 appear without s. to salvat.
10:6 in sacrifices for s. no pleas
8 off. for s. thou wouldest not
18 remission, no offering for s.
11:25 enjoy the pleasures of s.
12:1 lay aside s. doth beset us
4 not resisted, striv. against s.
13:11 bod. of beasts for s. burnt
Jam. 1:15 it bring. forth s. and s.
when finished, bring. death
2:9 if have respect to per. ye s.
4:17 not good, to him it is s.
1 Pet. 2:22 did no s. nor guile
4:1 suff. in flesh, ceased from s.
2 Pet. 2:14 eyes can. cease fr. s.
1 John 1:7 the blood of Jesus
Christ his son cleanseth us
from all s.
8 say, We have no s. we dece.
3:4 whoso comm. s. trans-
gresseth; s. is transgression
5 manifested, in him is no s.
8 committeth s. is of the devil
9 born of G. doth not commit s.
5:16 s. wh. is not to death, s.
17 all unrighteousn. is s. and
there is a s. not unto death
Great SIN.
Gen. 20:9 brought on me great s.
Ex. 32:21 bro. g. s. on them
30 M. said, Ye sinned a g. s. 31
1 sam. 2:17 s. of young men g.
2 K. 17:21 Jeroboam made them
sin a great s.
His SIN.
Lev. 4:3 bring for his s. a bullock
23 if h. s. come to knowl. 28
5:6 bring trespass-offer. for h. s.
1 K. 15:26 Nadab walked in h. s.
34 Baa. walked in way of h. s.
16:19 Zimri walked in his s.
26 Omri in his s.
2 K. 21:16 beside h. s. wherewith
made Judah

17 acts of Manasseh, and h. s.
2 Chr. 33:19 all h. s. bef. humbl.
Job 34:37 addeth rebellion to h. s.
Is. 27:9 fruit to take away his s.
Ezek. 3:20 shall die in h. s. 18:24
33:14 if he turn from his s.
Hos. 13:12 bound up, h. s. is hid
Mic. 3:8 full to declare to Is. h. s.
My SIN.
Gen. 31:36 what is my s. that th.
Ex. 10:17 forg. my s. this once
1 Sam. 15:25 I pray, pardon my s.
20:1 what my s. bef. thy father
1 K. 17:18 to call my s. to rem.
Job 10:6 thou search. after my s.
13:23 make me to know my s.
14:16 dost thou not watch my s.
35:3 if I be cleansed from my s.
Ps. 32:5 I acknowledged my s.
and thou forgavest my s.
38:3 nor rest because of my s.
18 iniqu. I be sorry for my s.
51:2 cleanse me from my s.
3 my s. bef. 59:3 not for my s.
Prov. 20:9 I am pure from my s.
Dan. 9:20 I was confessing my s.
Our SIN.
Ex. 34:9 pardon iniq. and our s.
Jer. 16:10 what o. s. we commit.
Their SIN.
Gen. 18:20 because t. s. is griev.
50:17 forgive their s. 2 Chr. 7:14
Ex. 32:32 if thou forgive their s.
34 when I visit, I will visit t. s.
Num. 5:7 they shall confess t. s.
Deut. 9:27 stubbornness, nor t. s.
1 K. 8:35 if they turn from their
s. 2 Chr. 6:26
Neh. 4:5 let not t. s. be blotted
Ps. 85:2 thou hast covered t. s.
Is. 3:9 they declare t. s. as Sod.
Jer. 16:18 recompense t. s. doub.
18:23 neither blot out their s.
31:34 rememb. their s. no more
36:3 that I may forgive their s.
John 15:22 have no cloak for t. s.
THY SIN.
2 Sam. 12:13 Lord put away t. s.
Is. 6:7 taken away, t. s. purged
Your SIN.
Ex. 32:30 atonement for your s.

Num. 32:23 y. s. wi. find you out
Deut. 9:21 I took y. s. the calf
John 9:41 theref. y. s. remaineth

SIN, Verb.

Gen. 39:9 do this, and s. ag. G.?
42:22 do not s. ag. the child
Ex. 20:20 fear, that thou s. not
23:33 lest make thee s. ag. me
Lev. 4:2 if soul s. thro' ignorance
3 if priest s. 13 if congregat. s.
27 if people s. thro' ignorance
5:1 if a soul s. and hear swear.
6:2 if a soul s. lie unto neighbor
Num. 16:22 s. wroth with all?
Deut. 20:18 should you s. ag. L.
24:4 shalt not cause land to s.
1 Sam. 2:25 if one man s. against
another; s. against the Lord
12:23 God forbid I should s.
14:33 people s. against Lord
34 s. not in eating with blood
19:4 let not king s. ag. servant
5 why s. ag. innocent blood?
1 K. 8:46 if they shall s. against
thee, 2 Chr. 6:36
2 K. 21:11 Man. made Judah s.
2 Chr. 6:22 if man s. ag. neighbor
Neh. 6:13 and do so, and s.
13:26 did not Solo. s. by these
Job 2:10 did not J. s. wi. his lips
5:24 visit habitation, and not s.
10:14 if I s. thou markest me
31:30 nei. suffered mouth to s.
Ps. 4:4 stand in awe, and s. not
39:1 take heed I s. not
119:11 I might not s. ag. thee
Ec. 5:6 mouth cause flesh to s.
Jer. 32:35 do this to cau. J. to s.
Ezek. 3:21 rig. s. not, doth not s.
Hos. 8:11 Ephraim hath made
altars to s. altars to him to s.
13:2 now they s. more and more
Mat. 18:21 L. how oft brot. s.?
John 5:14 s. no more, lest worse
8:11 nei. do I cond. s. no more
9:2 who did s. man or parents?
Rom. 6:15 s. bec. not under law?
1 Cor. 8:12 s. ag. breth. s. ag. C.
15:34 awake to righteous. s. not
Eph. 4:26 be ye angry and s. not
1 Tim. 5:20 them that s. rebuke

Heb. 10:26 if we s. wilfully after
1 John 2:1 I write unto you that
ye s. not, and if any man s.
8:9 can. s. bec. he is born of G.
5:16 any man see his brother s.

SING.

Ex. 15:21 s. to the Lord, 1 Chr.
16:23; Ps. 30:4; 95:1; 96:1, 2;
98:1; 147:7; 149:1; Is. 12:5
22:18 noise of them that s.
Num. 21:17 spring up, O well, s.
1 Sam. 21:11 did they not s. one
1 Chr. 16:9 s. unto him, s. psalms
33 the trees of the wood s. out
2 Chr. 20:22 they began to s. and
29:30 Hez. command. Lev. to s.
Job 29:13 I caused wid. heart s.
Ps. 21:13 so will we s. praise
33:2 praise the Lord, s. to him
3 s. to him a new so. Is. 42:10 '
51:14 s. of thy righteousn. 145:7
65:13 valleys shout, they also s.
66:2 s. forth honor of his name
4 earth s. to thee, they shall s.
67:4 let nations be glad and s.
68:32 s. to God, ye kingdoms
71:22 to thee will I s. 98:5
81:1 s. aloud to G. our strength
104:12 fowls s. among branches
105:2 s. to him, s. psal. unto him
137:3 s. us one of the songs of Z.
4 how shall we s. L. song in?
138:5 they shall s. in ways of L.
149:5 s. aloud upon their beds
Prov. 29:6 righteous s. and rej.
Is. 23:15 after 70 years sh. T. s.
24:14 they shall s. for maj. of L.
26:19 s. ye that dwell in dust
27:2 in that day s. ye to her
35:6 then sh. tongue of dumb s.
Is. 38:20 we will s. my songs
42:11 let inhabitants of rock s.
44:23 s. O ye heav. for L. 49:13
52:8 with the voice shall they s.
9 s. to the L. ye waste places
54:1 s. O barren, didst not bear
65:14 my servants sh. s. for joy
Jer. 31:7 s. with gladness for Ja.
12 they shall s. in height of Z.
51:48 all that is therein shall s.
Ezek. 27:25 ships of Tarsh. did s.

Hos. 2:15 sh. s. in days of youth
Zep. 2:14 their voice shall s.
  3:14 s. daugh. of Zion, Zec. 2:10
Jam. 5:13 any merry? let him s.
Rev. 15:3 they s. song of Moses
I will SING.
Ex. 15:1 I will s. to the Lord,
  Jud. 5:3; Ps. 13:6
P. 57:7 fixed, O God, I will s.
  9 I will s. to thee am. nations
59:16 I w. s. of thy power, 89:1
  17 unto thee, O my stre. w. Is.
101:1 I will s. of mercy and jud.
104:33 I will s. to the L. as long
144:9 I will s. a new song
Is. 5:1 now will I s. to well-belo.
Rom. 15:9 for this cause will I s.
1 Cor. 14:15 I will s. with the sp.
  I will s. with understanding
SINGED.
Dan. 3:27 nor w. hair of head s.
SINGER.
1 Chr. 6:33 Heman a s. son of J.
Hab. 3:19 to chief s. on instrum.
SINGERS.
1 K. 10:12 made psalteries for s.
  2 Chr. 9:11
1 Chr. 9:33 these are the s. 15:16
  15:19 s. were appoint. to sound
  27 Levites and s. had fine lin.
2 Chr. 5:13 trumpet. and s. were
  20:21 Jehoshaphat appointed s.
  23:13 peo. rejoiced also s. 29:28
  35:15 the s. the sons of Asaph
Ezr. 2:41 s. childr. of Asaph 128
  70 s. dwelt in cities, Neh. 7:73
7:7 some s. went up to Jerusa.
Neh. 7:1 the s. were appointed
  10:29 the s. clave to their bret.
  11:22 s. were over bus. of house
  23 portion for s. 12:47; 13:5
  12:28 sons of s. gathered thems.
  29 the s. builded them villages
  42 s. sang; 45 s. kept ward of G.
  46 in days of da. there were s.
  13:10 Levites and s. were fled
Ps. 68:25 s. went before
  87:7 as well s. as players
Ezek. 40:44 chamb. of s. in court
Men-SINGERS, women-
SINGERS.

Ec. 2:8 I gat men-s. and wo.-s.
SINGETH.
Prov. 25:20 so is he that s. songs
SINGING.
1 Sam. 18:6 wo. came out of Is. s.
1 Chr. 6:32 ministered with s.
  13:8 Dav. and Is. played with s.
2 Chr. 23:18 offer burnt-off. wi. s.
  30:21 s. with loud instru. to L.
Neh. 12:27 kept dedication wi. s.
Ps. 100:2 bef. presence with s.
  126:2 our tongue filled with s.
Cant. 2:12 time of the s. of birds
Is. 14:7 they break forth into s.
  16:10 in vineyards shall be no s.
  35:2 sh. blossom with joy and s.
  44:23 break into s. ye mount.
  48:20 flee from Chaldeans wi. s.
  49:13 break forth into s.
  51:11 redeemed sh. come wi. s.
  54:1 break forth into s. O bar.
  55:12 mount. shall break into s.
Zep. 3:17 joy over thee with s.
Eph. 5:19 s. in y. heart, Col. 3:16
SINGING-MEN, SINGING-
WOMEN.
2 Sam. 19:35 I hear s.-m. s.-w.
2 Chr. 35:25 the s.-m. spake of J.
Ezr. 2:65 200 s.-m. 200 s.-women
Neh. 7:67 245 s.-m. and s.-women
SINNED.
Ex. 9:34 Pharaoh s. yet more
  32:30 ye have s. a great sin, 31
  33 whosoever hath s. him will
Lev. 4:3 for sin he hath s. a bul.
  22 ruler s. 23; 28 one of peo. s.
  5:5 confess he hath s.
  6:4 bec. he hath s. shall restore
Num. 12:11 lay not s. wher. we s.
  32:23 ye have s. against the L.
Deut. 9:16 behold, ye had s. ag. L.
  18 your sins wh. ye s. in doing
Jos. 7:11 Isr. hath s. and trangr.
Jud. 11:27 I have not s. ag. thee
1 Sam. 19:4 he hath not s. ag th.
  24:11 I have not s. against thee
1 K. 8:33 they have s. against
  thee. 35; 2 Chr. 6:24, 26
  50 forgive peo. th. s. 2 Chr. 6:39
  15:30 Jer. which he s. 16:13, 19
  18:9 what have I s. that thou

224

2 K. 17:7 Israel had s. against L.
21:17 sin th. Manas. s. is writ.
Neh. 9:29 s. against thy judgm.
Job 1:5 Job said, My sons ha. s.
22 in this J. s. not, nor charg.
8:4 if chil. have s. against him
24:19 so doth grave who have s.
Ps. 78:17 they s. yet more, 32
Is. 43:27 thy first father hath s.
Jer. 2:35 sayest, I have not s.
40:3 because ye have s. 44:23
50:14 Babylon hath s. ag. Lord
Lam. 1:8 Jer. hath grievously s.
5:7 fathers have s. and are not
Ezek. 18:24 sin he hath s. in th.
28:16 violence, and thou hast s.
37:23 dwelling-p. wherein th. s.
Hos. 4:7 as they increased they s.
10:9 thou hast s. fr. days of G.
Hab. 2:10 thou hast s. ag. soul
John 9:3 neither this man s. nor
Rom. 2:12 as have s. with. law,
as have s. in the law
3:23 all have s. and come, 5:12
5:14 death over them had not s.
16 not as it was by one that s.
1 Cor. 7:28 if marry, hast not s.
2 Cor. 12:21 I bewail many that s.
13:2 I write to them wh. have s.
Heb. 3:17 was it not wi. them s.?
2 Pet. 2:4 G. spared not angels s.
1 John 1:10 if say, We have not s.

I have SINNED.
Ex. 9:27 Phar. said, I h. s. 10:16
Num. 22:34 Balaam said, I h. s.
Jos. 7:20 indeed, I h. s. ag. God
1 Sam. 15:24 Saul said, I have s.
30; 26:21
2 Sam. 12:13 Da. said to Na. I h.
s. 24:10, 17; 1 Chr. 21:8, 17
19:20 thy serv. doth know I h. s.
Job 7:20 I h. s. 33:27 say, I h. s.
Ps. 41:4 heal my soul, I have s.
51:4 against thee only have I s.
Mic. 7:9 I have s. against him
Mat. 27:4 Judas said, I have s.
Luke 15:18 prodi. said, I h. s. 21

We have SINNED.
Num. 12:11 sin, wherein we h. s.
14:40 for we have s. Deut. 1:41
21:7 we h. s. have spoken ag. L.

Jud. 10:10 we h. s. bec. we have
forsaken God, 1 Sam. 12:10
15 we h. s. do what seem. good
1 Sam. 7:6 and said, we have s.
1 K. 8:47 we h. s. done perversely
2 Chr. 6:37 we h. s. done amiss
Neh. 1:6 confess sins we have s.
Ps. 106:6 we h. s. with our fath.
Is. 42:24 L. ag. whom we have s.
64:5 thou art wroth, for we h. s.
Jer. 3:25 lie down in sh. we h. s.
8:14 given us gall, for we h. s.
14:20 acknow. wick. we have s.
Dan. 9:5 we h. s. committed ini.
15 we have s. done wickedly

SINNER.
Prov. 11:31 more wicked and s.
13:6 wickedn. overthroweth s.
22 wealth of s. laid up for just
Ec. 2:26 the s. he giveth travail
7:26 s. shall be taken by her
8:12 thro' s. do evil 100 times
9:2 so is s. and he that sweareth
18 one s. destroy. much good
Is. 65:20 s. being 100 years old
Lu. 7:37 wo. in city who was s.
15:7 joy in heaven over one s.
18:13 G. be merciful to me a s.
19:7 guest with man a s.
John 9:16 can s. do miracles?
John 9:24 gi. G. praise, man is s.
25 whe. he be a s. I know not
Rom. 3:7 yet judged as a s.?
Jam. 5:20 convert. s. save a soul
1 Pet. 4:18 where ungodly s. ap.

SINNERS.
Gen. 13:13 men of Sod. were s.
1 Sam. 15:18 utterly destroy s.
Ps. 1:1 stand. not in way of s.
5 nor s. in congre. of righteous
25:8 theref. will he teach s. way
26:9 gather not my soul with s.
51:13 s. sh. be converted to thee
104:35 let the s. be consumed
Prov. 1:10 if s. ent. consent not
13:21 evil pursueth s. to right.
23:17 let not thy heart envy s.
Is. 1:28 destr. of s. be together
13:9 destroy s. thereof out of it
33:14 the s. in Z. are afraid
Amos 9:10 s. shall die by sword

Mat. 9:10 many s. sat at meat
  with Jesus, Mark 2:15
  13 call right. but s. to repentance, Mark 2:17; Luke 5:32
  11:19 fri. of publ and s. Lu. 7:34
Luke 6:32 s. love those love them
  33 what tha. ha. ye? s. do same
  34 s. lend to s. to receive again
  13:2 suppose th. these were s. 4
  15:1 publicans and s. to hear
John 9:31 kn. G. heareth not s.
Rom. 5:8 wh. we were s. C. died
Gal. 2:15 Jews, not s. of Gentiles
  17 if we ourselves are found s.
1 Tim. 1:9 the law is made for s.
  15 Ch. Jesus came to save s.
Jam. 4:8 ye s. purify hearts
Jude 15 speeches s. have spoken

SINNETH.

1 John 3:6 whoso. abid. in him s.
  not, whoso. s. hath not seen
  8 devil s. from the beginning
  5:18 whoso. is born of G. s. not

SINNING.

Gen. 20:6 I withheld thee fr. s.
Lev. 6:3 man does, s. therein

SINS.

1 K. 14:16 give Is. up bec. of s.
  15:3 Abij. walked in s. of Reho.
  30 smote N. bec. of s. of Jero.
  16:13 s. of Baasha, and s. of El.
  31 light thing to wa. in s. of J.
2 K. 3:3 Jeho. cleaved to s. of J.
  10:29 from s. of Jeroboam Jehu
  13:6 Is. departed not fr. s. of J.
  17:22 Is. walked in s. of Jerob.
  24:3 remove Ju. for s. of Mana.
2 Chr. 28:10 are th. not wi. y. s.?
Neh. 1:6 confess the s. of Israel
Job 13:23 how many are my s.?
Ps. 19:13 keep thy servant fr. s.
  25:7 remem. not s. of my youth
Prov. 5:22 hold. with cords of s.
  10:12 strifes, love covereth all s.
  28:13 that covereth s. not prosp.
Is. 40:2 received double for her s.
  43:24 ma. me to serve wi. thy s.
  25 blot out, not remem. thy s.
  44:22 blot. out as a cloud thy s.
Jer. 15:13 I give to spoil for s.
  30:14 bec. thy s. increased, 15

50:20 s. of Judah sought
Lam. 3:39 for punishm. of his s.
  4:13 s. of her proph. and priests
  22 Edom, he will discov. thy s.
Ezek. 16:51 S. committed thy s.
  52 bear thine own shame for s.
  18:14 that seeth his father's s.
  21 if wicked turn from his s.
  23:49 shall bear s. of your idols
  33:16 none of his s. be mention.
Dan. 9:24 make end of s.
Mic. 1:5 for s. of house of Israel
  6:13 making desol. bec. of thy s.
Mat. 26:28 shed for remissi. of s.
Luke 24:47 remis. of s. preached
John 9:34 altogether born in s.
  20:23 s. ye remit, whose s. reta.
Acts 22:16 wash away thy s.
Rom. 7:5 s. did work in members
Eph. 2:1 who were dead in s. 5
Col. 2:11 putti. off the body of s.
1 Tim. 5:22 partakers of men's s.
  24 men's s. opened beforehand
Heb. 2:17 reconcilia. for s. of pe.
  5:1 gifts and sacrifices for s.
  7:27 for his own s. for people's
  9:28 Ch. off. to bear s. of many
  10:4 blood of goats take away s.
  12 offered one sacrifice for s.
Jam. 5:20 and hide multit. of s.
1 Pet. 2:24 dead to s. live to righ.
  3:18 Christ once suffered for s.
  4:8 charity cover multitude of s.
2 Pet. 1:9 was purged from his s.
1 John 2:2 the s. of whole world
Rev. 18:4 be not partak. of her s.
  5 her s. have reach. unto heav.

My SINS.

Ps. 51:9 hide thy face from my s.
  69:5 O G. my s. not hid fr. thee
Is. 38:17 cast my s. behind back

Our SINS.

1 Sam. 12:19 added to our s.
2 Chr. 28:13 int. to add to our s.
Neh. 9:37 ki. over us bec. of o. s.
Ps. 79:9 purge away our s.
  90:8 e. s. in light of countenance
  103:10 not dealt accord. to o. s.
Is. 59:12 our s. testify against us
Ezek. 33:10 if our s. be on us
Dan. 9:16 bec. of o. s. peo. beco.

1 Cor. 15:3 Christ died for our s.
Gal. 1:4 gave himself for our s.
Heb. 1:3 himself purged our s.
1 Pet. 2:24 his own self bare o. s.
1 John 1:9 if we confess our s.
3:5 manifest. to take away o. s.
Rev. 1:5 washed us from our s.

Their SINS.

Lev. 16:16 transgression in th. s.
Num. 16:26 consumed in all t. s.
1 K. 14:22 provoked with their s.
16:2 prov. me to anger with t. s.
Neh. 9:2 Israel confessed their s.
Is. 58:1 show house of Jacob t. s.
Jer. 14:10 vis. t. s. Hos. 8:13; 9:9
Mic. 7:19 cast all t. s. into sea
Mat. 1:21 save his peo. from t. s.
3:6 bapt. confes. t. s. Mark 1:5
Mark 4:12 t. s. should be forgiv.
Luke 1:77 salva. by remis. of t. s.
Rom. 11:27 shall take away t. s.
1 Thes. 2:16 to fill up t. s. alway
Heb. 8:12 I w. be merciful to t. s.
10:17 th. s. remember no more

Your SINS.

Lev. 16:30 may be clean fr. y. s.
26:18 punish you for y. s. 24, 28
Deut. 9:18 nor drink, bec. of y. s.
Jos. 24:19 G. will not forgi. y. s.
Is. 1:18 tho' your s. be as scarlet
59:2 your s. have hid his face
Jer. 5:25 y. s. withholden good
Ezek. 21:24 in doings y. s. appe.
Amos 5:12 know y. trans. and s.
John 8:21 seek me, die in y. s. 24
Acts 3:19 repent, that y. s. may
1 Cor. 15:17 raised, ye are in y. s.
Col. 2:13 you being dead in y. s.
1 John 2:12 y. s. are forgiven you

SISTER.

Mat. 12:50 same is brother, s.
John 19:25 stood by cross m.'s s.
Acts 23:16 Paul's s. son heard of
1 Cor. 7:15 s. is not under bond.
Col. 4:10 Marcus s. son to Barna.
2 John 13 children of thy elect s.

SISTERS.

Mat. 13:56 s. with us? Mark 6:3
1 Tim. 5:2 int. as s. with purity

SIT.

Mat. 8:11 many sh. s. with Abr.

20:21 sons s. one on thy ri. hand
23 but to s. on my right hand,
Mark 10:37, 40

SIX cities.

Num. 35:6 be s. c. for ref. 13, 15

SIX cubits.

1 Sam. 17:4 Goliah's height s. c.
Ezek. 40:5 measuring-reed of s. c.
41:1 measured posts s. c. broad
8 foundations were s. great c.
Dan. 3:1 breadth of image s. c.

SIX months.

Luke 4:25 heav. was shut three
years and s. m. Jam. 5:17

SIX sheep.

Neh. 5:18 prep. daily s. choice s.

SIX sons.

Gen. 30:20 I have borne s. s.
1 Chr. 8:38 Azel had s. s. 9:44

SIX things.

Prov. 6:16 s. t. doth Lord hate

SIX times.

2 K. 13:19 ha. smitten five or s. t.

SIX troubles.

Job 5:19 sh. deliver thee in s. tr.

SIX water-pots.

John 2:6 were set there s. wa.-p.

SIX wings.

Is. 6:2 seraphim, each had s. w.
Rev. 4:8 4 beasts had each s. w.

SKIN.

Job 2:4 s. for s. for all a man hath
7:5 s. broken, and loathsome

SLAIN, passive.

Prov. 22:13 sloth. sai. I sh. be s.
24:11 deliv. those ready to be s.
Is. 10:4 they shall fall under s.
32:2 thy s. men not s. with sw.
Is. 26:21 earth no more cov. her s.

SLAUGHTER.

Zec. 11:4 sai. L. Feed flock of s.
7 I will feed flock of s.
Rom. 8:36 counted as sheep to s.

SLAY.

Deut. 19:6 avenger pursue and s.
Jos. 13:22 Israel did s. Balaam
Prov. 1:32 turn. of simple sh. s.
Is. 11:4 with breath shall he s.

To SLAY.

Gen. 18:25 far fr. thee to s. right.
22:10 Abra. stretched hand to s.

227

37:18 they conspired to s. him
Ex. 2:15 Ph. sought to s. Moses
21:14 if come on neighbor to s.
Deut. 9:28 brou. out to s. them
27:25 taketh reward to s. inno.
1 Sam. 5:10 brou. the ark to s. us
19:5 why then sin, to s. David?
11 S. went to watch and s. him
2 Sam. 3:37 not of king to s. Ab.
21:2 Saul sought to s. them
1 K. 17:18 art come to s. my son?
18:9 deliv. me to Ahab to s. me
2 Chr. 20:23 utterly to s. and des.
Neh. 6:10 to s. th. in night to s.
Ps. 37:14 to s. such as be upright
32 watcheth righte. seek. to s.
Jer. 15:3 appoint sw. to s. dogs
18:23 know. their counsel to s.
Ezek. 13:19 to s. souls th. should
John 5:16 Jews, sou. to s. him
Acts 5:33 took counsel to s. apos.
9:29 they went about to s. him
Rev. 9:15 prep. to s. third part
SLEEP, Substantive.
Zec. 4:1 man wakened out of s.
Mat. 1:24 J. being raised from s.
SLEEP, Verb.
Gen. 28:11 Jacob lay down to s.
John 11:12 if he s. he sh. do well
1 Cor. 11:30 for th. cause many s.
15:51 we shall not all s.
1 Thes. 4:14 who s. in Je. will G.
5:6 let us not s. as do others
7 they that s. s. in the night.
10 that whether we wake or s.
SLEW.
Rom. 7:11 commandment s. me
1 John 3:12 C. who s. his brother
SLOTHFUL.
Jud. 18:9 be not s. to poss. land
Prov. 12:24 s. shall be under tri.
Rom. 12:11 not s. in business
Heb. 6:12 ye be not s. but follow.
SLUGGARD.
Prov. 6:6 go to the ant, thou s.
SMITE.
Gen. 32:8 to one comp. and s. it
Ex. 7:17 I will s. upon waters
12:23 not suffer destroyer to s.
17:6 thou shalt s. rock in Horeb
21:26 if a man s. eye of servant

Mat. 5:39 wh. sh. s. th. on cheek
SMITE, referred to God.
Zec. 9:4 L. will s. her power
12:4 I will s. ev. horse and rider
13:7 awake, O sword, s. Sheph.
Mat. 26:31; Mark 14:27
14:12 plague wherewith L. s. 18
SMOTE.
Mat. 26:51 Peter s. off his er
68 who is he s. thee, Lu. 22:64
SNARE.
Ps. 69:22 let their table become
a s. unto them. Rom. 11:9
91:3 deliver thee fr. s. of fowler
1 Tim. 3:7 lest he fall in s.
6:8 rich, fall into a s. and lusts
2 Tim. 2:26 may recover out of s.
SNOW.
Is. 1:18 sins as scar. white as s.
SOBER.
2 Cor. 5:13 whether we be s. it is
1 Thes. 5:6 let us watch and be s.
8 let us who are of day be s.
1 Tim. 3:2 bis. mu. be s. Tit. 1:8
11 deacons' wives must be s.
Tit. 2:2 that aged men be s.
4 teach young women to be s.
1 Pet. 1:13 gird loi. of mind, be s.
4:7 be ye s. watch unto prayer
5:8 be s. be vigilant, bec. you
SOBERLY.
Rom. 12:3 think s. acc. to faith
Tit. 2:12 teach. we should live s.
SOBER-MINDED.
Tit. 2:6 exh. yo. men to be s.-m
SOBERNESS.
Acts 26:25 speak forth words of s.
SOBRIETY.
1 Tim. 2:9 adom themse. with s.
15 continue in holiness with s.
SODOM.
Gen. 13:10 bef. Lord destroy. S.
Mat. 10:15 for land of S. 11:24;
Mark 6:11; Luke 10:12
Jude 7 even as S. and Gomorrah
Rev. 11:8 spiritually called S.
SOLD.
Gen. 25:33 Esau s. his birthright
Rom. 7:14 carnal, s. under sin
1 Cor. 10:25 whats. is s. in sham.
Heb. 12:16 for one morsel s. birt.

SOLDIER.

2 Tim. 2:3 end, as a good s. of C.
4 hath chosen him to be a s.

SOLDIERS.

2 Chr. 25:13 s. fell upon cities
Ezr. 8:22 I ashamed to regu. s.
Is. 15:4 armed s. of Moab cry
Mat. 8:9 having s. und. Luke 7:8
Acts 12:4 delivered Peter to s.

SOLOMON.

2 Sam. 5:14 there was born to
   David S. 1 Chr. 3:5; 14:4
12:24 he called his name S. and
1 K. 1:10 S. his brother, 19, 26
12 S. sh. reign after me, 17, 30
21 I and my son S. shall be
34 God save king S. 39, 43
37 wi. D. even so be he wi. S.
47 God make name of S. better
51 S. swear to me that he will
2:1 David charged S. his son, 23
3:1 S. made affinity with Phar.
3 S. loved Lord; 10 S. asked
1 K. 3:5 Lord appear to S. 9:2;
   2 Chr. 1:7; 7:12
4:22 S. provision for one day
29 God gave S. wisdom, 5:12
34 hear wis. of S. from all the
   kings, Mat. 12:42; Luke 11:31
5:1 Hiram sent servants to S.
13 king s. raised a levy out of
6:14 S. built house and finished
   it, 2 Chr. 7:11; Acts 7:47
John 10:23 Je. walked in S. por.
Acts 3:11 ran to them to S. porch
5:12 with one accord in S. por.

SON.

Gen. 17:16 I will give thee a s. of
   Sarah, 19; 18:10, 14
Ruth 4:13 Ruth bare a s.
Mic. 7:6 s. dishonreth father
Mal. 1:6 s. honoreth his father
Mat. 1:21 bring forth s. Luke 1:31
9:2 s. be of go. cheer, Mark 2:5
10:37 he that loveth s. or daug.
11:27 know. S. but Father, nor
   Father save S. Luke 10:22
13:55 the carpen.'s s. Mark 6:3;
   Luke 4:22
16:16 thou art Christ, S. of God
21:28 s. go work in my viney.

22:42 of Christ? whose s. is he?
Mark 12:6 having one s. beloved
13:32 hour knoweth not the S.
14:61 Christ, S. of the Blessed?
Luke 1:13 Elisab, shall bear a s.
32 be called S. of the Highest
3:23 Jesus s. of Joseph, s. of H.
7:12 only s. of his mother
10:6 if s. of peace be there
11:11 if a s. ask bread of any
12:53 father divided against s.
Luke 15:13 younger s. gathered
16:25 s. remember, in thy lifet.
19:9 forasmuch as he is s. of A.
John 1:18 only S. in bosom of F.
3:35 Father loveth the S. 5:20
36 beli. on S. believeth not S.
5:19 S. can do noth. of himself
21 S. quicken, whom he will
22 committed all judgm. to S.
23 men should honor S. he th.
   honor, not S. honor. not F.
26 given to S. to have life
6:40 ev. one who seeth the S.
42 is not this Jes. s. of Joseph
8:35 s. abideth; 9:19 is this s.?
36 if S. shall make you free
9:20 we kn. that this is our s.
14:13 Fa. may be glorified in S.
17:12 none lost but s. of perdit.
Acts 4:36 Barnabas, s. of consol.
23:6 Pharisee, s. of a Pharisee
16 Paul's sister's s. heard of
Rom. 9:9 Sarah shall have a s.
1 Cor. 15:28 then S. himself sub.
Gal. 4:7 no more serv. but a s.
Phil. 2:22 as s. he serv. in gospel
Col. 4:10 Marcus sister's s. to B.
2 Thes. 2:3 man of sin, s. of per.
1 Tim. 1:18 commit to thee s. T.
Heb. 1:5 he shall be to me a s.
8 to S. he saith, Thy throne
3:6 Christ as a s. over his own
5:8 tho' he were a s. yet learned
7:28 word of the oath maketh s.
11:24 refu. to be called s. of Ph.
12:6 scourg. every s. he receiv.
1 John 2:22 antic. deni. F. and S.
23 whosoever denieth the S.
   the same hath not the Fath.
24 continue in S. and in Fath.

4:14 Father sent S. to be Savi.
5:12 he that hath S. hath life
2 John 3 L. Je. Ch. S. of Father
9 hath both the Father and S.

SON of God.

Dan. 3:25 fourth is like s. of G.
Mat. 8:29 thou S. of G. Luke 8:28
14:33 of a truth th. art S. of G.
26:63 whether be Ch. S. of G.
27:43 he said, I am the S. of G.
54 was S. of G. Mark 15:39
Mark 3:11 art S. of G. John 1:49
Luke 1:35 sh. be called S. of G.
3:38 s. of Adam, was s. of G.
4:41 crying, Thou art Christ the
S. of G. John 6:69; 11:27
22:70 art th. then the S. of G.?
John 1:34 this is the S. of God
3:18 the only begotten S. of G.
5:25 shall hear voice of S. of G.
9:35 dost thou beli. on S. of G.?
10:36 I said, I am the S. of God
11:4 that S. of G. might be glo.
19:7 he made himself S. of God
20:31 beli. Je. is C. the S. of G.
Acts 8:37 J. Christ is the S. of G.
9:20 Christ, that he is S. of G.
Rom. 1:4 declared to be S. of G.
2 Cor. 1:19 the S. of G. was not
Gal. 2:20 by faith of S. of God
Eph. 4:13 knowledge of S. of G.
Heb. 4:14 high-pr. J. the S. of G.
6:6 crucify to themsel. S. of G
7:3 made like to the S. of God
10:29 trod. under foot S. of God
1 John 3:8 for this purp. S. of G.
4:15 shall confess Je. is S. of G.
5:5 believeth Jesus is S. of God
10 that believeth on S. of God
13 believe on name of S. of G.
20 know that S. of G. is come
Rev. 2:18 write, saith S. of God

His SON.

Mat. 21:37 last of all sent his s.
22:2 made a marr. for his s.
45 how is he then h. s.? Mark
12:37; Luke 20:44
John 3:16 gave h. only begot. S.
17 God sent not his S. to con.
Acts 3:13 God hath glori. h. S. J.
26 God having raised up h. S.

Rom. 1:9 serve in gospel of h. S.
8:3 God sending his own S. in
32 that spared not his own S.
Gal. 1:16 it pleas. G. to rev. h. S.
4:4 God sent forth his S.
1 Thes. 1:10 to wait for his S.
Heb. 1:2 spoken to us by his S.
Jam. 2:21 had offered Isaac his s.
1 John 1:3 fel. is with F. and h. S.
7 blood of Jes. Ch. h. S. clea.
3:23 believe on name of his S.
5:9 he hath testified of h. S.
10 beli. not rec. G. gave of h. S.
11 this life is in his S.
20 we are in him, even his S.

My SON.

2 Sam. 18:33 king said, O my s.
Absal.
Mat. 3:17 my beloved S. 17:5
Mark 9:17 I have brought my s.
Luke 9:38 Mast. look upon my s.
15:24 for this my s. was dead
1 Tim. 1:2 to Timothy my own s.
2 Tim. 2:1 my s. be stro. in grace
Tit. 1:4 to Titus mine own s.
Phile. 10 I beseech th. for my s.
Rev. 21:7 his God, he sh. be my s.

Thy SON.

Gen. 22:2 take t. s. thine only s.
24:5 must I needs bring thy s.?
37:32 know whe. it be t. s. coat
48:2 behold, thy s. Jos. cometh
Ex. 10:2 tell in the ears of thy s.
13:8 thou shalt show thy s.
14 wh. t. s. asketh, Deut. 6:20
Deut. 6:21 shalt say unto thy s.
7:3 nor daughter take unto t. s.
4 they will turn away thy s.
Jud. 6:30 bring out t. s. that he
8:22 rule over us, thou, thy s.
1 Sam. 16:19 send me David t. s.
1 K. 1:12 save life of thy s. Solo.
3:22 dead is t. s. 23 and thy s.
5:5 thy s. whom I will set upon
11:12 rend it out of hand of t. s.
17:13 for thee and for thy s.
19 give me t. s. 23 t. s. liveth
2 K. 4:36 he said, Take up thy s.
6:28 gi. t. s. that we may eat, 29
1 K. 16:7 I am thy ser. and thy s.
Prov. 19:18 chasten thy s. while

29:17 correct thy s. and he shall
Luke 9:41 Je. said, Bring thy s.
15:19 no more wor. to be t. s. 21
30 soon as this t. s. was come
John 4:50 thy s. liveth, 51, 53
17:1 glorify t. S. that t. S. may
19:26 saith, Woman, beh. thy s.

SONG.
Ex. 15:1 then sang Moses this s.
Ps. 28:7 with my s. will I praise
Rev. 5:9 they sung a new s. 14:3
14:3 no man could learn that s.
15:3 the s. of Moses and s. of L.

SONGS.
Col. 3:16 hymns, and spiritual s.

SONS.
Gen. 9:19 the three s. of Noah
Est. 9:10 ten s. of Ha. slew they
13 Ha.'s ten s. be hanged, 14
Ps. 89:6 who amo. s. of mighty?
144:12 our s. may be as plants

SONS of God.
Gen. 6:2 s. of G. saw daughters
Job 1:6 s. of G. came to pres. 2:1
38:7 s. of G. shouted for joy
Hos. 1:10 ye are s. of living God
John 1:12 power to bec. s. of G.
Rom. 8:14 Sp. of God, are s. of G.
19 manifestation of s. of God
Phil. 2:15 be harmless, s. of God
1 John 3:1 we be called s. of G.
2 beloved, now are we s. of G.

SORCERIES.
Rev. 9:21 nei. repented of th. s.
18:23 by s. were nations deceiv.

SORROW.
John 16:6 s. ha. fill. your hearts
20 your s. shall be turn. to joy
21 wo. when in travail hath s.
22 and ye now therefore ha. s.
Rom. 9:2 I have s. in my heart
3 Cor. 2:3 I sho. have s. from th.
7 swallo. up with overmuch s.
7:10 godly s. work. repentance,
but s of world worke. death
Phil. 2:27 lest I have s. upon s.
Rev. 18:7 s. give her, see no s.
21:4 be no more death, neith. s.

SORROW, Verb.
Jer. 31:12 shall not s. any more
51:29 land shall tremble and s.

Hos. 8:10 theyshall s. for burden
1 Thes. 4:13 s. not as others

SORROWFUL.
1 Sam. 1:15 woman of a s. spirit
2 Cor. 6:10 s. yet always rejoici.
Phil. 2:28 I may be the less s.

SOUL.
Gen. 2:7 man became a living s.
34:8 s. of son longeth for daugh.
35:18 as her s. was in departing
Lev. 4:2 if a s. sin thro' ignoran.
5:1 if a s. sin, and hear sweari.
6:2 if s. lie; 17:12 no s. eat blood
17:11 blood mak. atonem. for s.
22:11 if priest buy s.
23:30 whatso. s. doeth any work
Num. 21:4 s. of peo. discouraged
30:4 every bond she hath bound
her s. 5, 6, 7, 8, 9, 10, 11, 12, 13
31:28 one s. of five hund. for L.
Deut. 11:13 serve him with yo. s.
18 lay up th. words in your s.
13:3 wheth. you love L. with all
your s. Jos. 22:5; 1 K. 2:4
1 Sam. 18:1 s. of Jonathan knit
to s. of David
30:6 s. of the people was griev.
2 Sam. 5:8 blind hated of D.'s s.
13:39 s. of D. longed to go to A.
1 K. 8:48 return to thee with s.
17:21 let this child's s. come
2 K. 4:27 let alone, her s. is vex.
23:3 keep commandm. with s.
1 Chr. 22:19 set yo. s. to seek L.
2 Chr. 6:38 if they return with s.
15:12 seek the L. with their s.
Job 3:20 life giv. to bitter in s.?
12:10 hand is s. of every thing
16:4 if yo. s. were in my soul's
24:12 s. of the wounded crieth
Ps. 19:7 law perfect converting s.
33:19 deliver their s. from death
34:22 L. redeem. s. of his serva.
49:8 redemption of s. precious
72:14 he shall redeem their s.
78:50 spared not th. s. fr. death
86:4 rejoice s. of thy serv. O L.
94:21 gather against s. of right.
106:15 sent leanness to their s.
107:18 their s. abhorreth all me.
26 th. s. melted bec. of trouble

Prov. 10:3 not suff. s. of righteo.
11:25 liberal s. shall be made fat
13:2 s. of transgressors sh. eat
19 desire accom. is sweet to s.
16:24 pleasant words sweet to s.
19:2 s. without knowl. not good
15 idle s. shall suffer hunger
21:10 s. of wicked desireth evil
22:23 Lord will spoil s. of those
25:13 he refresheth s. of masters
27:7 full s. loathe. honey-comb.
to hungry s. bitter is sweet
Is. 3:9 woe to their s. they have
32:6 make empty s. of hungry
55:2 let yo. s. delight in fatness
3 hear, and your s. shall live
58:10 if thou satisfy afflicted s.
66:3 th. s. delighteth in abomi.
Jer. 4:10 the swo. reacheth the s.
20:13 he delivered s. of the poor
31:12 their s. shall be as a gard.
38:16 L. liveth, made us this s.
Lam. 1:11 for meat to relieve s.
2:12 wh. their s. was poured out
3:25 the Lord is good to the s.
Ezek. 18:4 as s. of father, so s. of
son, the s. that sinneth, 20
24:21 what your s. pitieth shall
Hos. 9:4 s. shall not come into
Mat. 10:28 fear th. can destroy s.
Mark 12:33 lo. him wi. he, and s.
Acts 2:43 fear came on every s.
3:23 eve. s. which will not hear
4:32 multitude believ. of one s.
Rom. 13:1 let every s. be subject
1 Thes. 5:23 that your s. and bo.
Heb. 10:39 believe to sving of s.
Jam. 5:20 he sh. save a s. fr. dea.
1 Pet. 2:11 lusts war agai, the s.
2 Pet. 2:8 Lot vexed righteous s.
Rev. 16:3 ev. living s. died in sea

His SOUL
Gen. 34:3 his s. clave to Dinah
Ex. 30:12 give ransom for his s.
Num. 30:2 sw. oath to bind h. s.
Jud. 10:16 his s. was grieved for
16:16 so that his s. was vexed
2 K. 23:25 Josiah turned to Lord
with all his s. 2 Chr. 34:31
Job 14:22 his s. within him
21:25 dieth in bittemess of h. s.

23:13 what his s. desireth, even
27:8 when God tak. away his s.
31:30 sin, by wish, curse to h. s.
33:18 keepeth back h. s. fr. pit
22 his s. draw. near unto grave
28 will deliver his s. from, 30
Ps. 11:5 violence, his s. hateth
24:4 who had not lifted up his s.
25:13 his s. shall dwell at ease
49:18 wh. he lived he bless. h. s.
89:48 sh. he deliver his s. from?
109:31 save fr. th. condemn h. s.
Prov. 6:30 if steal to satisfy h. s.
16:17 his way, preserveth h. s.
21:23 his mouth. keepeth his s.
22:5 that doth keep his s. shall
23:14 shalt deliver his s. fr. hell
29:10 but the just seek his s.
Ec. 2:24 shou. make his s. enjoy
6:2 wanteth nothing for his s.
3 his s. be not filled with good
Is. 29:8 awak. and his s. empty
44:20 he cannot deliver his s.
53:10 ma. his s. an offer. for sin
11 see of travail of his s.
12 poured out h. s. unto death
Jer. 50:19 his s. shall be satisfied
51:6 deliver every man his s. 45
Ezek. 18:27 right, he sh. sa. h. s.
33:5 waming, shall deliver h. s.
Hab. 2:4 his s. that is lifted up
Mat. 16:26 lose h. own s. give in
exchange for s.? Mark 8:37
Acts 2:31 his s. not left in hell

My SOUL.
Gen. 12:13 my s. sh. live because
19:20 let me escape, my s. shall
27:4 my s. may bless thee, 25
49:6 O my s. come not into their
Lev. 26:11 my s. sh. not abh. 30
1 Sam. 1:15 poured out my s. be.
24:11 thou huntest my s. to
26:21 beca. my s. was precious
2 Sam. 4:9 Lord who hath redeemed my s. 1 K. 1:29
Job 6:7 the things my s. refused
9:21 yet would I not kn. my s.
10:1 my s. is weary of life, I will
speak bitterness of my s.
19:2 how lo. will ye vex my s.
27:2 Alm. who hath vexed my s.

232

30:15 they pursue my s. as wind
16 my s. is poured out upon
25 was not my s. gri. for poor?
Ps. 3:2 who say of my s. There is
6:3 my s. is sore vex. but, O. L.
4 deliver my s. 17:13; 22:20;
116:4; 120:2
13:2 sh. I take couns. in my s.?
16:10 not leave my s. Acts 2:27
23:3 he restoreth my s. he lead.
25:1 unto th. O L. do I lift my s.
20 O keep my s. and deliver me
26:9 gather not my s. with sin.
30:3 brought my s. from grave
31:7 hast known my s. in adver.
34:2 my s. sh. make boast in L.
35:3 say unto my s. I am thy sa.
4 put to shame that seek my s.
7 have digged a pit for my s.
9 my s. shall be joyful in Lord
13 I humbled my s. with fast.
41:4 heal my s. I have sinned
42:4 I pour out my s. in me
5 cast down O my s.? 11; 43:5
6 O my G. my s. is cast down
54:4 L. is with that upho. my s.
55:18 delivered my s. in peace
56:6 when they wait for my s.
13 thou hast delivered my s.
57:1 be merciful, my s. trusteth
4 my s. is amo. lions and I lie
6 my s. is bowed down
59:3 they lie in wait for my s.
62:1 my s. waiteth upon God
5 my s. wait thou only upon G.
63:8 my s. followeth hard after
9 that seek my s. to destroy it
66:16 what G. ha. done for my s.
69:1 wa. are come in unto my s.
18 draw nigh to my s.
71:23 my s. shall rejoice
77:2 my sore ran, my s. refused
Ps. 84:2 my s. longeth for the L.
86:2 preserve my s. I am holy
4 O Lord, do I lift my s. 143:8
13 thou hast deliv. my s. from
88:3 my s. is full of troubles
14 why castest thou off my s.?
94:17 my s. had dwelt in silence
103:1 bless the Lord, O my s. 2,
22; 104:1, 35

109:20 them th. speak ag. my s.
116:7 ret. unto thy rest, O my s.
8 thou hast delivered my s.
119:20 my s. break. for longing
109 my s. is continu. in hand
129 therefore doth my s. keep
175 let my s. live and it shall
120:2 deliver my s. O Lord
6 my s. dw. wi. him that hate.
130:5 wait for the Lord, my s. 6
138:3 strengthen me in my s.
139:14 that my s. knoweth well
142:4 no man cared for my s.
7 bring my s. out of prison
143:11 bring my s. out of troub.
146:1 praise the Lord, O my s.
Ec. 7:28 which yet my s. seeketh
Cant. 1:7 wh. my s. lo. 3:1, 2, 3, 4
5:6 my s. failed when he spake
Is. 1:14 new moons my s. hateth
26:9 with my s. have I desired
38:17 in love to my s. deliv. it
61:10 my s. sh. be joyful in God
Jer. 4:19 hast heard, O my s.
5:9 my s. be avenged? 29; 9:9
6:8 instructed, lest my s. depart
12:7 beloved of my s. into hand
18:20 they dig. a pit for my s.
32:41 rej. over them my whole s.
Lam. 3:24 L. my por. saith my s.
58 pleased the auses of my s.
Mic. 6:7 body for sin of my s.?
7:1 my s. desired first ripe fruit
Mat. 12:18 in wh. my s. is pleas.
26:38 my s. is sor. Mark 14:34
Luke 1:46 my s. doth magnify L.
12:19 I will say to my s.
John 12:27 is my s. troubled
2 Cor. 1:23 for record upon my s.
Heb. 10:88 my s. sh. have no pic.
Our SOUL.
Num. 11:6 our s. is dried away
Ps. 33:20 our s. waiteth for Lord
44:25 our s. is bowed down
66:9 God who holdeth our s.
124:4 stre. had gone over our s.
Is. 26:8 the desire of our s. is
Own SOUL.
Deut. 13:6 friend as thine o. s.
Ps. 22:29 none can keep his o. s.
Prov. 6:32 destroyeth his own s.

8:36 sinneth, wrongeth his o. s.
19:16 commandm. keep. his o. s.
20:2 king, sinneth aga. his o. s.
29:24 partner with thief ha. o. s.
Mat. 16:26 if he shall gain world
and lose his o. s.? Mark 8:36
Luke 2:35 sword pierce thy o. s.

That SOUL.

Lev. 17:10 set face ag. t. s. 20:6
22:3 that s. shall be cut off from
23:30 that s. will I destroy from
Num. 15:31 t. s. sh. utter. be cut

Thy SOUL.

Gen. 26:19 thy s. may bless, 31
Deut. 4:9 keep thy s. diligently
29 if seek him with all thy s.
6:5 L. thy G. with all t. s. 30:6
10:12 serve Lord with all t. s.
12:15 whatso. t. s. lusteth, 14:26
26:16 do wi. t. s. 30:2 obey
with thy s.
30:2 obey wi. thy heart and t. s.
10 turn to Lord with all thy s.
1 Sam. 2:16 as much as t. s. desi.
20:4 whatsoever t. s. desireth
23:20 according to desire of t. s.
25:29 man risen to pursue t. s.
1 K. 11:37 reign according t. s.
Ps. 121:7 L. shall preserve thy s.
Prov. 2:10 know. is pleas. to t. s.
3:22 shall be life to thy s.
19:18 let not thy s. spare
22:25 and get a snare to thy s.
24:12 he that keepeth t. s. doth
14 knowl. of wisdom be to t. s.
29:17 he sh. give delight to t. s.
Is. 51:23 have said to t. s. Bow
58:10 draw out thy s. to hungry
11 Lord shall satisfy thy s.
Jer. 14:19 hath thy s. loathed Z.?
38:17 forth, thy s. shall live, 20
Ezek. 3:19 deliv. thy s. 21; 33:9
Hab. 2:10 hast sinned ag. thy s.
Mat. 22:37 love L. with all thy s.
Mark 12:30; Luke 10:27
Luke 12:20 thy s. be requ. of thee
3 John 2 even as thy s. prosper.
Rev. 18:14 fruits t. s. lust. after

SOULS.

Gen. 12:5 A. took s. th. had got
46:26 s. that came into Egypt

27 sons of Joseph in Egy. were
two s. all the s. of the house
of Jacob were 70 s. Ex. 1:5
Ex. 12:4 a lamb according to s.
30:15 atonement for your s. 16;
Lev. 17:11; Num. 31:50
Lev. 18:29 s. that commit them
20:25 not make your s. abomin.
Num. 16:38 sin. ag. their own s.
30:9 wherewith ha. bound th. s.
Jos. 23:14 know in all your s.
1 Sam. 25:29 s. of ene. shall sling
Ps. 72:13 shall save s. of needy
97:10 preserveth s. of his saints
Prov. 11:30 that win. s. is wise
14:25 a true witness deliver. s.
Is. 57:16 spi should fail, and s.
Jer. 2:34 in thy skirts is bl. of s.
6:16 rest for your s. Mat. 11:29
26:19 procure evil against our s.
44:7 why com. evil ag. your s.?
Lam. 1:19 sought meat to th. s.
Ezek. 7:19 sh. not satisfy their s.
13:18 hunt s. hunt s. of peo. 20
19 slay s. that should not die
14:14 should deliver their own s.
18:4 s. are mine; 22:25 devou. s.
Acts 2:41 added to them 3,000 s.
7:14 Jacob and his kindred 75 s.
14:22 confirming s. of disciples
15:24 troubled you, subvert. s.
27:37 we. in all in the ship 276 s.
1 Thes. 2:8 imparted our s. to you
Heb. 13:17 they watch for your s.
Jam. 1:21 word able to save yo. s.
1 Pet. 1:22 have purified your s.
3:20 that is, eight s. were saved
4:19 commit keep. of s. to him
Rev. 6:9 I saw s. of them slain
18:13 no man buyeth s. of men
20:4 I saw s. of them beheaded

SOUND, Adjective.

Tit. 1:9 be able by s. doctrine
13 that they may be s. in faith
2:1 things which become s.
doctrine
Tit. 2:2 th. aged men be s. in fa.
8 s. speech cannot be condem.

SOUTH.

Mat. 12:42 queen of s. shall rise
Luke 13:29 come fr. s. to sit do.

234

Acts 8:26 arise, and go toward s.
Rev. 21:13 on the s. three gates
SOW, Verb.
Luke 12:24 ravens nei. s. nor reap
19:21 reap. thou didst not s. 22
SOWETH.
Prov. 6:14 s. discord; 19 s. disc.
  11:18 that s. righteousn. a rew.
  16:28 a froward man s. strife
  22:8 s. iniquity. reap vanity
Mat. 13:37 that s. good seed is S.
Mark 4:14 sower s. the word
John 4:36 he that s. and reapeth
  37 true, one s. another reapeth
2 Cor. 9:6 s. sparingly, s. bounti.
Gal. 6:7 whatsoever a man s.
  8 that s. to flesh, reap corrup.
SPACE.
Rev. 14:20 blood by s. of 1,600 fur.
  17:10 must continue a short s.
SPARE.
Rom. 11:21 lest he also s. not
SPARED.
2 Pet. 2:4 if god s. not angels
  5 s. not old world, saved Noah
SPEAK.
Mat. 10:19 ye shall s. Mark 13:11
  20 not ye that s. Mark 13:11
12:34 can ye being evil s. good?
Act 2:11 hear them s. in tongu.
26:1 P. thou art permitted to s.
Rom. 15:18 I will not dare to s.
1 Cor. 3:1 I could not s. to you as
  12:30 do all s. with? 14:23 all s.
  14:35 sha. for women to s. in ch.
2 Cor. 2:17 in sight of God s. we
  4:13 we believe and therefore s.
  12:19 we s. before God in Christ
1 Thes. 1:8 so that we need not s.
  2:4 so we s. not as pleasing men
Tit. 3:2 put th. in mind to s. evil
Jam. 1:19 let ev. man be sl. to s.
1 John 4:5 theref. s. they of world
SPEAK, imperatively.
Jam. 2:12 so s. ye and do, as th.
I SPEAK.
Rom. 3:5 God unrighte.? Is. as
  6:19 I s. after manner, Gal. 3:15
1 Cor. 14:18 I s. with tongues
  19 I had rather s. five words
2 Cor. 11:17 that wh. I s. I s. not

Eph. 6:20 that therein I may s.
I will SPEAK, or will I.
Ezek. 2:1 stand on feet and I w. s.
  12:25 I will s. and word I speak
1 Cor. 14:21 wi. other lips w. I s.
SPEAR.
John 19:34 one of the soldiers
  with a s. pierced his side
SPECKLED.
Gen. 30:32 removing the s. cattle
SPIRIT.
Gen. 41:8 Phar.'s s. was troubled
  45:27 the s. of Jacob their fath.
Ex. 6:9 heark. not for angu. of s.
  35:21 whom his s. made willing
Num. 11:17 I will take of s. 25
  26 the s. rested on them
  29 L. wo. put his S. upon them
  14:24 he had ano. s. with him
  27:18 Jos. a man in whom is s.
Deut. 2:30 L. G. hardened his s.
Jos. 5:1 nor was th. s. in them
Jud. 15:19 drunk his s. came
1 Sam. 30:12 eaten his s. came
1 K. 10:5 no s. in her, 2 Chr. 9:4
  21:5 said, Why is thy s. so sad?
  22:21 th. came a s. 2 Chr. 18:20
2 K. 2:9 double portion of s. on
  15 s. of Elijah doth rest on El.
1 Chr. 5:26 Lord stirr. up s. of P.
  12:18 s came upon Amasai
  28:12 pattern of all he had by s.
Ezr. 1:5 wh. s. G. raised to go up
Neh. 9:30 by S. in thy prophets
Job 4:15 a s. passed bef. my face
  15:13 thou turnest thy s. ag. G.
  20:3 s. of my understanding
  26:4 whose s. came from thee?
  13 by his S. he garnished hea.
  32:8 there is a s. in man
  18 s. within me constraineth
  34:14 if he gather to hims. his s.
Ps. 32:2 in wh. s. there is no gu.
  51:10 renew right s. within me
  12 uphold me with thy free S.
  73:12 shall cut off s. of princes
  78:8 whose s. not stead. with G.
  104:30 thou sendest forth thy S.
  106:33 so they provoked his S.
  139:7 whit. sh. I go fr. thy S.?
  143:10 S. good, lead me to upr.

Prov. 14:29 he that is hasty of s.
15:4 perversen. is a breach in s.
16:18 haughty s. goeth bef. fall
Prov. 16:32 that rul. s. bet. th. he
18:14 s. of a man sust. infirmity
20:27 s. of a man is candle of L.
25:28 hath no rule over his s.
Ec. 3:21 s. of man, s. of beast
7:9 not hasty in s. to be angry
8:8 no power over s. to retain s.
10:4 if s. of ruler rise ag. thee
11:5 kno. not what is way of s.
12:7 the s. shall return to God
Is. 19:3 s. of Egypt shall fail
29:10 L. pour. on you s. of sleep
24 they th. erred in s. sh. come
31:3 their horses flesh and not s.
32:15 till S. be poured upon us
34:16 his s. it hath gathe. them
42:5 giveth s. to them that walk
48:16 L. G. and his S. hath sent
54:6 forsak. and grieved in s.
57:16 s. shall fail before me
61:1 S. of L. G. on me, Lu. 4:18
3 garment of praise for the s.
Jer. 51:11 L. raised s. of the king
Ezek. 1:12 whit. S. was to go, 20
2:2 the s. entered into me, 3:24
3:12 the s. took me up, 11:24
14 s. lifted me up, and I went
in heat of my s. 8:3; 11:1
13:3 proph. that follow own s.
21:7 every s. shall faint
Dan. 2:1 Nebuc. s. was troubled
4:8 in whom is S. of the holy
gods, 9, 18; 5:11, 14
5:12 excellent s. in Daniel, 6:3
Mic. 2:11 if man in s. and falseh.
Hag. 1:14 L. stirred s. of Zerub.
Zec. 7:12 sent his s. by prophets
12:1 form. s. of man within him
Mal. 2:15 had residue of S. 16
Mat. 4:1 Je. led up of S. Luke 4:1
14:26 say. It is a s. Mark 6:49
22:43 David in s. call him Lord?
26:41 s. is willing, Mark 14:38
Mark 1:10 S. descend. John 1:32
12 S. driveth him into wilder.
8:12 he sighed deeply in his s.
9:20 s. tare him; 26 s. cried
Luke 1:17 go before him in s.

80 child waxed st. in s. 2:40
2:27 he came by S. into temple
4:14 Je. returned in power of S.
8:55 her s. came ag. she arose
9:55 know not what s. ye are
10:21 in that hour J. rejoi. in s.
13:11 wom. had s. of infirmity
24:37 supp. they had seen a s.
39 s. ha. not flesh and bones
John 1:33 on wh. thou sh. see S.
3:34 G. giveth not S. by meas.
4:23 worship the Father in s.
24 G. is a S. worship him in
6:63 it is s. that quickeneth
words I speak, they are s.
7:39 spake of S. 11:33 groan. in
13:21 he was troubled in s.
Acts 2:4 spake as S. gave them
6:10 were not able to resist s.
8:29 the S. said to Philip, Go
10:19 S. said unto Peter, 11:12
11:28 Agabus signified by S.
16:7 the S. suffered them not
17:16 his s. was stir. within him
18:5 Paul was pressed in s.
25 and being fervent in the s.
20:22 bound in the S. to Jerusa.
21:4 said to Saul through the S.
23:8 Sadducees say th. is no s.
9 if a s. hath spoken to him
Rom. 1:4 Son of God accord. to s.
2:29 circumcis. is of heart in s.
8:1 walk not aft. flesh, but s. 4
2 law of s. of life made me free
5 after the S. things of the S.
9 flesh but s. if so be that S.
10 s. is life bec. of righteousn.
11 quick. your bodies by his S.
13 if ye through the S. mortify
16 S. beareth witn. with our s.
23 ourse. who have fruits of S.
26 S. also help. our infirmities;
but the S. maketh interces.
27 kno. what is the mind of S.
1 Cor. 2:4 in demonstration of S.
10 G. hath revealed th. unto us
by S. for S. searcheth all th.
11 s. of man which is in him
12 not s. of world, but s. of G.
5:3 absent in body, present in s.
5 s. be saved in day of Lord J.

236

6:17 joined to the Lord is one s.
20 glori. G. in your body and s.
7:34 may be holy in body and s.
12:4 gifts, but same S. S. 9, 11
8 given by S. word of wisdom
13 by one S. we are all baptiz.
been made to drink into S.
14:2 in s. he speaketh mysteries
15 sing with s. 16 bless with s.
1 Cor. 15:45 A. was ma. a quick. s.
2 Cor. 3:6 but of the s. letter killeth, but the s. giveth life
8 ministrations of s. be glorio.
17 L. is that s. where S. of L.
4:13 we having same s. of faith
7:1 from filthiness of flesh and s.
13 because his s. was refreshed
11:4 s. which ye have not recei.
12:18 walk. we not in same s.?
Gal. 3:2 receiv. ye S. by works?
3 foolish, having begun in s.?
5 he that ministereth to you S.
14 might receive promise of S.
4:6 G. sent forth S. of his Son
5:5 we thro' S. wait for hope
16 walk in S. 18 if led by S.
17 flesh lusteth against the S.
and the S. against the flesh
25 if we live in S. walk in S.
6:8 soweth to S. shall of S. reap
18 grace of our Lord be with
your s. Phile. 25
Eph. 2:2 s. that work. in child.
18 have access by one S. to F.
22 habitation of G. through S.
3:5 revealed to apostles by S.
16 strength. with might by S.
4:3 unity of s. in bond of peace
4 th. is one S. as ye are called
23 renewed in s. of your mind
5:18 not drunk, but filled wi. s.
6:17 sw. of S. is the word of God
18 praying with prayer in S.
Phil. 1:19 supply of s. of Je. Ch.
27 that ye stand fast in one s.
2:1 any fellowship of the S.
3:3 which worship God in the s.
Col. 1:8 declared your love in s.
2:5 yet am I with you in the s.
1 Thes. 5:19 quench not S. despise
23 I pray G. your s. soul, body

2 Thes. 2:2 neith. by s. nor word
8 L. shall consume with the s.
13 chosen thro' sanctific. of S.
1 Tim. 3:16 God justified in S.
4:1 the S. speaketh expressly
12 be thou an example in s.
2 Tim. 4:22 L. J. C. be wi. thy s.
Heb. 4:12 dividing of soul and s.
9:14 who through the eternal S.
Jam. 2:26 body witho. s. is dead
4:5 the s. in us lusteth to envy
1 Pet. 1:2 thro' sanctification of s.
22 in obeying truth through S.
3:4 the ornament of a meek s.
18 but quickened by S.
4:6 live accord. to God in the S.
1 John 3:24 s. he hath given us
4:1 beloved, believe not every s.
2 ev. s. that confesseth Je. Ch.
3 ev. s. that confesseth not Je.
13 bec. hath given us of his S.
5:6 S. beareth witn. S. is truth
8 wit. in earth, S. water, blood
Jude 19 sensual, not having S.
Rev. 1:10 I was in S. on L.'s day
2:7 what S. saith to churches,
11, 17, 29; 3:6, 13, 22
4:2 immediately I was in the S.
11:11 S. of life from G. entered
14:13 blessed are dead, saith S.
17:3 carried me in the S. 21:10
22:17 S. and bride say, Come
SPIRIT of adoption.
Rom. 8:15 ye have recei. s. of a.
SPIRIT of antichrist.
1 John 4:3 this is that s. of anti.
SPIRIT of bondage.
Rom. 8:15 have not rece. s. of b.
Born of the SPIRIT.
John 3:5 ex. man be b. of the S.
6 that which is born of the S.
8 so is ev. one that is b. of S.
Gal. 4:29 persec. him b. after S.
Broken SPIRIT.
Ps. 51:17 sacri. of G. are a b. s.
Prov. 15:13 sorrow of heart s. is b.
17:22 a b. s. drieth the bones
SPIRIT of burning.
Is. 4:4 blood of Jer. by s. of b.
SPIRIT of Christ.
Rom. 8:9 if man ha. not s. of C.

1 Pet. 1:11 S. of ch. did signify
SPIRIT of counsel.
Is. 11::2 s. of c. rest upon him
SPIRIT of divination.
Acts 16:16 possess. with s. of d.
Dumb SPIRIT.
Mark 9:17 son. who hath a d. s.
25 thou dumb s. I charge thee
Earnest of the SPIRIT.
2 Cor. 1:22 given us e. of t. S. 5:5
SPIRIT of error.
1 John 4:6 kn. we s. of tru. and e.
Faithful SPIRIT.
Prov. 11:13 he that is of faith. s.
SPIRIT of fear.
2 Tim. 1:7 ha. not giv. us s. of f.
Foul SPIRIT.
Mark 9:25 he rebuked the foul s.
Rev. 18:2 become hold of ev. f. s.
Fruit of the SPIRIT.
Gal. 5:22 f. of the S. is love, joy
Eph. 5:9 f. of t. S. is in all good.
Good SPIRIT.
Neh. 9:20 th. gavest thy good S.
Ps. 143:10 thy S. is g. lead me
SPIRIT of God.
Gen. 1:2 S. of G. moved on wat.
41:38 a man in wh. S. of God is
Ex. 31:3 Bez. wi. S. of G. 35:31
Num. 24:2 S. of G. came on Bal.
1 Sam. 10:10 the S. of God came
on Saul, 11:6; 19:23
19:20 S. of G. came on messen.
2 Chr. 15:1 S. of G. came on Aza.
Job 27:3 S. of G. is in my nost.
33:4 S. of God. hath made me
Ezek. 11:24 in vision by S. of G.
Mat. 3:16 saw S. of G. descend.
12:28 cast out devils by S. of G.
Rom. 8:9 S. of God dwell in you
14 many as are led by S. of G.
15:19 by the power of S. of G.
1 Cor. 2:11 no man, but S. of G.
14 recei. not things of S. of G.
3:16 S. of God dwelleth in you
6:11 sanctified by the S. of God
7:40 I think I have S. of God
12:3 no man speak. by S. of G.
2 Cor. 3:3 written with S. of G.
Eph. 4:30 grie. not holy S. of G.
1 Pet. 4:14 S. of God rest. on you

1 John 4:2 hereby kn. ye S. of G.
SPIRIT of glory.
1 Pet. 4:14 S. of g. resteth on you.
SPIRIT of grace.
Zec. 12:10 house of Da. S. of g.
Heb. 10:29 done desp to S. of g.
Humble SPIRIT.
Prov. 16:19 bet. to be of an h. s.
29:23 honor sh. uphold the h. s.
Is. 57:15 with him that is of h. s.
SPIRIT of jealousy.
Num. 5:14 s. of j. co. on him, 30
SPIRIT of judgment.
Is. 4:4 purged Jerusa. by s. of j.
28:6 L. shall be for a s. of jud.
SPIRIT of knowledge.
Is. 11:2 s. of k. sh. rest upon him
SPIRIT of meekness.
1 Cor. 4:21 come in s. of m.?
Gal. 6:1 such a one in s. of m.
My SPIRIT.
Gen. 6:3 my S. sh. not always
Job 6:4 poison drinketh up my s.
7:11 speak in anguish of my s.
10:12 visita. hath preserv. m. s.
21:4 sho. not my s. be troubled
Ps. 31:5 into hand I com. my s.
77:3 my s. was overwhelmed
6 my s. made diligent search
142:3 my s. overwhelmed in me
143:4 theref. is my s. overwhel.
7 hear me, O L. my s. faileth
Prov. 1:23 I will pour out my s.
Is. 26:9 with my s. will I seek
30:1 covering, but not of my s.
38:16 in th. things is life of m. s.
42:1 I ha. put my S. upon him
44:3 pour my S. upon thy seed
59:21 my S. that is upon thee
Ezek. 3:14 went in heat of my s.
36:27 my S. within you, 37:14
39:29 pour. my S. on house of I.
Dan. 2:3 and my s. was troubled
7:15 I dan. was griev. in my s.
Joel 2:28 I will pour out my S. on
all flesh, 29; Acts 2:17, 18
Hag. 2:5 my S. remain. am. you
Zec. 4:6 by power, but by my S.
6:8 quiet. my s. in north count.
Mat. 12:18 I will put my S. on
Luke 1:47 my s. hate rejoi. in G.

23:46 in thy hands I com. my s.
Acts 7:59 Lord Je. receive my s.
Rom. 1:9 wh. I serve with my s.
1 Cor. 5:4 when gath. and my s.
14:14 my s. prayeth, but my
16:18 they have refresh. my s.
2 Cor. 2:13 had no rest in my s.

New SPIRIT.
Ezek. 11:19 a n. s. in you, 36:26
18:31 a new heart and new s.

Newness of SPIRIT.
Rom. 7:6 we sho. serve in n. of s.

Patient SPIRIT.
Ec. 7:8 p. in s. bet. than proud

Perverse SPIRIT.
Is. 19:14 L. hath mingled a p. s.

Poor SPIRIT.
Mat. 5:3 blessed re poor in s.

SPIRIT of promise.
Eph. 1:13 sealed with H. S. of p.

SPIRIT of prophecy.
Rev. 19:10 testim. of J. is s. of p.

SPIRIT of slumber.
Rom. 11:8 G. given them s. of s.

Sorrowful SPIRIT.
1 Sam. 1:15 a woman of a s. s.

SPIRIT of truth.
John 14:17 S. of t. whom world
15:26 S. of t. which proceedeth
16:13 when S. of truth is come
1 John 4:6 hereby kn. we S. of t.

Unclean SPIRIT.
Zec. 13:2 cause uncl. s. to pass
Mat. 12:43 when the u. s. is gone
out of a man, Luke 11:24
Mark 1:23 synag. a man wi. u. s.
26 when u. s. had torn him
3:30 they said, He hath an u. s.
5:2 met him a man with u. s.
8 come out, th. u. s. Luke 8:29
7:25 whose daugh. had an u. s.
Luke 9:42 Jesus rebuked u. s.

SPIRIT of understanding.
Is. 11:2 the s. of u. sh. rest upon

SPIRIT of whoredoms.
Hos. 4:12 s. of w. caused to err
5:4 of w. is in midst of them

SPIRIT of wisdom.
Ex. 28:3 wh. I filled wi. s. of w.
Deut. 34:9 Joshua full of s. of w.
Is. 11:2 s. of w. sh. rest up. him

Eph. 1:17 G. may give s. of w.
Wounded SPIRIT.
Prov. 18:14 w. s. who can bear?
SPIRITS.
Num. 16:22 O God, the God of s.
27:16
Ps. 104:4 mak. angels s. Heb. 1:7
Prov. 16:2 Lord weighed the s.
Zec. 6:5 th. are four s. of heaven
Mat. 8:16 cast out s. with word
10:1 power ag. uncl. s. Mark 6:7
Mark 1:27 commandeth he the
unclean s. Luke 4:36
3:11 uncl. s. fell down bef. him
5:13 unclean s. entered swine
Luke 10:20 rejoice not that s. are
Acts 5:16 vexed with unclean s.
8:7 s. crying, came out of many
1 Cor. 12:10 to ano. discern. of s.
14:32 s. of proph. are subject to
1 Tim. 4:1 giv. heed to seduc. s.
Heb. 1:14 not all ministering s.
12:9 in subjection to Fath. of s.
23 to s. of just men made per.
1 Pet. 3:19 preach. to s. in prison
1 John 4:1 try s. wheth. they are
Rev. 16:13 I saw 3 unclean s. like
14 they are the s. of devils
SPIRITUAL.
Hos. 9:7 the s. man is mad
Rom. 1:11 impart to you s. gift
7:14 we know that the law is s.
15:27 partak. of their s. things
1 Cor. 2:13 comparing s. things
with s.
15 he that is s. judgeth all thi.
3:1 could not spe. to you as to s.
9:11 have sown unto you s.
10:3 did all eat same s. meat
4 same s. dri. drank of s. rock
12:1 concern. s. gifts, brethren
14:1 desire s. gifts; 12 zeal. of s.
37 if any man think himself s.
15:44 s. body, there is a s. body
46 that was not first whi. is s.
afterwards that which is s.
Gal. 6:1 ye which are s. restore
Eph. 1:3 blessed us with s. bless.
5:19 speak. to yours. in s. songs
6:12 wrestle against s. wickedn.
Col. 1:9 filled with s. understand.

3:16 admon. in psa. and s. songs
1 Pet. 2:5 built up a s. house, to
offer s. sacrifices

SPIRITUALLY.
Rom. 8:6 to be s. minded is life
1 Cor. 2:14 because are s. discer.

SPOIL, Substantive.
Ps. 68:12 tarried at home divi. s.
119:162 rejoice, as one findeth s.
Prov. 1:13 sh. fill houses with s.

SPOIL, Verb.
Is. 17:14 portion of th. that s. us
33:1 when shalt cease to s. thou
Zep. 2:9 residue of people shall s.
Mat. 12:29 s. goods? Mark 3:27
Col. 2:8 lest any man s. you

SPREAD.
Hos. 5:1 have been a net s. on T.
7:12 when they go, I will s. net
14:6 branches sh. s. his beauty
Mat. 21:8 multit. s. garments in
way, Mark 11:8; Luke 19:36

SPREAD abroad.
1 Thes. 1:8 faith to God-w. is s. a.

SPRINGS.
Jos. 10:40 smote country of s.
15:19 give me s. of water, gave
upper s. Jud. 1:15
Ps. 87:7 all my s. are in thee
Is. 35:7 land become s. of water

SPRING.
Ezek. 17:9 in all leaves of her s.

SPRING, Verb.
Ps. 85:11 truth sh. s. out of earth

SPRINKLING.
Heb. 9:13 the ashes of a heifer s.
11:28 thro' faith kept s. of blood
12:24 we are come to blood of s.
1 Pet. 1:2 s. of blood of Jesus Ch.

SPIES.
Gen. 42:9 said, Ye are s. 14, 16
34 then sh. I know ye are not s.

STAFF.
Ps. 23:4 thy god and s. comf. me

STALLS.
Hab. 3:17 there be no herd in s.

STAND, Verb.
Rom. 14:4 G. able to ma. him. s.
2 Cor. 1:24 joy, for by faith ye s.
Eph. 6:13 having done all to s.
Pet. 5:12 grace of G. wherein s.

Rev. 3:20 I s. at door and knock
6:17 who shall be able to s.?

STAND fast.
Gal. 5:1 s. f. in liberty Ch. made
Phil. 1:27 s. f. in sp. 4:1 s. f. in L.
1 Thes. 3:8 live, if ye s. f. in L.
2 Thes. 2:15 s. f. and hold trad.

STAND forth.
Mark 3:3 sa. to man, s. f. Lu. 6:8

STAND up.
Acts 10:26 Peter said, s. up, I am

STAND upon.
Ex. 33:21 thou shalt s. u. rock

STANDARD.
Is. 49:22 I will set up s. to peo.
59:19 L. sh. lift up a s. ag. him

STANDETH.
Jam. 5:9 judge s. before door
Rev. 10:8 angel who s. on sea

STAR.
Mat. 2:2 have seen his s. in east
9 lo. s. which they saw in east
Mat. 2:10 wh. they saw s. th. rej.
Acts 7:43 took up s. of your god
1 Cor. 15:41 s. differ. from ano. s.
Rev. 8:10 there fell a great s. 11
9:1 a s. fell from heaven to ear.

STARS.
Gen. 1:16 G. made lights, ma. s.
15:5 tell the s. if thou be able
37:9 sun, moon, and eleven s.
Rev. 8:12 third part of s. was
12:1 upon head a crown of 12 s.

STATURE.
Mat. 6:27 not add one cubit to
his s. Luke 12:25
Luke 2:52 Jesus increased in s.
Eph. 4:13 measure of s. of Christ

STATUTE.
Ex. 15:25 he made a s. and ordi.

STAYED.
Gen. 8:10 Noah s. seven days, 12

STEADFAST.
Job 11:15 yea, thou shalt be s.
1 Pet. 5:9 whom resist s. in faith

STEAL.
Mark 10:19 do not s. Luke 18:20
John 10:10 thief com. but to s.
Rom. 2:21 sho. not s. dost thou s.

STEPHEN.
Acts 6:5 chose S. a man full, S

7:59 they stoned S. calling on
8:2 devout men carried S. to his
11:19 abroad on perse. about S.
22:20 blood of thy martyr S.

STEPS.
Ps. 37:23 s. of a good man ordered

STERN.
Acts 27:29 cast 4 ancho. out of s.

STEWARD.
Gen. 15:2 and the s. of my house
43:19 they came near to the s.
1 K. 16:9 drunk in house of his s.
Mat. 20:8 L. of viney. saith to s.
Luke 8:3 wife of Chu. Herod's s.
12:42 who th. is that faithful s.
16:1 rich man who had a s.
2 thou mayest be no longer s.
8 L. commended the unjust s.
Tit. 1:7 bishop blameless s. of G.

STEWARDS.
1 Chr. 28:1 David assembled s.
1 Cor. 4:1 s. of mysteries of God
2 required in s. that a man
1 Pet. 4:10 good s. of grace of G.

STEWARDSHIP.
Luke 16:2 give account of thy s.
3 my lord taketh fr. me the s. 4

STICK, Verb.
Job 33:21 bones not seen, s. out
41:17 scales are joined, they s.
Ps. 38:2 thi. arrows s. fast in me
Ezek. 29:4 cau. fish to s. to scales

STICKETH.
Prov. 18:24 friend s. closer than

STICK.
2 K. 6:6 cut down a s. and cast it
Lam. 4:8 skin withered like a s.
Ezek. 37:16 one s. another s. 17

STICKS.
Num. 15:32 gath. s. on sabbath
1 K. 17:10 woman was gather. s.
12 behold, I am gather. two s.
Ezek. 37:20 s. whereon thou wri.
Acts 28:3 Paul gath. bundle of s.

STIFF.
Jer. 17:23 but made their neck s.

STIFF-HEARTED.
Ezek. 2:4 impud. child. and s.-h.

STIFF neck.
Deut. 31:27 I know thy s. neck
Ps. 75:5 speak not with a s. neck

STIFF-NECKED.
Ex. 32:9 this peo. is s.-n. peo.
5 say to Is. Ye are a s.-n. peo.
34:9 a s.-n. people, Deut. 9:13
Deut. 10:16 be no more s.-n.
2 Chr. 30:8 not s.-n. as your fath.
Acts 7:51 s.-n. ye resist H. Ghost

STILL.
Jer. 47:6 sw. of L. rest and be s.
Mark 4:29 to sea. Peace, be s.

STIR, Verb.
2 Tim. 1:6 thou s. up gift of God
2 Pet. 1:13 meet to s. you up, 3:1

STIRRED.
Dan. 11:10 his sons shall be s. up
25 king of south be s. up
Hag. 1:14 L. s. spirit of Zerubb.
Acts 6:12 they s. up the people
17:13; 21:27
13:50 Jews s. up devout women
14:2 unbelieving Jews s. Genti.
17:16 P. his spirit was s. in him

STOLE.
Eph. 4:28 let him th. s. steal no

STOMACH.
1 Tim. 5:23 use wine for s. sake

STONE.
Gen 11:3 they had brick for s.
28:18 Jacob set up a s. 22; 31:45
29:3 rolled s. from well's 8, 10
35:14 Jacob set up a pillar of s.
Ps. 91:12 lest thou dash foot ag.
a s. Mat. 4:6; Luke 4:11
118:22 s. wh. build. ref. is head
s. Mat. 21:42; Mark 12:10
Mat. 5:9 will give s.? Luke 11:11
21:44 whosso. shall fall on this
s. shall be brok. Luke 20:18
Mat. 24:2 not be left one s. Mark
13:2; Luke 19:44; 21:6
27:66 sealing s. setting a watch
28:2 angel came and rol. back s.
Luke 4:3 command this s. th. it
20:17 s. which builders reject.
Acts 4:11; 1 Pet. 2:7
22:41 withdr. fr. them a s. cast
24:2 fon. s. rolled away, Mark
16:4; John 20:1
John 1:42 Cephas, by inter. a s.
2:6 were set six water-pots of s.
8:7 let him first cast s. at her

241

11:38 a cave, a s. lay upon it
39 take away s. 41 they took s.
Acts 17:29 Godhead is like s. gra.
Rev. 16:21 hall fell ev. s. wel. of
18:21 angel took up s.
Precious STONE.
Ex. 24:12 I give th. t. of s. 31:18
34:1 hew two t. of s. Deut. 10:1
STONE, Verb.
1 K. 21:10 car. Nab. out, s. him
Ezek. 16:40 shall s. thee with st.
23:47 company shall s. them
Luke 20:6 the people will s. us
John 10:31 Jews took ston. to s.
32 for wh. of works do s. me?
11:8 Jews of late sou. to s. thee
Acts 14:5 assault made to s. th.
STONED.
Ex. 19:13 he shall be s. or shot
21:28 ox shall be surely s. 29, 32
Jos. 7:25 all Israel s. Achan
Acts 5:26 lest should have bee s.
7:58 they s. Stephen, calling, 59
2 Cor. 11:25 beaten, once was I
STONES.
Gen. 31:46 Jacob said, Gather s.
Mic. 1:6 pour down s. in valley
Zec. 5:4 consu. it with s. thereof
9:16 shall be as s. of a crown
Mat. 3:9 of these s. to raise up
children, Luke 3:8
4:3 command s. be made bread
Mark 12:4 at him they cast s.
13:1 see what manner of s. here
Luke 19:40 s. would immedi. cry
John 8:59 took s. to cast, 10:31
1 Pet. 2:5 as lively s. are built
Precious STONES.
1 Cor. 3:12 build on founda. p. s.
Rev. 18:12 no man buyeth p s.
21:19 founda. garnish. with p. s.
STOOD.
Acts 16:9 there s. man of Maced.
27:21 Paul s. forth in the midst
STOOD by.
Ex. 18:13 the people s. by Moses
Luke 19:24 said to them th. s. by
Acts 23:11 night fol. L. s. by him
27:23 there s. by me angel of G.
STOOD still.
Jos. 10:13 sun s. s. moon stayed

11:13 cities that s. s. in strength
STOOPED.
John 8:6 Jesus s. down, wrote, 8
STOP.
1 K. 18:44 that rain s. thee not
2 K. 3:19 s. all wells of water, 25
STOPPED.
Rom. 3:19 ev. month may be s.
Tit. 1:11 wh. months must be s.
Heb. 11:33 s. mouths of lions
STOREHOUSE.
Mal. 3:10 bring tithes into the s.
STORM.
Ezek. 38:9 shalt come like a s.
Nah. 1:3 Lord hath his way in s.
Mark 4:37 there arose a great s.
Luke 8:23 there came down a s.
STRAIGHT.
Mat. 3:3 make his paths s. Mark
1:3; Luke 3:4; John 1:23
Luke 13:13 she was made s. and
STRAIT.
Mat. 7:13 enter ye in at s. gate
14 bec. s. is gate, Luke 13:24
STRANGE.
Heb. 11:9 sojou. as in s. country
13:9 be not carried with s. doct.
1 Pet. 4:4 they think it s. ye run
12 think it not s. concerning
trial, as though s. thing
STRANGE woman.
Jud. 11:2 thou art son of a s. w.
Prov. 2:16 deliv. thee from s. w.
STRANGE women.
1 K. 11:1 king loved many s. w.
Prov. 22:14 mouth of s. w. is pit
23:33 th. eyes shall behold s. w.
STRANGER.
Deut. 1:16 judge righte. betw. &,
10:18 L. loveth the s. in giving
STRANGERS.
Heb. 11:13 confessed they were s.
13:2 not forgetful to entertain s.
STREET.
Acts 9:11 go into s. call. Straight
Rev. 11:8 dead bodies sh. lie in s.
21:21 s. of city was pure gold
22:2 in midst of s. tree of life
STREETS.
Jer. 5:1 run through s. of Jerus.
49:26 men shall fall in s. 50:30

Mat. 6:2 not sound a trum. in s.
5 pray standing in corners of s.
Mark 6:56 sick in s. Acts 5:15

STRENGTH.
Ps. 8:2 out of babes ordained s.
20:6 with saving s. of rig. hand
Prov. 8:14 I have s. 10:29 L. is s.
14:4 increase is by the s. of ox
Ezek. 30:15 fury on Sin. s. of Eg.
18 pomp of s. sh. cease. 33:28
Dan. 2:41 th. sh. be in it s. of iron
11:15 neit. shall there be any s.
Rom. 5:6 wh. without s. Ch. died
1 Cor. 15:56 s. of sin is the law
2 Cor. 1:8 we were pressed ab. s.
Heb. 11:11 Sarah herself recei. s.
Rev. 3:8 for thou hast a little s.
5:12 worthy is La. to receive s.
12:10 now is salvation and s.

His STRENGTH.
Rev. 1:16 count. as son in his s.

My STRENGTH.
Hab. 3:19 the Lord God is my s.
Zec. 12:5 be my s. in L. of hosts
2 Cor. 12:9 my s. is made perfect

Their STRENGTH.
Prov. 20:29 glory of men is t. s.
Is. 30:7 I cried, t. s. is to sit still
40:31 that wait on L. renew t. s.

Thy STRENGTH.
Mark 12:30 love the Lord with all
thy s. 33; Luke 10:27

STRENGTHEN.
Amos 2:14 strong sh. not s. force
Zec. 10:6 I will s. house of Judah
12 I will s. them in the Lord
Luke 22:32 when convert. s. bre.
1 Pet. 5:10 God stablish, s. you
Rev. 3:2 be watchful and s. thi.

STRENGTHENED.
Co. 1:11 s. with all might accord.
2 Tim. 4:17 Lord stood and s. me

STRETCH.
Ex. 7:19 s. out hand on waters
8:5 s. forth hand over streams

STRIFE.
Jud. 12:2 I and peo. were at s.
2 Sam. 19:9 people were at s.
Ps. 31:20 keep fr. s. of tongues
55:9 I have seen s. in the city
80:6 makest us a s. to neighbors

106:32 ang. him at watrs of s.
Prov. 15:18 a wrathful man stir.
s. slow to anger app. s. 29:22
Gal. 5:20 works of the flesh are s.
Phil. 1:15 some preach Chr. of s.
2:3 let nothing be done thro's
1 Tim. 6:4 wher. cometh envy, s.
Heb. 6:16 an oath is end of all s.
Jam. 3:14 bitter envying and s.
16 where s. is, there is confus.

STRIFES.
Prov. 10:12 hatred stirreth up s.
2 Cor. 12:20 envyings, wraths, s.
1 Tim. 6:4 quest. and s. of words
2 Tim. 2:23 knowing that they
gender s.

STRIPES.
Is. 53:5 with his s. we are healed,
1 Pet. 2:24
Luke 12:47 beaten with many s.
48 knew not, beaten wi. few s.
Acts 16:23 laid many s. upon th.
33 same hour, washed their s.
2 Cor. 6:5 in s. in imprisonments
11:23 in s. above measure
24 of Jews received I forty s.

STRIPPED.
Gen. 37:23 they s. Joseph of coat
Mat. 27:28 they s. Jesus, put on

STRIVE.
Mat. 12:19 he shall not s.
Luke 13:24 s. to enter strait gate
Rom. 15:30 s. wi. me in prayers
2 Tim. 2:5 if a man s. for maste.
2 Tim. 2:14 th. th. s. not ab. wor.
24 servant of Lord must not s.

STRONG.
Jud. 14:14 out of s. came sweet.
Ec. 9:11 battle is not to the s.
Cant. 8:6 for love is s. as death
Heb. 5:12 milk, not s. meat
11:34 out of weak. were made s.

Be STRONG.
Num. 13:18 see wheth. they be s.
28 people be s. that dwell in
Deut. 11:18 keep co. that ye be s.
Jos. 17:18 drive Canaa, tho' be s.
1 Sam. 4:9 be s. quit yourselves
2 Sam. 16:21 han. of all shall be s.
1 K. 2:2 be thou s. show thyself a
1 Chr. 28:10 L. chosen thee, be s.

2 Chr. 15:7 be s. work sh. be re.
25:8 do it, be s. for the battle
Ezr. 9:12 that ye may be s.
Ps. 144:14 that oxen be s. to lab.
Is. 35:4 th. of fearful heart, be s.
Ezek. 22:14 can thy hands be s.
Dan. 2:42 kingd. sh. be partly s.
10:19 peace to th. be s. yea, be s.
11:5 king of the south shall be s.
and he sh. be s. above him
32 pe. that know G. shall be s.
Hag. 2:4 be s. O Zerubabbel, be
s. O Joshua, be s. ye people
Zec. 8:19 let hands be s. ye that
13 but let your hands be s.
1 Cor. 16:13 quit you li. m. be s.
Eph. 16:10 brethr. be s. in the L.
2 Tim. 2:1 my son, be s. in grace

STRONG-HOLD, S.
Zec. 9:3 Tyrus did build a s.-h.
12 turn to the s.-h. ye prisons.
2 Cor. 10:14 mig. to pull. do. s.-h.

STRUCK.
Luke 22:64 they s. Jesus, John
18:22

STUDY.
1 Thes. 4:11 s. to be quiet
2 Tim. 2:15 s. to show thys. app.

STUMBLE.
Jer. 13:16 before your feet s. on
50:32 proud shall s. and fall
Dan. 11:19 he shall s. and fall
Mal. 2:8 have caused many to s.
1 Pet. 2:8 offence to them that s.

STUMBLING-BLOCK.
Rom. 11:9 made a trap, a s.-b.
Rom. 14:13 put s.-b. in br. way
1 Cor. 1:23 C. cruci. to Jews s.-b.
8:9 lest liber. of yours bec. s.-b.
Rev. 2:14 Bal. to cast s.-b. bef. Is.

STUMBLING, with stone.
Is. 8:14 be for a s. of s. to Israel
Rom. 9:32 stumbled at th. s.-s.

SUBDUE.
Phil. 3:21 he is able to s. all thi.

SUBJECT.
Luke 2:51 Jesus was s. to them
10:17 L. even devils are s. to us
20 rejoi. not spirits are s. to you
Rom. 8:7 it is not s. to law of G.
20 creature was s. to vanity

13:1 let eve. soul be s. to powers
5 wherefo. ye must needs be s.
1 Cor. 14:32 spirits of prophets
15:28 then sh. Son hims. be s.
Eph. 5:24 as church is s. to Chr.
Col. 2:20 are ye s. to ordinances
Tit. 3:1 put in mind to s. to pow.
Heb. 2:15 lifetime s. to bondage
Jam. 5:17 Elias was s. to passio.
1 Pet. 2:18 serv. be s. to masters
3:22 pow. being made s. to him
5:5 all of you be s. one to ano.

SUBJECTED.
Rom. 8:20 who s. same in hope

SUBJECTION.
1 Tim. 2:11 wom. learn with all s.
3:4 having his children in s.
Heb. 2:5 put in s. world to come
8 put all things in s. under feet
12:9 rather be in s. to Father
1 Pet. 3:1 be in s. to husbands, 5

SUBMIT.
1 Cor. 16:16 that ye s. yourselves
Eph. 5:22 s. to husb. Col. 3:18
Heb. 13:17 s. th. watch for souls
Jas. 4:7 s. yourselves theref. to G.
1 Pet. 2:13 s. to every ordinance
5:5 younger s. yourselv. to elder

SUBMITTING.
Eph. 5:21 s. yours. one to anoth.

SUBSTANCE.
He 10:34 ye have in heaven a s.
11:1 faith is s. of thi. hoped for

SUBTILTY.
Mat. 26:4 might take Jesus by s.
Acts 13:10 O full of s. and mischi.
2 Cor. 11:3 beguiled Eve thro's

SUBVERT.
Tit. 1:11 who s. whole houses
3:11 th. is such is s. and sinneth

SUCCESS.
Jos. 1:8 prosper and have good s.

SUDDENLY.
1 Tim. 5:22 lay hands s. on no m.

SUE.
Mat. 5:40 if any man s. thee

SUFFER.
Prov. 10:3 L. not s. righte. fam.
19:15 idle soul shall s. hunger
Mat. 3:15 Jesus said, s. it to be
8:21 s. me to bury, Luke 9:59

244

16:21 he must s. many things
17:12; Mark 8:31; 9:12; Lu.
9:22; 17:25
17:17 how long shall I s. you?
Mark 9:19; Luke 9:41
19:14 s. little children, Mark
10:14; Luke 18:16
23:13 neither s. ye them th. are
1 Thes. 3:4 told you, we should s.
2 Thes. 1:5 kingd. of G. for wh. s.
1 Tim. 4:10 we both labor and s.
2 Tim. 1:12 for wh. cause I also s.

SUFFERED.
Mat. 3:15 suf. it to be so, he s.
24:43 nor s. his hou. Lu. 12:39
27:19 I have s. many things this
Mark 1:34 he s. not dev. Lu. 4:41
5:19 Jesus s. him not, but said
26 s. many things of physici.
Luke 8:32 s. them to enter swine
51 he s. no man to go in.
13:2 because they s. such things
24:26 ought not Ch. to have s.?
Acts 13:18 about 40 years s. he
Heb. 5:8 learn, obed. by things he s.
1 Pet. 2:21 Christ s. for us. leav.

SUFFERETH.
1 Cor. 13:4 charity s. long, is kind

SUFFERINGS.
Rom. 8:18 I reckon that the s. of
2 Cor. 1:5 for as the s. of Christ
2 Cor. 1:6 endur. same s. wh. we
7 ye are partakers of the s.
Phil. 3:10 fellowship of his s.
Col. 1:24 who now rejo. in my s.
Heb. 2:10 Captain perfect thro' s.
1 Pet. 1:11 it testified the s. of Ch.
4:13 ye are prtakers of Ch.'s s.
5:1 I am a witn. of the s. of Ch.

SUFFICIENT.
Mat. 6:34 s. to the day is the evil

SUMMER.
Gen. 8:22 s. and winter, day and
Mat. 24:32 ye kn. that s. is nigh,
Mark 13:28; Luke 21:30

SUN.
Gen. 15:17 when s. went down
Jos. 1:4 tow. going down of s.
10:12 s. stand still upon Gibeon
13 s. stood still, moon stayed
Jud. 5:31 that love him be as s.

Ps. 19:4 set a tabernacle for s.
Ec. 1:5 s. riseth, s. goeth down
Cant. 1:6 be. s. looked on me
6:10 fair as moon, clear as s.
Is. 24:23 then s. sh. be ashamed
30:26 light of moon as s. light
49:10 nor heat nor s. smite th.
60:19 s. be no more li. by day
20 s. shall no more go down
Joel 2:10 s. be dark. 3:15; Mat.
24:29; Mark 13:24; Luke 23:45
31 s. sh. be turned to darkness
Mat. 5:45 maketh his s. to rise
13:43 then sh. right. shine as s.
17:2 his face did shine as the s.
Rev. 1:16; 10:1
Eph. 4:26 let not s. go down
Rev. 6:12 s. became as sackcloth
7:16 nor shall s. light on them
8:12 third part of s. was smit.
9:2 s. and the air were darken.
12:1 appeared wom. clo. with s.
16:8 angel poured out vial on s.
19:17 I saw angel standing on s.
21:23 city had no need of s. 22:5

SUNG.
Mat. 26:30 s. hymn, Mark 14:26
Rev. 5:9 they s. a new song
14:3 s. as it were a new song

SUPPER.
Luke 14:12 makest a dinner of s.
16 a cert. man made a great s.
24 none bid, shall taste of my s.
22:20 likewise also cup after s.
John 12:2 there they made Je. s.
13:2 s. ended; 3 Je. ris. from s.
21:20 disc. lean. on breast at s.
1 Cor. 11:20 not to eat Lord's s.
Rev. 19:9 that are called to the s.
17 come to s. of the great God

SUPPLICATION.
Phil. 4:6 but in every thing by s.

SUPPLICATIONS.
2 Chr. 6:21 hearken to s. of sery.
1 Tim. 2:1's be made for all men
5:5 continueth in s. and prayer
Heb. 5:7 he offered prayers and s.

SUPPORT.
Acts 20:5 ought to s. the weak,
1 Thes. 5:14

SURE.

John 6:69 are s. thou art Christ
16:30 are we s. thou knowest
Rom. 15:29 I am s. when I come
SURELY be put to death.
Jer. 38:15 w. not s. p. me to it?
SURETY.
Heb. 7:22 Je. made s. of a better
Of a SURETY.
Gen. 15:13 know of a s. thy seed
Gen. 26:9 of a s. she is thy wife
Acts 12:11 of a s. Lord sent ang.
SUSTAIN.
Prov. 18:14 spirit of man will s.
Is. 59:16 his righteous. it s. him
SWADDLING.
Luke 2:7 wrap. him in s. clo. 12
SWALLOW, Verb.
Jon. 1:17 Lord prep. a fish to s.
Mat. 23:24 stra. at gnat, s. camel
SWALLOWED.
Ezek. 36:3 they have s. you up
Hos. 8:8 Israel is s. up am. Gent.
1 Cor. 15:54 death is s. up in vic.
2 Cor. 2:7 lest such a one be s. up
5:4 that mortal. might be s. up
Rev. 12:16 earth s. up the flood
SWARE.
Jos. 6:22 br. out Rahab as ye s.
Heb. 3:18 to whom s. he that th.
7:21 Lord s. and will not repent
SWARM.
Jud. 14:8 a s. of bees and honey
SWEAR.
Jer. 4:2 thou shalt s. Lord liveth
5:2 Lord liveth, they s. falsely
7:9 murder, commit adultery, s.
12:16 s. by my name, as peo. s.
Mat. 5:34 s. not; 36 s. not by h.
28:16 s. by temple, s. by gold
18 whoso shall s. by altar
20 whoso theref. sh. s. by altar
21 s. by temple; 22 s. by heav.
26:74 be. to curse, s. Mark 14:71
Heb. 6:13 s. by no greater, he s.
Heb. 6:16 men verily s. by the gr.
Jam. 5:12 my brethren s. not
SWEARETH.
Ps. 15:4 that s. to his hurt
Is. 65:16 he that s. swear by G.
Mat. 23:18 whosoever s. by gift
20 s. by altar; 21 s. by temple

22 s. by throne of God
SWEARING.
Hos. 4:2 by s. lying, and steal.
10:4 s. falsely in making coven.
SWEAT.
Luke 22:44 s. as drops of blood
SWEET.
Jer. 6:20 nor your sacri. s. to me
31:26 my sleep was s. to me
Jam. 3:11 pl. s. water and bitte?
Rev. 10:9 in mouth s. as hon. 10
SWEET spices.
Ex. 30:34 take s. s. frankincense
37:29 he made pure inc. of s. s.
Mark 16:1 brou. s. s. anoint him
SWEET wine.
Mic. 6:15 s. w. not drink wine
SWEETER.
Jud. 14:18 what is s. th. honey?
Ps. 19:12 thy word s. th. honey
119:103 words s. than honey
SWIFT.
Mal. 3:5 a s. witn. ag. sorcerers
Rom. 3:15 feet s. to shed blood
Jam. 1:19 let every man be s.
SWIFTLY.
Ps. 147:15 his word runneth s.
Is. 5:26 behold, they sh. come s.
Dan. 9:21 Gabriel caused to fly s.
Joel 3:4 if ye recompense me s.
SWIM.
2 K. 6:6 and the iron did s.
SWINE.
Mat. 7:6 nei. cast pearls befo. s.
8:30 herd of s. feeding, Mark
5:11; Luke 8:32
31 go into herd of s. Mark 5:12
32 went into s. the herd of s.
ran, Mark 5:13; Luke 8:33
Mark 5:14 they that fed s. fled
Luke 15:15 he sent him to feed s.
16 filled belly with husks s. eat
SWORD.
Gen. 3:24 cherubim and flam. s.
Jos. 5:13 stood with his s. drawn
24:12 not with thy s. nor bow
1 Sam. 13:22 neither s. nor spear
2 Sam. 1:22 s. of S. returned not
1 Chr. 5:18 men able to bear s.
10:4 Saul took a s. fell upon it
5 his armor-bear, fell on the s.

21:5 a 100,000 that drew s.
12 or 3 days the s. of the Lord
16 the angel having a s. drawn
27 he put up his s. again
30 he was afraid of s. of angel
2 Chr. 20:9 wh. s. of judgm. com.
Ps. 7:12 if turn not will whet s.
149:6 a two-edged s. in th. hand
Prov. 5:4 her end as a two-edg. s.
12:18 speaketh like pierc. of s.
25:18 bear, false witness is a s.
Is. 2:4 nation not lift s. ag. nati.
31:8 the s. not of a mean man
34:6 s. of L. is filled with blood
49:2 made mouth like sharp s.
66:16 by his s. will Lord plead
Jer. 2:30 your s. devoured proph.
Mic. 4:3 nation not lift s. ag. na.
Nah. 2:13 s. shall devour lions
Mat. 10:34 not send peace, but s.
26:51 drew his s. struck serv.
Mark 14:47; John 18:10
52 put up ag. thy s. John 18:11
Luke 2:35 a s. sh. pierce thy soul
23:36 he that hath no s. let him
Acts 16:27 he drew his s. and wo.
Rom. 8:35 shall s. separate us
from the love of Christ?
13:4 he beareth not s. in vain
Eph. 6:17 s. of Sp. which is word
Heb. 4:12 sharp, th. two-edged s.
Rev. 1:16 out of mouth went a s.
2:12 the sharp s. with two edges
6:4 was given to him a great s.
19:15 out of his mou. goeth s. 21

With the SWORD.
Is. 1:20 sh. be devoured w. the s.
Mic. 5:6 waste Assyria w. the s.
Mat. 26:52 that take the s. shall
perish with the s.
Luke 22:49 sh. we smite w. t. s.?
Acts 12:2 Her. killed Jas. w. t. s.
Heb. 11:37 tempt. slain w. the s.
Rev. 2:16 I will fight th. w. the s.
6:8 and power to kill w. s. and

SWORDS.
Joel 3:10 beat ploughsh. into s.
Mat. 26:47 with Ju. great multi-
tude with s. Mark 14:43
Luke 22:38 beho. here are two s.

SWORN.

Gen. 22:16 by myself have I s.
saith L. Is. 45:23; Jer. 49:13;
51:14; Amos 6:8
Amos 8:7 Lord hath s. by Jacob
Mic. 7:20 perf. mercy th. hast s.
Heb. 4:3 I have s. in my wrath

SYCAMORE-TREE.
Luke 19:4 Zaccheus climbed s.t.

SYCAMORE-TREES.
1 K. 10:27 Solomon made cedars
as s.-trees, 2 Chr. 1:15; 9:27

SYNAGOGUE.
Mat. 12:9 he went into their s.
13:54 tau. in their s. Mark 6:2
Mark 5:22 Jairus, one of the rul.
of the s. 36, 38; Luke 8:41, 49
Luke 4:16 custom, went into s.
20 eyes of all in s. fast. on him
7:5 loveth nation, built us a s.
John 9:22 he sho. be put out of s.
12:42 lest they be put out of s.
18:20 I ever taught in s. temple
Acts 6:9 then arose cert, of the s.
Rev. 2:9 but are the s. of Satan
3:9 I will make them of s. of Sa.

SYNAGOGUES.
Ps. 74:8 they burned all s. of G.
Mat. 4:23 Je. went teaching in s.
9:35; Mark 1:39; Luke 13:10
6:2 as hypocrites do in the s.
5 love to pray standing in s.
10:17 scourge you in s. 23:34
23:6 love chief seats in s. Mark
12:39; Luke 11:43; 20, 46
Mark 13:9 in s. ye sh. be beaten
Luke 4:15 taught in s. glorified
44 he preached in s. of Galilee
12:11 they bring you unto s.
21:12 delivering you up to the s.
Acts 9:2 Saul desired letters to s.
20 he preached Christ in the s.
13:5 P. and Barn. preached in s.

SYRIA.
Jud. 10:6 Is. served gods of S.
2 Sam. 8:6 David put garrisons
in S. 1 Chr. 18:6
Mat. 4:24 went throughout all S.
Luke 2:2 Cyrenius governor of S.
Acts 15:23 to the brethren in S.
41 he went through S. and
18:18 sailed thence into S. 21:3;

Gal. 1:21

SYRIAN.
Gen. 25:20 daugh. of Bethuel S.
Lab. the S. 28:5; 31:20, 24
Luke 4:27 saving Naaman the S.

SYRIANS.
2 Sam. 8:5 when S. of Da. came,
David slew of S. 22,000
6 the S. became David's servants, 1 Chr. 18:5, 6

T.

TABERNACLE.
Ps. 15:1 L. who sh. abide in t.?
Amos 9:11 will I raise up t. of D.
Acts 7:46 desired to find a t. for G.
15:16 will build again t. of Dav.
2 Cor. 5:1 if house of t. be disso.
4 we th. are in th. t. do groan
Heb. 8:5 when Moses was to make
t.
9:2 there was a t. made, sanctu.
3 t. which is called holiest
6 priests went alw. into first t.
8 while as first t. was yet stan.
11 priest by greater and per. t.
21 sprinkled with blood the t.

TABLE.
Ps. 23:5 thou preparest t. be. me
78:19 can G. furn. t. in wildern.
128:3 child, like plants about t.
Prov. 3:3 wri. on t. of heart, 7:3
9:2 wisd. hath furnished her t.
Ezek. 39:20 ye shall be filled at my
t. 41:22 this is t. that is bef. Lord
Mat. 15:27 dogs eat crumbs from
their master's t. Mark 7:28
Luke 16:21 cru. fr. rich man's t.
22:21 betrayeth, is wi. me on t.
30 may eat and drink at my t.
John 12:2 L. was one th. sat at t.
1 Cor. 10:21 ye cannot be partakers of Lord's t. and t. of dev.

TABLES.
Ex. 32:19 cast the t. out of his h.
34:1 write on t. words in first t.
Mat. 21:12 he overthrew t. of the
money-changers, Mark 11:14
Mark 7:4 wash. of cups, pots. t.
Acts 6:2 leave word of G. serve t.
2 Chr. 3:3 not in t. of st. fleshly t.

TAKE.
Ps. 51:11 t. not thy Holy Sp. fr. me
Prov. 30:9 t. name of my God in
vain
Ezek. 24:5 t. choice of flock
Mat. 6:25 t. no thought for your
life,
28, 31, 34; 10:19; Mark 13:11;
Luke 12:11, 22, 26
15:26 it is not meet to t. children's bread, Mark 7:27
18:16 t. with thee one or two
20:14 t. that thine is, go thy w.
26:26 Je. took break, said t. eat,
Mark 14:22; 1 Cor. 11:24
1 Cor. 6:7 why not ra. t. wrong?
9:9 doth God t. care for oxen?
2 Cor. 1:20 if a man t. of you
1 Tim. 3:5 how t. care of church
1 Pet. 2:20 if ye t. it patiently
Rev. 3:11 that no man t. thy cro.
5:9 thou art worthy to t.
6:4 power to t. peace fr. earth
22:17 let him t. water of life

TAKE away.
Ezek. 36:26 I will t. a. stony heart
Mat. 5:40 t. away thy coat
Mrk 14:36 Father, t. a. this cup
Rom. 11:27 when I sh. t. a. sins

TAKE heed.
1 K. 2:4 if thy children t. heed to
their way,
Mal. 2:15 t. heed to your spir. 16
Mat. 6:1 t. h. do not alms bef. m.
18:10 t. h. that ye despise not
24:4 t. h. lest any man deceive
you, Mark 13:5
Mark 4:24 t. h. what you hear
Luke 8:18 t. h. the. how ye hear
11:35 t. h. that lig. be not dark.
21:8 t. h. ye be not deceived
Rom. 11:21 t. h. lest he spare not
1 Cor. 3:10 man t. h. how he bul.
10:12 standeth t. h. lest he fall
Gal. 5:15 t. h. ye be not consum.
Heb. 3:12 t. h. lest heart of unbe.
2 Pet. 1:19 ye do well to t. heed

TAKE up.
Mat. 9:6 t. up bed, Mark 2:9, 11;
Luke 5:24; John 5:8, 11, 12
16:24 t. up cross. Mark 8:34;

10:21; Luke 9:23
17:27 t. up fish that first cometh
TAKEN up.
Ex. 40:36 cloud was t. up from
Num. 9:17 w. cloud was t. up. 21
2 Sam. 18:9 Absalom was t. up
Luke 9:17 t. up of fragments
Acts 1:9 he was t. up, a cloud
  11 Jesus which is t. up fr. you
TAKETH.
Mat. 4:5 devil t. him up into ho.
  10:38 that t. not his cross, and
  12:45 t. sev. spirits, Luke 11:26
Mark 4:15 Safan cometh, and t.
  away word, Luke 8:12
Luke 9:39 a spirit t. him, he
suddenly John 1:29 Lamb of G. t.
away sin 10:18 no man t. it from
me

TABLEBEARER.
Lev. 19:16 shalt not go as a t.
Prov. 11:13 t. rev. secrets, 20:19
  18:8 words t. are wounds, 26:22
  26:20 where is no t. strife
TALENT.
Mat. 25:25 I went and hid thy t.
  28 take therefore the t. fr. him
TALENTS.
Mat. 18:24 one ow. him 10,000 t.
  25:15 to one he gave five t.
TALK, Verb.
1 Chr. 16:9 t. ye of all his won-
drous works, Ps. 105:2
Prov. 24:2 and their lips t. of
mischi.
Jer. 12:1 let me t. with th. of thy
TALKING.
Mat. 17:3 Mo. and Elins t. with
  him. Mark 9:4
TAME.
Mark 5:4 neith. could man t. him
Jam. 3:8 the tongue can no man t.
TARES.
Mat. 13:26 then appeared the t. also
TARRY.
Is. 46:13 my salvation sh. not t.
1 Tim. 3:15 if I t. long thou may.
Heb. 10:37 will come, and not t.
TARSUS.
Acts 9:11 inq. for one Saul of T.
TASKMASTERS.

Ex. 1:11 they set over them t.
TASTE, Substantive.
Ps. 119:103 sw. thy word to t.?
TASTE, Verb.
John 8:52 keep say. nev. t. death
Col. 2:21 touch not, t. not,
Heb. 2:9 sho. t. death for ev. man
TASTED, ETH.
1 Sam. 14:24 none t. 29 I t. hon.
Mat. 27:34 wh. he had t. thereof
John 2:9 ruler t. wat. made wine
Heb. 6:4 have t. of heavenly gift
1 Pet. 2:3 t. that L. is gracious
TATTLERS.
1 Tim. 5:13 not only idle, but t.
TAUGHT.
Deut. 31:22 Moses t. the childr. of
Is.
2 K. 17:28 t. them how to fear L.
2 Chr. 6:27 ha. t. them good way
  23:13 rejoiced, t. to sing praise
Ps. 71:17 hast t. me, 119:102
  119:171 hast t. me thy statues
Prov. 4:4 he t. me also, and said
  11 I t. thee in way of wisdom
Ec. 12:9 he t. people knowledge
Is. 54:13 thy child. shall be t. of G.
Jer. 32:33 tho' I t. them, rising early
Ezek. 23:48 women t. not lewdn.
Zec. 13:5 t. me to keep cattle
Mat. 7:29 he t. them as one hav-
  ing authority, Mark 1:22
Mark 10:1 as he wont he t. th. again
Luke 11:1 as John t. his disciples
  13:26 thou hast t. in our streets
John 6:45 they sh. be all t. of G.
  7:14 Je. went into temple, t. 28;
  Mark 12:35; Lu. 19:47; 20:1
  8:28 as my Father hath t. me, I
Acts 5:21 entered temple early and
t.
  20:20 I showed you and t. pub.
  22:3 t. accord. to manner of law
Gal. 1:12 nor t. but by revelation
1 Thes. 4:9 ye are t. of G. to love
TAXED.
Luke 2:1 a decree world sho. be t.
TEACH.
Job 21:22 shall any t. G. knowl.
  27:11 will t. you by hand of G.
  32:7 multitude of years t. wisd.

T

Ps. 25:8 he will t. sinners
9 meek will he guide and t.
Ps. 25:12 him t. fear. L. sh. he t.
34:11 I will t. you fear of the L.
51:13 t. transgress. thy ways
90:12 t. us to number our days
105:22 and t. his senators wisd.
Prov. 9:9 t. a just man, he incre.
Mat. 5:19 t. men so; 28:19 t. na.
Luke 11:1 Lord, t. us to pray
12:12 Holy Gh. t. what to say
John 7:35 t. Gent. 9:34 dost t.?
14:26 Holy Gh. t. you all things
Acts 1:1 Jesus began to do and t.
4:18 nor t. in name of Je. 5:28
5:42 ceased not to t. Jesus Chr.
16:21 t. customs wh. not lawful
1 Cor. 4:17 as I t. every where in
11:14 doth not nature itself t.
1 Tim. 1:3 charge t. no oth. doc.
2:12 I suffer not a woman to t.
6:3 if any t. otherw. he is proud
2 Tim. 2:2 men able to t. others
Tit. 2:4 t. yo. women to be sober
Heb. 5:12 need that one t. you
1 John 2:27 need not that any t.

TEACH me.

Job 6:24 t. me, will hold tongue
34:32 wh. I see not, t. thou me.
Ps. 25:4 t. me paths; 5 le. and t.
27:11 t. me thy way, O L. 86:11
119:12 t. me thy statutes, 26, 33,
64, 68, 124, 135
66 t. me judgm. 108 t. m. thy j.
143:10 t. me to do thy will

TEACH thee.

Ex. 4:12 I t. t. what th. sh. say
Job 33:33 hold peace, I sh. t. t. wisd
Ps. 32:8 will t. t. in way sh. go
45:4 ri. hand sh. t. t. t. ter. things

TEACH them.

1 K. 8:36 thou t. them good way
2 K. 17:27 let him t. t. manner of
Ezr. 7:25 t. ye t. that know not
Ps. 132:12 keep testimony I t. t.
Mat. 5:19 whoso shall do and t. t.
Mark 6:34 began t. t. many thi.
8:31 to t. t. Son of man suffer

TEACHER.

Rom. 2:20 confident thou art a t.
1 Tim. 2:7 t. of Gent. 2 Tim. 1:11

TEACHERS.

1 Cor. 12:28 proph. t. 29 all t.?
Eph. 4:11 evangelists, pastors, t.
1 Tim. 1:7 desir. to be t. of law
2 Tim. 4:3 heap to themselves t.
Tit. 2:3 women be t. of good thi.
Heb. 5:12 time ye ought to be t.
2 Pet. 2:1 sh. be false t. am. you

TEACHEST.

Ps. 94:12 blessed is man thou t.
Mat. 22:16 t. way of G. in truth,
Mark 12:14; Luke 20:21
Rom. 2:21 t. ano. t. not thyself?

TEACHETH.

2 Sam. 22:35 he t. my hands to
war, Ps. 18:34
Job 36:22 G. exalt. who t. like him?
Ps. 94:10 that t. man knowledge
144:1 which t. my hands to war
Prov. 16:23 hea. of wise t. his m.
Is. 9:15 the prophet that t. lies
48:17 I am thy G. which t. thee
Acts 21:28 man that t. all men
Rom. 12:7 he that t. on teaching
1 Cor. 2:13 wis. t. but wh. H. G. t.
Gal. 6:6 communi. to him th. t.
1 John 2:27 same anointing t. you

TEACHING.

Jer. 32:33 rising early and t. th.
Mat. 4:23 Jesus went about Galilee, t. 9:35; Luke 13:10
15:9 t. for doctrines commandments of men, Mark 7:7
Acts 5:25 the apostles t. the peo.
Rom. 12:7 he that teacheth on t.
Col. 1:28 warning and t. ev. man
3:16 t. and admonish. one ano.
Tit. 1:11 t. things they ought not
2:12 t. us, denying ungodliness

TEARS.

Ps. 116:8 hast delivered eyes from
t.
126:5 th. sow in t. sh. reap in joy
Ec. 4:1 behold the t. of such as
Is. 16:9 I will water thee with t.
25:8 the Lord will wipe away t.
Jer. 9:1 O that mi. eyes were t.1
Lam. 1:2 t. are on her cheeks
2:11 mine eyes do fail with t.
18 let t. run down like a river
Ezek. 24:16 neither sh. thy t. run

Mal. 2:13 cover. altar of L. wi. t.
Mark 9:24 father said with t. L.
Luke 7:38 to wash feet with t.
  44 she washed my feet with t.
Acts 20:19 serving the L. with t.
  31 cease not to warn with t.
2 Tim. 1:4 mindful of thy t.
Heb. 5:7 offered supplica. with t.
  12:17 he sought it caref. with t.
Rev. 7:17 G. sh. wipe away t. 21:4

TEETH.
Prov. 10:26 as vinegar to the t.
Jer. 31:29 children's t. are set on
  edge, Ezek. 18:2
Lam. 3:16 hath broken my t.

TEMPEST.
Mat. 8:24 there arose a t. in sea
Heb. 12:18 not co. to darkn. and t.
2 Pet. 2:17 clouds carried with a t.

TEMPESTUOUS.
Jon. 1:11 sea wrought and t. 13
Acts 27:14 arose ag. it t. wind

TEMPLE.
2 Sam. 22:7 he did hear my voice
  out of his t. Ps. 18:6
Ps. 48:9 kindness in midst of thy t.
Mal. 3:1 L. come sudd. to his t.
Mat. 4:5 set him on a pinnacle
  12:6 place is one greater than t.
  23:35 wh. ye slew bet. t. and altar
  24:1 show build, of t. Luke 21:5
  26:61 I am able to dest. t. of G.
  27:40 destroyest t. Mark 15:29
  51 veil of t. rent in twain, Mark
  15:38 ; Luke 23:45
Mark 14:58 destroy t. ma. with
  hands.
John 2:15 he drove them out of t.
Acts 3:2 laid daily at gate of t. to
  ask alms of them ent. t. 10
1 Cor. 3:16 that ye are t. of God
  17 if any man defile t. of G. him
  G. dest. t. holy, wh. t. ye are
  6:19 your body is t. of H. Ghost
Rev. 7:15 serve day and ni. in t.

In, or into the TEMPLE.
Neh. 6:11 go i. the t. to save life
Mat. 12:5 priests in t. prof. sabb.
  21:12 went into the t. to cast out
  them that sold in t. Mark
  11:15; Luke 19:45

  14 and lame came to him i. t. t.
  15 child, crying in t. Hosanna
  26:55 teaching in t. Luke 21:37
  27:5 cast down pieces of sil. i. t.
Mark 14:49 I was daily teaching
  in the t. Luke 22:53
Luke 1:21 tarried so long in t. t.
  2:27 he came by Spirit into t. t.
  46 found him in the t. sitting
  24:53 continu. in t. praising G.
Acts 2:46 with one accord in t. t.
  3:1 Peter and John went i. the t.

TEMPLES.
Hos. 8:14 forgot Maker, build. t.
Joel 3:5 into t. my goodly things
Acts 7:48 the M. H. dwelleth not
  in t. made with hands, 17:24

TEMPT.
Gen. 22:1 God did t. Abraham
Ex. 17:2 wheref. do ye t. Lord?
Deut. 6:16 ye shall not t. the L.
Mal. 3:15 that t. God are deliv.
Mat. 4:7 shalt not t. L. Luke 4:12
  22:18 why t. ye me?
Mark 12:15;
  Luke 20:23
Acts 5:9 ye have agreed to t. Sp.
  15:10 therefore why t. ye God?
1 Cor. 7:5 Sa. t. you not for your
  10:9 neither let us t. Christ

TEMPTATION.
Mat. 6:13 and lead us not into t.
  Luke 11:4
Mat. 26:41 that ye enter not into
  t. Mark 14:38; Luke 22:40, 46
Luke 4:13 wh. devil ended his t.
  8:13 in a time of t. fall away.
1 Cor. 10:13 no t. tak. you, wi. t.
Gal. 4:14 t. in flesh despised not
1 Tim. 6:9 that be rich fall into t.
Jam. 1:12 bless, that endureth t.

TEMPTATIONS.
Deut. 7:19 great t. th. eyes saw,
  29:3
Luke 22:28 contin. with me in t.
Acts 20:19 serv. G. with many t.
Jam. 1:2 joy when ye fall into t.
1 Pet. 1:6 are in heaviness thro' t.
2 Pet. 2:9 L. deli. godly out of t.

TEMPTED.
Ps. 106:14 lusted, t. God in desert

Mal. 4:1 wildern. to be t. of the
devil. Mark 1:13; Luke 4:2
1 Cor. 10:9 some t. were destroy.
13 not suffer you to be t. above
Gal. 6:1 lest thou also be t.
1 Thes. 3:5 by means tempter t.
Heb. 2:18 himself suff. being t.
4:15 in all points t. like as we
11:37 were sawn asun. were t.
Jam. 1:13 say wh. he is t. I am t.
of God, for God cannot be t.
14 ev. man t. wh. drawn of lust

TEMPTER.

Mat. 4:3 when t. came to him

TENTH.

Gen. 28:22 surely give t. to thee
Lev. 27:32 t. shall be holy to L.
Is. 6:13 yet in it shall be a t.

TENDER.

Deut. 28:56 the t. and delic. woman
2 K. 22:19 heart t. 2 Chr. 34:27
1 Chr. 22:5 Sol. young and t. 29:1
Prov. 4:3 t. and belov. in sight of
Luke 1:78 thro' t. mercy of God
Jam. 5:11 L. is pitiful, of t. mercy

TENDER-HEARTED.

2 Chr. 13:7 Reh. young and t.-h.
Eph. 4:32 be kind and t.-h.

TESTAMENT.

Mat. 26:28 this is my blood in
new t. Mark 14:24
Luke 22:20 this cup is the new t.
1 cor. 11:25
Heb. 7:22 surety of a better t.
9:15 he is mediator of new t. for
redemption under first t.
16 where a t. is, th. must death
17 t. is of force after men dead
20 this is blood of t. G. enjoin.
Rev. 11:19 in temple ark of t.

TESTIFY.

Luke 16:28 send Laza, that he t.
John 2:25 that any sho. t. of man
3:11 t. have seen; 5:39 t. of me
7:7 bec. I t. of it; 15:26 t. of me
Acts 2:40 wi. oth. words did he t.
10:42 t. it is he was ordai. of G.
20:24 to t. gospel of grace of G.
26:5 know they, if th. would t.
Gal. 5:3 I t. to ev. man circum.
Eph. 4:17 this I say, and t. in L.

1 John 4:14 we ha. seen and do t.
Rev. 22:16 I Jesus sent ang. to t.
18 I t. to ev. man that heareth

TESTIFIED.

Acts 8:25 wh. they t. and preach
18:5 P. t. to Jews that J. was C.
28:23 to whom he t. king. of G.
1 Cor. 15:15 bec. we ha. t. of G.
1 Thes. 4:6 we forewarned you, t.
1 Tim. 2:6 gave himself to be t.
Heb. 2:6 one in a certain place t.
1 Pet. 1:11 t. beforeh. sufferings
1 John 5:9 witness G. t. of his S.
3 John 3 t. of truth that is in th.

TESTIFYING.

Acts 20:21 t. both to Jews and G.
Heb. 11:4 witn. G. t. of his gifts
1 Pet. 5:12 t. this is grace of God

TESTIMONY.

Ex. 16:34 pot of manna bef. t.
25:16 sh. put into ark the t. 21
31:18 gave M. two tables of t.
Mat. 8:4 gift M. commanded for
a t. Mark 1:44; Luke 5:44
10:18 t. against them, Mark 13:9
Acts 13:22 to wh. also he gave t.
14:3 gave t. to word of his grace
22:18 they will not recei. thy t.
1 Cor. 1:6 as t. of C. was confir.
2:1 declaring unto you t. of God
2 Cor. 1:12 t. of our conscience
2 Thes. 1:10 bec. our t. was beli.
2 Tim. 1:8 not asham. of t. of L.
Heb. 3:5 t. of things which were
11:5 Enoch had t. he pleased G.

TESTIMONIES.

Ps. 25:10 keep coven. and his t.
78:56 keep not t. 93:5 t. sure
99:7 th. kept t. and ordinances
119:2 bles. are they th. keep t.
14 I rejoiced in way of thy t.
22 I have kept thy t. 167, 168
24 thy t. deli. 31 I stuck to t.
36 incline my heart to thy t.
79 have known t. turn to me
95 wick. waited, I consider t.
99 thy t. are my meditation
111 thy t. have I taken
119 I love thy t. 125 know t.
129 thy t. are wonderful

THANK.

Luke 6:32 those that love you
what t. have ye? 33:34

THANK, Verb.

1 Chr. 16:4 appoint. Lev. to t. L.
7 Da. delivered psalm to t. L.
23:30 stand ev. morning to t. L.
29:13 we t. thee, praise name
Dan. 2:23 I t. thee, praise thee
Mat. 11:25 Je. said, I t. thee, O
Fa. L. of heaven, Luke 10:21
Luke 17:9 doth he t. that serv.?
18:11 G. I t. th. not as oth. men
John 11:41 Father, I t. thee
Rom. 1:8 I t. my God, 7:25
1 Cor. 1:4 I t. G. on your behalf
14 I t. G. I bapt. none of you
14:18 I t. G. I speak with tong.
Phil. 1:3 I t. G. on rem. of you
1 Thes. 2:13 for this can. t. we G.
2 Thes. 1:3 are bound to t. God
1 Tim. 1:12 I t. Jesus Christ
2 Tim. 1:3 I t. G. whom I serve
Phile. 4 I t. God, mak. mention

THANKFUL.

Ps. 100:4 t. to him Col. 3:15
Rom. 1:21 glori. not, nor we. t.

THANKS.

Neh. 12:31 companies th. gave t.
Dan. 6:10 he prayed, and gave t.
Mat. 26:27 he took the cup, and
gave t. Luke 22:17
Mark 8:6 seven loaves and ga. t.
14:23 when he had given t. he
2 Cor. 1:11 t. may be given
Eph. 5:20 giving t. always for all
1 Thes. 3:9 what t. can we reder
Heb. 13:15 offer praise, giving t.
Rev. 4:9 give t. to him on throne

THANKSGIVING.

Lev. 7:12 if he offer it for a t.
13:15; 22:29
Neh. 11:17 to begin t. in prayer
12:8 which was over the t.
46 th. were songs of praise, t.
Ps. 26:7 publish with voice of t.
50:14 offer unto God t. pay vows
69:;4 30 I will mag. him with t.
95:2 come before his face wi. t.
100:4 enter into his gates wi. t.
107:22 let sacrifice sacri. of t.
116:17 offer to thee sacri. of tn.

147:7 sing to the L. with t. sing
Is. 51:3 t. and melo. found there
Jer. 30:19 out of them shall pro-
ceed t.
Amos 4:5 offer a sacrifice of t.
Jon. 2:9 sacrifice with voice of t.
2 cor. 4:15 thro' t. grace redound
9:11 causeth thro' us t. God
Phil. 4:6 wi. t. let your requests
Col. 2:7 abounding therein wi. t.
4:2 watch in the same with t.
1 Tim. 4:3 God to be rece. wi. t.
4 creature good if rece. with t.
Rev. 7:12 t. and hon. be to our G.

THANKSGIVINGS.

Neh. 12:27 keep dedication wi. t.
2 Cor. 9:12 abundant by many t.

THICKET.

Gen. 22:13 a ram caught in a t.

THIEF.

Ex. 22:2 if t. be found break. 7
Mat. 24:43 t. wo. come, Lu. 12:39
26:55 are ye come as ag. a t.?
Mark 14:48; Luke 22:52
Luke 12:33 wh. no t. approacheth
John 10:1 same is a t. and robber
10 t. cometh not but to steal
12:6 bec. he was a t. and had
1 Thes. 5:2 day of the L. cometh
as a t. 2 Pet. 3:10
4 day sho. overtake you as a t.
1 Pet. 4:15 let none suffer as a t.
Rev. 3:3 I will come as a t. 16:15

Any THING.

Gen. 18:14 is any t. too hard for L.?
Mat. 18:19 agree touching any t.

THINGS.

Mat. 22:21 render to Cesar t. that
are C.'s, to God t. that are God's,
Mark 12:17; Luke 20:25
Phil. 2:10 t. in hen. t. on earth, t.
und.

All THINGS.

Phil. 3:13 I can do all t. through
Chr.

These THINGS.

Mat. 6:33 all th. t. shall be added
unto you, Luke 12:31

THINK.

Eph. 3:20 above all we ask or t.
Phil. 4:8 if any praise, t. on these

Jam. 1:7 let not man t. he sh. re.

THINKEST.

2 Sam. 10:3 t. thou David doth
honor thy fath.? 1 Chr. 19:3
Job 35:2 t. thou this right, that
Mat. 17:25 What t. thou? 22:17
26:53 t. th. I cannot pray to my
Luke 10:36 wh. t. th. was neigh.
Acts 28:22 de. to hear what th. t.

THINKETH.

Prov. 23:7 as he t. in his heart
1 Cor. 10:12 let him that t. he st.
13:5 charity seek. not, t. no evil

THIRD time.

11 Sam. 3:8 L. called Samuel t. t.
Mat. 26:44 prayed t. t.
John 21:14 t. t. Je. showed hims.
17 saith t. t. Lovest thou me?
P. grieved, bec. he said t. t.

THIRST, Substantive.

Ps. 69:21 in t. gave me vinegar
Amos 8:11 not t. for water
13 young men shall faint for t.
2 Cor. 1:27 in hunger and t.

THIRST, Verb.

Is. 49:10 shall not hunger, nor t.
Mat 5:6 hung. and t. after right.
John 4:13 drink, of this water t.
14 drinketh, shall never t. 6:35
15 give me this wa. th. I t. not
7:37 any t. let him come to me
19:28 after this, Jesus saith, I t.
Rom. 12:20 if enemy t. gi. drink
1 Cor. 4:11 to present hour we t.
Rev. 7:16 th. sh. not t. any more

THIRSTETH.

Ps. 42:2 my soul t. for God, 63:1;
143:6

THIRSTY.

Prov. 25:21 if enemy t. gi. drink
25 as cold waters to a t. soul,
so good news
Mat. 25:35 I was t. ye gave drink
37 when saw we thee t.?
42 I was t. ye gave no drink

THOMAS.

Mat. 10:3 T. and Matthew, MArk
3:18; Luke 6:15; Acts 1:13
John 20:24 T. was not with them

THORNS.

Prov. 15:19 slothf. as hedge of t.

Mat. 7:16 do men gather grapes
of t.? Luke 6:44
13:7 fell among t. 22; Mark 4:7
18; Luke 8:7, 14
27:29 platted crown of t. put it
on, Mark 15:17; John 19:2

THOUGHT, Verb.

Neh. 6:2 th. t. to do me mischief
Acts 8:20 t. gift of G. be purcha.
10:19 while Peter t. on vision
12:9 but t. he saw a vision
1 Cor. 13:11 child, I t. as a child
Phil. 2:6 t. it not robberty to eq.
Heb. 10:29 pun. he be t. worthy

THOUGHT.

Deut. 15:9 not a t. in thy heart
1 Sam. 9:5 lest my father take t.
Mat. 6:25 take no t. for your life,
31:34; 10:19; Mark 13:11;
Luke 12:11, 22
Mat. 6:27 which of you by taking t. can add unto stature?
Luke 12:25
28 take t. for rai.? Luke 12:26
Acts 8:22 if t. of thy heart may
2 Cor. 10:5 bri. into captiv. ev. t.

THOUGHTS.

Ps. 139:17 how precious are thy t.
23 O God, try me, know my t.
146:4 in that very day his t. pe.
Prov. 12:5 the t. of the righteous
15:26 the t. of wicked are abom.
16:3 thy t. shall be established
Is. 55:7 let unrighteous forsake t.
8 my t. are not your t. saith L.
9 so are my t. higher th. yo. t.
65:2 peo. walketh after their t.
Mic. 4:12 they know not t. or L.
Mat. 9:4 J. knowi. their t. 12:25;
Luke 5:22; 6:8; 9:47; 11:17
15:19 out of heart proceed evil t.
Mark 7:21
Luke 2:35 the t. of many hearts
24:38 why do t. arise in hearts?
Rom. 2:15 their t. accusing
1 Cor. 3:20 the Lord knoweth t.
Heb. 4:12 God is a discerner of t.
Jam. 2:4 become judges of evil t.

THOUSAND.

2 Pet. 3:8 one day wi. L. is as a t.
years, a t. years as one day

THREATEN, ED.
Acts 4:17 let us straitly t. th. 21
1 Pet. 2:23 wh. he suff. he t. not
THREE times.
Dan. 6:10 he kneeled t. t. a day
THRICE.
Mat. 26:34 thou shalt deny me t.
75; Mark 14:30, 72; Luke
22:34, 61; John 13:38
THROAT.
Prov. 23:2 put a knife to t. if giv
Mat. 18:28 servant took him by t.
THRONE.
2 Sam. 3:10 to set up t. of David
7:13 stablish t. of kingdom, 16
1 K. 1:13 Solomon shall sit on
my t.
Jer. 17:25 sitting on t. of Da. 22:4,
30
Heb. 4:16 come boldly to t. of gr.
Rev. 22:1 a river proceeding out of
t. 3 t. of God and of the Lamb
THRONG, ED.
Mark 3:9 lest they should t. him
5:24 much peo. t. him, Luke 8:42
31 thou seest multitude t. thee
Luke 8:45 the multitude t. thee
THROWN.
Mat. 24:2 stone th. shall not be t.
down, Mark 13:2; Lu. 21:6
TIDINGS.
Luke 1:19 show thee glad t. 2:10
8:1 showing glad t. kingd. of G.
Acts 13:32 declare unto you glad t.
Rom. 10:15 bring glad t. of good
TIMBREL.
Ex. 15:20 Miri. took t. in hand
Job 21:12 they take t. and harp
Ps. 81:2 take psalm, bring t.
149:3 sing praises to him with t.
150:4 praise him with t.
TIMBRELS.
Ex. 15:20 wom. went out with t.
2 Sam. 6:5 house of Is. played
before Lord on t. 1 Chr. 13:8
Ps. 68:25 damsels play. with t.
TIME.
Ec. 3:1 t. to ev. purpose, 17; 8:6
Mat. 8:29 come to torment us bef.
t.?
Mark 13:33 ye know not wh. the t.

is
2 Thes. 2:6 might be revealed in t.
2 Tim. 4:3 t. come, will not end.
Rev. 1:3 for t. is at hand, 22:10
11:18 t. of ded. sho. be judged
Any TIME.
Lev. 25:32 Lev. redeem at any t.
Luke 21:34 a. t. hearts overchar.
John 1:18 no man see G. at a. t.
5:37 nor heard his voice at a. t.
Heb. 2:1 lest at any t. we should
1 John 4:12 no man se. G. at a. t.
TIMES.
Acts 1:7 not for you to kn. the t.
All TIMES.
Ps. 34:1 I will bless Lord at all t.
Prov. 17:17 a friend loveth all all t.
TIMOTHY.
2 Cor. 1:1 and T. our brother
TINKLING.
1 Cor. 13:1 I am bec. t. cymbal
TIP.
Luke 16:24 may dip t. of finger
TITHE.
Lev. 27:30 the t. of land is L.'s
Num. 18:26 off. a tenth part of t.
Deut. 12:17 not eat the t. of corn
14:23 eat t. in place the Lord
28 at end of three years bring t.
2 Chr. 31:5 they brought the t.
of all thin. 6, 12; Neh. 13:12
Neh. 10:38 Levites shall bring t.
Mat. 23:23 pay t. of mint, anise
TITHE, Verb.
Deut. 14:22 thou sh. t. increase
Luke 11:42 ye t. mint and rue
TITHES.
Gen. 14:20 Abr. gave Melchi. t.
Lev. 27:31 man redeem of his t.
Num. 18:24 t. I have given to L.
Deut. 12:6 ye sh. bring your t. 11
26:12 made end of tithing the t.
Amos 4:4 bring your t. Mal. 3:10
Mal. 3:8 ye have robbed me of t.
Luke 18:12 I give t. of all I poss.
Heb. 7:5 have command. to ta. t.
6 he received t. of Abraham
TITTLE.
Mat. 5:18 one t. shall in no wise
Luke 16:17 one t. of law to fail
TITUS.

2 Cor. 2:13 bec. I found not T.

TOGETHER.

Prov. 22:2 rich and poor meet t.
Ec. 4:11 if two lie t. then they
Is. 65:25 wolf and lamb sh. feed t.
Mat. 18:20 two or three gath. t.
19:6 what God hath joined t. let
not man put, Mark 10:9

TOIL.

Gen. 5:29 conc. our work and t.
41:51 God made me forget my t.

TOILING.

Mat. 6:28 they t. not, neither do
they spin, Luke 12:27
Mark 6:48 saw them t. in rowing

TOLERABLE.

Mat. 10:15 more t. for Sodo. and
Gommorrah, 11:24; Mark 6:11;
Luke 10:12
11:22 more t. for Tyre, Lu. 10:14

TOMB.

Job. 21:32 he shall remain in t.
Mat. 27:60 Joseph laid body in t.
Mark 6:29 laid John's corpse in t.

TOMBS.

Mat. 8:28 with devils com. out t.
Mark 5:2, 3, 5: Luke 8:27
23:29 ye build t. of the prophets

TONGUE.

Jud. 7:5 lappeth of water wi. t.
Prov. 6:17 hateth proud, lying t.
24 flattery of t. of stra. woman
10:29 t. of just as choice silver
31 froward t. shall be cut out
12:18 t. of the wise is health
19 a lying t. is but for a mom.
15:2 t. of wise useth knowledge
4 a wholes. t. is a tree of life
16:1 answer of t. is from the L.
17:4 liar giv. ear to naughty t.
20 perv. t. falls into mischief
18:21 dea. and life in pow. of t.
21:6 treasu. by lying t. is vanity
23 whoso keepeth t. keep. soul
25:15 soft t. breaketh the bone
23 angry counten. a backbit. t.
26:28 lying t. hateth th. afflicted
Prov. 28:23 he that flat. with t.
31:26 in her t. is law of kindne.
Zec. 14:12 t. consume in mouth
Mark 7:33 spit, and touch. his t.

35 his t. was loosed, Luke 1:64
Jam. 1:26 and bridleth not his t.
3:5 so the t. is a little member
6 t. is fire; 8 t. no man tame

MY TONGUE.

Luke 16:24 dip finger, cool my t.

TONGUE, for language, speech.

Gen. 10:5 every one after his t.
Ex. 4:10 slow of speech, slow t.
Deut. 28:49 whose t. not unders.
Is. 28:11 anoth. t. will he speak
Acts 2:8 how hear we in our own t
26:14 saying in Hebrew t. Saul
Rom. 14:11 every t. confess to G.
1 Cor. 14:2 speak in unkn. t. 4:27
9 by t. words easy understood
26 every one hath a psalm, a t.
Phil. 2:11 ev. t. confess. J. is L.

TONGUED.

1 Tim. 3:8 be gra. not double t.

TONGUES.

Gen. 10:20 sons of H. after th. t.
31 sons of Shem, after their t.
Ps. 31:20 keep th. fr. strife of t.
55:9 O Lord, and divide their t.
78:36 lied to him with their t.
140:3 sharpened t. like a serpe.
Is. 66:18 gath. all nations and t.
Jer. 23:31 use their t. and say
Acts 2:3 th. appeared cloven t. 4
11 hear in our t. works of God
10:46 heard them speak with t.
19:6 spake with t. prophesied
1 Cor. 12:10 divers kinds of t. 28
30 do do all speak with t.? do all
13:1 tho' I speak with t. of men
14:5 I would ye all spake wi. t.
6 if I come to you speak, wi. t.
18 I speak with t. more than
21 with men of other t. I speak
22 t. for a sign; 23 speak wi. t.

TOOK.

Gen. 5:24 En. was not, G. t. him
Num. 11:25 L. t. of Spirit on him

TOP.

Prov. 21:9 in corner of house-t.
25:24

TOPS.

Mat. 10:27 preach upon house-t.
Luke 12:3 proclaim. on house-t.

TORMENT.

Mat. 4:24 tak. wi. disease and t.
TORMENT, Verb.
Mat. 8:29 art thou come to t. us?
Mark 5:7 t. me not, Luke 8:28
TORMENTED.
Mat. 8:6 serv. lieth grievously t.
Luke 16:24 I am t. in this flame
25 he is comforted, thou art t.
Rev. 9:5 should be t. five months
11:10 two prophets t. them
14:10 he sh. be t. with fire and
20:10 shall be t. day and night
TORMENTORS.
Mat. 18:34 lord deliver. him to t.
TORN.
Hos. 6:1 hath t. he will heal
Mal. 1:13 bro. that which was t.
Mark 1:26 uncl. spirit had t. him
TOSSED.
Eph. 4:14 children t. to and fro
Jam. 1:6 waver, is like wave t.
TOUCH.
1 Chr. 16:22 t. not mine anointed,
Ps. 105:15
Jer. 12:14 that t. the inheritance
Lam 4:14 men could not t. gar.
15 it is unclean, depart. t. not
Hag. 2:12 if one with skirt t. br.
13 if one that is unclean t.
Mat. 9:31 if I but t. Mark 5:28
14:36 that they might t. the
hem, Mark 6:56; 8:22
Mark 3:10 to t. him, Luke 6:19
8:22 besou. him to t. blind man
John 20:17 Jesus saith, t. me not
1 Cor. 7:1 good not to t. a wom.
TOUCHED.
Mat. 8:3 and Jesus t. him, Mark
1:41; Luke 5:13
15 he t. her hand, the fever left
9:20 diseased with an issue t.
garm. Mark 5:27; Luke 5:13
29 then t. he their eyes, 20:34
14:36 many as t. him were made
whole, Mark 6:56
Mark 5:30 t. clothes, Lu. 8:45, 47
TOUCHING.
Ezek. 7:13 vision is t. multitude
Mat. 18:19 t. any thing they ask
Rom. 11:28 as t. elect. they are
1 Cor. 8:1 as t. things offer. idols

Col. 4:10 t. whom ye received
TOWER.
Gen. 11:4 let us build city and t.
High TOWER.
2 Sam. 22:3 God is my high t. Ps.
18:2; 144:2
TRAIN, Verb.
Prov. 23:6 t. ch. in way he sh. go
TRAITOR, S.
Luke 6:16 Iscariot which was t.
2 Tim. 3:4 in last days men be t.
TRANSFIGURED.
Mat. 17:2 t. bef. them, Mark 9:2
TRANSFORMED.
Rom. 12:2 be ye t. by renewing
TRANSGRESS.
Mat. 15:2 do disciples t. tradit. ?
3 why do ye t. comm. of God?
Rom. 2:27 by circumcis. t. law
TRANSGRESSED.
43:27 thy teachers ha. t. ag. me
TRANSGRESSEST, ETH.
Est. 3:3 why t. king's com.?
Prov. 16:10 mouth t. not in judg.
Hab. 2:5 because he t. by wine
1 John 3:4 committeth sin. t. law
TRANSGRESSING.
Is. 59:13 in t. and lying ag. Lord
TRANSGRESSION.
Job 7:21 why not pardon my t.
Prov. 12:13 wick. is snared by t.
17:9 covereth t. seeketh love
19:11 his glory to pass over t.
Rom. 4:15 wh. no law is. is no t.
Heb. 2:2 every t. receiv. recomp.
1 John 3:4 for sin is t. of the law
TRANSGRESSIONS.
Ps. 51:3 for I acknowl. my t. my sin
103:12 so far hath be removed i.
53:5 he was wounded for our t.
Gal. 3:19 law was add. bec. of t.
Heb. 9:15 for redemption of t.
TRANSGRESSOR.
Prov. 21:18 t. be ransom for upr.
Is. 48:8 called a t. from womb
TRANSGRESSORS.
Is. 53:12 he was numbered with t.
and made intercession for t.
Mark 15:28 he was numbered
with t. Luke 22:37
Jam. 2:9 are convin. of law as t.

TRANSLATE, D.
Col. 1:13 t. us into kingd. of Son
Heb. 11:5 Enoch was t. that he

TRAVAILING.
Is. 42:14 I cry like woman in t.
Hos. 13:13 sorrows of t. woman
Rev. 12:2 t. in birth, and pained

TRAVELLER.
Job 31:32 I open my doors to t.

TREACHEROUSLY.
Mal. 2:10 why do we deal t. eve.
15 let none deal t. against wife
16 take heed, th. ye deal not t.

TREAD.
Deut. 11:24 whereon your feet t.
Mal. 4:3 ye shall t. down wicked
Luke 10:19 power to t. on scorp.

TREASURE.
Ps. 135:4 chosen Is. for his pecu. t.
Prov. 15:6 in house of right. is t.
16 than great t. and trouble
21:20 there is a t. to be desired
Ec. 2:8 I gathered t. of kings
Is. 33:6 fear of the Lord is his t.
Mat. 6:21 where t. is, Lu. 12:34
12:35 a good man out of good t.
evil man of evil t. Luke 6:45
13:44 kingd. of heav. is like a t.
52 bring. out of t. new and old
19:21 thou sh. have t. in heaven,
Mark 10:21; Luke 18:22
Luke 12:21 so is he that lay. up t.
33 provide t. in the heavens
2 Cor. 4:7 t. in earthen vessels

TREASURES.
Prov. 2:4 if search. as for hid t.
Mat. 6:19 lay not up for yourselves
20 lay up for yoursel. t. in hea.
Col. 2:3 in wh. are hid t. of wis.
Heb. 11:26 greater riches than t.

TREASURY.
Mat. 27:6 not lawful to put in t.
Mark 12:41 Je. sat against t. and
beheld peo. cast mon. into t.
Luke 21:1 rich cast. gifts into t.
John 8:20 words spake Je. in t.

TREASURIES.
1 Chr. 28:11 gave Sol. pattern of t.
12
Neh. 13:12 brought tithe into t.

TREE.

Gen. 2:16 of every t. of the garden
2:17 of t. of knowl. not eat, 3:3
3:22 lest he take also of t. of life
Ps. 1:3 like a t. plant by rivers
Prov. 3:18 she is a t. of life to th.
Mat. 3:10 ev. t. that bringeth not
good fruit, 7:19; Luke 3:9
7:17 good t. bring. good fruit
cor. t. evil fruit, Luke 6:43
18 good t. cannot bri. evil fruit
12:33 make t. good and fr. good,
t. is kno. by fruit, Luke 6:44

TREES.
Is. 55:12 t. of the fields shall clap
61:3 be called t. of righteousn.
Luke 21:29 beh. fig-tree and all t.

TREMBLE.
John 2:19 the devils beli. and t.

TREMBLING.
1 Cor. 2:3 with you in much t.
2 Cor. 7:15 wi. fear and t. ye rec.
Eph. 6:5 serv. be obed. with t.
Phil. 2:12 work out salva. with t.

TRESPASSES.
Ezr. 9:15 before thee in our t.
Mat. 6:14 if ye forg. men their t.
15 if forgive not, t. neither will
your Fa. forgive yo. t. 18:35
Mark 11:25 Fath. may forgive t.
2 Cor. 5:19 not imputting their t.
Col. 2:13 having forg. you all t.

TRESPASS, Verb.
Mat. 18:15 if brother t. tell fault
Luke 17:3 if bro. t. rebuke him
4 if he t. ag. thee seven times

TRIAL.
Job 9:23 laugh at t. of innocent
Ezek. 21:13 it is a t. what if swo.
2 Cor. 8:2 how in t. of affliction
1 Pet. 1:7 t. of your faith might
4:12 not strange concerning t.

TRIBULATION.
Mat. 13:21 when t. ariseth, he is
Mat. 24:21 then shall be great. t.
29 immed. after t. Mark 13:24
John 16:33 ye shall have t.
Acts 14:22 we must thro' t. enter
Rom. 2:9 t. and ang. on eve. soul
5:3 know. t. worketh patience
8:35 shall t. separate us fr. Ch.?
12:12 rejo. in hope, patient in th.

2 Cor. 1:4 who comforte. us in t.
7:4 I am exceeding joyful in t.
1 Thes. 3:4 we should suffer t.
Rev. 2:9 I know thy works, and t.
  10 ye shall have t. ten days
  22 I will cast th. into great t.
7:14 they which came of great t.

TRIBULATIONS

1 Sam. 10:19 saved you out of t.
Rom. 5:3 but we glory in t. also
Eph. 3:13 faint not at t.
2 Thes. 1:4 for your faith in all t.

TRIBUTE.

Neh. 5:4 bor. money for king's t.
Prov. 12:24 slothful be under t.
Mat. 17:24 doth not mas. pay t.?
  25 of whom do kings take t.?
22:17 is it lawf. to give t. to Ce.?
  Mark 12:14; Luke 20:22
  19 show me the t. money, they
Luke 23:2 forbidding t. to Cesar
Rom. 13:6 for this cau. pay ye t.
  7 render t. to whom t. is due

TRIMMED, EST.

Mat. 25:7 arose, t. their lamps

TRIUMPH.

Job 20:5 that t. of wicked is short
Ps. 47:1 shout unto God with t.

TROUBLE, Substantive.

Ps. 9:9 L. will be a refuge in t.
  13 consider my t. wh. I suffer
10:1 why hid. th. thyself in t.?
Prov. 11:8 right, del. out t. 12:13
Is. 1:44 new-moons, they are a t.
8:22 look to earth and behold t.
17:14 behold at evening tide t.
26:16 L. in t. they visited thee
2 Cor. 1:4 able to com. them in t.
  8 not have you ignor. of our t.
2 Tim. 2:9 I suffer t. as evil-doer

TROUBLES.

Ps. 34:6 L. saved him out of t. 17

TROUBLE, Verb.

Dan. 4:19 let not interpr. t. thee
  5:10 let not thy thoughts t. thee
Acts 15:19 t. not G. turned to G.
2 Thes. 1:6 trib. to th. that t. you
Heb. 12:15 lest bitterness t. you

TROUBLED.

Dan. 2:1 Neb.'s spirit was t. 3
  4:5 visions of my head t. 7:15

Mat. 2:3 Herod was t. and Jerus.
  14:26 they were t. Mark 6:50
  24:6 not t. thi. must co. to pass,
Luke 1:12 Zac. was to. 29 Mary t.
  10:41 Martha t. about many thi.
  24:38 why are t. and why do
John 5:4 angel went and t. water
2 Cor. 4:8 are t. on ev. side, 7:5
2 Thes. 1:7 to you that are t. rest
  2:2 that ye be not t. nei. by sp.
1 Pet. 3:14 not af. of terror, nor t.

TRUE.

1 K. 10:6 it was a t. report I
  heard, 2 Chr. 9:5
22:16 tell me noth. but that is t.
Phil. 4:8 whatsoev. things are t.

TRUE God.

1 John 5:20 this is the t. God.

TRULY.

Num. 14:21 t. as I live, saith L.
Mat. 27:54 t. this was Son of g.
Luke 20:21 teachest way of G. t.

TRUMPET.

Ex. 20:18 peo. heard noise of t.

TRUMPETS.

Num. 10:2 make two t. of silver

TRUST.

Job 8:14 wh. t. sh. be a spider's
  15:15 putteth no t. in his saints
Ps. 40:4 that maketh Lord his t.
  71:5 O Lord God, thou art my t.
  141:8 in thee is my t. leave not
Prov. 22:19 thy t. may be in Lord
  28:25 that puts his t. in Lord
  29:25 who putteth his t. in Lord
Is. 30:3 t. in Egypt shall be conf.
  57:13 that putteth t. in me shall
Luke 16:11 com. to t. true riches
2 Cor. 3:4 such t. ha. we thro' C.
1 Tim. 1:11 gospel, com. to my t.
  6:20 keep that commi. to thy t.

TRUST, Verb.

Ruth 2:12 thou art come to t.
Prov. 31:11 her husband doth t.
Is. 12:2 I will t. not be afraid
Jer. 7:4 t. ye not in lying words
Ezek. 16:15 th. didst t. in beauty
Zep. 3:12 shall t. in name of L.
Mat. 12:21 in his name shall Gen-
  tiles t. Rom. 15:12
Mark 10:24 them that t. in riches

John 5:45 Moses in whom ye t.
Rom. 15:24 I t. to see you in my
1 Cor. 16:7 I t. to tarry a while
2 Cor. 1:9 sho. not t. in ourselves
10 in whom we t. that he will
10:7 if any man t. to himself
Phil. 3:4 if any think. hath to t.
1 Tim. 4:10 we t. in living God
6:17 they t. not in uncertain
2 John 12 I t. to come unto you
3 John 14 I t. I shall shortly see

TRUSTED.

Eph. 1:12 who first t. in Christ
13 in whom ye also t. after ye
1 Pet. 3:5 holy wom. who t. in G.

TRUSTETH.

Jer. 17:5 cursed be man t. man
Hab. 2:18 maker of work t. ther.
1 Tim. 5:5 th. is a widow, t. in G.

TRUTH.

Prov. 22:21 kn. certain. of words
Dan. 4:37 all whose works are t.
Gal. 2:5 t. of gospel might conti.
14 walked not according to t.
3:1 ye should not obey t. 5:7
4:16 enemy bec. I tell you t.?
Eph. 4:15 speak. the t. in love
21 taught by him as t. is in J.
5:9 fruit of Spirit is in all t.
6:14 hav. your loins girt with t.
2 Thes. 2:10 recei. not love of t.
12 damned who believe not t.
13 salvation thro' belief of t.
1 Tim. 2:4 come to knowl. of t.
7 I speak t. in Christ, lie not
3:15 the pillar and ground of t.
4:3 received of them wh. kn. t.
6:5 corrupt minds, destitu. of t.
2 Tim. 2:18 concern. t. ha. erred
25 repent. to acknowledg. of t.
3:7 to come to knowledge of t.
8 Jambres, so do these resist t.
4:4 turn away their ears from t.
Tit. 1:1 to acknowledging of t.
14 commandm. that turn fr. t.
Heb. 10:26 received knowl. of t.
Jam. 3:14 lie not against the t.
5:19 if any of you err fr. the t.
1 Pet. 1:22 purified in obeying t.
2 Pet. 2:2 way of t. evil spok. of
1 John 1:6 we lie, do not the t.

8 dec. ourselves, t. is not in us
2:4 t. not in him; 27 t. is no lie
21 because ye know not t. and
no lie is of the t.
3:19 we know that we are of t.
5:6 witness, because Spirit is t.
2 John 1 they that have known t.
2 for t. sake that dwell. in us
3 John 3 tes. of t. that is in thee
8 might be fellow-helpers to t.
12 good report of men and of t.

In TRUTH.

Jos. 24:14 serve Lord in t. 1 Sam.
12:24
Jud. 9:15 if in t. ye anoint me
Mat. 22:16 teachest the way of
God in t. Mark 12:14
John 4:23 in spirit and in t. 24
1 John 3:18 love in tongue, in t.
2 John 4 I found of thy children
walking in t. 3 John 4

Thy TRUTH.

Ps. 25:5 lead me in thy t. teach
John 17:17 sanctify th. thro' t. t.

Word of TRUTH.

Ps. 119:43 take not w. of t. out
2 Cor. 6:7 appr. ours. by w. of t.
Eph. 1:13 that ye heard w. of t.
Col. 1:5 ye heard bef. in w. of t.
2 Tim. 2:15 dividing word of t.
Jam. 1:18 begat he us by w. of t.

TRY.

Jer. 6:27 mayest kn. and t. way
9:7 melt and t. them, Zec. 13:9
17:10 Lord search heart, t. reins
Lam. 3:40 let us search and t.
Dan. 11:35 some fall to t. them
1 Cor. 3:13 fire t. ev. man's work
1 Pet. 4:12 trial wh. is to t. you
1 John 4:1 t. spirits whether of g.
Rev. 3:10 temptation to t. them

TRIED.

Ps. 12:6 as silver is t. in furnace
17:3 th. hast t. me, find nothing
66:10 hast t. us as silver is t.
105:19 word of the Lord t. him
Is. 28:16 I lay in Z. a t. stone

TRIEST, ETH.

Job 34:3 ear t. words as mouth
Ps. 7:9 righteous God t. hearts
11:5 the Lord t. the righteous

260

Prov. 17:3 but Lord t. the hearts
Jer. 11:20 O L. that t. the reins
20:12 L. of hosts that t. righte.
1 Thes. 2:4 but God who t. hearts

TRYING.

Jam. 1:3 t. of faith work. patien.

TURN.

2 Chr. 30:9 L. will not t. a his face
Prov. 29:8 wise men t. a. wrath

TURN to the Lord.

2 Sam. 15:4 in trou. did t. to t. L.
Ps. 22:27 world shall t. to the L.
Lam. 3:40 try ways, t. to the L.
Hos. 14:2 take words, t. to the L.
Joel 2:13 rend heart, t. to the L.
Luke 1:16 many sh. he t. to the L.
2 Cor. 3:16 when it sh. t. to the L.

TWELVE.

Mat. 9:20 a wom. was diseased t.
years, Mark 5:25; Luke 8:43
10:2 names of t. apos. Luke 6:13
Mark 14:20 it is one of t. that
dippeth
Luke 2:42 when Je. was t. years

TWINKLING.

1 Cor. 15:52 changed in t. of eye

TWO.

Mat. 6:24 no man can serve t.
masters, Luke 16:13
18:8 t. ha. or t. feet, Mark 9:43
9 having t. eyes, mark 9:47
19 if t. of you agree on earth
20 wh. t. or three are gathered
24:40 then shall t. be in field

U.

UNBELIEF.

Mat. 13:58 works, because of u.
17:20 not cast out bec. of yo. u.
Mark 6:6 marvel. bec. of their u.
9:24 I believe, help th. mine u.
16:14 upbraid. them with th. u.
Heb. 3:12 an evil heart of u.
19 could not enter bec. of u. 4:6

UNBELIEVERS.

1 Cor. 6:6 goeth to law before u.
2 Cor. 6:14 unequal. yoked wi. u.

UNBELIEVING.

1 Cor. 7:14 u. husband sanctified
15 u. if depart, let him depart
Tit. 1:15 unto u. is nothing pure

Rev. 21:8 u. have th. part in lake

UNCLEAN Spirits.

Mat. 10:1 power against u.
spirits, Mark 6:7
Mark 1:27 com. u. s. Luke 4:36
3:11 u. s. when they saw him
5:13 u. s. went and ent. swine
Acts 5:16 were vexed with u. s.
8:7 u. s. came out of possessed

UNDERSTAND.

1 Cor. 13:2 tho' I u. all mysteries

UNDERSTANDETH.

Mat. 13:19 hear. word, u. it not
23 that heareth word, and u. it

UNDERSTANDING.

Prov. 1:2 to perceive words of u.
2:2 thou apply th. heart to u.
3 if thou liftest up voice for u.
6 out of his mouth cometh u.
11 discretion pres. thee, u. sh.
3:5 lean not to thine own u.
13 happy is man th. getteth u.
19 by u. he establish. heavens
4:1 attend to kn. 5 get u. 7
5:1 bow thine ear to my u.
6:32 commit. adult. lacketh u.
10:13 that hath u. wisd. is found
14:29 is slow to wrath is of u.
33 wisdom in him that hath u.
15:14 heart of him that hath u.
32 that heareth reproof get. u.
16:16 better to get u. than silv.
22 u. is a well spring of life to
17:24 wisd. bef. him that ha. u.
18:2 fool hath no delight in u.
Luke 1:3 having had perfect u.
2:47 were astonished at his u.
1 Cor. 14:15 pray with u. sing with
u.
19 ra. speak five words with u.
Phil. 4:7 peace of G. pass. all u.
Col. 1:9 filled with all spiritu. u.

Void of UNDERSTANDING.

Prov. 7:7 a young man v. of u.
10:13 a rod for him th. is v. of u.

UNDERSTANDING, Adj.

Prov. 8:5 be of an u. heart

UNDERSTOOD.

Rom. 1:20 being u. by the things
1 Cor. 13:11 I u. as a child
14:9 ut. by tongue wor. to be u.

261

UNFEIGNED.

2 Cor. 6:6 by H. Ghost, by love u.
1 Tim. 1:5 pure heart, faith u.
1 Pet. 1:22 thro' Spi. unto u. love

UNGODLINESS.

2 Tim. 2:16 will increase unto u.

UNGODLY.

Ps. 1:1 walk. not in coun. of u.

UNITY.

Ps. 133:1 for bre. to dwell in u.
Eph. 4:3 endeavoring to keep u.
13 till we come in the u. of

UNMOVABLE.

Acts 27:41 forep. of ship rema. u.
1 Cor. 15:58 bret. be steadfast, u.

UNPREPARED.

2 Cor. 9:4 if come and find you u.

UNPROFITABLE.

Job 15:3 sh. reason with u. talk
Mat. 25:30 cast u. ser. into dark.
Luke 17:10 say, We are u. serv.
Rom. 3:12 are altogether bec. u.
Tit. 3:9 genealogies, u. and vain
Phile. 11 in time past was u.
Heb. 13:17 not wi. grief, th. is u.

UNPROFITABLENESS.

Heb. 7:18 the weakness and u.

UNPUNISHED.

Prov. 11:21 wicked sh. not be u.
16:5 the proud shall not be u.
17:5 glad at calamities not be u.
19:5 false witness not be u. 9
Jer. 25:29 utterly u. sh. not be u.
30:11 not leave thee altoget. u.
46:28 not leave thee wholly u.
49:12 sh. thou go u.? not go u.

UNQUENCHABLE.

Mat. 3:12 but burn the chaff with
u. fire, Luke 3:17

UNREASONABLE.

Acts 25:27 it seemeth u. to send
2 Thes. 3:2 delivered fr. u. men

UNRIGHTEOUS.

Ex. 23:1 put not hand to be u.
Job 27:7 riseth ag. me be as u.
Ps. 71:4 deli. out of hand of u.
Is. 10:1 woe to th. that decree u.
55:7 u. man forsake thoughts
Luke 16:11 not faithful in u. ma.
Rom. 3:5 is G. u. who tak. ven.?
1 Cor. 6:9 the u. shall not inherit

Heb. 6:10 God is not u. to forget

UNRIGHTEOUSNESS.

Lev. 19:15 do no u. in judgm. 35
Ps. 92:15 there is no u. in him
Jer. 22:13 buildeth house by u.
Luke 16:19 friends of mam. of u.
John 7:18 true, no u. in him
Rom. 1:18 u. of men who hold
the truth in u.
29 filled with all u. fornication
2:8 them that obey u. indigna.
3:5 if our u. commend righte.
6:13 yield mem. as instru. of u.
2 Cor. 6:14 wh. fellow. with u. ?
2 Thes. 2:10 wi. deceivab. of u.
12 beli. not, had pleasure in u.
Heb. 8:12 be merciful to their u.
2 Pet. 2:13 shall receive rew. of u.
15 Bal. who loved wages of u.
1 John 1:9 cleanse us from all u.
5:17 all u. is sin; th. is a sin not

UNRULY.

1 Thes. 5:14 warn th. that are u.
Tit. 1:6 not accused of riot. or u.
10 there are many u. and vain
Jam. 3:8 the tongue is an u. evil

UNSEARCHABLE.

Job 5:9 G. doeth great th. and u.
Ps. 145:3 L. his greatness is u.
Prov. 25:3 heart of kings is u.
Rom. 11:33 how u. are his judg.
Eph. 3:8 preach u. riches of Ch.

UNSEEMLY.

Rom. 1:27 work. that which is u.
1 Cor. 13:5 doth not behave u.

UNSPEAKABLE.

2 Cor. 9:15 thanks to G. for his u.
12:4 cau. up and heard u. words
1 Pet. 1:8 rejoice with joy u. full

UNSPOTTED.

Jam. 1:27 to keep himself u. from

UNSTABLE.

Gen. 49:4 u. as water, not excel
Jam. 1:8 doublemind. man is u.
2 Pet. 2:14 beguilling u. souls
3:16 are unlearned and u. wrest

UNTHANKFUL.

Luke 6:35 he is kind to the u.
2 Tim. 3:2 blasphem. u. unholy

UNWISE.

Deut. 32:6 thus requi. L. u. peo.

Rom. 1:14 debtor to wise and u.
Eph. 5:17 be not u. but underst.

UNWORTHY, ILY.

Acts 13:46 judge yourselves u. of
1 Cor. 6:2 are ye u. to judge the?
11:27 drink this cup of the L. u.
29 he that eateth and drink. u.

UPBRAID, ED, ETH.

Jud. 8:15 with wh. ye did u. me
Mat. 11:20 then began he to u.
Mark 16:14 he u. th. with unbel.
Jam. 1:5 giveth liberally, u. not

UPHOLD.

Ps. 51:12 u. me with thy free Sp.
119:116 u. me according to word
Prov. 29:23 honor sh. u. humble
Is. 63:5 I wondered was none to u.

UPHOLDETH.

Ps. 37:17 Lord u. the righteous

UPPER.

Mark 14:15 will show you an u.
room, Luke 22:12
Acts 1:13 went up into u. room

UPRIGHTLY.

Prov. 2:7 buckler to th. walk u.
10:9 walketh u. walketh surely
15:21 man of underst. walk. u.
28:18 whoso walk. u. be saved
Gal. 2:14 that th. walked not u.

UPRIGHTNESS.

1 K. 3:6 walked before thee in u.
Prov. 2:13 who leave paths of u.
14:2 walketh in u. feareth Lord
28:6 better is poor walketh in u.

UPROAR.

Acts 20:1 after u. was ceased, Paul

UPSIDE down.

Acts 17:6 have turn. world u. d.

URIAH, or URIJAH.

2 Sam. 11:3 Bath-sh. wife of U.?
6 say, Send me U. the Hittite
14 sent it by U. 21 U. is dead

V.

VAIN.

Job 11:12 for v. man would be wise
Ezek. 12:24 no more any v. vision
13:7 have ye not seen v. vision
Mal. 3:14 it is v. to serve God
Mat. 6:7 use not v. repetitions
Rom. 1:21 bec. v. in imaginatio.

Jos. 1:26 this man's religion is v.
2:20 know, O v. man, that faith

In VAIN.

Ex. 20:7 not take name of Lord
in v. Deut. 5:11
Prov. 30:9 take name of G. in v.
Rom. 13:4 bear. not sword in v.
1 Cor. 15:2 unless ye belie. in v.
2 Cor. 6:1 not grace of G. in v.
Gal. 2:2 lest I should run in v.
21 then Christ is dead in v.
Jam. 4:5 think scri. saith in v.?

VALLEY.

2 K. 2:16 Spirit cast him into v.
Ps. 23:4 I walk thro' v. of death

VALLEYS.

Ps. 104:8 go down by v. unto place
10 sendeth springs into the v.
Cant. 2:1 rose of Shar. lily of v.

VALUE.

Mat. 10:31 ye are of more v. than
many sparrows, Luke 12:7

VALUED.

Job 28:16 wisdom cannot be v.
19 nei. shall it be v. with gold

VANITY.

Prov. 13:11 wealth gotten by v.
21:0 treas. by lying tong. is v.
22:8 soweth iniq. shall reap v.
30:8 remove from me v. and lies
Ec. 9:9 with wife all the days of v.
Hab. 2:13 weary themsel. for v.

VANITIES.

Jon. 2:8 that observe lying v.
Acts 14:15 ye should turn from v.

VEHEMENTLY.

Mark 14:31 Peter spake more v.
Luke 6:48 beat v. on house, 49
11:53 Pha. began to urge him v.
23:10 stood and v. accused him

VENGEANCE.

Prov. 6:34 not spare in day of v.
Is. 34:8 day of v. 61:2; Jer. 51:6
35:4 your God will come with v.
Mic. 5:15 execute v. Ezek. 25:17
Nah. 1:2 Lord will take v. on his
adversaries
Luke 21:22 for these be days of v.
Acts 28:4 v. suffereth not to live
Rom. 3:5 unright. who tak. v.?
12:19 v. is mine, saith the Lord

2 thes. 1:8 flaming fire, taking v.
Jude 7 suffering v. of eternal fire

VENISON.

Gen. 25:28 because he eat of v.

VESSEL.

Ps. 31:12 I am like a broken v.
Mark 11:16 carry v. thro' temple
Luke 8:16 coverth candle wi. v.
Acts 9:15 a chosen v. unto me
  10:11 Pe. saw a certain v. 11:5
Rom. 9:21 make one v. to honor
2 Tim. 2:21 sh. be v. to honor
1 Pet. 3:7 to wife as to weaker v.

VESSELS.

Mat. 13:48 gathered good into v.
  25:4 but wise took oil in their v.
Rom. 9:22 v. of wr. 23 v. of mercy
Rev. 2:27 as v. of potter be brok.

VEXED.

Num. 20:15 Egyptians v. us and
Job. 27:2 Almighty v. my soul
Ps. 6:2 my bones v. 3 soul v.
  10 let enemies be asha. and v.
Is. 63:10 they rebelled and v. Sp.
Mat. 15:22 daugh. is v. wi. devil
  17:15 he is lunatic and sore v.
Luke 6:18 they that were v. with
  unclean spirits. Acts 5:16

VICTORY.

2 Sam. 19:2 v. th. day was turn.
  23:10 L. wrought a great v. 12.
1 Chr. 29:11 thine, O L. is the v.
Ps. 98:1 arm hath gotten him v.
Is. 25:8 will swallow up death in
  v. 1 Cor. 15:54
Mat. 12:20 send judgm. unto v.
1 Cor. 15:55 O gra. where thy v.?
  57 to God, who giv. us the v.
1 John 5:4 this is the v. even fai.
Rev. 15:2 had got. v. over beast

VIGILANT.

1 Tim. 3:2 a bishop must be v.
1 Pet. 5:8 be v. bec. your adverse.

VILE.

Jud. 19:24 do not so v. a thing.
Ps. 15:4 v. person is contemned
Rom. 1:26 G. gave them up to v.
Phil. 3:21 shall change v. body
Jam. 2:2 a poor man in v. raim.

VILEST.

Ps. 12:8 when v. men are exalted

VINE.

Mat. 26:29 not drink of fruit of v.
  Mark 14:25; Luke 22:18
John 15:1 I am the true v. 5
  4 bear fruit, exc. it abide in v.
Jam. 3:12 can a v. bear figs?

VINEGAR.

Prov. 10:26 as v. to the teeth
  23:20 as v. upon nitre, so is he
Mat. 27:48 took a sponge and
  filled it with v. Mark 15:36;
  Luke 23:36; John 19:29, 30

VINEYARD.

Gen. 9:20 Noah planted a v. and
Mat. 20:1 hire labor. into his v.
  4 he said, Go ye also into v. 7
  21:28 go work to day in my v.
  33 certain householder planted
  v. Mark 12:1; Luke 20:9
Luke 13:6 fig-tree planted in v.

VIPER.

Acts 28:3 v. fasten. on P.'s hand

VIPERS.

Mat. 3:7 O generation of v. 12:34;
  23:33; Luke 3:7

VIRGIN.

Gen. 24:16 Rebekah was fair, v.
Luke 1:27 angel was sent to a v.
1 Cor. 7:28 if a v. marry. not sin.
  34 difference betw. wife and v.
  37 that he will keep his v.
2 Cor. 11:2 pres. you as chaste v.

VIRGINS.

Acts 21:9 daught. v. prophesied

VIRGINITY.

Lev. 21:13 take a wife in her v.
Luke 2:36 A. lived 7 years fr. v.

VIRTUE.

Mark 5:30 v. had gone out of
  him, Luke 6:19; 8:46
Phil. 4:8 if there be any v.
2 Pet. 1:3 called us to glo. and v.

VIRTUOUS, LY.

Ruth 3:11 thou art a v. woman
Prov. 12:4 a v. wom. is a crown
  31:10 who can find a v. wom.?

VISIBLE.

Col. 1:16 all things created, v.

VISION.

Num. 24:4 v. of Almighty, 16
1 Sam. 3:1 there was no open v.

15 S. feared to show Eli the v.
2 Sam. 7:17 accord. to this v. did
　Nathan speak, 1 Chr. 17:15
Ps. 89:19 spakest in v. to H. O.
Prov. 29:18 wh. no v. peo. perish
Is. 1:1 the v. of Isa. son of Almoz
21:2 a grievous v. is declared
22:1 burden of valley of v. 5
28:7 they err in v. stumble in
29:7 be as a dream of a night v.
11 v. is become as a book seal.
Jer. 14:14 they proph. a false v.
23:16 sp. a v. of their own heart
Lam. 2:9 proph. find no v. fr. L.
Ezek. 7:13 v. is touching whole
26 they seek a v. of prophet
8:4 according to v. 11:24; 43:3
12:22 days are prolonged v. fail.
23 the effect of ev. v. is at hand
24 no more vain v. nor divina.
27 v. he seeth is for days
13:7 ha. ye not seen a vain v.?
Dan. 2:19 revealed to D. in a v.
7:2 in my v. four winds strove
8:1 a v. appeared unto me
16 make this man understa. v.
26 shut up v. 27 astonish. at v.
9:21 whom I had seen in v. 23
10:1 he had understanding of v.
7 I saw v. men saw not v. 8
14 yet the v. is for many days
16 by v. my sorrows are turn.
11:14 exalt themsel. to estab. v.
Mic. 3:6 ye shall not have a v.
Hab. 2:2 write v. make it plain
3 v. is for an appointed time
Zec. 13:4 prophets asha. of his v.
Mat. 17:9 tell the v. to no man
Luke 1:22 perc. he had seen a v.
24:23 had seen a v. of angels
Acts 10:17 Peter doubted of v. 19
11:5 I saw a v. a vessel descend
12:9 but thought he saw a v.
16:9 v. appeared to Paul, 18:9
26:19 I was not disobedi. to v.

In a VISION.
Gen. 15:1 L. came to Ab. in a v.
Num. 12:6 make myself kn. in v.
Ezek. 11:24 brought me in a v.
Dan. 8:2 I saw in a v. by river
Acts 9:10 to An. said L. in a v.

12 S. hath seen in a v. a man
10:3 Cor. saw in a v. an angel
VISIONS.
Gen. 46:2 God spake to Is. in v.
2 Chr. 9:29 written in v. of Iddo
26:5 Z. had understanding in v.
Ezek. 1:1 I saw the v. of God
8:3 he bro. me in v. of G. to J.
13:16 which see v. of peace
Hos. 12:10 I have multiplied v.
2 Cor. 12:1 come to v. and revela.
VISIT.
Jer. 3:16 they shall v. ark of L.
Jer. 29:10 v. you and perf. my word
Jam. 1:27 v. fatherl. and widows
VISITATION.
Mic. 7:4 thy v. cometh, perplex.
Luke 19:44 knew. not time of v.
1 Pet. 2:12 glorify G. in day of v.
VISITED.
Gen. 21:1 Lord v. Sar. as he said
Mat. 25:36 v. me; 43 v. me not
VISITING.
Ex. 20:5 v. iniquity of fathers,
31:7; Num. 14:18; Deut. 5:9
VOICE.
Deut. 4:30 if thou be obedi. to v.
2 Sam. 22:14 M. High uttered v.
1 K. 18:26 was no v. nor any, 29
19:12 after fire a still small v.
Ps. 47:1 shout to G. wi. v. of trium.
98:5 sing to L. with v. of psalm
Prov. 2:3 if liftest up v. for understa
Is. 40:3 v. th. crieth in wilder. Mat.
3:3; Mark 1:3; Luke 3:4
6 v. said, Cry; 48:20 v. of sing.
50:10 obeyeth v. of his servant
51:3 thanksgiving, v. of melody
52:8 wi. v. together sh. th. sing
Ezek. 1:24 I heard v. of Almighty
10:5 as the v. of Almighty God
23:42 a v. of multitude at ease
33:32 one that hath a pleas. v.
43:2 v. li. noise of wat. Rev. 1:15
Dan. 4:31 there fell v. fr. heaven
10:6 v. of words like v. of mult.
Joel 2:11 L. utter v. before army
Jon. 2:9 with v. of thanksgiving
Mat. 3:17 a v. fr. heaven, Mark
1:11; Luke 3:22
17:5 a v. out of cloud, this is

my S. Mark 9:7; Lu. 9:35, 36
John 1:23 v. of one cry. in wild.
10:4 follow, for they kn. his v.
 5 know not v. of strangers
12:28 then came a v. saying, I
18:37 that is of truth hear. my v.
Acts 9:7 hear. v. seeing no man
10:13 a v. say. Rise, 15; 11:9
12:14 when she knew Peter's v.
 22 it is v. of a god, not of man
10:34 with v. cried, Great is Di.
1 Thes. 4:16 with v. of archangel
Heb. 12:26 whose v. shook earth

VOICE, with hear.

Ps. 5:3 my v. shalt thou hear
27:7 hear, O Lord, when I cry
wi. my v. 28:2; 64:1; 119:149;
130:2; 140:6
55:17 cry aloud, he shall h. my v.
95:7 to-day if ye will hear his v.
 Heb. 3:7, 15; 4:7
Mat. 12:19 neither any h. his v.
John 5:25 dead h. v. of Son, 28
10:3 sheep hear his v. 16, 27
Rev. 3:29 if any man hear my v.

VOICE, with hearken, ed.

Ex. 15:26 if diligently h. to v. of L.
Deut. 15:5 if thou carefully h. to v.
 of L. 26:17; 28:1, 2; 30:10
28:15 if th. wilt not h. to v. of L.
Ps. 5:2 h. to the v. of my cry
81:11 peo. would not h. to my v.

VOICES.

Rev. 11:15 there were v. in heaven
 19 temple opened, th. were v.

VOID.

Gen. 1:2 earth with. form and v.
Ps. 89:39 made v. the covenant
Prov. 11:12 v. of wisd. despiseth
Is. 55:11 word not ret. to me v.
Acts 24:16 conscien. v. of offence
Rom. 3:31 do we make v. law?
4:14 be heirs, faith is made v.
1 Cor. 9:15 make my glorying v.

VOLUNTARY.

Lev. 1:3 off. it of his own v. will
7:16 a v. offering shall be eaten
Col. 2:18 a v. humility, worship

VOMIT, ED, ETH.

Lev. 18:25 land v. inhabitants
Job 20:15 swallo. riches, v. them

Prov. 23:8 morsel eaten shalt v.
 25:16 filled with honey and v. it
Jon. 2:10 the fish v. out Jonah

VOMIT, Substantive.

Prov. 26:11 dog return. to his v.
Is. 19:14 man stagger. in his v.
28:8 tables are full of v. filthin.
2 Pet. 2:22 dog is turned to his v.

VOW.

1 Sam. 1:11 Hannah vowed a v.
 5 better thou shouldest not v.

VOWEST.

Ec. 5:4 when thou v. a vow
 5 better thou shouldest not v.

W.

WAGES.

Luke 3:14 be cont. with your w.
John 4:36 that reapeth receiv. w.
Rom. 6:23 the w. of sin is death
2 Pet. 2:15 B. lov. w. of unright.

WAIL.

Mic. 1:8 I will w. and howl

WAILING.

Ezek. 27:31 they sh. weep wi. w.
Mat. 13:42 w. and gna. teeth, 50
Rev. 18:15 merchants stand w. 19

WAIT, Verb.

Is. 8:17 I will w. on the Lord

WAITED.

Acts 10:7 Corn. called sol. th. w.
17:16 while P. w. his spirit was
1 Pet. 3:20 long-suffer. of G. w.

WALK, Verb.

Lev. 18:3 nor w. in ordin. 20:23
26:3 if ye w. in my statut. 1 K.
 6:12; Ezek. 33:15; Zec. 3:7
Deut. 5:33 shall w. in ways of L.
 13:4; 28:9; Ezek. 37:24
Jos. 22:5 take heed w. in ways
Jud. 5:10 ye that w. by the way
1 K. 3:14 if wilt w. to keep my
 comman. as Da. did w. 8:25;
 9:4; 11:38; 2 Chr. 7:17
8:23 servants that w. before
 thee, 2 Chr. 6:14
 36 teach them way wherein
 they should w. 2 Chr. 6:27
Ps. 23:4 though I w. thro' the val.
 26:11 will w. in mine integrity
116:9 I will w. before the Lord

Is. 2:3 w. in his paths, Mic. 4:2
5 let us w. in light of the Lord
42:5 giv. spirit to them that w.
59:9 but we w. in darkness
Jer. 3:17 nor w. aft. imagination
13:10 peo. which w. in imagina.
of heart, w. 16:12; 18:12
Lam. 5:8 Z. desolate, foxes w.
Ezek. 11:20 they w. in my statu.
Joel 2:8 w. ev. one in his path
Amos 3:3 can two w. ex. agreed?
Mic. 4:5 ev. one w. in name of G.
Nab. 3:15 thou didst w. thro' sea
Zep. 1:17 they sh. w. like blind
Zec. 6:7 th. might w. to and fro
Mat. 11:5 the lame w. Luke 7:22
Rom. 4:12, w. in steps of faith
8:1 who w. not after the flesh, 4
2 Cor. 5:7 we w. by faith
6:16 dw. in them and w. in th.
10:3 tho' we w. in flesh, not war
Gal. 6:16 as many as w. accord.
Eph. 2:10 we should w. in them
4:1 w. worthy of the vocation
WALK, imperatively.
Mat. 9:5 say, Rise, and w. Mark
2:9; Luke 5:23; John 5:8, 11,
12; Acts 3:6
Rom. 13:13 let us w. honestly
Gal. 5:16 w. in the Spirit, 25
Eph. 5:2 w. in love, C. loved us
Col. 2:6 received C. so w. in him
4:5 w. in wisdom toward them
WALKED.
Gen. 5:22 Enoch w. wi. God, 24
6:9 a just man, and w. with G.
Is. 9:2 people th. w. in darkness
Eph. 2:2 time past ye w. Col. 3:7
1 Pet. 4:3 we w. in lasciviousness
He WALKED.
Mat. 14:29 Peter w. on the water
WALKEST.
3 John 3 even as thou w. in truth
WALKETH.
Ps. 1:1 w. not in couns. of ungo.
Mic. 2:7 to him that w. upright.
Mat. 12:43 spirit is gone out, w.
thro' dry places, Luke 11:24
WALKING.
Dan. 3:25 men loose, w. in fire
Mark 8:24 I see men as trees w.

Acts 3:8 lame man w. leaping, 9
9:31 w. in the fear of the Lord
2 Cor. 4:2 not w. in craftiness
2 Pet. 3:3 w. after lusts, Jude 16
2 John 4 thy children w. in truth
WALL.
Jos. 2:15 Rah. dwelt on town-w.
Dan. 5:5 fingers wrote on the w.
Rev. 21:14 w. of city had 12 fou.
18 the w. of it was of jasper
WALLS.
Heb. 11:30 w. of Jeri. fell down
WANDERING.
Jude 13 w. stars to wh. is reser.
WANT, Substantive.
Ps. 34:9 no w. to them that fear
Prov. 6:11 w. as arm, man, 24:34
10:21 fools die for w. of wisdom
WANTING.
Dan. 5:27 weighed and found w.
Tit. 1:5 set in order the things w.
WAR.
1 Chr. 5:10 made w. with H. 19
Ps. 27:3 tho' w. rise against me
Dan. 7:21 made w. with saints
WAR, Verb.
Jam. 4:1 lusts that w. in memb.
2 fight and w. yet ye have not
WARFARE.
2 Cor. 10:4 weap. of w. not carnal
1 Tim. 1:18 might. war a good w.
WARN.
2 Chr. 19:10 sh. w. they tresp. not
Ezek. 3:18 to w. the wicked, 33:8
19 yet if thou w. wicked, 33:9
21 w. righteous; 33:3 w. peo. 7
Acts 20:31 I ceased not to w. ev.
1 Cor. 4:14 beloved sons I w. you
1 Thes. 5:14 w. that are unruly
WARNED.
2 K. 6:10 man of God w. him
Ps. 19:11 by them is servant w.
Ezek. 3:21 live, because he is w.
33:6 and the people be not w.
Mat. 2:12 Joseph being w. of G.
3:7 O generation of vipers, who
hath w. you? Luke 3:7
Acts 10:22 Cornelius w. from G.
Heb. 11:7 Noah w. prepared ark
WARNING.
Ezek. 33:4 tak. not w. 5 took not w.

267

Col. 1:28 w. every man, teaching
WASH.
Gen. 18:4 w. y. feet, 19:2; 24:32
Ex. 2:5 daught. of P. came to w.
Ruth 3:3 w. thyself, and anoint
1 Sam. 25:41 servant to w. feet
2 Sam. 11:8 go down and w. feet
2 K. 5:10 go w. in Jordan 7 times
Job 9:30 if I w. myself wi. water
Ps. 26:6 I will w. my hands in
51:2 w. me from mine iniquity
7 w. me and I sh. be whiter th.
58:10 w. feet in blood of wicked
Is. 1:16 w. ye, make you clean
Ezek. 23:40 thou didst w. thyself
Mat. 6:17 when fastest, w. face
15:2 they w. not when they eat
Mark 7:3 exc. they w. eat not, 4
Luke 7:28 began to w. his feet
John 9:7 w. in pool of Siloam, 11
13:5 began to w. disciples' feet?
8 never w. my feet, if I w. not
14 ought to w. one ano.'s feet
Acts 22:16 and w. away thy sins
WASHED.
Gen. 43:24 water, they w. feet
31 Joseph w. face and went out
Jud. 19:21 concub. w. their feet
2 Sam. 12:20 David arose and w.
Ps. 73:13 I w. hands in innocen.
Cant. 5:3 I have w. my feet
12 his eyes are w. with milk
Is. 4:4 w. away filth of daughters
Ezek 16:4 nor wast w. in water
9 I thorou. w. away thy blood
Mat. 27:24 Pilate w. his hands
Luke 7:44 she hath w. my feet
11:38 marvelled he had not, w.
John 9:7 he went and w. 11, 15
13:10 is w. need, not save to
14 Master have w. your feet
Acts 9:37 wh. when they had w.
16:33 he took them, w. stripes
1 Tim. 5:10 if she w. saints' feet
Heb. 10:22 having our bodies w.
Rev. 1:5 that w. us fr. our sins
7:14 have w. their robes white
WASHING, S.
Mark 7:4 w. of cups and tables, 8
Eph. 5:26 cleanse wi. w. of wat.
Heb. 9:10 stood in meats and w.

WASTE, Substantive.
Mat. 26:8 to what purpose is this
w.? Mark 14:4
WASTE, Adjective.
Hag. 1:9 because my house is w.
WASTED.
Luke 15:13 prodig. w. substance
Gal. 1:13 persecu. church and w.
WATCH, Substantive.
Jud. 7:19 middle w. had set w.
Mat. 24:43 wh. w. thief wo. come
WATCH, Verb.
Mat. 24:42 w. therefore, 25:13;
Mark 13:35; Luke 21:36;
Acts 20:31
26:38 Jesus said, w. with me
40 could ye not w.? Mark
14:34, 37
41 w. and pray, Mark 13:33;
14:38; Col. 4:2
1 Cor. 16:13 w. stand in faith
1 Thes. 5:6 let us w. 1 Pet. 4:7
2 Tim. 4:5 w. th. in all things
Heb. 13:17 th. w. for your souls
WATCHED.
Dan. 9:14 Lord w. on evil
Mat. 24:43 man of house would
have w. Luke 12:39
27:36 sitting down they w. him
Mark 3:2 w. whether he would
heal on sab. Luke 6:7; 14:1
Luke 20:20 th. w. and sent spies
Acts 9:24 w. gates day and night
WATCHETH.
Ps. 37:32 wicked w. righteous
Rev. 16:15 blessed is he that w.
WATCHFUL.
Rev. 3:2 be w. strengthen things
WATCHING.
2 Cor. 6:5 in labors, in w. in fast.
WATER, Substantive.
Gen. 16:7 angel found Ha. by w.
18:4 let a little w. be fetched
Ex. 17:6 shall come w. out of rock
2 K. 3:11 Eli. poured w. on Elijah's
Hab. 3:10 overflow. of w. passed
Mat. 3:11 bapt. you wi. w. Mark
1:8; Luke 3:16; John 1:26
16 J. went out of w. Mark 1:10
10:42 giv. cup of w. Mark 9:41
14:28 bid me come to thee on w.

268

27:24 Pilate took w. and washed
Mark 14:13 bearing pitcher of w.
  Luke 22:10
Luke 8:23 ship was filled with w.
  24 rebuked w. 25 w. obeyed
  16:24 may dip his finger in w.
John 2:7 fill water-pots with w.
  3:5 except a man be born of w.
  23 because there was much w.
  4:10 living w. 11; 15 give me w.
  46 came wh. he made w. wine
  5:3 waiting for moving of w.
Acts 1:5 J. bapt. with w. 11:16
  8:36 here is w. 38 went into w.
Jam. 3:12 yield salt w. and fresh
1 Pet. 3:20 8 souls saved by w.
Rev. 21:6 give of fount. of w. of life
  22:1 show. me a pure river of w.
  17 let take w. of life freely

No WATER.
Luke 7:44 thou gavest me no w.

WATERS.
2 K. 2:8 smote w. 14 Elisha.
Is. 48:21 caused w. flow out of rock
Jer. 2:13 fountain of living w.

WAVERETH.
Jam. 1:6 he that w. is like wave

WAVERING.
Heb. 10:23 hold faith without w.
Jam. 1:6 ask in faith, nothi. w.

WAY.
Prov. 2:8 preserveth w. of saints
  6:23 w. of life, 15:24; Jer. 21:8
Is. 43:19 I will make w. in wildern.
Mal. 3:1 prepare w. before me
Mat. 7:13 broad is w. to destruc.
  14 narrow is w. lead. unto life

By the WAY.
Deut. 6:7 walkest by t. w. 11:19

In the WAY.
Prov. 22:6 train up a child in the w.
he

My WAY.
Gen. 24:56 Lord prospered my w.
2 Sam. 22:33 maketh my w. perfect, Ps. 18:32

Own WAY.
Prov. 1:31 eat fruit of their c. w.
  20:24 can man unders. his o. w.?

Their WAY.
1 K. 2:4 if children take heed to

t. w. 8:25; 2 Chr. 6:16

This WAY.
2 K. 6:19 Elisha said, t. is not w.

His WAYS.
Ps. 128:1 blessed that walk. in h. w.
  145:17 Lord is right. in all h. w.
Is. 45:13 I will direct h. w. saith L.
Jam. 1:8 is unstable in all his w.

My WAYS.
Ps. 119:5 O that my w. were direct.
  26 I have declared my w. and
  59 I thought on my w. turned
Prov. 8:32 bles. that keep my w.
  23:26 let thine eyes obs. my w.
Is. 55:8 neit. your ways my w.
  9 my w. higher th. your ways
  58:2 delight to know my w.
Zec. 3:7 if wilt walk in my w.
Mal. 2:9 have not kept my w.

Thy WAYS.
Deut. 28:29 not prosper in thy w.
1 Sam. 8:5 walk not in thy w.
Job 4:6 the uprightness of thy w.
Ps. 25:4 show me thy w. O Lord
  51:13 teach transgressors t. w.
  91:11 to keep thee in all thy w.
Prov. 3:6 in t. w. acknowl. him
  4:26 let all t. w. be established
  31:3 not t. w. to that wh. destr.
Rev. 15:3 just and true are t. w.

WEAK.
Joel 3:10 let w. say, I am strong
Mat. 26:41 flesh w. Mark 14:38
Acts 20:35 ye ought to supp. w.
Rom. 4:19 being not w. in faith
  8:3 law was w. through flesh
  14:1 that is w. in faith recei. ye
  2 another who is w. eat. herbs
  21 broth. stumb. or is made w.
  15:1 ought to bear infirm. of w.
1 Cor. 1:27 w. things to confound
  8:12 wound their w. conscience
  9:22 to the w. I became w. that
  11:30 for this cause many are w.
2 Cor. 11:29 who is w. and I am
  12:10 when I am w. then strong

WEAKNESS.
1 Cor. 1:25 w. of God is stronger
  2:3 I was with you in w.
  15:43 sown in w. raised in pow.
2 Cor. 12:9 strength is perf. in w.

Heb. 7:18 going before for the w.
11:34 out of w. were made stro.

WEALTH.

2 Chr. 1:11 th. hast not asked w.
Ps. 44:12 dost not increase w.
49:6 trust in w. boast in riches
10 and leave their w. to others
112:3 w. and riches in his house
Ec. 5:19 God hath given w. 6:2
Acts 19:25 by this craft have w.
1 Cor. 10:24 seek every man another's w.

WEAPON.

Is. 54:17 no w. form. sh. prosper

WEAPONS.

1 Sam. 21:8 neither sword nor w.
2 Cor. 10:4 w. of warf. not carnal

WEAR.

Mat. 11:8 that w. soft clothing

WEARETH, ING.

John 19:5 Jesus came w. purple
1 Pet. 3:3 let it not be w. of gold
Jam. 2:3 him that w. gay cloth.

WEARY.

Gen. 27:46 Rebek. said, I am w.
Prov. 3:11 be not w. of L.'s cor.
25:17 lest he be w. of thee
Is. 40:28 G. fainteth not, nei. is w.
Gal. 6:9 let us not be w. in well-
doing, 2 Thes. 3:13

WEARIED.

Mal. 2:17 w. Lord, wherein have
we w. him?

WEATHER.

Job 37:22 fair w. com. out of nor.
Mat. 16:2 fair w. for sky is red

WEEK.

Luke 18:12 I fast twice in the w.

WEEP.

Luke 6:21 blessed are ye that w.
Jam. 5:1 ye rich men, w. and howl

WEEPEST.

1 Sam. 1:8 Han. why w. thou?
John 20:13 wom. why w. th.? 15

WEEPETH.

2 Sam. 19:1 behold the king w.

WEEPING.

Mat. 8:12 there sh. be w. 22:13;

WEIGHED.

Ezr. 8:25 priests w. sil. and gold
Dan. 5:27 thou art w. in balance

WEIGHT.

Lev. 26:26 deliver your bread by w.
Deut. 25:15 thou sh. have just w.
Prov. 16:11 a just w. and bal. are L's
Ezek. 4:10 thy meat sh. be by w.
Zec. 5:8 w. of lead on mouth
Heb. 12:1 let us lay aside ev. w.

WEIGHTS.

Lev. 19:36 just w. shall ye have
Deut. 25:13 sh. not ha. divers w.
Prov. 16:11 w. of bag his work
20:10 divers w. are abomina. 23

WEIGHTY.

Prov. 27:3 stone heavy, sand w.
2 Cor. 10:10 let. say they, are w.

WEIGHTIER.

Mat. 23:23 omitted w. matters

WELFARE.

Gen. 43:27 asked th. of their w.
Ex. 18:7 asked each other of w.
1 Chr. 18:10 sent to inq. of his w.
Neh. 2:10 man to seek w. of Is.
Ps. 69:22 sho. have been for w.
Jer. 38:4 seeketh not w. of peo.

WELL, Substantive.

Gen. 21:19 she saw a w. of water
30 witness I have dig. this w. Num
21:17 spring up, O w. 18 dig. w.
2 Sam. 17:18 man that had w.
23:15 give me drink of water of
w. of Beth. 1 Chr. 11:17, 18
Ps. 84:6 passing Baca make it w.
Prov. 5:15 wat. of thine own w.
10:11 a righte. man is w. of life
John 4:6 Jacob's w. was there
11 w. is deep; 12 J. gave us w.

WELLS.

Gen. 26:15 w. Abr.'s serv. digg.
18 Isaac digged ag. w. of water
Num. 20:17 drink of water of w.
Deut. 6:11 w. thou diggedst not
2 K. 3:25 they stopped all w. of
wat.
Is. 12:3 draw out of w. of salvat.
2 Pet. 2:17 are w. without water

WELL-SPRING.

Prov. 16:22 und. is a w.-s. of life
18:4 w.-s. of wisdom as a brook

WELL, Adverb.

Jer. 22:15 it was w. with him, 16
40:4 and I will look w. to thee

270

42:6 that it may be w. with us

Mat. 25:21 w. done, th. good and
faithful serv. 23; Luke 19:17

Luke 20:39 Master, thou hast w.
said, John 4:17

1 Tim. 5:17 elders that rule w.
be counted worthy

WEPT.

Gen. 21:16 Hag. w. 27:38 Es. w.
29:11 and Jacob w. 33:4; 37:35;
Hos. 12:4

42:24 Joseph w. 43:39; 45:2,, 14,
15; 46:29; 50:1, 17

Jud. 14:16 Samson's wife w.

Ruth 1:9 kissed daughters, w. 14

1 Sam. 1:7 Hannah w. not eat, 10

20:41 Jonathan and David w.

24:16 S. lifted up his v. and w.

2 Sam. 3:32 Da. w. at grave of A.

12:22 child alive, I fast, and w.

Mat. 26:75 P. w. bitterly, Mark
14:72; Luke 22:62

Mark 16:10 Mary told them as th.
w.

Luke 19:41 beheld city and w. over
it

John 11:35 Jesus w. 20:11 M. w.

Acts 20:37 w. fell on P.'s neck

1 Cor. 7:30 weep as tho' w. not

Rev. 5:4 w. because no man was

WHALE.

Mat. 12:40 Jo. was 3 days in w.

WHEAT.

Mat. 13:25 enemy sowed tares am.
w.

23 lest ye root up w. wi. them

30 gather the w. into my barn

Luke 22:31 Satan may sift you as w

Acts 27:38 cast w. into the sea

Rev. 6:6 meas. of w. for a penny

18:13 merchand. of w. is depart.

WHIRLWIND.

2 K. 2:1 take up Elijah by a w. 11

WHITE.

Dan. 7:9 garm. was w. as snow

Mat. 5:36 make hair w. or black

WHOLE, for sound.

Mat. 9:12 th. that be w. need not
a physic. Mark 2:17; Lu. 5:31

21 I shall be w. Mark 5:28

12:13 and his hand was made w.

Mark 3:5; Luke 6:10

15:28 her daugh. was made w.

31 wond. saw maimed to be w.

Mark 5:34 faith hath made th. w.
go, be w. Luke 8:48; 17:19

Luke 7:10 found the servant w.

John 5:6 wilt th. be made w.? 14

Acts 9:34 J. C. maketh thee w.

WHOLESOME.

Prov. 15:4 w. tongue tree of life

1 Tim. 6:3 cons. not to w. words

WHORE.

Lev. 21:7 not take wife that is a w.

Prov. 23:27 a w. is a deep ditch

WICKED.

2 Chr. 7:14 if my peo. turn fr. th. w.
Ways, Ezek. 18:21; 33:11, 19

Neh. 7:6 adversary is w. Haman

9:25 Haman's w. device sh. ret.

Ps. 17:13 deli. my soul fr. the w.

26:5 I will not sit with the w.

Prov. 15:29 Lord is far from the w.

Mal. 3:18 discern between righteous and w.

Mat. 12:45 more w. than himself,
so to this w. gen. Luke 11:26

13:49 angels sh. sever w. fr. just

16:4 w. generation seek. a sign

1 Cor. 5:13 put away w. person

Of the WICKED.

Eph. 6:16 qu. fiery darts of t. w.

2 Pet. 3:17 led away with error of
t.w.

WICKEDNESS

Job 20:12 tho' w. be sweet in mouth

27:4 my lips shall not speak w.

Jer. 4:14 wash thy heart from w.

8:6 no man repented of his w.

Mark 7:22 out heart proceed. w.

Luke 11:39 inw. part is full of w.

Acts 25:5 man, if any w. in him

Rom. 1:29 being filled wi. all w.

1 John 5:19 wh. world lieth in w.

Their WICKEDNESS.

Mat. 22:18 Jesus perceived t. w.

Thy WICKEDNESS.

Is. 47:10 hast trusted in thy w.

Jer. 3:22 polluted land with t. w.

Acts 8:22 repent of this thy w.

WIDE.

Mat. 7:13 w. gate to destruction

WIDENESS.
Ezek. 41:10 chambers w. 20 cub.
WIDOW.
Ex. 22:22 sh. not afflict any w.
2 Sam. 14:5 I am a w. woman
Mal. 3:5 those that oppress w.
Mark 12:42 w. threw in 2 mites
Luke 2:37 Anna was a w. ah. 84
1 Tim. 5:4 if any w. have child.
  5 she is a w. ind. trust. in God
  9 let not w. be taken into num.
WIDOWS.
Ex. 22:24 your wives shall be w.
Job 22:9 hast sent w. aw. empty
  27:15 bur. in death, w. not weep
Jer. 49:11 child. let w. trust in me
Lam. 5:3 our mothers are as w.
Mat. 23:14 ye devour w. houses
  Mark 12:40; Luke 20:47
Acts 6:1 bec. w. were neglected
1 Tim 5:11 but the younger w. refuse
  16 if any have w. relieve them
Jam. 1:27 religion is to visit w.
WIFE.
Gen. 11:29 Abram's w. was Sarai,
  21:21 Hag. took w. for Ishmael
Jud 14:16 Samson's w. wept bef. him
Prov. 5:18 rej. with w. of youth
  16:22 a w. findeth a good thing
  19:13 contentions of w. dropp
  14 a prudent w. is from the L.
Jer. 6:11 husb. and w. sh. be taken
  16:2 shalt not take thee a w.
Ezek. 16:32 as w. commit. adult.
  18:11 and defiled his neighbor's w. 22:11; 33:26
Hos. 1:2 take a w. of whoredoms
  12:12 Israel served for a w. kept
Mal. 2:14 witness bet. th. and w.
Mat. 14:3 H. bound J. for Phillip's w.
Luke 14:20 I have married a. w.
  17:32 remember Lot's w.
1 Cor. 7:3 husb. render to w. due be nevolence, likew. w. to hus.
  4 w. hath not power over body
  10 let not w. depart from hus.
  14 w. is sanctified by husband
  16 what knowest thou, O w.

27 loosed fr. w. seek not a w.
34 difference bet. w. and virgin
39 w. is bound as long as hus.
Eph. 5:23 husband is head of w.
  33 let very one love his w.
  and w. see she rever. husb.
1 Tim. 3:2 hus. of 1 w. 12; Tit. 1:6
  5:9 the w. of one man
1 Pet. 3:7 giving honor to w. as
His WIFE.
Gen. 2:24 a man sh. cleave to his w. Mat. 19:5; Mark 10:7
  19:26 his w. look. back fr. behind
  24:67 she bec. h. w. 1 Sam. 25:42
  25:21 Isa. entreated L. for h. w.
Num. 5:14 if he be jealous of his w. 30
  30:16 statu. bet. man and his w.
Deut. 24:5 he shall cheer up his w.
Jud. 15:1 Samson visited his w.
Est. 5:10 Haman called his w.
Jer. 3:1 if a man put away his w. Mat. 5:31, 32; 19:9; Mark 10:11; Luke 16:18
Mat. 8:14 saw his w. mother sick
  19:3 is it lawful for a man to put away his w.? Mark 10:2
Luke 14:26 and hate not his w.
1 Cor. 7:2 let ev. man have h. w.
  11 let not husb. put away h. w.
  33 how he may please his w.
Eph. 5:28 loveth h. w. lov. hims.
  31 join. to h. w. 33 love his w.
My WIFE.
Gen. 20:11 will sl. me for my w.
  29:21 Jacob said, Give me my w.
Ex. 21:5 I love my w. and chil.
Luke 1:18 my w. is strick. in yrs.
Thy WIFE.
1 Cor. 7:16 thou sh. save thy w.
To WIFE.
Gen. 12:19 taken her to me to w.
  34:4 get me this damsel to w.
  8 I pray, give her him to w. 12
Lev. 21:24 take a virgin to w.
Deut. 22:16 I gave my dau. to w.
Jos. 15:16 give Achsah my daug.
In the WILDERNESS.
Deut. 8:2 forty years in the w.
  29:5; Jos. 5:6; 14:10
Is. 40:3 voice of him that crieth in

the w. Mat. 3:3; Mark 1:3;
Luke 3:4; John 1:23
Luke 15:4 leave 99 sheep in t. w.
Into the WILDERNESS.
Lev. 16:21 by a fit man i. the w.
22 sh. let go the goat i. the w.
Ezek. 20:10 I bro. them i. the w.
35 I will bring you into the w.
Hos. 2:14 I will bri. her in the w.
Luke 8:29 driven of devil i. the w.
Rev. 12:6 woman fled i. t. w. 14
WILES.
Num. 25:18 th. vex you with w.
Eph. 6:11 able to stand ag. w.
WILL.
Luke 2:14 good w. toward men
John 1:13 not of w. of the flesh
4:34 my meat is to do w. of him
5:30 I seek the w. of my Father
6:39 this is the Father's w. 40
His WILL.
Luke 12:47 nei. accord. to his w.
John 7:17 if any do h. w. sh. kn.
1 John 5:14 ask accord. to his w.
Thy WILL.
Ps. 40:8 I delight to do thy w.
143:10 teach me to do thy w.
Mat. 6:10 t. w. be done, Luke 11:2
26:42 not pass, thy w. be done
Heb. 10:7 I come to do thy w. 9
WILL, Verb.
Prov. 21:1 heart whither. he w.
Dan. 4:17 giveth it to whomso-
ever he w. 25, 32; 5:21
Mat. 8:3 and said, I w. be thou
clean, Mark 1:41; Luke 5:13
26:39 not as I w. Mark 14:36
WILLING.
Mat. 26:41 spirit is w. flesh is weak
2 Cor. 5:12 if there be first a w.
mind
Heb. 6:17 w. to show heirs of pr.
2 Pet. 3:9 not w. any sho. perish
WILLINGLY.
Neh. 11:2 that w. offered thems.
Prov. 31:13 work, w. with hands
John 6:21 they w. received him
2 Cor. 9:17 if I do this w. a rew.
2 Pet. 3:5 they are w. ignorant
WIN, NETH.
Prov. 11:30 he that w. souls

Phil. 3:8 that I may w. Christ
WINDS.
Mat. 7:25 blew, beat house, 27
8:26 rebuked the w. Luke 8:24
27 even the w. and sea obey
him? Mark 4:41; Luke 8:25
WINDOW.
Jos. 2:15 Rah. let spies thro' w.
WINDOWS.
Gen. 7:11 w. of heav. were open.
Joel 2:9 enter in at w. like thief
Mal. 3:10 if I will not open w. of
WINE.
Luke 7:33 J. neither drinking w.
John 2:3 saith, They have no w.
9 tasted water made w. 4:46
Eph. 5:18 be not drunk with w.
1 Tim. 3:3 and not given to w. 8;
Tit. 1:7; 2:3
5:23 use w. for stomach's sake
1 Pet. 4:3 walked in excess of w.
WINGS.
Ex. 19:4 bare you on eagle's w.
Ps. 63:7 in shadow of w. will I rej.
Is. 40:31 mount up with w. eagles
Mat. 23:37 as a hen gathereth her
chick, under w. Luke 13:34
WIPE.
Is. 25:8 Lord will w. away tears
fr. all faces, Rev. 7:17; 21:4
Luke 7:38 woman did w. th. with
hairs, 44; John 11:2; 12:3
WISDOM.
1 K. 4:29 God gave Solomon w.
5:12;
2 Chr. 1:12
30 Solomon's w. excelled w.
of Egypt, 34; 7:14; 10:4, 23
24; 2 Chr. 9:3, 22, 23
1 Chr. 22:12 Lord give thee w.
Ps. 37:30 mouth of righ. speak w.
51:6 shalt make me to know w.
90:12 apply our hearts to w.
104:24 in w. hast th. made wor.
105:22 and teach his senators w.
136:5 him th. by w. made heav.
Prov. 1:2 kn. w. 7 fools desp. w.
20 w. crieth, 8:1; 2:2 ear to w.
2:6 Lord giveth w. 3:21 keep w.
7 he layeth up w. for righteous
10 when w. entereth into heart

3:13 happy man that findeth w.
  19 Lord by w. founded earth
4:5 get w. 7;
8:5 unders. w. 9:1 w. buildeth
  12 I w. dwell with prudence
  14 counsel is mine sound w.
Prov. 14:8 w. of prudent is to understa.
  33 w. resteth in heart of him
16:16 better to get w. than gold
17:16 in hand of fool to get w.
23:9 a fool will despise w. of wor.
29:3 whoso loveth w. rejoiceth
  15 the rod and reproof give w.
Ec. 1:18 for much w. is much grief
2:3 acquaint. my heart with w.
  12 I turned myself to beho. w.
  26 G. give. w. 7:12 w. giv. life
7:19 w. strengtheneth the wise
  25 I applied heart to seek w.
9:10 there is no w. in the grave
Jer. 9:23 let not wise glory in w.
Dan. 2:20 blessed be G. w. and might
  21 he giveth w. to the wise
Mat. 12:42 came fr. utterm. parts
  to hear w. of Sol. Luke 11:31
Luke 21:15 give you a mouth and w.
Acts 6:3 seven men full of w.
7:10 God gave Joseph w. in the
1 Cor. 1:17 not with w. of words
  19 destroy the w. of the wise
  20 God made foolish the w. of
Col. 4:5 walk in w. tow. them that
Jam. 1:5 any lack w. let him ask
Rev. 5:12 the Lamb to receive w.
  7:12 glory, and w. be to our God
WISDOM, joined with Is..
Prov. 4:7 w. is principal thing
Jer. 8:9 lo, th. have rejected the
  word, what w. is in them?
49:7 is w. no more in Teman?
Dan. 5:14 excellent w. is found
Mat. 11:19 but w. is justified of
  her children, Luke 7:35
Mark 6:2 wh. w. is giv. to him?
Jam. 3:17 w. from above is pure
Rev. 13:18 here is w. let him that
Of WISDOM.
1 Cor. 2:1 of speech or of w.

12:8 by Spirit the word of w.
Col. 2:3 are hid all treasu. of w.
  23 have indeed a show of w.
Jam. 3:13 show with meek. of w.
WISE.
Gen. 3:6 a tre to make one w.
Ps. 2:10 be w. now, O ye kings
19:7 making w. the simple
Prov. 1:5 w. man at. w. counsel
9:12 be w. thou shall be w. for
10:1 a w. son maketh a glad father, 15:20
  5 gathereth in summer is w.
  19 he that refrai. his lips is w.
11:29 servant to the w. in heart
  30 he that winneth souls is w.
Prov. 23:15 be w. my hea. sh. rej.
  24 begetteth a w. son have joy
24:6 by w. coun. make thy war
  23 these things belong to w.
25:12 w. reprover on obedi. ear
26:5 answer a fool, lest he be w.
  12 a man w. in his own conceit
28:7 whoso keep. law is w. son
Ec. 2:15 why was I more w.?
Ec. 9:1 w. are in the hand of God
Is. 5:21 woe to them that are w.
Dan. 2:21 God giv. wisdom to w.
12:3 they that be w. shall shine
Mat. 10:16 be ye w. as serpents
  11:25 because th. hast hid these
  things from w. Luke 10:21
24:45 who is faith. and w. ser.?
25:2 five virgins w. five foolish
  4 w. took oil in their vessels
Rom. 1:14 I am debtor to the w.
12:16 be not w. in your conceits
1 Cor. 1:19 destroy wisdom of w.
  27 chosen foolish th. to con. w.
3:18 be w. let him become a fool
  20 L. knows thoughts of the w.
Any WISE.
Lev. 19:17 shall in a. w. rebuke
WISE men.
Gen. 41:8 Phar. called for magicians and w. men, Ex. 7:11
In no WISE.
Mat. 5:18 shall in no w. pass
10:42 he shall in no w. lose rew.
Luke 18:17 he shall in now. enter therein. Rev. 21:27

WISE woman.
Prov. 14:1 ev. w. w. buil. house
WISELY.
2 Chr. 11:23 Rehoboam dealt w.
Ps. 58:5 charming never so w.
Prov. 16:20 handleth a matter w.
Luke 16:8 becau. he had done w.
WISER.
1 K. 4:31 Sol. was w. th. all men
Prov. 9:9 and he will be yet w.
26:16 slug. is w. in his conceit
Luke 16:8 in their generation w.
1 Cor. 1:25 fool. of G. w. th. men
WISH.
Rom. 9:3 co. w. myself accursed
2 Cor. 13:9 we w. even your per.
3 John 2 I w. th. mayest prosper
WISHED.
Jon. 4:8 and w. himself to die
Acts 27:29 cast anch. w. for day
WITCH.
Ex. 22:18 not suffer a w. to live
Deut. 18:10 not be am. you a w.
WITCHCRAFT.
1 Sam. 15:23 rebelli. as sin of w.
2 Chr. 33:6 Manasseh used w.
Gal. 5:20 works of flesh are w.
WITCHCRAFTS.
2 K. 9:22 Jezebel's w. are many
WITHDRAW.
1 Sam. 14:19 S. said to priest w.
Job 9:13 if God will not w. anger
Prov. 25:17 w. fr. neigh.'s house
Ec. 7:18 fr. this w. not thy hand
1 Tim. 6:5 cor. minds w. thyself
WITHDRAWN.
Ezek. 18:8 w. his hand from iniq.
Hos. 5:6 L. w. himself from them
Luke 22:41 was w. a stone's cast
WITHDRAWETH.
Job 36:7 w. not from righteous
WITHER.
Is. 19:6 reeds and flags shall w.
7 thing sown by brooks sh. w.
40:24 blow upon them, shall w.
Jer. 12:4 shall herbs of field w.?
WITHERED.
Jon. 4:7 smote gourd that it w.
Mat. 12:10 man wh. had his hand
w. Mark 8:1, 3; Luke 6:6, 8
13:6 hav. no root, w. Mark 4:6

21:19 fig-tree w. 20; Mark 11:21
WITHERETH.
Is. 40:7 grass w. the flower fad-
eth, 8; 1 Pet. 1:24
Jam. 1:11 the sun w. the grass
Jude 12 trees w. without fruit
WITHHELD.
Ec. 2:10 I w. not my heart
WITHHOLD.
Ps. 40:11 w. not thy mercies
84:11 no good thing will he w.
Prov. 3:27 w. not good
23:13 w. not correct. from child
WITNESS.
Ps. 89:37 a faithful w. in heaven
Prov. 14:5 faithf. w. will not lie
25 a true w. delivereth souls
Rom. 1:9 God is my w. I serve
Heb. 2:4 God bear. w. with signs
10:15 the Holy Ghost is w. to us
WITNESSES.
Mat. 18:16 mou. of two or th. w.
Rev. 11:3 give power to my w.
WIVES.
1 K. 11:3 Solomon had 700 w.
Eph. 5:22 w. submit to your hus-
bands as unto the Lord, Col.
3:18; 1 Pet. 3:1
24 so let w. be to th. husbands
1 Tim. 4:7 refuse old w. fables
Their WIVES.
Eph. 5:28 love t. w. as th. bodies
1 Tim. 3:11 so must t. w. be gr.
Your WIVES.
Mat. 19:8 suff. to put away y. w.
Eph. 5:25 love your w. Col. 3:19
WIZARD.
Lev. 19:31 nor seek after w.
WOE.
Rev. 8:13 w. w. w. to the inhabi-
ters of the earth; 12:12
9:12 one w. past; 11:14 sec. w.
WOE unto me.
1 Cor. 9:16 w. u. me if I preach.
WOE to them.
Mic. 2:1 w. to t. devise iniquity
Mat. 24:19 w. to t. wh. are with
chi. Mark 13:17; Luke 21:23
Jude 11 w. to t. gone way of Cain
WOMAN.
Gen. 2:22 rib of man made he w.

275

23 she shall be called w.
3:15 enmity between th. and w.
Prov. 6:24 keep thee fr. evil w.
7:10 there met him a w. subtile
9:13 a foolish w. is clamorous
12:4 virtu. w. is a crown, 31:10
14:1 ev. wise w. buildeth house
21:9 brawling w. in house, 19
31:10 who can find a virtu. w.?

30 w. that fears L. be praised
Hos. 3:1 love w. beloved of friend
sh. come up. him, Mic. 4:9, 10
Mat. 5:28 whoso looketh on a w.
John 4:9 askest of me, a w. of
Sama.

39 many belie. for saying of w.
8:3 brought w. taken in adult. 4
10 when Jesus saw none but w.
19:26 mother, w. behold thy son
Acts 9:36 w. was full of works,
17:34 a w. named Damaris beli.
Rom. 1:27 men leaving use of w.
7:2 w. that hath husb. is bound
1 Cor. 7:1 good not to touch a w.
2 every w. have her own husb.
7 w. is glory of the man, 8, 9
10 w. ought to have power, 11
12 as w. is of man, so it by w.
13 is it comely for w. to pray
15 if a w. have long hair
Gal. 4:4 sent his S. made of a w.
1 Thes. 5:3 com. as travail on w.
1 Tim. 2:12 suff. not w. to teach
14 w. being deceiv. in transgr.
Rev. 2:20 suff. w. Jezeb. to teach
12:1 appear. w. cloth with sun
6 w. tied; 16 earth helped w.
17 dragon was wroth with w.
17:3 I saw a w. sit on a beast
6 w. drunken; 7 mystery of w.

WOMB.
Is. 44:2 Lord formed thee from
the w. 24; 49:5
Luke 1:31 sh. conceive in thy w.
41 babe leaped in her w. 44
2:21 bef. he was conceiv. in w.

WOMEN.
Gen. 24:11 w. go to draw water
Ex. 15:20 w. went after Miriam
35:25 w. wise-hearted spin, 26
Lev. 26:26 ten w. sh. bake bread

Num. 31:15 have saved w. alive
Jos. 8:35 Jos. read law before w.
Jud. 5:24 blessed above w. Jael
Est. 1:9 made a feast for the w.
2:17 A. loved Esther above w.
3:13 little children and w. 8:11
Job 42:15 no w. fair as Job's dau.
Ps. 45:9 among thy honorable w.
Prov. 31:3 give not stren. to w.
Cant. 1:8 fair, among w. 5:9; 6:1
Is. 3:12 peo. w. rule over them
4:1 sev. w. ta. hold of one man
19:16 Egypt shall be like to w.
27:11 w. come. set them on fire
32:9 ye w. that are at ease

10 careless w. 11 w. be troub.
Jer. 7:18 w. knead their dough
9:17 mourning and cunning w.
20 yet hear word of L. O ye w.
38:22 w. left be brought to king
44:24 Jer. said to w. Hear word
50:37 they sh. become w. robbed
51:30 men of Ba. became as w.
Lam. 2:20 shall w. eat children?
Ezek. 8:14 w. weeping for Tam.
23:2 two w. daughters of one

45 after man, of w. shed blood
Hos. 13:16 w. with child be rip.
Amos 1:13 ripped w. with child
Mic. 2:9 w. of people ye cast out
Nah. 3:13 people in midst are w.
Zec. 5:9 there came out two w.
8:4 old w. shall dwell in Jerus.
14:2 houses rifled, w. ravished
Mat. 11:11 th. are born of w. not
greater than Bapt. Luke 7:28
14:21 5,000 men, besi. w. 15:38
24:41 two w. grind. Luke 17:35
27:55 w. were beholding afar off
Luke 1:28 blessed among w. 42
24:22 w. made us astonish. 24
Acts 1:14 conti. in prayer wi. w.
13:50 Jews stirred up devout w.
16:13 speak to w. wh. resorted
17:4 of w. not a few believ. 12
Rom. 1:26 th. w. did change use
1 Cor. 14:34 let w. keep silence
35 shame for w. to speak in ch.
Phil. 4:3 help w. which labored
1 Tim. 2:9 w. adorn in mod. ap.
10 becom. w. professing godli.

11 let w. learn with subjection
5:2 entreat elder w. as mothers
14 I will that young. w. marry
2 Tim. 3:6 captive w. laden with
  sins
Tit. 2:3 aged w. behave as beco.
  4 teach younger w. to be sober
Heb. 11:35 w. receiv. dead raised
1 Pet. 3:5 manner holy w. adorn.
Rev. 9:8 had hair as hair of w.

WONDERFULLY.
Ps. 139:14 for I am w. made

WONDERS.
2 Thes. 2:9 com. in signs and w.
Heb. 2:4 witn. with signs and w.

WOOL.
Dan. 7:9 hair like w. Rev. 1:14

WORD.
2 Sam. 3:11 not answer Ab. a w.
Mark 4:14 sower soweth the w.
  14:72 Pe. called to mind the w.
  16:20 confirming w. with signs
Luke 4:36 amaz. what w. is this1
John 1:1 in beginn. was the W.
  14 the W. was made flesh
Eph. 5:26 clea. with water by w.
Phil. 1:14 speak w. without fear
1 John 1:1 handled w. of life
  5:7 Father, W. and Holy G. one
Rev. 3:10 kept w. of my patience

WORD of God.
1 Sam. 9:27 I show thee w. of G.
1 K. 12:22 w. of G. came to She.
1 Chr. 17:3 w. of G. came to Na.
Prov. 30:5 every w. of G. is pure
Is. 40:8 w. of G. stand for ever
Mark 7:13 w. of God of no effect
Luke 3:2 w. of G. came unto J.
  4:4 not by bread but by w. of G.
  5:1 pressed to hear w. of God
  8:11 the seed is the w. of God
  21 breth. th. wh. hear w. of G.
  11:28 they that hear w. of God
John 10:35 gods to wh. w. of G.
Tit. 2:5 w. of G. be not blasph.
Heb. 4:12 w. of G. qui. and pow.
  6:5 tasted the good of God
  11:3 worlds framed by w. of G.
2 Pet. 3:5 by w. of G. heav. were
1 John 2:14 w. of G. abid. in you
Rev. 1:2 bare record of w. of G.

6:3 were slain for w. of God
19:13 name is called W. of God

His WORD.
Luke 4:32 his w. was with power
John 4:41 many beli. his own w.
Acts 2:41 that gladly rec. his w.
Tit. 1:3 hath manifested his w.
1 John 2:5 whoso keepeth his w.

My WORD.
Num. 11:23 my w. come to pass
1 K. 6:12 perfor. my w. with th.
Is. 55:11 so sh. my w. that goeth
29:10 perf. my good w. to. you
Mat. 24:35 my w. not pass away

This WORD.
Jos. 14:10 L. spake t. w. to Mos.

Thy WORD.
1 K. 3:12 done accord. to thy w.
8:26 let thy w. be verified
18:36 done all th. things at t. w.
22:13 let thy w. speak what is
  good, 2 Chr. 18:12
Ps. 119:11 thy w. ha. I hid in my
heart

WORDS of God.
Ezr. 9:4 trembleth at w. of God
Ps. 107:11 rebelled ag. w. of God
John 3:34 G. sent speak. w. of G.
8:47 that is of G. hear. w. of G.
Rev. 17:17 until w. of G. be fulf.

His WORDS.
Dan. 9:12 he hath confirm. h. w.
Amos 7:10 not able to bear h. w.
Mark 10:24 astonished at his w.

My WORDS.
Mic. 2:7 do not my w. do good to
Zec. 1:6 my w. did they not take
Mark 8:38 ashamed of my w. of
  him Son be asha. Luke 9:26
13:31 my w. shall not pass away,
  Luke 1:20 thou believ. not my w.
John 5:47 how believe my w.?
12:47 if any man hear my w.

Their WORDS.
Ps. 19:4 their w. to the end of the
  world, Rom. 10:18
Luke 24:11 t. w. seemed as tales

These WORDS.
1 Thes. 4:18 comfort one another
  with these w.
Rev. 21:5 t. w. true and faithful

WORK.

Ezek. 15:3 shall wood do any w.?
1 Cor. 3:13 ev. man's w. be manif.
14 if w. abide; 15 if w. burnt
2 Tim. 4:5 w. of an evangelist
Jam. 1:4 let patience ha. perf. w.

WORKS of God.

Rom. 14:20 for meat destroy not
the w. of God

His WORK.

Ps. 62:12 renderest to ev. man
according to h. w. Prov. 24:29
111:3 h. w. is honorable, glorious
Prov. 21:8 for the pure h. w. is right
Is. 5:19 let him hasten his w.
40:10 his w. is before him, 62:11

WORK, Verb.

Dan. 11:23 he sh. w. deceitfully
Hab. 1:5 I will w. a work in your
days, Acts 13:41
Hag. 2:4 w. for I am with you
Mal. 3:15 w. wicked. are set up
Mat. 21:28 go w. in my vineyard
Luke 13:14 wh. men ought to w.
Rom. 7:5 sin did w. in our mem.
98:28 all thi. w. togeth. for good
Phil. 2:12 w. out your salvation
1 Thes. 4:11 to w. with hands
2 Thes. 2:7 mys. of iniq. doth w.

WORKS.

Dan. 4:37 him wh. w. are truth
Mat. 11:2 John heard w. of Chr.
John 5:20 show him greater w.
John 10:37 if I do not w. 38 be-
lieve w.
Gal. 2:16 man is not justi. by w.
Eph. 2:9 not of w. lest any boast
Col. 1:21 enemies by wicked w.
1 Thes. 5:13 estem for w. sake
2 Tim. 1:9 saved us, not accord-
ing to our w. Tit. 3:5
Heb. 1:10 heav. w. of thy hands
Jam. 2:14 not w. can faith save?
17 faith with. w. is dead, 20:26

His WORKS.

Prov. 24:12 render to ev. man ac. to
h. w.? Mat. 16:27; 2 Tim. 4:14

Their WORKS.

Ex. 5:4 let people from their w.
Ps. 33:15 he considereth their w.
Is. 29:15 t. w. are in the dark

41:29 vanity, t. w. are nothing
Amos 8:7 nev. forg. any of t. w.
Mat. 23:3 do not ye after t. w.
5 t. w. do to be seen of men
2 Cor. 11:15 end accord. to t. w.
Rev. 14:13 t. w. do follow them

Thy WORKS.

2 Chr. 20:37 L. hath broken t. w.
Is. 57:12 I will declare thy w.
Jer. 48:7 thou trusted in thy w.
Jam. 2:18 sh. faith without t. w.
Rev. 2:2 I know thy w. 9, 13, 19;
3:1, 8, 15
3:2 I have not found t. w. perf.

Wonderful WORKS.

Acts 2:11 hear in tongues w. w.

WORKETH.

Ex. 3:9 what profit he that w.?
Is. 44:12 the smith w. in coals
Dan. 6:27 w. signs and wonders
John 5:17 my Fath. w. hitherto
Acts 10:35 he that w. righteous.
Rom. 2:10 to every one w. good
4:4 to him that w. is reward
5 him that w. not, but believ.
15 because the law w. wrath
5:3 tribulation w. patience
13:10 love w. no ill to neighbor
1 Cor. 12:6 it is same G. that w.
2 Cor. 4:12 then death w. in us
Gal. 3:5 he that w. miracles
5:6 but faith which w. by love
Eph. 1:11 who w. all things
Phil. 2:13 it is God w. in you
Col. 1:29 wh. w. in me mightily
1 Thes. 2:13 effectually w. in you
Jam. 1:3 try. of faith w. patience
Rev. 21:27 whosoe. w. abomina.

WORKING, Participle.

2 Thes. 3:11 w. not, busybodies
Heb. 13:21 w. th. wh. is pleasing
Rev. 16:14 spi. of devils w. mira.

WORKING, Substantive.

Is. 28:29 Lord excellent in w.

WORKMAN.

2 Tim. 2:15 a w. not to be asha.

WORKMANSHIP.

Eph. 2:10 we are his w. in C. Je.

WORKMEN.

Ezr. 3:9 set w. in house of God
Is. 44:11 the w. they are of men

WORLD.

Ps. 9:8 he shall judge the w. in
  righteousness, 96:13; 98:9
Ps. 17:14 deliver from men of
  the w.
19:4 to end of w. Rom. 10:18
22:27 ends of w. shall remember
24:1 the earth and the w. is the
  Lord's, 98:7; Nah. 1:5
33:8 inhabit. of w. stand in awe
49:1 give ear, inhabitants of the
50:12 for the w. is mine.
77:18 lightnings light. w. 97:4
89:11 founded w. and its fulness
90:2 form. the earth and the w.
93:1 the w. also is established
96:10 w. also sh. be established
Prov. 8:26 not made dust of w.
Ec. 3:11 set w. in their heart
Is. 13:11 I will punish w. for evil
14:17 is this he made w. wild.?
  21 nor fill face of w. wi. cities
24:4 the w. languisheth away
27:6 Is. sh. fill the w. with fruit
34:1 let world hear, and all that
Mat. 4:8 the devil showeth him
16:26 what profit. gain w. lose
  soul? Mark 8:36; Luke 9:25
John 1:10 he was in w. the w. was
  made by him, Acts 17:24
  29 L. of G. takes away sin of w.
3:16 God so loved the w. that
4:42 C. Savi. of w. 1 John 4:14
6:33 bread of G. giv. life to w.
  51 my flesh, I give for life of w.
12:47 I co. not to jud. but save w.
14:27 I give, not as the w. giveth
  31 the w. may know I love Fa.
15:18 w. hate you, 1 John 3:13
  19 of w. the w. love his own
16:20 but the w. shall rejoice
  33 I have overcome the w.
17:5 glory I had before w. was
  14 w. hated th. bec. not of w.
  16 not of w. as I am not of w.
  25 the w. hath not known me
18:20 I spake openly to w.
Acts 17:6 turned w. upside down
19:27 Diana, Asia and w. worsh.
Rom. 1:8 faith is spo. of thro' w.
  3:6 for how shall G. judge w.?

1 Cor. 1:21 w. by wis. kn. not G.
3:22 w. or life, or death, yours
6:2 kn. th. saints sh. judge w.?
7:33 careth for things in w. 34
11:32 not be condemned with w.
2 Cor. 5:19 C. reconc. w. to hims.
2 Tim. 1:9 in Christ before w.
Heb. 2:5 in subjection w. to come
  6:5 tasted powers of w. to come
  11:38 of wh. w. was not worthy
Jam. 1:27 unspotted from the w.
1 John 2:2 propitia. for sins of w.
  15 love not w. 16 is of the w.
  17 the w. passeth away
1 John 3:1 the w. knoweth us not
  4:5 they are of the w.
  5:4 born of G. overcometh w.

In or into the WORLD.

Ps. 73:12 ungod. wh. pros. i. t. w.
Mat. 26:13 this gospel be preached in the whole w.
Mark 10:30 and in the w. to come
  eternal life, Luke 18:30
John 1:9 man that comes . the w.
  10 he was in the w.
  3:17 sent not his Son into the w.
  19 light is come into the w.
  6:14 should come i. t. w. 11:27
  9:5 as long as I am in the w.
1 Tim. 1:15 Christ Jesus came
  into the w. to save sinners
3:16 and believed on in the w.
Heb. 10:5 when he cometh i. t. w.
1 Pet. 5:9 afflict. that are in t. w.
1 John 2:15 love not thi. in t. w.
  4:1 false prophets gone i. t. w.
  3 now already is it in the w.
  4 greater th. he that is in t. w.
  9 sent his Son into the w. that
2 John 7 many deceivers i. t. w.

This WORLD.

Mat. 12:32 not forgi. him in t. w.
13:22 cares of this w. choke the
  word, Mark 4:19
Luke 16:8 children of this w. are
20:34 children of this w. marry
John 8:23 ye are of this w.
  9:39 for judg. I come into t. w.
12:25 that hateth life in this w.
  31 now is judgment of this w.
13:1 should depart out of t. w.

14:30 prince of this w. cometh
16:11 prince of this w. is judged
18:36 kingdom is not of this w.
Rom. 12:2 not conformed to t. w.
1 Cor. 1:20 wh. is disp. of t. w.?
2:6 speak not wisdom of this w.
3:18 if man seem. wise in t. w.
19 wisd. of t. w. foolish. wi. G.
5:10 not with fornicat. of t. w.
7:31 use t. w. as not abusing it
2 Cor. 4:4 god of t. w. blinded
Gal. 1:4 deli. us fr. t. present w.

WORLDLY.

Tit. 2:12 ungodlin. and w. lusts
Heb. 9:1 first cov. had w. sanct.

WORLDS.

Heb. 1:2 by whom he made w.
11:3 w. were fram. by word of G.

WORM.

Ex. 16:24 neither any w. therein
Ps. 22:6 I am a w. and no man
Jon 4:7 a w. smote the gourd

WORMS.

Mic. 7:17 out of holes like w.
Acts 12:23 Herod was eaten of w.
Rev. 8:11 name of star called W.

WORSE.

Jer. 7:26 w. th. their fath. 16:12
Dan. 1:10 see faces w. liking?
Mat. 12:45 last state of that man
is w. than first, Luke 11:26
27:64 last error w. than the first
2 Tim. 3:13 seducers sh. wax w.

WORSHIP.

Gen. 22:5 I and the lad will go
and w.
Ex. 34:14 thou shalt w. no other G.
Deut. 4:19 lest th. be driven to w.
8:19 if thou w. other gods,
11:16; 30:17
1 Sam. 1:3 man went up to w.
1 K. 12:30 the people went to w.
2 K. 5:18 w. in house of Rimmon
17:36 L. ye fear, him sh. ye w.
18:22 shall w. bef. this altar in
Jeru. 2 Chr. 32:12; Is. 36:7
1 Chr. 16:29 w. L. in the beauty
of holiness, Ps. 29:2; 66:4;
96:9; Mat. 4:10; Luke 4:8
Is. 2:8 w. work of han. 20; 46:6
27:13 w. Lord in holy mount

Jer. 7:2 enter th. gates to w. 26:2
25:6 go not after oth. gods to w.
Mic. 5:13 thou shalt no more w.
work of thine hands
Zep. 1:5 that w. host of heaven
Zec. 14:16 w. Lord of hosts, 17
Mat. 2:2 and come to w. him
John 4:20 in Jerusal. is the place
wh. men oug. to w. Mark 7:7
22 ye w. ye know not what
23 w. the Father in spirit, 24
Acts 17:23 whom ye ignorantly w.
18:13 persuaded men to w. God
24:11 Paul came to Jerus. to w.
1 Cor. 11:25 he will w. God
Phil. 3:3 which w. God in spirit
Heb. 1:6 let angels of G. w. him
Rev. 3:9 and w. before thy feet
4:10 w. him that liveth for ever
9:20 they should not w. devils
11:1 and them that w. therein
13:8 all that dwell on earth shall
w. beast, 12
15:4 nations come. w. bef. him
19:10 I fell at his feet to w. 22:8;
22:9 w. God

WORSHIPPED.

Gen. 24:26 Abraham w. Lord, 48
Deut. 17:3 served other gods, and
w. 29:26; 1 K. 9:9; 2 K.
21:21; 2 Chr. 7:22; Jer. 1:16;
8:2; 16:11; 22:9
1 Sam. 1:19 Hannah w. before L.
2 Sam. 12:20 D. arose w. 15:32
2 K. 17:16 they w. host of heav-
en, 21:3; 2 Chr. 33:3
Neh. 8:6 all people w. Lord, 9:3
Dan. 2:46 king w. 3:7 w. image
Mat. 2:11 wise men fell, w. Christ
8:2 leper w. him, 9:18 a ruler w.
14:33 that were in ship w. him
15:25 woman of Canaan w. him
18:26 servant fell, w. his lord
28:9 held him by feet, w. him
17 disciples w. him, Lu. 24:52
Mark 5:6 ran out of tombs, w.
15:19 spit on him, bowing, w.
John 4:20 our fath. w. in mount.
9:38 man believed, and w. him
Acts 10:25 Cornelius w. Peter
16:14 Ly. w. God; 18:7 Justus w.

Rom. 1:25 w. creature more than
Heb. 11:21 Jacob w. Rev. 7:11
  w. God
Rev. 5:14 twenty-four elders w.
  11:16; 19:4
  13:4 they w. dragon, w. beast
  19:20 deceiv. that w. his image

WORSHIPPERS.

John 4:23 w. sh. worship in spirit
  9:31 if any man be a w. of God

WORTHY.

Gen. 32:10 I am not w. of merci.
Mat. 3:11 I am not w. to bear
  8:8 Lord, I am not w. Luke 7:6
  16:37 loveth more, he is not w. 38
Luke 3:8 fruits w. of repentance
  10:7 laborer is w. of his hire
Rom. 8:18 not w. to be compared
Eph. 4:1 th. ye walk w. of voca.
Col. 1:10 ye might walk w. of L.
Heb. 11:38 world was not w.
Jam. 2:7 blasph. that w. name?
Rev. 3:4 walk in white, are w.
  4:11 w. to receive glory, 5:12
  5:2 who is w. to open the book

WOULD.

Rom. 7:15 what w. that I do not

WOULD God.

2 Cor. 11:1 w. to G. bear wi. me

WOULD not.

Rom. 7:16 do that whi. I w. not
  19 evil that I w. not that I do
2 Cor. 12:20 such as ye w. not

WOUNDS.

Jer. 6:7 before me is grief and w.
  30:17 I will heal thee of thy w.
Zec. 13:6 are th. w. in thy hands?
Luke 10:34 Samari. bound up w.

WOUNDED.

Prov. 18:14 a w. spirit who can
  bear?
Zec. 13:6 w. in house of my frie.
Mark 12:4 w. him, Luke 20:12

WRAPPED, or WRAPT.

Mat. 27:59 Jos. w. body in linen,
  Mark 15:46; Luke 23:53

WRATH.

Ps. 37:8 forsake w. 55:3 w. hate
Prov. 14:29 slow to w. of great
  under.
  27:4 w. is cruel, anger is outrage.

  29:8 wise men turn away w.
Is. 13:9 day of L. cometh with w.
Zec. 8:14 fathers provoked me to
  w.
Mat. 3:7 flee from w. to come,
  Luke 3:7
1 Tim. 2:8 lift, hands without w.
Heb. 11:27 not fearing w. of king
Jam. 1:19 slow to spe. slow to w.

Day of WRATH.

Zep. 1:15 that day is a day of w.
Rom. 2:5 treasu. w. ag. d. of w.
Rev. 6:17 great d. of w. is come

WRATH of God.

2 Chr. 28:11 w. of God upon you
Rom. 1:18 w. of God is revealed
Eph. 5:6 w. of God com. Col. 3:6

His WRATH.

2 K. 23:26 L. turned not fr. h. w.
2 Chr. 29:10 his fierce w. may
  turn from us, 30:8
Rom. 9:22 G. will. to show h. w.
Rev. 16:19 cup of wine of his w.

My WRATH.

Ex. 22:24 my w. shall wax hot
Heb. 3:11 I sware in my w. they

WREATHS.

2 Chr. 4:13 400 pomegranates on
  two w. two rows of pomeg. on w.

WRESTLE.

Eph. 6:12 we w. not against flesh

WRESTLED.

Gen. 30:8 have I w. with sister
  32:24 there w. a man with him
  25 thigh out of joint as he w.

WRETCHED.

Rom. 7:24 O w. man that I am

WRITE.

Ex. 34:1 will w. on ta. Deut. 10:2
  27 L. said to Mo. w. th. words
Num. 17:2 w. every man's name
Deut. 6:9 w. them on posts, 11:20
  24:1 let him w. her a bill of divorcement, 3; Mark 10:4
  27:3 w. the words of this law, 8
  31:19 w. ye this song for you
Hab. 2:2 w. the vision on tables
Luke 1:3 it seem. good to w. th.
  16:6 w. fifty; 7 w. fourscore
John 1:45 Mos. and prop. did w.
2 Cor. 9:1 it is superfluours to w.

you

1 John 1:4 th. thi. w. we to you
2:7 I w. no new commandment
8 a new commandm. I w. you
Rev. 2:1 angel of ch. of Ephe. w.
3:12 I will. w. on him new name
14:13 w. bles. are dead die in L.
21:5 w. words true and faithful
WRITING.
Mat. 5:31 let him give her a w.
of divorcement. 19:7
John 19:19 w. was, Jesus of Naz.
WRITTEN.
Ex. 31:18 w. with the finger of
God, Deut. 9:19
Mark 11:17 w. my hou. be called
15:26 his accusation was w. K.
of J. Luke 23:38; John 19:20
Luke 4:17 place where it was w.
10:20 your names are. w. in hea.
2 Cor. 3:2 epistle w. in hearts
3 w. not with ink, but S. of G.
Rev. 1:3 things wh. are w. ther.
2:17 in stone a new name w.
13:8 whose names are not w.
14:1 Fa.'s name w. in foreheads
Rev. 17:5 up, head was w. Myst.
19:12 name w. on his thigh, 16
21:12 names w. on the gates
It is WRITTEN.
Jos. 8:31 as it is w. in the law of
Moses, 1 K. 2:3; 2 Chr. 23:18;
25:4 ; 31:3; 35:12 Ezr. 3:2, 4;
6:18; Neh. 8:15; 10:34, 36;
Dan. 9:13
1 Cor. 15:45 it is w. first man A.
1 Pet. 1:16 it is w. be ye holy
WRONG.
1 Cor. 6:7 why do ye not rather
take w.?
8 ye do w. defraud brethren
2 Cor. 7:12 his cause th. done w.
12:13 burdensome, forg. this w.
Col. 3:25 doth w. receive for w.
WRONGFULLY.
Job 21:27 devices ye w. imagine
Ps. 35:19 let not enemi. w. rejoi.
1 Pet. 2:19 grief, suffering w.
WROTE.
Ex. 24:4 Moses w. all the word
of the Lord, Deut. 31:9

Rom. 16:22 I Terti. who w. this
1 Cor. 5:9 Paul w. in an epistle,
2 Cor. 2:3, 4; 7:12; Eph. 3:3;
Phile. 21
3 John 9 I w. to the church
WROTH.
Gen. 4:5 and Cain was very w.
6 L. sa. to C. Why art th. w.?
31:26 Jacob was w. 34:7 sons w.
40:2 Pharaoh was w. 41:10
Lam. 5:22 th. art very w. ag. us
Mat. 2:16 Her. was exceeding w.
Rev. 12:17 the dragon was w.
WROUGHT, actively.
Neh. 4:16 my serv. w. in work
17 every one with hand w.
Ezek. 20:9 I w. for my name's
sake, 14, 22, 44
WROUGHT, passively.
Ec. 2:17 work w. under sun
John 3:21 manif. th. are w. in G.
WRUNG.
Lev. 1:15 blood sh. be w. out. 5:9
Y.

YEA.
Mat. 5:37 conve. be y. Jam. 5:12
2 Cor. 1:17 sho. be y. y. and nay
YEAR.
Lev. 16:34 atonement once a y.
YEAR by YEAR.
Deut. 14:22 tithe inc. of thy seed
field bringeth forth y. by y.
YEARLY.
1 Sam. 1:3 E. went y. to worship
YEARS.
Gen. 1:14 for sesons, days, y.
1 K. 1:1 David was stricken in y.
1 K. 17:1 not dew nor rain th. y.
Is. 21:16 accord. to y. of hireling
Joel 2:2 y. of many generations
Heb. 1:12 thy y. shall not fail
Rev. 20:2 bound Satan a thou. y.
YESTERDAY.
Ps. 90:4 a thou. years, but as y.
Heb. 13:8 same y. and for ever
YIELD.
Joel 2:22 fig-tree y. strength
Hab. 3:17 altho' fields y. no meat
Rom. 6:13 y. yourselves to God
16 that to whom ye y. yoursel.

19 y. members to righteousn.
Jam. 3:12 no fount. y. salt water
YIELDED.
Rom. 6:19 ye have y. your mem.
YOKE.
Jer. 2:20 of old time brok. thy y.
Lam. 1:1 4 y. of my transgressions is bound
Mat. 11:29 take my y. upon you
30 my y. is easy, burden light
YOKED.
2 Cor. 6:14 be not unequally y.
YOKE-FELLOW.
Phil. 4:3 I entreat thee, true y.-f.
YOUNG.
Is. 40:11 those that are with y.
Mark 7:25 y. dau. unclean spirit
John 21:18 y. thou gird. thyself
YOUNG unicorn.
Ps. 29:6 and Sirion like a y. u.
YOUNG women.
Tit. 2:4 teach y. w. to be sober
YOUNGER.
1 Tim. 5:1 entreat y. as brethren
2 the y. women as sisters, with
11 y. widows refuse, for when
14 I will that y. women marry
1 Pet. 5:5 y. submit to the elder
YOURS.
2 Chr. 20:15 battle not y. God's
YOUTH.
Ps. 25:7 remember not sins of y.
Ec. 11:9 rejoi. O man, in thy y.
10 childhood and y. are vanity
Mat. 2:14 and the wife of thy y.
15 treach. again. wife of his y.
Mat. 19:20 th. have I kept fr. my
y. Mark 10:20; Luke 18:21
1 Tim. 4:12 no man desp. thy y.

Z.

ZACCHEUS.
Luke 19:5 Z. haste, come down
ZACHARIAH, ZECHA-
RIAH.
Luke 1:5 Z. a priest of the course
13 fear not, Z. 59 called him Z.
ZEAL.
Rom. 10:2 they have a z. of God
ZEALOUS.
Acts 21:20 they are all z. of law

1 Cor. 14:12 z. of spiritual gifts
Tit. 2:14 people, z. of good works
ZEBULUN.
Gen. 30:20 L. alled his name Z.
35:23 Reuben, Simeon, Jud. Z.
46:14 the sons of Z. Num. 1:30;
26:26
Tribe of ZEBULUN.
Num. 1:31 numbered of t. of Z.
ZEDEKIAH.
1 K. 22:11 Z. made, 2 Chr. 18:10
ZEPHANIAH.
2 K. 25:18 took Z. Jer. 52:24
Zep. 1:1 the word came to Z.
ZERAH.
Gen. 36:13 sons of Reuel, Z.
ZERUBBABEL.
1 Chr. 3:19 son of Pedaiah, Z.
ZERUIAH.
2 Sam. 2:18 three sons of Z.
ZIBA.
2 Sam. 9:2 art thou Z.? 10 Z. had
ZIDON.
Gen. 49:13 border shall be to Z.
Jos. 11:8 chased th. to great Z.
ZILPAH.
ZIMRI.
Gen. 29:24 Lab. gave to Leah Z.
Num. 25:14 th. was slain was Z.
ZION.
2 Sam. 5:7 David took strong
hold of Z. 1 Chr. 11:5
Ps. 51:18 thy good pleas. unto Z.
Is. 1:27 Z. shall be redeemed
12:6 shout, th. inhabitant of Z.
In ZION.
Ps. 9:11 sing praises to L. who
dwell. in Z. 76:2; Joel 3:21
Is. 4:3 that is left in Z. shall be
10:24 O my peo. dwellest in Z.
Jer. 8:19 is not the Lord in Z./
Amos 6:1 that are at ease in Z.
Rom. 9:33 in Z. a stumbl. stone
Mount ZION.
Mic. 4:7 reign over th. in m. Z.
Heb. 12:22 are come unto m. Z.
Rev. 14:1 Lamb stood on m. Z.
Out of ZION.
Ps. 14:7 come out of Z. 53:6
Joel 3:16 L. shall roar out of Z.
Rom. 11:26 come out of Z. deliv.

Y

Z

Look for these Convenient
DUGAN
HANDYBOOK Titles

- Everything You Need to Know About Social Security

- The Consumers' Amortization Guide

- The Dugan Bible Dictionary

- The Cruden's Condensed Concordance

- Daily Prayer Journal

- Bible Stories from the Book of Acts

- Journals

- Bible Questions and Answers

- Serenity Promises

- Glossary of Legal Terms

D·U·G·A